AF657754

GREAT MEN
OF
INDIA

BY COURTESY OF THE VICTORIA AND ALBERT MUSEUM, LONDON

BABUR, HUMAYUN AND AKBAR

The First Three Mogul Emperors.

GREAT MEN OF INDIA

Edited by

L.F. RUSHBROOK WILLIAMS

QUONDAM FELLOW OF ALL SOULS COLLEGE

BHARATIYA KALA PRAKASHAN

DELHI (INDIA)

Indian Edition 2007

Published by **C.P. Gautam**
BHARATIYA KALA PRAKASHAN
3421-A, IInd Floor, Narang Colony, Tri Nagar, Delhi-110035
Phone : 27393083, 32967505
E-mail : bkp3421@yahoo.co.in

ISBN : 81-8090-139-4

Printed by
BDH Printer at Salasar Imaging System,
Delhi-35

CONTENTS

5

INTRODUCTION

OF India, it may perhaps be said, more truly than of many other countries, that through the centuries, time and again, her destiny has rested in the hands of one man. This is of itself remarkable, for no man, however great, has possessed the advantage of a field clear of rivals and competitors. Where numerous kingdoms flourish it needs a more than ordinarily great king to conquer and to hold so great a stretch of territory. Where there are many statesmen, it calls for very remarkable qualities in any one of them to impress his ideas of government upon the others. Where there are many creeds, it is only a very great teacher whose precepts can stand the test of centuries. Where poets flourish, it takes a very great genius to compose epics which are accepted as national.

This book is an attempt to tell the story of some of the greatest of the men who have made and are making Indian history. In the eighteenth and early nineteenth centuries, India herself tended to forget her great and splendid past. The legacies of her cultures, her art, her literature, the records of her history were neglected. But during the last fifty years India's national spirit has revived, and with that revival has arisen a new generation of Indian leaders.

The subjects of this book are divided into eight sections according to the varied manifestations of their genius. Yet they might well be divided into two parts only, for any classification of the great men of India falls naturally into two main groups. There are the men who made the India of the past with its rich culture, its deep philosophical wisdom, and its stirring examples of courage and chivalry. There are the men of to-day who, turning again for guidance to the history of their land, are taking the best from the past, and making of it a foundation on which to build an even greater India of the future.

Though there has been no attempt to make this book in any way a history of India, we cannot study the lives of her great men over a period of more than two thousand years without learning much of her history and progress. Thus it is that the biographies in this book serve to illuminate, and in some sort even to recount, the history of the great land in which they lived.

Looking back over the centuries it is not hard to assess the spiritual debt India owes to these great figures of the past. Buddha has given to the world one of its greatest religions. The debt that Hinduism owes to Sankaracharya and Ramanuja is incalculable. In later times the work of Raja Rammohan Roy has world-wide significance—the list might be increased almost infinitely.

The lives of Indian kings and emperors are full of colour. We study in turn Chandragupta Maurya, the first great emperor, the splendid age of the Gupta kings, Harsha and the last blaze of glory before the sun finally set on the Golden Age. This glory is revived in the splendour of the Mogul dynasty, who ruled on the whole strongly and well, and came nearer to uniting India under one monarchy than any before or after them. The whole romance of the Rajput clan is packed into the story of Rana Pratap Singh fighting his lost cause gallantly and fiercely until he drew his last breath. We see also Shivaji the Maratha hero; Haidar Ali and his son Tippu Sultan, who might have changed Indian history had they not in the end become pawns in the contest between England and France, fought to its end on Indian soil. Last of the glittering pageant is Ranjit Singh who, while he lived, saved himself and the Sikhs from a similar fate.

Such were some of the great figures of the past. Time has proved them and has shown their worth. When we come to the great men of to-day it is noticeable that though widely varying in their activities, their methods of working and their points of view, an underlying national spirit unites them all. They strive, not for separate causes, as did their heroes of the past, but for one—even though they may apprehend that cause diversely—their Motherland, India. There are among them men who have discarded agelong traditions of caste and creed. There are men who have sacrificed great careers for their convictions. There are men who have given up the prizes the world can offer. There are men who have come, through patient toil, to fame they did not seek. The ranks include scientists, scholars, poets, authors, founders of universities and schools, princes and great ministers. They are all of them in their own way working for the advancement of India. Many are presented in this book by people who know or have known them intimately, and welcome the opportunity of reminding the people of India of the debt of gratitude they owe to these architects of the country's future.

Whether of the past or of the present, India's great men are such as would do honour to any country known to history. Of such as these was the Hebrew preacher thinking when he exhorted:

"Let us now praise famous men, and our fathers that begat us. The Lord manifested in them great glory, even His mighty power from the beginning. Such as did bear rule in their kingdoms, and were men renowned for their power, giving counsel by their understanding, such as have brought tidings in prophecies: leaders of the people by their counsels, and by their understanding men of learning for the people; wise were their words in their instruction: such as sought out musical tunes, and set forth verses in writing: rich men furnished with ability, living peaceably in their habitations: all these were honoured in their generations, and were a glory in their days."

L. F. RUSHBROOK WILLIAMS.

Rye House,
Silchester.

EDITORIAL NOTES AND ACKNOWLEDGMENTS

FOR assistance and advice in the task of collecting illustrations for this book, we would like especially to acknowledge our gratitude to:

The Superintendent of Records and the Librarian of the India Office, who have given us access to the various paintings hanging in the India Office: to material from The Johnson Collection and the Archæological Survey of India, photographs from which are acknowledged A.S.I. in the text.

K. de. B. Codrington, Esq., of the Victoria and Albert Museum (Indian Museum).

Basil Grey, Esq., of the Department of Oriental Antiquities, the British Museum.

H. G. Rawlinson, Esq.

The Times of India.

The Statesman, Calcutta.

H. L. O. Garrett, Esq.

We would also like to express our gratitude to the many contributors who, both in India and England, have placed at our disposal photographs in their private possession, or have taken great personal trouble to procure material for us.

In the case of some old and valuable prints included for their historical interest, the printed reproduction is below the standard of the rest of the book. We regret this is unavoidable.

Finally, although we have taken every possible care to trace the copyright of all illustrations used, to give proper acknowledgment, and to request permission where necessary, we would point out that illustrations have come from many and varied sources, so that if we should inadvertently have used material without due permission and acknowledgment we trust copyright owners will accept this explanation.

F. HENLE

JAIN TEMPLE AT SRAVANA BELGOLA

Tradition says that Chandragupta, having conquered Southern India, abdicated and lived as a pious Jain ascetic at Sravana Belgola, where eventually he died.

CHANDRAGUPTA MAURYA

THE KING WHO DEFEATED THE GREEKS

c. 323-299 B.C.

BY RADHA KUMUD MOOKERJI, M.A., PH.D.

CHANDRAGUPTA was one of the greatest rulers of India. He ruled over an India more extensive than British India, with its boundaries extended beyond the frontiers up to the borders of Persia. He was the first Indian ruler to bring together the valleys of the Indus, Ganges and Jumna under one political authority. He was also the first to add to this political unification of northern India the further achievement of uniting in one Empire both North and South across the barrier of the Vindhyas. He was again the first to face the consequences of a European invasion, the conditions of depression and disorganisation it had created, and to achieve the distinction of liberating his country from the yoke of Greek rule. Alexander's invasion of India lasted for about 3 years, May, 327–May, 324 B.C., while Chandragupta was able to rid the country of all vestiges of Greek authority by 323 B.C. Chandragupta was also great in achieving so much within a short time, a reign of only 24 years, as stated in the *Purānas* (the well-known Sanskrit historical works). Thus he reigned from 323 B.C. to 299 B.C. and was succeeded by his son Bindusāra, who reigned for 25 years and was succeeded by the great Asoka in 274 B.C. These dates gathered from the *Purānas* fit in with the known chronology of Asoka's reign.

Chandragupta's early life has been the subject of much romance and conflicting traditions. Quite a cycle of legends has grown round it. It is difficult to separate fact from fiction in their mixture.

According to the *Purānas* the Sūdra dynasty of Nandas, who had exterminated the Kshatriya kings of the time, was overthrown by the Brahman Kautilya (or Chānakya), who anointed Chandragupta as king and inaugurated the rule of the Mauryas.

The well-known work *Artha-Sāstra* of Kautilya echoes this tradition by stating that it was left to Kautilya to free the country, its culture, science and arts (*Sāstra* and *Sastra*) from the stranglehold of the unlawful Nanda Kings.

The implication of this tradition is that Chandragupta was a true-born Kshatriya prince utilised by Chānakya as a fit instrument for his mission of restoring the country to lawful Kshatriya rule in accordance with Varnāsrama-dharma, which reserved royalty to Kshatriyas.

But the drama of *Mudrārākshasa*, however (which is later by more than seven centuries than the time of Chandragupta), is supposed to insinuate that he was a low-born connection of the Nandas themselves. He is dubbed in the drama by epithets like Vrishala or Kulahīna (of low lineage). The insinuation may be explained away, because *Vrishala* literally means "a *vrisha* or bull among kings, the best of kings," in a passage (III, 18) in the drama itself. The term is also used in the drama as one of endearment by Chanakya for his pupil, Chandragupta, and the epithet *Kula-hīna* may refer not to *low*, but *lowly* lineage, as contrasted with the epithet *prathita-Kula*, "famous lineage," applied by the drama to the Nandas whom it was out to exalt and extol. Dramatic partisanship is not history. It was left to the commentator

WHERE THE GREEKS RULED

Ruins of the famous old city of Taxila, which became the centre of the Greek rule in India.

Dhundirāja of the eighteenth century to describe Chandragupta definitely as the son of Maurya, the offspring of the Sūdra wife, *Murā*, of his father named Sarvārthasiddhi, who had another son named Nanda by his wife Sunandā. This is the only passage in Sanskrit literature which definitely ascribes a base birth to Chandragupta. Perhaps it was suggested by the commentator on the *Purāna*, who explained *Maurya* as one born of *Murā*, but even he does not state that Murā was a Sūdra woman. His grammar, however, is wrong, because Murā leads to the derivative *Maureya* and not *Maurya*. He is thus innocent of both grammar and of libel against Chandragupta.

It should further be noted that the Kashmiri works, *Kathāsaritsāgara* of Somadeva, and *Brihatkathāmanjarī* of Kshemendra, suggest a different lineage for Chandragupta. They describe him as the son of *Pūrva*-Nanda, a previous Nanda King, distinguished from the other Nanda called *Yoga*-Nanda.

Moreover, Buddhist tradition is quite certain about the noble pedigree of Chandragupta. He is stated to be the scion of the Kshatriya clan of *Moriyas*, an offshoot of the noble and sacred sept of the S'ākyas who gave the Buddha to the world. Instead of the term *Maurya*, Buddhist works use the form *Moriya*, derived from *Mora*, *Mayūra*, peacock. The story is that the *Moriyas*, separating from the parent community of S'ākyas, to escape from the invasion of the cruel Kosala King, Vidudhava, found refuge in a secluded Himalayan region full of peacocks, whence they also became known as *Moriyas*, i.e. those belonging to the place of peacocks. Another version of the story derives *Moriya* from the city called *Moriya-nagara*, as it was built with "bricks coloured like peacocks' necks." The people who built the city became known as *Moriyas*.

According to Jain tradition (*Paris'-ishtaparvan*, p. 56), Chandragupta was born of a family who reared peacocks.

The Greek accounts of Alexander's campaign mention an Indian tribe called *Mories* after the allied term *Moriya*.

The canonical Buddhist work *Dīgha-Nikāya* (II, 167) refers to the *Moriyas* of Pipphalivana. The *Mahāvamsa* (Geiger's Tr., p. 27) describes Chandragupta as being born of Moriyas who were Kshatriyas. The *Divyāvadāna* (Cowell's ed., p. 370) describes Chandragupta's son Bindusara and also his grandson Asoka as a Kshatriya.

The connection of peacock, *Mayūra*, with *Moriya* or *Maurya* dynasty is attested beyond doubt by singular archæological evidence. One of the Pillars of Asoka, that at Nandangarh, bears at bottom the figure of a peacock as the dynastic emblem of the *Moriyas* or *Mauryas*, while the same Mayūra symbol is repeated in some sculptures on the Great Stūpa at Sanchi, which are associated with Asoka on the basis of the stories of his life which they translate into stone.

Perhaps the true facts of Chandragupta's lineage were gathered by the Greeks. Justin (XV, 4) states that "he was born in *humble* life." Plutarch (Ch. LXII) makes Chandragupta report to Alexander that the then Nanda King of Magadha was unpopular for "his wickedness and meanness of origin." A descendant cannot cast aspersion on his own ancestry. Ancestral meanness will also be *his* by descent!

The fact of Chandragupta's humble life is also borne out by Buddhist tradition. (See *Mahawamsa*, ed. Turnour, p. x.) According to this tradition his father, the chief of his tribe, was killed in a border fray. The helpless widow escaped to Pushpapura (Kusumapura-Pātaliputra) where she gave birth to Chandragupta. The boy was spirited

A STUPA AT TAXILA

It is believed that as a boy Chandragupta visited the city, a centre of learning, and saw Alexander the Great.

away by a cowherd, who brought him up in his cowpen and then sold him to a hunter by whom he was employed to tend cattle. The story goes that at the village common, the boy Chandragupta took instinctively to the game of playing the King (rāja-krīdā) with his companions, administering justice in a mock court got up for the purpose. It was at one of these plays that Chandragupta was first seen by Chānakya. Chānakya saw in that rustic child the promise and signs of royalty and at once bought him from his foster-father for the sum of 1,000 *Kārsha-panas*, brought him to Taxila, his own native city (*Takshasilānagara-Vāsī*), and had him educated there for 7 or 8 years. These details explain the reference of Justin to Chandragupta's "humble life" at the beginning. They also explain the other very interesting and important fact that Chandragupta, when a mere youth, had seen Alexander in the course of his campaigning in India (Plutarch, Ch. LXII). It was possible for a youth brought up at Taxila.

According to the Buddhist text (*Mahāvatsa-tīkā*), Chānakya, after the completion of Chandragupta's education at Taxila, proceeded to "recruit an army locally and made Chandragupta its commander." According to Justin also (XV, 4), Chandragupta "collected a band of *robbers*." As pointed out by McCrindle (*Invasion of India by Alexander*, p. 406), these "robbers" were the republican peoples of the Panjab, the Ārāttas or Arāshtrakas, "kingless" peoples. Baudhāyana, in his *Dharma-Sūtra* (*c.* 400 B.C.), calls the Panjab the country of the *Ārattas.* The *Mahābhārata* (VIII, 44, 2056–2070; 45, 2100) also defines the *Āratta* as the people of the *Pañchanada* country, "the land of five rivers," and also calls them *Vāhikas*, along with peoples named Prasthala, Madra, Gandhāra, Khasa, Vasāti, Sindhu, and Sauvīra. Alexander saw some of them, such as the Vasāti, whom he calls Ossadii, or the Arāttas, whom he calls Adraistai. Alexander's invasion brought to light the many free peoples who resisted it at different centres in the Panjab, with all their might and resources. A large part of the Panjab, according to Arrian (IV, 21), was then held by "independent Indian tribes," "fierce nations" ready to fight Alexander "with their blood" (Curtius, IX, 4).

There were, then, magnificent military material and possibilities available in the Panjab among her small republican peoples and States. Their heroic defence of their liberties against Alexander's invasion failed, probably because it lacked leadership, organisation, unity of direction and pooling of resources. Alexander was able to deal with each State separately and to subdue it easily. The multiplicity of States prevented a united front against a common enemy and caused the collapse of opposition.

It was left to the genius of Chānakya and Chandragupta to exploit and organise this local military material and spirit of resistance, which they had seen with their own eyes, for a more successful endeavour for the achievement of the country's freedom from Greek control. They knew how to produce out of this material an army fit for freedom's battle.

Indian literature throws some light on the composition of the army which Chandragupta had got together for fighting his battles. The *Mudrārākshasa* speaks of an alliance which Chānakya had arranged with a Himalayan chief called Parvataka. The *Sthavirāvalicharita* also states that "Chānakya went to Himavatkūta and entered into alliance with Parvataka, the king of that region"; and Buddhist accounts also mention a Parvata as a close associate of Chānakya. Thus three traditions testify to this alliance. It is extremely probable, as F. W. Thomas has suggested (in *Cam-*

bridge History of India, Vol. I), that this Parvataka was no other than King Poros of the Greeks. He filled such a large place in the politics of the Panjab that no adventure in that region was possible without him at that time.

The *Mudrārākshasa* further informs us that as a result of this Himalayan alliance, Chandragupta got together a composite army recruited from the different peoples of the region.

Apart from his military preparations, the internal conditions of the country helped Chandragupta and were not favourable to Greek rule. The course of Alexander's invasion did not itself run smooth. Rebellion was rearing its head in his rear and sometimes even among his own people. Popular opinion on the situation was conveyed to Alexander by an Indian ascetic, who asked Alexander to tread on a piece of dry hide and made him observe that as he placed his foot on one end its other end would fly up. This was a visible image of the uncertain and unstable consequences of campaigns carried on in countries too far from "the centre of his dominion" (McCrindle's *Invasion*, p. 315). The prospects of his enterprise did not appeal very much to the Greeks themselves. Alexander's policy was to plant colonies of Greek veterans at suitable centres to mark the progress of his conquest (Arrian v, 27, 5). Such colonies were set up first in Bactria and Sogdiana; but the moment there was a rumour of Alexander's death, 300 of these colonies left for home (Diodorus, XVII, 99). Alexander himself thought of these colonies as penal settlements, to which the Greeks convicted of disloyalty were committed (Justin XII, 5, 8, 13).

Then, again, to consolidate his conquests, Alexander divided Greek India into six Satrapies, three on the west side of the Indus and three on the east. The three western Satrapes were Greek: Peithon posted as Governor of Sind, Nicanor, of the province called "India West of the Indus," comprising lower Kabul valley and hill-tracts up to Hindu Kush with its capital at Pushkalāvatī (Charsadda), assisted by a Macedonian garrison under Commandant Philip and Oxyartes, governor of Paropanisadae province (Kabul valley). Alexander could not post Greek governors to the east of the Indus. Here the three Satrapes were placed under Indian Kings, Āmbhi, King of Taxila, the King of Abhisāra country, and Paurava (Poros), Alexander's worst enemy, now installed as ruler of the largest territory comprising "15 republican peoples, 5,000 considerable cities and villages without number" (McCrindle, p. 309).

The position of the Greek governors rapidly became precarious. First Kandahar revolted under the instigation of an Indian Chief called Samaxus or Damaraxus. Next, the Asvakas killed their Greek governor or Nican (Arrian, v, 20, 7). The Eastern Asvakas threatened the Indian Agent of Greek imperialism, Sisikottus (Sasīgupta), who had to ask Alexander for help.

All this trouble was brewing in 326 B.C. when Alexander was in the thick of his campaigns. He was even falling short of men. He had to wait for Thracian reinforcements from distant Iran to be able to advance beyond the Chenab, but the Beas proved the limit of his advance. Koinos conveyed to Alexander the spirit of revolt among the Greek soldiery, "of whom few were left with their bodily strength and spirits no longer as before" (McCrindle).

The place of Nicanor, murdered by the Indian "Mutineers," was taken by Commandant Philip, who became the most powerful Greek Governor. He was already acting as Alexander's agent at Taxila to keep watch over the activities of his old and powerful enemy Paurava

(Poros). He was further selected by Alexander to guard the rear of his advance down the Hydaspes and, later, to take charge of the territories of the free peoples, the Mālavas (Malloi) and Kshudrakas (Oxydrakai), conquered by Alexander, as far south as the confluence of the Indus and the Chenab. Philip, therefore, held the key-position of Greek rule in India. The assassination of such a man was a fatal blow to that rule. He was murdered on his return to headquarters after he had seen Alexander off on his return journey down the Jhelum. According to Arrian (VI, 27, 2), Philip fell a victim to jealousy between Greeks and Macedonians of his garrison, but the incident was "symptomatic of a more deeply seated trouble" (*Cambridge History of India*, Vol. I). Alexander received the news of his murder before he had reached Carmania, on his westward march, but he was quite helpless to avenge it. All that he could do was to seek the good offices of his Indian ally, the King of Taxila, to whom he sent despatches asking him kindly to "assume the administration of the Province previously governed by Phillipus until he could send a Satrap to govern it" (Arrian, VI, 27). That Satrap was never sent. On the contrary, an Indian King was helped to extend his authority beyond the Indus and the frontiers up to the Kabul valley and Hindukush. A Thracian, named Eudamus, was left as the sole Greek agent in charge of the garrison at Pushkalāvatī (modern Charsada) to deal with the scattered Greek and Macedonian troops and colonists who lingered on in India.

Then followed the death of Alexander in 323 B.C., when the Greek situation in India became extremely critical. The two years 325-323 B.C. that intervened between the death of Philip and that of Philip's master were fateful years for the revolutionary movement that was silently

THE PEACOCK

The peacock carved on the Sanchi gateways, reputed to be work of Asoka.

going on behind the scenes for achieving India's freedom from foreign subjection.

Chandragupta appears on the scene as the leader of this movement. What was then happening may be gathered from the following statement of Justin (XV, 4), the only available evidence on the subject. "India, after Alexander's death, as if the yoke of servitude had been shaken off her neck, had put this Prefect to death. Sandrocottus (Chandragupta) was the leader who achieved this freedom. . . . He was born in humble life. . . . Having collected a band of 'robbers,' he instigated the Indians to overthrow the existing (Greek) government. . . . He was thereafter preparing to attack Alexander's Prefects, mounted on an elephant which fought vigorously in front of the army." The "Prefects" mentioned here must be the Satraps Nicanor and Philip, who were both assassinated, as already related.

His success in the Panjab in ridding it of foreign rule made him turn confidently to the main mission of his life, viz., to rid his own country of its wicked ruler, Nanda. We have not much evidence on the details of Chandragupta's conquest of Magadha, but it was a sensational episode and roused popular interest. It passed into folklore and tradition. The Buddhist texts relate

ON SANCHI GATEWAY

The peacock was the crest of the house of Maurya. Asoka was Chandragupta's grandson.

that Chandragupta's movement was from the frontier to the interior of India, towards Magadha and Pātaliputra and that he had first made mistakes in strategy. "In his ambition to be a monarch, without beginning from the frontiers and taking the towns in order as he passed, he invaded the heart of the country and found his army surrounded by the people on all sides and routed: like a child eating the middle part of a cake and not eating from the edges, which were thrown away." Next, he tried another method. He commenced operations from the frontiers (*Pachchantato Patthāya*) and conquered many *rāshtras* and *janapadas*, States and peoples, on the way; but his mistake was not to post garrisons to hold the conquests. The result was that the people left in the rear of his advance were free to combine, to encircle his army, and defeat his designs. Then the proper strategy dawned on him. He had garrisons stationed at the *rāshtras* and *janapadas* as they were conquered (uggahitanayā balam samvidhāya) and, crossing the frontiers of Magadha with his victorious army, encountered the Nanda army, besieged Pātaliputra and killed Dhana-Nanda (*Mahāvamsatīkā*).

A similar comment on strategy is also contained in the Jaina work, *Sthavirāvalicharita*, which states: "Like a child burning his finger which he greedily puts in the middle of the dish, instead of eating from the outer part which was cool, Chānakya had been defeated because he had not secured the surrounding country before attacking the stronghold of the enemy. Profiting by this advice, Chānakya went to Himatvatkūta and entered into alliance with Parvataka, the king of that place . . . they opened the campaign by reducing the provinces."

These stories only point to the fundamental fact of Indian history that all movements of conquest in India have been from the frontier to the interior, from the north to the south, from the highlands to the plains. It is only in the case of the British as a sea-power that the movement has followed a different course, from the sea upwards.

It is also apparent from the stories that the conquest of Nanda's Empire was the result of several attempts, because it was so powerful. Curtius records that its army comprised 200,000 infantry, 20,000 cavalry, 2,000 four-horsed chariots, and 3,000 elephants. It was very large, extending as far as the Panjab. Paurava II, retreating before Alexander's invasion of his country between the Chenab and Ravi, found shelter in the Nanda dominions (McCrindle's *Invasion*, p. 279). The Purānas describe the first Nanda "as a second Parasurāma, who exterminated all Kshatriyas," and mentions as the contemporary Kshatriya dynasties the Aiksvākus, Pañchalas, Kāsīs, Haihayas, Kalingas, Asmakas, Kurus, Maithilas, Sūrasenas and Vītihotras. The Greeks describe him as the ruler of peoples called Gangaridæ and Prasii, i.e. the peoples of the Ganges valley and the Prāchyas or Easterns, peoples living to the east of the "Middle Country" such as the Pañchālas, Sūrasenas, Kosalas and the like. The Purānas again call him Mahāpadma, which literally means "lord of immense army and wealth, 100,000 millions." Thus Nanda had untold resources in both men and money. What he lacked was popularity. Chandragupta himself reported to Alexander that Nanda was "hated by his subjects" and this report Alexander got confirmed by the Indian Kings Paurava and Bhagalā (Phegelas). The Greek writers record that Nanda's unpopularity was due to the original sin of his ancestor who was a barber and a paramour of the wife of his royal master, whom he murdered, together with the royal children, and seized the throne for his son by the guilty Queen (Diodorus and Curtius cited in McCrindle's *Invasion*).

Thus the Nanda dynasty was born in sin, which Hiṇdu social opinion could not tolerate. The *Purānas* dub the dynasty as "immoral." The Buddhist texts call Nanda as Dhana-Nanda for his rapacity. The *Mahāvamsatīkā* (Turnour, *Introduction to Mahāwanso*, p. xxxix) has a different tradition about the first Nanda, whom it calls by another name, Ugrasena. He started as a marauder and formed a gang of dacoits with his other brothers and later seized Magadhan sovereignty (*cf. Mahābodhivamsa*). Perhaps the Greek version is more reliable as being based upon first-hand reports. It is echoed in Bāna's *Harshacharita*, which states that "Kākavarnī Saisunāgī was killed by a dagger thrust into his throat in the suburb of his city"—pointing to the treacherous murder of his royal master by the Queen's paramour, the barber, the sinful progenitor of the Nanda dynasty. A similar tradition is recorded in Jain works. The *Parisishtaparvan* (p. 46) describes Nanda as the son of a barber by a courtesan, which implies a double degradation due to both parents being tainted. The *Āvasyakasūtra* (p. 690) describes the Nanda king as "begotten of a barber" (nāpitadāsa).

There are different traditions as to the circumstances which led to a clash between Chandragupta and Nanda. According to Justin, Chandragupta "by his insolent behaviour had offended King Nandrus and when ordered by that king to be put to death, he had sought safety by a speedy flight." The text of Justin has the name Alexandrum, which is taken to be a mistake for Nandrum, i.e. Nandra. The *Mahāvamsatīkā*, however, relates that it was not Chandragupta but Chānakya who had offended Nanda. Chānakya had come all the way from his native city of Taxila to Pātaliputra to try his wits at disputation at the court of Dhana Nanda, who was now a changed man, his avarice being replaced by a love of giving. His charities were organised through an institution called Dānasālā, administered by a Samgha, of which Chānakya was appointed president with liberty to give up to a crore, but the king, unable to stand his look and manners, relieved him of his office. The insulted Chānakya now became his mortal enemy and escaped in the disguise of an Ājīvika ascetic. Then he came across Chandragupta as a foundling and brought him to Taxila, as already related. The *Mudrārākshasa* also supports this tradition in stating that Nanda had insulted Chānakya by expelling him publicly from his place of honour in his court. It represents Chānakya as the primary enemy of Nanda, and Chandragupta only as his instrument. The drama opens with the statement of Chānakya that he has already destroyed the Nanda family and will not spare a single offshoot thereof. The *Milinda-pañho* (SBE. Vol. XXXVI, p. 147) gives the information that the general of Nanda's army was Bhaddasāla and mentions the colossal carnage of the war at which were killed "100 kotis of soldiers, 10,000 elephants, 1 lac of horses and 5,000 charioteers."

The subsequent career of Chandragupta may be gathered from the following statement of Plutarch (*Life of Alexander*, Ch. LXII) as the only evidence on the subject. "Not long afterwards, Androkattos (Chandragupta), who had by that time mounted the throne, presented Seleukos with 500 elephants and overran and subdued the whole of India with an army of 600,000." "The throne" here refers to the throne of Magadha, which Chandragupta had won by defeating the Nanda king. His conquest of the Magadhan Empire was followed by two other achievements, first, the defeat of Seleukos and, secondly, the conquest of southern parts of India which were not included in the Nanda Empire. In the struggle for power among his generals, following Alexander's death, Seleukos emerged victorious in 312 B.C., and later thought of recovering Alexander's conquests in India. Crossing the Indus in 305 B.C., he found a new India, strong and united, under Chandragupta, with whom he had to come to terms. He ceded to Chandragupta the four Greek provinces of Paropanisadæ (Kabul), Aria (Herat), Arachosia (Kandahar) and part of Gedrosia, making up modern Afghanistan and Baluchistan. Chandragupta on his part presented Seleukos with 500 elephants, which he found helpful in his war with his rival Antigonos. By this treaty of 303 B.C. Chandragupta was the first Indian King to extend the frontiers of India to the borders of Persia.

There is no evidence to prove Chandragupta's conquest of the south, except the passage from Plutarch cited above. A Jain tradition (*Rājāvalikathe* cited in *IA.* 1892, p. 157) relates that Chandragupta abdicated and settled down at Sravana Belgola in Mysore as an ascetic. It stands to reason that he chose for his retirement a place which was not outside his vast dominion, while his grandson, Asoka, tells in his *Inscriptions* that his immediate "neighbours" in the south (Antah) were Cholas, Pāndyas and others. So the Maurya Empire had included Sravana Belgola within its limits.

Some ancient Tamil authors like Mamulanar or Paranar mention Mauryas advancing up to a hill in Tinnevelley district, led by a warlike clan called Kosar. There are also late Mysore inscriptions referring to Chandragupta's rule in Mysore (Rice, Mysore and Coorg from the *Inscriptions*, p. 10). Nāgakhanda in Shikarpur Taluka, Mysore, is stated to be included in the kingdom of

Chandragupta. The Mauryas are supposed to have penetrated into Southern India through the Konkan.

To sum up, Chandragupta is to be credited with achievements which include the overthrow of the Greek occupation and conquest of the Panjab; the conquest of the Empire of Magadha; the victory over the western king, Seleukos, and the extension of empire beyond the Indian frontiers; and the conquest of the South and the political unification of North and South under one paramount sovereignty.

The government of such a vast empire was necessarily based upon a system of decentralisation. The empire was divided up into a number of Provinces and Vice-royalties and each of these was of the time-honoured pattern of the Hindu State, comprising the ruler or governor at the top, heads of departments, a hierarchy of officials in different grades of jurisdiction and the self-governing village communities at the foundation of the structure. In the inscriptions of Asoka, under whom the Maurya Empire was seen at its best, there are mentioned cities like Taxila, Ujjain, Kosambi, Girnar, Tosali, and Suvarnagiri as the seats of the provincial governments. The evidence for the reign of Chandragupta on these matters is very meagre. We know only from a later inscription of Rudradāman (of *c.* A.D. 150) of the western province of Chandragupta's empire, which was then called Surāshtra and had its capital at Girinagara (Girnar). It was administered by the governor (*Rāshtrīya*), named Pushyagupta Vaisya. The province was known for the "beautiful reservoir" called Sudarsana Tatāka (Lake).

The provincial government in the traditional Hindu polity rested on a hierarchy of officers of different grades and jurisdictions, planned on what may be called the decimal system, comprising the village (*grāma*) as the smallest unit under the officer called *Grāmanī* and groups of 10, 20, 100 and 1,000 villages under officers called, respectively, *Dasī*, *Vimsī*, *Satesa* and *Sahasresa*, in an ascending order of authority, culminating in the provincial governor called *Adhipati* (*cf. Manu*, VII, 115-125). These several authorities received revenue, dealt with the returns of crime and passed them on from one to the next higher till revenues and reports focused in the king, the lord of all. Towns grew out of villages as centres of protection and prosperity. Every ten villages were served by a market-town called Samgrahana; 300 or 400 villages had their county towns called Kharvataka and Dronamukha (located at a river's mouth); and, lastly, there were the great city, Nagara, or Pura, the port or Pattana and the capital or Rājadhānī (*Artha-Sāstra*, p. 46).

At the foundation of the structure was the village community functioning like a self-governing corporation or republic. The villagers were free to legislate for themselves through the groups to which they belonged, the Kula or family, the Jāti or caste, the Srenī or guild and the Janapada, the locality. The king's duty was to recognise and enforce the laws laid down for themselves by these self-governing groups, communities, and corporations, and the laws of different localities (*Manu*, VIII, 41, 46).

As regards the administration, a vast body of valuable and concrete evidence is furnished by the epoch-making Sanskrit work, the *Artha-Sāstra* of Kautilya. Although the exact date and authorship of the work cannot be ascertained with certainty (as in the case of most Sanskrit works which are products of schools and not of individual authors and hence open to additions), scholars are agreed that the contents of the work reflect the conditions of Maurya India.

The main source of information

regarding India under Chandragupta Maurya is the account of Megasthenes who, after the Treaty of 303 B.C., was sent as an envoy by Seleukos to the court of the Indian king, where he spent a number of years and had several times visited the Maurya capital.

He describes Pātaliputra as situated at the confluence of the Son and Ganges, protected by a massive timber palisade (of which fragments have been recently excavated), pierced by 64 gates, crowned by 570 towers, and surrounded by a moat 600 feet broad and 30 cubits deep, filled from the waters of the Son.

The palace was of timber, with gilded pillars adorned with golden vines and silver birds. The king was carried in a golden palanquin adorned with tassels of pearls, and was clothed in muslin embroidered with gold. Public amusements were fights of bulls, rams, elephants, rhinos, and other animals, gladiatorial contests, ox-races and the like. The chief royal amusement was the chase. The king was attended by armed female guards. He attended court to administer justice, "remaining there all day thus occupied, not suffering himself to be interrupted even though the time arrives for attending to his person" (Strabo, III, 106-107).

Megasthenes brings the Indians under seven classes with reference to their occupations: (1) The *Philosophers*, i.e. the Brahmans, who performed sacrifices privately for individuals and publicly for kings; (2) the *Agriculturists* who formed the bulk of the population and were exempt from military service and were often found freely working in the fields, in sight of a battle raging close by; (3) *Herdsmen* and *Hunters*; (4) *Traders*, *Artisans* and *Boatmen*. Armourers and ship-builders were to work for the State, and not for private individuals. The admiral of the king's navy hired out ships to private individuals for the transport of goods and passengers. (5) *Soldiers*, who received pay even in peace time; (6) *Inspectors* forming the Intelligence Department, who watched what was going on and reported to the king, and were known for their probity; and (7) the *King's Ministers*, the class from whom were recruited "the magistrates, the chiefs of districts, the deputy governors, the keepers of the treasury, the army superintendents, the admirals, the high stewards, and the overseers of agriculture."

Megasthenes gives some facts about the educational system of the country. Its leaders are called "Philosophers," who were both Brahmans and "*Sarmanes*," S'ramanas, ascetics. The Brahman students spent 37 years in studentship, living with their teacher "in a grove near the city, using beds of leaves and skins, living sparely, practising celibacy and abstinence from flesh-food, listening to discourse, and admitting others to discussion. This points to the Hindu system of education based on *Brahmacharya*. The *Sramanas* 'lived in the forests on leaves and wild fruits, wearing barks of trees' and always meditating and worshipping gods. These were probably the *Sannyāsīs* in the fourth stage or *āsrama* of a Hindu's life. Some of these were 'Medical philosophers,' 'treating people by diet and not by medicines' and preferring medicines to be applied externally 'to drugs.'" (Megasthenes, *Frag.* 40=Strabo, XV, C. 711f). Strabo mentions another class of philosophers called *Pramanai*, the *Prāmānikas*, who believed in *pramāna* or reasoning as a means of knowledge. Being rationalists, they laughed at ritualist Brahmins (Strabo, XV, C. 719). It is also stated that the 'Philosophers' were assembled by the king on New Year's Day to make their suggestions for improving the conditions of the country and sound recommendations were rewarded by the king by granting exemptions from taxation.

FRITZ HENLE

THE IRON PILLAR AT DELHI

The Iron Pillar at Delhi, standing within the Kutb Minar enclosure, is one of the most famous of the Gupta monuments. It bears an inscription showing that it was erected in A.D. 415 *by Kumaragupta I to commemorate the exploits of his father. It is believed that the pillar was brought to Delhi by a Tomara Rajput king, from Bihar, the old Magadha, and that it originally stood before a Vishnu temple.*

THE IMPERIAL GUPTAS

THE GOLDEN AGE OF ART

A.D. 300-500

BY ROBERT BRYAN

THE fourth century in Europe saw the disintegration of the greatest empire that the world had yet known, and in the succeeding two hundred years the lamps of civilisation which the Romans had either inherited from Greece or kindled themselves were extinguished by barbarian hordes. Only in the far south-east of the continent did the Byzantines gallantly, precariously, preserve the great Greco-Roman tradition.

We turn our gaze eastwards to be met by one of history's greatest contrasts; for while Europe was plunging into barbarian obscurity, India was emerging from her dark ages into a period, nearly three hundred years long, which, together with the reign of Harsha which followed after a short interval, has rightly come to be looked upon as the golden age of Hinduism, the period of the imperial Guptas.

The Indo-Scythian empire, the rulers of which had controlled north-west India and exercised some sort of sovereignty over the Ganges valley, was in A.D. 300 a thing of the past. For about eighty years there had been no paramount power in north India, and groups of small states had struggled intermittently and anarchically with each other without gaining any mastery. From the very scarcity of records of this period it is safe to assume that it lacked outstanding personalities, culture, or achievement. Prominent among these states was Magadha, whence centuries earlier had sprung the first of India's great dynasties, the Maurya, and where now the family of Gupta held power; and prominent also in that region was the tribe of the Lichchavi, who held sway at Vaisali and who had appeared in history as early as the days of Buddha.

Of the origins of the Gupta family nothing is known for certain; it has been conjectured that they were of low birth or alternatively that they came from non-Hindu stock. They emerge into historical certainty only in the beginning of the fourth century in the person of the founder of the dynasty and the era that bears their name, Chandragupta I. He was ruling at Pataliputra about 318, and at that date succeeded in marrying a princess of the Lichchavi tribe, Kumara Devi.

COURTESY BRITISH MUSEUM

COINS OF THE GUPTA KINGS

Left: a coin of Chandragupta I. Right: a coin of Chandragupta II.

TWO VYALAKAS——

These two Hippogryphs from the sculptures at Sarnath are typical examples of Gupta Art.

The effects of this union were far-reaching and of the utmost importance to India. At the date of his marriage Chandragupta was ruler of a small principality—one among many; at his death, which probably occurred about 335, he was reigning over a wide, fertile stretch of territory comprising all the modern districts of Oudh, Tirhut and Bihar—lands that all through the ages have had a better claim than any others to be called the heart of India. To his own skill much of this achievement was doubtless due, but the prestige that came to him with his marriage must also have been a powerful factor in making it possible. Kumara Devi's family was an old and honoured one, the Guptas were new-comers, vigorous but without tradition; vigour and tradition allied could accomplish great things. At his accession Chandragupta styled himself Maharaja, but after his marriage he was Maharajadhiraja; and on February 26, A.D. 320, there came into existence, for the purpose of reckoning dates, a new era, the Gupta era, which continued to be used even after the power of the dynasty had waned, and which is vital evidence of the power which by then Chandragupta must have achieved. Coins exist too, to-day, bearing the joint images of Chandragupta and Kumara Devi, struck probably by their son, Samudragupta; they show how highly that ruler estimated his mother's importance, as does the fact that he described himself as "the son of the daughter of the Lichchavi."

Chandragupta chose as his successor

A. S. I.

——FROM SARNATH

They combine the characteristic grace and elegance with simplicity and boldness of design.

MEDALLIONS AT BHARHUT

Four medallions typical of Early Buddhist work. They illustrate scenes from the Jatakas, the stories dealing with Buddha's previous incarnations.

Samudragupta, who was to prove the greatest in a great line of rulers. In the famous inscription at Allahabad recording the events of this reign we find the choice described:

"'Here is a noble man.' With these words the father embraced him with shivers of joy that spoke of his affection, and looked at him with eyes heavy with tears and overcome with love—the courtiers breathing freely with joy and the kinsmen of equal grade looking up with sad faces—and said to him, 'Protect then this whole earth.'"

Having chosen, the father made his son promise that his first task should be the *digvijaya*, the conquest of the Four Quarters, a task imposed by tradition on all Kshatriya rulers who aspired to greatness.

The Allahabad inscription tells how the promise was redeemed. Master of

GUPTA TEMPLE AT SANCHI

At Sanchi, in Central India, are to be found many of the most notable Buddhist remains, among which this Temple of the Gupta period upon the Chandra Hill is notable. Buddhist art in all its forms benefited by the great cultural renaissance that took place in the Gupta Era.

the central Ganges plain, Samudragupta first "violently uprooted" the neighbouring Gangetic rulers and annexed their territories. Secure at home, he then embarked on his most famous campaign, which, having as its first object the conquest of the "kings of the forest country" (probably the tribes of Orissa), was extended, after this had been achieved, so that he reached the Madras coastline and may even have crossed southern India and invaded Malabar, Maharashtra and Khandesh. It has been estimated that in the course of three years' campaigning he covered three thousand miles, a feat almost comparable to the exploits of Alexander.

Whether because he was defeated by the Pallavas in southern India—which is not certain—or because he was more far-sighted than any other would-be conqueror of the south, he made no attempt to annex any territories south of the Narbada river. The material gains of his great campaign were confined to booty and tribute. Its effect nevertheless was immense. Samudragupta had proved himself to be supreme in India, without a serious rival. As a result the rulers of the states bordering his dominions paid homage to him, and with neighbouring kingdoms he established diplomatic relations. Chief among these were the surviving Kushan kingdom of Kabul and the kingdom of Ceylon. To the ruler of the latter he granted permission to build a great monastery for Buddhist pilgrims to Bodh Gaya. His fame had spread, too, further afield, and in his reign contact was made both with the Roman Empire and, more fruitfully, with China.

Shortly after his great campaign Samudragupta performed the rite known as the Horse Sacrifice (*Rajasuya*). The full tradition of this ritual is to be found in the Mahabharata. In anticipation of a campaign a horse, distinguished by certain natural markings, is set free to wander. It is followed by the would-be conqueror, who challenges to battle the ruler of any state into which the horse goes. If victorious the challenger proclaims himself emperor and returns to his capital, where the horse is sacrificed to the gods. Samudragupta's performance of the last part of this ritual, the actual sacrifice, was his boast that he was supreme over all those he wished to conquer. The Horse Sacrifice is evidence, too, that in the Gupta empire Buddhism was giving way to the orthodox Hinduism of the Brahman caste. Samudragupta was known as the "Restorer of the Horse Sacrifice," the reason being that since the days of Asoka Buddhism had been predominant in India and animal sacrifice was abhorrent to Buddhist principles. Its revival speaks for itself.

BUDDHIST MEDALLION FROM AMARAVATI

Yet Samudragupta was tolerant of Buddhism as a branch of Hinduism; the Monastery at Bodh Gaya shows this, as more forcibly does the fact that he chose a Buddhist, Vasabandhu, as his chief councillor.

BUDDHIST CAVE-TEMPLE AT ELLORA

The Buddhist caves of Ellora are, together with those at Ajanta, the most famous of their kind. They were constructed in the Gupta Era.

Samudragupta was both poet and musician—many of the coins of his reign show him playing on a lyre. Of more importance to India was the fact that he was a patron of art in all its forms. In the latter part of his reign there was peace throughout his dominions, and poetry, music, and drama had the opportunity to flourish. The chief literary figure was Harishena, the court poet. He specialised in the *Kavya* (Court Epic) and his verse plays were frequently performed. In addition, he was the author of the Allahabad inscription. Inscribed on one of Asoka's pillars, it tells the story of the triumph and glory of Samudragupta in war, a story contrasting strangely with the ideals which Asoka had preached to his subjects, but showing clearly, even when we allow for exaggeration, the greatness of its hero. Northern India under Samudragupta was powerful, settled, and prosperous; the stage was set for the Golden Age of Hinduism, even if it had not already begun.

That Age approached its zenith in the reign of his son Chandragupta II. Samudragupta died in about 380, bequeathing to his son a great inheritance. The father created an empire, the son consolidated and in two important respects enlarged it. He conquered eastern Bengal, gaining an outlet to the eastern sea, and on the iron pillar at Delhi it is recorded how he crossed the "seven mouths of the Indus." Finally in the last ten years of the century he conquered and annexed what are now Kathiawar and Gujerat and the country round Ujjain. This last campaign far exceeded the others in importance, for it brought to him a footing on the western seaboard, the seaports of Broach and Cambay and the opportunity of renewed intercourse with Egypt and the west.

BY COURTESY OF THE BRITISH MUSEUM

LATE GUPTA PAVINGS

Ivory carvings found at Brahminabad, Sind, dating from the Sixth Century.

BY COURTESY OF THE BRITISH MUSEUM

HAMSA AND MAKARA

Carved stone decorative panels of the Gupta period.

THE AMARAVATI SCHOOL

This concentrically designed medallion shows the amazing skill of Buddhist carving at its best.

Much of the great prosperity that the Gupta empire enjoyed in the fifth century was due to the use made of this opportunity.

Thus by the year 400 the Gupta empire stretched from the modern boundary of the Punjab in the north-west to the Ganges delta in the east and from the Himalayas southwards to the line of the river Narbada, excluding Sind and most of Rajputana. Chandragupta changed the capital from Pataliputra to Ayodha, near the modern Lucknow and connected with the story of Rama. It was the largest empire to be created in northern India since the days of Asoka, and, as far as effective control of territory was concerned, it was not to be exceeded until the days of Akbar. The conditions that prevailed therein—and particularly in the Ganges valley—have been vividly described in the journal kept by the Chinese pilgrim, Fa Hien.

This remarkable traveller entered India by the dangerous route over the Pamirs and the Hindu Kush in the year 405, and remained in India until 411, sailing finally from the mouth of the Ganges. His object was to study in, and collect manuscripts from, the land that gave birth to his faith. His accounts of what he saw relate mainly to his fellow Buddhists, who by this time had become a dwindling minority. Not all that he says applies to the majority of the population, but his account of the general conditions under which people lived is true of all northern India. It forms a glowing testimony to the wisdom, tolerance and strength of the early Gupta emperors, all the more glowing because it is unconscious. Of conditions in the Ganges valley he says:

"The people are numerous and happy; they have not to register their households or attend to any magistrates and their rules; only those who cultivate the royal land have to pay a portion of the gain from it. If they want to go they go; if they want to stay on they stay. The king governs without decapitation or other corporal punishment; criminals are simply fined, lightly or heavily, according to the circumstances. Even in repeated attempts at wicked rebellion, they only have their right hands cut off. The king's bodyguard and attendants all have salaries."

And again: "The heads of the Vaisya families establish in the cities houses for dispensing charity and medicines. All the poor and destitute in the country, orphans, widowers and childless men, maimed people and cripples, and all who are diseased, go to these houses and are provided with every kind of help, and doctors examine their diseases. They get the food and medicines which their cases require and when they are better they go away of themselves."

During the whole of his Indian travels Fa Hien was never once molested, and according to his own words the only dangers he was likely to encounter were from wild beasts. Here is evidence both of a land well policed and of a people trained to practise lawful and orderly behaviour, evidence also that Buddhists were as free and unmolested as any other members of the great Hindu family.

As trade increased in volume to and from the newly acquired western seaports, so did Ujjain, centrally situated between the Ganges valley and the coast, grow in importance. It is probable that for much of his reign Chandragupta held his court there, and the "Raja Bikram" of Hindu legend at whose court flourished the "Nine Gems" of literature, was certainly this emperor. The "Nine Gems" are also legendary figures, but they illustrate the truth that in the reigns of Chandragupta and his successor Kumaragupta Hinduism achieved in literature its classical age. At the emperor's court Kalidasa, the greatest of all Hindu poets and dramatists, composed poems such as the *Ritu Samhara* (Cycle of Seasons) and the *Magadhuta* (Cloud Messenger) and the dramatic masterpiece *Sakuntala*. In lighter vein

THE MATHURA BUDDHA

This sandstone image of Buddha of the Gupta Era was dedicated by the Monk Yasadinna.

BODHISATTVA AT SARNATH

This figure of the Bodhisattva Avalokiẽesvara is one of the masterpieces of Gupta Art.

was the *Sringara Sataka* (Century of Love), written by Bhartrihari, and from the pens of many writers came *Kavyas* written in the style of Harishena. In science in the fifth century Arybhata was maintaining that the earth rotated on its axis, and a little later Brahmagupta was stating that "All things fall to earth by a law of nature," a fact that was new to Newton a thousand years later.

This age is of unique importance to India for two further reasons. It saw the final adoption of Sanskrit as the general language of the educated classes and it was the first period in which writing came into general use. The importance of the change over from oral tradition to the written word cannot be over-estimated.

To what use were these two innovations put? To aid a great burgeoning of literary genius, as we have seen, but even more to help in the crystallisation of the orthodox Brahman view of the Hindu "Way of Life." The Gupta era marks the triumph of orthodox Brahmanism, a triumph shown particularly in the codification and explanation of those strict rules which govern the life of every Brahman and those principles which guide all Hindu conduct. The Mahabharata, which in its original oral form was an Indian equivalent of a Homeric epic, was recast so that it was given religious significance; into it was incorporated for the first time the magnificent *Bhagavad Gita*. The Dharmasastras were compiled and written down, as were the writings of Yajnavalkya, and, perhaps most important of all, a code entitled the laws of Manu was produced, wherein are laid down for each caste its duties and necessary observances. During the Gupta era, and particularly during the period of settled prosperity that Chandragupta and his successor gave to northern India, Brahmanism, after a long period in the wilderness, reasserted itself; it has never since been supplanted.

Chandragupta II died about 415. At his accession he had styled himself proudly *Vikramaditya* (Sun of Valour), and by his achievements he substantiated the boast. The coins struck in his reign show him usually on horseback, often in combat with a lion. Like his father he was a warrior king, a man of action, a true Kshatriya; but he was something much more as well, a wise ruler, a patron of the scholars that abounded in his dominions, and of the Arts.

His successor, Kumaragupta, reigned for some forty years. His reign, according to one inscription, was one of "increasing victory," and it is known that he performed the Horse Sacrifice. During at least the first part of his reign the Hindu renaissance gathered further momentum, and by about 440 northern India had enjoyed a hundred years of settled, enlightened and successful government.

But the Gupta Empire, like the Moslem Empire which centuries later may in many ways be regarded as its Indian counterpart, was destined to disintegrate when still apparently at the height of its power. In the latter years of the reign of Kumaragupta, who died about 454, India was threatened, as was western Europe, by the terrible menace of the Huns. They swept down through the passes of the Hindu Kush, and Kumaragupta, opposing them, was defeated and slain. His son, Skandagupta, however, stemmed for a while the tide of invasion. According to an inscription at Bhitari he slept a night on the bare ground preparatory to avenging his father's death; and he is described, at the end of a campaign, galloping into the courtyard of the palace at Ayodha where his mother resided to bring to her the news of a great, and for the time being, decisive victory. In 465, however, the Huns reappeared, and after Skandagupta's death in 480, they rapidly overran all the north-western part of the empire. By the beginning of the sixth century the descendant of the great Guptas ruled over only Magadha.

Not for a hundred years was Hinduism, under the emperor Harsha, to re-emerge as a great political force; barbarism swept over great portions of India. But, save on the field of battle, it gained no real victories. Hinduism lived on, awaiting its further opportunities. It was the rule of the great Guptas that made this possible, and herein lies their true greatness. As regards their personal qualities they are shadowy figures—Fa Hien does not in the whole course of his narrative mention the emperor by name—their appearance and characteristics we can learn only from inscriptions, coins and the flattering references made about them by writers whom they patronised; but their achievements cannot be belittled. They built up the greatest purely Hindu empire that India has ever known, they consolidated it, and after their triumphs they gave to their subjects that material prosperity and security which is one of the best of all forcing houses for intellectual genius.

Kalidasa has been called the Indian Shakespeare, and the age which he adorned has much in common with the Elizabethan age in England. Both periods are towering peaks on the map of civilisation. We have touched upon the age's intellectual achievements; in architecture the secret of massive stone building was fully discovered, and the iron work of the age still remains a marvel. The famous iron pillar at Delhi is larger than anything achieved in Europe until the nineteenth century. The Gupta Age represents in fact, together with the age of Harsha, the highest consummation of the Hindu spirit. Great Hindus there have been since in profusion, but there have been no such great Hindu empires. This fact alone is justification enough for placing the Gupta emperors, little as we know for certain of their personal qualities, among the galaxy of great Indians.

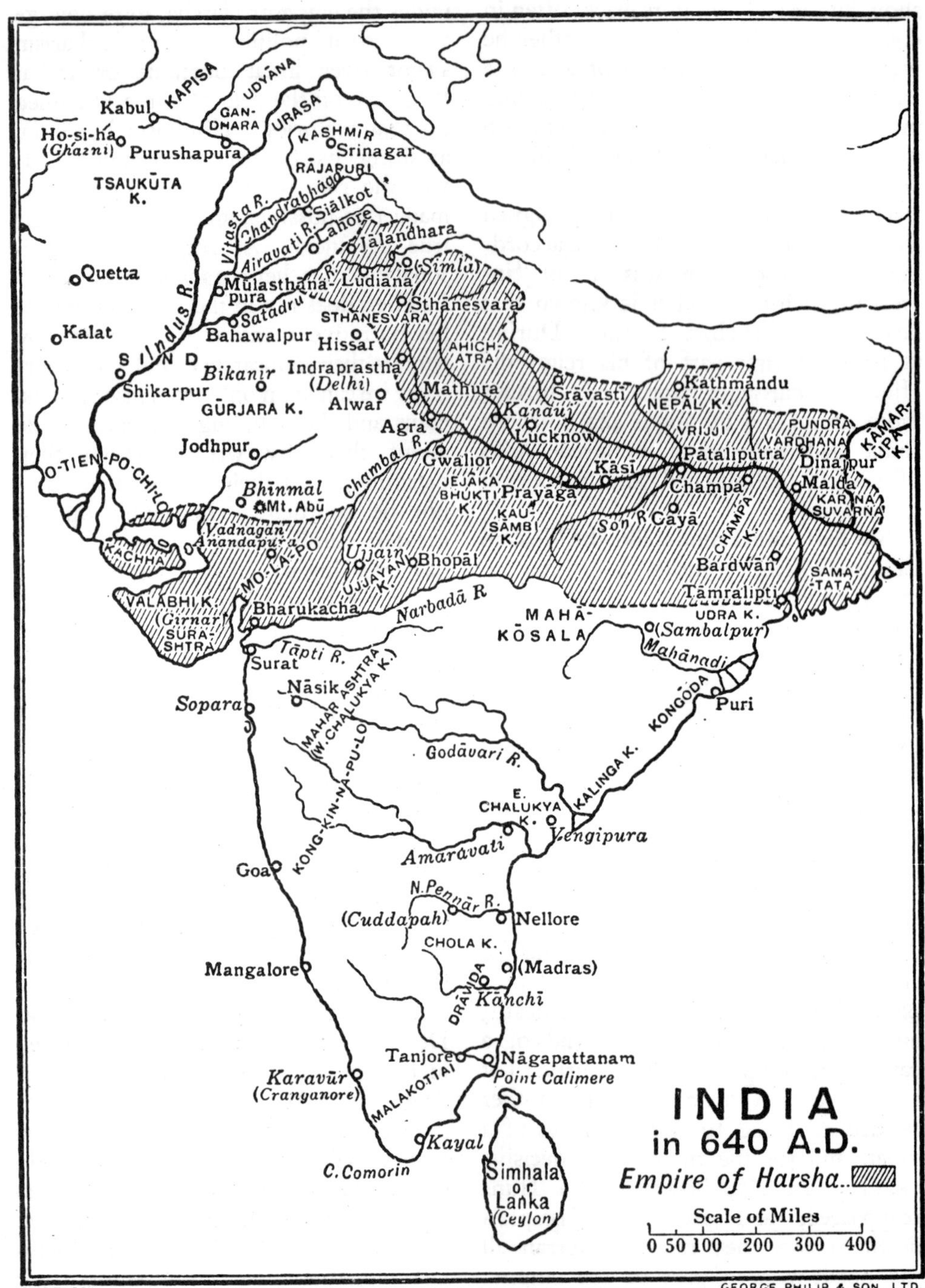

WAXTYPE

GEORGE PHILIP & SON, LTD.

COURTESY OXFORD HISTORY OF INDIA

HARSHA'S EMPIRE

Map showing the extent of King Harsha's territory.

KING HARSHA OF KANAUJ

LAST GREAT EMPEROR OF ANCIENT INDIA

A.D. 606–647

BY CHARLES KINCAID, C.V.O.

IN A.D. 605 Prabhakar Vardhan, raja of Thanesar, died leaving two sons, Rajya and Harsha. The death of Prabhakar was closely followed by the assassination of Rajya by the king of Malwa, Karnasuwarna. At this time Harsha was only sixteen and was about to enter a Buddhist monastery. When the news of Rajya's death reached Thanesar, the chief ministers and magistrates sent for Harsha and called him to the throne. The prince replied modestly that the government of a country was a responsible and difficult office and before accepting it he must consult a statue of Buddha on the banks of the Ganges, already famous for miracles. He went to it and fasted and prayed. The statue assumed a human form and asked what it was that the prince sought. He replied, "I have suffered a great affliction. My father is dead; my brother has been odiously murdered. In the presence of these calamities I humble myself as one of little virtue; nevertheless the people would exalt me to the royal dignity, to fill the high place of my illustrious father. In my trouble I ask your holy counsel."

Buddha answered, "In your former existence you lived in this forest as a hermit and by your earnest diligence and unremitting attention you inherited a power of religious merit, which resulted in your birth as a king's son. Karnasuwarna has overturned the law of Buddha. Now when you succeed to the royal estate, you should in the same proportion exercise towards it the utmost love and pity. If you give your mind to compassionate the condition of the distressed and to cherish them, then before long you shall rule over the five Indies. If you would establish your authority, attend to my instructions and by my secret power you shall receive additional enlightenment, so that not one of your neighbours shall be able to triumph over you."[1]

Acting on this divine advice, Harsha accepted the crown of Thanesar and shortly afterwards inherited that of Kanauj. This he made his capital, probably because of its more central position. From being a quiet, devout youth, he became suddenly a most active and capable soldier. For the

[1] *Beal's Buddhist Records of the Western World. Bk. V, p.* 213.

THE SIGNATURE OF KING HARSHA

CENTRE OF BUDDHIST PILGRIMAGE

Pilgrims entering the Buddha temple at Buddh-Gaya. The temple was standing when Hiuen Tsang visited Harsha at Buddh-Gaya in A.D. 635.

next six years he led his armies from east to west "subduing all who were not obedient. During this time the elephants were not unharnessed, nor were the soldiers unhelmeted."[1] So effectively did he conduct his campaigns that after six years of warfare he was able to reign for thirty years in profound peace. His dominions included the whole Gangetic valley from the mouth of the Ganges and extended to the west as far as the Sutlej, embracing Central India, Gujarat and Kathiawar; his influence was everywhere dominant as far south as the Vindhya mountains. He assumed the title of Emperor of the Five Indies and would gladly have added southern India to his possessions; but here he was foiled by a king as able as himself, namely, Pulakesi II of the Chalukya house. The following passage from the account of the contemporary Chinese traveller Hiuen Tsang (translated into French by M. Julien) describes Pulakesi II's successful opposition.

"The kingdom of Maharashtra has a circumference of 6,000 li. To the west of the capital runs a big river; the circumference of the town is thirty li. The soil is rich and fertile and yields a great harvest of corn. The climate is hot. The manners of the people are simple and honest. They are tall and proud and distant. Whoever does them a kindness can count on their gratitude. But he who does them an injury never escapes their vengeance. If anyone insults them they risk their life to wash out the affront. If anyone in distress begs their help, they forget their own safety in their efforts to assist him. When they have an insult to avenge they never fail to warn their enemy beforehand. In battle they pursue the fugitives, but never kill those who surrender. When a general has lost a battle, they do not inflict on him corporal punishment. They make him dress in women's clothes and thus force him to commit suicide. The State keeps a body of fearless champions. Every time they get ready for a fight they get drunk and, once drunk, a single champion, lance in hand, will challenge ten thousand foes. If he kills anyone as he goes to battle, the law does not punish him. Every time the army sets out on a campaign, the chosen body leads the way with drums beating. Besides these picked troops, there are hundreds of fierce war elephants. When the battle is about to open, the elephants are given strong liquor to drink. They then rush forward and trample down everything underfoot. The king, proud of his soldiers and his war elephants, despises and insults the neighbouring kingdoms. He is of Kshattrya stock; his name is Pulakesi. His views are broad and profound and he dispenses as far as the most distant spots his kindliness and his favours. His subjects serve him with absolute devotion.

"To-day the great king (Harsha) bears from the east to the west his victorious arms; he conquers distant races and makes the nations near him tremble; but those of Pulakesi's kingdom are the only men who have never yielded to him. Although several times he has put himself at the head of all the forces of the Five Indies, although he has called to his aid the bravest generals of all countries, although he has himself marched to punish the men of Maharashtra, he has not yet overcome their resistance. From this fact alone it is possible to judge their warlike habits and customs. The men love study and practise at the same time heresy and truth. There are a hundred monasteries, which contain about five thousand monks. There are a hundred temples

[1] *Buddhist Records of the Western World. Bk. V, p.* 213.

to the gods. The heretics of the different sects are very numerous."

This Hiuen Tsang was the most famous of the Chinese pilgrims, who from time to time made their way to India. One of the earliest was Fa Hian, who was in India from A.D. 405 to 411. Hiuen Tsang reached India in A.D. 630. It had taken him over a year to make the journey from China to Gandhara, and he encountered the gravest dangers. Undaunted he made his way to king Harsha's residence at Ujjain. He spent altogether fifteen years in India; of these he passed eight in Harsha's empire. He has left a striking account of contemporary Indian life.

"The Kshattriyas and Brahmans are cleanly and wholesome in their dress and they live in a homely and frugal way. There are rich merchants, who deal in trinkets. They mostly go barefooted; a few wear sandals. They stain their teeth red or black; they bind up their hair and pierce their ears. They are very particular in their personal cleanliness. All wash before eating; they never use food left over from a former meal. Wooden and stone vessels must be destroyed after use; metal ones must be well polished and rubbed. After eating they cleanse their mouth with a willow stick and wash their hands and mouths."

The ordinary people Hiuen Tsang described as upright and honourable, although naturally frivolous. They were straightforward in commerce and the magistrates were merciful in the administration of justice. The Indians dreaded the retribution of a future state of existence and made light of their present world. They were neither deceitful nor treacherous and they kept alike oaths and promises.[1] In their rules of government there was unusual rectitude, while they behaved with gentleness and sweetness.

Criminals and rebels were few in number and only rarely troublesome. When the laws were broken or there was a rebellion against the ruler, then the matter was carefully sifted and the offenders were punished. Corporal punishment was unknown; but the guilty were not counted as men and were left to live and die without interference. If a man was immoral or unjust or dishonest or a bad son, his nose and ears were cut off and he was expelled from the city to die in the jungle. Other faults were punished by a small fine. Torture was not used to extort confessions. Frank admission by the accused reduced the penalty; but if he obstinately denied the fault he was tried by ordeal.

As the administration was founded on benign principles, wrote Hiuen Tsang, the executive was simple. The families were not entered on registers nor was there any forced labour. The crown lands were divided into four parts. The rents of the first part were for the State treasure. Those of the second were for paying ministers and officers of the crown; the third for rewarding men of genius; those of the fourth were allotted to the religious communities. The merchants circulated freely and ferries and tolls kept the roads and rivers open.

Hiuen Tsang's description of Harsha's army might well have been that of an Indian State fifty years ago:

"The military guard the frontiers and put down disturbances. They mount guard at night round the palace. The soldiers are levied according to the requirements of the service. They are promised certain salaries and publicly enrolled. The royal forces were divided into infantry, cavalry, chariots and

[1] *Beal's Buddhist Records of the Western World* (*quoted by Rawlinson in "India; a short cultural history"*).

FAÇADE OF THE AJANTA CAVES

The entrance to the Ajanta caves which are excavated in the side of a deep ravine. The temples and monasteries of Ajanta date from the time of Asoka (about 273–232 B.C.) to the time of Harsha, when Hindu influence was becoming overwhelmingly strong and Buddhism, despite the piety of the King, was waning.

elephants. The commanding officer rode in a chariot drawn by four horses abreast, his bodyguard around him and a charioteer on either hand. The elephants wore armour plate; the infantry depended chiefly on their long spears and large shields. The army advanced protected by a cavalry screen."[1]

The empire of Harsha struck Hiuen Tsang as extremely prosperous. The people lived well. They sometimes paid their debts in kind, but they could also pay in the gold and silver coins and cowrie shells in circulation. The soil was fertile and highly cultivated. Wheaten cakes, parched grain, sugar, ghi and milk were the staple diet; but fish, venison and mutton were also eaten. Beef, however, was forbidden then as now.

Education was imparted by Brahman preceptors and the student often continued his studies until he was thirty years old. Learning was immensely esteemed and many wealthy men refused honours and high office that they might pass their lives in unbroken study. Hiuen Tsang spent five years in the Nalanda University in Bihar. From all parts of the East students flocked there, but only those who passed an entrance test were allowed to remain. Once admitted the disciple was first treated as a guest and then assigned a place in the monastery. The student was subjected to a severe discipline. He had to live according to the maxims of the Buddhist scriptures and breaches were punished severely. To break the rules of the community was to incur a public rebuke. For a slight fault the student was condemned to silence; for a graver fault he was expelled. Once expelled he could not return to the monastery. Usually he resumed the work that he had done before joining the college.

[1] *Beal's Buddhist Records, pp.* 83, 84, *quoted by Rawlinson in "India."*

WOMAN AND CHILD

One of the best-known paintings from the famous Ajanta Frescoes.

The full course included grammar, mechanics, medicine, logic and metaphysics, and the students were encouraged not only to learn but to discuss and criticise their teachers' conclusions. When a man had acquired a high reputation he was entitled to summon an assembly for discussion. He would then judge the abilities of those who took part in it. Where one of the disputants had distinguished himself by his subtlety and his ornate as well as skilful diction, he would be mounted on an elephant and covered with jewels and conducted by a host of admirers to the gates of the monastery. On the other hand, woe betide the disputant who failed in his argument or whose eloquence did not reach a sufficiently high standard. The audience covered him with mud and threw him into a ditch.

Hiuen Tsang did not go to Harsha's court immediately on his arrival in India. Kumara, king of Assam, sent him a pressing invitation to visit his country and this the pilgrim accepted. Harsha, however, deemed that the eminent Buddhist teacher should have visited his court first. He was encamped near Patna at the time and he sent an order to Kumara, who was his vassal, to send him Hiuen Tsang. Kumara was very reluctant to lose his honoured guest and sent back word that he would willingly give to his suzerain his head, but not his guest. Harsha, however, was in no mood for concessions. "Very well," he replied, "I insist on having your head." This literal interpretation of his words was too much for Kumara. Greatly as he valued the presence of Hiuen Tsang at his court, he valued his life more. He obeyed his overlord's command and accompanied the pilgrim towards Harsha's camp.

On the arrival of the king the emperor forgave him his previous insolence. He received him with courtesy and asked where the Chinese pilgrim was. Kumara had left Hiuen Tsang in his last camp, installed in a temporary palace built especially for him. He explained this to Harsha, who impatiently asked why he had not brought him. Kumara answered with gentle malice that it would not have been fitting to make "The Master of the Law visit first the emperor, great although he was." Harsha took the rebuke in good part and said that next day he would call on the Chinese pilgrim himself. His interview over, Kumara returned to the temporary palace and warned his guest that Harsha had promised to visit Hiuen Tsang the following day, but that he would probably call on him that very night.

THE MONKEYS. FROM THE FRESCOES AT AJANTA

Everything, therefore, should be ready for the emperor's visit. King Kumara's guess proved accurate, for in the first watch of the same night Harsha arrived in great state. He was preceded by thousands of torchbearers and a hundred drums.[1] The sounding of drums on the march was an imperial privilege and Harsha allowed none of the vassal monarchs to enjoy it.

The emperor on meeting Hiuen Tsang prostrated himself before the sage and kissed his feet. Then he asked him why he had not come before, although invited. Hiuen Tsang made suitable excuses and then described the exceeding great merits of his own sovereign the emperor of China. After some time Harsha withdrew and next day Kumara and Hiuen Tsang returned the imperial visit. The emperor went to meet his guest with twenty attendants. After exchanging the customary compliments, Harsha asked Hiuen Tsang whether he had not written a treatise on Buddhism. The pilgrim admitted that he had and produced it. He supported the Mahayana doctrine and such was his ability that he converted to his views the emperor, who until then had been a follower of the Hinayana school of Buddhism. In this change of doctrine Harsha was supported by his widowed sister, an extremely intelligent lady, who listened to the treatise throughout. It must be admitted that the discussion was one-sided; for Devasena, the emperor's previous teacher, had before the arrival of the illustrious foreigner gone on a pilgrimage to Vaisali. He pretended that he wished to see its sacred buildings. The emperor's comment on his conduct was severe but not unjustified: "I have recognised by his behaviour that the masters of his school are alike without knowledge or capacity."

The same day, according to our pilgrim, the emperor sent messages to all parts of his dominion, ordering all those learned in the sacred books to assemble at Kanauj to listen to lectures and, if needs be, to discuss them with the Master of the Law from China. The subsequent gathering must have been the most splendid ever seen at Kanauj. In the last month of that year Hiuen Tsang reached that city. He and Harsha went up the Ganges together and no less than eighteen Indian kings, three thousand holy men, learned in both the Greater and the Lesser Vehicles, two thousand Brahmans and other heretics and a thousand monks from the monastery of Malanda accompanied them. Each of these persons had his own suite of attendants. Some came on elephants, some in palanquins and on all sides were to be seen their standard and banner bearers. To receive his visitors the emperor had had built two enormous buildings roofed with thatch. In the centre rose a mighty statue of Buddha. The rest of the space was allotted to the guests. The emperor's own camp was at a distance of five li. On the first day of the assembly he had a gold statue of Buddha placed on his largest elephant. Then assuming the garb of the god Indra, Harsha walked, a fly whisk in his hand, on the elephant's right. His vassal Kumara, in the garb of the god Brahma, walked on the elephant's left. He carried a parasol, made of rich cloth. Both sovereigns wore tiaras, from which hung flowers and ribbons decked with precious stones. Behind them walked two other elephants laden with baskets of rare flowers, which their attendants showered down as they walked.

Hiuen Tsang, the chief officer of State and the feudal princes found seats on three hundred elephants collected for that purpose, and led by Harsha and Kumara they went in procession to the great buildings erected for the guests.

[1] *Julien's "Vie et voyages de Hiuen Tsang," p.* 237.

The gold statue of Buddha was placed on a costly throne and Harsha, the pilgrim and the chief guests, did homage to it. Thereafter food was served to the whole vast multitude and presents distributed. Then the emperor invited Hiuen Tsang to preside over the conference. The Chinese saint had written a discourse, but he did not read it himself. He ordered one of the attendant monks, Vidyabhadra, to do so. He also had a copy affixed to the main entrance. Underneath he wrote: "If anyone finds in the document a single error and shows himself capable of refuting it, I shall cut off my head to prove to him my gratitude." No one, however, dared take up the challenge.

Harsha was delighted with Hiuen Tsang's assurance and accepted everything said by him as gospel truth. Next day he had the pilgrim brought to the foot of the golden statue of Buddha and honoured him then and for several days afterwards; but if these attentions pleased the Chinese saint, they were by no means pleasing to the followers of the Lesser Vehicle or of Hinduism. They began to plot against Hiuen Tsang's life. The vigilance of Harsha's police was too great for the discontented sectaries. The police discovered the plots and informed their master. He thereupon issued the following proclamation:

"The partisans of error darken the truth, as I have long seen. They say evil of the holy doctrine and unworthily seduce the people; but for sages of superior merit, how could their lies be discovered? The Master of the Law of China, who is gifted with rare intelligence and whose conduct commands respect and esteem, travels in the kingdom to uproot mistakes, to throw light on the Sublime Law and to save mortals from the darkness that envelops them. Nevertheless the partisans of the most monstrous heresies instead of blushing with shame dare to weave odious plots and to threaten his life. To tolerate such conduct would be to promise immunity to the most horrible crimes.

"If in the multitude a single man attacks or wounds the Master of the Law, I shall cut off his head; and I shall cut out the tongue of anyone who speaks evil of him or abuses him. All those who trusting to my justice wish to explain their views with moderation, will enjoy perfect liberty to do so."[1]

In spite of the indulgence promised in the second paragraph of the imperial proclamation, the partisans of error decamped with all speed; and for no less than eighteen days no one dared to open his mouth or begin a religious discussion.

As a result of Hiuen Tsang's preaching and probably still more of the imperial favour that he enjoyed, countless multitudes abandoned the doctrine of the Lesser Vehicle and accepted that of the Greater Vehicle. Harsha would have showered countless gifts on the Chinese sage—ten thousand gold pieces, thirty thousand silver pieces and all sorts of precious clothes. The emperor's eighteen feudal chiefs would have done likewise, but Hiuen Tsang with rare moderation refused all presents. Nevertheless the emperor insisted on accompanying him part of the way to Prayag, which was the pilgrim's next goal.

It is unnecessary to follow Hiuen Tsang on his remaining journeys. It will suffice to say that he eventually reached China safely and there died a natural death in his own land. The emperor was not so fortunate. He had always been a Buddhist, but at the beginning of his reign he had been eminently tolerant.

In public he worshipped the Hindu gods Shiva and Surya as well as Buddha. The visit of Hiuen Tsang seems to have

1 *Julien's "Vie et voyages de Hiuen Tsang."*

MARTIN HURLIMANN

THE GREAT BUDDHA OF AJANTA

The colossal seated Buddha in Cave No. 1 at Ajanta. It is probable that this cave was constructed during Harsha's reign.

had the unfortunate effect of increasing his religious enthusiasm and lessening his tolerance. The result was that the persecuted Hindus and so-called Buddhist heretics retaliated by plots against Harsha's life. On one occasion a fire broke out in the thatched pavilion over the palace gateway; and when the emperor went to see what had happened, a man rushed out, knife in hand. The officers were paralysed with fright or may possibly have sympathised with the would-be murderer. In any case they made no attempt to stop him. Harsha, with consummate coolness, seized, disarmed him and handed him over to the magistrates, directing them not to harm him. Afterwards he questioned the miscreant himself. "What have I done," he asked, "that you attempted such a deed?" The man confessed that he had been hired by the Brahmans, who were jealous of the partiality shown by the emperor to the Buddhists. The conspirators had planned to fire the assembly-room and in the subsequent confusion to assassinate Harsha. The fire had not spread as the traitors had hoped and so they had sent the assassin to stab Harsha without further delay.

Harsha's reign is doubly interesting. We have a contemporary account of him as he appeared to an enlightened foreigner of the time; but he claims our attention also in that he is the last great emperor of ancient India. Although separated from some of them by many centuries and not connected with any of them by blood, Harsha was really the successor of Chandragupta and Asoka and of the wonderful series of Gupta autocrats.

I have mentioned how in his later years Harsha grew more fanatical and this was the cause of his murder. After Hiuen Tsang's departure he sent a Brahman envoy to the Chinese court. In return the Chinese emperor sent a distinguished mandarin to Kanauj. Harsha loaded the ambassador with presents; and the envoy was on his way back to China when Harsha's minister, Arjuna, organised a revolution. He killed his master and tried to overtake the mandarin and seize his wealth. The latter escaped into Nepal. There he complained to the king of Thibet, who was the son-in-law of the Chinese emperor. A Thibetan army at once took the field, invaded India, defeated Arjuna and put him to death.

Harsha left no male heirs and on his death darkness settled on India, a darkness that endured two centuries. When it lifted India had completely changed. Buddhism had all but gone, Hinduism was once more supreme. The rulers, too, of the new India were as different as possible from the Mauryas, the Guptas and Harsha. The subcontinent was split up into small kingdoms dominated by strange, fierce, romantic clans, who in no way resembled the Indians of Harsha's time. During the "black out" a flood of Central Asian warriors, Huns, Gurjaras and others, had swept over India and had been absorbed into Hinduism. They called themselves Rajputs, or sons of kings, and the Brahman genealogists skilfully traced their origin to the various heroes of the Hindu epics; but so far from being unwilling to take life, the only occupations deemed fit by them for a warrior were the battle and the chase. Still they approved their new genealogies, provided they were allowed to lead their lives as they wished and to die gloriously on the field of battle. They regarded themselves as the appointed defenders of India and right well they did their duty. In fact, they have profoundly influenced the course of Indian history down to the present day. Mediæval and modern India, in fact, began with the emergence of the Rajput clans.

DUTUGEMUNU—THE GREAT HERO

A portrait carved out of stone and weathered by time, of the national hero of Ceylon, who expelled the invaders and brought peace to his people.

DUTUGEMUNU

CEYLON'S NATIONAL HERO

161–137 B.C.

BY DENIS CLARK

IN 543 B.C., when the prince Vijaya sailed south from Bengal to find and colonise Ceylon, he deserted the mass of fair-skinned northern invaders and became separated from them both by sea and a strong wedge of dark, warlike tribes. On the island his descendants' position was never too desperate so long as they kept their old fighting traditions, exercised by forays against the aboriginal "Yakko" and "Naga" tribesmen. But once local peace was secure they began to devote themselves only too diligently to their natural genius for agriculture. They brought rice-growing with them (if the aboriginals cultivated at all, it can only have been *chena* work, burning off patches of forest, sowing, reaping, and then moving on), they excavated great tanks. Under their care the fertile island gave splendid return of rich crops. But meanwhile the Sinhalese people completely forgot to keep watch against those who beheld it with envy across the narrow sea. When Asoka sent his son Mahinda to convert Ceylon to Buddhism, the gentle, *ahimsa* doctrine, newly revived by the war-weary despot, undermined their last powers of defence. The ranks of the Buddhist *bhikkus* were crowded, but for soldiers their kings imported mercenary troops from the mainland.

It was small wonder, then, that in 237 B.C. they suffered their first invasion. Sena and Guttika, leaders of "Damila" legions installed for the island's defence, rebelled and with help from their kinsmen in Malabar themselves took the throne of Ceylon. Only after twenty years did King Asela manage to drive them away. But during his reign the Damilas came back again under their raja, Elara. Asela was slain and Elara settled himself to rule at the royal city of Anuradhapura in the north.

Elara styled himself raja of Madura and the Cholas, but the "Damilas" (Tamils) he led, although consistently referred to under this term in the *Mahawansa* (Ceylon's historical Pali record kept by the monks), actually included warriors from several different martial Hindu tribes, from Malabar chiefly but also perhaps from as far north as Cuttack. They seem to have been quite uninfluenced by Buddhism or Asoka's widespread crusade of pacifism and tolerance. Before them the wretched Sinhalese fled to the jungle-clad south, or stayed behind in their towns, unwilling subjects to Elara. Once more the ancient faith of the Brahmins prevailed in Ceylon and, though, as appears from their writings, Elara did not persecute its monks, the new and popular teaching suffered eclipse.

Down in the far south-east, in the province known as Rohana, reigned a little king who was nephew to Devenampiya Tissa, the ruler who had received the monk-prince Mahinda, planting the sacred Bodhi Tree sent by Asoka. This petty king, Kakavanna ("Crow-coloured") Tissa by name, was son to a prince forced by a palace intrigue to fly from his brother's court, to carve out his own tiny kingdom in the south-eastern jungles. His city of Mahagama was to be the cradle of the revolt which drove the Damila invaders out of Ceylon; but not through Kakavanna, who seems to have been a monarch of very poor spirit or very superior caution. He made no attempt whatever to re-establish his race's dominion. Rather than that, he paid tribute to the usurper and endeavoured to make his sons promise "never to take up arms against the Damilas."

These sons were two, Gemunu and Saddha Tissa. Of these Gemunu, the elder, exhibited manly characteristics notably lacking in both his father and brother. Perhaps he inherited these from Vijaya, grandson of the warrior-bandit, "the Lion," from whom the Sinhalese people derive their name. Or they may have come from his mother Vihara-Devi, daughter of a valiant and singularly ruthless chief. At his father's command Gemunu willingly promised always to honour the monks and to love and live in peace with his brother Saddha. But when the king sought to extort the pacifist oath, he hurled the food (on which it was to be sworn) on the ground and ran in a rage from the room. To his mother who sought him and found him bent up on his bed he complained: "How can I stretch myself when these accursed Damilas confine us so closely!"

In adolescence Gemunu's whole aim was centred on raising an army of vengeance. Before his birth such a destiny had been augured. The pregnant queen had suffered from curious cravings, one of which entailed a clandestine journey by a warrior, Velusumana, who had entered the raja's palace, stolen his war-horse and cut off the head of his army's commander-in-chief. The head was brought back for the queen to use as a footstool while "*she drank the water which washed the blood from Velusumana's sword.*" The

ELSPETH HUXLEY

THE ANCIENT CAPITAL

Ruins of a palace and a small dagaba in the background. Dutugemunu's most famous monument. Ruanweli was of the same construction. Now all that is left is a crumbling mound.

ELSPETH HUXLEY

MOONSTONE AT ANURADHAPURA

Semicircular moonstones paved the entrances to temples at Anuradhapura. Because the worshippers went in barefooted, the stones are little worn, and the carved animals are wonderfully clear.

Mahawansa abounds in such quaint legends as this, but even so it is generally acknowledged as a fairly trustworthy account of historical events. There seems little doubt that prophecies of a "Deliverer" existed, which applied to Gemunu and which the young prince fulfilled. Another auspicious event was the capture of a young elephant of the "royal" caste, which was named Kandula and was fated to play a large part in Gemunu's ultimate victory.

Young Gemunu gathered about him ten young chiefs, distinguished for valour and prowess. Through these he raised his own army, despite the king's disapproval. Regular troops had been maintained as a guard on the northern frontier, at Dighavapi near the great east-flowing river Mahawelliganga, which served as a boundary between Damila and Sinhalese kingdoms. In fear that his warlike son might provoke new trouble between the two races, King Kakavanna sent him to keep watch there, against such of their unwelcome neighbours as crossed the river to raid. He was content to go on paying tribute but Gemunu grew wildly impatient. He implored his father to allow him to take an army against Elara, and, when he would not consent, sent him an insulting token, a woman's bracelet, with the bitter advice to wear it, since his behaviour fitted him for the part of a woman.

This provocation so enraged the nerve-ridden king that he ordered his eldest son to be bound with chains and prevented from further mischief. But Gemunu escaped and fled up to the mountains which stand in the island's southern centre, called at that time "the Malaya." There Gemunu, henceforward known to all men as Dutugemunu,

GUARD STONE

This "Naga-rajah," carved dwarf and elephants is a typical sculpture of Anuradhapura.

which means "the unfilial," dwelt in exile for some years. Legends about his presence and doings still exist in the valley of Kotmale, now surrounded by tea estates. Peasants there tell tales of his exploits, and even recently would display weapons and furniture which, they said, he had used. For them, as for all Sinhalese, he is still the national hero, an epic figure of ancient chivalry, comparable with Europe's Bayard or Roland. His solitude was only broken by the news of his father's death. Saddha Tissa, discounting his oath of fraternal affection, had seized the throne, the queen-mother's person, and the "state-elephant Kandula."

Without hesitation Dutugemunu returned to lay claim to his rights. His reception was not encouraging. His ten chiefs had been sworn by the late king not to take part in any such family strife as had now arisen. His brother had whole-hearted support from the monks, with whom Saddha Tissa had always been popular; and Dutugemunu, with what poor following he was able to muster, suffered a defeat of arms. Nothing discouraged, he gave what last trinkets were left him, a pair of gold earrings, to two penurious *theras* and went into battle again. This time he was more successful. Saddha came out to meet him, mounted on Kandula. Dutugemunu rode with his scanty troops, himself engaging the elephant. Enraged by the swift-turning horse and rider, Kandula set off after them, rushing recklessly under a tree. The *howdah* with Saddha inside it crashed into a branch. Saddha fell on to the ground with its fragments, and ran for his life to a neighbouring monastery where the monks gave him shelter. They smuggled him out past his victorious brother, prone on a bier, with a monk's yellow robe draped to hide him. Dutugemunu saw through the ruse but remembered his oath to his father to honour the monks. He let them take him away.

The elder prince's next move, after his triumphal entry into the city, was to call an assembly of monks and warriors with the purpose of holding a general council of war. In the midst of the banquet accompanying this conclave an ancient *thera* entered, leading one "in rags and shame," the treacherous Saddha, now penitent and come to beg for forgiveness. Dutugemunu freely gave it, thereupon delivering an outspoken speech to the monks on the encouragement shown by them to his erring brother. Much mortified by such straight words as had never yet smitten their ears, the Order suggested he should lay some penance upon them. The young man agreed. A certain number, he said, should accompany him and his army, giving them spiritual support against the Damilas.

He was crowned. Wasting no time, he mustered his troops. With a holy relic in the mast of his war-chariot, Dutugemunu set forth, sending men ahead to clear a road for his passage through the dense local jungle. His way passed close by to the ancient forest temple of Kataragama, sacred to Skanda, where, in spite of his Buddhist upbringing, the new king called halt to pay reverence. At the ford of Mahiyanganga the first engagement took place and the Damila outposts retired. The Sinhalese progress was held up by forts on the opposite bank of the Mahawelliganga, but the chief of one fortress was decoyed from its shelter and captured, the southern army obtaining a footing at last in the enemy territory. One after the other Elara's forts, lined on the river's north bank, fell to Dutugemunu's assault. One pitched battle was fought in the open, sword, spear, war-quoit and arrow all playing their part, while the chariots dashed to and fro, and the elephants led by Kandula broke through the Damila soldiers. At last Nalika, the local commander, was slain. His army broke and was driven into the marshes. Dutugemunu's warriors pressed on.

Several fortified towns now stood in their way. At Vijitapura a long siege took place. Kandula led a valiant attack on the gate, but the rampart's resourceful defenders poured boiling pitch from a turret, temporarily putting that doughty beast *hors de combat.* While its wounds were dressed fires, vinegar, hammers and crowbars established a breach, and at length the gate was thrown down. Vijitapura was taken and the tank nearby dyed red with the blood of the slain.

ELSPETH HUXLEY

THE BRAZEN PALACE

These great stone pillars are all that remains of Dutugemunu's famous Brazen Palace, which originally was nine storeys high and contained 1,600 gilded pillars.

Dismayed by Dutugemunu's successes Elara sent over to India for his nephew Bhalluka to aid him with reinforcements. But before Bhalluka had come, Dutugemunu's army broke through the earthworks raised to repel its progress and marched on Anuradhapura. Elara himself now came out to meet him, leading his garrison troops. Dutugemunu gave orders by beat of drum that no one but he alone should fight with the Damila raja. The two war-elephants circled, charging and thrusting, outside the walls of the city, while the men on their backs in the open battle-howdahs cast javelins at each other. At last Kandula's tusks pierced deep in the side of the other. As it sank to the ground Dutugemunu's spear struck the raja a mortal blow.

This incident, so full of chivalry, was completed when the victor caused a great tomb to be raised where Elara had died.

No music should ever play there, he decreed; and many centuries later the kings of Ceylon still dismounted to honour that place. Dutugemunu entered the ancient city, which had been his ancestors' capital. But his campaign was not yet over. Bhalluka had brought an army from Malabar, which now marched down to attack. Dutugemunu led his soldiers to meet it. Another great battle was fought, in which the king all but lost his life. Bhalluka was slain by an arrow shot from the bow of Phoosadeva, a chief who rode with Dutugemunu on Kandula's back.

After this peace was restored. The Damilas quitted Ceylon and Dutugemunu reigned there wisely and long. Records of dates are not always exact but it seems that he spent about twenty years as a ruler, during which time he performed many good and some notable works. He furnished his people with hospitals and free food for the aged and needy. He built monasteries for the monks. But his chief fame lies in the mighty buildings he raised to honour the Buddha. The "Brazen Palace," nine-storeyed and standing on sixteen hundred pillars of stone, was built to fulfil a prophecy made long ago, that, "*King Tissa's son, the Great Deliverer, shall build a splendid dagaba and a most magnificent pagoda, such as never before have been seen.*" It was sheathed from top to bottom in sheets of bright, burnished copper, and its rooms were furnished in most extravagant fashion. "*Even the bowl for the rinsing of feet was of gold.*" Its chambers were frescoed with wonderful carvings and paintings. In it the Order took up their abode: *arahats* on the verge of Nirvana using the topmost rooms, novices down at the bottom. Admittedly much of its splendour, its coral balconies, its pearl-draped halls and myriad jewel-carved flowers, are sufficiently conventionalised to make one suspect its monk-recorders of using the "Brazen Palace" as a peg on which to hang a lavish example for the eyes of less generous monarchs. But its sixteen hundred stone pillars stand to this day, a wonder for visiting pilgrims.

After the palace Dutugemunu set himself to the building of the vast Ruanweli Dagaba, "the Shrine of the Golden Dust." The *Mahawansa* describes its erection in detail, telling how its design was derived (though Devenampiya Tissa had already exploited the dome-shape) from the form of a bubble; how from Kashmir, Benares and Persia, and as far away as the cities where the Greeks lived, the king summoned monks to its foundation ceremony: and how his proposed site was of so vast a perimeter that a *thera* warned him he would never live to see the dagaba's completion. All the work done was to be at his own expense. No compulsory labour was used. In it were bestowed the Buddha's own sacred begging-bowl, with so many of his bones that no such collection of relics had ever been brought together in one place until now.

Before it was finished a fever struck the king down. In dread that the *thera's* words might come true, he sent for Saddha, his brother, to come from where he looked after the excavation of tanks and hurry on with the building. Months passed however, and, though the dagaba towered one hundred and eighty feet high, still it was not completed. The king fell into such a state of nervous distress lest he might never see it finished that the monks and Saddha were forced to resort to a ruse to make his mind easy. They said the dagaba was finished.

At once, to their consternation, Dutugemunu insisted on going to view it. They begged for a few days' grace to prepare his way, and set desperately to work, completing the dome with a painted cap of white linen and a gilded spire of bamboo.

So, when Dutugemunu was carried there in his palanquin, his sickness-dimmed eyes could not perceive the deception. He died contented, lying midway between his two great memorials, the "Brazen Palace," and the Ruanweli Dagaba. Though the Damilas soon returned to the island after his death maltreating his race and tearing down his fine palace, whose foundations only are left, the Ruanweli Dagaba still looms tremendous in the jungle.

SKANDA ON HIS PEACOCK

Skanda, the six-armed war god: his temple at Katuagamu in the south-east jungle was endowed by Dutugemunu to commemorate his victory over the Damilas.

KING PARAKRAMA OF CEYLON

This massive stone image of Parakrama, holding the book of Law inscribed on palm leaves, can be seen amid the ruins of the city of Polonnarua.

PARAKRAMA BAHU THE GREAT

CEYLON'S MOST ILLUSTRIOUS RULER

REIGNED A.D. 1153–1186

BY F. A. BEAUMONT

It is nearly eight hundred years since Parakrama Bahu reigned in Ceylon, but his colossal statue at Polonnarua is still revered by the Sinhalese as the memorial of the most illustrious ruler their race has ever known—as brave as Dutugemunu and as pious as Devanampiya Tissa.

He rose to manhood in a country torn by civil wars and at the mercy of invaders. Authority was openly flouted, religion had fallen into decay. But before he died in A.D. 1186 he had united the entire island into a realm that could defy its foreign enemies; law and order had been established, and the Buddhist faith restored throughout Ceylon.

When Parakrama Bahu was born, four "lords of the land" held sway over "Lanka" (Ceylon), according to a native chronicle. Vikrama Bahu ruled the region known as the "King's Country" with its capital at Polonnarua, two brothers, Siri Vallabha and Siri Megha, divided Ruhuna between them, while the "Southern Country" was in the

A FLORAL ALTAR

The curved pillars surrounding this altar for flowers in the ruins of Polonnarua are unique in Sinhalese Art. The altar and pillars are enclosed in a stone post-and-rail fence.

CIRCULAR RELIC HOUSE AT POLONNARUA

On the walls of this Ota-dagé (relic-house) which surround the central dagaba are carved floral patterns as well as dwarfs and heraldic lions.

power of a third brother, Manabharana, the father of Parakrama Bahu.

Not one of these four overlords made any more attempt to govern than was necessary to extort heavier and heavier taxes from their oppressed subjects, "even as the mill squeezes juice from the sugar cane." Vikrama Bahu's tyranny did not spare even the priests, who fled to Ruhuna with the sacred tooth and bowl relics of Buddha after he confiscated the lands dedicated to their creed. Crime and disorder were rife; wandering bands of soldiers plundered and burned village after village, servants rose against their masters, and workers seized arms and went out on the highways to rob travellers.

Parakrama Bahu was born at Punkhagama in the "Southern Country." Soothsayers at his father's palace foretold that he would become a prince blessed by fortune, and would conquer not only the whole of Lanka but all India as well. The boy was accordingly trained from early childhood for the rôle of a great prince. He learnt both the arts of war and the laws of Buddhism, studied theology, medicine, poetry and music, became skilled in the use of sword and bow, and in the management of elephant and horse. Tales of the heroes of older times were read to him and aroused in him a burning ambition to rule over all Lanka and free his beloved country from the anarchy into which it had fallen.

His father died while he was still a boy, and his uncle Siri Megha became lord of the "Southern Country." Parakrama Bahu went to live for some time with his other uncle, Siri Vallabha, who now ruled the whole of Ruhuna. When he grew up, the young prince returned to the "Southern Country" and lived at Siri Megha's court.

Parakrama Bahu's restless ambition made him very dissatisfied with his lot. He knew that on the death of Siri Megha he would succeed to the rule of the "Southern Country," but he was far from content with the prospect of spending the rest of his days as the lord of a minor principality.

He determined to bring all the people of Lanka under his sway, and to restore to the island all its ancient greatness and prosperity. But how was this formidable task to be accomplished?

He would have to conquer both Ruhuna and the "King's Country." Which should he attempt first? Ruhuna presented fewer difficulties. On the other hand, there was an old saying that he who reigned at Polonnarua, the capital of the "King's Country," was the true king of the Sinhalese. Moreover, Vikrama Bahu, its warlike and vigorous ruler, had died, leaving the throne to his weak, irresolute son, Gaju Bahu, of whom even his own father had said "he can neither get what he has not, nor keep that which he has."

Eventually, Parakrama decided upon the bolder course of overthrowing Gaju Bahu and seizing the "King's Country," before advancing against Ruhuna.

But first it would be necessary to discover the strength of his opponent's position. What forces were at his command? What were his resources in money and grain? Was he liked by his people, or could they be persuaded to rebel against him?

Parakrama Bahu might have sent agents into the "King's Country" to obtain this information for him, but he knew that in order to find out all he wanted to know, he would have to play the part of a spy himself. So at dead

CARVED WITH THE LIONS OF CEYLON

In contrast to the circular building illustrated on page 56 this relic house, also at Polonnarua, is square in shape. Its base carries an animal frieze.

of night he stole out of his uncle's palace, eluded the guards stationed to watch the roads, and met a number of his followers at an appointed place near Badulla.

They went on to Batalagoda, where the governor of the district became suspicious and tried to detain Parakrama Bahu while word was sent to Siri Megha. Parakrama Baru had the governor killed. Siri Megha now began to fear that an untoward incident might precipitate a crisis with the "King's Country" and dispatched troops with orders to capture the young prince and bring him back. But Parakrama Bahu made a swift detour which enabled him to cross the frontier into the "King's Country" before Siri Megha's soldiers could reach him—though it is said that he twice narrowly escaped death at the hands of his uncle's spies.

Gaja Bahu was angered and perplexed by the presence of his impetuous young visitor. He assembled a conference of his ministers and, after much anxious discussion, it was decided that it would be unwise to offend Parakrama Bahu. Perhaps he had come to complain against the rule of Siri Megha, and in any case it would be more politic to assume for the time being that this was his motive. So Gaja Bahu sent costly gifts to the young prince, then went out himself to receive him with all due ceremony.

Parakrama Bahu became a guest in the royal palace. He seemed to have no other concern than to enjoy the pleasures of the court, and such was his friendliness and charm of manner that before long Gaja Bahu had ceased to suspect him of intriguing against his power. But meanwhile Parakrama Bahu lost no chance of learning all he could about the strength of his host's position. On hunting expeditions, while he apparently had no other thought than for the delights of the chase, he was taking exact note of the country's defences and the stations of the guards. It is said that he was in the habit of going to and fro in the streets with a fiery-spirited elephant and then pretending that it chased him into the houses of men of high rank, whose friendship he courted and won by splendid presents; also that he talked freely with every man he met, learning his character, and the measure of his loyalty or disloyalty to Gaja Bahu.

Nor were his followers idle in spying out the land. They disguised themselves as traders, musicians, snake-dancers, physicians and monks. Many people of importance received them into their homes as teachers of religion. They got all the information they could, and overlooked no opportunity to encourage discontent with the rule of Gaja Bahu.

Parakrama Bahu became so popular with all classes that Gaja Bahu began to grow jealous. His bravery, in particular, aroused admiration wherever he went. It is recorded for example that on one occasion he was being carried through Polonnarua on his palanquin when a wild buffalo charged along the road, killing or wounding all in its path. His bearers fled in terror, but Parakrama Bahu rose from his palanquin and shouted at the buffalo so loudly that it turned and ran away.

When he knew more about the "King's Country" than Gaja Bahu did himself, Parakrama Bahu returned to the court of Siri Megha who now had grown very old and soon afterwards died. Parakrama Bahu succeeded him and began to plan war against Gaja Bahu. But first he resolved to make his own country prosperous and orderly for the coming struggle.

Realising that large stores of food might be needed for a prolonged campaign, he began transforming great tracts of wild, uncultivated land into rice-fields and groves of fruit-trees.

THE GIANT BUDDHA

Twice the natural size of a man, this giant statue of Buddha stands amid the ruins of the "house of eight relics" at Polonnarua.

MARTIN HURLIMANN

THE LAST GLORIES

The Thuparama: this is a brick temple built in the later days of Parakrama, when the glories of Polonnarua were on the wane.

The irrigation system was poor and faulty; many old tanks were choked with weed and jungle or had crumbled into ruins. Parakrama Bahu cleared and repaired them, and built many new ones, obtaining supplies of water for them either by damming rivers or digging canals from them.

He reorganised the administration of the country. Hitherto, two ministers had shared this task between them. To ensure a more efficient collection of the bigger revenue needed for war purposes, Parakrama Bahu placed the royal villages and "all the lands of great value" in the charge of a third minister and appointed officials in all districts who had to render a full account of all taxes they obtained.

Parakrama Bahu meanwhile had been assembling and drilling an army of invasion. Youths of noble family were trained in his palace as its officers. Thousands of soldiers were enrolled and armed, including regiments of Tamils, and probably of savage Veddahs from the jungle as well. Manœuvres and mock battles were held throughout the countryside. Troops were stationed at all strategic points.

He required now only a pretext for declaring war and this was not long in forthcoming. Gaja Bahu had invited to his court a number of foreign princes. Parakrama Bahu, in real or simulated anger, protested that one of these might inherit the "King's Country" on Gaja Bahu's death, though not one of the royal visitors was a Buddhist.

After having carefully planned his campaign, Parakrama Bahu opened hostilities by annexing Dumbara, and some of the nearby hill country. In the fighting which followed, his generals won battle after battle, the area of intensest conflict being what is now known as the Matale District. Finally, Parakrama Bahu advanced on Polonnarua. It is said that the gates of the capital were opened to his army by spies he had left behind. Whether this was so or not, Parakrama Bahu managed to storm Polonnarua and capture Gaja Bahu, whom he held as a prisoner in his palace.

Disobeying Parakrama Bahu's stern orders, the victorious army began to loot and riot in the streets of the capital. Gaja Bahu appealed for help to Manabharana, who had succeeded his father, Siri Vallabha, as ruler of Ruhuna. Manabharana joined his army to what was left of Gaja Bahu's and inflicted a severe defeat on Parakrama Bahu's forces, then set Gaja Bahu at liberty. But Gaja Bahu soon found that he was in a worse plight than before, for Manabharana now plotted to seize his throne, and was trying to kill him by poisoning his food. The king implored Parakrama Bahu to come to his rescue; war broke out afresh, the king fled into hiding, and this time Parakrama Bahu triumphed over Manabharana and those of the king's generals who were aiding him.

Priests from Gaja Bahu now came to Parakrama Bahu with a bold request. The king was too ill to live long and had no sons to succeed him. Would Parakrama Bahu allow him to reign for the little that remained of his days, and in return Gaja Bahu would leave him the throne? It says much for Parakrama Bahu's generous and noble nature that he at once granted this plea and withdrew to his own country.

Manabharana now sent gifts to Gaja Bahu and tried to persuade him into an

ELSPETH HUXLEY

POLONNARUA—THE COUNCIL CHAMBER

The terrace of the Council Chamber is covered with carvings of elephants and dwarfs. The latter motif runs through much Sinhalese sculpture of the 12th century.

HOUSE OF EIGHT RELICS ELSPETH HUXLEY

All that is left of what is perhaps the most famous of the relic houses—two chambers in an outer enclosure with a standing Buddha at one end.

alliance against his deliverer. But Gaja Bahu rejected his overtures, went to a vihara—a Buddhist monastery—and made a public announcement that Parakrama Bahu would inherit his country. He caused these words to be inscribed on stone so that after his death there could be no dispute as to his intention.

It was not long before he died, and Parakrama Bahu hurried to Polonnarua and was crowned. Meanwhile, a group of ministers in the capital had sent an urgent summons to Manabharana. In the fierce war that followed, the issue was for some time in doubt, but ultimately Parakrama Bahu triumphed, and Manabharana fled to his own country and died.

The victor was now crowned a second time as the monarch of all Ceylon, and Parakrama Bahu entered upon his long reign from A.D. 1153 to 1186 that was to justify by its achievements in peace and war his title of "the Great."

Three years after he ascended the throne, Sugala Devi, the mother of Manabharana, organised a revoit in Ruhuna. Parakrama Bahu is said to have "smiled sweetly" when he heard that she was making ready for war, but it was only with great difficulty, after a long and arduous campaign in which thousands of his soldiers perished, that he succeeded in crushing the rebellion, and capturing Sugala Devi. The tooth and bowl relics were taken from her charge and sent to Polonnarua, where a magnificent Feast of Lights was held to celebrate the victory.

In the twelfth year of his reign, Parakrama Bahu showed that when the interests and prestige of Ceylon were menaced, he was not afraid even to send an army overseas to defend them.

Trouble arose with the king of Aramanna—a country in the south of Burma which for a long time had been on the friendliest terms with Ceylon. Enemies of Parakrama Bahu spread false reports about him at the court of Aramanna. For this or other reasons, the king began to insult Parakrama Bahu's ambassadors, stopped the trade in elephants with Ceylon, and forbade Sinhalese ships to call at his ports. Finally, he enraged Parakrama Bahu by capturing a princess on her way from Ceylon to the king of Cambodia.

Parakrama Bahu appointed a general, Kit Nuvaragiri, in command of an expeditionary force which embarked in a fleet assembled at Paluvaktota, on the coast north of Trincomalee. The southwest monsoon had begun; but the fleet sailed, and a landing party stormed the city of Kusumiya—the modern Cosmin on the River Pegu. After five months' heavy fighting, the invading army triumphed, the king of Aramanna was killed, and the peace terms included a grant of land to Kit Nuvaragiri which is recorded in an inscription on a rock at Devanagala in the Kegalla District of Ceylon.

War in southern India followed about two years later. Kulasekhara, the king of Chola, invaded Pandya. The king of Pandya, Parakrama Pandya, sent an urgent appeal for help to Ceylon. Parakrama Bahu responded by immediately dispatching an army under his general, Lankapura. Before it arrived at the coast, however, Pandya was killed, and the Cholas had occupied his capital, Madura.

The Sinhalese army landed and fought battle after battle with the Cholas in the country around Ramnad. After a long and arduous campaign, during which they erected a fortress called Parakramapura, they defeated the Chola king, and crowned Vira Pandya, son of the Pandyan king, in Madura. Some of the Chola prisoners were sent to Ceylon and put to work on repairing the Ruanweli Dagaba—the Sinhalese had not forgotten that this shrine of Buddhist relics had been ruined by the Cholas during their earlier domination of the island.

The Sinhalese chronicle *Mahavansa* records further triumphs by Lankapura, but these are uncertain, for Chola annals declare that later the Sinhalese army was defeated and the heads of Lankapura and his officers nailed to the gates of Madura.

By A.D. 1165 Parakrama Bahu was able to devote himself mainly to the arts of peace. Hitherto, he had been chiefly concerned with the problems facing a brave and skilful general intent on suppressing civil war in his country, unifying it, and making it powerful enough to resist the threat of foreign invasions. Nevertheless, he had not allowed the turmoil of war to prevent him from improving the internal administration of his country. Immediately he gained the throne, he had begun to introduce the reforms he had tried out with success during his earlier rule of the "Southern Country." He had divided the island into twelve provinces, each under the charge of a governor; eighty-four rulers of smaller districts were also appointed, and chiefs with powers of military and civil jurisdiction controlled the borders.

Inscriptions of Polonnarua reveal particulars of the council he had created to aid him in the task of administration. On his right hand sat the Mapa or sub-king, the Epas or princes, the Senevirad, or commander-in-chief of the army, the "Principal Chiefs" and the chief secretary with his assistants. On his left hand were the governors of provinces, the chiefs of districts and the leading merchants.

We know very little about the functions of this council, but some indication of the law and order it maintained throughout Ceylon may be obtained from an inscription on the rock of Dambool which states that "even a woman might traverse the island with a precious jewel and not be asked what it was."

Parakrama Bahu was a devout Buddhist and he determined to restore religion to its former supremacy in the lives of his people. There were three sects of priests—the Maha Vihara, the Jetavana Vihara and the Abhayagira Vihara—which had been separated and unfriendly for hundreds of years. The king went to great trouble to unite the three orders, appointed a council to settle points of difference, and at last succeeded in his aim. During the long period of indifference to religion which had preceded his reign, many priests had become careless of their duties; they sought only comfort and worldly ease, and had forgotten their vows. Parakrama Bahu disrobed them and revived the earlier strictness and purity of their brotherhood. He built for them the Jetaranarama Temple at Polonnarua, the Lankatilake Vihara and the Gal Vihara; new preaching and image rooms were established for them in many places, and rest houses for their journeys throughout the land.

It is also recorded that his tolerance was such that he erected a house of worship for Brahmans, so as to afford the comforts of religion even to his Malabar enemies.

For the people, he built almonries where the poor could be cared for, and hospitals staffed by physicians, wherein he himself often superintended the nursing of the sick.

His love of magnificence found ex-

BUDDHA RECUMBENT

Carved from the living rock, this huge statue, now to be seen in the ruins of Polonnarua, measures 43 *feet in length.*

pression in the many palaces with which he adorned his capital, and in the fine gardens "resembling the paradise of the God-King Sakkraia, with trees of all sorts bearing fruits, and odorous flowers." He founded schools and libraries, built public baths and halls for music and dancing, and repaired shrines and temples at Anuradhapura.

Perhaps his most spectacular achievement, however, was the construction of new irrigation works throughout the island. The building or repair of more than a thousand tanks is attributed to him, including the famous "Sea of Parakrama," usually identified by modern historians with the great chain of tanks along the Angamedilla Ela.

"Thus was the whole island of Lanka," says the *Mahavansa*, "improved and beautified by this King, whose majesty is renowned in the annals of good deeds, who was faithful in the religion of Buddha, and whose fame extended abroad as the light of the moon."

Parakrama Bahu died in A.D. 1186 after ruling for thirty-three years. Sinhalese writers of to-day still refer to his reign as "the glorious era" and more than one declares that whatever native institutions, manners and habits still survive in Ceylon are largely due to his efforts.

ELSPETH HUXLEY

THE MOURNING DISCIPLE

A further view of the recumbent Buddha, with his favourite disciple, Ananda, shown mourning for his master. The Buddha lies in the attitude in which he received enlightenment under the bo-tree.

THE EMPEROR BABUR
Mogul School.

BABUR

"THE TIGER" OF THE MOGULS

1482–1530

BY H. G. RAWLINSON, C.I.E.

ZAHIR-UD-DIN MUHAMMAD, surnamed Babur, "the Tiger," was born in A.D. 1482. He was a Jaghtai Turk by race, and descended from two of the greatest conquerors in history, the mighty Timur-el-leng on his father's side and Chingiz Khan on his mother's. His ancestral home was in Ferghana, what is now Russian Turkestan, a pleasant country of vales and mountains lying between the Oxus and the Syr Darya rivers, abounding in roses, melons, apricots and pomegranates and full of game to give sport to the hunter. His father, Shaikh Umar, was a companionable man, inclined, as Babur tells us in his Memoirs, to corpulence, and apt to burst open his tunic if he moved too hastily after a meal. He was fond of backgammon, and could on occasion turn out tolerable verses. He was frank and honest, but had a violent temper; he was very skilful with his fists, and never hit a man without knocking him down. "His generosity was large, and so was his whole soul; he was of a rare humour, genial, eloquent, and sweet in his discourse, yet brave withal and manly." Babur's uncle, the King of Samarkand, was a great soldier and a bit of a dandy. He always wore his turban with the fold tied exactly over the eyebrow, and was so well-mannered that on one occasion he sat for hours on a bone rather than uncross his legs in the presence of his preceptor. He had, however, the family failing for strong drink, and on occasion would carouse with his courtiers day and night without a break for twenty or thirty days on end. Babur himself was a true child of his race, handsome, affable and fearless; he was an expert polo-player, and a deadly shot with the bow. He would plunge into an ice-cold mountain torrent and swim it, and could run along the battlements of Samarkand with a man under each arm, leaping the embrasures as he went.

In 1494 Shaikh Umar died. He was inspecting a pigeon-cote on the cliff-side, when it collapsed and fell over the precipice, carrying him with it. Immediately anarchy broke out in Samarkand, and Babur had to flee; but three years later, at the age of twelve, he returned, routed his rivals and restored order. Samarkand was in his hands, however, for only a short time. While he was away on an expedition his enemies seized the city, and he found himself once more an exile. After wandering about the country for another three years, in 1500 he suddenly swooped down again on Samarkand with a handful of followers, two hundred and forty in all. Some hardy spirits scaled the wall and threw open the gates. "The city was asleep. Only some shopkeepers, peeping out, discovered what had happened and gave thanks to God. Soon the news spread, and the citizens, with great joy and congratulations, fraternised with my men." The boy king was seated on the throne under the Royal Arch in the beautiful home of his fathers, with its orchards and pleasure gardens, the Kiosk adorned with pictures of Chinzig Khan's exploits, the China House with its blue tiles, its

BABUR AND HIS ELDEST SISTER

Mogul School.

college and observatory, and the famous Palace of the Forty Pillars.

But his triumph was destined to be short-lived. In the following year, Shahi Beg, the great Khan of the Uzbegs, advanced to expel him. Babur, who was still only a headstrong boy, rashly accepted battle with his more experienced opponent, who turned his flank and drove him in disorder to take shelter behind the walls of the town. Samarkand was besieged, and so close was the blockade that the poor were reduced to eating dogs and donkeys, and the horses browsed on the branches of trees.

There was no help for it, and Babur soon found himself again once more a wanderer on the face of the earth. But nothing daunted his spirits. "On the road," he writes, "I had a race with Kambar Ali and Basim Beg. My horse got the lead. As I turned round on my seat to see how far I had left them behind, my saddle turned, the girth being slack, and I fell right on my head. Though I sprang up and remounted, I did not recover the full possession of my senses until the evening." At the time of the evening prayer they halted and killed a horse, from which they cut some steaks. At nightfall they came to a village where they were given some fine fat meat, sweet melons and grapes, and so they passed "from the extremity of famine to plenty, and from calamity to peace and ease." "In all my life," Babur says, "I never enjoyed myself so much. Enjoyment after suffering, abundance after want, come with increased relish and afford more exquisite delight."

This was in 1502, and the next two years Babur spent roaming about the countryside with a tiny body of followers, mixing freely with the shepherds and peasants, who accorded to him the hospitality always forthcoming in the East. It was the kind of life he loved, and on one occasion, to his delight, he stayed with a village elder whose old mother, aged one hundred and eleven, could remember talking to soldiers who had served in the army of his great grandfather, Timur, when they raided India in 1398. Perhaps this first put into Babur's head the idea of a similar exploit, for he was already meditating all sorts of wild schemes, including a visit to China. He visited an uncle, and joined him in an expedition against an old rival, Beg Ahmad Tambal. It resulted in some bonny fighting. On one occasion he met his foe in single combat. "Except for his horse, Tambal was completely in mail. I had on my cuirass, and carried my sabre and bow and arrows. I drew up to my ear and sent my arrow right at his head, when at the same instant an arrow struck me on the right thigh and pierced me through and through. Tambal rushed in, and with the great Samarkand sword I had given him smote me such a blow on my steel headpiece as to stun me. Though not a link of the cap was cut, my head was severely bruised. I had neglected to clean my sword, so that it was rusty and I lost time in drawing it. I was alone, solitary, in the midst of foes. It was no time for standing still, so I turned my bridle, receiving another sabre stroke on my quiver."

On another occasion, when he was fighting a chieftain named Shaikh Bayazid, he suddenly ran into his opponent in a narrow lane. "Kuli Kukildash struck down one foot-soldier with his mace and had passed another, when the fellow aimed an arrow at Ibrahim Beg, who baulked him by shouting 'Hai! Hai!' and went on; but the man, being no further off than the porch from the hall, let fly an arrow which hit me under the arm. I had on a Kalmak mail, and two of its plates were pierced and shivered by the shot. Then he fled, and I sent an arrow after him which caught a foot-soldier who happened just then to be flying along the rampart, and pinned his cap to the wall, where it stood transfixed. A man on horseback passed close by me. I gave him the point of my sword on the temple; he swerved over as if to fall, but caught the wall and, thus supported, recovered his seat and escaped." Once when he was lying exhausted, with closed eyes, he heard two men arguing with one another which of them should strangle him. He looked up and said, "That's all very well, but I am curious to see which of you dares to approach me first." His would-be assailants promptly changed their minds and decamped!

But at length Babur was forced to acknowledge that Samarkand could not be retaken. With a heavy heart he turned his face southward. One of his many uncles had been King of Kabul; he had lately died, leaving the state in disorder. Why not carve out a kingdom for himself there? "I here entered my twenty-third year," he notes, "and had begun to use the razor to my face. The followers who still clave to me, great and small, were more than two hundred and less than three. Most of them were on foot, with brogues on their feet, clubs in their hands, and tattered cloaks over their shoulders. So poor were we that we had only two tents. My own I gave to my mother, and they pitched for me at every halt a felt tent of cross poles, in which I took up my quarters." As he marched, men began to flock to his standard, and at last the force, moving by night up the high passes of the Hindu Kush, reached the summit and saw beneath them the Promised Land. A brilliant star was shining overhead. "Surely that cannot be Suhail (Canopus)?" cried Babur; and one of his companions answered in an extemporised couplet—

"*O Suhail, how far dost thou shine, and in what distant sky dost thou rise?*
Good hap to the storm-beaten wanderer shines bright in the light of thine eyes."

Kabul was occupied early in October, 1504. Babur was enraptured with his new kingdom. There were melons in abundance, and fresh flowers and birds to study. Babur, with the keen interest which he always felt in natural history, tells us that he counted thirty-three distinct species of tulips. He describes how the local sportsmen lassoed herons and netted shoals of fish by stupefying them, and he knew that birds could be caught in thousands when exhausted by their migration over the Hindu-Kush. His favourite spots were the Garden of Fidelity, with its lake bordered by oranges and pomegranates, and the Fountain of Three Friends, where he loved to sit and discourse with his boon companions. "When the flowers are in bloom, the yellow mingling with the red, I know no place on earth to compare with it." On the hillside, near Kabul, he cut out a cistern which he lined with granite. It was filled with red wine, and on the sides he inscribed the following stanza:

"*Give me but wine and lovely girls,*
All other joys I freely spurn;
Enjoy them, Babur, while you may,
For youth once past will ne'er return."

Here Babur loved to sit, with his group of "noble and illustrious drinkers," passing round the wine-cup, capping verses and watching the dancing-girls, on the rare occasions when he was not fighting, hunting, playing polo, or laying out parks and gardens to beautify his new capital.

BY COURTESY OF THE VICTORIA AND ALBERT MUSEUM, LONDON

ENCAMPMENT AT KABUL

In his twenty-third year Babur started to carve out his great career by seizing the kingdom of Kabul. Here he is encamped before the gates of the city.

BY COURTESY OF THE VICTORIA AND ALBERT MUSEUM, LONDON

AT THE HEAD OF HIS ARMY

Babur leading his army into battle at Panipat in 1524. He conquered the forces of Ibrahim Lodi, Afghan emperor of Delhi, and became master of all Hindustan.

The Afghans were a turbulent and independent race, as fond of war as their descendants are to-day. It took a hard campaign to bring them to their senses, and many a good man and true "drank the wine of martyrdom" ere they were quelled. But at length he beat them so thoroughly that the leaders prostrated themselves before him, "with grass between their teeth, as who should say, 'I am thine ox.'" He varied his warlike expeditions by a visit to Herat, the chief centre of culture in the Middle East, with its hundred colleges, its poets, musicians and artists. Here Babur, with his usual gusto, vastly enjoyed the dinner-parties and the cultured society of the *jeunesse dorée*, until alarming tidings arrived of a revolt at Kabul. It was mid-winter and the passes were covered with snow, but there was no help for it. During this terrible journey an incident occurred which goes far to explain the devotion with which Babur inspired his followers. The force was lost in a snowdrift and seemed likely to perish. A cave was discovered, but Babur refused to take shelter in it. "I felt that for me to be in a warm dwelling and in comfort while my men were in the midst of snow and drift—for me to be within, enjoying sleep and ease, while my followers were in trouble and distress, would be inconsistent with what I owed them, and a deviation from that society of suffering that was their due. So I remained sitting in the snow and wind in the hole that I had dug out, with snow four hands thick on my head, back and ears." The next morning a path was discovered, and all found their way down to safety. The revolt was easily crushed, and in 1512 there appeared to be a chance of retaking Samarkand. But Babur's triumph was short-lived. After holding the city for eight months he was compelled to evacuate it and return to Kabul. But Babur could never sit still for long, and he was already meditating fresh conquests. If the north was barred to him, why not carve out a fresh empire in the rich valleys of the Indus and the Ganges?

"From the year 910 (A.D. 1504), when I obtained the principality of Kabul, I had never ceased to think of the conquest of Hindustan. But I had never found a suitable opportunity for undertaking it, hindered as I was, sometimes by the apprehensions of my Begs, sometimes by disagreements between my brothers and myself. Finally all these obstacles were happily removed. Great and small, Begs and Captains, no one dared to say a word against the project. So in 1519 I left at the head of my army and made a start by taking Bajaur. From this time to 1525–26 I was always actively concerned in the affairs of Hindustan. I went there in person at the head of an army five times in the course of seven or eight years. The fifth time, by the munificence and liberality of God, there fell beneath my blows an enemy as formidable as Sultan Ibrahim, and I gained the vast empire of Hind. As it was always in my heart to possess Hindustan, and as these several countries had once been held by the Turks, I pictured them as my own, and was resolved to get them into my own hands, whether peacefully or by force. For these reasons, it being imperative to treat the hillmen well, this order was given: 'Do no hurt or harm to the flocks and herds of these people, nor even to their cotton-ends and broken needles!'"

On Friday, November 17, 1525, "when the Sun was in Sagittarius," Babur finally set out for Hindustan. His whole force only numbered 12,000, including camp-followers, but he had been promised the help of Daulat Khan, the Governor of Lahore, who was in rebellion against Ibrahim Lodi, the Afghan

BABUR GIVES A

The great Mogul emperor entertaining Rapi-uzzaman Mirza in a tent beside the Murghab illustrated Memoirs of Babur: *Mogul*

BY COURTESY OF THE VICTORIA AND ALBERT MUSEUM, LONDON

FORMAL ENTERTAINMENT

river in 1516. *These and the other illustrations in this article are taken from the School of painting, executed about* 1590.

Sultan of Delhi. When he reached the Punjab, the faithless Daulat Khan changed his mind, but was easily defeated. Babur then, to quote his own words, "placed his foot in the stirrup of resolution and his hand on the reins of confidence in God, and marched against Sultan Ibrahim, the son of Sultan Iskander, the son of Sultan Bahlol Lodi Afghan, in whose possession the throne of Delhi and the dominions of Hindustan at that time were; whose army in the field was said to amount to a hundred thousand men and who, including those of his Amirs, had nearly a thousand elephants."

The two armies met on April 21, 1524, at Panipat, the historic battle-ground in the gap between the mountains and the desert, where the fate of India has been so often decided. Babur's force was only a tenth that of his enemy's, but while at Kabul he had acquired a number of firearms, a weapon hitherto almost unknown in the East. These consisted of cannon, swivel-guns and matchlocks, under the command of a master-gunner named Ustad Ali Kuli. The traditional Mongol manœuvre was to lager the waggons, and while the enemy was assaulting them, to counter-attack simultaneously on both flanks with swift masses of cavalry. Babur adopted these tactics. Resting his right flank on the walled town of Panipat, he made a lager of waggons in front, with guns at regular intervals, while his left was protected by an *abattis* of logs. His opponent, a rash and unskilful young man, was tempted into making a frontal attack, hoping by means of his elephants to crush down the rough defences in front of him. This was just as Babur desired. Withholding his fire until the elephants were at point-blank range, he suddenly opened on them with all his guns. The poor brutes stampeded and spread confusion in their own ranks, whereupon the Mongol cavalry sallied forth and took the enemy in flank, pouring in volleys of arrows from horseback and then charging home.

By midday the battle was over. Sultan Ibrahim and 20,000 men lay dead on the field. The spoils were immense. Gold and silver, cloth and jewels and slaves were heaped upon the officers of the victorious force, and every soul in Kabul received a silver piece. To the share of Babur's son, the young prince Humayun, fell the fairest prize of all, the great Koh-i-Nur diamond, once reputed to have belonged to the Pandava princes, and said to be the most wonderful jewel in the world. Before the enemy could recover the invaders were knocking at the gates of Delhi. The capital surrendered and Babur's name was read from the pulpit of the Great Mosque in the Friday Prayers as Emperor of Hindustan.

It was now the height of the hot weather, and the climate was well-nigh unendurable to men born and bred in the hills. Their idea was to descend into the plains to gather plunder and then to return to their mountain homes; to settle in this strange and unprepossessing country was more than they bargained for. But Babur won them over in a statesmanlike speech.

"I told them that empire and conquest could not be acquired without the materials and means of war; that royalty and nobility could not exist without subjects and dependent provinces; that by the labour of many years, after undergoing great hardships, measuring many a toilsome journey and raising various armies, and after exposing myself and my troops to circumstances of great danger, to battle and bloodshed, by the divine favour I had routed my formidable enemy, and achieved the conquest of the numerous provinces and kingdoms which we at present held: 'And now,

BY COURTESY OF THE VICTORIA AND ALBERT MUSEUM, LONDON

A TERRIBLE JOURNEY

Babur passing the Minai Hill near Kabul in a heavy snowstorm, 1506. *He was on his way to check the revolt in Kabul.*

what force compels, and what hardship obliges us, without any visible cause, after having worn out our life in accomplishing the desired achievement, to abandon and fly from our conquests, and to retreat back to Kabul with every symptom of disappointment and discomfiture? Let not anyone who calls himself my friend ever henceforward make such a proposal. But if there is any among you who cannot bring himself to stay, or to give up his purpose of returning back, let him depart.' Having made them this fair and reasonable proposal, the discontented were of necessity compelled, however unwillingly, to renounce their seditious purposes."

As a matter of fact, he had himself a very poor opinion of India and its inhabitants, and his remarks on the subject are couched in his usual shrewd and penetrating manner.

"Hindustan is a country that has few pleasures to recommend it. The people are not handsome. They have no idea of the charms of friendly society, of frankly mixing together, or familiar intercourse. They have no genius, no comprehension of mind, no politeness of manner, no kindness or fellow-feeling, no ingenuity or mechanical invention in planning or executing their handicraft works, no skill or knowledge in design or architecture; they have no horses, no good flesh, no grapes or musk-melons, no good fruits, no ice or cold water, no good food or bread in their bazaars, no baths or colleges, no candles, no torches, not a candlestick. Beside their rivers and standing waters, they have some running water in their ravines and hollows; but they have no aqueducts or canals in their gardens or palaces. In their buildings they study neither elegance nor climate, appearance nor regularity. The chief excellency of Hindustan is, that it is a large country and has abundance of gold and silver. The climate during the rains is very pleasant. On some days it rains ten, fifteen and even twenty times. During the rainy season inundations come pouring down all at once and form rivers, even in places where at other time there is no water. While the rains continue on the ground the air is singularly delightful, insomuch that nothing can surpass its soft and agreeable temperature. Its defect is, that the air is rather moist and damp. During the rainy season you cannot shoot even with the bow of our country and it becomes quite useless. Nor is it the bow alone that becomes useless: coats of mail, books, clothes and furniture all feel the bad effects of the moisture. Their houses, too, suffer from not being substantially built. There is pleasant enough weather in the winter and summer, as well as in the rainy season; but then the north wind always blows, and there is an excessive quantity of earth and dust flying about. When the rains are at hand, this wind blows five or six times with excessive violence, and such a quantity of dust flies about that you cannot see one another. A convenience of Hindustan is that the workmen of every profession and trade are innumerable and without end. For any work, or any employment, there is always a set ready, to whom the same employment and trade have descended from father to son for ages."

Babur at once set to work to make life more tolerable by planting gardens with his favourite flowers and fruits, and by employing Hindu builders to erect palaces after the manner of those in his native country.

But an even greater danger loomed ahead. He had found it a comparatively easy matter to deal with his Afghan co-religionists, but now he heard that the Rajput clans had been called together by the Rana Sangram Singh, the "Sun of

BY COURTESY OF THE VICTORIA AND ALBERT MUSEUM, LONDON

THE BIRTH OF AN HEIR

Babur receiving congratulations and gifts on the occasion of the birth of Humayun, his son and heir to the throne, in 1506.

Mewar," to drive the infidel intruders from the sacred soil of India. The Rajput army, 80,000 horse and 500 elephants, commanded by one hundred and twenty chieftains of ancient lineage, were the flower of Hindu chivalry. The Rana himself had beaten the Afghans in eighteen pitched battles. He was a mere "fragment of a man," who had lost an arm and an eye in the field. Babur advanced from Agra to a place called Kanua to await the approach of his opponents. He adopted the Mongol tactics which had proved so successful against Ibrahim Lodi. His waggons were bound together with iron chains, with the cannon at intervals, and, in addition, he had mounted his matchlocks on wheeled tripods which could be moved quickly to any threatened point. His flanks were protected by deep ditches and entanglements.

Babur's men became nervous as the mighty Rajput host approached, but their leader never lost heart. Ever since he became King of Kabul he had taken to the habit of drinking heavily, in defiance of the precepts of Islam. Now he took a vow that, if God gave him victory, he would never touch strong drink again. All his beautiful drinking-cups were collected and broken to pieces in front of the army, and the wine spilt on the ground. Then he addressed his men:

"Noblemen and soldiers! Every man that comes into the world is subject to dissolution. When we are passed away and gone, God only survives, unchangeable. Whoever comes to the feast of life must, before it is over, drink from the cup of death. He who arrives at the inn of mortality must one day inevitably take his departure from that house of sorrow, the world. How much better is it to die with honour than to live with infamy!

"The Most High God has been propitious to us, and has now placed us in such a crisis, that if we fall in the field we die the death of martyrs; if we survive, we rise victorious, the avengers of the cause of God. Let us then, with one accord, swear on God's Holy Word that none of us will even think of turning his face from this warfare, nor desert from the battle and slaughter that ensues, till his soul is separated from his body."

The army, inspired by these noble words, swore an oath on the Koran to conquer or die. On March 16th, 1527, scouts brought word that the enemy were approaching. Babur immediately drew up his men in three bodies, with a strong reserve, and galloped down the line with words of advice and encouragement. The attack began soon after. Wave after wave of Rajputs threw themselves upon the line, and Babur's artillery did terrible execution. When the enemy had exhausted himself in these fruitless charges, Babur ordered a simultaneous advance in the centre and on either flank. At length the gallant Rajputs began to yield ground, and were pursued relentlessly to their camp, losing enormous numbers of men. A ghastly minaret of heads was erected on the battle-field, and Babur took the title of Ghazi, or Victor in a Holy War. There was still much work to be done, but in the following year the great stronghold of Chanderi was captured, thanks chiefly to Ustad Ali's heavy artillery, and Babur then undertook expeditions for the purpose of overthrowing the independent Afghan Kingdoms in Bihar and Bengal. By the end of the year he was master of Hindustan, and the foundations of the Mogul Empire were well and truly laid.

He did not, however, live long to enjoy his triumph. His few remaining months of life were spent in organising his new kingdom. The more settled lands were given as *jagirs* or fiefs to his

BY COURTESY OF THE VICTORIA AND ALBERT MUSEUM, LONDON

THE GARDENS AT AGRA

Babur, like all the Moguls, loved gardens. Here he is seen receiving a deputation in the gardens he laid out himself at Agra.

BY COURTESY OF THE VICTORIA AND ALBERT MUSEUM, LONDON

HUMAYUN'S ACCESSION DURBAR

The great Babur died in 1530, and his last act was to call his nobles together to pay homage to the heir, his beloved son Humayun.

officers, who paid a fixed sum to the Crown, which they recovered by means of land-taxes levied on the peasants, duties on merchandise, and the *jaẓiah* or poll-tax on non-Muslims. In outlying districts the zemindars or landholders, Hindu and Muslim, were left undisturbed. Hindu masons and gardeners were hard at work beautifying his new capital at Agra, where, in December, 1529, he gave a grand Durbar, attended by ambassadors from Persia, Herat and Bengal. There were fights between elephants and camels and rams, wrestling matches and jugglers and dances by nautch-girls.

But Babar was happiest with his family, his beloved son Humayun, and his three daughters, "Rosy-face," "Rose-blush" and "Rose-body." In December, 1530, Humayun was taken ill with fever, and lay at the point of death. Babur was distracted, and determined to lay down his life for him if he could. The wise men begged him to sacrifice anything—his riches or even the great Koh-i-nur diamond. "Is there any stone," he answered, "that can be weighed against my son?" Walking thrice round the sick-bed, he prayed, "On me be the sickness." Then suddenly he cried joyfully, "I have prevailed! I have taken it!" And from that moment Humayun gradually recovered, but Babur sickened and died. He passed away on December 26, 1530. One of his last acts was to call the nobles together and put their hands in Humayun's in token of investiture. He was indeed "a very perfect, gentle knight," dauntless in adversity, merciful in the hour of victory, a lover of beauty and a loyal friend. He sleeps in a garden on the hillside in Kabul, by the flowers and the running stream where he once delighted to sit and gaze on the beautiful world. "His permanent place in history," says Professor Lane, "rests upon his Indian conquests." He laid the first stone of the splendid fabric which his grandson, Akḅar, achieved. But his place in biography and literature is determined rather by his daring adventures and the delightful *Memoirs* in which he related them. Soldier of fortune as he was, Babur was not the less a man of fine literary taste and fastidious critical perception. In Persian, the language of culture, the Latin of Central Asia, he was an accomplished poet, and in his native Turki he was master of a pure and unaffected style, alike in prose and verse. As his cousin, himself an excellent historian, writes: "No one of his family before him ever possessed such talents, nor did any of his race perform such amazing exploits or experience such strange adventures."

RANA PRATAP SINGH

RANA PRATAP SINGH

THE RAJPUT HERO

REIGNED 1572–1597

BY ISHWARI PRASAD, M.A., D.LITT.

TOWARDS the close of the fifteenth century a fiery and spirited youth was wandering from place to place in Transoxiana pursued by his own hostile kinsmen and Uzbegs of Sharbani Khan who allowed him no respite. Unable to recover the throne of his ancestors, he betook himself to the snowy regions of Kabul, where among a fierce and fanatical people he established himself, and now that he was driven away for good from the west, he began to look about for fresh fields and pastures new. The Afghan empire of India was in a bad condition; it lacked the elements of cohesion and development and its strength was sapped by the feuds of nobles and the imprudence of kings. The malcontents invited Babur to invade the country and Rana Sanga of Mewar joined in the request. Babur grasped at the opportunity with joy and with his warlike Chaghtais came and overpowered the Afghans and Rajputs alike in two bloody battles at Panipat and Khanua. The old dynasty tumbled down and a new one was put in possession of Delhi and Agra.

THE ARMS OF THE HOUSE OF MEWAR

The rulers of the House of Mewar claim to be descended from the Sun itself, which is symbolised on their coat of arms.

THE MAJESTIC RUINS

All that remains of the great fort of Chitor, perhaps the most historic place in Rajputana.
than surrender. Akbar finally took Chitorgarh in 1567, the cowardly Udai Singh

MARTIN HURLIMANN

OF CHITORGARH

It was sacked three times in its long history, and each time the Rajputs sought death rather having fled, leaving his generals to carry on the gallant traditions of the Rajputs.

THE PLACE OF SACRIFICE

The temple in the Fort of Chitor where the Rajput women performed sacrificial rites before throwing themselves into the flames sooner than be captured by their enemies.

But Indian fatalism remained unmoved, and beneath the bright sun and brilliant sky the Mogul conquerors forgot, for the present, the lands of the Oxus and decided to settle down in Hindustan.

Babur's health soon gave way under the strain of ceaseless fighting and manœuvring and he died in 1530. His son Humayun, a kindly man of weak will and unsteady temper, found it hard to maintain himself on his throne owing to the jealousy of his brothers and the revival of Afghan power. He was expelled from India, and it was after 15 years' exile that he regained his kingdom, leaving it soon after to his young son, who was born under the sheltering care of a Hindu in the desert of Umarkot. Like the fragrance of the musk, which the fugitive emperor had distributed among his nobles to celebrate the birth of an heir, his fame spread to all parts of India and Asia. His bold imperialism was not merely the challenge of his physical prowess but also the expression of an eager soul that aimed at bringing the whole of India under its sway by fusing together the diverse elements of the population. He planned a new synthesis of creeds, which were all, according to him, different routes leading to the same goal.

It was a noble dream originally conceived by the great mystics of India who had preceded the mighty Mogul. They had condemned polytheism and bigotry and emphasised the need for a pure faith. A stir was created and idol worship and effete symbolism were alike denounced as futilities which could lead neither to spiritual advancement nor to human happiness. Thus a new environment was created, of which Akbar was a typical product. As lord of Hindustan, he dreamed of an empire in which the Hindu and the Moslem would be equal partners. The policy of universal peace (Sulh-i-Kul) would unite all, and for the first time the Rajput princes were confronted with a man who conquered to love and cherish. Political subjection lost its sting and defeat its bitterness. The princess of Amber, whom Akbar had married at Sanganir, became a golden link in the chain of this new imperialism. The fusion of the Rajput and the Mogul, who had so far fought *à outrance*, augured well for the future; but there was one sad thought that troubled the minds of the exponents of this policy, entirely unknown as it was to the previous Moslem rulers of India. Would the Sisodia house of Mewar accept the policy which Akbar had enounced and Amber had seconded? Who could foresee at this time the crop of miseries and the wails of broken hearts which were to be the lot of the men and women of Mewar, of high and low degree? Pride and prejudice alike tended to confirm the Sisodias as the forlorn hope of Rajput resistance to this new orientation of imperial policy.

The land of Mewar has rightly been regarded as the breeding place of heroes and heroines in history. Situated in the Aravalli hills it is a beautiful country, intersected by mountain torrents and covered with abundant vegetation in many places and forests stretching for miles abounding in all kinds of game. Parts of it are rocky and barren, and

GATEWAY TO THE FORTRESS

One of the six gateways to the fort of Chitor, which is still in existence.

THE LAST SACK

In 1567 Akbar advanced against Chitorgarh. Though he conquered, even he admitted and Patta, who led the Rajputs in

BY COURTESY OF THE VICTORIA AND ALBERT MUSEUM, LONDON

OF CHITOR

that the greater glory rested with the Rajputs, and especially with the two heroes, Jaimal the absence of their ruler Udai Singh.

THE CASTLE OF AMBER MARTIN HURLIMANN

The powerful state of Amber formed an alliance with Akbar and did not support Rana Pratap Singh in his struggle against the Moguls.

this physical aspect has made the people hardy and vigorous and capable of enduring privations. The seat of political power in the sixteenth century was Chitor, famous alike in legend and history as the nursery of heroes. It is now a small town on the border of a vast plain, and is overlooked by the fort, which stands on a mass of rock three miles and a quarter long and about 1,200 yards wide in the centre. The circumference at the base is more than eight miles and the height some four or five hundred feet. In the sixteenth century the city was situated on the summit of the hill where now desolation reigns supreme, except for a few humble dwellings of poor cultivators who are the only remnants of what must have been a fairly busy and populous town, adorned with palaces, houses, temples and markets. As we stand on the lofty hill looking down below, the great figures of history pass before our eyes and we perceive the meaning of Tod's well-known description.

"With the wrecks of ages around me, I abandoned myself to contemplation. I gazed until the sun's last beam fell upon 'the ringlet of Cheetore,' illuminating its grey and grief-worn aspect, like a lambent gleam lighting up the face of sorrow. Who could look on this lonely, this majestic column, which tells in language more easy to interpret than the tablets within, of

'deeds which should not pass away,
And names that must not wither,'

and withhold a sigh for its departed glories? But in vain I dipped my pen to record my thoughts in language; for, wherever the eye fell, it filled the mind with images of the past, and ideas rushed too tumultuously to be recorded. In this mood I continued for some time, gazing listlessly, until the shades of evening gradually enshrouded the temples, columns, and palaces; and as I folded up my paper till the morrow, the words of the prophetic bard of Israel came forcibly to my recollection: 'How doth the city sit solitary that was full of people! how is she become as a widow! she, that was great among the nations, and princess among the princes, how is she become tributary!'"

The entrance to the fort is by a gate which is succeeded by six others through which we have to pass. The last is the Rampol gate, a large and handsome structure, erected in the Hindu style, towards the west. Between these gates are many spots rendered famous by the sacrifice of the sons of Mewar, and in moving accents the lonely guide still relates their story to the tourist and the visitor. Some of the buildings are impressive—Mira's temple and the Jayastambha, or pillar of victory, which was reared by Rana Kumbha in the fifteenth century to commemorate his success over the Sultans of Malwa and Gujarat.

The Rajputs of Mewar were a gallant tribe. Brave and undaunted, they were always ready to lay down their lives for the honour of their race. The bards recount their virtues with fervour, and sober history sees no reason to dissent from their patriotic panegyrics. Mewar has the unique distinction of being a state in Rajasthan which has produced in the past great rulers and warriors and in awful crises her women have behaved like their men. The chronicles are replete with the deeds of valour performed by the heroes of Mewar. But it was her misfortune to be ruled by a man who was neither a great soldier nor a statesman at the time when the sceptre of Delhi and Agra was swayed by the mightiest of Moslem kings—the man who was to shatter the patriarchal system of Rajasthan and to draw the little states into an imperial union based on reciprocal trust and goodwill.

Rana Udai Singh, father of the celebrated Pratap, had come to the *gaddi* in 1537. According to Tod he had not one quality of a sovereign and lacking in martial virtue, the common heritage of his race, he was destitute of all. He might have frittered away his life in sloth and ease, secure in the fastnesses of his native mountains, had it not been for Akbar, who was now developing a scheme of bringing the whole of Rajasthan within the orbit of his empire. In 1562 he had allied himself with Amber by marriage and cemented his friendship further by elevating to high office Raja Man Singh, nephew of Raja Bhagwan Das, the heir of Beharimal, a man of rare abilities, who afterwards rose to be the supreme general and commander of the imperial forces. This done he turned against Mewar. As descendants of Bappa Rawal, her Ranas were recognised as pre-eminent among the various clans and were accorded universal esteem in Rajasthan. Their subjugation was bound to make an impression upon the other princes. Besides, the acquisition of such fortresses as Chitor and Ranthambhor would establish his hold on northern India.

In 1567 the imperial armies marched towards Mewar and on hearing the news Udai Singh retired into the hills, leaving the fort to be defended by Jaimal and Patta with 8,000 Rajputs. It was an act of cowardice unworthy of the Sisodia clan and well does the historian of Rajasthan observe that it would have been better for Mewar had the poniard fulfilled its intention, and the annals never recorded the name of Udai Singh in the catalogue of her princes. The Moguls besieged Chitor and laid their batteries around the fortress. Jaimal and Patta heroically defended themselves, and the fair damsels in the inner apartments saved themselves from dishonour by performing *Jauhar*—an act of self-immolation to which the Rajput women resorted in the last extremity of danger. Akbar entered the Fort at midday and ordered a general massacre. If tradition is to be believed the sacred threads of those who perished weighed 74½ mans, a figure still marked on the banker's letter in Rajasthan by which is invoked "the sin of the slaughter of Chitor" on those who violate the sanctity of the letter by opening it. Akbar returned to Ajmer and offered a thanksgiving service at Khwaja Muinuddin Chishti's shrine. Udai Singh also emerged from his mountain retreat after the departure of the imperialists and busied himself in completing the palaces which he was constructing at the time of the invasion.

After Udai Singh's death in 1572, Rana Pratap succeeded to the *gaddi* of Mewar. The poetic fancy of the bards described Chitor after the desolation as a "widow" despoiled of all that added to her loveliness. Brave and warlike, a true Kshatriya in whose veins flowed the blood of Bappa Rawal, Pratap was the very embodiment of Rajput chivalry and honour. The humiliation of Chitor poured iron into his soul and he longed for revenge. His noble spirit was deeply stirred by what had happened and he desired the vindication of the honour of his house. Like his forefathers he resolved, in the language of the bard, "to make his mother's milk resplendent." The task was difficult. His state was small; it did not possess resources enough to contend against the might and majesty of the empire over which Akbar ruled. Secondly, the Rajput Princes of Amber, Marwar, Bikaner and Bundi had become the allies of his Moslem foe and were ready to help him against their own compatriots.

But Pratap's ardour was not damped by the magnitude of the peril. He denied to himself all luxuries, slept on a straw bed, eschewed rich food and laid aside the plates of gold and silver from which royalty had so far eaten in Mewar. The kettledrums no longer sounded in the van of battle or processions. Like the Italian patriot, Mazzini, Pratap felt deeply the woes of his native land and regarded no sacrifice as too great in its service. Often was he heard to exclaim in sorrow: "Had Udai Singh never been born or none had intervened between him and Rana Songa, no Turk should have ever given laws to Rajasthan." His soul revolted at the thought of entering into a matrimonial alliance with the Moslem emperor and he determined not to bow his head before him in submission. To him the conduct of his fellow princes was indefensible; it meant degradation and dishonour. With a singleness of purpose that has no parallel in Rajput annals, Pratap resolved to carry on the battle of freedom against the empire.

The first thing he did was to strengthen his small state. He reorganised the Government, properly garrisoned the forts and entrusted them to capable officers. He commanded his subjects to retire into the mountain country when they were attacked by the Moguls. Raja Man Singh was deputed by Akbar to see the Rana after the conquest of Gujarat. The latter accorded to the Prince of Amber a warm reception but refused to listen to his overtures for an imperial alliance. An anecdote which is widely prevalent in Rajasthan shows the dislike which Pratap felt for such a union. Before his departure, Man Singh was invited to dinner by the Rana, and when the dishes were served, he himself did not turn up and excused

WITHIN THE FORT OF CHITOR WITH THE TOWER OF VICTORY IN THE BACKGROUND

himself on the ground that he was too ill from stomach-ache to be present. Man Singh understood the hint; he rose up in great agitation and said that he well knew the remedy for the Rana's ailment and that he would have to pay dearly for this affront. Unperturbed by this threat, the Rana replied that he should always be happy to meet him, but as Raja Man leapt on horseback, uttering some more comment upon his host's behaviour, an indiscreet Rajput remarked from behind that he should not forget to bring his *phupha* (father's sister's husband) Akbar with him. This was a biting allusion to what the Mewar heroes regarded as a *mésalliance* between the house of Amber and the Mogul. The spot on which the plates were laid for Man Singh was sprinkled with Ganges water and the chiefs bathed and changed their clothes as if they had been contaminated by the presence of one who had allied himself with the Mogul by marriage. Raja Man was mortally offended at this insult and he persuaded the emperor to humble the pride of Pratap.

It is not necessary to examine the *casus belli* between the emperor and Rana Pratap. The court historian, Abul Fazl, writes that the motive was to chastise him for his "arrogance, presumption, disobedience, deceit and dissimulation." The Rana's offence was that he was proud of his lineage and was determined to preserve the independence of his country. Nothing could draw him into an alliance with the Turk. Such were the sentiments of Rana Pratap, and it can be easily imagined how they must have galled the emperor as well as his Rajput satellites who in their heart of hearts desired the ruin of the Rana in order to avoid the odious comparison between him and themselves. Akbar, on his part, was bent on the Rana's humiliation and the extinction of Mewar's independence. The struggle between these two men representing different ideals of imperial expansion and insular freedom was bound to be a bitter one, and no wonder if it evoked the finest qualities in those who pitted themselves against a foe of matchless wealth and power. The better mind of Rajasthan approved of Pratap's action as is shown by the fervour with which the tale of his heroic achievements is still recounted before admiring listeners by bards.

Akbar chose Man Singh, whom he had exalted by the title of *Farzand* (son), to lead the campaign against the Rana, obviously in the hope that being a Rajput, whose ancestors had been vassals of Mewar, he would provoke his great antagonist to a mortal combat in which he would be killed. Accompanied by many nobles, Moslem and Rajput, and five thousand horse, Man Singh started for Mewar in April, 1576, and soon reached Mandalgarh where he began to organise his army. The Rana marched from Kumbhalgarh to Goganda and desired to give battle at Mandalgarh, but his nobles advised him to wait and encounter the enemy from the mountains. The imperialists encamped on the bank of the river Banas near Haldighat and marching from his place the Rana also posted himself at a distance of six miles from Man Singh's camp. He was assisted by a number of Rajput chiefs, and it is significant to note that among his allies was Hakim Khan Sur who had joined with his auxiliaries. Here was fought the great battle which has immortalised Pratap in history and has exalted Haldighat to the rank of Thermopylæ in Greece.

Abdul Qadir Badaoni, the historian, who was present on the field of battle as a follower of the Mogul commander, Asaf Khan, has given a graphic account of it. It was the hottest part of June

THE TANK AT CHITORGARH

In the background are the ruins of the palace of Rani Padmani. Akbar removed the famous gates of this palace, and they are now in Agra fort.

COURTESY OF THE BRITISH MUSEUM

MAN SINGH OF AMBER

Man Singh of Amber married Akbar's sister and became one of the Mogul emperor's most trusted generals.

and the scorching sun made the air like a furnace which made men's brains boil in their skulls. The troops were organised in battle array and Man Singh, seated on an elephant, posted himself at the centre, accompanied by Khwaja Mohammad Rafi Badakhshi, Ali Murad Uzbeg, Raja Lon Karan and others. The right, left and van were similarly placed under veteran commanders. The Rana advanced from behind the pass with his 3,000 Rajputs whom he divided into two sections. One of these under Hakim Khan Sur attacked the imperial vanguard and threw it into confusion. The Rajputs in the left wing, under Lon Karan, fled like sheep and offered no resistance. At this time Badaoni asked Asaf Khan how he could distinguish the friendly from the enemy Rajputs and was told in reply: "Go on shooting arrows. On whichever side they may be killed, it will be a gain to Islam." Badaoni acted as advised and was glad to have this opportunity of slaying the "infidels."

The second division of the Rana's army commanded by himself fell upon Qazi Khan at the entrance of the pass and scattered it. The battle raged fiercely from morning till midday and both sides engaged in a death grapple. In a combat of elephants Man Singh displayed great gallantry, but the Rana's elephant, Ram Prasad, fought with undaunted vigour until, his keeper being wounded, he was seized by the imperialists. The Rana could no longer hold on and left the field. Nearly five hundred men lost their lives, and the soldiers were so dispirited that they did not pursue the Rana in his flight. Badaoni writes with pleasure that the son of Jaimal, the hero of Chitor, "went to hell" and there was much other "good riddance of bad rubbish."

Next day the imperialists marched to Goganda where they had to endure great privations. There was a dearth of provisions and the soldiers had to subsist on animal flesh and mangoes which abounded in the country. The parching wind made the soldiers sick and their strength and vigour ebbed disastrously. Badaoni was sent by Asaf Khan to convey the despatch of victory to court and at the same time offer the elephant of the Rana which was captured in battle. The brave animal was presented to Akbar and renamed Pir Prasad, and Badaoni's services were recognised by the reward of 96 *asharifs*. Apparently the Mulla was satisfied.

The Rajput annals are in agreement with the official chronicler who has recorded the details of the battle. There was a desperate encounter between Raja Man and Rana Pratap. The latter attacked Man Singh in person with his spear and the forelegs of his horse Chaitak struck against the sword fastened to the trunk of the Kachwaha's elephant. The Rana hastily drew back but the noble charger was badly wounded and at a distance of two miles from Haldighat, he fell exhausted and died. The grateful master raised a platform in his honour which exists to this day.

Both sides claimed the victory and a temple inscription at Udaipur dated May, 1562, records the flight of Man Singh's army before the onset of Pratap's valiant sword. Even according to Moslem chronicles the plight of the imperial army was terrible. The fleeing soldiers looked back in fear lest the Rana should suddenly attack them from behind and at Goganda they took special precautions to defend themselves. The Rana seized the passes and cut off the supplies of the imperialists and reduced them to sore straits. Four months passed in this condition. At last, fighting the Rajputs at every stage, the imperial army pushed on to Ajmer,

BY COURTESY OF THE VICTORIA AND ALBERT MUSEUM, LONDON

DEATH OF JAIMAL AND PATTA

Akbar slays the two Rajput heroes. A scene from the siege of the fort of Chitor.

leaving their *thansa* to be captured by the enemy.

The Rana utilised this interval to increase his resources. He won over to his side the rulers of Sirohi, Jalor and Idar and with their help began to raid the Mogul outposts. The emperor sent punitive expeditions against the rulers of Sirohi and Jalor with the result that they submitted to him. His attempts to check the Rana's exploits proved unsuccessful.

Hearing of these audacious attempts Akbar marched from Ajmer to Goganda and remained in the Rana's country for six months, but the latter took no notice of him. When he left for Banswara, the Rana came out of the hills and blocked the road to Agra. The imperial officers, Raja Bhagwan Das, Raja Man Singh, Mirza Khan and Qasim Khan, did their best to catch the Rana but in vain. He wandered from hill to hill raiding the Mogul camp and on one occasion it so happened that the *haram* of Mirza Khan fell into the hands of the Crown Prince but the chivalrous Rana treated the ladies like his own daughters and sent them to their husband with every mark of honour.

But nothing served to induce Akbar to desist from his attempts to bring about the Rana's destruction. He sent Shahbaz Khan against him with a considerable force in October, 1578, assisted by the Rajputs of Amber. But the latter were sent back by the imperial general who had no faith in their loyalty. Shahbaz Khan seized Kelwara and then proceeded to Kumbhalgarh but the Rana evacuated the fortress leaving it in charge of one of his chiefs. The Mewar garrison offered a desperate resistance and every inch of ground was contested, but they were overpowered by the Moguls, and Shahbaz Khan captured Goganda and Udaipur and seized enormous booty. The Rana had retired to Chavand, where he took up his abode and built a small temple which exists to this day.

In these days of difficulty the Rana received great help from his minister, Bhamashah, who brought much booty from Malwa and placed at his master's disposal twenty-five lacs of rupees and twenty thousand *asharifs*. The condition of the army was improved, and the raids were begun with redoubled vigour. Kumbhalgarh fell into his hands and a little later the princes of Banswara and Dungarpur were repulsed in an attack and made to acknowledge the Rana's sovereignty. Shahbaz Khan appeared once again at the head of a large army but he had to return unsuccessful. The Rajputs followed their usual tactics. The Rana fled into the hills. He forbade cultivation in the plains and ordered the farmers not to pay a single pice to the Moslem tax-collectors. The object was to reduce the country to such a desolate condition that it would not be worth while for the Moguls to waste their energy in conquering it. The beautiful valley presented a melancholy aspect: brambles and thorns grew along the road side; wild animals prowled about in search of prey; the human habitations were deserted; from the Aravallis to the eastern plateau the whole country became a wild waste. Such was the method by which Rana Pratap tried to check the aggressive designs of Mogul imperialism.

The events of Rana Pratap's life savour of romance and the bards have woven legends round his personality which have made his name a dear possession in Rajasthan. Years rolled away in hardship and misery, and at times he felt anxious for the safety of his family. Yet he bore up against it all with a fortitude which is worthy of the highest praise. Mirza Khan was touched by the Rana's valour and perseverance and sent him verses in his own tongue to the following effect:

"All is perishable in this world; power and pelf will disappear but the virtue of a great name will live forever." What sustained him in all these trials was his own faith and the example of the brave sons of Mewar. At times his children had to go without food and even the elderly princes and princesses found the sorrows of a never ending exile unbearable. At one time the wife of Amar Singh asked her husband how long all this misery was going to last, and the prince's reply that his sire was engaged in a fruitless struggle against a mighty empire, caused much grief to the noble warrior and he felt anxious for the future. Tradition says that on one occasion the Rana, much vexed by his misfortune, wrote a letter to Akbar in which he prayed for a relaxation of his severities. But Prithiraj of Bikanir, who admired Pratap's heroism, sent to him a few couplets asking him not to deviate from his path, and the substance of these is given by Colonel Tod. The Rana stuck to his resolve and never agreed to bow his head before the Mogul. God helped him to wear his moustache high and avoid all contact with the Turk. Prithiraj was satisfied.

But Akbar could never forgive the Rana's faults. In 1584 he again sent Jaganath Kachwaha and Zafar Beg to deal with the Rana, but even they realised that his subjugation was a wild goose chase. Circumstances became more favourable; the emperor was detained in the Punjab for a number of years owing to troubles on the north-west frontier. He found no time to look to the affairs of Mewar. Rana Pratap recovered all his places and at last died in 1597, invincible and indomitable to the last moment of his life.

The last scene has been pathetically described by Tod. The noble warrior is lying in a humble dwelling, surrounded by his chiefs, the comrades of his many fights who had literally borne him to victory on the edges of their swords, waiting for the shuffling off of his mortal coil, when a groan came from the depth of his heart and Salumbar enquired: "what afflicted his soul that it would not depart in peace?" The proud spirit replied: "It lingered for some consolatory pledge that his country should not be abandoned to the Turk." With his expiring breath he related an incident, alluded to before, which created a doubt in his mind whether Amar would carry on the struggle for freedom and forsake the humble dwellings for the luxuries of palaces. "These sheds," said he, "will give way to sumptuous dwellings, thus generating the love of ease; and luxury with its concomitants will ensue, to which the independence of Mewar, which we have bled to maintain will be sacrificed; and you, my chiefs, will follow the pernicious example." They pledged with one voice to hold aloft his banner and assured him of the prince's devotion to his ideals. The soul of Pratap was satisfied and he expired with joy.

Rana Pratap lived and died like a true hero. He was an undaunted patriot. A brave warrior, a lover of freedom and a man whose self-respect was superb, he dedicated his life to an ideal in the pursuit of which he recked nothing of danger or death. He suffered much to maintain the honour of his house and the purity of his blood, and while the other Rajputs chose to bask in the sunshine of imperial favour, he held aloft the banner of freedom and challenged the greatest power in Hindustan. Every art that was employed to wean him from his ideals was treated with scorn, and every intrigue that was set on foot to frustrate his plans was foiled by his valour and enterprise. There is no other name in the Rajputs' Saga which is mentioned with greater honour and reverence. Lapse of time has not bedimmed the splendour of Pratap's achievements, and his epic heroism is as much an object of admiration to-day as it was in the sixteenth century. Even Akbar, on hearing the news of his death, was moved and admitted that his was an example worthy of the highest praise. The Moslem empire has vanished into the unknown; the great palaces and council-halls of Agra and Delhi lie tenantless, the Moslem and Rajput imperialists, who marched against the Rana to tame his proud spirit, are mere phantoms across the pages of history, but Pratap lives a charmed life. Even to-day his name is to all ardent lovers of liberty a cloud of hope by day and a pillar of fire by night. To those whose lot it is to engage in righteous but forlorn causes it is an abiding source of inspiration.

But, along with Pratap, history must accord its meed of praise to the men who fought and suffered with him. Abul Fazl and other court chroniclers have not a word of sympathy to offer for these hapless victims of imperial ambition who made their glory possible. Indeed in this drama of Mewar's struggle, as Vincent Smith remarks, the vanquished are greater than the victors, for their sacrifice and idealism added to the dignity of life, and enriched the pages of history as nothing else could have done. They fought for the honour of Rajasthan and unheeded the contagion of example. Unlike others of their tribe they chose poverty and exile as their lot in life. The race owes something to these men of noble minds and brave hearts, and if their foes added to the glory of the empire, they contributed to those graceful virtues without which wealth and power tend to turn men into brutes. Amidst much that is sordid and mean, their example stands like that of the Greeks and Romans of old who courted ruin in the service of the cause which they held dear. The deeds of such men are the salt of history and as long as man appreciates high aspiration and the endeavour to realise it, their remembrance shall remain a precious heritage of our race.

THE JAI MAHAL ON THE AMBER ROAD

BY PERMISSION OF THE SECRETARY OF STATE FOR INDIA

SHER SHAH

A reputed portrait of the great Afghan Emperor. From the Johnson Collection in the India Office.

SHER SHAH

THE GREAT AFGHAN LEADER

1486?–1545

BY CHARLES KINCAID, C.V.O.

THE real name of this eminent adventurer was Farid the son of Hasan. He was a member of the Afghan tribe of Sur, who claimed descent from the princes of Ghor. His grandfather, Ibrahim Khan, first entered the imperial service when Bahlul Lodi was emperor of Delhi. To Bahlul Lodi succeeded Sikandar Lodi, and in his reign Jamal Khan, the governor of Jaunpur, took into his service Ibrahim's son, Hasan Khan, and eventually conferred on him the districts of Sasaram and Tanda in Behar for the maintenance of five hundred horse.

Hasan Khan had eight sons, of whom only two, Farid Khan and Nizam Khan, were the legitimate sons of an Afghan mother. The other six were illegitimate and by different mothers. Hasan Khan so neglected his wife that when Farid grew up, he left home and enlisted as a private soldier in the service of Jamal Khan, the governor of Jaunpur. His father wrote to Jamal asking that he should send Farid back to be educated. To this young Farid objected that Jaunpur had better schools than Sasaram; at the same time he showed himself to be in earnest by committing to memory all Sheikh Sadi's Persian poetry and by becoming proficient in the other sciences and learning of the day. Three or four years later Hasan Khan visited Jaunpur. Through the offices of family friends he and his son become reconciled and Hasan appointed Farid manager of his Sasaram estate, while he himself settled at Jaunpur. Farid when accepting the post is reported to have said: "That the stability of every administration depended on justice and that it would be his greatest care not to violate it, whether by oppressing the weak or by permitting the strong to infringe the laws with impunity." This promise, which sounded like a pompous platitude, Farid kept alike as manager of his father's jaghir, as king of Bengal and as emperor of Delhi.

Unfortunately Farid's merits could not protect him from zanana intrigue. Hasan Khan's favourite concubine had borne him two sons, Suleiman and Ahmad. She used all her charms to secure the Sasaram jaghir for Suleiman. Hasan Khan was very reluctant to turn out Farid; but the young manager, to avoid further unpleasantness, voluntarily resigned his office and with his full brother, Nizam, went to Agra, where he obtained service with Daulat Khan Lodi. While Farid was at Agra his father, Hasan, died, and through Daulat Khan's influence Farid obtained the Sasaram jaghir. In 1526 Babur, the first Mogul emperor, invaded India with a small but veteran army and an admirable train of Turkish artillery. He defeated and killed the emperor Ibrahim Lodi and made himself master of the Delhi empire. Farid at first joined one Bahar or Bahadur Khan Lohani, who, under the title of Mahomed Shah, had proclaimed himself king of Behar. It was at this time that Farid changed his name. One day his master was charged, when out hunting, by a tiger and was in grave danger. Farid rushed at it and killed it with a blow of his sabre. For this act of loyal daring Mahomed Shah conferred on the young adventurer the title of Sher Khan, which he ever afterwards used.

In spite of his obligation to Sher Khan, Mahomed Shah allowed himself to be so prejudiced against him by tale bearers that he ordered him to surrender his jaghir to his brother Suleiman and sent a large body of troops to enforce the order. Sher Khan at first resisted, but afterwards fled to Sultan Janid, whom Babur had appointed governor of Karra and Manikpur. Obtaining troops from his new patron, he defeated Mahomed Shah and not only recovered his own jaghir, but seized several other districts, which he professed to hold from the new emperor Babur. He supported his professions by waiting in the train of Sultan Janid on the emperor, who confirmed him in his holdings and gave him a military command in Behar.

The imperial favour did not last long. While he was in the Mogul camp, Sher Khan was indiscreet enough to say to a friend that it would not be difficult to drive the foreigners out of India. The friend asked him his reasons. He replied that the emperor had ability, but that he left all his affairs to corrupt ministers and that if the Afghans united they could drive out the Moguls. He added that, if fortune favoured him, he regarded himself as equal to the task. Some time later Babur remarked in Sher Khan's hearing:

"This Afghan is not disconcerted by trifles: he may become a great man yet."

Sher Khan suspected that his rash words had been repeated to the emperor and that night he fled from the imperial camp to his estate.

The following year Mahmud Shah Lodi, a son of the dead king Sikandar Khan Lodi, conquered Behar with the help of a Rajput army. Sher Khan joined him, but the Rajput forces were defeated and dispersed by Babur and Sher Khan had no alternative but to make his submission to the Mogul. The magnanimous Babur pardoned him but offered him no post, so Sher Khan returned to Mahomed Shah Lohani, the self-appointed king of Behar. His patron died soon afterwards, but Sher Khan so won the affections of his widow, Sultana Lodi, the mother of the minor heir, Jalal Khan, that she bestowed on him and his supporters all the key positions in the Behar government. On her death the administration fell wholly into his hands. Unfortunately the increased power of his chief minister roused Jalal Khan's jealousy. He implored the help of the hereditary king of Bengal, Mahmud Shah Purbia. A Bengal army invaded Behar, but the military skill of Sher Khan triumphed over superior numbers. The invading army was destroyed, its general, Ibrahim Khan, killed and the minor Jalal Khan forced to flee an exile to Bengal.

Sher Khan thus became master of Behar, to which he shortly afterwards added the stronghold of Chunar and its dependent lands. The commandant was one Taj Khan, who held it as his own, although nominally for the Lodi family. He had two or three wives, one of whom was barren; by the others he had several children. The barren wife, Ladu Malika, in spite of her childlessness contrived to keep Taj Khan's affections. The other wives, who had borne Taj Khan sons, resented this preference. One of them urged her son to murder Ladu Malika. He struck her so clumsily that he inflicted only a slight wound. Taj Khan heard her cries and rushed at his son with drawn sword, only to fall slain in her defence. Ladu Malika roused the neighbourhood; and the local landholders, disgusted with the parricide, appointed Ladu Malika to manage the estate. Sher Khan, learning this, offered the widow marriage. She accepted the offer, so the Chunar fortress, its wide lands and immense treasure passed into the hands of Sher Khan. Afterwards,

THE WALLS OF PURANA QILA, BUILT BY SHER SHAH

THE MOSQUE OF SHER SHAH AT DELHI

I regret to say, he neglected the widow and left her a bare subsistence:

"Sher Khan took from the Bibi 300 mans of gold to equip his army and gave her two parganas for her support, besides leaving her some ready money for her immediate expenses."

In December, 1530, Babur died and his son, Humayun, succeeded him as Mogul emperor. For the first nine years of his reign Humayun was sufficiently occupied with the rebellions of his brothers and the conquest of Gujarat. In 1539 he resolved to check the rising power of Sher Khan. The latter had on two occasions sent contingents to the imperial army, but each time their commander, Sher Khan's son, had deserted at a critical moment with results disastrous to the Moguls. At the same time Sher Khan had in person invaded Bengal and shut up the king of Bengal, Mahmud Shah Purbia, in Gaur, his capital. Closely invested, Mahmud Shah saw his supplies run low. He tried to evacuate Gaur with his garrison, but he was overtaken and a battle forced on him. His army was defeated and he himself severely wounded. He fled and abandoned to Sher Khan the wealthy kingdom of Bengal.

While Sher Khan was still engaged in the siege of Gaur, Humayun marched on Bengal. On the road lay the fortress of Chunar which Sher Khan had strongly garrisoned. The Mogul officers pressed the emperor to take Chunar before proceeding. With greater wisdom his Indian officers urged him to mask it and press on to the relief of Gaur. Unfortunately for himself the emperor followed the advice of his Mogul officers and sat down before Chunar. The fortress held out beyond all expectation and by the time Chunar had fallen Gaur had also surrendered. As Humayun marched towards Gaur, he met near Patna the unhappy Mahmud Shah, who, still suffering from his wounds, implored the emperor's assistance in the recovery of his kingdom.

Sher Khan's forces were neither sufficiently disciplined nor numerous to meet the Mogul armies in the field. He, moreover, wanted time in which to store the captured treasures of the king of Bengal. He wished to deposit them in Rohtas, a strong place in the hilly tract to the south-west of Bengal. Rohtas did not belong to Sher Khan, but that mattered little to the resourceful adventurer. It was the capital of the Raja of Rohtas. To him Sher Khan sent a letter with valuable presents. He described his own distressful condition and begged the prince to give to the families of the Afghan soldiers shelter within his citadel. Sher Khan also took the precaution of sending a large bribe to the Raja's Naib or prime minister, a Brahman named Churaman. The latter accepted the bribe and acting as Sher Khan's advocate obtained the Raja's consent to receive the Afghan women and children. Afterwards the Raja Hari Krishna Rai changed his mind and revoked his consent. Sher Khan thereupon sent a still larger present (no less than six maunds of gold) to Churaman, begging him again to plead his cause. At the same time he threatened Hari Krishna Rai that he would make terms with Humayun and lead the Moguls in a joint attack on Rohtas if the Raja persisted in his refusal. Churaman took even stronger measures. He threatened to commit suicide. "If you do not admit," he said, "these families into the fort, I shall take poison and die at your doors."[1] Fearing to incur the blood guilt of a Brahman's death, Hari Krishna Rai reluctantly consented.

On obtaining the Raja's consent, Sher

[1] "*Sher Shah*," *by Kalikaranjan Qanungo, p.* 147.

Khan collected some twelve hundred litters. In the first dozen or two he seated old women. All the others he filled with picked Afghan soldiers, fully armed. As the litters entered the fort gates the sentries looked inside them and found them to contain only old women. Sher Khan then sent a message to the Raja, begging him to discontinue the examination of the litters. The sentries, he said, had satisfied themselves that they contained only old women. It would be highly indecorous that his Afghans' wives should be exposed to the gaze of common sepoys. The Raja was taken in by this mendacity and ordered the sentries to let the remaining litters pass without examination. When they had all entered, the Afghans sprang out and seized the fort gates. Sher Khan, who unobserved had brought a body of troops close to the fortress, rushed them inside. The Raja and his garrison resisted gallantly, but they were overcome. The prince escaped with difficulty through a postern gate at the back of the fortress, leaving Sher Khan master of his stronghold and of his family treasures. (March, 1538.)

While Sher Khan was securing Rohtas, Humayun marched in a somewhat leisurely fashion on Gaur, which he occupied without difficulty. He rested his army in the Bengal capital for three months when he learnt that his brother, Hindal Mirza, whom he had left in northern Behar, had seized Agra, put to death Humayun's loyal officer, Sheikh Bahlul, and had proclaimed himself a sovereign prince. It was no longer possible for the emperor to remain where he was, yet a march northwards was full of difficulty. The monsoon was at its height. The Gangetic Delta

MARTIN HURLIMANN

PURANA QILA

One of the gateways of the Old Fort.

was one vast sheet of water and brooks dry in the summer had become unfordable torrents. Sickness raged in the imperial army and the disheartened soldiers deserted in thousands. When progress became possible, it also became possible to Sher Khan. While Humayun's forces had shrunk, the Afghan's army had grown and he now became as bold as formerly he had been cautious. To clear the road for the march of the main body the emperor sent a strong vanguard under Khani Khan Lodi, a veteran officer trained in the school of Babur. Khani Khan Lodi reached Mungir without opposition and sending word to Humayun of his safe arrival, cantoned his troops until the imperial army should join him. A few weeks later Sher Khan's lieutenant, Khawas Khan, made a night attack on Mungir, surprised Khani Khan Lodi, took him prisoner and captured or killed his entire contingent.

Humayun was thunderstruck when the news of the disaster reached him. Leaving a garrison of five thousand men under Jahangir Kuli Beg in Gaur, he marched northwards. He reached Buxar safely, but at Chounsa or Jhusa he met Sher Shah, for the enterprising Afghan, confident in his past victories, had taken the title of Shah and pretended to the imperial throne itself. He had marched thirty-five miles to prevent Humayun from crossing the Ganges. The two armies entrenched themselves respectively on opposite banks of the river and watched each other for two months. Humayun collected boats and tried to make a bridge by which to convey his troops across. When the bridge was all but ready, Sher Shah took action (June, 1539). He hid his movements by leaving his camp standing and enough troops in it to conceal his departure. With a picked force he secretly crossed the river and shortly before daybreak fell on the imperial camp. Humayun's army was completely surprised and hardly resisted.

The emperor, who did not lack courage, fought until his chief officers insisted on his flight. He rode across the bridge of boats until he reached the still remaining gap. He then plunged his horse into the Ganges. The horse, exhausted by the current and the weight of its panoplied rider, sank and was drowned. Humayun would have shared its fate had not a water-carrier, who was at the time crossing on the inflated skin from which he distributed water, gone to the emperor's aid and brought him safely to the farther bank. In later years, as it is pleasant to read, Humayun, once more master of Delhi, sent for the water-carrier and, as a reward, bade him exercise the full imperial power for two hours. The water-carrier, undismayed by his sudden rise, spent the two hours profitably in providing himself and his relatives with extensive jaghirs.

Although Humayun did not perish in this disastrous action he lost almost his entire army. His empress, Bega Begum, fell into Sher Shah's hands. He treated her with the utmost courtesy and attention, and sent her at the first opportunity to a place of safety. Humayun with a dwindling retinue made his way first to Calpi and thence to Agra. The garrisons that he had stationed at Jaunpur and Chunar left their posts to join him. Sher Shah occupied the abandoned fortresses and proclaimed himself king of Bengal, Behar and Jaunpur; but he took no immediate steps to pursue the emperor. He feared that any such action might cause the emperor's brothers to join Humayun with their forces.

Sher Shah's proclamation of his assumption of the triple throne was an elaborate affair. He had the royal umbrella of the king of Bengal opened over his head. The *Khatba* was read in his name and he took the additional title of Al Sultan ul Adil or the Just Sultan. Abbas Sarwani's description is as follows:

"For seven days drums were beaten in token of rejoicing. Afghan youths came in troops from every tribe and danced according to Afghan custom. Gifts were made to the musicians and the servants of Sher Shah sprinkled saffron and musk, mixed with rose water and ambergris of various colours, upon the heads of the dancing youths. Delicious dishes emitted sweet scents that suggested the perennial flavour of the dinner table of heaven and drinks which suggested the sweetness of the Divine Love were distributed among the revellers." [1]

For eight months Humayun strove to raise another army. He was hampered by the treachery of his brother Kamran. The latter had heard that Humayun had been killed at Chaunsa and was bitterly disappointed at his safe arrival in Agra. He had marched on that town hoping to seize the imperial throne, but Humayun was already there. So Kamran, after months of useless discussion, retreated to Lahore, leaving with the emperor a draft of a thousand men. In April, 1540, Humayun, hearing that Sher Shah had reached the Ganges near Kanauj, marched to meet him. Indeed the constant desertions of his troops left the emperor no alternative. On the road Sultan Mirza, a general of the house of Timur, basely changed sides. Still Humayun thought it best to advance. On the 17th May, 1540, Sher Shah attacked the emperor at Bilgram. He had only fifteen thousand men, while the imperial

[1] *Quoted by Kalikaranjan Qanungo in "Sher Shah" p.* 206.

SHER SHAH'S TOMB MARTIN HURLIMANN

The mausoleum of the Afghan emperor at Sasaram. It is one of the most magnificent tombs in all India.

army numbered some forty thousand; but the latter had degenerated into a mob. As the Afghans advanced the Mogul soldiers broke and fled and Sher Shah seems to have won the battle without the loss of a single man.

In the pursuit the Moguls suffered heavy losses. Humayun, whose horse was wounded, could not swim the Ganges. He asked a mahout to take him across on his elephant. The mahout refused. Humayun knocked him off the elephant's back and put a eunuch in his place. The eunuch drove the elephant into the river, which it swam; but it could not mount the opposite bank. The emperor would have been drowned had not two soldiers tied their turbans together and thrown one end to their master and dragged him to safety. Humayun made his way back to Agra where two of his brothers, Hindal and Askari, joined him with contingents. Humayun did not linger at Agra. He collected his treasure and stores and retreated to Lahore, where Kamran reluctantly received him.

Sher Shah followed the fugitive, but Kamran did not wish to fight his brother's battles. He ceded the Panjab to the victor and fell back on Kabul. Forced to leave Lahore, Humayun tried in vain to establish himself in Sind first and then in Jodhpur. At last he found a refuge at Amarkot, the chief of which, Rana Prasad, received him hospitably. At Amarkot his wife gave birth to the famous Akbar. She was a Sindi, with the beauty for which Sindi women are still renowned, and she was called Hamida. He met her at an entertainment given in his honour by his step-mother, the mother of Prince Hindal. Against the family's wishes Humayun insisted on marrying Hamida and she bore him a son destined to raise the Mogul fortunes to their zenith. It was usual at the birth of a child for the father to give presents to his friends; but Humayun was absolutely destitute. All he could do was to break open a packet of musk, distribute fragments of it among those near him and express the hope that his son's fame would be diffused through the world like the odour of the perfume. Humayun again tried hard to establish himself in Sind, but again failed. At last he quitted the empire in despair and took refuge in Kandahar (1543). It was not until 1555 that he made his victorious return to Delhi.

The flight of Humayun left Sher Shah in possession of the Mogul empire; but before he could exercise complete control he had to reduce a number of powerful barons, who had like Sher Shah himself taken advantage of the general unrest to make themselves independent. A certain Rajput, Puran Mal, had established himself in Malwa or Central India and had treated the Moslems there with intolerant cruelty. His chief stronghold was Raisin. In January, 1543, Sher Shah's son, Jalal Khan, marched against Puran Mal. After Humayan's flight Sher Shah joined his son; but the Rajput prince defended himself with obstinate courage. At last Puran Mal offered to evacuate the fort, if he and his troops and their families were granted a safe conduct and the honours of war. The Afghan emperor agreed and withdrew his troops to a distance of two marches and swore solemn oaths that he would in no way molest the Rajput retirement.

It is probable that Sher Shah meant honourably to keep the terms of peace; but he had not counted on the savage temper of his followers. Directly the Afghan soldiery saw the Rajputs marching through the open plain they disregarded completely their leader's commands. At the same time the Moslem priests pressed on Sher Shah the wickedness of keeping a treaty with the unbelievers.

Sher Shah had to watch helplessly while a division of his Afghan troops set out in pursuit of Puran Mal. The Rajputs met their assailants with their usual splendid courage. They first killed their wives and children. They then clothed themselves in saffron to show that they would neither give nor take quarter and, charging the Afghans, died fighting to a man.

From Central India Sher Shah marched against Jodhpur in Rajputana; but it was no light task to conquer the Rahtor cavalry in their own plains. The military skill of the Raja Maldev checked Sher Shah's advance at Mairta, some seventy miles north-east of Jodhpur. The two armies entrenched, but Sher Shah had far greater difficulty in obtaining supplies than the Rahtors. Soon the Afghans were in a desperate plight. Sher Shah extricated his men by a ruse that should have deceived no one. He forged letters in the name of the Raja's nobles and caused them to be dropped near the tent of Maldev's vakil. The latter sent them to his prince. Completely hoodwinked, Maldev ordered an instant retreat. It was in vain that the nobles swore to their loyalty by the most solemn oaths; the Raja fled, panic-stricken, to Jodhpur.

Some of his chiefs with twelve thousand men vindicated their honour by attacking, unsupported, the entire Afghan army in position and died fighting. Thereafter Sher Shah rapidly overran the whole of Rajputana and even Mewar made no resistance. Having accepted the submission of the Rajput chiefs, Sher Shah returned to Central India. There he invested Kalinjar (November, 1544). He first offered the Raja easy terms which the Rajputs, mindful of the Afghan treachery at Raisin, contemptuously rejected. The emperor then sat down before the fortress. To quote the words of the Tarikh-i-Daudi:

"Sher Shah encircled Kalinjar and began to construct mines and a lofty tower for mounting a battery and covered approaches. The latter reached the fort and the tower was built so high that the land within the fort could be overlooked from its top. For the space of seven months the soldiers and camp-followers laboured day and night."[1]

On the 22nd May a general assault was ordered. The first attempt was defeated by the heavy stones rolled down by the defenders. Sher Shah ordered a second attack, led by grenadiers carrying hand bombs. In his eagerness he went part of the way with them to encourage them. Unhappily, one of the bombs fell short and striking the parapet of the wall rebounded and exploded close to a powder magazine, which instantly blew up. Several of the generals were hurt but Sher Shah was mortally injured. In spite of his sufferings he still directed the assault. When the fortress was finally carried, the emperor exclaimed "Thanks be to God!" and never spoke again.

So ended the life story of this brilliant soldier of fortune. From the rank of a private he rose to be emperor of India. A most skilful and active general, he yet found time to bring order into his territories and he constantly sought to improve the civil government. He made roads with rest-houses at every stage and he dug wells at intervals of a mile or two miles. By the roadside he planted innumerable trees and he compelled the owners of the land through which the roads passed to suppress brigandage and to see to it that travellers could journey in safety. His early death was a heavy loss to India, for he left no posterity capable of continuing the great traditions of his reign.

[1] *Quoted by Kalikaranjan Qanungo in "Sher Shah," p. 339.*

AKBAR

Two impressions of the Great Mogul. The top right-hand sketch is from the Johnson Collection in the India Office; (below) a head taken from a painting of Abdur Rahim with inset portraits of Akbar and Jahangir.

BY COURTESY OF THE SECRETARY OF STATE FOR INDIA AND THE BRITISH MUSEUM

AKBAR

THE GREAT MOGUL

1542–1605

BY ROBERT BRYAN

In the month of November, 1542, Humayun, son of Babur, and successor to the power which that great soldier had built up in northern India was a fugitive, hunted and harassed, in the parched and arid desert of Sind. Indolent and pleasure-loving, he had lost in a few years all that his father had won, and Sher Shah, the Afghan, now ruled at Delhi while Humayun depended precariously on the chance hospitality of various chiefs, upon whose mercy he threw himself.

In that month he was the guest of the friendly Raja of Umarkot; he lay in camp with a small body of horsemen some distance from the little walled fortress, while within it his wife Hamida awaited her confinement. On a night of the full moon she gave birth to a son, and the next morning messengers reached Humayun's camp with the news. Normally such a day would have been spent in celebrations and the giving of presents, but Humayun was penniless. Yet some sort of pretence at ceremony there must be, so he collected all the valuables that the camp possessed and solemnly presented them to their rightful owners. Then, seated in his tent, he broke a pod of musk over a plate and distributed the grains among his personal followers. "This is all the present I can afford to make you on the birth of my son, whose fame will I trust one day be expanded over all the world, as the perfume of the musk now fills this tent." He named the child Akbar, which means "Great."

The first years of Akbar's life afforded little hope that his father's wish would be fulfilled; indeed seldom can a child have been born into such a hazardous environment. Within a year he had been separated from his parents, captured by his uncle, Askari, while Humayun fled westwards to Persia, and taken to Kandahar where his uncle ruled. Thence he was moved to the court of his other uncle Kamran at Kabul. That neither uncle chose quietly to murder him for fear he might be a potential rival to their ambitions was a lucky exception to the general practice of those days.

Two years later, in 1545, Humayun, with Persian aid, defeated both his brothers and entered Kabul in triumph, where he ruled for the next nine years. But his position was for long insecure and he had to make frequent expeditions to quell revolts. During one of these Kamran reoccupied Kabul, and it is told how, while Humayun was trying to retake the city, Akbar was held aloft on the ramparts as a target for his father's artillery. If the story is true luck was with him, as it was to be so often, for he escaped unscathed.

Humayun was a man of culture, a lover of art and learning, but for long it appeared as if his son would have none of these things. He was given tutors, but obstinately he refused to learn either to read or write. He seemed happy only when he was with animals. Over wild beasts he developed early an extraordinary power and there were few, however savage, that he could not tame to his will. The life that, during these years in Afghanistan, he chose whenever possible to lead was that of a tamer of beasts rather than of the heir to empire. At

BY COURTESY OF THE VICTORIA AND ALBERT MUSEUM, LONDON

THE BUILDING OF FATEHPUR SIKRI

In 1569 Akbar's son and heir Salim was born at Sikri. To commemorate the event he started to build there his new and magnificent capital Fatehpur Sikri.

BY COURTESY OF THE VICTORIA AND ALBERT MUSEUM, LONDON

AKBAR INSPECTING HIS NEW CITY

The Mogul emperor himself inspecting the work on the Royal City. Scenes from the illustrated Akbarnamah (History of Akbar). Mogul School, 16th century.

the age of twelve there were few signs of the embryo statesman, but perhaps those around him wondered what would happen if some day he chose to exert his abnormal will-power over men as well as over animals. For the moment, however, he was, or seemed, no more than a wild untutored boy.

Humayun had never given up hope of regaining his lost empire, and in 1554 he found his opportunity. The Afghans who ruled in his stead at Delhi were quarrelling among themselves; Humayun, accompanied by Akbar, crossed the Indus in December, recovered the Punjab, and finally re-entered Delhi, which he had left in flight fifteen years earlier. He made Akbar governor of the Punjab under the tutelage of Bairam Khan, his ablest and most faithful supporter; then, suddenly, a year later he died.

So, at the age of thirteen, Akbar was proclaimed emperor. Emperor of what? It is the question that has faced every man who has aspired to make himself ruler in India, and which was to face Akbar, the greatest of them all, to the day of his death. The answer in January, 1556, was "Of very little." Two armies still held the field in overwhelming superiority against the Moguls, and behind, in Afghanistan, was open insurrection. One defeat and Akbar would become, like his father before him, a hunted fugitive. Bairam Khan acted with great resolution and marched at once against the vast Hindu-Afghan army under the command of the Hindu Hemu, which had occupied Agra and Delhi. The armies, small but compact against vast but unwieldy, met on the historic field of Panipat, three times the scene of battles decisive in Indian

TOMB OF SHEIKH SALEM CHISHTI

The holy recluse who had prophesied the birth of Akbar's sons lies in this splendid tomb at Fatehpur Sikri.

BY COURTESY OF THE VICTORIA AND ALBERT MUSEUM, LONDON

THE BIRTH OF SALIM

Rejoicings at the birth of Akbar's son and heir Prince Salim. From the Akbarnamah. Mogul School, 16th century.

history. Hemu's army was routed and Hemu himself, blinded and unconscious, was dragged before the young emperor. What followed is uncertain; Akbar was bidden by Bairam Khan to strike off the head of his helpless enemy, but whether, as some say, he obeyed eagerly or whether he shrank in disgust from such a deed, will never be known. Hemu, by whatever means, was killed and with his defeat and death resistance collapsed. Akbar was emperor now in more than name; the Mogul power was foremost in northern India.

For the next four years Bairam Khan ruled the country and Akbar's foster-mother, Maham Anaga, ruled the palace. Akbar seemed content to remain in the background, a cipher emperor. But all the time he was developing, and learning. To the day of his death he remained illiterate, but now he was eager that people should read to him, above all his favourite works—those of the Sufic mystic poets. The choice was significant, showing the growth of a mind at once highly intelligent and at times despairing of the world as it was. It contrasted strangely with the wild, animal side of his nature, unsubjected as yet to any self-restraint. An incident when he was fifteen illustrates the contrast. Suddenly violent and self-willed, he demanded one day his favourite horse, vicious and high-mettled, and galloped away alone and furiously into the empty plain that lies around Agra. As suddenly, he dismounted. He fell into a trance and in his own words "communed with God." Presently he awoke to normality, to find himself alone; his horse had galloped away. He waited, uncertain what to do; then he saw in the distance his horse galloping across the

PANCH MAHAL: FATEHPUR SIKRI

GLORIES OF FATEHPUR SIKRI

The famous carved pillar which stands in the centre of the Diwan-i-Khas (Hall of Private Audience), Fatehpur Sikri.

plain to him. It was a sign that he must return to the world and find his life's work therein. The story is Akbar's; what is important is that he believed in it.

He was learning about people too. Often after night had fallen he would slip out disguised from the palace, to mingle with the crowds in the bazaar, watching their behaviour, particularly the behaviour of the Hindus. More than any other Mogul ruler he came to realise the point of view of his Hindu subjects. And in the palace he watched the intrigues, the plots and counter-plots of the courtiers who surrounded him, though he gave as yet no sign that he noticed them. Bairam Khan and Maham Anaga regarded him still as a boy; the court's main fear was lest his reckless bravery should lead to disaster. He would have two elephants goaded into savagery, then ride one against the other, so that it seemed he must be killed; but no beast was too violent and vicious for him to control. Such was Akbar in 1560.

Court intrigues came to a head in that year. Maham Anaga had grown jealous of the power of Bairam Khan, wishing his place to be held by her own son, Adham Khan. The young Akbar listened to her advice and, moving for safety's sake to Agra, issued from there a command that Bairam Khan should go on pilgrimage to Mecca. The message that he sent was curt and uncompromising. "I have determined to take the reins of government in my own hands, and it is desirable that you should make the pilgrimage to Mecca, upon which you have been so long intent." Addressed to one who had served both Akbar and his father so long and on the whole so well, it might have been intended deliberately to provoke disobedience. Such was its effect, but Bairam Khan's rebellion was short-lived. Akbar pardoned him—an almost unheard-of occurrence in those days—but on his way to Mecca the old warrior was murdered. His son, Abdurrahmin, was brought to Akbar, protected by him, and became one of his most faithful supporters.

THE DESERTED CAPITAL

A general view of the red sandstone city of Fatehpur Sikri to-day, showing the Buland Darwaza (Great Gate) and the Hiran Minar (Deer Minaret).

BY COURTESY OF THE VICTORIA AND ALBERT MUSEUM, LONDON

PRINCE SALIM

The eldest son and heir of Akbar, who came to the throne as Jahangir.

FROM THE AKBARNAMAH—

BY COURTESY OF THE VICTORIA AND ALBERT MUSEUM, LONDON

SCENES SHOWING AKBAR HUNTING

Maham Anaga thought herself triumphant; her son would now succeed to the position of first soldier in the land. Akbar seemed to acquiesce in this arrangement, and Adham Khan led an army to subdue the kingdom of Malwa. He succeeded in his task, but he failed to send to Akbar either the booty or the captured women. For the first of many times Akbar acted with unexpected, overwhelming swiftness. Before his foster-brother knew that he had left Agra he appeared in his camp. Taken unawares Adham Khan begged forgiveness and on the entreaties, of Maham Anaga, received it; but Akbar did not forgive him.

Adham Khan hastened his own doom. His mother grew jealous of a new minister whom Akbar had appointed; Adham Khan stabbed him to death in the palace at Agra. Roused at dead of night from the harem where he was sleeping, Akbar confronted the murderer. Adham Khan raised his sword against him, whereupon Akbar struck him senseless with a single blow on the face. He commanded that he be thrown from the wall of the fort into the moat below. When the servants picked him up from the ground he was not quite dead. Akbar ordered that he be thrown down again and watched while the man who had been his boyhood's constant companion was hurled again to his death. Maham Anaga, prostrated by grief, died six weeks later.

Akbar had asserted himself; those who had sought to dominate him had paid dearly for the attempt. At the age of twenty, emerging—in the words of Abul Fazl, his historian and devoted servant—"from behind the veil," he assumed absolute control of his government, never to let it go. In the previous two years he had displayed ingratitude and an almost barbarous cruelty, but he had also shown unsuspected powers of swift, decisive action which had brought him to a position which at the time of his father's death had seemed quite beyond his grasp.

To that power of swift action, allied to great physical strength and to bravery that in anyone else would have been wanton recklessness, he owed the unbroken series of military successes that marked his reign. He seemed always to think quicker, act quicker than his opponents. The semi-independent States of central India—even Chitor, the proudest and most stubborn of them all—came under his effective control, and Gujerat, bringing an outlet to the sea. Bengal was his, and Gondwana and Orissa. He never knew defeat in battle and only when in his last years, like his successors and as unwisely, he crossed the river Narbada to add the Deccan to his dominions, did he suffer any sort of check. Such achievement alone would have been sufficient to rank him with the great conquerors of India, but it is as great soldier, statesman and religious enquirer combined that Akbar is unique in Indian history, and in the fact that he realised that India must be united by consent as well as by force if his empire was to survive him.

The keystone of his statesmanship was his conciliation of his Hindu subjects. No previous Moslem conqueror had even thought of such a policy, yet Akbar had already, in 1561, married a princess of Amber, a leading Rajput house. Rapidly he pursued his policy. For many years every Hindu had been forced to pay a pilgrim and a poll tax; both these were now swept away. Hindu princes sat in places of honour at the court at Agra; Tan Sen, the great singer of Gwalior, became one of Akbar's intimates; later, Todar Mal was to reorganise the finances of the empire, and Man Singh was to become Akbar's most trusted general. Though

BY COURTESY OF THE VICTORIA AND ALBERT MUSEUM, LONDON

ADHAM KHAN PAYS HOMAGE

Adham Khan having conquered Malwar, failed to send to Agra either booty or women. Akbar appeared suddenly in his camp, and the terrified Adham Khan pleaded for mercy.

he ruthlessly crushed those who opposed his desire to conquer, as when the gallant Rajputs of Chitor were massacred because they had resisted so long and so bravely, he nearly always conciliated after he had crushed. He caused statues to be erected in Delhi to Jaimal, Chitor's chief defender, and to Patta, the young prince who had perished in the siege.

His most perilous and spectacular military exploit in these early years of his power was his famous march to Gujerat. Rebellion had flared up after that province's conquest in 1572. It was midsummer and the rebels had no thought that Akbar would attempt the 600 miles march from Agra to Ahmedabad through the stifling heat of Rajputana. Within eleven days he was upon them. At once, though outnumbered, he attacked. In his impetuosity he outdistanced his followers, found himself, a river at his back, almost alone and faced by a large force of rebels. Without hesitation he charged, and, astounded and terrified, his opponents fled. In a few hours the city had capitulated. Henceforth his enemies in battle were to regard him always as more than human.

In the early years of his reign Akbar made Agra his capital. There two sons were born to him and died in infancy. He grew to hate the place and to be fearful of having no heir. A Moslem holy man living in the barren neighbourhood of Sikri prophesied for him three further sons. Shortly afterwards his Hindu wife became pregnant. Akbar sent her to Sikri, where his child and heir, Salim, was born in 1569. Akbar, who did nothing in half measures, began to build there at phenomenal cost the city which for fifteen years was to be his capital, the scene of the richest life, the most splendid court, some of the finest architecture of the age. Even to-day, deserted for 350 years, Fatehpur Sikri, with its ruined red sandstone walls and palaces, remains one of the wonders of the East.

In the royal stables of this city, bigger than the London of that century, were 5,000 elephants; at the court, painters, richly rewarded, evolved that exquisite style of painting, half Persian, half Hindu in origin, which we know as the Mogul school; within the city walls it is said that 5,000 women inhabited the Zenana, awaiting Akbar's pleasure, while young nobles played polo by night with specially illuminated balls. Fatehpur Sikri became the setting for a display of imperial splendour and at times excess that has seldom been rivalled.

It was the scene also of Akbar's greatest experiment—the founding of a new religion. He had favoured the Hindus; as the years advanced he came to a hatred of the fanatically orthodox Moslems who aspired to a monopoly of religion. His enquiring, semi-mystic mind revolted against their absolute acceptance of the words of the Koran, and he saw them as the real obstacle in the way of the unification of his empire. Also, and less worthily, he wanted to be its religious as well as secular head.

In 1575 he started religious discussions between the various Moslem sects, at which he was the audience. Each speaker drove him further from the religion of his fathers. He preferred what the Hindus taught; it approached nearer to his own secret mysticism; but for a while he preferred to any other doctrine the exciting new creed of Christianity, brought to him by Portuguese missionaries from Goa. In 1577 the Jesuit Father, Pereira, visited the Mogul court and in 1580 there arrived the first formal mission, led by Aquaviva and Monserrate. Meanwhile Akbar had had himself proclaimed Imam-i-Adil (spiritual head of the empire) and had passed laws forbidding the building of new mosques and the appointment of new

BY COURTESY OF THE VICTORIA AND ALBERT MUSEUM, LONDON

ARREST OF BAIRAM KHAN

Bairam Khan, once minister to Humayun, was accused of intrigue by Maham Anaga, Akbar's foster mother. He was assassinated as he journeyed towards Mecca on pilgrimage.

Moslem judges. He thereby jeopardised the loyalty of strict Moslems.

For a time it seemed that he would make Christianity his religion. Christian worship was encouraged at Fatehpur Sikri; the Jesuit Fathers were offered riches and honours—which they declined—and Murad, Akbar's second son, was given instruction in the Christian faith. The Fathers themselves thought that they were gaining a convert. But Christianity seemed to Akbar, on closer acquaintance, as intolerant of other faiths as Islam; it was dogmatic, and his mind revolted from dogma of every kind; moreover, it demanded from him a spirit of humility and obedience which he was not in the least prepared to give. The Fathers insisted that he should give up the excesses of his daily life, and on occasions he was himself revolted by them. In the middle of an enormous hunt, when the beasts had been driven in by beaters from a radius of 40 miles, he suddenly ordered the hunt to cease, letting all the animals go free and unharmed. But he was not prepared to forego his pleasures at the command of others, pleasures that were as much a part of him as his occasional mystical experiences.

So he rejected Christianity, as he did every other established religion, though he encouraged the Jesuits to remain. Dissatisfied with them all, he invented a religion of his own, which he called the Din Ilahi.

Its principles, never very clear, seemed to derive mainly from Hinduism. There was to be one impersonal God, the sun, stars and fire being his manifestations. The objects of all men were to be the conquest of evil and the practice of virtue. In practice it became almost at once a glorification, then a deification of Akbar himself. It survived until Akbar's death, but it survived only through the personality of its founder. Its active supporters numbered only a handful—Abul Fazl and his brother Faizi, Hindus close to the throne like Raja Birbal and Todar Mal, and, unwillingly, Abdurrahmin and Man Singh—its opponents were many and bitter. It provoked serious rebellions in Bengal and Afghanistan, which it took all Akbar's military genius to quell, and opposition to it rallied its opponents round Salim, the heir to the throne. It was in fact a failure, but it was a magnificent failure, the mistake of a great man who had overreached himself.

Religion was not Akbar's sole preoccupation during these brilliant middle years at Fatehpur Sikri. He did much to improve and stabilise the administration of his empire. Unafraid to surround himself with able men as his ministers, he went far towards abolishing the corrupt feudal Jagirdar system. Taxation was no longer farmed out, communications became safer, and later, by giving full rein to the genius of Todar Mal, he allowed the evolution of a system of taxation that was copied centuries later by the British. Judged by the standards of the day, Akbar's administration was a marvel of enlightened government. There were hideous poverty and wretchedness, but there was a measure of justice and enlightenment, as in Akbar's ban on the burning of widows.

The fifteen years in the "rose-red city" marked the zenith of Akbar's glory. He lives for us in numerous paintings by Mogul artists of his day, and in the writings of his contemporaries. Almost fair in complexion, burly but not tall, he had small regular features, intensely mobile, a flashing eye, a head carried slightly on one side. The keynote to his temperament was energy that on occasions exploded into unbridled excess of violence. It has been said of him that "in whatever assemblage of

BY COURTESY OF THE VICTORIA AND ALBERT MUSEUM, LONDON

AKBAR WELCOMED HOME

Akbar, returning to his capital of Fatehpur Sikri, is welcomed by his three sons. Prince Salim kisses his stirrup. Behind him stand Murad and Daniyal.

men, he is recognisably the king." Whether giving audience, gorgeously arrayed, to his nobles or appearing, as he did every day, before the common people, his was an overmastering personality, incalculable but great.

Incalculably he deserted Fatehpur Sikri and made Agra once again his capital. There he was to retain his power and much of his prestige, but his glory was to be dimmed. Success, it is true, still attended him, and Sind and Kashmir were added to his empire, but Moslem discontent grew steadily, as did the disloyalty of Salim. Akbar, like his descendants after him, suffered cruelly from the behaviour of his sons. Murad died from delirium tremens; Daniyal, for long the favourite, became a worthless degenerate; Salim, moody, uncouth, and bitterly jealous of his father, became an open rebel.

By 1593 India north of the river Narbada was Akbar's; there remained only the Deccan to conquer. In that year Akbar demanded from the ruler of Ahmednagar acknowledgment of his paramountcy, and on the latter's refusal sent his armies southwards to enforce his demands. It was three years before they achieved any success, and though Ahmednagar then ceded the province of Berar no conclusive victory was achieved. In 1599 Murad, joint commander in the Deccan, died, and Akbar, who had hitherto remained at Agra, took command in person. As always his presence brought victory. The great fort of Asirgarh was taken amid scenes of horrible cruelty and Ahmednagar itself, gallantly defended by the Princess Chand Bibi, fell in 1600.

But if his presence brought victory, his absence from Agra brought open rebellion by Salim, who proclaimed himself emperor at Allahabad. Akbar left Abul Fazl in command in the Deccan and returning northwards forestalled Salim's march on Agra. There followed a stunning blow; Abul Fazl, returning north, was ambushed and murdered at Salim's instigation and his head brought in triumph to Allahabad. In all Akbar's triumphs and schemes Abul Fazl had been nearest to him of all, his most staunch and unwavering supporter, his dearest and constant friend. Akbar raged against Salim, but either he could not or he would not advance against him. There followed negotiations, at the end of which father and son were officially reconciled, but Salim still plotted while a party at court was planning to supplant Salim by his son, Khusru. Finally Akbar, hearing news of a new plot, commanded his son to come before him; Salim refused and Akbar marched against him. In vain his mother, the aged Hamida Begum, pleaded for her grandson, but less vainly, while Akbar was marching, did she die. Akbar turned back to mourn her (according to Hindu fashion, by shaving his head) at Agra. There he heard also that his third son, Daniyal, was dead.

How could he march against his only surviving son? He relented and Salim was persuaded to submit; but at their meeting Akbar's pent-up rage and resentment overcame him and he struck him, cursing him, across the face. Salim, cowed before him, was put under arrest, but in a few days Akbar's rage turned to forgiveness. Salim was pardoned and went free, though not yet assured of the succession to the imperial throne. He had not, however, long to wait. Men who live violently, vividly and emotionally often die suddenly. Akbar was taken ill with dysentery in 1605; the tragedies of the previous years may have hastened his end. In October it became known that he was dying. Some of his last visitors were Jesuit Fathers, still welcome at his court; but he was not to be converted. Finally

BY COURTESY OF THE VICTORIA AND ALBERT MUSEUM, LONDON

BURNING OF THE RAJPUT WOMEN

Scene from the siege of Chitorgarh. When it was realised that the fort was lost the Rajput women cast themselves into the flames, while the men marched out to meet certain death.

F. HENLE

AKBAR'S TOMB

In the middle of a great garden at Sikandra, not far from Agra, stands the fine mausoleum of the Emperor Akbar. It is built of red sandstone, inlaid with marble.

Salim was summoned. When he reached the sick bed, Akbar could no longer speak, but he made signs that Salim should clothe himself in the imperial turban and gird on the sword of Humayun. The succession was assured. Then after a while, on October 27, he died.

But his empire lived on after him, to be destroyed only by the mad bigotry of his great-grandson, Aurangzeb. The wonder of his age, he does not diminish in stature with the passage of time. Part mystic, part man of action, gentle and cruel, tolerant and self-willed, ascetic and voluptuary, he astonishes us to-day by the complexity, but still more by the intense force of his character. The hope expressed by his father, that his fame would spread through all the world, has been fulfilled. The child born in poverty and flight in the desert of Sind became Akbar the Great Mogul, one of the great men of the world.

BY COURTESY OF THE BRITISH MUSEUM

AKBAR AND SALIM (JAHANGIR)

BY COURTESY OF THE BRITISH MUSEUM, LONDON

THE EMPEROR JAHANGIR

The fourth Mogul emperor sitting under a canopy drinking wine. By Manohar.

JAHANGIR

"WORLD GRASPER"

1605–1627

BY H. G. RAWLINSON, C.I.E.

On October 27, 1605, the great Emperor Akbar passed to his rest. One of his last acts was to signify to the nobles gathered round his bedside that Prince Salim should be invested with the royal turban and the sword of Humayun. Salim was the Emperor's eldest and favourite son, the offspring of his marriage with the sister of the Rajput chief, Raja Bihari Mal of Amber, whom he had espoused in the hope of welding the Hindu and Moslem peoples into a single nation. Salim was born, so his father believed, in answer to the prayers of the famous saint Shaikh Salim Chishti of Sikri, 23 miles from Agra, where Akbar afterwards founded his dream-city. This was in 1569, so Salim was 36 years old at the time of his father's death. He had received a liberal education, partly at the hands of the gallant Jesuit Fathers who had come from Goa to Akbar's Court, and at one time it seemed possible that he might be converted to Christianity. He had, however, proved to be a wayward and unstable young man, and declined the position of Viceroy of the Deccan in order that he might not be deprived of the luxuries of life in the capital. In 1600, in a fit of jealousy at his father's preference for his other son, Prince Daniyal, he retired in a dudgeon to Bengal, where he started a rebellion. Two years later, he almost broke Akbar's heart by hiring a ruffian to assassinate his trusted friend and counsellor, Abul Fazl, whom Salim hated and feared. But in 1604, father and son were reconciled.

As soon as he ascended the throne, Salim assumed the title of Jahangir or World Grasper. He issued a proclamation assuring his subjects that he would protect the Mohammedan religion, and promising various reforms such as a general release of prisoners, the abolition of barbarous punishments, the suppression of highway robbery, the prohibition of the sale of intoxicants, and the confirmation of noblemen and religious bodies in their estates. This, however, did not prevent popular risings in favour of his son Khusru, a gentle and enlightened young man, who is described as "a gentleman of a very lovely presence and fine carriage, exceedingly beloved of the common people." Khusru had been confined in Agra fort, but he escaped to the Punjab, where he raised the standard of rebellion. He was joined by an army of peasants, and the Sikh Pontiff Arjun gave him a sum of money and his blessing, "not because he was a prince, but because he was needy and friendless."

The rebellion was easily put down. The governor of Lahore refused to open the gates of the city to the insurgents, and Khusru and his chief adherents were captured and brought before the Emperor. Jahangir describes the punishment he meted out to the two ringleaders. "I ordered these two villains to be enclosed in the skins of a cow and an ass, and to be paraded round the city. As the skin of a cow dries quicker than the skin of an ass, Hussain Beg only lived to the fourth watch. Abdul Aziz, who was in the ass's skin, lived for twenty-four hours and was then released. To strengthen and confirm

BY COURTESY OF THE BODLEIAN LIBRARY

"LIGHT OF THE WORLD"

A reputed portrait of Nur Jahan, the only wife of Jahangir. A strong-minded woman, she grasped the reins of government and kept them in her capable hands.

our rule, I directed that a dense row of stakes should be set up from the garden to the city, and that the rebels should be impaled thereon and thus receive their deserts in this most excruciating punishment." The Emperor, on a gorgeously caparisoned elephant, rode between the lines of his writhing victims followed by the unhappy Khusru, trembling and weeping at the horrible fate which had overtaken his adherents. Another distinguished sufferer for his share in the rebellion was Arjun who, though he was the Fifth Guru of the Sikh sect and compiler of their Adi Granth or Bible, was tortured to death for refusing to pay the fine imposed upon him; the Sikhs never forgot this act. Khusru himself was blinded with hot irons and imprisoned for life. After a time he partly recovered his sight, and was made the catspaw of contending factions until his death, caused, as everyone believed, by his brother Khurram, in 1622. It was a tragedy that Khusru never succeeded to the throne for, had he done so, the history of the period would have been a very different story. "If Sultan Khusru prevail," wrote Sir Thomas Roe, our Ambassador and a very shrewd observer, "this kingdom will be a sanctuary for Christians, whom he loves and honours, favouring learning, valour and the discipline of war, abhorring all covetousness, and discerning the base custom of taking, used by his ancestors and the nobility." He was looked on by the common folk as a martyr to their cause and wherever his body halted on its way to its last resting-place in the garden named after him in Allahabad, a shrine was erected to his memory, surrounded by a tiny plot of grass.

Unlike other Mohammedans of his day, he had refused to contract numerous alliances, and had married only a single wife, to whom he was devoted.

Such enlightened souls as Khusru had, alas, but a very small chance of surviving in those hard and cruel times.

BY COURTESY OF THE VICTORIA AND ALBERT MUSEUM, LONDON

MINISTER OF JAHANGIR

Wazir Asaf Khan, brother of Nur Jahan, who was Jahangir's chief minister.

At the beginning of his reign, in spite of his promises, Jahangir showed marked favour to the Jesuit Fathers. He decorated his throne room with pictures representing biblical subjects, and portraits of the Pope and the King of Spain. Church processions with full Catholic ceremonial were to be seen in the streets of Agra and Lahore, and, to the great scandal of the orthodox, the Emperor sealed official documents with a signet bearing the effigies of Christ and His Mother. In 1607, however, the Jesuits received a severe set-back on the arrival at Agra of Captain William Hawkins of the newly-formed East India Company, with a letter from James I of England, asking for the grant of trade facilities. Hawkins had learnt Turkish in the Levant, and this was so closely allied to Turki, Jahangir's mother-tongue, that they could converse without an interpreter. Hawkins was a jovial Elizabethan toper, and Jahangir had the family weakness for drink; the consequence was that Hawkins rose to high favour, and the two sat carousing together until a late hour every night. Hawkins was made a "Commander of 400," with a salary of 30,000 rupees a year, and this so incensed the Jesuits, says Hawkins, that they became "like madde dogges," and, if we can credit his story, even tried to poison him. The Emperor provided him with an Armenian wife to cook his food. Hawkins went home in 1611, and in the following year the Portuguese, who had sent a large fleet to turn the English out of their newly-acquired factory in Surat, were completely defeated by two tiny English merchantmen. "The Great Mogul, which before thought none comparable to the Portuguese at sea, much wondered at the English resolution." From this event we may reckon the beginning of British ascendancy in India. Hawkins gives a fascinating account of Jahangir's daily life:

SHALIMAR GARDENS, KASHMIR

The Shalimar Bagh, most lovely of all the gardens Jahangir laid out. To Kashmir he went when his health failed and amid these gardens he died.

BY COURTESY OF THE VICTORIA AND ALBERT MUSEUM, LONDON

JAHANGIR HOLDING COUNCIL IN A GARDEN

"First in the morning about the break of day he is at his beads with his face turned to the westward. The manner of his praying when he is in Agra is in a private fair room, upon a goodly jet stone, having only a Persian lamb-skin under him; having also some eight chains of beads, every one containing four hundred. At the upper end of this jet stone the pictures of Our Lady and Christ are placed, graven in stone; so he turneth over his beads and saith 3,200 words, according to the number of his beads, and then his prayer is ended. After he hath done, he showeth himself to the people, receiving their salames or good-morrows; unto whom multitudes resort every morning for this purpose. This done, he sleepeth two hours more, and then dineth, and passeth his time with his women; and at noon he showeth himself to the people again, sitting till three by the clock, viewing and seeing his pastimes and sports made by men and fighting of many sorts of beasts, every day sundry kinds of pastimes.

"Then at three of the clock all the nobles in general (that be in Agra and are well) resort unto the Court, the King coming forth in open audience, sitting in his seat royal, and every man standing in this degree before him, his chiefest sort of nobles standing within the red rail, and the rest without. They are all placed by his lieutenant-general. This red rail is three steps higher than the place where the rest stand; and within this red rail I was placed, amongst the chiefest of them all. The rest are placed by officers, and they likewise be within another very spacious place railed; and without that rail all sorts of horsemen and soldiers that belong unto his captains and all other comers. At these rails there are many doors kept by many porters, who have white rods to keep men in order. In the midst of the place, right before the King, standeth one of his sheriffs, together with the master hangman, who is accompanied by forty hangmen, wearing on their heads a certain quilted cap different from all others, with hatchets on their shoulders; and others with all sorts of whips being there ready to do what the King commandeth. The King heareth all causes in this place and stayeth some two hours every day.

"Then he departeth towards his private place of prayer; his prayer being ended, four or five sorts of very well dressed and roasted meats are brought him, of which as he pleaseth he eateth a bit to stay his stomach, drinking once of his strong drink. Then he cometh forth into a private room, where none can come but such as himself nominateth (for two years I was one of his attendants there). In this place he drinketh other three cupfuls, which is the portion that the physicians allot him. This done, he eateth opium, and then he ariseth, and being in the height of his drink he layeth him down to sleep, every man departing to his own home."

Hawkin's account may be compared with that of another Englishman, Sir Thomas Roe, who came out as ambassador from James I in 1615, and stayed until 1619. His Diary is an invaluable commentary on all that he witnessed:

"I went to Court at 4 in the evening to the Durbar, which is the place where the Mogul sits out daily to entertain strangers, to receive petitions, to give commands to see, and to be seen. To digress a little from my reception and to declare the customs of the Court will enlighten the future discourse. The King hath no man but eunuchs that comes within the lodgings or retiring rooms of his house. His women watch within and guard him with manly weapons. He comes every morning to a window called the *Jharokha* (Window of Audience) looking into a plain before his gate, and

TOMB OF ITMAD-UD-DAULAH

The tomb which Jahangir built for his father-in-law at Agra. It is one of the masterpieces of the emperor's builders.

shows himself to the common people. At noon he returns thither and sits some hours to see the fight of elephants and wild beasts; under him, within a rail, attend the men of rank; from whence he retires to sleep among his women. At afternoon he returns to the Durbar before mentioned. At eight after supper he comes down to the *Ghuzlkhana* (private apartments), a fair court where in the midst is a throne erected of free-stone, wherein he sits, but sometimes below in a chair; to which are none admitted but of great quality, and few of those without leave; where he discourses of all matters with great affability. There is no business done with him concerning the state, government, disposition of war or peace, but at one of these two last places, where it is publicly propounded and resolved and so registered, which if it were worth the curiosity might be seen for two shillings, but the common base people know as much as the council, and the news every day is the King's new resolutions tossed and censured by every rascal. This course is unchangeable, except sickness or drink prevent it; which must be known, for as all his subjects are slaves, so is he in a kind of reciprocal bondage, for he is tied to observe these hours and customs so precisely that if he were unseen one day, and no sufficient reason rendered, the people would mutiny; two days no reason can excuse, but that he must consent to open his doors and be seen by some to satisfy others. On Tuesday at the *Jharokha* he sits in judgment, never refusing the poorest man's complaint, where he hears with patience both parts; and sometimes sees with too much delight in blood the execution done by his elephants.

"At the Durbar I was led right before him at the entrance of an outer rail, where met me two principal noble slaves to conduct me nearer. I had required before my going leave to use the customs of my country, which was freely granted, so that I would perform them punctually. When I entered within the first rail I made an obeisance; entering in the inward rail another; and when I came under the King a third. The place is a great court, whither resort all sorts of people. The King sits in a little gallery overhead; ambassadors, the great men, and strangers of quality within the inmost rail under him, raised from the ground, covered with canopies of velvet and silk, under foot laid with good carpets; the meaner men representing gentry within the first rail, the people without in a base court, but so that all may see the King."

In 1611, Jahangir married the famous Nur Jahan, or Light of the World, with whom he had long been in love. This remarkable woman was the daughter of a Persian refugee, and Jahangir became enamoured of her while he was still Prince Salim. Akbar, who did not approve, married her off to one of his officers, Ali Kuli, surnamed Sher-afgan or Tiger-thrower, who was made governor of Bardwan in far-off Bengal. The details are obscure, but apparently it was the old story of David and Bath-sheba: after Jahangir's accession, Sher-afgan was attacked and killed by one of the Imperial envoys, and the lady brought back. For a long time she resisted her royal lover's importunities, and when at last, after four years, she consented to accept him, she was thirty-four, an age when women in the East are usually long past their prime. But Nur Jahan was singular in this as in other respects, and she soon obtained complete mastery over her husband. Her father, Itmad-ud-daulah, and her brother, Asaf Khan, became the leading figures in the court. She married her daughter by her former husband to Jahangir's younger son, Prince Shahryar, and her niece, afterwards the Empress Mumtaz Mahal, who sleeps in the famous mausoleum which bears her name, to Prince Khurram, afterwards the Emperor Shah Jahan. She thus made her position completely unassailable.

The weak and self-indulgent emperor allowed his strong-minded consort to gain entire ascendancy over him, and the empress was the *de facto* ruler of Hindustan. She used her power wisely and well. She curbed her husband's craving for drink. She sat daily at the Audience Window, with a veil over her face, hearing the grievances of her subjects and personally redressing them. She spent much of her private fortune in finding dowries for orphaned girls. She even had her name stamped on the coinage. She was a great horsewoman and a mighty *shikari*; contemporary pictures show her playing polo, and on one occasion she brought down four tigers in four successive shots. The nobles were intensely jealous, and on one occasion Mahabat Khan, one of the most powerful of them, actually attempted to kidnap the emperor and empress when they were encamped on the bank of the Jhelum river. Surrounding their camp with a body of Rajputs, he forced his way into the Royal tent, and compelled Jahangir to mount an elephant which he held in waiting. The reason for this action, he said, was that the empire was being ruled by a woman, and that Jahangir was a mere puppet in the hands of his wife and her faction. But Mahabat Khan had reckoned without his hostess. The doughty Nur Jahan forced her way through the ranks of her would-be captors amid a shower of arrows, one of which wounded a female attendant in the arm, and forded the

BY COURTESY OF THE VICTORIA AND ALBERT MUSEUM, LONDON

EUROPEAN ENVOY AT THE COURT OF JAHANGIR

Painted by a court artist of Jahangir.

river on her elephant. She then took such effective counter-measures that Mahabat Khan was glad to release his royal prisoners and take refuge among his friends in Rajputana.

Jahangir's reign was not distinguished by any great military exploits. He had little appetite for martial glory, and was a scholar and connoisseur rather than a soldier. His son, Prince Khurram, brought to an honourable conclusion the war against the Rana of the Rajput state of Mewar, which had defied the efforts of Akbar himself. The families of many of the nobles were captured, and at length the Rana submitted. It was agreed that the fortress of Chitor should not be fortified, but on the other hand, the Rana was not to be asked to send his women-folk to the Imperial harem. The Mogul troops took the great fortress of Kangra on the Kashmir border, but Shah Abbas of Persia was allowed to capture the important fortress of Kandahar, commanding the highroads to Central Asia. In the Deccan, which was destined to be the grave of the Mogul Empire, Malik Ambar, the Minister of Ahmadnagar, had discovered the fact that the famous Maratha light horsemen were more than a match for the clumsy and unwieldy Mogul army. The hardy Marathas, subsisting on nothing more than a bag of grain suspended from the saddle-bow, and what they could get from the surrounding country, hung on the flanks of the Imperial troops, cutting off stragglers, intercepting supplies, and refusing to be drawn into a pitched battle until their opponents were completely exhausted. Moreover, Jahangir, like all the Mogul Emperors, was unlucky in his sons. With the exception of Khusru they were dissolute and quarrelsome, and instead of supporting their father and assisting in the administration of the far-flung provinces of his great empire, spent their time in fighting among themselves and intriguing against Nur Jahan and her faction. In 1626 Jahangir's health was failing, and in March of the following year the Court moved up from Lahore to Kashmir in order that he might recover his health among the gardens that he loved so well. Here he seemed for a time to recover, but on his way down to the plains at the beginning of the cold weather, on November 7th, 1627, he passed away at the age of fifty-eight. His body was taken to Lahore and buried in a garden; over the grave his widow erected a magnificent mausoleum, in which, under a severely simple marble tomb, that great and masterful woman was in due time also laid to rest at her consort's side. It bears the inscription,

> Let neither lamp nor rose adorn
> my poor grave,
> To save the moth from courting
> death and the nightingale a song.

Jahangir's character is a curiously complex one, and Terry, Sir Thomas Roe's chaplain, summed him up acutely when he observed, "for the disposition of the king, it ever seemed to me to be composed of extremes; for sometimes he was barbarously cruel, and at other times he would seem to be exceeding fair and gentle." He was exceedingly fond of children and animals, and once, when his little grandchild was sick unto death, he vowed he would give up hunting if the child recovered. Unlike his father, he was a good scholar, and his *Memoirs*, written in elegant Persian, are second only in interest to those of Babur. He was a keen naturalist, and made a special journey to the passes of Kashmir in order to make a catalogue of the spring flowers growing there. He had a large zoological collection, and his artists have preserved realistic portraits of his favourite beasts. He tried experiments in breeding birds in capitivity, and in his passion for knowledge he personally carried out dissections of various animals.

All the Persians loved gardens, and it was the custom of every Mohammedan nobleman to design one for himself, where he might take his ease during the heat of the day, and find a last resting-place when he died. These gardens were of a formal type, with cypresses, marble channels for water, fountains and cascades. Jahangir and his consort are responsible for many lovely gardens at Lahore and in Kashmir. Most beautiful of all of them is the Shalimar Bagh in Kashmir, with its immense cheenar trees, its shady walks and beds of many-coloured flowers, and its rippling streams, all set against the incomparable background of the silver waters of the Dal Lake and the snowy mountain-ranges in the distance. Jahangir's love of Kashmir is recorded in many striking passages in his *Memoirs*, of which one may suffice:

"Its pleasant meads and enchanting cascades are beyond all description. There are running streams and fountains beyond count. Wherever the eye reaches, there are verdure and running water. The red rose, the violet and the narcissus grow of themselves; in the fields there are all kinds of flowers and all sorts of sweet-scented herbs more than can be calculated. In the soul-enchanting spring the hills and plains are filled with blossoms; the gates, the walls, the courts,

BY COURTESY OF THE VICTORIA AND ALBERT MUSEUM, LONDON

ELEPHANT IN JAHANGIR'S ZOO

the roofs, are lighted up by the torches of the banquet-adorning tulips. What shall we say of these things or the wide meadows and the fragrant trefoil?"

Jahangir was not a great builder, like the other Moguls, but his few works are of a rare loveliness. He completed the tomb of Akbar at Sikandra, and he erected another for his father-in-law, Itmad-ud-daulah, which is a masterpiece. Standing in an enclosure of red sandstone, its dazzling marble, exquisitely fretted and inlaid, is in striking contrast to its surroundings. "Whether regarded as an architectural composition of matchless refinement," says a recent critic, "or as an example of applied art displaying rare craftsmanship, or as an artistic symbol of passionate devotion, the tomb of Itmad-ud-daulah expresses in every part of it the high æsthetic ideals that prevailed among the Moguls of that time."

In the realm of art, however, Jahangir's chief contribution was to painting. Of this he was a connoisseur of rare ability. He says in his *Memoirs*, "as regards myself, my liking for painting and my practice in judging it have arrived at such a point that when any work is brought before me, either of deceased artists or of the present day, without the names being told me, I say on the spur of the moment that it is the work of such and such a man. And if there be a picture containing many portraits, and each face be the work of a different master, I can discover which face is the work of each. If any other person has put in the eye and eyebrow of a face, I can perceive whose work the original face is, and who has painted the eye and eyebrows." There was, of course, an indigenous school of painting in India long before the coming of the Moguls, and Akbar blended the Rajput and Persian styles by encouraging Hindu and Moslem artists to collaborate. A third influence was added when Jahangir introduced his painters to the copies of the Italian masterpieces brought to Agra by the Jesuits. In this way Indian painting attained to its zenith. Jahangir's two chief painters were Ustad (Master) Mansur, and Abul Hasan, "The Wonder of the Age." These artists copied a miniature belonging to Sir Thomas Roe so skilfully that he was at a complete loss to know which was the original and which the copy. Jahangir also struck a series of coins of exceptional artistic merit.

It is difficult to say what Jahangir's religion was. Probably, like his father, he was a mystic, holding the tenets of the Sufi sect, who regard all creeds as imperfect shadows of the same underlying truth. His leaning towards the Catholicism of the Jesuits has already been noted, and he encouraged religious debates between the Fathers and the Moslem doctors. He loved talking about philosophy to Hindu ascetics, but he regarded popular Hinduism as a "worthless religion." Unlike many of his contemporaries, he was completely tolerant and never persecuted a man for his beliefs.

As a ruler, Jahangir was proud of his even-handed justice. "God forbid," he exclaims, "that I should consider princes, far less noblemen." "A king has no relations," is another of his sayings. The lack of communications made it difficult to keep a check on distant officials, but corruption and extortion were severely punished when detected, and anyone who could do so was at liberty to petition the Emperor personally at his daily Audience. The sale of intoxicating liquor and drugs was stopped, and customs such as Suttee and infanticide were forbidden. Compensation was paid for damage done by troops on the march, and when one of the famines so common

BY COURTESY OF THE VICTORIA AND ALBERT MUSEUM, LONDON

PURSUIT OF ASAF KHAN

TOMB OF JAHANGIR

Jahangir lies in this simple dignified tomb at Lahore, which for many years was his capital.

in pre-British India broke out, he did his best to alleviate it by free kitchens and remissions of revenue. No execution could take place till sunset, in order to give time for the arrival of a reprieve. The horrible punishments inflicted for political crimes, though revolting to modern sentiment, were no worse than the disembowellings, quarterings and breaking on the wheel of contemporary Europe.

In his personal appearance and the pleasures of the table, Jahangir was as fastidious as he was in everything else. He records the delight of eating freshly-plucked figs, and the excellence of Kabul cherries. He is perfectly frank about his unhappy fondness for strong drink, which marred what might otherwise have been an excellent character, and was responsible for most of his failings. He tells us that he commenced taking wine at the age of eighteen, and when this ceased to intoxicate him, he had recourse to raw spirits and drugs. At one time his hand shook so violently that he could not hold a cup, but Nur Jahan partially reformed him. Altogether, Jahangir, though by no means the greatest of his line, is an interesting character, who, like his grandfather, Humayun, only just failed to be a good ruler owing to an unfortunate weakness which he was unable to overcome.

BY COURTESY OF THE VICTORIA AND ALBERT MUSEUM, LONDON

JAHANGIR'S JADE DRINKING CUP

BY COURTESY OF THE VICTORIA AND ALBERT MUSEUM, LONDON

SHAHJAHAN

A portrait of the fifth Mogul Emperor. Shahjahan's love of precious stones is shown by the exquisitely wrought jewellery that adorns his dress and person.

SHAHJAHAN

THE BUILDER OF THE TAJ

1592–1666

BY DR. B. P. SAKSENA

ABUL MUZAFFAR SHIHABUDDIN SHAHJAHAN GHAZI SAHIB QIRAN SANI, the fifth sovereign in the line of the Great Moguls, is known to the world as the "Builder of the Taj." Born at Lahore on the night of Thursday, the 5th of January, 1592, during the lifetime of his grandfather Akbar, he was destined to a life of unprecedented glory and magnificence. He grew up under the fostering care of his childless grandmother, Ruqiah Sultan Begum, who became deeply attached to him. As a boy he was called Khurram or "joyous," this name having been given to him by his doting grandfather, who always kept him by his side.

Exactly on the date when Prince Khurram became four years, four months and four days old, in strict accordance with the age-long custom which obtained among the Chaghtai Moguls, he was put to school, the occasion being celebrated with much pomp and festivity. Akbar made a very liberal provision for his education. He appointed well-known and competent teachers, who were not narrow-minded theologians, but who had imbibed the theosophical spirit pervading the Mogul Court and the Mogul society of the later sixteenth century. Among his tutors mention should be made of the distinguished scholar Sufi Mulla Qasim Tabrezi, of Hakim Ali Gilani, of Shaikh Sufi, and of Shaikh Abul Khayr, brother of Shaikh Abul Fazl.

Akbar had carried out many experiments in the field of education and he wanted to make Khurram a cultured prince of comprehensive imagination, agile intellect, and of a practical and resourceful bend of mind. His son Salim had not shaped after his heart. He, therefore, longed to see that the defects in the equipment and culture of the latter were not repeated in his grandson. And his delight was boundless when he found the boy-pupil making a quick response to the liberal instruction imparted to him by his teachers. Khurram, unlike his father Salim, proved to be a man of this world. He formed noble ideals; his own ambition was to follow the example of his illustrious grandfather in every walk of life.

Khurram did not develop into a scholar, but his intellectual interests were varied, and it was his early cultural education which led him as a king to patronise and promote art and culture. Unlike his father he did not cultivate interest in Zoology and Botany, but he was gifted with an eye for appreciating a work of art or a beautiful sight of nature. Jahangir all his life remained a student eager to learn and acquire knowledge, but Khurram (Shahjahan) cultivated the art of understanding men and how to control them. The one was a passive scholar, the other an active politician. That was what Akbar wanted him to be.

Nature had endowed Prince Khurram with a sturdy constitution which he improved by taking part in all sorts of games and sports. He was a skilful shot both with rifle and bow and arrow, an indefatigable rider, an excellent swordsman and an adept in all sorts of knightly exercises. The Rajput blood which ran in his veins made him bold, ambitious, and utterly regardless of danger.

At the tender age of 15, he was, in A.D. 1607, betrothed to Arjumand Banu Begum, daughter of Itiqad Khan, the future Asaf Khan. The celebration of marriage was postponed to a later date. Meanwhile, two years after, Jahangir betrothed him to the daughter of Mirza Muzaffar Husain Safavi and performed the marriage ceremony on October 28, 1610. It was not till March, 1612, that the nuptials of his first engagement were performed. This was the red letter day in the life of the prince. The silken tie brought him spiritual happiness and temporal advancement. Arjumand Banu Begum, as a queen surnamed Mumtaz Mahal or Taj Mahal, proved a loving and devoted wife. As she was the niece of the celebrated Nur Jahan, her husband became the favourite of the new party led by Asaf Khan and Itimad-ud-daulah, the brother and father of the imperious queen who dominated Jahangir.

BY COURTESY OF THE VICTORIA AND ALBERT MUSEUM, LONDON

SHAHJAHAN

The companion miniature of the emperor himself. These two miniatures were painted in the late eighteenth century by a European artist.

MUMTAZ MAHAL

A miniature of the dearly loved Mumtaz Mahal for whom Shahjahan built the Taj.

When Prince Khurram was in the Deccan leading the Imperial army against the redoubtable Abyssinian Malik Amber in August, 1617, he married the daughter of Shahnawaz Khan, the son of the Commander-in-Chief Abdur Rahim Khan Khanan. This was a political alliance, and it strengthened his position by bringing to his side a number of trustworthy adherents.

Of the three, Prince Khurram loved his second wife most. She bore him fourteen children, of whom seven died in infancy. Of the remaining seven, four sons and two daughters played important rôles in the politics of the Mogul Empire. These were Dara, Shuja, Aurangzeb, Murad, Jahanara Begum and Roshanara Begum.

His political genius and skilful military leadership brought uninterrupted success to Prince Khurram during the life-time of his father. He usually succeeded where others had failed. The first test of his ability was in the field of Mewar. Even the concentrated resources of the Mogul Empire, directed as they were by a man of such supreme abilities as his grandfather Akbar, could not bring to his knees the valiant Chief of Mewar. Chitor had been occupied, but the Sissodias still held their heads high. They were unbeaten. Jahangir after his accession deputed general after general to achieve that which had remained unaccomplished during the reign of his predecessor. But their efforts proved in vain, and their tactics useless. At length, the choice of the emperor fell on Prince Khurram. He was deputed to the Mewar front. Fortune smiled on him. By a proper disposition of the army at his command he reduced the enemy to the verge of starvation. The "war-wearied" nobles of Rana Amar Singh "earnestly counselled peace." And Prince Khurram won the crown of glory. He was hailed as a great general and a consummate politician. Veteran war-lords of the Mogul Empire yielded honour to him. "The Mogul historians went into raptures over the submission of the last of the Rajputs."

From Mewar he was transferred to the Deccan. Here too a number of generals had been tried, but the genius of Malik Amber had thwarted their designs and rendered success elusive. Prince Khurram was anxious to score another point over his elders in experience. "Loaded with honours and presents" and having been ennobled with the title of Shah, a title which no other Timurich prince had ever received, "he left for the

PONTING

THE TAJ MAHAL

The white marble tomb of Mumtaz Mahal at Agra, whose ethereal beauty is a lasting reminder of Shahjahan's love for his wife.

PONTING

INSIDE THE TAJ

The exquisite white marble screen which encloses the cenotaphs of Mumtaz Mahal and Shahjahan who lies beside her.

Deccan at the head of a splendid train of nobles and troopers." His arrival at the scene of activity changed the entire situation. The Deccan Confederacy crumbled away. The Adil Shah waited on the Prince with a magnificent present. Malik Amber returned all the territory which he had seized and, in addition, delivered the keys of the fort of Ahmadnagar and of other strongholds. Thus he solved the Deccan problem within the short space only of six months, which increased the affection and esteem of his father for him. "I increased," says Jahangir, "my favours and kindness to him and made him sit near me." "He was promoted to the rank of 30,000 Zat and Suwar, styled Shahjahan and entitled to a chair near the throne in darbar." This was the height of honour to which a Mogul prince could aspire.

For the next three years Shahjahan remained by the side of his father. During this period he found new friends, and began to realise that it was possible for him to stand on his own legs, without the support of Nur Jahan. Conditions for a clash between him and his ambitious patron were slowly coming to a head. Meanwhile a crisis developed in the Deccan which required the presence of a strong man there. Again the choice of the Emperor fell on him. He obeyed the command and, as usual, performed his duties satisfactorily. Once more the Deccan rulers yielded to superior force. But this time his success was not celebrated with as much show as on the previous occasion.

The "Light of the World" (Nur Jahan) was growing cold towards him. She was waiting for an opportunity to ruin his reputation and prestige. Just at this moment Jahangir received the unwelcome news of the occupation of

F. HENLE

THE JASSAMINE TOWER

The Musamman, or Saman Burj, at Agra fort, which is usually known as the Jassamine Tower. This pavilion was once the apartment of the chief Sultana.

Qandahar by Shah Abbas of Persia. He asked Shahjahan to proceed to the West and retrieve the Mogul honour. But when he insisted on the fulfilment of certain conditions, precedent to his departure to Qandahar, the Mogul Emperor flew into a rage. The outcome was Shahjahan's rebellion which kept the Empire in commotion for a number of years. He was deprived of his rank, was hounded from place to place, till he sought the protection of his erstwhile rival Malik Amber, who allowed him to stay at Junnar. It was here that he received the news of the death of his father and the summons of his father-in-law asking him to hasten to Agra and proclaim himself the Emperor of India.

Shahjahan's advent to the throne heralded an era of unprecedented peace and prosperity in the Mogul Empire. His reign saw an uninterrupted round of military victories inside the country. His armies fought on every front of the Empire and, with the partial exception of the west and the north, success attended his plans both military and diplomatic.

Three serious outbreaks occurred during his reign. The first to raise the standard of revolt was Khan Jahan Lodi, a favourite of the late Emperor Jahangir and a partisan of Nur Jahan, who saw in Shahjahan's rise into prominence complete ruination of his position and power. Though reconciled in the beginning to the new order of things, he remained suspicious and moody. At length in October, 1629, all of a sudden he fled from the Court, and escaped to the Deccan. The Emperor himself supervised the operations against the rebel, whose cause was taken up by Murtaza Nizam Shah, the ruler of Ahmadnagar. Khan Jahan was pursued from pillar to post, and he died fighting desperately. But the repercussions of his rebellion proved to be serious with regard to the politics of the Deccan.

The second disturbance occurred in Bundelkhand where the Bundela Chief Junjhar Singh had forcibly occupied Chauragadh in spite of the warning of the suzerain power. On his refusal to disgorge the ill-gotten booty, his country was attacked on the ground that "he had outraged the Imperial dignity and had broken the traditional rules of conduct." Bundelkhand was devastated. The rebels were hunted down like wild beasts. In all about ten million of rupees were credited to the royal exchequer, and numerous places of strategic importance were occupied.

A similar case, when a feudal baron was pressed to account for his excesses against another local chief, is that of Jagat Singh, Zamindar of Mau-Nurpur. He had encroached upon the territories of the Chamba State and refused to comply with the summons to appear at court to explain his conduct. This was tantamount to rebellion. Several armies converged from all sides on the seat of his power. Driven to straits Jagat Singh threw himself at the mercy of the Emperor. He was pardoned and reinstated in his former rank.

Among the events of minor importance mention should be made of the suppression of Portuguese piracy in Bengal, of the subjugation of recalcitrant chiefs or petty rajas "like Bhagirath Bhill (1632), and Marvi Gond (1644), in Malwa, Raja Pratap of Palamau (1642) in Chitra-Nagpur, and the turbulent border tribes on the frontiers." To this record should be added the reduction of Little Tibet, the annexation of Kuch Bihar and Kamrup, and the fixing of definite boundaries and resumption of trade relations with Assam.

But the most daring exploit of the reign was the conquest, though only temporarily, of Balkh and Badakhshan.

BY COURTESY OF THE VICTORIA AND ALBERT MUSEUM, LONDON

SHAHJAHAN RECEIVING ENVOYS IN A PALACE GARDEN AT AGRA

Mogul School.

PEARL MOSQUE AT AGRA

F. HENLE

The Moti Masjid at Agra, built by Shahjahan, has been described as "one of the purest and most elegant buildings of its class to be found anywhere."

On this tract of land the Great Moguls laid ancestral claims. To occupy it had been the cherished aim of Akbar and Jahangir, but they did not have a favourable opportunity to achieve it. The outbreak of civil strife between Nazr Mohammad Khan, ruler of Bokhara and his son Abdul Aziz afforded Shahjahan a tempting chance to try his luck in Trans-Oxiana. In June, 1646, he sent to Balkh an army of 50,000 horse and 10,000 foot under the command of Prince Murad. The city was occupied without a blow, and the Imperialists were rewarded by the capture of a treasure worth 12 lacs of rupees, 2,500 horses and 300 camels. But the flight of Nazr Mohammad Khan to Persia defeated the object of the enterprise. To Murad a stay in those inhospitable regions was irksome and he abandoned his post of duty in spite of the threats and warnings of the Emperor. He was replaced by Aurangzeb, a man of steady character and ambitious ideals. His bravery and cool courage won him the admiration of his enemies, but this did not help him in maintaining his hold on Balkh. He had to retire.

Another direction where the Mogul armies suffered severe reverses was Qandahar. It had been recovered by the Persians during the second part of Jahangir's reign. But a combination of circumstances and diplomacy had yielded its possession in 1638 to Shahjahan. For the next ten years the Persians were not in any position to attempt its recovery. When in 1642 Shah Abbas II came to the throne of Persia, he expressed a keen desire to score a point over his contemporary, the Mogul Emperor of India. For so long as he was a minor, nothing substantial could be done. But when in 1648 he took the reins of government into his own hands, he chalked out plans for the consummation of his cherished design. And he succeeded in occupying Qandahar. This was a severe blow to the pride of Shahjahan and he made frantic efforts to undo the success that had attended the armies of his Persian contemporary. Two campaigns were led by Aurangzeb, and one by Dara Shikoh. They were assisted by the most experienced generals of the Empire. They had enormous resources at their disposal. And yet humiliation and defeat were their lot. The three sieges of Qandahar cost the Imperial Exchequer about 120 millions of rupees.

If the Imperial army failed in the west, it achieved distinct success in the south. Advance towards the Deccan had become the keynote of the Mogul policy ever since the occupation of Khandesh and the partial reduction of Ahmadnagar during the later years of Akbar's reign. Under Jahangir not much of territorial gains accrued to the Mogul Empire. Malik Amber had proved a tower of strength to the Nizam Shahi Kingdom. And though he had to face the Mogul military storm twice, by yielding diplomatically to its fury he had succeeded in saving the integrity of the kingdom of Ahmadnagar.

But his death in A.D. 1626 unchained serious rivalries in the Nizam Shah's court. His son and successor Fath Khan was neither respected nor trusted. And when Murtaza Nizam Shah cast his lot with the rebel Khan Jahan Lodi, the fate of Ahmadnagar was sealed. Fath Khan imprisoned his master, put him to death, read the Khutba and struck coins in the name of the Mogul Emperor. He was allowed to retain possession of Daulatabad which proved a storm-centre. Thanks, however, to the genius of Mahabat Khan the crisis was averted. Fath Khan and the puppet Nizam Shah were sent away to the Imperial Court, the latter to be imprisoned in the fort of Gwalior.

Daulatabad was occupied by the Moguls. But a little indiscretion on the part of Mahabat Khan and the consequent humiliation which caused his death unsettled the political settlement in the Deccan. The activities of Sahu, a Maratha Chief, encouraged and abetted as they were by the Adil Shah of Bijapur, threatened the prestige and the stability of the Mogul possessions in the Deccan. The situation became so critical as to induce the Mogul Emperor himself to lead the campaign of chastisement. Shahjahan arrived with a large army in the Deccan. He overawed his enemies. Sahu was driven to bay and compelled to forsake the country of his birth. The Adil Shah submitted and agreed to pay an indemnity of twenty lacs in jewels and elephants, etc. As to the Qutb Shah, "when the Imperial envoy approached Golconda, he came forth from Kos to receive him, and conducted him to the city with great honour. . . . He had the Khutba read aloud in the name of the Emperor." Thus the Deccan problem was solved satisfactorily by Shahjahan in 1636.

Aurangzeb was now appointed Viceroy of the Deccan. For eight years to come he strove hard to administer a difficult tract. He succeeded in keeping it under control, nay even added to the Imperial possessions by annexing Baglana, and by exacting tribute from the Chief of Deogadh. He was dismissed from this post in 1644.

After serving as Governor of Gujerat and Multan, and the leader of military campaigns in Balkh and Qandahar, Aurangzeb returned to the Deccan in 1653 to find the province financially bankrupt and administratively a prey to maladministration, bribery and corruption. Once more he devoted himself, with all the enthusiasm that he could gather, to the task of reorganising the province in his charge. Under the able guidance of Murshid Quli Khan the revenue department was thoroughly overhauled and the Northern method of revenue assessment was introduced into the Deccan. His inspector-general of Ordnance, Shamsuddin Mukhtar Khan, carefully looked into the efficiency of the military department, and greatly pleased the Viceroy with his ability and received many favours from him.

The Deccan being a poor province, Aurangzeb began to look around to improve his resources.

He invaded and extorted tribute from the States of Deogadh and Jawahir. Then he turned his attention to Bijapur and Golconda. The ruler of the latter was in arrears of tribute. Further, his relations with his prime minister, Mir Jumla, were very strained and the Qutb Shah had interned the members of his family. Aurangzeb ordered the Qutb Shah to clear off the arrears of tribute immediately and to release the family of Mir Jumla. He succeeded in so manipulating the situation that even Shahjahan felt no hesitation to sanction the invasion of Golconda. The fabulous riches of that kingdom were plundered, and Aurangzeb would have annexed the entire kingdom but for the countermanding command from the Emperor. Peace was concluded with the Qutb Shah, who married his daughter to Aurangzeb's son, Mohammad Sultan, and Mir Jumla was admitted into the Imperial service.

Next it was the turn of Bijapur to suffer. The death of Mohammad Adil Shah in 1656 provided for Aurangzeb the long sought-for opportunity to invade that kingdom. Again he secured the permission from Shahjahan "to settle the affairs of Bijapur in any way he thought fit." The Mogul armies flooded the territories of Bijapur. The forts of Bidar and Kalyani were occupied, and but for the intervention of the

BY COURTESY OF THE VICTORIA AND ALBERT MUSEUM, LONDON

THE THREE BROTHERS

This, one of the most charming portraits of the period, shows the three younger sons of Shahjahan out riding. Artist Balchand. Mogul School, 1635.

BY COURTESY OF THE VICTORIA AND ALBERT MUSEUM, LONDON

SHAHJAHAN, WHEN PRINCE KHURRAM, RIDING WITH AN ESCORT

Mogul School, 1618.

Emperor, the Adil Shahi kingdom would have met the same fate as threatened the Qutb Shahi kingdom of Golconda. The Sultan agreed to pay an indemnity of 1½ crores.

But a sudden calamity changed the whole course of the Imperial politics. On 6th September, 1657, Shahjahan suddenly fell ill of "strangury and constipation. For one week the royal physicians toiled in vain. The malady went on increasing. . . . The daily durbar was stopped; the Emperor even ceased to show his face to the public from the Jharoka every morning; the courtiers were denied access to sick-bed. A rumour spread that the Emperor was dead. It filtered to the various provinces of the Empire." Conditions were thus ripe for a struggle for the throne.

The fratricidal war of succession among the four sons of Shahjahan, Dara, Shuja, Aurangzeb, and Murad, was the most sanguinary that was ever fought in the Mogul period. The result was the humiliation and execution of Dara and Murad, and the pathetic disappearance of Shuja. Aurangzeb came out victorious, and he proclaimed himself king. Shahjahan was detained in the fort of Agra as a prisoner, where he passed the remaining years of his life.

It is not possible, at such distance of time, even to imagine the extent of misery and mental affliction caused to the ex-emperor of Delhi in the changed circumstances of his life. Perhaps Napoleon had to suffer less at St. Helena than Shahjahan in the fort of Agra. The former was quite cut off from the scene of his former glory and grandeur. On the other hand, every nook and corner in the Agra fort must have brought to Shahjahan bitter memories of thirty years of regal life, when high and low, rich and poor, all alike looked up to him for favours, and when everyone was ready to lay down his life at his bidding. The Agra fort represented the most glorious period of his life, when he knew only how to command. Here he was accosted as "Lord of the World" and "Master of the Universe." Now, even for a change of his apparel he had to depend upon the favours of a low-placed eunuch. Really it must have been terrible.

Manucci, the Italian, writes: "Going several times into the fort I noted that the imprisonment of Shahjahan was closer than could be expressed. There passed not a day, while I and others were in conversation with the Governor, that there did not come under-eunuchs to whisper into his ear an account of all the acts and words of Shahjahan." (*Storia de Mogor*, Vol. II, 77.) But the French physician, M. Bernier, unfolds a different story: "Although Aurangzeb kept his father closely confined in the fortress of Agra and neglected no precaution to prevent his escape, yet the deposed monarch was otherwise treated with indulgence and respect. He was permitted to occupy his former apartments, and to enjoy the society of *Begum Sahib* and the whole of his female establishment including the singing and dancing women, cooks, and others. In these respects no request was ever denied him." (*Travels in the Moghul Empire*, p. 166.)

The fact is that Aurangzeb regarded the ex-emperor with much suspicion and distrust. He was fairly conversant with the sympathies of the fallen monarch and he knew that if he gave even the least latitude to him there was the possibility of outbreak of serious mischief. To him Shahjahan was no longer a father but a dangerous political enemy. Hence the rigour and severity of the watch kept over him.

It took some time for Shahjahan to accustom himself to the new mode of

F. HENLE

TOWER IN THE FORT

When Shahjahan was imprisoned he would gaze on the Taj Mahal from a tower of the fort. Tradition says it was the last thing he looked on as he lay dying.

life. During the first year of his captivity he carried on an acrimonious correspondence with Aurangzeb. At last he resigned himself to the will of God. And "though blow after blow fell on his stricken heart, to the last day he maintained his endurance and steadiness." "Religion gave him solace. His constant companion now was Sayyid Muhammad of Qanauj. . . . Another no less saintly, but more tender, comforter he had in his daughter Jahanara, whose loving care atoned for the cruelty of all his other offspring." On the 7th of January, 1666, he was seized with a fever which was complicated by strangury and griping of the stomach. "Retaining full consciousness to the last and gazing on the resting-place of his beloved and long-lost Mumtaz Mahal," he repeated the Moslem formula of faith, and "sank peacefully into eternal rest," full fifteen days after the commencement of his illness.

The death of the ex-emperor was universally mourned and public grief was sincere. Jean Baptiste Tavernier remarks: "This great monarch reigned more than forty (thirty) years, less as a king over his subjects than as a father of a family over his house and children." (Vol. I, 325.) Elphinstone describes his reign as "the most prosperous ever known in India." Manucci remarks: "Not only did Shahjahan do justice against those guilty of great crimes: he also dealt with the nobles whenever he found an opportunity. . . . His object was to make the governing of his kingdom easier." At another place he observes, "He (Shahjahan) upheld the maxim of his father that true justice must be enforced, rewarding the meritorious and punishing the guilty. He kept his eye on his officials, punishing them rigorously when they fell short in their duty." And the Italian gunner has described numerous instances of the clever way in which the Mogul Emperor detected crime and awarded punishment to the guilty. He bestowed so much care on the development of the prosperity of his people and to securing them even-handed justice, that no wonder he was universally loved and respected. At his death "the cry of lamentation rose up from every house in the lanes and market-places alike."

To his contemporaries Shahjahan was great because of his love of justice and his concern for their peace and prosperity; to posterity he is great because he has left a record more enduring, more glorious, and greater than could be unfolded by oriental historians or their commentators. He lived for an ideal at once grand and noble. He loved magnificence, not grotesque or bizarre, but refined and cultured. He aimed at the unsurpassable. The buildings which he constructed at Agra and Delhi are the best illustrations of his refinement and culture. What Jahangir achieved on paper, Shahjahan achieved in brick and mortar. The one loved painting; the other architecture—an architecture in which the grace and beauty of painting could be faithfully reproduced.

The Mogul miniatures present before our eyes "realms of gold." But Shahjahan's buildings elevate us to a higher region. "If there be a Heaven upon earth, it is this—it is this!" wrote Shahjahan on his palace walls at Delhi. "We still read, and still endorse the proud assertion." "At every point, in these buildings, one's imagination is caught and enchained, and not unoften their sight throws us into ecstasies." Shahjahan's reign marks the "golden age" of the Mogul architecture.

The building which is "unique in its evasive loveliness, and which is "so difficult to define in architectural terms, but most expressive of the builder's intentions," is the Taj. Its undiminished charm extorts universal admiration. It is symbolic of the grace of Indian womanhood and of the chaste devotion of Shahjahan to his beloved wife. It is a lyric in marble. According to Bernier "the edifice has a magnificent appearance, and is conceived and executed effectually. Nothing offends the eye; on the contrary it is delighted with every part, and never tired with looking." Further he remarks, ". . . the mausoleum of Taj Mahal is an astonishing work. It is possible I may have imbibed an Indian taste, but I decidedly think that this monument deserves much more to be remembered among the wonders of the world than the pyramids of Egypt." Tavernier says: "I witnessed the commencement and accomplishment of this great work, on which they have expended twenty-two years during which twenty-thousand men worked incessantly; this is sufficient to enable one to realise that the cost of it has been enormous." Fergusson observes: "It is the combination of so many beauties, and the perfect manner in which each is subordinate to the other, that makes up a whole which the world cannot match, and which never fails to impress even those who are most indifferent to the effects produced by architectural objects in general." Havell calls it "a living thing with all the æsthetic attributes of perfect womanhood, more subtle, romantic, and tender in its beauty than any other building of its kind." And it was the Taj at which Shahjahan fixed his gaze during the last hours of his life. It is one of the wonders of the world.

The Moti Masjid or Pearl Mosque was built in Agra fort between A.D. 1645 and 1653. It has been described as "a fervent stone." It is a sanctuary in which "a mysterious soul throbs between bliss and ecstasy." Built on a high pedestal and in a corner, it provided peace and seclusion to the Emperor to pray to the Almighty for the blessings of his life. No *pietra dura* work is needed to enhance its beauty. Simplicity is its charm, and the purity of its white marble its chief attraction. It does not look imposing from outside, but the moment one enters it one is overwhelmed with its grandeur. If fine ornamentation, floral designs and the intricate trellis work form the main charm of the Taj, the very absence of these suits the grace and grandeur of Moti Masjid. It is really a "pearl" of the finest water without a flaw in it.

Shahjahan shifted the capital of the Empire from Agra to Delhi which he renamed Shahjahanabad. Here Shahjahan gave full vent to his building propensity. The construction of the Lal Qila or Delhi fort was started in April, 1639, and it took nine years to finish it. Its entire walls are built of red sandstone; in shape it is an irregular octagon with its two long sides on the east and west and the six smaller ones on the north and south. The construction work was done under the supervision of *ustads* (master builders) Hamid and Ahmad. A vaulted arcade leads from the Lahore Gate to the Naubat Khana, which served as the main entrance to the court of the Diwan-i-Am or Hall of Public Audience. It is built throughout of red sandstone and measures 80 feet by 40 feet. In the centre of its east wall is a recess about 21 feet in width and "faced with the most exquisite designs in *pietra dura* work, representing trees, flowers and birds." The Asad Burj, the Mumtaz Mahal, the Rang Mahal, the Tasbih Khanan, the Khuabgah, the Baithak, the Musamman Burj or Octagonal Tower are some of other smaller buildings inside the fort. But the most remarkable and heavily decorated one is the Diwan-i-Khas or the "Hall of Private Audience." It was also known as Shah Mahal.

Fergusson considers it "if not the most beautiful, certainly the most highly ornamented of all Shahjahan's buildings." "*Pietra dura* work is freely used on the lower portions of the arch-piers, the upper portion being treated with gilding and painting." A marble water-channel (the Naha-i-Bihisht) runs through the centre of the Hall, and gives it a look of Paradise as visualised by man. The marble dais is said to have supported the famous Peacock Throne of Shahjahan.

Outside the fort, and built on a very high pedestal, is the Jama-Masjid or the Masjid-i-Jahan Numan. It was built in A.D. 1650 under the superintendence of the prime minister Sadullah Khan and the Mir Saman Fazil Khan. Five thousand men worked at it daily for 6 years, and it cost the Imperial Exchequer ten lacs of rupees.

But Shahjahan's patronage did not extend to architecture alone. He encouraged other fine arts as well. According to V. Smith, "The portraits of Shahjahan's time, which are far from the stiffness common in the preceding and succeeding ages, are wonderfully life-like and often perfectly charming." The paintings of his time display brilliance of colour, lavish use of gold, and create an impression of great splendour and superb luxury which we associate with the "Grand Mogul."

Manucci remarks: "His (Shahjahan's) usual diversion was to listen to various instruments, to verses and poetry, and he was very fond of musicians, especially of one who was not only a graceful poet but also a buffoon." His favourite tune was Dhurpat and he loved to hear it sung by Lal Khan *Gun-Samudra* the son-in-law of the famous Tan Sen. He also patronised Jagannath the best Hindu musician.

Shahjahan had collected a vast hoard of precious stones. He displayed them in his own way. Some he wore on his person while others he used in the construction of articles of furniture. And the Peacock Throne was one of them. Tavernier gives a detailed description of its design and construction. "The underside of the canopy is covered with diamonds and pearls, with a fringe of pearls all round; and above the canopy, which is a quadrangular-shaped dome, there is to be seen a peacock with elevated tail made of blue sapphires and other coloured stones, having a large ruby in front of the breast, from whence hangs a pear-shaped pearl of 50 carats or thereabouts and of somewhat yellow colour." He estimates its cost at one thousand and seventy lacs of rupees. Bernier puts the figure at 4 crores of rupees. Thevenot says that "the throne was reputed to be worth 20,000,000 in gold," but he adds that a true estimate could only be arrived at by a careful examination of precious stones with which it was adorned.

Thus a sovereign who knew how to conquer extensively, who was keen to extend his liberal patronage to art and literature, and who devoted his attention and energy to extending the prosperity of his subjects, may with justice be counted among the Great Men of India.

BY COURTESY OF THE BODLEIAN LIBRARY

THE EMPEROR AURANGZEB

A portrait of the sixth and last of the great Mogul emperors. After his reign the dynasty declined rapidly. Painted by Anupchater.

AURANGZEB

LAST OF THE GREAT MOGULS

1618–1707

BY ELIZABETH D'OYLEY

Akbar, "Guardian of Mankind," greatest and wisest of the Mogul emperors, had been dead thirteen years; at Agra—which he had built—his son Jahangir reigned in his stead; far to the southward, beyond the Vindhya and Satpura Mountains, Prince Khurram, Jahangir's heir, ruled as Viceroy of the Deccan, when, at Dhud on the night of November 4, 1618, his favourite wife, Mumtaz-Mahal, gave birth to their third son. The child came not only of the blood of Akbar: the blood of the great Tamerlane was in his veins: Timur or Tamerlane whom men had called "The Scourge of God."

Mahomed was the name chosen for the child, a name his father later changed to Aurangzeb (Throne-Ornament). It might have been thought that a third son was born to no happy destiny. The younger sons of Mogul emperors were dangerous rivals for the throne, and death or imprisonment was their usual fate. Even the heir troubled the Emperor's peace. Jahangir had rebelled against Akbar. Prince Khurram rebelled against Jahangir.

AURANGZEB'S MOSQUE

The Mosque of Aurangzeb in the city of Aurangabad which was his capital during his viceroyalty in the Deccan.

MAUSOLEUM OF AURANGZEB'S WIFE

The tomb of Rabi'a Daurani, Aurangzeb's wife, is a copy of the Taj Mahal, and counted one of the finest Mogul buildings in the Deccan.

Aurangzeb was two years old then. What happened to him during the years of his father's warfare is not known, but in 1625 the boy had his share in paying the price of it. As hostages for Prince Khurram's future loyalty, his eldest son Dara and seven-year-old Aurangzeb were sent to Jahangir at Agra. Jahangir, the drunkard—so strong was his liquor that it made the English ambassador cough and sneeze—the fierce-tempered, must have seemed a strange man to his young grandson Aurangzeb. Pictures of the Christians' Madonna found a place in his palace at Agra, not because Jahangir was tolerant, as Akbar had been, of all religions, but because he cared for none of them. In Aurangzeb there was something of the saint and much of the ascetic which even in these early days may have made him turn in revolt from the luxury and profligacy of his grandfather. For two years he lived in Jahangir's Court, watched by the quick eyes of Nur-Jahan, his grandmother and virtual ruler of the Empire.

It seems that the boy's education was entrusted to an ordinary Moslem schoolmaster. From him Aurangzeb learnt to write in a hand that was exquisite. He learnt the *Koran* so thoroughly that he could recite it from memory. He learnt Arabic, wasting—as later he complained—the precious hours of his youth "in the dry, unprofitable and never-ending task of learning words." Rather should he have been taught the duty of a King to his people, he said, and by his people to their King. Aurangzeb was his own best schoolmaster.

In the November of 1627, Jahangir

BY COURTESY OF THE BODLEIAN LIBRARY

COURT OF AURANGZEB

The Emperor Aurangzeb receiving an Ambassador to his Court.

MUSIC ROOM, BIDAR
The fine existing "Musician's gallery" in the old fort of Bidar.

died suddenly, and two months later Prince Khurram was at Agra—Emperor, with the title of Shah Jahan or King of the World. No Mogul Emperor was ever loved as Shah Jahan. Prosperity came to the Empire, leaving him free to earn his title of "the Magnificent." Unsurpassed splendour surrounded young Aurangzeb. Agra was no longer the chief residence of the Court. On the banks of the Jumna, Shah Jahan built his city of Shahjahanabad, or New Delhi. Along the riverside ran the battlements of his palace where, in the Diwan-i-Am or Hall of Audience stood the Peacock Throne, which had taken seven years to complete (Tamerlane began and Shah Jahan finished it). Plated with gold inlaid with diamonds, emeralds, pearls and rubies, it stood upon feet of gold. Twelve pillars covered with emeralds supported an enamelled canopy, and each pillar bore two peacocks encrusted with gems standing on either side of a tree covered with diamonds, emeralds, rubies and pearls. In Agra, too, Shah Jahan built magnificently: not a palace for the living, but a tomb for the dead: the Taj Mahal, which to this day bears witness to his love for the mother of Aurangzeb.

She had been dead five years when, in May, 1636, he was appointed Governor of his father's old Viceroyalty of the Deccan. He was only eighteen, and the coercing of that coveted territory, with its exhaustless wealth in gold and diamonds, was in reality left to older hands. But Aurangzeb had emerged from the Courts of Jahangir and Shah Jahan with thoughts more on heaven than on earth. The flame of religion burned in him, and while, in obedience to his father, he was bringing the territory of Baglana into subjection, he longed to cast off his greatness and, arraying himself in the rags of a fakir, seek God in solitude. In June, 1644, he boldly announced his intention to discard the world. His father raged, deprived him of his income, his title, his Viceroyalty of the Deccan. Willingly he let them go. Dara his brother scorned him as "saint," but for nearly a year he hid himself in the wilds of the Western Ghâts, mortifying his body and communing with God.

The phase passed. He came back to the world, to spend his unwearying energies as leader of armies, but to the end of life there went with Aurangzeb the Emperor, Aurangzeb the ascetic, who reckoned the Faith of Islam worth all the empires in the world.

Within three years of his return, his

father had sent him to rule the provinces of Balkh and Badakhshan, which Ali Mardan and Aurangzeb's younger brother, Murad Bakhsh, had conquered two years earlier. Shah Jahan, thus extending his conquests beyond the Hindu Kush, dreamt of recovering Tamerlane's city of Samarkand. But Aurangzeb saw that the ramparts of the Hindu Kush made land beyond them impossible to hold. He gave back the useless provinces to the King of the Uzbegs, and determined on retreat. October had come when he set off across the mountains. The hillmen hung on his flanks, cutting off whole companies of stragglers. For five days snow fell without ceasing. The unhappy beasts of burden—elephants, camels, horses—died like flies. Five thousand men perished, and only a miserable remnant of Shah Jahan's magnificent army staggered into Kabul.

Dara, perhaps, jeered at the "Saint," but in Aurangzeb had been lit a lust for conquest that was destined to sweep Dara himself from his path. Thirteen years were to run before that came to pass, years in which Aurangzeb, learning generalship under his father's finest fighting men—Ali Mardan, Jai Singh, S'ad Allah—proved himself a stoic under untold hardships, and of such coolness and "incomparable courage," that in the midst of a battle he would dismount at the hour of evening prayer and prostrate himself before God. "To fight with such a man," cried the King of the Uzbegs, "is self-destruction."

Two unsuccessful attempts—in May, 1649, and in the spring of 1652—to

GATE OF THE FORT

The Fateh Gate within the fortress wall of Bidar. Aurangzeb conquered Bidar with the help of Mir Jumla.

regain Kandahar which the Persians had captured, and Aurangzeb was back in his old province of the Deccan, there to take up a task which, with one full-fraught interval, was to be his for the rest of his life: the task of recovering for the Mogul Empire the whole of the Deccan. Two centuries earlier, Muhammad-ibn-Taghlak had won it, and named there his Daulatabad or Empire-City. But with his death the Bahmani Kings swept over his conquest. Wise Akbar, wanting only as much of the Deccan as would serve for frontier guard, took Khandesh, Berar and the fortress of Ahmadnagar, and asked from the Kings of Bijapur and Golconda no more than tribute. But to Aurangzeb the Deccan Kings were heretics to be rooted out, and not until the whole Empire of Muhammad-ibn-Taghlak lay under the foot of Islam would he rest.

Nearly twenty years had gone since he first came to the Deccan as a lad of eighteen. He came now as a man of thirty-seven, his iron will determined on its subjugation. Already he must have known that it could not be long before he was drawn into another fight. Shah Jahan grew old, and Dara had his ear. Dara was the eldest son, but the Mogul Crown went to him that could win it.

The winning of the Deccan was for the moment the game in hand, and Aurangzeb's first move in it was to pick a quarrel with 'Abdallah, king of Golconda. Against the fortress of Golconda, high on its granite ridge, he launched his attack. Mounted on his war elephant he led his Mogul Horse in a fierce charge which drove in the King's first sally. In vain 'Abdallah tried to appease his enemy with baskets of gems and gorgeously-caparisoned horses and elephants. For two months the siege went on, while at Agra, Dara stirred his father to suspicion of Aurangzeb's growing power. Aurangzeb would hear of no truce between him and his foe, until Shah Jahan, urged by Dara, sent peremptory orders for him to raise the siege. With the hard conditions that 'Abdallah should set Shah Jahan's name on his coinage, pay an annual tribute of a crore of rupees, and give his daughter as a wife for Aurangzeb's son Muhammad, the Prince drew off to Aurangabad.

He was well aware that he owed this check to Dara, and meant it to be no more than a check. By the hand of Mir Jumla, his ablest ally, he sent his father a priceless diamond—the famous Koh-i-nur or Peak of Light—from the mines at Kollur. With this as earnest of the country's wealth, Mir Jumla urged upon Shah Jahan the conquest of the Deccan. Never should the Great Mogul rest, he said, until his empire stretched from the Himalayas to Cape Comorin.

Fear of the fate of every Mogul Emperor—to see war with his sons or among his sons—had come upon Shah Jahan. To keep them occupied far from him and from each other, he had sent them South, East and West: Aurangzeb to the Deccan, Shuja his eldest son to Bengal, Murad Bakhsh the youngest to Gujarat. Only Dara (the Chosen One) remained with him, "Lord"—as he had named him—"of Exalted Fortune." In a robe sewn with diamonds and pearls, a great ruby shooting fire from his turban, Dara rested on a couch at the foot of the Peacock Throne, the only person permitted to be seated in the presence of the Emperor.

More troops were what Aurangzeb has asked for, and—though Dara offered strong opposition—was to have. It was little reassurement for Dara that the Emperor stipulated that Mir Jumla and not Aurangzeb should have command of these troops. Dara gained nothing by that, for Mir Jumla at once joined forces with Aurangzeb, and with him captured

BIJAPUR

The fine old archway in the walls of Bijapur, another stronghold of the Deccan conquered by Aurangzeb during his viceroyalty.

the fortress of Bidar. Success followed success, and the whole kingdom of Bijapur was within their grasp when news that the Emperor had fallen ill called Aurangzeb to the fight for the Peacock Throne.

In Agra, as day followed day and Shạh Jahan came no more to the seat overlooking the Hall of Audience—where each day a Mogul Emperor must show himself to his people or risk rebellion—rumour cried that he was dead. Panic reigned. The shops shut. The whole Court was in confusion. Dara, on guard against his brothers, gathered his fighting men. In Bengal, Shuja gave out that Shah Jahan had been poisoned by Dara, had himself proclaimed Emperor and set out on his march to Delhi. In Gujarat, Murad Bakhsh engraved his name on the coinage, had the Prayer for the Emperor offered in his own name, and laid siege to Surat.

Only Aurangzeb made no open move. He knew that just as Shah Jahan had killed his brother, so would any of his own three brothers kill him. Warily he played his game; waiting while Dara, making a false move, divided his forces to deal with both Shuja and Murad Bakhsh at once. Dara was well aware which of his three brothers he had most to fear. Jaswant Singh, marching against Murad Bakhsh, had orders to cut the communications between him and Aurangzeb.

Watchful, Aurangzeb waited, until in December, Shuja, surprised in his camp at Benares, was put to flight; waited still, until a month later Surat fell to Murad Bakhsh. Then he showed his hand.

"Whatever course you have resolved upon in opposition to the shameless and unrighteous conduct of our abandoned brother (Dara)," he wrote to Murad Bakhsh, "you may count on me as a staunch ally."

In the eyes of Aurangzeb—the zealous follower of Islam—Dara an idolater and Shuja a heretic, were both unworthy of the Crown. Only Murad Bakhsh—he professed to think—was fit to ascend the Peacock Throne. As for himself—he told Murad Bakhsh—he desired nothing but the life of a fakir. Nevertheless he would join with him. And he invoked "the word of God as his bail for this compact."

The end of March had come when he set out from Burhampur on his march to Agra. By the river Narbada he and Murad Bakhsh met, and thither came messenger after messenger from Shah Jahan, assuring Aurangzeb that he was well, and commanding him back to the Deccan. It was too late to turn back. The two Princes believed, or pretended to believe, that their father was dying, and that his letters were forged by Dara. If indeed he lived, they said, then would they deliver him from the tyranny of that apostate.

On April 25, Murad Bakhsh forded the river under a storm of javelins and arrows from the Imperial host. Kasim Khan, who shared with Jaswant Singh the Imperial command, fled ingloriously from the field. Jaswant Singh, thus left to bear the brunt of the onslaught alone, fought till only six hundred of his eight thousand Rajputs remained. Then dismay fell upon him. He too fled, leaving victory to the man to fight with whom—as the King of the Uzbegs had long ago said—was self-destruction.

Dara was determined there should be no compromise between his father and his brothers. With an army finer than any that had trod the plains of Hindustan he marched out of Agra to entrench himself on the bank of the river Chambal. But Aurangzeb had already crossed

THE DELHI OF AURANGZEB

A view showing the Moti Masjid, the famous gate, and the Diwan-i-Khas.

PONTING

THE JAMI MASJID, DELHI

The great mosque at Delhi, the largest mosque in the world, was begun in 1644 *during the reign of Shah Jahan, and completed in the year Aurangzeb deposed his father.*

lower down, leaving his empty tents to deceive the enemy. Beside the river Jumna, with men refreshed, he waited for Dara.

On June 7th the two armies were face to face at Samugarh,[1] five leagues from Agra. For some days they lay in sight of each other, while in the intense heat of an Agra summer men fainted and died under weight of their armour, and Shah Jahan urged Dara to await the arrival of his son, Sulaiman Shukor, fresh from his victory over Shuja. But Dara wanted glory for himself alone. He answered Shah Jahan: "In three days I will bring my brothers bound hand and foot to receive your judgment."

It was early in the morning when Aurangzeb launched his attack. To his son Muhammad he had given the van; to Murad Bakhsh the left wing; to Bahadur Khan the right, reserving the centre for himself. No fiercer fight was ever waged. Muhammad and his advance guard were driven back. Bahadur Khan was only saved from destruction by reinforcements from Aurangzeb. Dara, mounted on a beautiful Ceylon elephant, led his cavalry in a fierce charge against the enemy's weakened centre, captured the guns and put the camel corps to flight. Showers of arrows darkened the sun until every man's quiver was empty. The fight became one of swords then as men battled hand to hand. Aurangzeb, mounted like Dara on an elephant, saw his men give way, break, fly, till barely a thousand remained.

Flight was not for Aurangzeb. Indomitable, iron-willed, cool, he cried to his wavering few:—

"*Dili, Yarana!* Take heart, my friends! *Khuda-he!* There is a God! What hope have we in flight? Know ye not where is our Deccan? *Khuda-he! Khuda-he!*"

And he cried to his servants to chain

[1] *Renamed later Fathabad—Place of Victory.*

the legs of his elephant together that retreat might be impossible.

Then it was that Dara, courageous though he was, made his first mistake. The moment had come for the annihilation of Aurangzeb's centre, which would send dismay through all his host. Instead Dara flew to succour his left wing, which was heavily beset by Bahadur Khan, while his right waged furious battle with Murad Bakhsh. With a string of pearls about his head, and his Rajputs all in yellow, Raja Ram Singh charged down upon the elephant of Murad Bakhsh, crying to the Prince:

"Dost *thou* contest the throne with Dara Shukoh?"

Hurling his javelin at Murad Bakhsh, he tried to cut the elephant's girths, shouting to the *mahout*: "Make him kneel! Make him kneel!" But Murad Bakhsh, wounded though he was, cast his shield over his little son who sat beside him, and sent an arrow through the Raja's brain. One after the other the Rajputs dropped at the elephant's feet, until the ground all about him was yellow as a field of saffron.

The day was going against Aurangzeb despite his valorous fight. Then Dara made his second mistake. Aloft for all to see, Aurangzeb sat upon his elephant. Murad Bakhsh, with howdah stuck as thick with arrows as a porcupine with quills, sat upon his. But Dara—whether because he was startled by a rocket which struck his howdah, or because he was urged by treacherous Khalil-Allah—dismounted, and the sight of his empty place sent panic running through his host. Some cried that he was dead. Others that they were betrayed. Fear of Aurangzeb's vengeance upon those who had fought against him seized on all. They fled. Dara fled, leaving Aurangzeb to dismount from his besieged elephant and prostrate himself before God in thanksgiving for the victory.

Three or four days later he and Murad Bakhsh were in a garden outside one of the gates of Agra. Aurangzeb knew better than to trust himself within the fortress where Shah Jahan still remained. The old man had sent his victorious son a sword inscribed *'Alamgir*—World-Compeller, but Aurangzeb was aware that he had also sent to Dara two elephants loaded with rupees and had bidden the Governor of Delhi to furnish him with a thousand horses from the royal stables. On June 18, Aurangzeb's son Muhammad, on the pretext of bearing a message from his father, entered the fortress with a handful of men, overcame the guards and made the old Emperor captive.

Only Murad Bakhsh, it seems, remained still unsuspicious of Aurangzeb, who flattered him with "Your Majesty." Together the two set off in pursuit of Dara. At Muttra, thirty miles on the road to Delhi, they halted, and supped, Aurangzeb, with gentle hand, wiping the dust and sweat from his brother's face. When, at the end of the meal, delicious wines were brought, Aurangzeb, strict follower of the Prophet, would not touch them. He slipped softly away, leaving his brother, whose weakness for wine he knew, to drink himself to sleep.

Then, stepping as softly as his grandfather, came six-year-old A'zam, the son of Prince Muhammad, bribed by promise of a jewel to steal the sleeping man's sword and dagger.

"Oh, shame and infamy!" cried Aurangzeb, stirring his brother with his foot, "Thou a King and yet possessing so little discretion! What will the world now say of thee, and even of me? Let this wretched and drunken man be bound hand and foot, and removed there within to sleep away his shame."

That night—the night of July 5th, 1658—Murad Bakhsh was carried to the

F. HENLE

THE MOTI MASJID, DELHI

The Pearl Mosque at Delhi was built by Aurangzeb in 1659. The decorations lack the exquisite fineness and delicacy which mark the best period of Mogul architecture.

outwork-fortress of Salimgarh, whence, across the river, he could see the lovely city of Delhi where he had thought to reign. He must have known that his days were numbered.

Marching day and night, sleeping on the bare ground, with dry bread and bad water for his only fare, Aurangzeb followed in the wake of Dara. Only when he learnt that Dara, making yet another mistake, had turned aside from Kabul—where he might have strongly fortified himself—and gone south to Sind, did he leave the pursuit to others, and return to Agra. There was yet another brother to be dealt with: Shuja, who was once more in arms.

Well had the King of the Uzbegs said that to fight with Aurangzeb was self-destruction. In less than a year, Shuja had fled, never to be heard of more, and Dara, betrayed by a treacherous host, was his brother's prisoner. Dressed in dirty clothes, and mounted on a miserable elephant, he was paraded through the streets of Delhi. The lamentations of the people sealed his fate. Not many days later Aurangzeb held in his hands the head of his brother.

Only Murad Bakhsh remained. From Salimgarh he had passed up the long stairway and through the Elephant Gate into the fortress of Gwalior. But men had not forgotten his valour and his good fellowship, and songs were made in praise of him. He had done his own share of killing. Aurangzeb chose to remember one incident and to call it murder. When the dead man's sons, diplomatically incited thereto, demanded the murderer's head, he gave it. Shah Jahan lived on, given by his strange son all that he desired save freedom. The fortress of Gwalior held Dara's sons, the son of Murad Bakhsh, and Aurangzeb's own son Muhammad, who in a reckless moment had joined his uncle Shuja. Aurangzeb, World-Compeller, had reached the Peacock Throne.

For nearly fifty years he held it: one of the greatest of the Mogul Emperors. "A faint-hearted man," he told his father, "cannot carry out the great duty of government. Sovereignty is the guardianship of the people, not self-indulgence and profligacy. . . . He is the truly great King who makes it the chief business of his life to govern his subjects with equity."

To the Mohammedan he is a saint, whose zeal for the Faith of Islam washes clean the bloodstained path by which he reached the throne. It would have been better for the Empire had he had the tolerance of Akbar. Not blindly, but with conviction and courage, he followed his narrow path, led on by hope of laying all Hindustan at the foot of the Prophet; great, just, careful of his people, unsparing of himself, suspicious, ascetic, unloved.

Ascetic though he was, he kept, for the sake of the Empire, the Emperor's pomp. Bernier, the French traveller, describes him in the first days of his succession, seated in the dazzling splendour of the Peacock Throne, his sons and his amirs about him. His vest was of white, delicately-flowered satin. His turban of cloth of gold was adorned with an aigrette whose base was fashioned of diamonds and an opal whose lustre was that of the sun. And a rope of enormous pearls hung from his neck.

Magnificence laid aside, there remained Aurangzeb the austere, to whom music and dancing were such abominations that he issued edicts against them. One day as he was going to the Mosque, he saw a great crowd of singers following a bier, their voices uplifted in lamentation. He sent to ask whose funeral it was, and was answered "The funeral of Music, killed by the Emperor's edicts."

"I approve their piety," he answered.

MARTIN HURLIMANN

AURANGZEB'S MOSQUE, BENARES

With its two slender minarets rising above the other buildings, the Mosque of Aurangzeb is a conspicuous landmark in Benares, as the Emperor intended.

"Let her be buried deep, and never heard again."

By day and by night, in public and in private, he offered his prayers, fasted when he should fast, kept vigils. To the Palace in Delhi he added for his own use that gem in black and white marble, the Pearl Mosque. He dared not make the Pilgrimage to Mecca, lest he should lose his throne in his absence. All else that a follower of Islam should do he did, even obeying the Prophet's precept that every Moslem should practise a trade: he made skull caps.

Less wise than Akbar his great-grandfather, he could not see that no power on earth can make men think alike, and that God is to be reached by many ways.

O God (wrote Abu-l-Fazl, friend of Akbar) in every temple I see people that see thee, and in every language I hear spoken, people praise thee.

Polytheism and Islam feel after thee.

Each religion says, "Thou art one, without equal."

If it be a mosque, people murmur the holy prayer; and if it be a Christian Church, people ring the bell from love of thee.

Sometimes I frequent the Christian cloister, and sometimes the mosque.

But it is thou whom I seek from temple to temple.

Thy elect have no dealings with heresy or with orthodoxy: for neither of them stands behind the screen of thy truth.

Heresy to the heretic, and religion to the orthodox.

But the dust of the rose-petal belongs to the heart of the perfume-seller.

"Heresy to the heretic" was not Aurangzeb's creed. For the sake of Islam he persecuted the Hindus, thus alienating the great Rajputs who were the pillars of his throne, and woke in the South that Maratha power which was ultimately to bring the Empire to destruction.

Small, sturdy men, the Marathas inhabited the inaccessible fastnesses of the Western Ghâts: peaceful, frugal, hard-working Hindus, subject to the King of Bijapur. By the time of Jahangir, numbers of them had joined the army of their Bijapur ruler. As horsemen none surpassed them. Many rose to be officers. One of them, Shahji Bhosla, became Governor of Poona and Bangalore, and to him—when Aurangzeb was nine—there was born a son, Shivaji.

The blood of the wild ran in Shivaji's veins. Mixing with the people of the Western Ghâts, he came to know every path and lurking place of that precipitous region. A born leader of men, before he was twenty he had gathered the hillmen to his standard, and turned the military knowledge learnt at Poona against his teachers. Fort after fort in the hills, left neglected by the King of Bijapur, fell before Shivaji and his Marathas. Forces sent to crush him were themselves defeated. By 1660 he could put 50,000 men into the field, and was threatening Aurangzeb's city of Aurangabad. For three years the Emperor's Viceroy, Shayista Khan, tried to subdue him. Aurangzeb's son, Prince Mu'azzam, in company with Jaswant Singh, next essayed the task. Shivaji, undaunted, sacked Surat, the Gate of Mecca, and every Moslem cried out against the sacrilege.

Aurangzeb tried new generals, Raja Jai Singh and Dilir Khan, and in five months "the mountain rat" was cornered. Then the Emperor made a mistake worthy of Dara the Unfortunate. Shivaji, ready to be his vassal, came to Delhi to do homage for the Viceroyalty of the Deccan. No other man could give Aurangzeb such help in conquering that long-desired territory. But the

WALLS OF GOLCONDA

The fortress of Golconda, the keystone of the defence of the Deccan against Aurangzeb. It was besieged for over two months, but not utterly conquered.

Great Mogul in his bigotry scorned to ally himself with a Hindu mountain robber. He let him stand unnoticed in the Hall of Audience, and Shivaji, raging at the humiliation, slipped away without taking leave. Soon, despite the Imperial guards posted at his door, he had made his escape in a basket carried on a porter's back.

By 1671 he had sacked Surat once more. For another nine years he held sway, pushing his raids as far North as Baroch, subduing all the Konkon, save what the English, Portuguese and Abyssinians held, and forcing the army of Aurangzeb to raise the siege of Bijapur. Then death took him.

Shivaji was dead, but he had created a nation. In 1681—some six months after Shivaji's death—Aurangzeb himself arrived at Burhanpur to take the Deccan in hand. Little did he dream that he had looked his last on Delhi, that twenty-five years hence he would still be here, with a demoralised army and the Marathas more powerful than ever.

He began by despatching his sons Mu'azzam and A'zam to lay waste the Konkon. The wise Marathas cut down all the grass, then left the Princes to go their way. The country would destroy them more effectively than they themselves could do. When Mu'azzam and A'zam reached the end of their task, they had scarcely a horse to carry them, and no more than a starving remnant of the army they set out with. No sooner were they gone than Shivaji's son, Sambhaji, swept down with his horsemen on Burhanpur, fired it, and set all the surrounding country in a blaze.

Aurangzeb had marched south to Ahmadnagar by then, his aim being to cut off the resources of the Maratha by reducing the kingdoms of Golconda and Bijapur, which Shivaji had long ago forced to pay tribute to him. Twenty-eight years had gone since, with Mir

Jumla, Aurangzeb had so nearly conquered them. Now the conquest should be complete. When Prince A'zam failed to reduce Bijapur to obedience, Aurangzeb, in the August of 1685, appeared before the doomed capital. For fifteen months he laid siege to it. By November, 1686, the keys were in his hands, and its king, brought before him fettered with silver chains, was sent captive to Daulatabad.

Two months later the iron-willed Emperor drew his line about Golconda. Day by day, in spite of a ceaseless fire from the beleaguered city, the encircling host closed in. At last the ditch was reached, and Aurangzeb himself sewed the first of the sacks which, filled with earth, were thrown into it. But all about the Imperial army the Marathas had laid waste the country. Plague came to add to the horror of famine. For three days rain fell ceaselessly, washing away much of Aurangzeb's entrenchments. Twenty-eight years ago, 'Abdallah, King of Golconda, had sought to appease Aurangzeb with baskets of gems. Now Abu-l-Hasan his successor showed his prisoners the riches of his granaries, and offered both grain and an indemnity if the Emperor would raise the siege.

"Abu-l-Hasan," Aurangzeb answered, "must come to me with clasped hands, or he shall come bound before me. I will then consider what mercy I can show him."

Treachery gave Aurangzeb his will at last. A bribe unlocked a postern gate, and the Moguls poured in. But the Emperor did not forget the valour of his enemy. When Prince A'zam brought Abu-l-Hasan before him, he treated him with courtesy, then sent him to join the King of Bijapur in Daulatabad.

Now at last Aurangzeb seemed master of the Deccan. But there still remained the Marathas. He had thought to weaken them by destroying Golconda and Bijapur. He found he had strengthened them, for the vanquished went to swell their numbers. He might push his military occupation as far as Mysore, and drive the Marathas to their hills. Sambhaji, captured, might be put to death, but not even the great Emperor Aurangzeb, with all his armies, could wipe out the nation Shivaji "the mountain rat" had raised.

Year followed year, and still the Emperor strove with his hopeless task. No hardship was too great for him to bear: heat, famine, pestilence, floods. He had been sixty-three when he marched out of Burhanpur. Careri, the Neapolitan traveller, saw him fourteen years later in camp at Galgala: an old white-bearded man, slender and stooping but still indomitable. Four years after that, at the siege of Sattara, when a mine exploded, he made a ravelin with the bodies of his dead, and only with great difficulty was persuaded from leading the attack himself.

Lonely, suspicious, the fate of all Mogul Emperors to fear his own sons did not pass him by. Muhammad the eldest had died in his prison at Gwalior. Mu'azzam, unjustly suspected, had suffered seven years of rigorous captivity. A'zam, Akbar, Kam-Bakhsh, one after the other fell under suspicion, but were forgiven, and for Kam-Bakhsh, the youngest, son of the only woman for whom he ever felt passion, he had true love.

As he looked back along his life, he felt the years had been profitless, and that he himself was bowed beneath the burden of his sins. Many a time, awake in the darkness of the Deccan night, he must have remembered Shah Jahan, whom he had kept captive in Agra. He must have seen again the blood-stained head of Dara in his hands, and Murad-Bakhsh fighting so gallantly at Samugarh. In the fort at Delhi he still had the howdah which, stuck as full of arrows as a porcupine with quills, had shielded Murad Bakhsh that day. A poor reward he had given to Murad Bakhsh. Did he repent of it as he repented of the treatment he had given to Shah Jahan? Was this earthly Empire worth all that he had given for it? He had failed, he told himself. The Deccan for which he had striven all these years was a desert and his army but the shadow of itself. Openly the Marathas scoffed at him. At home in Delhi rebellion was raising head. Failure everywhere, he thought, as, pursued by parties of Maratha horsemen, he led the remnant of his army back to Ahmadnagar.

"Peace be with you and yours," he wrote to A'zam. "I am grown very old and weak, and my limbs are feeble. Many were around me when I was born, but now I am going alone. . . . The army is confounded and without help, even as I am: apart from God, with no rest for the heart. They know not whether they have a King or not. . . . Farewell, farewell, farewell."

To beloved Kam-Bakhsh he wrote: "Soul of my Soul. . . . Now I am going alone. I grieve for your helplessness. But what is the use? Every torment I have inflicted, every sin I have committed, every wrong I have done, I carry the consequence with me. Strange that I came with nothing into the world, and now go away with this stupendous caravan of sin. . . . Wherever I look I see only God. . . . I have greatly sinned, and I know not what torment awaits me. . . . I commit you and your sons to God's care, and bid you farewell. I am sorely troubled. Your sick mother, Udaipuri, would fain die with me. . . . Peace."

Haunted by remembrance of his own treatment of Shah Jahan, he kept all his sons away from him. But what would happen after he was gone? Muhammad and Akbar were dead: there remained three of his sons, Mu'azzam, A'zam and Kam-Bakhsh. He would prevent war between them if he could, and so he drew up a paper stating that he would have Mu'azzam recognised as Emperor, but that A'zam should share the Empire with him, one taking Delhi, with the Northern and Eastern Provinces, and the other Agra, with all the country to the South and South-west of it, including all the Deccan, save Golconda and Bijapur; these he left to Kam-Bakhsh.

He died on March 4th, 1707, and near Daulatabad was buried as he had desired: "Carry this creature of dust to the nearest burying place and lay him in the earth with no useless coffin."

The bloodshed that he feared followed. A'zam, as soon as he heard of his father's death, came to Daulatabad and had himself proclaimed Emperor. At Kabul Mu'azzam did the same. On the plains of Agra the rival forces met, and the battle raged fiercely. A'zam and his two eldest sons were killed, and his youngest, a baby, was captured. Kam Bakhsh, who had acknowledged A'zam as Emperor, refused to yield obedience to Mu'azzam. No concessions would win him, and Mu'azzam finally marched into the Deccan against him. Near Haidarabad a battle was fought, and Kam Bakhsh died of his wounds.

Well might the old Emperor feel all was failure. Mu'azzam, with the title of Bahadar Shah, reigned only five years. Not thirty years later Nadir Shah of Persia swept over Hindustan, sacked Delhi and carried off the Peacock Throne. Henceforth the Mogul Emperors were but puppets. In 1803 when General Lake—fighting the Marathas—entered Delhi, he was shown a miserable blind old man, sitting under a tattered canopy. It was Shah-Alam, "King of the World," and captive of the Marathas. Courteously the Englishman raised his hand in salute to the Emperor.

BY COURTESY OF THE BIBLIOTHÈQUE NATIONALE, PARIS

SHIVAJI AND HIS ARMY

A portrait of the great Maratha ruler with his followers: from a print in the Bibliothèque Nationale.

SHIVAJI BHOSLE

LIBERATOR OF THE MARATHA NATION
1627–1680

BY CHARLES KINCAID, C.V.O.

On the 10th of April, 1627, was born Shivaji the liberator of the Maratha nation. His father, Shahaji Bhosle, claimed descent from Sajansing the grandson of that Rana Lakhmansing of Chitor, who had fallen in defending his capital from the Afghan emperor Ala ud din Khilji. The Bhosles took their name from the family fief of Bhosawat in Udaipur. Sajansing emigrated to the Deccan and his descendants became soldiers of fortune in the service of the king of Ahmadnagar. Babaji, Shivaji's great-grandfather, became patil or headman of the village of Verul near Daulatabad. His two sons, Maloji and Vithoji, founded the greatness of the family. Led, as they believed, by the goddess Parwati, they discovered in an ant heap a hidden treasure. Using it wisely they equipped a body of troops and hired their services to Jagpatrao Nimbalkar, the ancestor of the present chief of Phaltan. Eventually Maloji married Nimbalkar's sister Dipabai. Childless for some years Maloji and his wife went on a pilgrimage to the shrine of a Moslem saint, known as Shah Sharifji. The result crowned their hopes and in 1594 Dipabai gave birth to Shahaji Bhosle, Shivaji's father.

When Shahaji was ten years old, Maloji conceived the ambitious design of marrying him to Jijabai, the daughter of the first noble in Ahmadnagar, namely Lakhoji Jadhavrao, who claimed descent from the ancient Yadava kings of Devgiri. Events favoured him. He took Shahaji with him to celebrate the Holi at Lakhaji's house. Jijabai was present and she and Shahaji began to mimic their elders and squirt red-coloured water over each other's clothes. Lakhoji, his heart warmed by the gay scene and attracted by the beauty and sturdy build of Shahaji, exclaimed: "What a fine pair they will make!" Maloji turned to the other guests and called them to witness that the boy and girl were formally betrothed. Lakhoji reluctantly agreed, but his wife strongly opposed the match. Eventually through the mediation of Murtaza Nizam II the wedding was celebrated.

The marriage of Shahaji and Jijabai seems at first to have been happy enough. In 1623 she bore her husband a son called Sambhaji. Thereafter, so a legend runs, Shahaji was so engaged in fighting the Moguls on behalf of the Ahmadnagar king that he found no time to pay his wife conjugal attentions. One night he dreamt that a Hindu anchorite, clad in rags and smeared with yellow ashes, put a mango in his hand and said: "Share the fruit with your wife and you will be the father of a son, who will be an incarnation of the god Shiva." When Shahaji awoke from his dream, he found a mango in his hand, visited his wife and shared it with her. The offspring of this reunion was the birth of a little boy. Convinced that the anchorite whom he had seen in his dream was the god Shiva, Shahaji called his son Shivaji, just as he himself had been called Shahaji after the saint Shah Sharif.

In 1633, while Shivaji was still a little boy, an enemy of Shahaji named Mhaidar Khan deserted to the Moguls, then attacked Ahmadnagar, and out of spite betrayed to them Shahaji's wife,

SHIVAJI

From an old Dutch print.

Jijabai. They imprisoned her in Kondana fort, now known as Sinhgad, but her servants contrived to conceal Shivaji. At last peace came through the partition of Ahmadnagar between Delhi and Bijapur. Jijabai was allowed to rejoin her son; but in the meantime Shahaji had entered the service of the Bijapur state and had contracted a second marriage with Tukabai, a girl of the Mohite family. Jijabai would not share her husband with a second wife, so her relations with Shahaji became merely formal.

In 1637 Shivaji was ten years old and the question of his marriage became important. Jijabai took him with her to Bijapur. There he was married to Saibai, the little daughter of Vithoji Newaskar. Shivaji, however, had been hunted during his infancy by Moslems. His mother had been imprisoned by them; and not unnaturally he had conceived a violent dislike for them. He refused to bow to the king of Bijapur according to the prescribed etiquette; and he made so violent a protest against the killing of cows that a riot ensued. Shahaji hastened to send Jijabai and her son back to his distant fief of Poona and Supa. To help her in its management, he appointed a trusted Brahman officer called Dadaji Kondadev.

Unfortunately the fief was utterly desolate. In Shahaji's absence armed bands of Moslem soldiers and of Hindu brigands had overrun the estate. The peasants had fled, the land had gone out of cultivation and the village itself had been razed to the ground and the site ploughed up by a Mogul captain. Out of his own savings Dadaji enlisted hillmen to guard the peasants, whom he tempted back. On the right bank of the Mula river, where now stretches the municipal garden, he built a home for Jijabai and her son. So well indeed did Dadaji administer the ruined property that Shahaji added to it the talukas of Indapur and Baramati, recently conferred on him by the Bijapur government. The rich black soil of the new lands soon repaid Dadaji what he had spent and gave him besides a handsome balance for development. His financial difficulties surmounted, Dadaji gave his mind to Shivaji's education. Round the growing lad he gathered other boys of his own age, the sons of the petty landholders of the neighbourhood, and bade them explore the folds of the Sahyadri mountains and the tracks that led through them, so that in the future Shivaji might know how to defend his inheritance. As a veteran soldier, Dadaji had Shivaji taught martial exercises and as a scholar he told him stories of the heroes of the Ramayana and the Mahabharata. In fact he cared for the young Maratha noble as if he had been his own son. Thus at eighteen Shivaji was a man, tireless, fearless and deeply inspired with the resolve to free his country from the rule of Bijapur.

In the monsoon of 1646 Shivaji began his life's work by seizing the Bijapur hill fort of Torna to the southwest of Poona. It is a beautiful spot in summer and winter, but very dreary during the monsoon. A custom had grown up by which during the rainy season the commandant and his entire garrison left the fort for the village at its foot, returning at some date in November. Shivaji took advantage of this breach of discipline and occupied the fort during the commandant's absence and seized the garrison's arms and treasure chest. The commandant complained to Bijapur, but Shivaji used the plunder to bribe the court officials. He was nominated governor of the fortress, and his victim not only lost his post but received a reprimand. Shivaji's next step was to fortify Morbad hill, six miles away, and rename it Rajgad. These two strongholds guarded the south-western frontier of his fief, but its southern frontier could not be deemed safe until the fortresses of Kondana and Purandar were his. In the former his mother, Jijabai, had been confined. Shivaji secured it by bribing its commanding officer, and renamed it Sinhgad. Purandar became his through a lucky chance. The commandant had recently died and his three sons were quarrelling over the succession. They called in Shivaji as arbitrator. As he passed through the fort gates, the garrison tumultuously acclaimed him as their leader. He accepted the office and satisfied the claims of the brothers by lands elsewhere.

Shivaji now owned four great fortresses, but he had emptied his treasure chest. This he had to refill somehow. Not long afterwards he surprised the treasure train of the Moslem governor of Kalyan. It is a wealthy town near Thana and the treasure was proceeding under armed guard to Bijapur. Rich once again, Shivaji took by storm no less than nine forts to the west of Poona and occupied Kalyan itself. The indignant king of Bijapur ordered Shivaji to present himself at court. The young rebel replied that he would do so, if the king conferred on him all the lands in his possession.

The Moslem courtiers insinuated that Shivaji was merely his father's tool, although Shahaji had really written to his son a letter of censure. The king, through the treachery of another Maratha noble, Baji Ghorpade, arrested Shahaji and ordered him to be bricked up in a wall. A small aperture was left open, so that he might breathe and he was allowed to send word to Shivaji. If the son failed to surrender, the aperture would be closed and the father would be suffocated. Shivaji met the situation with consummate skill. He offered to become a feudatory of Shah Jahan. The Mogul emperor grasped eagerly at the chance of meddling in Bijapur affairs and ordered Shahaji's immediate release. The Bijapur court at once freed Shahaji from his brick prison, ordering him not to leave the capital. They did not, however, overlook Shivaji's conduct. They induced Balaji More, Raja of Jaoli, to connive at his assassination. The plot failed and Shivaji, after vainly attempting to win over Balaji More, attacked and took possession of his fief and treasure. With this new wealth he fortified a neighbouring hill, which he renamed Pratapgad.

In the meantime Shah Jahan's third son Aurangzeb was vigorously attacking Bijapur, and Shivaji, having declared himself a Mogul feudatory, joined the prince's army with a contingent. Before any decision could be reached, the emperor fell ill. Prince Aurangzeb abandoned the Bijapur campaign and hastened north to fight for the throne against his brothers. Shivaji, left alone to face the wrath of Bijapur, tried to seize their naval base at Janjira, but failed. Encouraged by his enemy's repulse, the young Bijapur king called for volunteers to destroy the rebel's growing power once for all. The queen's brother, Afzul Khan, who knew the country round Jaoli well, asked for the command, promising to bring Shivaji back a prisoner. Made commander, he desecrated as he marched the Hindu temples that lay along his route. At the same time he bragged openly that he would bring Shivaji back in a cage of wickerwork that he had prepared for the purpose. Shivaji's spy Vishwasrao Korekar overheard this boast and warned his master. When Afzul Khan entered Jaoli limits he sent his secretary Krishnaji Bhaskar to lure Shivaji to a conference. For all the secretary's silver speech, the young rebel distrusted Afzul Khan's proposal. That

SON OF SHIVAJI

Sambhaji, who deserted to Aurangzeb and was eventually imprisoned by Shivaji.

night he secretly visited Krishnaji and implored him, by all that a Hindu held sacred, to disclose the Khan's real intentions. With great reluctance Krishnaji at last confessed that nothing but treachery was in his master's mind.

Armed with this information, Shivaji resolved to turn the tables on his lying enemy. He agreed to meet Afzul Khan on the slopes of Pratapgad; but under his tunic he put on a coat of chain mail, under his turban a steel helmet and concealed a dagger in his sleeve. To his left hand he fitted steel points, known as *sagh nak* or tiger claws. In the meantime Afzul Khan marched vaingloriously to the foot of Pratapgad hill. Thence he was carried in a palanquin to the meeting place, where Shivaji had put up a reception tent. The two commanders, attended by only two orderlies each, met inside the reception tent. As Shivaji appeared to be unarmed, Afzul Khan thought that his chance had come. With his left arm he caught Shivaji round the neck and tried to drive his sword into the Maratha's stomach. The coat of mail turned the point. Shivaji, unable to free his neck from the Khan's powerful grip, drove with his right hand his dagger into Afzul Khan's back and tore open his belly with the tiger claws in his left hand. Afzul Khan broke away and struck a mighty sword blow at Shivaji's head. The steel helmet under the turban broke its force; nevertheless he received a slight cut on his head. The Moslem's attendants tried to help their master, but they were overpowered and the Khan was seized and beheaded. At the same moment Shivaji's soldiers fell on the unsuspecting Bijapur army and completely destroyed it.

FATHER OF SHIVAJI

Shahaji Bhosle, the father of Shivaji. From "History of the Maratha People." By Kincaid and Parasnis.

The news of this disaster merely roused the Bijapur king to fresh efforts. A second force under Sidi Johar, an Abyssinian mercenary, marched to avenge Afzul Khan. Shivaji occupied Panhala, but it was invested with such strictness that he was in grave danger of capture. With great skill he slipped from the fortress and made his escape to Vishalgad. The place was impregnable. Sidi Johar was relieved of his command and the Bijapur army retreated.

Shivaji thought this a favourable moment for punishing Baji Ghorpade for his treacherous arrest of Shahaji. Ghorpade was moreover very hostile to himself. With three thousand men he stole one night out of Vishalgad, surprised Ghorpade and, killing him, returned laden with booty.

Bijapur was in despair. Shivaji was unconquerable and always the Mogul peril threatened from the north. At the same time, however, Shivaji was menaced from the same quarter. Shahaji, intensely proud of his son's achievements, offered himself as mediator. Father and son met at Jejuri, a celebrated Hindu shrine, and together they rode to Poona, where they negotiated a treaty. Shivaji was left in possession of his conquests. In exchange he promised to aid Bijapur against foreign aggression. At Shahaji's advice his son moved his capital to the great fortress of Raygad.

Safe from attack by Bijapur, Shivaji planned to free the Marathas under Mogul dominion. About the same time Aurangzeb directed Shayiste Khan, the governor of the Deccan, to take active measures against the new power in the south. Shivaji, driven from Poona, retired to Rajgad. There he planned a raid on the Mogul general. Two hundred picked soldiers, disguised as a marriage procession, obtained leave to enter Poona. There they were met by five hundred others, disguised as Mogul infantry. That night, with Shivaji at their head, they raided Shayiste Khan's residence, killed his son and most of his servants and slashed off his thumb. Thinking they had killed the Mogul captain, the Marathas dispersed and escaped to Sinhgad. The disgusted emperor replaced Shayiste Khan by his own son, Prince Muazzim. The latter's inactivity gave Shivaji a chance of carrying the war into the enemy's country.

He hid his movements by a pretended attack on the Portuguese province of Bassein, on the frontiers of which he erected two large camps. Then suddenly, on the fifth January, 1664, he appeared before Surat with four thousand picked cavalry. The Mogul governor made no attempt to defend the town but withdrew his garrison inside the castle, leaving the town to the invaders. Unmolested the Marathas collected or dug up the property and jewels of the rich and timid Gujarati merchants. Only the English Factory resisted them successfully. On January the tenth, hearing of the advance of a Mogul relief force, he loaded the treasure of the unfortunate inhabitants on their own horses and ponies and brought it safely to Rajgad.

Shahaji had been killed hunting during the raid on Surat and Shivaji assumed the hereditary title of Raja conferred on him by the king of Ahmadnagar. He felt deeply his father's death but he was at once called on to face a new Mogul army, led by Jai Sing and Diler Khan, two skilful and experienced veterans. Diler Khan invested Purandar while Jai Sing blockaded Sinhgad. Shivaji, fearing a simultaneous attack from Bijapur, sued Jai Sing for peace and eventually obtained it on the rendition of all his recent conquests from the Moguls and of all the territory that had once belonged to Ahmadnagar. He was allowed to retain his gains from Bijapur and allowed a free hand against that state. In return he was to visit Agra and do homage to the emperor Aurangzeb.

The emperor, however, had no intention of keeping the treaty. Directly Shivaji appeared at Agra he was publicly insulted and given a lower place than that to which he was entitled. Eventually he was detained in a bungalow on the outskirts of the town. From this prison house he escaped with extraordinary skill and acuteness. He hid himself in a brickwork basket especially made for sending sweetmeats to friends and then rode as fast as he could to Mathura. There he and his comrades assumed the garb of anchorites and made their way to Benares, Allahabad and Gaya. Thence they turned back and travelling through Central India arrived safely at Poona. Shivaji's young son Sambhaji, who had been left at Mathura, was able to join his father some months later. Not long afterwards Bijapur, Delhi and Shivaji entered into a threefold treaty of peace.

The treaty remained unbroken for two years. Then Aurangzeb ordered his son, Prince Mu'azzam, the new governor of the Deccan, treacherously to seize Shivaji. The prince, however, liked the Maratha and warned his agent at Aurangabad. Shivaji acted on the warning and was soon out of reach of Mogul treachery. On the advice of his mother Jijabai he retaliated by retaking the great forts of Sinhgad and Purandar. The former was escaladed by his lifelong friend, Tanaji Malusre, who fell in the undertaking. The latter was stormed by Tanaji's brother Suryaji. The king tried but failed to capture Shivner and Janjira and then again turned his attention to Surat. Once more he took valuable plunder from the Gujarati merchants, and on his way back to Rajgad defeated a Mogul army sent to intercept him.

These successes, followed as they were by further inroads into the crumbling kingdom of Bijapur, led Shivaji to have himself formally crowned at the hands of a Benares priest. He enjoyed indeed the hereditary title of Raja conferred on his grandfather Maloji by the king of Ahmadnagar, but that kingdom had ceased to exist. He had been confirmed in the title by the emperor; but he had finally renounced his fealty to the Moguls. He had therefore no real dignity to raise him above the level of the wellborn and highspirited nobles who shared his campaigns. On May 21, 1674, and on the succeeding days he had himself crowned with splendid ceremonial at his capital, Rajgad. He was invested with the sacred thread by Gaga Bhat, a high priest of Benares, and anointed after the manner of the ancient Kshattrya kings. When Shivaji had been duly installed, he had himself weighed against gold coins, which he distributed among the Brahmans, who had flocked to see the great king's coronation. On the following day he received an embassy from Bombay. The English merchants there were anxious to have their rights admitted by a regular treaty and they claimed, with great firmness, compensation for losses suffered by them from Maratha raids on their factories or branches at Rajapur and Hubli. The English were led by Oxenden, who presented a diamond ring and received in return a robe of honour. The king granted the English ten thousand pagodas for their losses at Rajapur, but refused their Hubli claim. He allowed them to trade in his dominions on paying two and a half per cent. duty, to build trading factories in Rajapur, Dabhol, Chaul and Kalyan. He also agreed to let English money circulate throughout his territories and to restore all English ships wrecked on his coasts.

Shortly after the coronation Shivaji's

mother, Jijabai, died to his great sorrow. He sought distraction in a second attack on Shivner, where she had given him birth. Failing again to take it by storm, he determined to conquer the great stretch of southern territory that Bijapur had acquired on the break up of the Vijayanagar empire. It was no mere land hunger that prompted him, but a full understanding of the danger that threatened him from the north. He realised that once Aurangzeb brought against him the full strength of his empire, he would be lost unless, by retreating to the extreme south, he could so lengthen the enemy's line of communications that he could face their fighting front with some chance of success.

The plan was born of statesmanship and executed with triumphant skill. Under pretence of going to Tanjore to claim his share of Shahaji's estates, he marched across Bijapur to the eastern coast, paying for his supplies as he went. There he formed an alliance with the king of Golconda and then turning southwards he conquered not only Tanjore, but the whole south as far as Mysore. It was this magnificent campaign that later enabled his descendants to keep at bay and finally to overthrow the whole strength of the Delhi empire.

The last years of the great king were embittered by the turbulence of his eldest son Sambhaji. After reducing Bijapur to helplessness, he resolved to protect it from the renewed Mogul attack. After winning an important battle at Sangamner, he had returned to Panhala. There he learnt that Sambhaji had deserted to the enemy and had been received with the greatest courtesy by the Mogul commander Diler Khan. Aurangzeb, who always distrusted his subordinates, ordered that the prince should be at once sent to Delhi. Samb-

PRATAPGAD FORT

One of Shivaji's famous hill fortresses. From "Indian Historical Studies." By H. G. Rawlinson, M.A.

haji escaped and returned to Shivaji, who imprisoned him in Panhala. The king then forced the Moguls to raise the siege of Bijapur, and at the invitation of the king Sikandar Ali Shah went there in state.

In 1680, Shivaji, angry at the help given by the English to the Moguls, ordered his admiral to destroy the shipping in Bombay; but his fleet was no match for the English vessels. The *Revenge* sank five gunboats of the enemy, one after the other. This was Shivaji's last important military effort, for on the 28th March, 1680, on his return from a raiding expedition, a painful swelling appeared on his knee joint. Fever followed, and after a seven days' illness the great king died at Raygad on the third of April, 1680. I shall close this monograph by quoting the just and admirably chosen words of Orme on p. 94 of his Historical Fragments:

"In personal activity he (Shivaji) exceeded all generals of whom there is record. For no partizan appropriated to service of detachment alone ever traversed as much ground as he at the head of armies. He met every emergency of peril, however sudden or extreme, with instant discernment and unshaken fortitude; the ablest of his officers acquiesced in the imminent superiority of his genius, and the boast of the soldier was to have seen Shivaji charging sword in hand."

THE FACTORY AT SURAT

Surat, at which there was an important English trading station or "factory," was besieged by Shivaji in 1664. He secured a great deal of treasure before being forced to withdraw, but did not molest the possessions of the English, owing to their stout resistance, which appealed to his sense of chivalry. From "Ovington's Voyage to Surat." Edited by H. G. Rawlinson, M.A.

HAIDAR ALI

From a drawing by J. Leister, of Madras, 1776.

HAIDAR ALI

DICTATOR OF SOUTHERN INDIA

1717–1782

BY CHARLES KINCAID, C.V.O.

It must be borne in mind that Haidar Ali was never a sovereign prince. He was what nowadays would be called a dictator or "leader"; in fact, he occupied a position not dissimilar from that occupied by Signor Mussolini in Italy to-day. There was always a raja of Mysore as there is a king of Italy, but the raja was as eclipsed by Haidar Ali as the king of Italy is to-day by the Duce.

Mysore formed part of the great Vijayanagar empire that was irretrievably destroyed at the battle of Talikota in 1565. The Wodiar or Viceroy of Mysore retreated from the battlefield, abandoned his overlord and made himself an independent prince. In 1609 his descendant, Raj Wodiar, seized Seringapatam and made it his capital. The Wodiars increased in power until in 1699 the emperor Aurangzeb bestowed on the ruling prince, Chikka Devaraj, the title of "raja" and "Jaga Deva" and gave him an ivory throne, ever afterwards used for the installation of his successors. Chikka Devaraj was a gallant soldier and a most competent ruler; but, unfortunately, his descendants had little or no ability. The result was that, as in the case of the later Merovingians, the royal power fell into the hands of the king's ministers. The direct line of the Wodiars failed in 1736 and thereafter their successors were adopted as the caprice of the Dalwai or commander-in-chief willed. It was this state of things that made possible the rise of Haidar Ali.

The courtly learning of the Mysore genealogists sought to prove the descent of Haidar Ali from the Koreish, the family of the prophet Mahomed. According to their story a certain Hasan, descended from Yahya, left Baghdad and came to Ajmir. His son, Wali Mahomed, went farther south to Gulbarga. Thence Wali Mahomed's son, Ali Mahomed, migrated to Kolar in eastern Mysore. In 1678 he died, leaving four sons, of whom the youngest was Fateh Mahomed. He was the father of Haidar Ali, who, born in 1717, rose to be dictator of Mysore.

In 1749 Haidar obtained employment in the Mysore army through the influence of his eldest brother Shahbaz, who had risen from the ranks to a command of twelve hundred men. Haidar was absolutely fearless and his courage soon attracted the notice of Nanjraj, the Mysore chief minister, who gave him his first promotion. The young soldier went with a Mysore force to help Nasir Jang, who had seized the throne left vacant by the great Nizam of Hyderabad. Nasir Jang was defeated by the French and then treacherously murdered. The Mysore troops retreated, but in the confusion Haidar Ali contrived to seize part of Nasir Jang's treasure, and thus skilfully founded his own fortunes. He collected some 1,500 cavalry and 3,000 infantry and took into his service as secretary a Deccan Brahman named Khanderao. In 1755 he was raised to the governorship of Dindigul, which he at once converted into a powerful arsenal with the help of French officers from Pondicherry. At this time he conceived an immense liking for the French that never left him.

STRONGHOLD OF THE ENGLISH

Fort St. George, Madras, as it appears to-day. Haidar Ali marched on Madras, and came so near that the Madras Government sued for peace.

In 1757 the new Nizam Salabat Jang, accompanied by his French adviser, M. de Bussy, marched on Mysore to collect tribute. Nanjraj, though hampered by the hostility of his brother Devaraj, still contrived by plundering the temples to buy off Salabat Jang with a payment of eighteen lakhs. No sooner had the Nizam gone than the Marathas, led by the third Peshwa in person, Balaji Bajirao, appeared. They were bought off by a payment of five lakhs in cash and the mortgage of several valuable districts. These payments emptied the Mysore treasury, and the unpaid troops mutinied. Nanjraj sent for Haidar Ali. Khanderao, at his orders, examined carefully the military accounts, reduced the demands of the mutineers to a reasonable figure and, disbanding four thousand men, paid the rest by plundering the property of their leaders. The army reduced to obedience, Haidar Ali denounced the treaty with the Peshwa. A Maratha force under Gopalrao Patwardhan reappeared. Haidar Ali went to meet it and by his skill and energy foiled all the efforts of Patwardhan to occupy the pledged districts. Eventually Patwardhan retired on receiving sixteen lakhs in cash and the promise of a similar sum later. The young adventurer returned to Mysore in triumph and the grateful raja Chikka Krishnaraj conferred on him the title of Fateh Haidar Bahadur.

The raja and his mother had grown weary of the ascendancy of Nanjraj and induced Haidar to drive him out; but the court soon found their new master harsher than the old one. They persuaded Khanderao to turn against his employer. Khanderao, whose country of origin was the Deccan, turned to the

Marathas, and with their help surprised and dispersed Haidar's force. He rallied some of the fugitives and attacked Khanderao at Nanjangad but was again beaten. In despair he threw himself at Khanderao's feet and actually won his forgiveness and was again appointed commander-in-chief. He once more rebelled and was again defeated. As a last hope he forged letters in Nanjraj's name to Khanderao's leading officers, asking them to surrender the Deccan Brahman, as they had promised. The letters were allowed deliberately to fall into Khanderao's hands. He read the fabricated documents and believing them to be genuine fled panic-stricken to Seringapatam. Haidar Ali then appeared and won over the leaderless army. Marching on the capital he recovered control of the administration and demanded of the raja the surrender of Khanderao, who had hidden in the royal palace. At the same time he promised that he would not only spare the fugitive's life, but would cherish him like a tota or parrot. On these conditions Khanderao was surrendered. Haidar Ali kept his promise in the letter, if not in the spirit, by confining his prisoner in an iron cage and feeding him until his death on rice and milk.

In 1763 Haidar Ali added Bednur to his possessions. The ruling chief, Baswappa Naik, had died leaving his widow, Virammaji, as guardian of an adopted son named Chenna Baswaia. The widow and her paramour murdered the boy; but an impostor presented himself at Haidar Ali's camp, claiming to be Chenna Baswaia and the lawful heir to the throne of Bednur. Haidar Ali adopted his cause and with the help of the dead chief's former minister surprised the town and its treasures and sent widow,

HILL FORT, BELLARY

The fort at Bellary rebuilt by Haidar Ali, and the stronghold of his campaign against the Nizam of Hyderabad's French supporters.

paramour and pretender to various prisons in Mysore.

Aware that the Marathas would sooner or later return to avenge the check of Gopalrao Patwardhan, he made extensive preparations to meet them; but the new Peshwa, Madhavrao, was a most capable prince and in spite of Haidar Ali's skilful generalship defeated him severely at Rattahalli. The adventurer sued for peace and obtained it on the surrender of most of the lands that he had recently conquered and an indemnity of thirty-two lakhs of rupees. To repair his broken fortunes Haidar Ali cast his eyes on the Malabar coast, alleging that its inhabitants, the Nairs, were subjects of the Bednur principality. A legend ran that the whole court was once ruled over by a viceroy of the Chera dynasty. In A.D. 825 the last viceroy turned Moslem and resolved to go to Mecca. Before going he divided his lands among his principal chiefs. To the ruler of Kolattiri he left his regalia and the northern part of his territory; to the ruler of Travancore the southern part; to the chief of Perimpatappa Cochin; and to the Zamorin of Calicut he gave his sword and as much country as the crow of a cock could be heard over. The chief of Kolattiri supported Haidar Ali, but the Nairs resisted the invader vigorously and only submitted after a fierce struggle. Haider Ali insured against further rebellions by deporting them wholesale to the Mysore plains, where most of them died of hunger.

Haidar Ali had hitherto fought Indian princes. From 1767 to 1769 he was engaged in a war against the English of Madras and their ally, Mahomed Ali the Nawab of Arcot. The Nizam of Hyderabad, Nizam Ali, had at first joined the English, but he soon changed sides and joined Haidar Ali. The opposing armies fought a number of actions without any decisive result. The English won a hard-fought battle at Trinomalais, but Haidar Ali's activity enabled him to overrun and lay waste a large extent of territory, thus cutting off the supplies of the more slowly moving English forces. Near Erode he and his general, Fazl Ullah Khan, overwhelmed an English detachment under Captain Nixon. The recovery of such districts as the English had won followed, and Haidar Ali marched to within five miles of Madras. This daring move was completely justified by its success. The Madras government sued for peace and entered into a defensive alliance with Mysore, both sides restoring their recent conquests.

No sooner had Haidar Ali imposed an advantageous treaty on the Madras government than he had again to face a Maratha invasion. In 1767 the Peshwa, Madhavrao, had extorted from him thirty-five lakhs of rupees. In 1769 the Peshwa demanded a crore, or ten million rupees, as indemnity. Haidar Ali called on his allies, the Madras government, to assist him, but they sent him nothing but fair promises. Madhavrao's advancing troops carried everything before them, including the fort of Nijagul, the only place indeed that resisted. He would probably have succeeded in completely humbling Haidar Ali had not consumption, the hereditary sickness of his family, compelled his return to Poona. He made over the command to his uncle Trimbakrao, who advanced victoriously to Chirkuli. There the Marathas inflicted so severe a defeat on the Mysore troops that had they pushed on at once to Seringapatam, they might well have taken it; but fortunately for Haidar Ali they wasted so much time plundering the temple of Melukot that the active adventurer was able to put the capital in a state of defence and resist successfully Trimbakrao,

HAIDAR ALI'S TOMB

The magnificent mausoleum of Haidar Ali and his son, Tippu Sultan, at Seringapatam. The tomb is in the Lalbagh, two miles from the fort

when at last he besieged it. Both sides became weary of the struggle and the Marathas accepted fifteen lakhs in cash and a promise of another fifteen lakhs later, as the price of their withdrawal. Haidar Ali vented his ill temper on his unfortunate master, the raja Nanjraj, who had succeeded his father, Chikka Krishnaraj, in 1766. Charging him with having made secret overtures to the Marathas, Haidar Ali had the young prince strangled. In his place he raised his brother Chamraj to the throne.

Political events in Poona enabled Haidar Ali to recover the districts pledged to the Marathas for the second fifteen lakhs and also to make himself master of Coorg. The able and gallant Peshwa, Madhavrao I, died in 1772. His younger brother Narayanrao succeeded him, but in the following year he was murdered by his guardsmen, incited thereto, as it was supposed, by the Peshwa's uncle, Raghunathrao. The latter assumed the Peshwaship, but his claim was frustrated by the birth of Narayanrao's posthumous son, Madhavrao II. Raghunathrao would not give up his title and to secure Haidar Ali's help he connived at his recovery of the districts won back by Madhavrao I and reduced the tribute payable by Mysore to six lakhs a year. Safe from Maratha interference Haidar Ali overran Coorg, a thickly wooded province on the edge of the Sahyadris.

Since his conquest of Bednur Haidar Ali had claimed a suzerainty over Coorg. A disputed succession enabled him to make his claim effective. In 1770 Lingraj, one of the claimants, asked for the dictator's help. He was not free to act until 1773. Intriguing with both claimants Haidar Ali reached Merkara, the capital, unopposed. One of the claimants, Devappa, fled, but was caught and imprisoned in Seringapatam. To the other Haidar Ali gave the principality as a feudal appanage of Mysore. Then marching through the passes of the Sahyadris he completed the subjugation of Malabar.

In 1776 the young raja Chamraj died. Although he despised the royal house, Haidar Ali resolved to continue it as a political necessity. To find a successor to Chamraj, who had left no son, the dictator had recourse to the following expedient. He collected the youngest children of the royal family, and then threw in front of them a variety of toys and trinkets. One of the children, also called Chamraj, seized a dagger, attracted no doubt by its jewelled handle. Haidar Ali declared that this act proved the child's capacity for kingship and made the late sovereign's widow adopt the little boy as her son. He became the father of Maharaja Krishnaraj of Mysore, whom the English in 1799 acknowledged as ruler of Mysore. He reigned for sixty-eight years, dying in 1868.

The year 1776 witnessed one of Haidar Ali's most brilliant campaigns. The palegar or hill baron of Bellary, a petty chief under the Nizam of Hyderabad, suddenly renounced his allegiance to his sovereign and asked the help of Mysore. The Nizam sent a French officer, M. Lally, to besiege Bellary, but Haidar Ali by forced marches reached the town in five days, entered the fort, surprised the attacking party and all but captured M. Lally, who escaped with difficulty to Hyderabad. From Bellary the dictator marched sixty miles eastwards to the fortress of Gutti, the headquarters of Murarirao Ghorpade. He was the descendant of Santaji Ghorpade, the commander-in-chief of Shivaji's son, king Rajaram. Thinking that his master would be taken inside Jinji fort by the Moguls, Santaji had, without orders, seized the stronghold of Gutti in the valley of the Tungabhadra. Thereafter he and his descendants had ruled there as independent princes. Haidar Ali,

THE MASJID-I-ALA

The Mosque of Haidar Ali in Seringapatam. It is built in a style different from anything in Northern India.

however, claimed to levy tribute from Murarirao on behalf of the raja of Mysore. Murarirao rejected the demand but was at last forced to surrender through want of water. Haidar Ali sent the Maratha's family to Seringapatam, but he imprisoned Murarirao in Kabaldrug, where he soon afterwards died. Nor was Haidar Ali less successful in checking the advance of a new Poona army sent by the regent, Nana Phadnavis, to punish him for allying himself to the pretender Raghunathrao, whose cause the English in Bombay were supporting. With the Marathas marched a considerable contingent from Hyderabad. Haidar Ali's general, Mahomed Ali, met the allied army at Saunsi, some ten miles north of Savanur. By a feigned retreat—a ruse often effectively used by the Marathas themselves—he led them into an ambush where they suffered heavily from the Mysore artillery. The rainy season put a stop to further operations and the contending forces withdrew to their respective headquarters.

The withdrawal of the Poona and Hyderabad armies gave Haidar Ali a breathing space. He used it in an attempt to reduce to servitude the Bedar chief of Chitaldrug. The ancestor of this ruler had been appointed commandant of Chitaldrug by the king of Vijayanagar, but when Vijayanagar fell, the Bedar chief declared himself independent. His claim, however, was contested by both the Marathas and Haidar Ali. The former claimed tribute from Chitaldrug as the successors of the Bijapur kings, while Mysore claimed it as the owner of the Sira district. When Sira had been held by the Moguls, the Bedar chief had, it appeared, paid them tribute. When Haidar Ali attacked Chitaldrug the Bedar chief appealed to the Marathas and defended himself gallantly while they marched to his aid.

During the cold weather of 1777–1778 the regent and his ministers sent sixty thousand horse and foot under Hari Ballal Phadke and Parashrambhau Patwardhan to relieve Chitaldrug. Haidar Ali, on their approach, raised the siege in return for a cash payment and a vague promise of military support in the future.

As he marched to meet the Marathas Haidar Ali, with the help of Bajirao Barve, a Konkanastha Brahman and a connection of Raghunathrao, contrived to bribe several of the Maratha leaders. The most important of these was Manaji Shinde, a very brave Maratha soldier, who had been acclaimed by his troops as Phadke, or the gallant. He received six lakhs and undertook to desert with his men at the first general action. Patwardhan heard of Shinde's treachery just before Haidar Ali attacked him near the Tungabhadra. Patwardhan at once cut the traitor's division to pieces before it could change sides, Shinde escaping with only thirty horsemen. Patwardhan then broke off the action. On enquiring into the conspiracy he found so many of his other officers involved that he no longer dared continue his march. He retired to Poona, harassed all the way by the Mysore light cavalry.

On his enemy's retirement Haidar Ali reduced all the country between the Krishna and Tungabhadra rivers and took after a long siege the fortress of Dharwar on the edge of the Marathi-speaking Deccan. He then remembered the chieftain of Chitaldrug, who not unnaturally had not sent him any help against the Marathas. The Bedar resisted heroically, but a band of three thousand Moslem mercenaries in his pay went over to Haidar Ali and made any further defence impossible. The chief surrendered and was imprisoned with his family in Seringapatam. Haidar Ali transplanted twenty thousand Bedars to lands near the capital. All the Bedar boys whom he captured he converted to Islam and turned them into janissaries under the name of Chela Battalions.

The next victim of the dictator's land hunger was the Nawab of Kadappa. Against him Haidar Ali sent his brother-in-law, Ali Raza Khan, and after the capture of Chitaldrug joined his lieutenant in person. Kadappa was well defended by its Afghan cavalry, but eventually yielded to superior forces. Haidar Ali spared the life of the Nawab, but forced him to give him in marriage his beautiful sister, Bakshi Begum. He took also into his service the Nawab's Afghan cavalry. This act nearly cost the conqueror his life. Eighty Afghan troopers burning with hatred tried one night to murder him in his tent. They cut down his guards, but the lucky dictator escaped. The mutinous Afghans were killed or executed. Warned by this peril, Haidar Ali showed himself more indulgent towards the Nawab of Savanur, a powerful feudatory of the Nizam. The Nawab's eldest son was married to Haidar Ali's daughter and the Nawab's daughter to the dictator's second son, Karim. The marriages were celebrated with great splendour in Seringapatam.

During the marriage festivities an envoy came to Haidar Ali from Poona. He invited the Mysore government to join with the Nizam and the Marathas in expelling the English from Madras. In 1778 a Bombay army had marched on Poona to install Raghunathrao as Peshwa but had been forced to capitulate at Wadgaon. The Madras government had enraged the Nizam by occupying one of his districts, Guntur, and by binding themselves to support against him his brother, Basalat Jang. Haidar Ali was angry with the English because in spite of their alliance they had steadily refused to send him any support against the Marathas and had always helped against him Mahomed Ali, the treacherous and incompetent Nawab of Arcot. In return for military aid Nana Phadnavis offered to confirm the dictator in possession of all territory occupied by him between the Krishna and Tungabhadra rivers, and to reduce his tribute for Mysore to eleven lakhs. Haidar Ali and the Nizam both joined the alliance. The Nizam did little, but Haidar Ali's attack was of the most formidable kind. In July, 1780, he marched on Madras with an army of eighty-three thousand men, officered in many cases by gallant French adventurers. Having isolated the capital he sought out the English armed forces. On September 10 he surprised a detachment of 3,700 men commanded by Colonel Baillie and after a hard fought battle forced it to surrender.

This grave defeat threatened seriously the whole British dominion in India. Fortunately Warren Hastings was governor-general in Calcutta and he took into his own hands the conduct of the war. His first step was to appoint as commander-in-chief of the Madras army, Sir Eyre Coote, then commanding in Calcutta. This distinguished soldier had first served in 1745 against the Scottish insurgents. He had been a divisional general at Plassey and it is believed that it was his insistence that led Clive to attack the enemy in spite of overwhelming odds. In 1760 he defeated de Lally at Wandewash and took Pondicherry in 1761. He had then returned home and had entered Parliament, but in 1779 had accepted the commander-in-chiefship of Bengal and although not the Eyre Coote of 1760 he was still far the most competent English soldier in India.

At the same time Warren Hastings detached Nizam Ali from the confederacy by ordering the immediate rendition of Guntur. He also undertook vigorous action against the Marathas in Central India. Captain Popham escaladed Gwalior, and Colonel Carnac defeated

FORT AT SERINGAPATAM

Part of the old walls in Haidar Ali's capital fort.

Madhavrao Sindia's army at Seronj. The English thereafter so wasted Sindia's territories that on October 13 the Maharaja not only agreed to remain neutral, but promised to press the Poona government to make peace with the English. Mudhoji Bhosle, the Maratha captain established in the Central Provinces, was won over by a large cash subsidy and the cession of the districts of Karra and Mandela. The Poona government waited to see how Haidar Ali was faring before they took definite steps. Coote had won several actions against Mysore, but had also suffered some reverses. His most successful battle was at Porto Novo. For some months previously he had lost the initiative owing to the sudden appearance of the French fleet off Madras. He had attacked the fort of Chilambrun at first without success; but on the arrival of an English fleet and the departure of the French he again attacked the stronghold. Haidar Ali by a forced march to its relief compelled the English commander to raise the siege and meet him in the open. The Mysore troops were confident of victory, but the English artillery was so well served that Haidar Ali's infantry and cavalry were first checked and then defeated with a loss of ten thousand men near the town of Porto Novo, that gave its name to the battle. This victory enabled Coote to effect a junction with a reinforcement from Bengal, to raise the siege of Wandewash and capture the stronghold of Tirapasur. On August 27 Haidar Ali again attacked the English on the very spot where he had in the previous year overwhelmed Colonel Baillie. This time the English were more numerous and also better led and equipped and Haidar Ali was forced to retire.

Weary of the war and disappointed at his failure to destroy Haidar Ali's army in a pitched battle, Sir Eyre Coote resigned; but the governor of Madras, Lord Macartney, persuaded him to withdraw his resignation and march to the relief of Vellore. Its garrison was in serious straits, for the siege had been pressed under the guidance of skilled French engineers, and Haidar Ali regarded its fall as certain. Coote's advance surprised him, while his guns were unharnessed and their bullock trains grazing at some distance from their camp. Haidar Ali rallied his troops with great rapidity, but after the loss of five thousand men he was obliged to abandon the siege and withdraw from the field.

The Mysore government at this time received a welcome ally in the Dutch governor of Negapatam. In 1781 the Dutch were at war with the English; and for the assistance of his troops, Haidar Ali offered the Dutch governor the English district of Nagur then in Mysore occupation. Colonel Braithwaite was detailed to crush this combination, but after taking Nagur and storming Negapatam, he was surprised by Haidar Ali's heir, Tipu Sultan, his little army destroyed and he himself taken prisoner.

In spite of this success the Poona government decided that Haidar Ali would never succeed in driving the English out of southern India; and on May 17, 1782, the regent Nana Phadnavis signed with them the treaty of Salbai. By it the English agreed to abandon the pretender Raghunathrao, but were allowed to retain the province of Salsette, near Bombay. Their other conquests they agreed to restore. Haidar Ali thus found himself deserted both by the Nizam and the whole Maratha confederacy. On the other hand he received a reinforcement of twelve hundred French infantry commanded by M. de Bussy. On June 2, 1782, Haidar Ali and Sir Eyre Coote fought their last battle. Coote had tried to surprise Arni, the chief arsenal of the Mysore forces below the western Ghats. The surprise failed and an indecisive action followed, which led to Coote's retirement.

In August the Bombay government sent an expedition under Colonel Humberstone to invade Malabar. The Bombay troops took Calicut, but were forced to take post at Ponani, near the coast, where they were protected by the guns of two British men-of-war. Tipu and his French general de Lally attacked Humberstone without success. Suddenly to the surprise of the English Tipu retreated with all speed. The reason was adequate. He had learnt of the death of his father, Haidar Ali. The dictator had long suffered from cancer in the back. It suddenly took a more malignant form, and on December 7, 1782, he died in his camp near Chittur.

It is impossible to deny the greatness of Haidar Ali. A penniless adventurer, he raised himself to the first position in his country and made Mysore greater than it has ever been before or since. Illiterate, he yet restored the finances of his country, and left to his successor a full treasury and an efficient army. His judgment of men can be gauged by his liking for the French, who rendered him the most valuable services both as officers and engineers. Although a Moslem, he was no bigot and cared not a jot to what religion his subordinates belonged so long as they did their duty. He would gladly have been allies of the English, and had he met Warren Hastings those two great men would probably have become fast friends. It was their common misfortune that Haidar Ali's dealings were always with the Madras government who, subservient to the faithless Mahomed Ali, Nawab of Arcot, were quite untrustworthy. I shall conclude by copying a few of the great adventurer's reflections recorded by Wilks and quoted in Bowring's admirable work on Haidar Ali and Tipu Sultan:

"I have committed a great error. I have purchased a draught of country liquor at the price of a lakh of pagodas. Between me and the English there were grounds for mutual dissatisfaction, but no sufficient cause for war, and I might have made them my friends in spite of Mahomed Ali, the most treacherous of men. The defeat of many Baillies and Braithwaites will not destroy them. I can ruin their resources by land but I cannot dry up the sea. I ought to have reflected that no man of common sense will trust a Maratha and that they themselves do not expect to be trusted. I have been amused by idle expectations of a French force from Europe; but supposing it to arrive and to be successful here, I must go alone against the Marathas and incur the reproach of the French for distrusting them; for I dare not admit them in force into Mysore."

TIPPU SULTAN

The son and successor of Haidar Ali.
From an original picture in the possession of the Marquis Wellesley.

TIPPU SULTAN

"THE TIGER OF MYSORE"

1753–1799

BY H. H. DODWELL

Tippu Sultan was a man evidently destined to struggle against adverse circumstances. Inheriting a great position from his father, he found that mysterious causes were hindering him from maintaining that position by the methods which his father had employed with striking success, and despite all his efforts to retrieve his situation, to reorganise his kingdom, and to set off power against power, he perished in a vain endeavour to preserve his independence of the new political forces which had gathered such weight and momentum even during his own lifetime. Nor was he unlucky only in the circumstances of his career. He has been unlucky in his historians. Many men have defied the evident will of the gods, and yet received the admiration of humanity for the heroism of their struggle. But Tippu Sultan has been commemorated by Moslem chroniclers of the old school, following the traditional ways and seeking to glorify him as a martyred champion of Islam, the steadfast enemy of the infidel, no matter whether Hindu or English, or by English writers who naturally regarded him as the obstinate enemy of their own people, and reckoned his fall as the culmination of their triumphs in Southern India. The first show him as the indifferent and unsympathetic master of his Hindu subjects; the second ascribe to the faults of his character and intelligence the failure of his political management. A truer estimate may perhaps be reached by

THE DARA DAULAT BAGH

The Summer Palace of Tippu Sultan, Seringapatam.

recollecting that he was surrounded by forces which he could not analyse or even evaluate, and that therefore his efforts were necessarily blind and almost inevitably fruitless.

Tippu Sultan succeeded at the close of 1782 to the power of his great father, Haidar Ali, in the midst of the second war in the Carnatic. He was then thirty years of age, and had already enjoyed considerable experience of both war and administration. He had taken a conspicuous part in the campaigns which had been in progress since 1781 against the East India Company, and had on more than one occasion displayed his fondness for swift movement and unexpected attack in the field. His education had been carefully attended to. He spoke and wrote Persian with ease and fluency. He was a practised horseman, incessantly in the saddle. At the moment of his father's death, which occurred in the Mysorean camp near Arcot, Tippu was engaged in repelling the advance of a body of English troops which had landed on the Malabar coast. His position was embarrassing. He had to choose between continuing his Malabar campaign or hastening eastwards to take over the charge of the kingdom. At Arcot was his younger brother, whom malcontents might easily attempt to set up as Haidar's successor. If that happened, then Tippu would be confronted by a war of succession as well as by a foreign war. He was forced therefore to quit his campaign in Malabar and hurry across the peninsula to take personal command of the army in the Carnatic. Fortunately almost all Haidar's chief officers faithfully held to the declared wish of their late master. Tippu arrived and assumed with the command of the army the government of Mysore.

The conduct of the war was the foremost problem before him. Already the position was beginning to be less unfavourable to the English. Warren Hastings' insight and fortitude had brought Mahadaji Rao Sindia to make the Treaty of Salbai, by which the Anglo-Maratha war was brought to a practical though not immediately to a formal conclusion. Thus resources were freed by which Hastings' plan of attacking the Mysore territories on the Malabar coast might be carried into more effective operation than had been possible earlier. The change involved a certain loss of initiative on the part of Tippu. Whereas Haidar in the Carnatic had been free to accept or refuse battle, Tippu had no choice but to seek out and destroy the invaders of his territory. The region was, moreover, that in which Tippu's power was least consolidated. The numerous petty chiefs who had recently been reduced to submission were naturally restless and discontented, and ready to afford help to any invader. An expedition from Bombay had therefore small difficulty in landing and seizing a couple of seaports and in invading the province of Bednur, where they speedily occupied the capital.

With swift decision Tippu moved against this unexpected and indeed dangerous thrust at a vulnerable point. Fortunately for him the English expedition was ill commanded. It had been entrusted to a Company's officer, General Matthews, who was in himself overconfident of success, and who, moreover, was hampered by the jealousy of the King's officers serving under him. Tippu succeeded in surprising the English before they had concentrated to meet him and quickly recovered Bednur. He then laid siege to Mangalore in order to complete their expulsion from the territory.

To aid in this affair he had brought with him a detachment of his French allies under the command of an officer named Cossigny, and he had expected

COMMEMORATING A VICTORY

Mural paintings in the Tippu's Summer Palace. They depict the victory of his father over Colonel Baillie at Polilore, near Conjeeveram.

considerable aid in the siege operations from the skill of French engineers. But while the siege was still in progress orders came from the Coromandel coast, where was the main body of the French forces, announcing that the preliminaries of peace between France and England had been signed in Europe, and directing the French with Tippu to desist from acting against the English. This meant not only the neutralisation of Tippu's French contingent at Mangalore, but also that the English forces in the south were set free to act against his southern provinces.

Luckily the governor and council at Madras were little inspired by Warren Hastings' principle of seeking peace by making war terrible to the enemy. They were undoubtedly in need of peace, though not quite so acutely as they thought they were. They were also in great difficulties owing to internal disputes with the Nawab of Arcot, with their own military officers, and with the government of Bengal. They resolved therefore after a brief interval to seek peace by negotiation rather than by pressing their advantages in the south. The proposal was far from unwelcome to Tippu himself. He needed peace in order to carry into effect his plans for reorganising his kingdom; but he also felt sure that in policy he ought to carry the siege of Mangalore to a successful conclusion, were it only to convince the Malabar chiefs that they had nothing to hope from intriguing with the English. He therefore agreed to receive the proposed mission, but took care that it should move so slowly through his territories that he would be in possession of the besieged place before their arrival. The Treaty of Mangalore was signed on March 11, 1784.

Tippu's treatment of the mission has long been the object of peculiar misrepresentation. The story ran that it was subjected to extraordinary indignities; that the commissioners were in danger of their lives; that gibbets were erected opposite their tent-doors; that they attempted to escape to the British vessels lying off Mangalore; and that the treaty was negotiated and signed under duress. The facts were very different. In the course of the siege Tippu had discovered a correspondence going on between Colonel Campbell, who commanded in Mangalore, and Muhammad Ali, an officer high in the Mysore service. The details are unknown, but Campbell regarded the intrigue as securing "one half of the Nabob's army to our side" and bidding fair "for the overturning of the present government." The discovery of the plot had led to the execution of a number of persons believed to have been concerned. Tippu had hanged them on gibbets set up on the high ground surrounding Mangalore, presumably in order that the English garrison might see what had become of their promised friends. When the English ambassadors arrived, they desired their tents to be pitched on an eminence from which they could communicate by signal with the ships in the roads. Although they did not choose a spot closely adjacent to any of the gibbets, it seems that from the shipping their tents did appear to be close to these memorials of Tippu's justice. Hence, in the excited state of men's minds, a story which spread to Bombay and thence to Calcutta, to find prominent record in the pages of Colonel Wilks.

Another matter of the same kind is

BY COURTESY OF THE SECRETARY OF STATE FOR INDIA

THE ASSAULT OF SERINGAPATAM

East India Company troops advancing on Seringapatam, 1799. From a painting in the India Office.

afforded by the alleged treatment of the English prisoners in Mysore. They are represented to have been treated with extraordinary severity. Many are said to have been forcibly converted to Islam, many others put to death, and a large number detained in slavery after the conclusion of the treaty, which stipulated for the release of all prisoners of war. In this respect too there was evidently misunderstanding and misrepresentation. Normally between two European nations the private soldiers taken prisoners in war were put in confinement, but the officers would only be imprisoned if they refused to give their parole not to attempt to escape. That was not the established Indian custom. The prisoners taken by Haidar and Tippu were all imprisoned, and, though officers and privates were generally separated, the case of the officers at all events was much harder than it would have been in Europe. Again, attempts to escape led to prisoners being placed in irons, a great hardship indeed, but perhaps the only way in which the prisoners could be securely kept. The allowance made to them for food was small. Altogether there can be no doubt but that their lot was very miserable. But this is as far as one can truthfully go. The standards of the time considered, they were treated severely, not barbarously. The severity of treatment led to a high mortality among those whose constitutions were unable to resist the depressing conditions in which they had to live. But this is a very different thing from the deliberate massacre of prisoners with which contemporary English opinion charged Tippu Sultan. No evidence survives which confirms that opinion.

The case is much the same as regards the conversion to Islam. Among the private soldiers a miserable confinement might well induce a certain number to be willing to exchange their religion for liberty, even at the cost of circumcision and a foreign service from which they could never return. Tippu, moreover, was certainly anxious to recruit such men as might be useful either as artificers in equipping or as instructors in training his army. His gaolers were not wanting in offering inducements such as good pay and easy employment to those willing to embrace Islam. There is no reason to believe that there were any converts other than those who elected thus to purchase their freedom.

The case of those prisoners detained in Mysore after the peace almost certainly follows out the facts regarding conversion. A convert to Islam would necessarily be regarded not merely as having abandoned his former faith, but also as having accepted the sovereignty of the sultan and having renounced his British allegiance. The sultan would not regard such men as prisoners of war; they had ceased to be so; and it may be argued quite reasonably that he never understood the clause in the treaty stipulating for the surrender of prisoners of war as including men who had become his subjects.

But if the Treaty of Mangalore was not so humiliating and its execution not so evasive as has been supposed, so also it was a truce rather than a settlement. It certainly left Tippu Sultan with the belief that he could meet the armies and negotiators of the East India Company on equal terms. Nor was he favourably impressed by the past unsteadiness of the Company's policy. He did not realise that in great part this was due to the defective organisation which had left the management of external policy in the hands of three separate authorities at Madras, Bombay and Calcutta respectively. He failed to understand that this was the major cause why he and his father had twice been able to ravage the

Carnatic and defy its English protectors. He fell into the grievous error of under-estimating the power of his late enemy; and believed that with a trifle of good political management he could over-throw them altogether. In this belief he was certainly encouraged by the French, who, though not prepared at once to renew their efforts to dominate India, earnestly hoped that the next war in Europe would enable them to do so and used every effort to keep alive every spark of hostility to the English at every court in India. But this evident intimacy with Pondicherry inevitably made Tippu's policy suspect in English eyes; nor was their suspicion weakened by the fact that Tippu controlled a great stretch of the western sea-board, and so might receive support and assistance from the French. He was destined to receive none. But even if he could have looked into the future and seen how slender was the actual aid he was to receive from the French, it may well be doubted if his conduct would have been materially changed. His mind was too active, his nature too independent, for him ever to have been willing to sink into subordination to another power.

These qualities are clearly to be seen in the projects for internal reorganisation which mark his reign and which must be regarded as, in the main, his own work. Within the scope of his vision he was a realist. For example, under Haidar Ali the coin of Mysore had borne the name and titles of Shah Alam, the Delhi emperor. This was of course no more than a polite make-belief. The English were doing, and for many years continued to do, the same in Bengal. Early in 1786, when on the verge of war with his northern neighbours, the Marathas, Tippu resolved to abandon this practice. He assumed the title of Padshah. He caused his own name to be inserted in the Friday prayers in all the mosques of Mysore, and ordered a new coinage to be struck and issued bearing his own name and title. As he himself wrote with complete truth, Shah Alam was the prisoner of Sindia and could be deemed a sovereign by none but idiots. Again, he was extensively busied with drawing up a code of regulations for the guidance of his officials. He abolished the Moslem calendar with its lunar year, so inconvenient administratively, since the harvests and the periods of assessing and collecting the revenue had to follow the courses of the sun. He drew up a series of revenue instructions, largely embodying the traditional usage of the country. He prepared a body of commercial regulations, many of which seem to anticipate the policy of self-sufficiency which has been adopted as an economic ideal by many modern states. He discouraged foreign trade, except that portion of it conducted by his officials for the profit of the State. He set up a board of nine persons to conduct this, and invited his subjects to participate by a method of deposits, on which a share of the profits was to accrue to the subscribers. He endeavoured to abolish the local bankers, to take over their functions of internal remittance, and to substitute State money-changers for the *shroffs* who till then had driven a profitable trade in every bazaar. Wilks is much inclined to turn all this to ridicule. But that is absurd. In some of these matters Tippu was following in the wake of Akbar. In others he was seeking, so far as he understood it, to follow the example of the East India Company. He was the first Indian sovereign to seek to apply Western methods to his administration. That the effort was unsuccessful is neither here nor there. Tippu had to meet two great difficulties. He did not really understand the principles which he was seeking to apply, and could not command the services of officials who understood them. But his mind was evidently alert, and he was eager to learn by experiment. Nor was his treatment of his Hindu subjects what Wilks had described. In the *Historical Sketches of Southern India* we read of mass circumcisions, of the destruction of temples, the confiscation of temple lands. But Dr. Surendranath Sen has shown that on occasion Tippu championed the cause of the Hindus, and reaches the sound conclusion that where Tippu used severity his motive was political and not religious. In fact a rational consideration of his career shows him not the bigoted tyrant of tradition, but an active, enterprising man, moving in a world in which new forces had recently been let loose, forces beyond his control and to some extent beyond his comprehension.

What conclusions, for instance, could Tippu Sultan, or any other Indian prince of his day, draw from the passing of the India Act and the appointment of Cornwallis as Governor-General of Bengal (possibly he never heard of the first and missed quite completely the significance of the second)? Yet they marked a change that was to be of decisive influence upon his fate. They meant that at Calcutta would govern one man with a control over English policy and English power in India as complete (save for the shadowy authority of London on the other side of the world) as that exercised by an Indian prince, and, because his organisation was much more strongly knit, incomparably more efficient. The third war between the Moslem rulers of Mysore and the East India Company proves how completely and inevitably Tippu misread the portents of the time. He was eager to

BY COURTESY OF THE SECRETARY OF STATE FOR INDIA

LAST STAND OF TIPPU SULTAN

From a painting in the India Office.

complete his control of the Malabar coast by the conquest of Travancore. The raja had been seeking to strengthen his northern frontier by the purchase of certain fortresses which had long been in the possession of the Dutch and which the Dutch had conquered from the Portuguese. A complication lay in the fact that the raja of Travancore was declared to be an ally of the East India Company by the Treaty of Mangalore. But Tippu almost certainly knew that the governor of Madras was averse to acting in defence of Travancore. For that reason, I think, he decided upon the attack, supposing that the authority of the Company was lodged in the governor. But it was not. The governor was suspended. Another took his place. Cornwallis was resolute to defend his Hindu ally, and the third Mysore War ensued. In both the former contests Tippu's northern neighbours, the Marathas and the Nizam, had been either neutral or hostile to the Company. But Cornwallis swiftly concluded alliances with each, so that, for the first time in a war with the English, Tippu had to defend his northern frontier. Nor was that the only fundamental change. When, at the outset, Tippu's rapidity of movement checked and constricted the English attack, Cornwallis came down in person from Calcutta, assumed the direction of the war, penetrated into Mysore, captured Bangalore and laid siege to Seringapatam itself. The outcome was the Treaty of 1793, by which Tippu was obliged to pay a heavy indemnity and sacrifice a large part of the additions which he and his father had made to the Mysore territory.

This severe set-back led Tippu closely to consider the ways and means by which his position might be restored. He could not meet the combined attack of the triple alliance which Cornwallis had formed against him. The Nizam perhaps counted for little. But the Marathas must not join the English again; and might not the French be brought in to set right the balance? He had already sent one embassy to Paris, and, although he had got out of it little save a few French artificers and plenty of kind words, war had now broken out between the French and English. A second embassy went therefore to the new Revolutionary government. The numerous Frenchmen in his service were allowed to form a Revolutionary Club. Tippu himself patronised it. "Citoyen Tipou" the Frenchmen called him. He was in close and regular correspondence with Pondicherry. He sent a mission to the governor of Mauritius seeking French recruits, and the governor recklessly put out a proclamation inviting all zealous French subjects who could be spared to join Tippu and drive the English out of India.

These steps were taken in 1798. At almost the same moment there arrived in India a new governor-general, Richard Wellesley. He learnt of this Mauritius proclamation, of the arrival at Mangalore of a small number of French recruits and of Napoleon's invasion of Egypt. In his eyes the question of Mysore must be settled before any considerable French expedition could reach India. He persuaded the Nizam to dismiss his French brigades and accept instead a body of the Company's troops. That settled, he invited Tippu to enter into an alliance with the Company. Tippu sought to lead the negotiations into those elaborate by-ways beloved of statesmen who are playing for time. But Wellesley would admit of no delays. He reckoned that no French force could reach India before the middle of May, 1799. At the close of 1798 he had gone down to Madras, in order to have complete control of the situation. In January he despatched an ultimatum. Tippu sought refuge in a

WHERE TIPPU SULTAN FELL

The wicket gate in the old fort at Seringapatam where Tippu Sultan was cut down.

hunting expedition and returned no answer. Then again Mysore was invaded by the Company's troops. Their movements from Bombay by way of the Malabar Coast, from Hyderabad, and from Madras, converged on the capital. Their instructions were to concentrate on Seringapatam without delay. If Tippu offers battle, fight and march on. If he seeks negotiation, receive his envoys, discuss his proposals, offer him terms, but march on. In April the siege of Seringapatam was formed. On May 2 the defences of the city were stormed, and Tippu Sultan was slain by a chance shot in the conflict.

In this final struggle he was clearly out-manœuvred, out-generalled, outclassed. He might still have found safety in an agreement only a little more onerous than that which Ranjit Singh chose to accept a few years later. But he did not desire mere safety. He was too proud. He could not see the danger of his position—which of the two, Tippu Sultan or Richard Wellesley, could best estimate the probability of French assistance coming by a specified time? Moreover the English supremacy on the high seas made a policy of hostility fatal to those Indian states that adopted it. Tippu, in fact, was caught in the interaction of forces which he could not appraise. But what really led him to his downfall were his own qualities—his bold spirit, his persistent and unwavering hostility to the fast-rising power of the East India Company. A less resolute and adventurous ruler might well have saved his throne and dynasty.

BY COURTESY OF THE BRITISH MUSEUM

RANJIT SINGH

A portrait of the great ruler of the Sikhs who took part in his first battle when he was ten, and succeeded his father when he was twelve.

RANJIT SINGH
AND THE SIKH EMPIRE

1780–1839

BY H. G. RAWLINSON, C.I.E.

THE rise of the Sikhs from an obscure and persecuted religious sect in the Punjab to a great and formidable Empire is one of the most dramatic episodes in Indian history. In the middle of the fifteenth century, Nanak, the founder of the movement, was born not far from Lahore in the Punjab. Nanak in due course grew up and, renouncing the world, became a wandering religious teacher. Like his predecessor Kabir, he was anxious to find a common bond between Hinduism and Islam. "God is one," said Kabir, "whether we worship Him as Ali or as Rama. The Hindu God lives at Benares, the God of the Moslems at Mecca; but He who made the world lives not in a city made by hands." The same spirit stirred in the breast of Nanak. When questioned by the Mohammedan governor about his religious views, he is said to have replied in the following stanza:

Make love thy mosque, sincerity thy
prayer-carpet and justice thy Koran;
Modesty thy circumcision, courtesy thy
Kaaba, truth thy guru, charity thy
creed, and the will of God thy rosary.

THE LILY GATE, LAHORE

RANJIT SINGH IN COUNCIL

The great Sikh ruler holds a Council of State. Facing Ranjit Singh standing are his European officers, Court, Allard, Ventura, Avitabile, Foulkes, and Argond. From "European Adventurers in Northern India." By C. Grey and H. L. O. Garrett.

When reproached for sleeping with "his feet towards God" (i.e. Mecca), he replied, "show me where God is not." Nanak went round preaching in Mohammedan mosques and Jain temples, and to the great crowds assembled at Hindu places of pilgrimage, and he gradually collected a body of followers who called themselves Sikhs or disciples, and acknowledged him as their Guru or religious teacher. While retaining the Hindu doctrine of *Karma* and transmigration, he rejected caste, idolatry and, above all, the authority of the Brahmans. On the evils of caste he uttered a famous saying, which reminds us of Christ's words of rebuke to the Pharisees:

Evilmindedness is the low caste woman, cruelty is the butcher's wife, a slanderous heart the sweeper woman, wrath the pariah woman; what availeth it to have lines drawn round thy cooking-place, when these three sit ever with thee?

In due course, Nanak was gathered to his fathers, and as he felt his end approaching, he heard his disciples disputing whether his body should be burnt as a Hindu or buried as a Mahommedan. According to a beautiful legend, he asked that flowers be heaped at his right side by his Hindu followers, at his left by the Moslems. Those whose flowers were fresh in the morning could claim his body. Next day both heaps were still fresh, and when they lifted the winding-sheet the body had disappeared.

Before he died Nanak nominated his successor. The first four Gurus were peaceful religious teachers, with an ever-growing following. The great Emperor Akbar granted the fourth Guru a piece of land on the banks of a lake known as Amritsar or the Pool of Immortality, and here he built a shrine, the precursor of the famous Golden Temple. The fifth Guru, Arjun, compiled the Adi Granth or Sikh bible, from the inspired sayings of his predecessors. Arjun, unfortunately, came to blows with the authorities. For taking part in the rebellion of Prince Khusru, the son of Jahangir, the Emperor had him put to death. This changed the whole outlook of the Sikhs.

When Arjun's successor, Hargobind, was about to be invested with the turban and necklace which were the badges of office of the Sikh pontiffs, he declared, "My necklace shall be my sword-belt, and my turban shall be adorned with the royal aigrette." Teg Bahadur, the ninth Guru, was seized by the Emperor Aurangzeb, and thrown into prison. When he was accused of the crime of gazing from the top of his gaol at the abode of the Royal Harem, he is said to have replied, "Emperor Aurangzeb, I was not gazing at thy apartment or thy Queen's. I was looking in the direction of the people who shall come from the West to tear down thy Purdahs and destroy thy Empire."

Teg Bahadur was put to death, and his son Govind, the tenth and last Guru, fled to the hills. In due course he returned, and thousands flocked to his banner. Govind made the Sikhs into a militant sect, known as the Khalsa or Elect, dedicated to unrelenting war against the Mogul Empire. Converts were admitted to the order by a mystic ceremony, in which they drank water stirred with a sword, and ate in solemn communication cakes prepared from consecrated flour. They took the surname of Singh or Lion, and were distinguished by the five badges of long hair and beard, short breeches, a comb, a dagger and an iron discus. After Govind's death, the struggle was continued by a leader

BY COURTESY OF THE BRITISH MUSEUM

A SIKH COURT

Sikh School, Nineteenth Century.

named Banda, who carried on a relentless campaign until his capture and execution.

During the Great Anarchy—which was the result of the break-up of the Mogul Empire in the eighteenth century—the Punjab was in a state of constant turmoil, invaded by the Afghans from the north-west and the Marathas from the south, until it became a kind of no man's land. The Sikhs had now become split into twelve great *misls* or clans, each jealous of its neighbour. The Sikh character had greatly deteriorated. Strong drink and drugs, in defiance of the prohibition of the Gurus, were freely consumed, and the only law in the Punjab was that of the sword.

At this crisis in the national fortunes, Ranjit Singh was born in 1780. His father, Mahan Singh, was head of the powerful Sukarchakia confederacy, which was at constant war with the rival clan of the Bhangis. At the age of ten, seated upon his father's war-elephant, he saw his first battle and he was nearly killed by one of the opposing side, who climbed into the howdah and was on the point of despatching the child when he was cut down. Two years later, in 1792, Mahan Singh died, and Ranjit Singh was left, at the age of twelve, to control the destinies of his turbulent and unruly clansmen. Soon after, he nearly lost his life in a flood, which swept away his camp, with a number of men, horses and camels. His first object was to shake off the "petticoat government" of his mother and mother-in-law, two fierce and warlike ladies, who led their armies in person. Both of them were, after some show of resistance, captured and sent to honourable confinement in fortresses.

Ranjit Singh was now master of his own house, and a lucky chance enabled him to occupy

BY COURTESY OF THE BRITISH MUSEUM

THE SON OF RANJIT SINGH

Sikh School, Nineteenth Century.

RANJIT SINGH ON HORSEBACK

Ranjit Singh had a great love of good horses. He risked the attack on Peshawar to obtain Laili, reputed to be the finest steed in Asia.

From "European Adventurers in Northern India." By C. Grey and H. L. O. Garrett.

Lahore, the capital of the Punjab. Shah Zaman, the Amir of Afghanistan, had been making one of his periodical raids on the country, when he was cut off by a rising of the Jhelum river. He was forced to abandon twelve of his guns, and in those days artillery had an enormous value in the eyes of Indian commanders. Ranjit Singh undertook to salve the guns and forward them to Peshawar, provided that he were recognised as ruler of Lahore. The offer was accepted, and Ranjit Singh duly marched on the city and occupied it, in July, 1799. He followed up his success three years later by appearing in front of Amritsar, the sacred city of the Sikhs, held by the rival clan of the Bhangis, and demanding the surrender of the Zam Zam gun, which was looked on as the "Luck" of the Sikh nation. This famous cannon, which now stands outside the Lahore Museum, was originally cast from copper water-pots collected in lieu of *jaziah* or poll-tax by the Mohammedans from the Hindus, and had a romantic history. It had passed from hand to hand, and had been at one time in the possession of Ranjit Singh's grandfather, Charrat Singh.

Ranjit Singh's master passions were for guns and horses. "The Raja's attachment to guns," wrote Metcalfe, "and his opinion of their weight, are so great, that he will never miss an opportunity of obtaining a gun. If he learns there is a gun in any fort, he cannot rest until he has taken the fort to get the gun, or until the gun has been given up to him to save the fort." The Bhangis put up a poor resistance, and with the capture of Amritsar and its coveted weapon, Ranjit Singh became the leading chief in the Punjab and assumed the title of Maharaja.

BY COURTESY OF H. L. O. GARRETT

TOMB OF ANARKALI, LAHORE

It was given to General Allard as quarters by Ranjit Singh. From 1853–1877 *it was St. James' Church. Now it is the Record Office.*

BY COURTESY OF H. L. O. GARRETT

LAHORE IN THE TIME OF RANJIT SINGH

An old print showing General Allard's quarters (right) *and those of General Ventura* (left), *now the Secretariat of the Punjab Government.*

It was at this juncture that Ranjit Singh came into contact with the English. The defeat of Holkar by Lord Lake had brought the British power to the banks of the Sutlej, and they had taken under their protection the Phulkian Sikh chieftains in the cis-Sutlej districts. Ranjit Singh, on the other hand, wished to bring all the Sikhs under his rule, and in 1806 he crossed the Sutlej with a large force in order to intervene in a dispute between the chiefs of Jind and Patiala. For a time it looked as though his action would result in war, but the British Government wished to utilise the Sikhs as a buffer between themselves and possible invaders, French or Russian, from the north-west. Ranjit Singh, on the other hand, was not anxious to cross swords with the formidable power which had beaten Tippu Sultan in the south and had routed the Marathas. He knew that he was surrounded by a ring of enemies, and while he was fighting beyond the Sutlej he would be attacked in the rear by Afghans and Gurkhas, as well as by his rivals in the Punjab. He therefore welcomed the arrival of Charles Metcalfe, a rising young political officer who was sent by Lord Minto in 1808 to negotiate with him at Amritsar. The result was an agreement by which Ranjit was left in possession of his territories south of the Sutlej, but was to leave the cis-Sutlej chiefs alone, while the Company undertook not to interfere north of the river.

An incident occurred during the visit which was destined to have momentous consequences. The little escort of two companies of Indian infantry which accompanied Metcalfe was attacked by a raging mob of Akalis, puritan fanatics armed with steel quoits and two-handed swords, and beat them off with ease. This convinced the Maharaja of the advantages enjoyed by disciplined troops trained in the European manner, and he decided to engage a number of foreign officers to build up a regular army for him. Of these the most important were Generals Ventura and Allard (soldiers of fortune who had fought under Napoleon, and after his downfall had offered their services to the Shah of Persia), Colonel Court, and an Irish artillery officer named Gardner. Later they were joined by a Neapolitan general of the name of Avitabile. Hitherto, all Sikhs had fought in the cavalry, and service on foot was despised. Ventura raised a regular brigade of all arms known as the Fauj Khas, and on this model the Maharaja built up a magnificent force of 29,000 men and 192 guns, known as the Army of the Khalsa. This he steadily enlarged as his resources grew.

Armed with this formidable weapon he proceeded to make himself complete master of the country. His first objective was Multan, a stronghold ruled over by Nawab Muzaffar Khan, an Afghan chief of ancient family, who refused to pay tribute and defied all attacks. In January, 1818, Ranjit Singh laid siege to Multan, and brought up the Zam Zam gun to batter down the walls with her huge stone missiles. But as fast as a breach was made it was filled up, and the storming parties were driven back in hand-to-hand fighting. Month after month the siege dragged on, and the garrison was reduced to 300 men. At length, on June 2, a party of Akalis seized an important bastion and an entrance was effected. But still the old Nawab, conspicuous by his white beard, held out, with his eight sons and the remnants of the garrison. Time after time the attackers were driven off, unable to face the Afghan swordsmen. "Come on," cried the defenders, "and let us perish like men." But the Sikhs preferred to pick them off with their matchlocks, and Muzaffar Khan and five of his sons, refusing quarter, fell dead. The other three surrendered. Multan brought the Maharaja spoils estimated at two million pounds.

A more notable exploit was the conquest of the large and beautiful province of Kashmir. The Maharaja had originally planned to undertake this in conjunction with the Afghans. But the Sikhs were poor hands at mountain-warfare; the Afghan general stole a march on them, and refused to give his allies their share of the plunder. Ranjit Singh in retaliation seized the fortress of Attock, commanding the chief ford over the Indus. This led to a pitched battle between the Afghans and the Sikhs at Hardaru, on July 13, 1813. Prince Dost Mahommed Khan, afterwards ruler of Kabul, broke the Sikh line by a brilliant cavalry charge, but was in his turn defeated by the Sikh general, Diwan Mokham Chand, who brought up his reserves at the critical moment. The following year, however, Ranjit Singh's army suffered a severe reverse in the mountain passes of Kashmir, and had to retreat after the monsoon had burst and rendered the roads and rivers impassable. It was not till 1823 that the country was subdued, and even after that there was fierce fighting with the Hazaras and other mountain tribes.

The conquest of the Punjab was rounded off by the capture of Peshawar, which was held by an Afghan general named Yar Mahommed Khan. One of Ranjit Singh's reasons for attacking Peshawar was in order to get possession of Laili, an Arab mare renowned for her beauty throughout Afghanistan and the Punjab, and said to be the finest steed in Asia. She was not surrendered until the Afghan general was arrested and told that he would stay in prison till she was given up. Ranjit Singh boasted that she cost sixty lakhs of rupees and 12,000 good men. Baron Von Hügel, the German traveller, describes her as a grey with black points, sixteen hands high and magnificently caparisoned. She lived in a silver-plated stall, with golden bangles round her fetlocks. No horse since the fall of Troy, it has been said, had been the source of so much suffering.

The Maharaja, though, like the Emperor Akbar, Shivaji the Maratha and many other great Indian empire-builders, he had had little or no formal education, was an enlightened man with an enquiring mind. His Court was the resort of men of all religions and nationalities. His Chief Minister was a Mohammedan from Bokhara named Fakir Azizuddin, a physician by profession, whom Ranjit Singh consulted on all important occasions and left in charge of the Government when he went on his campaigns. Azizuddin was an adherent of the mystic Sufi sect, and when asked whether he was a Moslem or a Hindu by religion, replied, "I am a man floating in the midst of a mighty river. I turn my eyes towards the land, but can distinguish no difference in either bank." He was an accomplished Persian and Arabic scholar, and maintained a college at his own expense.

Fakir Azizuddin was Foreign Minister. The Finance Minister was a Rajput named Raja Dina Nath, one of three brothers of great talent and personal bravery who had all made their names in the Court of Lahore. Raja Dina Nath was responsible for organising the revenue systems which supplied Ranjit Singh with the funds for building up his army, no light matter in a fierce and lawless country, where for years taxes had been collected at the sword's point. Azizuddin, unlike Raja Dina Nath, was pro-British in his outlook. The Maharaja was at first deeply suspicious of the ever-advancing tide of English supremacy, and there is a well-known story that, on looking at a map of India, he exclaimed, *Sab lal hojayega* ("It will soon be all red"). But fortunately, the wise counsels of the Foreign Minister prevailed, and there was no clash in Ranjit Singh's lifetime. Another outstanding figure was Lehna Singh, a Sikh, the Master of Ordnance, who was responsible for casting the artillery of the Khalsa, and was a mechanical inventor of distinction. By arranging that his councillors, civil and military, should be drawn from these widely differing nationalities and classes, Ranjit Singh shrewdly and effectually prevented any plotting against his authority. Mention has been made of the European military officers in his employ, and visitors and travellers from the West always received a ready welcome at the Court; they included the intrepid traveller Moorcroft, who afterwards died while exploring the mountain fastnesses of the Hindu Kush, the French botanist Victor Jacquemont, the German Baron Carl von Hügel, and several others.

When Lord William Bentinck came out to India in 1831 the British Government was still perturbed about the advance of Russia in Central Asia, and the new Governor-General was ordered to enter into negotiations with the Lion of the Punjab. The two met at Rupar on the Sutlej and here for some days a grand durbar was held, which recalled the Field of the Cloth of Gold. The scene was picturesque in the extreme; the

BY COURTESY OF THE BRITISH MUSEUM

HUNTING WILD BOAR AT NIGHT
Sikh School, Nineteenth Century.

regular infantry, looking like a wall of scarlet, made a striking contrast to the irregular cavalry, with their shirts of mail, their helmets inlaid with gold and decked with heron's plumes, their small round shields and their bows or matchlocks. The members of Ranjit Singh's own bodyguard were gaily attired in red and yellow satin, with pink turbans and gold-embroidered swordbelts. Sports and tourneys were held, in which the Maharaja, in spite of his paralysis, displayed his superb horsemanship to the admiration of all. The result was a treaty of amity between the two nations, which was renewed seven years later at a meeting between the Maharaja and Bentinck's successor, Lord Auckland.

The British authorities, still dominated by fear of the Russian bogey, had now resolved upon prosecuting their unlucky policy of deposing Dost Mahommed, the able and gallant ruler of Afghanistan, and placing on the throne his brother, Shah Shuja, as a puppet ruler in his place. Shah Shuja had long been an exile in the Punjab, and Ranjit Singh had the poorest opinion of him. When he first took shelter in Lahore, the Maharaja, hearing that he had in his possession the historic diamond known as the Koh-i-nur or Mountain of Light, had persecuted him mercilessly until he gave it up.

The meeting between Ranjit Singh and Lord Auckland has been picturesquely described by the Governor-General's sister, Miss Emily Eden, in her charming volume of letters entitled *Up the Country*. As the two state elephants came alongside, Lord Auckland, in his uniform of diplomatic blue, was seen to take a bundle of crimson cloth out of the state howdah, and it was known that the Lion of the Punjab was then seated on the elephant of the English ruler. In a minute the little, tottering, one-eyed man, who had founded a vast empire on the banks of the fabulous rivers of the Macedonian conquests, was leaning over the side of the howdah, shaking hands with the principal officers of the British camp as their elephants were wheeled up beside him.

Miss Eden describes him as looking like a little old mouse, with his grey whiskers and his plain red coat bordered with squirrel's fur. The negotiations ended in a Tripartite Treaty between Lord Auckland, Ranjit Singh and Shah Shuja, by which the latter was to be installed at Kabul. The whole plan was fundamentally unsound, and the Maharaja himself viewed it with grave misgiving. But he loyally supported his English allies, though at the time his health was rapidly deteriorating. He died in June, 1839. A life of almost continual exertion in the field, coupled with hard drinking in defiance of his physician's advice, had undermined his iron constitution, and he had already had more than one paralytic stroke. Before his death he distributed his jewels and horses of state among various shrines. Two Ranis accompanied him to the funeral pyre. He was only fifty-nine at the time of his death.

Ranjit Singh was by far the greatest Indian of his generation. He found the Punjab a warring confederacy, a prey to its factions and chiefs, pressed by the Afghans and Marathas, and ready to submit to English supremacy. He consolidated the numerous petty states into a kingdom, he wrested from Kabul the fairest of its provinces, and he gave the potent English no cause for interference. He found the militia of his country a mass of horsemen, brave indeed, but ignorant of war as an art, and he left it mustering fifty thousand disciplined soldiers, fifty thousand well-armed yeomanry and militia, and more than three hundred pieces of cannon. Victor Jacquemont spoke of him as an extraordinary man, a Bonaparte in miniature;

in versatility, religious and racial tolerance and organising ability, he came near to Akbar. He is described as a little man, careless in his dress, with a wrinkled face pitted with smallpox, a grey beard and long arms. Only on horseback, riding at the head of his army with his small black shield slung over his shoulder, did he appear the man he really was. Miss Eden says, "he made himself a great king; he conquered a great many powerful enemies; he is remarkably just in his government; he hardly ever takes away life, which is wonderful in a despot, and is excessively beloved by his people." It was impossible to rule the haughty and martial races of the Punjab with kid gloves on, and General Avitabile, the Warden of the Northern Marches, ruthlessly hung marauders at the gates of their villages or blew them from guns.

But in the settled districts, government was strict but just. Ranjit Singh, says Cunningham, took from the land as much as it could readily yield, and from the merchants as much as they could profitably give. He put down open marauding; the Sikh peasantry enjoyed a light assessment, and no local officer dared to oppress a member of the Khalsa. If elsewhere the farmers of the revenue were resisted in their tyrannical proceedings, they were more likely to be changed than to be supported by battalions, for Ranjit Singh never arrogated to himself the title or powers of a despot or a tyrant. The Maharaja himself toured indefatigably, and punished officers who abused their powers. Villages near which a robbery took place were taken to account and made to pay for the value of the goods stolen, and booty taken by his soldiers was ordered to be returned. Time was when Sikh and robber were synonymous terms, but now few thefts were heard of, to say nothing of the forays to which the chiefs were formerly addicted. Remissions of revenue were made in cases of famine, and the records teem with instances of the ruler's acts of generosity, irrespective of caste or creed. Affable and unassuming as he was, Ranjit Singh was every inch a king, and his personality overawed all who came near him. Early in life he had lost an eye from smallpox, and Azizuddin was once asked which eye it was. "Such is the splendour of his face," replied the diplomatic Minister, "that I have never dared to look close enough to discover."

The sequel must be briefly told. After the death of the great Maharaja, the commanders of the Army of the Khalsa became completely out of control. The prestige of England was at its lowest ebb owing to the evacuation of Kabul and the annihilation of the British force

A SIKH SEPOY

Najib or Musalman Sepoy, 1838.

From "European Adventurers in Northern India." By C. Grey and H. L. O. Garrett.

BY COURTESY OF THE SECRETARY OF STATE FOR INDIA

RANJIT ṢINGH
From a portrait in the India Office.

BY COURTESY OF THE BRITISH MUSEUM

SUTTEE OF RANJIT SINGH'S RANIS
Sikh School. About 1840.

during its return, and in 1845, the Sikhs, in defiance of the treaty, crossed the Sutlej. They were defeated in four pitched battles, and a peace was patched up. But it did not last, and in 1849 war once more broke out. "The Sikh nation has called for war," said Lord Dalhousie, "and upon my word, they shall have it with a vengeance." The fighting was the fiercest in the history of British India; but at Gujrat, on the Chenab, the flower of the Sikh army was annihilated. The Sardars laid their swords at the conquering general's feet. The cavalry, with bitter pain in their hearts, surrendered the horses which were their pride; and man after man, filing past, flung sword and matchlock on the ever-growing heap of weapons.

Aj Ranjit Singh mar gya, "To-day Ranjit Singh is dead," exclaimed a grizzled warrior, as he lifted his hands in a last salute to the glittering cairn of arms which symbolised that the glory had departed from the last great Indian principality.

H.H. MAHARAJA GANGA SINGHJI
Twenty-first ruler of Bikaner.

THE RULER OF BIKANER

SOLDIER, STATESMAN, INNOVATOR

BORN IN 1880

BY SARDAR K. M. PANIKKAR

His Highness Maharaja Ganga Singhji is the 21st ruler of Bikaner, one of the premier states of Rajputana. The Bikaner House represents one of the Imperial Dynasties of India, the Rashtrakutas or the Rathores, who play a most prominent part in Indian history from at least the eighth century A.D. The Bikaner State (area 23,317 square miles) was founded by Rao Bikaji, son of Rao Jodhaji of Jodhpur, in the middle of the fifteenth century. As independent rulers in their own right and at the Mogul Court successive Maharajas of Bikaner achieved great distinction, especially Maharajas Rai Singhji and Anup Singhji, who were entrusted with the highest offices of the Empire as viceroys, generals and ambassadors by the Great Moguls. The state concluded a treaty of alliance with the British Government in 1818, and has since been recognised as one of the most loyal and progressive states of India.

Maharaja Ganga Singhji was born in 1880, and succeeded his brother, Maharaja Dungar Singhji, at the age of seven. His early education was at the Mayo College, Ajmer, where his precocious ability earned him many distinctions. In view, however, of the fact that the Maharaja had to assume the responsibility of governing his state early, his further training was entrusted to an English official of high distinction, Mr. (now Sir) Brian Egerton, who as guardian and tutor to the Maharaja brought him up in a manner fitted to his high responsibilities. The Maharaja also received military training in 1898 at Deoli, where he was attached to the Deoli Regiment.

In 1899, at the age of eighteen, Maharaja Ganga Singhji assumed full powers as the ruler of Bikaner. The time was far from auspicious. An unprecedented famine overtook the state. The rains failed completely and over the entire area of Bikaner a calamity such as never had happened before threatened the life of man and beast. The regency council which had managed the affairs of the state during the minority of the Maharaja had left the state in no position to meet such an emergency. It was the young Maharaja's personal initiative and ability that saved the situation. Though hardly nineteen, he took the entire work on himself and was his own famine officer. He organised relief works over the entire state, and though attacked by cholera at a critical time, insisted on supervising all the arrangements himself. The success that attended the Maharaja's efforts drew encomiums from Lord Curzon himself who, in awarding the Kaisar-i-Hind Gold Medal for this humanitarian work, publicly expressed his appreciation of the extraordinary ability displayed by the Maharaja. Sir Denzil Ibbetson, who under Lord Curzon's direction was in charge of famine work all over India, in his report also stated:

> "The personal attention which His Highness the Maharaja of Gwalior and His Highness the Maharaja of Bikaner have paid to the organisation of relief in their respective states is not only highly creditable to themselves as rulers, but is also contributing largely to the success which has attended that organisation."

VICEROY'S VISIT TO BIKANER

State procession through the capital on the occasion of the visit of the Viceroy, the Marquis of Linlithgow, to H.H. the Maharaja of Bikaner.

The Maharaja also displayed early in life that desire for personal service in the cause of the Empire which was to become so marked a characteristic of his reign. In 1901 the intervention of powers following the attack on the Legation led to troops from India being sent to China. The Maharaja was the first to offer his personal services and, in fact, was the first ruler to go to foreign lands on military duty for the Empire. On return from China he was accorded a ceremonial reception at Calcutta. The Maharaja was also invited to be present as a guest of His Majesty at the Coronation of King Edward VII.

It was after his return from the Coronation of King Edward VII that the Maharaja applied himself to the task of reorganising the state. His state was very extensive from the point of view of area, but most of it was arid desert. There were only 87 miles of railway when the regency council handed over charge to him. The machinery of government was almost mediæval: the feudal nobility lived in a semi-independent state in their desert castles. There was no properly organised judiciary or police. Medical and educational facilities hardly existed. Moreover, the income of the state was totally inadequate to the needs of government.

The Maharaja recognised the great handicaps under which he had to labour; but he was determined to overcome them. First of all he set himself to reorganise the executive machinery of government: to establish a secretariat which could efficiently cope with the problems of modern administration; to enforce law and order throughout the state; to have the lands properly settled and assessed; to encourage the peasantry by introducing new crops and by improving agriculture. A railway policy

THE ROYAL PALACE

Lalgarh Palace, the residence of the Maharaja, lies just outside the city. It is a fine building of red sandstone designed by the late Sir Swinton Jacobs.

was enunciated, the object of which was to connect Bikaner, till that time an inaccessible area, with the surrounding territories. A scientific exploitation of the mineral resources was taken in hand. Within a few years' time the young Maharaja converted what was in effect a mediæval administration into a modern state capable of many-sided activities in the interests of the people.

It was not to be expected that such important reforms would not meet with opposition. The chiefs and nobles of the state, who had for generations set the authority of the central government at nought, viewed these changes at first with suspicion. A few of them even attempted to organise an open rebellion against the reforming zeal of the Maharaja. The movement was put down with a firm hand. While the Maharaja appreciated the strength that a loyal aristocracy gave to the state and encouraged the nobles to take their full share in the work of government, he made it clear that the days of feudal anarchy were past and could not be revived by threats or intimidation. From the side of the officials of the government of India also the Maharaja did not in his earlier years receive unqualified support. But it should be added that when once the paramount power had been satisfied that the reforms were beneficial and that the Maharaja's activities were exclusively for the welfare of his people, the suspicion with which the political officers at first viewed his reforms gave place to wholehearted support.

By 1912, when the Maharaja's Silver Jubilee was celebrated, Bikaner had become a modern and progressive state taking its place among the most advanced principalities in India. The revenue had more than doubled. Schools, hospitals, improved communications, an efficient police, a trained magistracy, and a chief court (the first in Rajputana), bore witness to the steady advancement of Bikaner during the first decade of the century. A notable announcement at the Silver Jubilee was the Maharaja's decision to establish a Legislative Assembly in the state. He was the first ruler in northern India to introduce the beginnings of representative institutions. It was a courageous and statesmanlike act, as the Rajput kingdoms, conservative *par excellence*, had an unbroken tradition of personal and semi-feudal government. Besides, it was an entirely voluntary act, as the subjects of the Maharaja had not evinced any desire for political advance in the direction of representative institutions. The Maharaja, in fact, correctly anticipated the developments in India and realised that the strength of a ruler in the future would lie only in a close association of his people with the government.

In the years that followed the Jubilee, the activities of the Maharaja became more and more associated with all-India and Imperial politics. As soon as the Great War of 1914 was declared he placed the entire resources of the state at the disposal of His Majesty and offered his personal services together with those of the Bikaner army in the cause of the Empire. The Maharaja left for France in September, 1914, and served first with the Meerut division of the Indian army and was later attached to the Staff of Sir John (later Viscount) French. In 1915 the continued ill health (which proved fatal) of his daughter compelled him to return, but not before he had an opportunity of taking personal part at the head of his own troops in the campaign against the Turks in the neighbourhood of the Suez Canal. The Maharaja was in fact the only one among

VIEW OF THE OLD FORT

The building of the fort at Bikaner was begun by Raja Rai Singh, one of the Akbar's generals. Inside its walls are the old palaces of the rulers of Bikaner.

the princes of India who could claim to have been personally engaged in warfare in the service of the King-Emperor.

On his return to India the Maharaja addressed himself seriously to the question of creating an organisation for the princes of India, so that in matters of common interest to them and to the Empire the rulers of Indian states may consult among themselves and make their influence felt at the centre. The need for this was all the greater as the princes had their own legitimate grievances; and in their disorganised condition had been unable to resist the encroachments on their sovereignty by the officials of the paramount power. The Maharaja was able to convince Lord Hardinge of the wisdom of his proposal; and the first official conference of the princes of India met in Delhi in 1916 under the presidency of Lord Chelmsford. The Maharaja was elected Honorary General Secretary, a post he continued to hold for five years until the conference itself was converted into a Chamber of Princes and the Maharaja was elected its first chancellor.

In 1917 the Maharaja, along with Sir Satyendra (later Lord) Sinha, was nominated to represent India at the Imperial War Cabinet and Conference. He was the first Indian prince to take part in the inner councils of the Empire, and his work in that capacity was spoken of in the highest terms by Mr. Lloyd George. The war-time Prime Minister has recorded in his Memoirs:

> "'Bikaner,' as he was familiarly and affectionately called—the Indian Prince—was a magnificent specimen of manhood of his great country. We soon found that he was one of 'the wise men that came from the East.' More and more did we come to rely on his advice, especially on all questions that affected India."

The winter of 1917–18 was a crucial year for India. The British Government had come to realise the strength of popular feeling in India in favour of political reforms. During the Maharaja's stay in London as a member of the Imperial War Cabinet, he had not hesitated to urge before the authorities the necessity for immediate action. From Rome on his way back, the Maharaja sent to Mr. Austen Chamberlain, then Secretary of State for India, a detailed note suggesting a generous measure of constitutional reform and an early announcement on behalf of His Majesty's Government of the policy in relation to India. An announcement on the lines of the Maharaja's note was made in Parliament on August 20, 1917, which is still regarded as the Charter of Indian Self-Government. Following the announcement, Mr. E. S. Montagu, who had succeeded Mr. Chamberlain at the India Office, came to India to study conditions locally and report to the Cabinet. The Maharaja was among the first to realise that political reforms in British India would affect the position of the princes materially, and he therefore took the lead in the discussions among his brother princes which formulated specific proposals to safeguard the sovereign character of the states. The suggestions then put forward were incorporated in Chapter X of the Montagu-Chelmsford Report.

At the special request of the Prime Minister, the Maharaja was nominated in 1918 as one of India's representatives at the Peace Conference. In this capacity he took part in the discussions so far as they affected India at the Versailles Conference; and was in a large measure responsible for the admission of India as an original member of the League of Nations. The Maharaja, along with his colleague, Lord Sinha, also very strongly urged the point of view of Indian Moslems in regard to Turkey, and with the support of the Secretary of State fought hard against the allocation of Smyrna to Greece and for the retention of Constantinople in Turkish hands. As both his colleagues were absent from Paris at the time that the final decision about the membership of the League of Nations was taken, the brunt of the fight to get India admitted fell on the Maharaja. There was strenuous opposition from many quarters to the admission of India, and it was only the vigilant attitude of the Maharaja and his timely intervention with the chiefs of the British delegation that secured for India her membership of the League of Nations. The Maharaja was one of the plenipotentiaries who signed the Treaty of Versailles.

Another notable incident which marked out the Maharaja as one of the leading personalities in imperial politics was his courageous and outspoken championship of the cause of Indian political reforms. The Reform Bill of 1919 had been attacked vigorously on the ground that the princes of India were alarmed at the change and opposed to it. The appointment of Lord Sinha, the Maharaja's colleague at the Versailles Conference, as Under-Secretary of State for India, had also been criticised on the same ground. The Maharaja utilised the occasion of a banquet given by him in honour of Lord Sinha to define authoritatively the attitude of the princes towards political reforms in India. It is not too much to say that this timely and forceful intervention saved the Montagu - Chelmsford Reforms from being wrecked by the opposition of reactionary elements in India and in England.

As an integral part of the Montagu-Chelmsford Reforms, His Majesty constituted by a proclamation the Chamber of Princes as the accredited organisation of the Sovereign Princes of India. At the very first meeting, the Maharaja, then General Secretary of the Princes' Conference, was elected chancellor. For five successive terms the Maharaja was elected to this post by his brother princes, and was in that capacity responsible in a very large measure for initiating and carrying on the negotiations for recovering to the states the ground which they had lost through the imperceptible encroachment of paramountcy.

In 1926, after ten years of uninterrupted work in the interests of his brother princes, the Maharaja, in spite of persuasion, decided not to offer himself for election as chancellor. Very urgent affairs in the state required his attention. A great scheme for irrigating no less than 1,000 square miles of his territory had been taken in hand. This had been one of the Maharaja's most cherished ambitions; and so early as 1906 he had put forward proposals to that effect. In 1911 the government of India agreed to the participation of Bikaner in the project; but for one reason or another the scheme was finally sanctioned only in 1921. The Bikaner territory is in the main desert land; but the northern part of it is rich and fertile and with adequate supply of water could be made a granary for the rest of the state. But the canal scheme was a costly project; the estimated expenditure was over £2 million. The risk involved was by no means insignificant, as any failure would have totally ruined the state. But the Maharaja considered the risk worth taking, and supported by the technical advice of his revenue minister, the late Mr. G. D. Rudkin, he planned out every detail of a great colonisation scheme for the area which was to be watered by the new system of canals. In 1927 Lord Irwin (now Viscount Halifax) opened the sluice in the Gang Canal and the Maharaja saw the realisation of his cherished ambition to bring water to the parching deserts of Rajputana.

WEIGHED AGAINST GOLD

H.H. the Maharaja being weighed against gold during the celebrations which in 1937 marked his Golden Jubilee. He ascended the throne at the age of seven.

ON A TIGER SHOOT

H.H. the Maharaja about to take aim from an elephant's back during a tiger shoot.

The Gang Canal area is now a flourishing colony of about 1,000 square miles. The area which the desert once claimed is now a smiling garden where cotton, sugar cane, wheat and other staple products grow in plenty. A well-laid-out system of railways serves the district which is now the veritable granary of Bikaner. The population has jumped from a bare 28,957 to 145,259. Towns, markets and industrial areas have sprung up, and the Maharaja, who devotes special attention to the development of the colony, has not stinted money for the provision of modern facilities in the way of schools, hospitals, and local government institutions for the benefit of those who, trusting in his justice and wisdom, have invested money and labour for its development. Though the original estimates have been greatly exceeded and the world depression has affected in no small measure the prosperity of the colonists, the Ganganagar Colony has more than paid its way. In fact it has been not only one of the biggest ventures of the kind in any state in India but the most successful—a striking tribute to the foresight and planning of the Maharaja, who not only conceived the idea but worked out every detail of the scheme.

In 1930 the Mahajara was invited to lead the Indian Delegation to the League of Nations. He was the first prince to be entrusted with this honour. He was also one of India's representatives at the Imperial Conference held in London that year; and Mr. Ramsay MacDonald justly described him as the doyen of the

THE BAG

H.H. the Maharaja photographed with the lion which he shot.

conference, being the only one who had taken part in the conference of 1917. The same year also witnessed the historic Round Table Conference on India in London and the Maharaja's part in it was described by Lord Sankey, who as Lord Chancellor presided over the work of the main committee, in the following terms:

"We should place on record our great thanks to His Highness of Bikaner for the assistance and advice which he has given us throughout these proceedings, not only now (at the second Round Table Conference) but on the last occasion when we had the pleasure of meeting him. He is gifted, if he will allow me to say so, with great powers of speech and great powers of expression; but I know that he has had to work very hard in the evenings and in the early mornings, in order to place before us his views which have been so very helpful. It reconciles us a great deal to the difficulties we have had when we remember the courtesy and the skill with which he has endeavoured to solve them."

His contribution to the discussions that have since been going on for the satisfactory settlement of the Indian problems has been recognised to be pre-eminent. A staunch fighter for the special rights and sovereign position of the States of India, he has shown himself a wise and farseeing statesman anxious to further the political progress of the Motherland and desirous of India attaining the position that is her due in the Councils of the Empire.

In 1935 the Maharaja visited England by special invitation for the Jubilee of His late Majesty King George V and in 1937 for the Coronation of His Majesty King George VI.

In October, 1937, the Golden Jubilee of his own reign was celebrated with éclat in Bikaner, when princes from all over India, leaders of public opinion and

FORDING THE RIVER

H.H. the Maharaja is a keen sportsman. He is seen here fording a flooded river during a shooting trip.

THE ENTRANCE HALL TO LALGARH PALACE

friends from England came in large numbers to offer personal congratulations to one who had so nobly served the States of India and the Empire.

The Maharaja's career, viewed as a whole, shows four main interests:

As ruler of the state of Bikaner;

as a prince interested in the welfare of his brother princes;

as an Indian patriot and statesman desiring to see India attain, through ordered stages of political evolution, equality with other units in the British Commonwealth; and

as a devoted ally of the British Empire, always ready to serve it to the utmost limit of his abilities.

What he has done for the State may best be realised from the statistics given below showing the increases under the different heads during the 38 years of the Maharaja's active reign:

	1899	1937
1. *Irrigation*	5,000 acres	376,000 acres
2. *Educational progress*		
Schools	28	421
Expenditure	Rs. 20,230	349,612
3. *Medical Relief*		
Hospitals and Dispensaries	14	42
Expenditure	Rs. 35,183	373,410
4. *Railways*		
Mileage	85·15	795·85
Gross Earnings	Rs. 174,539	3,832,805
5. *Revenue*	Rs. 2,144,410	Rs. 13,519,021

His work for the princes and states in general has been no less outstanding. The substantial recovery of the position and authority of the princes during the last quarter of a century has been in the main due to his efforts. The Conference of Princes was organised by him; he is the recognised father of the Chamber of Princes, and again only recently he has been devoting his energies to the reorganisation of that body to make it fully representative of the States of India. In all the struggles during the last 25 years for maintaining the position of the states he has taken the leading part.

As an Indian patriot and statesman his work, though less known to the public, has been substantial. His contribution to the Montagu-Chelmsford Reforms, his strenuous fight for the admission of India to the League of Nations, the notable part he played at the first Round Table Conference and in the subsequent discussions entitle him to be ranked high among those responsible for India's present political position.

In the service of the Empire his record has been unique. He has personally taken part in wars in China, Egypt and France, and held aloft the honour of Rajputs in the battlefield. As a member of the Imperial War Cabinet and twice of the Imperial Conference, he has been in the inner councils of the Empire. During the recent crises, which preceded the Munich Agreement, he was the first Indian prince to place at the disposal of His Majesty the entire resources of the state in a spirit of voluntary service to the Empire. An elder statesman of the British Commonwealth of Nations, the Maharaja by the achievements in his own state, by the notable contribution he has made to the settlement of the Indian problems, and by his unyielding championship of the rights of the states, may justly be considered one of the most remarkable personalities that modern India has produced.

BIKANER CAMEL CORPS

Part of the famous Camel Corps passing the Viceroy and H.H. the Maharaja during a review.

PANDIT MADAN MOHAN MALAVIYA
The great supporter of Hindu Orthodoxy.

PANDIT MADAN MOHAN MALAVIYA

UPHOLDER OF THE HINDU FAITH

BORN 1862

BY C. F. ANDREWS

I CAN best begin to describe the character of Pandit Madan Mohan Malaviya by a short story of what happened in my own experience long ago; for though outwardly it was of very little consequence, it seemed to open out to me a world of human kindness beneath the forbidding exterior of his scrupulous Hindu orthodoxy, and for this reason it may be worth repeating.

Mr. Gokhale had come back from South Africa, in 1912—ill both in body and mind. In the following year he had been profoundly stirred to action in India itself by the news of the heroic struggle that Mr. Gandhi was carrying on to obtain the barest elementary rights for the distressed Indian labourers suffering under the indenture system. In October, 1913, the passive resistance struggle in South Africa had at last reached its final stage. Indians were brutally treated as they tried to leave the estates, and there was a serious danger of violence breaking out on an extensive scale. Mr. and Mrs. Gandhi, along with their sons, were in prison, and thousands of Indians, both men and women, had gone to prison also. The moral support of India was behind Mr. Gokhale in seeking to prevent the movement from being crushed through any lack of public support. At this time W. W. Pearson had volunteered to accompany me to South Africa in order to take part in the struggle. We had said good-bye to Mr. Gokhale at Delhi, and intended to wait for a few hours at Allahabad in order to see Pundit Madan Mohan Malaviya. We were on our way to Calcutta, where we were to embark for Durban.

Mr. Gokhale had wired to Malaviya to meet the train. He was a personal friend, and we well knew his orthodox Hindu mode of life. He had prepared food for us in his own home; but the train was running very late and we had no time to leave the station. So instead he insisted, in spite of all our protests, in taking us to the refreshment room (where meat was usually served) and sat with us while we took the vegetarian dishes which he had ordered. The European passengers, who were having their breakfast, wondered who this strange Indian was with his immaculately white *pagri* and *chaddar* and his very distinguished features. One or two recognised him. But he used every moment of his time in sending messages through us to the heroic passive resisters in South Africa. His own caste scruples had been laid on one side for our sakes in order to show us this last act of hospitality before we sailed.

It would be difficult to explain the significance of this in England where caste scruples are not understood, but here in India the story, simple as it is, can be easily appreciated. It happened nearly thirty years ago; and things have moved very far forward since those days.

More, perhaps, than any other national leader of the present generation, Pundit Madan Mohan Malaviya has stood out for Hindu orthodoxy in its most binding religious form. This scrupulous exactness of religious observance has made him undergo incredible hardships in the name of his religion which he holds so dear.

In his extreme Hindu outlook lies the main difference between himself and every other leader of first rank in Indian politics to-day. I do not know any outstanding personality who carries his orthodoxy as far as Malaviya. He is conservative to the last degree in everything where Hinduism is concerned, while at the same time in national affairs he is in many respects an advanced thinker. For this reason a conflict is always going on within, between his Hindu orthodoxy and his Indian Nationalism. Divided loyalties tear him asunder; but whenever it comes to a tug of war, Hinduism wins. More and more, as he has grown older, Hindu loyalty has prevailed and Indian Nationalism, as such, has tended to recede into the background.

It may be argued that he has recently stood in the very forefront of the battle for the removal of untouchability, which was one of the standing disgraces of popular Hinduism. But on that subject Panditji had already shared the opinion of Mahatma Gandhi, that such a custom was not Hindu at all. It could not be found—so he asserted—in any of the Hindu Scriptures; furthermore, it was historically unknown in the earliest Sanskrit period. In long arguments I have often heard him argue this point again and again. He would quote passage after passage to show that men of the lowest caste, on account of their purity of character and nobility of life, had been the preceptors of members belonging to the highest castes, teaching them religious truths. How could such men have ever been regarded as polluted and untouchable by those whom they instructed? Thus he would argue; and when the tide of reform swept over the country, and millions of these very people were already wavering in their allegiance towards Hinduism, he anticipated the rapidly impending crisis and pronounced in favour of the complete abolition of this hateful and inhuman custom, using himself the strongest words about it and causing a great sensation. Indeed, as a Brahman, he went so far as to receive back into Hinduism, by a purifying ceremony, large numbers of those who had left it for other religious faiths.

Yet when, on the other hand, another injurious custom within Hinduism, called "Child Marriage," was brought forward in the Central Assembly for legislative action he objected vehemently to any State legislation on the subject. In this matter he seems to have believed, along with many Pundits of the south, that such child marriages had the sanction of the sacred Hindu scriptures. Any legislation, therefore, was regarded by him as an act of religious persecution, or at least an interference with religion—if the State declared such marriages to be illegal.

Wherein, then, lies the real greatness of this orthodox Pundit, who can still remain thus, in a mediæval atmosphere, antagonistic to many necessary reforms and blocking the way, time after time, to any further advance?

His importance surely lies in the fact that just because of his conservative character, with regard to all these articles of his own Hindu faith, he has kept touch with many millions of his fellow countrymen who are conservative also. He is unwilling to surrender the past at the imperious bidding of the modern age. He stands out for extreme simplicity of life: a diet which is bare almost to the limit of the ascetic, a supreme value set on the sanctity of marriage, a sense of the vastness of truth and right and harmlessness as the supreme things in religion. Those who know his own personal character, with its freedom from the baser passions, cannot help but feel that he is preserving something good. He is a model, in the modern age, of what the Brahman in ancient India aspired to be.

There is also one factor, which must always be taken into account, that comes out clearly in the story I have related above. In certain sudden emergencies, when the call of his country came to him with compelling force, he was ready to throw even his own strict Hindu orthodoxy aside and take steps which led him into forbidden paths. Such a new step was taken when he decided to cross the sea and go to London in order to attend the Round Table Conference. Few in England can realise what a dramatic action that was. He would of course perform the necessary purifications afterwards; but it meant a very great deal, in his old age, when he had lived all the while in one atmosphere, suddenly to change the whole character of his daily life in such a novel manner. It may also be said, to his credit, that with regard to the age of marriage, he *has* raised it voluntarily in his own family. What he objected to was any form of State compulsion which interfered with religion.

A danger, which Punditji himself had foreseen, has now loomed larger and larger, namely, the tension between Hinduism and Islam. It may well be doubted whether the founding of the Hindu University at Benares has not increased that tension. While he has astonished the whole world by the way in which he has got the rich men of India to subscribe for the University, there has always been the hidden anxiety, beneath this outward success, lest its communal basis should increase the separation between the two religious cultures.

There have been very fine efforts made to save the Hindu University from

WITH HIS FAMILY

Pandit Malaviya with a group of his friends and relations at Benares.

such a fate, but the whole character of our times has tended to set the bias strongly in the sectarian direction; and in consequence the Aligarh University in the north-west of the United Provinces, and the Benares University in the south-east, have both been almost forced to become centres of propaganda for the two rival creeds, to the detriment of union and good-fellowship. What the future holds in store is very difficult to anticipate. Much will depend on Malaviyaji himself. But it would probably be true to say that the most dangerous feature in the life of modern India is this communal tension which has broken out again and again recently in riots ending in bloodshed and an increase of bitter hate.

With the advent of the Non-Co-operation Movement, the pathway forward of Pundit Madan Mohan Malaviya was strewn with difficulties. He had gone up, at the earliest possible moment, to the Punjab, in August, 1919, after the martial law had been withdrawn; and his account of what he had seen and heard, when he proclaimed it to the world, was the first direct information from a non-official source which had reached the world press and had become world news. He was able, also, to speak at length in the Legislative Council, at the Centre of the Government of India, in such a manner as to carry the conviction right home to the hearts of men that a terrible blunder, which was worse than a crime, had been committed. Above all, he made clear the humiliation, more shameful even than death, which had been forcibly imposed in Amritsar.

But when the National Congress, under Mahatma Gandhi's leadership, had launched out on the full course of non-co-operation, his mind would not allow him to follow all the way. Above all, he was not ready to accept the Congress mandate with regard to the abandonment of the legislatures. He refused at the same time to leave the Congress; for he had an intense loyalty towards it as an institution which he had cherished from his youth up. He felt towards it a devotion which everyone deeply respected. When he stood out again and again, at the full Congress Sessions, and refused to vote in unison with the vast majority of delegates, he was always heard with the deepest respect and he retained in a very remarkable manner the affection of those who differed from him. But he could not change their own attitude towards Non-Co-operation; nor could they in the least degree alter his own fundamental ideas. Everyone knew that he would be the first to offer to go to prison, if his conscience would allow it: but his conscience for a long time did not move him in that direction. No one for a moment questioned his sincerity or his courage. In the end, however, he offered civil resistance and went to prison along with the rest.

There were probably two things which all the while moved him, subconsciously, though he would hardly think consciously about them. The former was his responsibility towards the Hindu University, which had received large emoluments from the Government of India. The second was his position, as the leading spirit in the Hindu Mahasabha, which also tied his hands to a considerable extent. He was not prepared that this whole communal organisation, containing many of the most eminent men in India, should be swung over to a definite position of antagonism to the Government.

Thus, while he had the utmost sympathy with the protest that was being made against what was called by Mahatma Gandhi "The Punjab Wrong" committed at Amritsar, and had condemned in the strongest manner the Government of India for not taking more drastic action against those who did the wrong, he was not prepared at first to go the whole length with Mahatmaji as to the method whereby the wrong should be set right. The fact that Non-Co-operation was succeeded very rapidly by the terrible Moplah Rising in the south, wherein many Hindus were brutally circumcised and thus "converted" to Islam in Malabar, made it impossible for him as an ardent Hindu to support the Khilafat Movement in the same whole-hearted way that Mahatma Gandhi did. Thus the conflict within his own soul became more and more acute, and he hardly knew, during the most anxious days in 1921 and 1922, where he stood.

No one was more pleased than Pundit Madan Mohan Malaviya when C. R. Das and Motilal Nehru broke away from the extreme form of Non-Co-operation and determined to fight the battle out *within* the Councils. But even here his own pathway was beset with difficulties. Pundit Motilal Nehru's position, as head of the Swaraj Party within the Congress, was not the same as his own. Motilal at the beginning was more determined on what were called "wrecking" tactics than was Malaviyaji himself, and he could never renounce the separate platform of his Hindu faith. Indeed, as we have seen, his Hinduism always occupied the first place in his mind, whenever the direct conflict came between Nationalism and Religion.

Added to this there was in him, as I have constantly discovered from my own experience of his inner mind, an intense belief in the liberalism expressed by Mr. Gladstone, whom he regarded as the greatest of all Englishmen in the nineteenth century. This admiration continually kept his mind dwelling rather on the "liberal" past than on the "socialist" future. Indeed, his whole idea of the Legislative Council at Simla and New Delhi was associated with that of the British Parliament in the great period when Gladstone was Prime Minister. He believed that it gave him a platform from which he could address the whole world; and so he prepared his speeches at various times with the utmost care. He had even a kind of reverence for the procedure of Parliament which others did not share. He delivered his set speeches with an eloquence which was quite remarkable, when we consider the fact that the language he used was not his own mother tongue.

In a measure these large hopes were justified; for his speech delivered on behalf of the "Abolition of Indentured Labour," and that which I have already referred to on the "Punjab Disturbances," carried their full weight both inside and outside of the Council Chamber.

When Pundit Motilal Nehru came in at the head of the poll as the leader of the Swaraj Party everybody expected Pundit Madan Mohan Malaviya, as an old congress man, to join that party. But he decided instead to form one of his own, which was called the Nationalist Party. Malaviyaji's leadership was typically confined to Hindus. The strongest member under him was his old and trusted friend, Lala Lajpat Rai of the Punjab. When any vote of censure of Government bearing a national character was going to be proposed, both parties in the Assembly could be counted upon to vote together. In lesser matters, however, especially where some point that touched Hinduism was concerned, there was no such unanimity of opinion.

This constitutional attitude of what may be called responsive co-operation was broken at last by the events that happened in 1930. In that fateful year of non-co-operation Pundit Madan Mohan Malaviya at last broke through all his earlier self-imposed restraints and offered himself again and again for imprisonment. I was not in India at the time but the story reached me in America how, after the arrest of Mahatma Gandhi for breaking the Salt Act, a number of new ordinances were passed and acts of which everyone was afterwards ashamed occurred during the *Lathi* charges in Bombay. An extraordinary all-night sitting of Malaviyaji, along with members of the Working Committee, took place in the streets of Bombay while the police blocked their path and tried to move them on. They, on their part, were attempting to resist by non-violence what they regarded as an arbitrary and illegal order. During the years that followed, in spite of his old age and the immense respect that was paid to him on every side, the Government of India found it difficult to refrain from imprisoning him and he was sentenced many times over, but not for long periods.

Of one of these imprisonments Jawaharlal Nehru wrote as follows:—"Pandit Madan Mohan Malaviya was also transferred to Naini from some other gaol. He was kept separately, not in our barrack, but we met him daily, and

BENARES UNIVERSITY

University College, Benares. Part of the great centre of Hindu culture, whose cause Pandit Malaviya has done so much to further.

perhaps I saw more of him there than I had done outside. He was a delightful companion, full of vitality and a youthful interest in things. He even started, with Ranjit's help, to learn German, and he showed quite a remarkable memory. He was in Naini when news of the floggings came, and he was greatly upset and wrote to the Acting-Governor of the Province. Soon afterwards he fell ill. He was unable to bear the cold in the conditions that prevailed in prison. His illness grew serious, and he had to be removed to the city hospital, and later to be discharged before his term was over. Happily, he recovered in hospital."

Again we find him arrested, along with Swarup Rani, Jawaharlal Nehru's mother, in 1933, but I cannot find out what happened after his arrest, or what sentence was passed. No one could have more bravely offered himself for imprisonment on all these occasions than Pundit Madan Mohan Malaviya.

It remains to try to sum in a few words his character, which all who have known him intimately have found so gentle and winning. No one, not even Mahatma Gandhi himself, is dearer to the vast majority of the Hindu public. He has also a great record of devotion to public national service, which places him very high indeed among those Indian leaders who are still living in our own times. There is in him a bravery of spirit which is equal to his tenderness of heart; and his religious faith is as simple as that of a child. Behind all is a personality so attractive that he has won the hearts of millions who have never even seen him, but have only known his great sacrifices both on behalf of his motherland and his Hindu faith.

BAL GANGADHAR TILAK

BAL GANGADHAR TILAK

"RESPECTED OF THE PEOPLE"

1856–1920

BY ROBERT BRYAN

THE period covered by the last decade of the nineteenth and the first decade of the twentieth centuries was marked in India by the growth of agitation in every sphere of life against the British rule and domination. Through the medium of the Indian-owned press, of the Indian National Congress, of the speeches and actions of Indians who visited or lived in England, of English people themselves like Charles Bradlaugh and later Mrs. Besant and C. F. Andrews, and, more reprehensibly, of the activities of terrorists in Bengal and the Bombay Presidency, the claims of Indians first to be associated on terms of equality in the government of their country, later to be granted home rule and a status equal to the self-governing portions of the British Empire, were ceaselessly and forcefully advanced. The force of this agitation took the Government of India, and many Indians as well, completely by surprise; it owed its origin and sustained continuance, more than to any other single factor, to the personality of Bal Gangadhar Tilak.

Before, however, the influence and the career of this remarkable man are discussed, it is necessary to get clear the background of past history against which he worked and which throughout his life so profoundly affected his thoughts. The crushing of the Indian Mutiny had led to a complete cessation of overt agitation against or dissatisfaction with British rule. Outwardly the years after 1858 were ones of internal peace. From open rebellion the British had nothing to fear. The Mutiny had, however, left a feeling of bitterness in many Indian minds which neither time nor the British did much to dispel. The latter gave to Indians an efficient, but impersonal, administrative system, but only intermittent prosperity; a large measure of justice, but only in rare cases any real understanding; above all, remembering always the Mutiny, they tended to treat Indians not only as their inferiors but also as people who could not be trusted. It was not surprising that resentment persisted in the minds of educated Indians.

But whereas in the pre-Mutiny era—the heyday of the Brahmo-Samaj—the educated classes had been at one in embracing Western ideals, after 1858 they split into two camps, of which one maintained that though Western education should be utilised to the full, yet all that was best in thought and action was contained in the tenets of orthodox Hinduism. This point of view was typified by the Arya Samaj and the "Back to the Vedas" movement, its upholders execrated the foreigners ("mlecchas"), displayed a harsh intolerance towards everything that was not Hindu; pre-eminent among them, at least during the early years of his prominence, was Tilak, though it is one of his main claims to greatness that he moved finally a considerable distance from this attitude.

Bal Gangadhar Tilak was born at Ratnagiri on the Konkan Coast in 1856. He was by birth a Brahman, which was to be an important factor in his life, and the sect to which he belonged was the Chitpavan, which was the predominant influence controlling his early activities. The Chitpavan Brahmans had been in the 18th and the early part of the 19th centuries *de facto* rulers of the Maratha kingdom, which had its capital at Poona —and the resistance of the Marathas to the English power had been at once more skilfully conducted, more stubborn and more prolonged than that of any other Indian kingdom, Hindu or Moslem. Towards their alien English rulers who had deprived them of their power and pre-eminence many of them felt an animosity more bitter, sustained and purposeful than was to be found anywhere else in India.

Tilak was brought up in the strictly orthodox Brahman tradition: as a Chitpavan he had behind him a tradition of politics and public service; as a Maratha he was told the stories of the glorious days of Shivaji and the Maratha Empire, the days when "the foreigners"—in this case the Moslems—were driven in ignominy from Maharashtra. He went as a young man to Poona, the centre of Maratha irredentism, where, as soon after the Mutiny as 1862, an abortive conspiracy had sought to re-establish the power of the Peshwas. There he was appointed professor of mathematics in the New English School, and there, after a while, he became the founder and proprietor of two journals, the *Maratha*, printed in English, and the *Kesari*. The latter, which was the first one printed in a vernacular—Marathi—to gain any noticeable circulation among educated Indians, was destined to gain fame throughout the peninsula. Hitherto education and day-to-day information had been assimilated through the medium of the English tongue. Tilak's earliest ideal—to which he gave practical expression by helping to found National Schools independent of government control, which, however, were later suppressed—was that English should take second place to, if not altogether be supplanted by, the vernacular in the sphere of education as well as of the press.

When Tilak was twenty-nine years old the first session of the Indian National Congress was being held in Bombay. Presided over by an Englishman, Allan Hume, regarded with benevolence as something harmless by the Viceroy, Lord Dufferin, it was mildly liberal in tone and nowhere expressed hostility to the British connection. Tilak was not present at this first meeting, though he had already made his mark in the Bombay Presidency. Violent in speech and print, he had already, in the Poona Sarvajanik Sabha and the Education Committee of which he and Ranade were the leading lights, proved himself the intolerant champion of Hinduism, often in a reactionary form.

He was, however, a delegate to the fifth session of the Congress at Bombay in 1889. His speeches in this and succeeding sessions, particularly his demand that the attitude of "mendicancy," the habit of begging favours from the British, should be abandoned, did much to drive Congress into opposition to the established government; his famous cry, "Freedom is my birthright, and I will have it," awoke an emotional echo throughout India. His attitude, however, aroused misgivings among many of the Moderates. Ranade, and later even Gokhale and Surendrenath Banerjea, not only viewed with alarm the violence of his language but also began to suspect that he spoke and acted first as a Brahman, second as a Maratha, and only incidentally as a man with a vision of a united India of the future.

It must be admitted that his actions, during the closing years of the nineteenth century, did much to justify these suspicions. In 1890 the Government of India introduced the Age of Consent Bill, forbidding the consummation of a marriage before the wife was twelve years old. Its provisions commanded assent from all those who clung to the ideals of the Brahmo Samaj, but Tilak, the orthodox Brahman, violently opposed it. His attitude won him praise from strictly orthodox Hindus, who abounded in Maharashtra, and from all those who welcomed any gesture of defiance to the British. Through the columns of the *Kesari*—which was to attain the then altogether remarkable circulation of 20,000 copies—he could already address a large public, and his personality, as well as the note of challenge and defiance in his writings and speeches, brought him an immense and unquestioning following. Outstanding in intellect, subtle as well as forceful in argument, he could rouse in those with whom he came into contact the same violent emotions, whether of enthusiasm or hatred, which he himself felt. On any given issue he was passionately sincere and he had the gift that was to be later pre-eminently Gandhi's, of inspiring unquestioning devotion. He was given, by common consent, the name of Lokamanya, "respected by the people."

Tilak in these early years bent all his efforts to re-awake in the Maratha people a sense of their past greatness with a view to future independence. He went among the poor villagers of the Deccan as well as the townspeople of Poona, urging the revival of celebrations in connexion with Ganpati, the elephant-headed God known to every village in India, and in 1893 he organised in Poona the first public festival in the God's honour. He founded Ganpati Societies, banded the students in the towns and the youths in the villages into *melas* and gymnastic societies, giving to them a corporate feeling and a sense of their own importance, the while he urged them in the columns of the *Kesari* to deeds of self-denial and valour—and by implication, violence—in defence of their ancient glory against the hated foreigner. In the same year he founded the Anti-Cow-Killing Society, a direct challenge to Moslems which he followed up by demanding, at meetings of the Sarvajanik Sabha, from the Government the lifting of the ban on the playing of music by Hindu processions in front of mosques. As a result the Moslem members of the Sabha resigned, but Tilak acquired fresh popularity as the champion of the Hindus.

Further to consolidate Maratha sentiment and activity Tilak determined to revive the worship of the greatest of all Maratha heroes, Shivaji, the founder of the Maratha power. In 1895 he organised and presided over the first great Shivaji festival at Raigarh, Shivaji's first capital. There was recited by one of Tilak's followers a poem written specially for the occasion, the sense of which was as follows:

> "Let us be prompt like Shivaji to engage in desperate enterprises. Take up your swords and shields and we shall cut off countless heads of enemies. Listen! Though we shall have to risk our lives in a national war, we shall assuredly shed the life-blood of our enemies."

There also Tilak himself spoke. In Shivaji's life there had been one incident—the killing with the notorious "tiger's claw" of Afzul Khan, the opposing general with whom he was in peace-conference—which laid him open to the charge of treachery. Tilak's way of treating the incident was highly significant.

> "It is needless to make further researches into the killing of Afzul Khan. Let us even assume that Shivaji deliberately planned and executed the murder. . . . Did Shivaji commit a sin in killing Afzul Khan?

The answer to this question can be found in the Mahabharata itself. The divine Krishna teaching in the Gita tells us we may kill even our teachers and our kinsmen, and no blame attaches if we are not actuated by selfish desires. . . . God has conferred on the foreigners no grant of Hindustan inscribed on imperishable brass. Shivaji strove to drive them forth out of the land of his birth, but he was guiltless of the sin of covetousness. Do not circumscribe your vision like frogs in a well. Rise above the Penal Code into the rarefied atmosphere of the sacred Bhagavad Gita and consider the action of great men."

There could be no clearer incitement to violent action, no clearer indication of that policy of condoning, if not actually inspiring, assassination, which he was shortly to adopt.

The years 1896 and 1897 were marked by an appalling famine not only in the Deccan but throughout India. Tilak was untiring and selfless in his efforts to relieve the distress, but neither voluntary service nor the measures which the various administrations were able to put into effect prevented untold suffering and a heavy mortality rate. Widespread bitterness was felt at the inability of the British to do more, and this bitterness was increased tenfold by the first outbreak, in Bombay Presidency in 1897, of bubonic plague in India. Once again Tilak displayed great energy and unselfishness. He refused to leave Poona, where the disease was raging and whence many who could afford to had fled, and organized relief on a wide scale. He worked through the Sarvajanik Sabha—with whom the British authorities unwisely refused to co-operate—and started Hindu Plague Hospitals throughout the city. At the same time he carried on a series of bitter attacks on the British in the *Kesari*. The measures which officials had to take to combat the plague ran counter to many Hindu religious customs and inborn prejudices. Tilak took full advantage of this, accusing the administration not only of incompetence but of deliberate and unnecessary interference in matters that good Hindus held sacred. Utterly sincere in his hatred of British domination, he was careless of what means he employed to achieve his end, and he inflamed the sentiments of his listeners and readers to a dangerously explosive emotional point.

In June, 1897, two British officials, Rand and Ayerst, were assassinated in Poona by a young Chitpavan, Damodar Chapekar. There is no shred of evidence that Tilak either planned the assassination or directly incited the assassin, but the deed was the inevitable consequence on an emotional youth of the tone of his articles in the *Kesari*. On account of these articles he was prosecuted for sedition, convicted on a majority vote of six European jurors against three Indians, and sentenced to eighteen months' imprisonment.

The murder of Rand and Ayerst is a landmark in Indian history for two reasons. It marked the start of organised terrorism and it resulted, owing to his subsequent conviction, in the final emergence of Tilak as a popular hero. His term of imprisonment was widely regarded as a martyrdom in the cause of Indian freedom and on his release he became at once the leader of the extremist party in Congress. For that position he was eminently fitted, for no single man had done more in the previous years to awaken in Indians, educated and uneducated, the desire to govern themselves and the feeling that they were fitted so to do. In its early days Congress had been mainly a body of intellectuals thinking in terms of the intellect. Tilak had been the first Indian to bring political agitation to the masses; now after the famine and the plague, which had affected not only Maharashtra, but the whole of India, the time was ripe to direct their thoughts into anti-British channels. Tilak was not the man to lose the opportunity.

Between moderate Congressmen like Naoroji, Gokhale and Surendrenath Banerjea and Tilak and his two chief allies, Bepin Chandra Pal and Arabindo Ghose there was always fundamental agreement on the end to be achieved, the governing of India by Indians. That Tilak was now recognised as more than a champion of orthodox Maratha Brahmanism is proved by his close collaboration with Bepin Chandra Pal, a Bengali of convinced reformist views. But upon the way of achievement the two wings of Congress came increasingly to differ. Hating violence, bearing no animosity against individual Englishmen, the Moderates were opposed to terrorism in all its forms. Tilak, on the other hand, who had become secretary of the Standing Committee for the Deccan, maintained that discussion and the passing of resolutions would achieve nothing, that only by direct action could they hope to achieve their goal—and by direct action he meant the use of the boycott weapon and the encouragement of political assassination. His ideas, which had already found acceptance in the Deccan, took root now even more effectively in Bengal, which took and in future held the lead in terrorist activities. To some extent the Government of India played into the extremists' hands; the partition of Bengal in 1905, against the clearly expressed wishes of its inhabitants, strengthened Tilak's position. To the demand for *Swadeshi*—which he had earlier put forward to Congress—he now added a demand for the complete boycott of British goods.

At the Congress meeting at Benares in 1905 the principle of the boycott was partially accepted; in 1906 at Calcutta the President, Dadabhai Naoroji, himself a Moderate, spoke more firmly than ever before. "We do not ask for any favours, we want only justice . . . the whole matter can be comprised in one word—"self-government" or "*Swaraj*." It was the standpoint taken up by Tilak many years before. The tone of this presidential speech, however, raised false hopes that the Moderates might in the following year adopt the full boycott policy, with all that it might entail. At Surat, where Congress assembled in 1907, it became obvious at once that no such change of heart had taken place. A violent scene developed, Surendrenath Banerjea being constantly interrupted by Tilak's party, and the second day Congress broke up in confusion. Not for ten years was Tilak, or those who thought with him, to attend its meetings.

The split in the Congress ranks that occurred at Surat was a blow to the ideal of Indian unity; a main factor contributing to it was Tilak's own uncompromising attitude. At Surat there was a dangerous recrudescence of the cleavage between Maharashtra and the rest of India. But neither his break with Congress nor the civil and criminal proceedings in which in the previous years he had been involved, did anything to lessen his popularity. In the Tai Maharaj case he was accused, as an executor, of forgery, perjury and corruption. On the criminal proceedings he was at first found guilty, but on appeal the conviction was set aside. In the civil proceedings brought against him on the same issue three trials were necessary, but again finally, before the Privy Council sitting in London, judgment was given in his favour. In the political field he had found a new outlet for his activities in the mill-hands of

Bombay. Miserably housed and miserably paid, they reacted at once to his propaganda which once again was compounded of disinterestedness—as in his efforts to curb the evils of drunkenness—and hatred of the British. That he, an orthodox Brahman, should condescend to come among the poor millhands, should strive to better their conditions, was a thing to make them wonder and then worship, and in his controversy with the Moderates it was he whom they regarded as their champion.

In the meantime he continued his control of the *Kesari*, which had now found many imitators throughout India, and it was again one of his articles therein that for a second time caused him to be tried, convicted and imprisoned. In 1908 Mrs. and Miss Kennedy were killed in Bengal by a bomb thrown by a terrorist. Tilak in the *Kesari* applauded the latter's action, comparing it with that of Chapekar eleven years earlier and praising both. The article was clearly intended to be an incitement to further similar deeds and Tilak, despite a speech in his own defence that lasted for 21½ hours, was sentenced to six years' transportation; this was commuted to imprisonment at Mandalay. Such was Tilak's popularity, that riots, breaking out in Bombay after news of the sentence, continued for six days.

With his imprisonment the most important part of his career was ended. He had already done more than any other man to raise active opposition to the British, first in Maharashtra, then in Bengal, and in lesser degree throughout the rest of India. He has been called "the Father of Indian Unrest," and the title is an apt one. As such he had come to enjoy immense popularity and prestige among Hindus of all castes. He had become something much more than a Maratha leader. When his term of imprisonment was over, though he was past middle age and had lived a turbulent life, he resumed many of his former activities. He found a new and powerful ally in Mrs. Annie Besant, and in 1915 formed a Home Rule League. In 1916 he attended, for the first time for ten years, the annual session of the Congress, held at Lucknow. The tone of that session, in the course of which the Moderates and the Extremists joined in demanding from the British an announcement that "it is the aim and intention of British policy to confer self-government on India at an early date," was the predominant cause of the introduction of the reforms embodied in the Government of India Act of 1919. The prestige of Congress was immensely strengthened by the return of Tilak; it is at least possible that if there had been no reconciliation, the British Government might have ignored its demands, or that the demands would not have been made.

After the armistice Tilak took a leading part in demanding that India should be represented on terms of equality with the other Dominions at the Peace Conference, and in anticipation of this he was chosen by Congress, together with Mr. Gandhi and Syed Hasan Imam, as a delegate thereto. When the British Government refused to grant him a passport, he wrote to M. Clemenceau, Premier of France and President of the Peace Conference, claiming that "with her (India's) vast area, enormous resources, and prodigious population, she may well aspire to be a leading power in Asia, if not in the world. She could therefore be a powerful steward of the League of Nations in the East for maintaining the peace of the world and the stability of the British Empire against all aggressors and disturbers of peace whether in Asia or elsewhere." India,

Tilak would in fact maintain, as at this time did Gandhi, aspired to freedom, but freedom as a partner in the British Empire.

In 1919 Tilak did visit England as the leading member of a deputation sent by Congress to put its point of view with regard to the new Government of India Act. Tilak appeared before the Joint Select Committee of Parliament, and was active in reorganising the British Committee of the Congress so that it could more effectively put the Congress point of view before the British public. He became involved in a libel action against Sir Valentine Chirol who had, after Tilak's imprisonment in 1908, published some severe strictures on him in *The Times*, which were reprinted in book form. It was after losing this action that he returned to India.

He was still a force in Indian political life, though events had moved far from the days of the *Kesari*. He himself had broadened and mellowed in outlook. By taking a leading part in bringing about the Lucknow Pact with the Moslem League in 1916 he had shown that he no longer classed Moslems as "foreigners," and he incited his followers no more to violence. But though a force, he was no longer the chief force, in Indian Nationalism; his mantle as a popular leader rested on the shoulders of Mahatma Gandhi. At the Amritsar Congress in 1919, which both attended, it was to Gandhi that members looked for leadership. In 1920 Congress adopted Gandhi's plan of non-violent non-co-operation; August 1 was the day fixed for the putting into practice of the new principle of *Satayagraha*, a principle so alien to the temperament of at least the Tilak of earlier years. On that same day, the day on which Gandhi arrived in the city, Tilak died in Bombay. A vast crowd, which included Gandhi and Jawaharlal Nehru, followed the funeral procession.

It is, frankly, difficult for an Englishman to form a just estimate of the measure of Tilak's greatness; though in his later years he grew more moderate, he had, through all the most active years of his life, been ruthless in his hatred of British rule, and it is not easy for a member of that race to condone the acts of terrorism in the Deccan and Bengal which he did so much to inspire. Yet that there were elements of real greatness in his character is not to be denied. He was, in fact, much more than a politician: he was a leader. Many aspects of his leadership were deplored not only by the British but also by many of his fellow Indians who were just as disinterested as he in the service of their country, but this salient fact remains: more than any man of his generation he was the cause of the great re-awakening of self-respect and self-confidence that came to India in the years before the war, and in his later years he was a powerful factor in the creation of an All-India opinion.

It must be held greatly to Tilak's credit that he, who in the nineteenth century could do his utmost to inflame Hindu opinion against the Moslems, should be a prime mover in effecting the considerable step forward towards Hindu-Moslem unity marked by the Lucknow Pact. After his death his great successor in the public esteem, Mahatma Gandhi, strove ceaselessly to the same end. Between the methods used by these two men to establish a free India there is a wide gulf fixed; to Gandhi the use of bullet, dagger or bomb is anathema. Yet this they have in common: to both was accorded by millions in India a hero-worship which is only given to those who, according to their lights, are doing their utmost to ensure the greatness of their country.

SIR SURENDRANATH BANERJEA

SIR SURENDRANATH BANERJEA

AWAKENER OF INDIAN POLITICAL CONSCIOUSNESS

1848–1925

BY SIR VERNEY LOVETT, K.C.S.I., M.A. (*Oxon*)

SURENDRANATH BANERJEA was born in 1848, the year in which Lord Dalhousie became Governor-General, six years before the Educational Despatch of Sir Charles Wood laid the foundations of a great change in the government of India, and nine years before the outbreak of the Mutiny. His grandfather was an orthodox Kulin Brahman of Calcutta; his father was a doctor who had studied Western medicine in the first Calcutta Medical College. He tells us in his Autobiography[1] that at his home "Eastern orthodoxy and Western culture strove together for mastery." The grandfather was predominant as long as he lived; but the father saw that his son was educated on Western lines and sent him to a school founded mainly by the generosity of Captain Doveton of the Nizam's service and attended chiefly by Anglo-Indian pupils. He matriculated at the Calcutta University, which had been established only a few years before, at the age of fifteen, and studied hard with the assistance of Anglo-Indian and European professors and teachers to whom in after years he expressed warm gratitude. While a student he was attracted by the addresses of Keshub Chandar Sen of the Brahmo Samaj to whom he listened with "ever increasing admiration," perceiving "the power of oratory over the Indian mind." His father attended to his physical as well as to his mental development. He ascribes the exceptional health enjoyed by members of his family "to the absence of child marriage for many years among them." When he took his B.A. degree, by the advice of the Principal of his College his father decided to send him to England to compete for the Indian Civil Service. But in spite of the paternal approval, the enterprise required considerable courage. "I started," he writes, "with Romesh Chandar Dutt and Bihari Lal Gupta. We were all young, in our teens, and a visit to England was a more serious affair than it is now. It not only meant absence from home and those near and dear to me for a number of years but there was the grim prospect of social ostracism, which for all practical purposes has now happily passed away. We all three had to make our arrangements in secret, as if we were engaged in some nefarious plot of which the world should know nothing." In such circumstances Indian competition was naturally negligible and confined entirely to a few youths from the then very limited classes that had turned to English education, the commercial, medical, legal and clerical professions in the sea-port towns, mostly Hindus. Surendranath and his two friends passed the Open Competition of 1869 and proceeded to a probationary period in the University of London. He writes with much appreciation of its professors and teachers and of the hospitable and kindly treatment that the three received. They passed out at the Final Examination of 1871, and travelling leisurely over Europe sailed by an Italian steamer for Bombay and arrived at Calcutta in September 1871. A big reception was held in their honour in a public garden, but they had still to contend with conservative Hindu pre-

[1] *A Nation in Making*—1925.

judice, and Surendranath's family was at first "practically outcasted" for receiving him. Perhaps if his enlightened father had been alive, things would have been easier, but he had died during Surendranath's absence in England. His stay in Calcutta was short, as he was posted to Sylhet as Assistant Magistrate and Collector in November, 1871. After a brief career under a District Officer whom he found unsympathetic he fell into trouble over the trial of a case and was reported to the High Court and the Bengal Government. The matter was, under the rules, investigated by a special commission of three senior officers whose report was unfavourable; and eventually he was dismissed by the Secretary of State in Council on the recommendation of the Government of India with a compassionate allowance of Rs50 per month. He tells his own story and supports it by quoting the opinion of A. O. Hume, "the father of the Indian National Congress." There was, of course, the government side to it. But it all happened nearly seventy years ago and the full circumstances cannot be adjudicated on now.

He had presented himself in London to plead his own cause and on being informed of the verdict decided to return to India as a barrister. During his previous stay in England he had kept eight terms at the Middle Temple. He continued to eat his dinners, but in 1875 the Benchers declined to call him to the Bar as he had been dismissed from the Indian Civil Service. This was a heavy blow, and he writes that he felt that he had suffered as an Indian, "a member of a community that lay disorganised, that had no public opinion, and no voice in the counsels of their government." There can be no doubt that this idea influenced his subsequent career. During the whole of his stay in England he studied hard, reading books which he thought would assist him to become instrumental in promoting an altered state of things. He returned to India in June, 1875, and beginning as Professor of English in the Metropolitan Institution gradually rose in the educational world of Calcutta, attaining great influence among the students to whom he lectured upon such subjects as Indian Unity, the study of History, the life of Mazzini and the life of Chaitanya.[1] He had resolved to stir them out of their indifference to politics "while protecting them from extreme fanatical views," and with this object he assisted in the organisation of a Students' Association. He further became a very active member of the new "Indian Association" established in July, 1876, by advanced members of the Calcutta middle class of Hindus with the idea of eventually bringing all India upon a common political platform. Its ideals were (1) the creation of a strong body of public opinion in the country; (2) the unification of the Indian races upon the basis of common political interests; (3) the promotion of friendly feelings between Hindus and Moslems; (4) the inclusion of the masses in public movements. Prominent among its members, Surendranath travelled into provinces outside Bengal developing his unusual oratorical talent, and discovering that "a common system of administration had prepared the ground for the realisation of one of our most cherished ideals, namely, united action by the different Indian provinces for the fulfilment of our national aims and aspirations."

I have followed Surendranath Banerjea through his formative years, and have shown the main influences to which his eager, impressionable character was subjected. It must be remembered that under the legislation of 1861 India was then governed by a Governor-General in Council on which no Indian

[1] *A Hindu poet and saint.*

sat, that Indians were not represented on any provincial executive Council, that for legislation not less than six nor more than twelve additional members were summoned to assist the central Executive, not less than half of whom were non-officials. As railways, education, commerce, roads, contact with Europe increased, it was inevitable that English-educated Indians should ask for a larger share in the government of the country. But the English view was that for good government, and for the general content of all the many sections of an enormous society of varied races and religions, it was impossible to abdicate effective control; or to delegate to any class or minority the duty of providing for so vast a congerie of peoples "marching in uneven stages through all the centuries from the fifth to the twentieth."[1] Politically-minded Indians were as yet few in number and mainly Hindu, but with spreading education and persistent agitation they began to increase among the English-educated professional class. Surendranath gradually became conspicuous as a vehement agitator. His influence was increased by his opposition to the Vernacular Press Act of 1878, passed by Lord Lytton's Government and repealed by Lord Ripon's, as well as by his tours in country districts to stimulate interest in Lord Ripon's local self-government policy—intended not with a view to improvement in administration but "as a measure of political and popular education." He tells us that the Indian Association regarded this measure as a first stepping-stone to a demand for a representative government. By this time he had become editor and proprietor of the *Bengalee* which he converted from an insignificant weekly into a successful daily newspaper. Civil imprisonment for two months for contempt of Court, at the time when the Ilbert Bill controversy was agitating Calcutta, increased the popularity which it is evident that he greatly enjoyed. After the Legislative Councils were enlarged in 1892 by an Act which recognised the elective principle he was elected to the Bengal Council and sat on it for eight years from 1893 to 1901, representing three different constituencies. He very strongly opposed the 1899 bill for reforming and "officialising" the Calcutta Corporation in conformity with the views of Lord Curzon, and refused to sit further on that body when this measure became law.

In the meantime the Indian National Congress had for some years recognised Surendranath as one of its leading members and appointed him to its deputation to England in 1890. It remained essentially and mainly a Hindu body. The great Moslem leader, Sir Saiyid Ahmad, had warned his co-religionists that a parliamentary system would subject them to the predominantly numerous Hindus, and that loyalty to Britain was their soundest policy. Within the circle of the Congress leaders there was difference of opinion as to the participation of students in politics. Surendranath favoured this idea, holding that students might even "take part in political work, subject to proper control and guidance." As we shall see, he afterwards acted on this principle vigorously in the agitation against the partition of Bengal; but after that and subsequent experiences, writing on the subject in his last years, he observed that while he still held his former views, "some of our young men have displayed an unpardonable intolerance of views opposed to their own"; there have been "demonstrations of rowdiness." Although "discipline is the soul of student life," its bonds had been relaxed and a spirit of disorder was gaining ground. He could only hope that this would be a

[1] *Lord Morley.*

temporary and passing phase. But in those earlier years he continued to lecture and speak as an educationist and politician. He remarks: "My professional work greatly helped me in my public speeches as I had to teach the classics of the English language. Among them were the speeches and writings of Burke, Froude, Lord Morley and others. I thus lived in constant association with the great masters of the English language and in close familiarity with their vocabulary and methods of thought, and to none do I owe a greater debt than Edmund Burke, whose political philosophy has so largely moulded my own views about government and society."

But with the advent of Bal Gangadhar Tilak into the Congress leading circles came a strong wind of reactionary Hinduism from Western India, and the beginnings of political extremism. Nowhere did Tilak's methods and organisations attract more attention than in Bengal. This was plainly to be seen later on in the anti-partition agitation. On July 26, 1899, before Lord Curzon had been a year in the country he observed in a private letter[1]—"There is no doubt that a sort of quasi-metaphysical ferment is going on in India, strongly conservative and even reactionary in its general tendency. The ancient philosophies are being re-exploited and their modern scribes and professors are increasing in number and fame. What is to come out of this strange amalgam—with European ideas thrown as an outside ingredient into the crucible—who can say?" As Lord Ronaldshay writes, "Curzon turned from these insoluble problems of the spirit to the more pressing problems of administration, to which it was no idle boast to say that he habitually devoted ten hours out of every twenty-four." Yet, curiously enough, he largely underrated the potential influence of the Congress, and even as late as December, 1900, believed that it was "tottering to its fall," and represented only a small section of the community. But in those days the wars and disturbing world-developments of the new century were hidden from the eyes of us all. Three acts of Curzon's government were particularly repugnant to Surendranath and other leaders of the Congress: the curtailment of the power of the elected element on the Calcutta Corporation, already referred to; the Universities Bill, which came too late and ran too sharply against popular prejudices and vested interests to effect much real improvement; and last but not least the partition of the old overgrown province of Bengal, Bihar and Orissa in such a manner as to split Bengal itself into halves, an operation which synchronised with the close of the Russo-Japanese war. In each of these bitter controversies Surendranath took a prominent part, and encouraged students and schoolboys to take part in picketing during the boycott movement. The results were lamentable and far-reaching. The whole boycott movement exacerbated Hindu and Moslem relations to an extreme degree in Eastern Bengal, and when at last Surendranath began to perceive the error of his ways, enormous mischief had been done. A significant incident is related on pp. 223–4 of his autobiography. He was approached by two young men with a proposal to shoot Sir Bamfylde Fuller, the Lieutenant-Governor of the new province of Eastern Bengal and Assam, because of a newspaper story. He deterred them from the idea and about this time awoke to the fact that the agitation was covering the operations of thorough-going revolutionaries. There is a note of personal reminiscence in some of the last words which he addressed to his countrymen (*in A Nation Making*—p. 402): "Talk

[1] *Ronaldshay, II, p.* 199.

not of revolutions, or of tactics, such as obstruction, which are allied to revolutionary movements. You would then stand upon a dangerous precipice and might be hurried, despite yourselves, into the abysmal depths of a real revolutionary movement with all the terrible consequences, the bloodshed and the reaction that follow in its train. Pray do not play with fire. When a movement has been set on foot, forces gather round it of which perhaps you had not the faintest conception, and impart to it a volume and momentum beyond the ideas of the originators who are now powerless to control it."

At Surat, in 1907, he took a leading part in preventing the Extremists from dominating the Congress; and when in 1909 his friend Ashutosh Biswas, public prosecutor, was murdered by a revolutionary he spoke in the Calcutta Town Hall in strong denunciation of the crime. The split at Surat between Moderates and Extremists had left the Moderates in possession of the Congress. They had declared its objective to be self-government within the Empire, to be obtained by constitutional means. They accepted the Minto-Morley reforms which a Bengali deputation to the Viceroy pronounced to be "a step worthy of the noble traditions of the Government which has given us liberty of thought and speech, high education and good government." The most prominent moderate leaders were in Bengal, Surendranath, and in Western India, Gopal Krishna Gokhale. But even by Moderates in Bengal the partition was still denounced, and on the stream of revolutionary crime the reforms produced no effect. A confederacy of revolutionary conspirators drew its recruits from the schools and colleges of Bengal and, in spite of a Press Act passed in 1910, was encouraged by the tone of some newspapers. In 1911 came the visit of King George V and Queen Mary to India, which was a brilliant success and distinctly influenced the general attitude of the country on the outbreak of the War. At the Coronation Durbar of December, 1911, it was announced that the partition of Bengal would be modified in such a manner as to leave that province intact, and that the capital of India would be moved from Calcutta to Delhi. But revolutionary conspiracy did not cease in Bengal even in August, 1914, when princes, politicians and people rallied strongly to the Empire's cause. As one who witnessed and rejoiced in the unity of those days, I can testify to its reality. When the Imperial Legislative Council passed with eager unanimity a resolution of "unswerving loyalty and enthusiastic devotion to their King-Emperor and unflinching support to the British Government," Surendranath said: "We aspire to colonial self-government, then we ought to emulate the example of the Colonials and try to do what they are doing."

But with the long strain of the War and the Home Rule Movement led by Mrs. Besant and Tilak came a certain political reaction. The Congress and the Moslem League, the latter largely moved by pro-Turkish influences, held simultaneous meetings at Lucknow in December, 1916, and each declared for colonial self-government, agreeing on separate electorates for the Mohammedans. In these consultations Surendranath took a prominent part. The Moderates had, to their subsequent embarrassment, readmitted the Extremists into the Congress fold. Later on, in August, 1917, came the declaration of a new policy by the Secretary of State for India—"increasing associations of Indians in every branch of administration; and the gradual development of self-governing institutions, with a view to the progressive realisation of responsible government in India as an integral part of the British Empire." The visit of Mr. Montagu eventuated in the publication of the Montagu-Chelmsford proposals for wide constitutional reforms which immediately produced a definite and lasting split between political Moderates and Extremists. The former left the Congress; the latter remained in possession. In the Viceroy's Legislative Council Surendranath Banerjea, as leader of the Moderates, moved a resolution approving generally of the new proposals, subject to minor criticisms, and inviting his countrymen to "grasp with alacrity and enthusiasm the hand of fellowship and friendship held out to them and in co-operation with British statesmen to move forward to those high destinies which, under the Providence of God, are reserved for our people." The resolution was carried with only two dissentients; and Surendranath justly claims that it saved the new scheme. I was present on this occasion and felt that the attitude of the non-official members was one of genuine cordiality. A resolution moved by a non-official member recommending that consideration and disposal of the Report of the Sedition (Rowlatt) Committee be kept in abeyance was rejected by 46 to 2 votes. But these fair beginnings of a new era were, as is well known, marred by much that followed. It is sufficient here to say that although Surendranath and the other Moderate members of the Imperial Legislative Council opposed the anti-revolutionary conspiracies legislation of February and March, 1919, yet when bitter agitation outside the Council increased and Mr. Gandhi inaugurated the policy of civil disobedience by communicating to the Press a pledge signed by himself and others, the Moderates countered by a manifesto expressing disapproval of this innovation. It was pointed out in one of their newspapers that the principle involved in the proposed pledge was extremely dangerous and might lead anywhere. The bill passed; the riots of April, 1919, and severe repression followed; and shortly afterwards Surendranath spent four months in England in order to attend the sittings of the Joint Parliamentary Committee that was considering the Government of India Bill of 1919. He returned in September but received a somewhat chilly welcome from his old followers. "Non-co-operation," he says, "had done its work by creating a profound sense of mistrust in British promises and pledges among a certain section of our people despite evidence of earnest efforts to redeem them." He notes that when it became clear to its authors that non-co-operation was marked by unrest and rowdyism and sometimes by bloodshed, that it achieved nothing constructive, it was converted into a policy of entry into the reformed Councils for the purpose of obstructing and wrecking them. This policy he strongly opposed. At a meeting of the Rotary Club in Calcutta he appealed to the members "to stand with us, to co-operate with us in ensuring the success of the great experiment upon which the honour of England is staked, and the future of India so largely depends. I am sure," he added, "that I do not appeal in vain. I am strengthened in this note by the cordiality of your reception and the kind and sympathetic hearing which you have accorded to me and for which I am truly grateful." He certainly did not appeal in vain.

He was knighted on January 1, 1921, and became a Minister in the Reformed Provincial Executive Council, accepting the portfolio of local self-government and the medical department. He writes warmly of his relations with the Governor, Lord Ronaldshay, with his colleagues in the government, both Hindu and Moslem, and with the Services, of the loyal help which he received from his secretary, Mr. O'Malley. He quotes the letter "of great regret in severing connection" which he received from the Surgeon-General of Bengal when his term of office came to a close in January, 1924.

But there was another side to the picture which he describes in language of sorrow. "The Press of Bengal was saturated with the spirit of non-co-operation and was Extremist in its views and utterances. The reception accorded to us was cold and hostile." Even friendly critics expected impossibilities, not recognising that "the work in its most difficult and controversial aspects necessarily resolved itself into a series of compromises." He framed and passed on March 7, 1923, a new Calcutta Municipal Act which superseded the Act passed by Lord Curzon in 1899, and restored supreme authority over the affairs of the City to the Corporation, four-fifths of whose members were to be elected by the ratepayers. Both the Mayor and the chief executive officer were to be its nominees, subject only to confirmation by the government. Surendranath calls the measure "a veritable Swaraj in the government of the second city of the Empire," and in the Provincial Legislative Council appealed for co-operation for its success. "Let no party spirit," he said, "mar the fruition of this great object." The new Corporation, however, was captured by his Swarajist adversaries, and his bitterest opponent became Mayor. At the Council election of 1923 he was defeated and practically excluded from public affairs for the rest of his life. He expresses, however, his faith that eventually a civic government will be established in Calcutta "not for the benefit of a party or clique but for the benefit of the people and worked through the people."

On retiring from office he finished his Memoirs and died on August 6, 1925. His memoirs are of great interest for they are a very human document and show clearly the ambitions and principles which guided his public life. He goes out of his way to pay warm tribute to old friends and colleagues and to some of the masters of English literature from whose writings he derived so much inspiration. His tone towards old antagonists is generally void of bitterness. We see the ideas that animated his political strivings, sometimes carrying him further than he cares directly to admit. "For self-government," he says, "I have worked step by step, stage by stage. I worked for it when the government treated it as a fantastic dream. Our efforts have changed all this, and even the view-point of the government. The message of August 20, 1917, is the tribute to our success." He ends by pleading earnestly with his countrymen for a policy of co-operation. "There is no standing still in this world of God's providence. Move on we must with eyes reverently fixed on the past, with a loving concern for the present, and with deep solicitude for the future. We must in this onward journey assimilate from all sides into our character, our culture, our civilisation, whatever is suited to our genius and is calculated to strengthen and invigorate it and weave it into the texture of our national life. Thus, co-operation and not non-co-operation, assimilation and not isolation must be a living and growing factor in the evolution of our people. Any other policy would be suicidal and fraught with peril to our best interests. That is my message to my countrymen, delivered not in haste or impatience, but as the mature result of my deliberations and of my life-long labours in the service of the Motherland."

CHITTA RANJAN DAS

CHITTA RANJAN DAS

THE FRIEND OF HIS COUNTRY

1870–1925

BY DR. J. C. GHOSH

CHITTA RANJAN DAS, political leader, lawyer, poet and journalist, was born on the 5th of November, 1870, in Calcutta. He was the eldest son of Bhuban Mohan Das and Nistarini Devi. The Das family was one of the most distinguished and cultured in Bengal, and belonged to that sect of reformed Hindus known as the Brahmo Samaj. Bhuban Mohan was a solicitor by profession and an amateur journalist and writer of songs. It is possible to argue that Chitta Ranjan's journalistic and poetic leanings were inherited from his father.

Chitta Ranjan was educated at the London Missionary Society's School at Calcutta, whence he matriculated at the Calcutta University in 1886. He then joined the Presidency College, and took the Bachelor's degree in 1890. Shortly after he came to England to study law and to compete for the Indian Civil Service. He joined the Middle Temple, and was called to the Bar in 1892. In the previous year he had taken the Civil Service examination, but had failed to secure a place in the list of successful candidates. During his stay in England he made several political speeches, notably in support of the parliamentary candidature of Dadabhoy Naoroji, the first Indian to be elected to the House of Commons.

Returning to India in 1893, he commenced practice as a barrister in the High Court of Calcutta, but for many years had little success. He also went through a period of acute financial trouble. Bhuban Mohan, who was then in declining health, had contracted several debts on his own account and, what was worse, stood security for a friend of his for a very large sum of money. The friend not being able to redeem the security, both Bhuban Mohan and Chitta Ranjan—who had assumed joint responsibility with his father—were financially ruined and had to seek the relief of the insolvency court in 1906. It should be said, however, that as soon as his circumstances permitted it, Chitta Ranjan took the unusual procedure of applying for the annulment of the insolvency order and paid back the entire amount of his and his father's debts. The debts had become time-barred, but Chitta Ranjan considered himself under the moral obligation to pay them. This act of honesty, which has very few parallels in any country, is one of the many instances of the magnanimity and large-heartedness that he always showed in all matters connected with money. It made a great impression and was applauded all over the country.

Between 1893 and 1906 the chief events of his life were his marriage, in 1897, to Basanti Devi, and the publication of the first two volumes of his poems, the *Malancha* and the *Mala*. The opportunity should be taken here to mention his work as a poet and a journalist, since no account of his life will be complete otherwise, and for the special reason that his reputation as a political leader and lawyer has somewhat eclipsed the reputation he deserves to have as a poet. Chitta Ranjan never regarded poetry as his calling, but there can be no doubt that some of his poems will find an abiding place in Bengali literature. He does not possess very great originality and does not introduce many strikingly novel themes or forms of expression. Nor does he evince, except in rare moments, the magical power of creation. But the bulk of his work is highly cultured, distinctive, competent, and impregnated with deep thought and feeling. Though very few of his poems touch the highest water-mark of genius, there are very few poets in Bengal, leaving out Tagore, whose average performance sustains such a high level as Chitta Ranjan's. This is because of the high seriousness of his purpose and the abundant vitality of his mind and senses. His themes are almost always profound—questionings on God and on the meaning of life, love and death—but they never remain abstract, and are rendered poetic by the intensity of his emotional fervour and the acuteness of his sense-perception. His poems possess the additional interest of a highly illuminating spiritual documentary. They describe the process by which he gradually cast off the puritanism and the sectarian outlook of the Brahmo Samaj, and the intellectualism, atheism and hedonism that he had imbibed with Western education, and found ultimate rest and happiness in the Vaishnava ideal of love. As Vaishnavism is the finest and the most characteristic flowering of the Hindu spirit in Bengal, Chitta Ranjan's spiritual pilgrimage may be described as his travelling away from the West to the ideals of his native land, and from the sect into which he was born to the larger life of the entire Bengali people whose political leader he was. The note of intellectual revolt, which in such early works as the *Malancha* had led him to the rejection of God, gradually subsides, and gives place, in such later works as the *Kishore Kishori* and the *Antaryyami*, to that ecstatic love of the Vaishnava which is at once carnal and spiritual, and realises, through its own intensity of pleasure and pain, the infinite and the immortal in the finite and the mortal. In his concluding years he wrote some devotional songs after the manner of the Vaishnava poets of Bengal. His conversion to Vaishnavism was not only the fulfilment of a religious need, it was also intimately connected with his political nationalism. For he stood for a synthesis which would unite the political nationalism of a country with its cultural and spiritual heritage in a harmonious whole. He held that the spirit of nationalism in Bengal should not, and could not, thrive in isolation, as if it were entirely a matter of politics and economics; but must be deeply interwoven with, and draw nourishment from, the cultural and spiritual heritage of that country. His most remarkable poems, inasmuch as they are the most original and have the greatest claim to permanence, are to be found in the collection known as *Sagar Sangit* (translated into English as *Songs of the Sea* by the author and Aurobindo Ghose). The poet's soul and the sea are found there as mutual counterparts, and bound to each other, in their manifold aspects of tranquillity and disturbance, by a bond that is basal and preordained.

Unhoped for, wondrous one, ever elusive,
Wait awhile that I weave thee in my song.
The calm sea lapped in dreams
Trembles to-day in the pale light of the moon!
If it be that thou hast truly come,
Then, O smiling mystery! dwell in my heart,
What time I weave thee into song!
Stay yet awhile,
And with the melodies of the sea and the free soundless rhythm of my heart

I will thee enrhythm in manner yet passing beyond all rhythm!
Bound then thou wilt be in the enduring solitudes of my heart!
Wilt thou there not abide,
O thou with the circling robe of dream,
Held fast in that music and stay in thy fulfilment,
Eternal, unmoving?

Chitta Ranjan kept himself in touch with all the important literary movements and organisations of the country, and presided over the Literary Conference of Bengal in 1915. His presidential address was on Bengali lyric poetry. He gave much time and attention to journalism at many periods of his life, and was one of the founders, and a member of the editorial board, of the *Bande Mataram*, an English daily started in 1906. His most important journalistic activities were the founding and editing of the *Forward* and the *Narayana*. The former, a daily paper in English, was the official organ of the Swaraj party of Bengal, and had a brilliant and stormy career for many years. The *Narayana*, a monthly in Bengali, was chiefly devoted to Vaishnavism and literature.

As lawyer Chitta Ranjan first came into prominence in 1908 as counsel for defence in the trial of Aurobindo Ghose, the editor of the *Bande Mataram*. The partition of Bengal in 1905 had let loose a tremendous wave of nationalist agitation and revolutionary activity, and the Government resorted to unusual measures. The *Bande Mataram* was the foremost nationalist paper of the day, and Aurobindo Ghose was tried on the charge of sedition before the Chief Presidency Magistrate of Calcutta. Chitta Ranjan's brilliant advocacy at once brought him into the limelight, but a still greater opportunity came to him the same year. This was the Manicktolla Bomb Case, one of the most sensational political trials in history. Following a bomb outrage in Muzafferpur, the police unearthed a bomb factory in Manicktolla, a suburb of Calcutta. Thirty-six young Bengalis were put on trial for conspiring and waging war against the King and for acquiring arms for that purpose. Aurobindo Ghose, whose brother was one of the leaders of the terrorist organisation, was put on trial too. The case lasted for a long time, more than two hundred witnesses were examined, four thousand documents filed, and there were so many as five hundred exhibits—bombs, revolvers, detonators, ammunition, etc. Chitta Ranjan, who conducted the defence for practically no remuneration, covered himself with fame by his brilliant forensic skill and power of cross-examination. He also endeared himself to the heart of nationalist Bengal, which regarded the accused as great, though misguided, patriots. This case was the starting point of his tremendous success in his profession. His practice was perhaps the largest and the most lucrative ever enjoyed by any lawyer in India, and his earnings sometimes verged on the record figure of £50,000 per year. His success was chiefly made in criminal cases—the most sensational of which, in addition to the aforementioned, were the Dacca Conspiracy Case and the Munitions Board Case—but he showed great ability in many civil suits as well. The most notable of these was the Dumraon Raj Adoption Case.

Chitta Ranjan had been associated with the new nationalist movement that began with the partition of Bengal, and with its two organs, the *New India* and the *Bande Mataram*. He had also joined the Indian National Congress as a delegate in 1906. But he took no active part in politics until 1917, when he was invited to preside over the Bengal Provincial Conference of the Congress in Calcutta. His connection with politics which began in this way continued uninterrupted until his death. His presidential address before the Bengal Provincial Conference was more in the nature of a sentimental rhapsody than a considered political speech. He painted a highly romantic picture of Bengal's golden past, and attributed the present suffering of the people to their fall from the spiritual ideals of ancient India and to their adoption of the materialist values of the West. He suggested as remedies village reconstruction, return to the soil and the renouncing of industrialism. But his practical sagacity and political acumen asserted themselves in the evidence he gave, in the same year, before the Montagu-Chelmsford Reforms Commission, which was then touring India with the object of ascertaining what measure of self-government should be introduced in the proposed reforms scheme. In his evidence Chitta Ranjan demanded popular control of finance as well as of all the services, but left the army, the navy and the railways as reserved subjects for the time being. In the same year he played an important part in the controversy that arose in the Congress Working Committee over the election of Mrs. Annie Besant as the president of the Calcutta Session of the Congress. Chitta Ranjan threw in his weight with the left wing, and the schism that thus began in the Congress ultimately resulted in the formation of a new party in India—the Moderate, or as it was later called, the Liberal Party, representing the older and the conservative section of Indian political opinion. Before the Congress met in Calcutta in 1917 Chitta Ranjan went on a lecturing tour in East Bengal and addressed large and enthusiastic meetings in every place he visited. In the Congress session he delivered an impassioned speech on India's right to develop her political constitution according to her needs, and independently of dictation from Whitehall.

In 1918 he succeeded, in the Congress session at Delhi, in carrying through the demand for complete and immediate provincial autonomy against the opposition of the Moderates led by Mrs. Besant. His other great activity in that year was directed against the proposed Defence of India Act (also called Rowlatt Act). He stirred up a tremendous amount of public opinion against the Act and condemned it in a big meeting in the Town Hall of Calcutta.

The Indian situation became more critical than ever in 1919, the black year of the Amritsar tragedy and of martial law in the Punjab. Chitta Ranjan did extremely able work in the committee set up by the Congress to inquire into the Punjab affairs. He met Mahatma Gandhi for the first time on this committee, and he supported the Mahatma when the latter launched *Satyagraha* (passive resistance) against the Defence of India Act. A complete *hartal* (public mourning and cessation of business) was declared and observed all over India on the 6th of April, the second Sunday after the Act had received the Viceroy's assent. In the Congress session at Amritsar that year he came out as one of the principal leaders of that section, called at the time the Extremist, which considered the proposed Montagu-Chelmsford reforms as "wholly inadequate, unsatisfactory, and disappointing." He also advocated for the first time the policy of obstructing the Government in order to achieve home rule for India. "Co-operation," he said, "when necessary to advance our cause, but obstruction when that is necessary for the advancement of our cause."

The next year was the most eventful in the history of Indian politics. At the special congress session in Calcutta

Mahatma Gandhi presented his five-fold programme of non-co-operation with the Government. Chitta Ranjan, who was a believer in the policy of obstruction from within the legislatures, opposed the Mahatma's resolution, but the Congress adopted it. Three months later, at the session of the Congress at Nagpur, Chitta Ranjan accepted the Mahatma's programme after entering into a pact with him by which each reserved to himself the freedom of future action. Chitta Ranjan's conversion to the policy of non-co-operation was a personal triumph for the Mahatma. In pursuance of its policy the Congress now proclaimed that all candidates for the provincial councils and the central assembly should withdraw from contest, all government servants should give up their posts, lawyers should suspend their practice in the British law courts, and students should leave government-aided schools and colleges. Chitta Ranjan threw himself wholeheartedly into the non-co-operation movement and gave up his immensely lucrative profession as lawyer. Henceforth he renounced all the comfort and luxury that wealth can give and lived the live of a political and spiritual *sannyasi* (ascetic). He was a *bon viveur*, and had almost perfected the art of high living since he achieved success in his profession. But his conversion to the simple life, when it came, was equally complete. A few years later he made over his entire property to the nation for the institution of a medical school, and a hospital for women. The heart of India was deeply moved by these acts of sacrifice, and he was lovingly called *deshabandhu*, the friend of his country. No one in India or elsewhere had a greater right to that title.

From now on his life was one continuous political activity and a succession of triumphs. Students left their schools and colleges by the hundreds at his call, and lawyers suspended their practice. National schools and colleges sprang up in many places, and Chitta Ranjan founded a national university at Dacca in 1921. The strike of the Assam Bengal railwaymen and the exodus of the coolies from the tea plantations of Assam engaged his attention for some time, but his chief activity in 1921 was the organising and directing of the Congress Volunteer Corps. To accelerate the non-co-operation movement the All-India Congress Committee asked for the recruitment of ten million national volunteers and for the raising of ten million rupees. In Bengal, Chitta Ranjan's appeal was answered by hundreds of young men and women. The picketing of Government offices, law courts, schools and colleges and of shops selling British goods, the sale of *Khaddar* (hand-made Indian cloth), and every other item of the non-co-operation programme were carried out with great efficiency. The volunteer corps swelled rapidly and showed signs of developing into a tremendous mass movement. The Government declared the movement subversive and put a ban on public meetings. Congress retaliated by deciding to disobey the law, and was supported in its decision by the Khilafat Committee. Thus arose a struggle between the Congress and the Government, and thousands of pickets and demonstrators obstructed the police and courted arrest and imprisonment. Chitta Ranjan's wife, son and sister were arrested, and he himself was arrested and sentenced to six months' imprisonment. Meantime he had been elected President of the Congress Session of 1921, but could not preside as he was an under-trial prisoner at the time when the Congress met.

Congress workers having resorted to violence in some parts of India, Mahatma Gandhi called off civil disobedience, and was soon after put into prison. The non-co-operation movement was on the decline when Chitta Ranjan was released in July, 1922, and he gave it the *coup de grace* with his new policy of "non-co-operation from within." According to this policy the Congress should contest the elections to the provincial and central legislatures and enter them with the object of obstructing and wrecking them from within. Chitta Ranjan enunciated his policy when he presided over the Congress Session of 1922, but was unable to carry it. But he gathered round him a sufficient number of followers to form the nucleus of a new party, later called the Swaraj Party, and succeeded in having his policy of council entry accepted by the Congress in 1923.

From now on until his death he was the leading figure in Indian politics. His policy was amply justified in Bengal and some other provinces. In Bengal, in spite of the shortness of time, Chitta Ranjan organised the Swaraj Party with marvellous efficiency and led it to victory as the largest single party in the Bengal Council. He declined to form a ministry, and under his lead the Council refused to vote the ministers' salaries in 1924 and 1925, and smashed the constitution introduced by the Montagu-Chelmsford Reforms. Another triumph of 1924 was the almost complete capture of the Calcutta Corporation by the Swaraj Party in the first election held under the new Calcutta Municipal Act. Chitta Ranjan was elected the first Mayor of Calcutta, and re-elected in 1925. In 1924 he conducted a successful campaign of civil disobedience against the maladministration and corruption prevalent in the Hindu shrine at Tarakeswar in Bengal.

The Swaraj Party was now all-powerful, and Chitta Ranjan the dictator of Bengal, though he never stooped to dictatorial methods. The struggle with the Government began with renewed intensity after the murder of an inoffensive Englishman by a Bengali youth named Gopinath Shah, who had mistaken him for a person of prominence. The Government promulgated an ordinance under which eighty young men—the number subsequently increased to several hundreds—were interned for suspected complicity in revolutionary activity. In 1925 the main provisions of the Ordinance were embodied in the Bengal Criminal Law Amendment Bill. Under Chitta Ranjan's leadership the Bengal Council threw out the Bill, but it was passed by certification by the Governor. Indignation in the country ran high, and the Bengal Provincial Conference of 1924 passed a resolution extolling Shah's patriotism and self-sacrifice, and Chitta Ranjan supported it. In a speech before the Calcutta Corporation, after denouncing the method of violence adopted by the Bengali revolutionaries, he said: "But so far as their enthusiasm for liberty is concerned, I am with them. So far as their love of freedom is concerned, I am with them." His attitude towards the revolutionary movement was widely misunderstood in India and England; but before long he made clear his position. In 1925 he issued two manifestoes strongly denouncing the use of violence as a political weapon: "I am opposed on principle to political assassination and violence in any shape or form. It is absolutely abhorrent to me and to my Party. I consider it an obstacle to our political progress. It is also opposed to our religious feeling." At the same time he appealed to the Government "to cause a searching enquiry to be made into the causes which have brought about the revolutionary movement in India and then to set about applying the proper remedy, so that there may be a radical and permanent cure of the disease. The Government should recognise that, however mistaken the revolutionaries may be, however wrong and futile their methods and however criminal and reprehensible their acts, the guiding principle of their lives is sacrifice for the attainment of political and economic freedom for their country. The moment they feel that at any rate the foundation of our freedom is laid by the Government, I venture to assert that the revolutionary movement will be a thing of the past. I suggest in all humility that there should be a distinct and authoritative declaration by the Government at the earliest opportunity." These utterances were considered by the Government as the first step towards a new era of co-operation, and negotiations took place between Chitta Ranjan and representatives of the Governments of Bengal and India. In the Bengal Provincial Conference in May, 1925, Chitta Ranjan declared his position as one of willingness to negotiate for co-operation on honourable terms. This might have led to a turning point in Indian politics, but his death intervened on the 16th of June.

His body was brought down from Darjeeling to Calcutta by train, and a procession, over two miles long and consisting of nearly three hundred thousand men and women with Mahatma Gandhi at their head, followed his body to the cremation ground.

As a political leader Chitta Ranjan possessed great organising and fighting power, and was one of the cleverest tacticians the world has seen. But the unique quality of his leadership came from his personality, from the personal love and reverence he inspired, and from the complete confidence he enjoyed among both the Hindu and Moslem communities. No other Hindu leader has been trusted by the Indian Moslems as he was. The Hindu-Moslem Pact promulgated by him was inspired by the highest statesmanship and by a generous recognition of the rights of the Moslem community. In his conception of self-government he was ahead of his time and regarded it as freedom and well-being not only for the privileged few, but for the toiling masses of India. In his later years he took increasing interest in working-class movements and presided over two annual conferences of the Indian Trades Union Congress. No words of his have greater significance for the future of India than the following, uttered at the Congress Session at Gaya in 1922: "Many of us believe that the middle class must win Swaraj for the masses. I do not believe in the possibility of any class movement being ever converted into a movement for Swaraj. If to-day the British Parliament grants provincial autonomy in the provinces with responsibility in the central Government, I for one will protest against it, because that will inevitably lead to the concentration of power in the hands of the middle class. I do not believe that the middle class will then part with their power. How will it profit India if, in place of the white bureaucracy that now rules over her, there is substituted an Indian bureaucracy of the middle classes? . . . My ideal of Swaraj will never be satisfied unless the people co-operate with us in its attainment. Any other attempt will inevitably lead to what the European socialists call the 'bourgeois' government. . . . If to-day the whole of Europe is engaged in a battle of freedom, it is because the nations of Europe are gathering their strength to wrest this power from the hands of the middle classes. I desire to avoid the repetition of that chapter of European history."

GOPAL KRISHNA GOKHALE

GOPAL KRISHNA GOKHALE

FOUNDER OF "SERVANTS OF INDIA SOCIETY"

1866–1915

BY CHARLES KINCAID, C.V.O.

GOPAL KRISHNA GOKHALE[1] was born on May 9, in the little village of Katluk in the Chiplun taluka of the Ratnagiri district on the western coast of the Bombay Presidency. He was by caste a Chitpawan Brahman and he spoke his mother-tongue Marathi with the peculiar elegance of his fellow castemen. A strange legend is related of the Chitpawans, which I have told in the History of the Maratha people. It is as follows:[2]

Once Parashu Rama, the Brahman incarnation of the god Vishnu, to avenge the murder of his father Jamadagni by the Kshattriya king Sahasrarjuna, cleared the earth twenty-one times of the Kshattriya caste. Thereafter he was so reeking with blood that no other Brahmans would eat with him. He therefore went to the summit of the Sahyadris and stood gazing at the sea, which then washed the foot of the mountains, and pondering where he could find Brahmans with whom he could dine. As he looked he saw floating on the surface of the water the corpses of fourteen Mlecchas or barbarians. He dragged them ashore, built a great pyre and burnt them to ashes. From the ashes he created fourteen new Brahmans, who had no scruples about eating with their creator. The meal over, the fourteen Brahmans begged Parashu Rama to give them a land wherein they might live. The hero drew the mighty bow given him by the god Shiva and shot an arrow into the Arabian Sea. He then commanded the ocean to go back within its borders as far as the arrow had fallen. It did so, thus leaving bare the Konkan. This reclaimed land Parashu Rama bestowed on the fourteen Brahmans. They went to dwell there and built themselves a town called Chitpolan or the Town of the Burnt Heart, which in course of time was corrupted into Chiplun. To themselves they gave the name of Chitpawans or Brahmans purified by the Funeral Pyre.

Whatever truth may underlie this romantic tale and whatever the real origin of the Chitpawan community may be, they have produced a greater number of eminent men than any other in India. The talented Peshwas or hereditary prime ministers of the Maratha empire were Chitpawans. So too were Ranade the great High Court judge, Paranjpye the distinguished mathematician, Tilak the famous journalist and politician and Apte the greatest of Indian novelists. So when Gokhale rose to eminence, he was in excellent company.

Gopal Krishna Gokhale was connected with the aristocratic house of Raste and his ancestors had held responsible office under the Peshwas. His father Krishnarao Gokhale was educated at Kolhapur, where he became a school friend of Ranade. Unhappily Krishnarao Gokhale was poor and his poverty

[1] *I have been greatly indebted, when preparing this slight monograph, to the admirable work of Mr. John S. Hoyland, M.A.*

[2] *Various authors have inferred from this story that the Chitpawans were originally foreign immigrants from Arabia, Egypt or even Scandinavia. In my view the legend contains no truth whatever. Exactly the same tale is told by the Ben-i-Israel or Indian Jews to explain their presence in the Bombay Presidency.*

forced him to give up his studies and accept a small post in the service of the Maratha prince of Kagal, a kinsman of the Maharaja of Kolhapur. Gopal Gokhale's mother was the daughter of Bhaskar Oka, a well-to-do Brahman of the same taluka. She was illiterate, but after the manner of so many Maharashtra ladies, she was strongwilled and deeply religious and she made a faithful wife and a devoted mother. The early years spent by Gopal in the countryside gave to him what so many other Indian politicians lacked, a first-hand knowledge of the Maratha peasant's difficulties.

When Gopal was ten years old he and his elder brother Govind were sent to Kolhapur for their secondary education; but three years later their father died in Kagal and his income died with him. Thus Govind at eighteen had, as his father had done before him, to leave school and give up all hopes of high office. He accepted a small post in the Kolhapur state on fifteen rupees a month. Out of this tiny income he not only supported his mother and sisters, but sent eight rupees a month to Gopal. Unable to complete his own education, he determined that his younger brother should not similarly suffer.

On eight rupees a month Gopal contrived to subsist and learn; but the struggle must have been appalling. He had to reduce his meals to one and cook it himself, and to read his textbooks by the street lamps because he could not pay for oil. Fortunately he had a retentive memory, a facility for mathematics and a fine constitution. In 1881 he matriculated and as an undergraduate went first to the Rajaram college of Kolhapur, thence to the Deccan college in Poona, and finally graduated in the Elphinstone college in Bombay. There he took a second class in mathematics and won a post-graduate scholarship of twenty rupees a month. He was now independent of his generous brother and accepted an assistant mastership in English at the New English High School in Poona. His salary was only thirty-five rupees monthly; but to a youth trained to live on eight rupees, his salary, added to his scholarship, seemed wealth beyond the dreams of avarice. He sent part of his earnings to his brother towards the liquidation of his debt; at the same time he kept terms as a law student and coached pupils for their public service examination.

Some years previously two distinguished Brahmans, Messrs. Tilak and Agarkar had founded the Deccan Education Society. It controlled a number of schools, but anyone who joined it had to bind himself for twenty years never to ask from the society more than seventy-five rupees a month for his services. This self-denying rule appealed to the young Gopal and he resolved to become a member of the society. The chief obstacle was his brother. Govind had during the best years of his life denied himself not merely luxuries but bare necessities; and he wished in return that Gopal should exploit for the family's benefit his great abilities. Nevertheless the young man stuck to his point and Govind gave way. They were right, for if Gopal never reached affluence, he won immortality.

In 1884 the Deccan Education Society decided to turn the New English school into the Fergusson college and the first classes were opened in 1885. Gokhale was appointed one of the professors of English; but English was only one of the many subjects that his versatile mind enabled him to teach. He had taken his degree in mathematics and he had published an excellent textbook on arithmetic; so he was soon teaching mathematics as well as English. At other times he was required to lecture on history and political economy. In fact, one cannot but think that his seniors exploited somewhat ruthlessly their junior's many-sided ability. Gokhale, however, was no bookworm. As a boy he had been a useful if not an outstanding cricketer and he was an excellent billiards, chess and card player.

While Gokhale was still a master at the New English school he made the acquaintance of his father's old school friend, Mr. Justice Ranade, in a somewhat unusual way. To celebrate some academic function the New English school had invited all the most prominent Poona citizens. The youthful Gokhale was posted at the door with strict instructions to prevent "gate crashing"; he was only to admit would-be entrants who could produce tickets. Suddenly a guest presented himself without a ticket. He had left it at home by mistake, he said. Gokhale jumped to the conclusion that here was the very type of intruder against whom he had been warned. Coldly he told the visitor that there was no admittance without a ticket. Unfortunately the reputed "gate-crasher" was no less a personage than Ranade, the greatest Indian then living. Flabbergasted for the moment, he looked round for an acquaintance who might help him. He found one in Mr. Sathe, who put matters right and introduced Ranade to the conscientious doorkeeper. The great man was far too magnanimous to bear ill-will towards the young obstructionist, and Gokhale became not only Ranade's firm friend but his devoted pupil, and to be a pupil of Ranade was no sinecure. In the following passage Mr. Shahani (Gokhale, p. 59) has described Gokhale's training:

"Under instructions from Mr. Ranade, the disciple set to work with intense application. Many were the dreary hours spent in hunting up materials; many were the nights when sleep was denied the young man, because work had a stronger claim. Even fever was not admitted as an excuse. 'Fevers would go away if medicine were taken, the exacting master would say, 'but a Wednesday lost could not be reclaimed' (Wednesday being the day when they usually met for their work). . . ."

This was no doubt an excellent training for one gifted with immortal youth, but the strain of it may well have been partly responsible for Gokhale's early death.

For the time being, however, all was well. Ranade honoured Gokhale by making him one of the secretaries of the Sarvajanik Sabha of Poona, then the chief political association in India. Its communications were always acknowledged and answered by the Bombay government. Under the care of Ranade the young secretary wrote drafts for the Sarvajanik Sabha's letters. Thus he had the advantage of writing English and moderate and restrained criticism under the eyes of a master. Unfortunately between 1889 and 1891 the Deccan Education Society passed through stormy times. The two founders Messrs. Tilak and Agarkar quarrelled. Mr. Tilak was a staunch upholder of the old-fashioned Hindu orthodoxy and tried to keep all his pupils free from modern influences. Mr. Agarkar inclined towards the liberal unorthodoxy of Ranade, who had waived his objections to eating and drinking with his English acquaintances. Eventually the differences between the two friends became acute. Mr. Tilak left the Education Society and the Fergusson college and took with him Mr. Namjoshi, to whom had been entrusted the organisation and collection of the college funds. This was a great loss to the staff, for Mr. Tilak was the senior mathematical tutor and Mr. Namjoshi had been very successful in his somewhat ungrateful duties. The all-too-willing Gokhale was directed to take their places, and he became permanent professor of mathematics and bursar as well as professor of English and political economy. Such labours would have overwhelmed the ordinary man; yet Gokhale still made time for weekly articles in the *Sudharak*. In fact the English articles were all by him and the Marathi articles by Mr. Agarkar. For this extra toil Gokhale refused payment, since his journalism, as he explained, was a labour of love for his country.

In 1890 Gokhale first entered politics. When only twenty-three he was called upon to speak at the Congress in support of a resolution to reduce the Salt tax. He did so with great effect, and he continued to inveigh against this impost until its practical abolition in 1906. In the Congress of 1892 he spoke strongly on the Indianisation of the public services and his speech brought him prominently before the public eye; but while Indians outside Maharashtra were coming to regard Gokhale as one of their chief political leaders, he was unhappily becoming more and more without honour in his own land. Gokhale's sympathies were with reformers like Ranade and Agarkar, but accident had put him in an unfortunate position. His first wife was found shortly after their marriage to be suffering from an incurable disease. Pressed thereto by his relatives and with his wife's consent he married a second lady. He thus incurred the wrath of the Hindu reformers who were preaching monogamy. On the other hand his support of the claims of the untouchable castes and, above all, his partaking of refreshments at the headquarters of a Poona mission brought down on his head the resentment of the orthodox party. Mr. Tilak took advantage of Gokhale's difficulties and stirred up the Poona mob against him. This was particularly the case at the Ganpati festivals, organised by the extremist wing in opposition to the Muharram celebrations. The students vied with each other in composing verses in derision of the moderate group. Unfortunately both "Gopal" and "Gokhale" lent themselves readily to Marathi rhyme, so that in every poem the owner of these names came in for jeers and jibes, always offensive and often obscene. Some years later this literary campaign reached its climax in the appearance of a play called "Kichak Wadh" or "The killing of Kichak" in the principal theatre of Poona. The author was Krishnaji Khadilkar, the chief leader writer on the *Kesari* staff. The play was based on an incident in the Mahabharata. The disguised Pandava brothers and their joint wife Draupadi took refuge in Viratnagar. Unfortunately Draupadi's beauty roused the passion of Kichak, the queen's brother, and he resolved to make her his mistress. She fixed a meeting with him, but sent instead the giant Bhima the second of the five brothers. When Kichak appeared Bhima killed him. In Mr. Khadilkar's play the eldest brother Yudhishthira preached patience. Bhima was full of a just wrath and advocated violence. The author intended that Yudhishthira should stand for the moderate party and its leader Gokhale; Bhima stood for Tilak and his followers; and Draupadi stood for India. The actors made Yudhishthira utterly contemptible and Bhima admirable. The play proved extraordinarily popular, but one strange circumstance led to its suppression by the Bombay government. Unexpectedly, the public took Kichak to stand for Lord Curzon. The actors played up to the public and every night Kichak's appearance led to a demonstration against the famous viceroy. The suppression of the play followed, but it continued to be read and enjoyed for many years afterwards by Gokhale's political opponents.

In 1896 Gokhale went with Sir Dinshaw Wacha to England to give evidence before the Welby Commission. His chief theme was the growth of Indian expenditure in excess of the growth of Indian revenues. While he was absent in England the bubonic plague attacked western India with fury. The Bombay government, anxious at all costs to check the horrible disease, were led by their doctors into measures that were not tolerable to the orthodox inhabitants of Poona. Great feeling was roused by the inspection of plague-ridden houses by English soldiers, and friends of Gokhale wrote to him exaggerated accounts of the sufferings of the Indian public at the hands of unclean barbarians. The climax was reached when Mr. Rand and Lieutenant Ayerst were shot when driving to Government House at Ganeshkhind by two excited young fanatics. Gokhale, not doubting the accuracy of his correspondents' letters, made wild charges against the Bombay government. An official enquiry was ordered; but when Gokhale, on his return to India, called on his informants to substantiate their statements, they one and all implored him not to reveal their identity. The unfortunate bringer of charges was thus unable to prove them. He had been deceived. The stories told him were either false or greatly distorted and he had unwisely accepted them as true. After grave thought he decided that he was in honour bound to apologise to the Bombay administration. In this decision he was strongly supported by Ranade and under his guidance he sent a full and frank apology to the Governor in Council. This action greatly increased the respect in which he was held by Indian and English officials; but the extremists were furious. Their papers described him as a mean and time-serving poltroon. Their view—to which Tilak cordially subscribed—seems to have been that when one brings an unfounded charge against the administration, one should stick to it at all costs; but Gokhale was too great a gentleman to adopt this course. He bore patiently his enemies' attacks in the sure consciousness that time was on his side. He proved right. The government appointed a commission to go into the question of plague and inoculation, and they nominated Gokhale as a member.

The journeys necessitated by the work of the Plague commission on the top of his journey to England changed considerably Gokhale's outlook. Before his western voyage he had been a Maharashtra Brahman and probably hoped for nothing more than the restoration of the Peshwa's rule; but whereas Tilak, for all his ability, continued to his death to hold this view, Gokhale became more and more an All-Indian and less and less a Chitpawan Brahman in his opinions. Indeed he was all for joining hands with the Moslems, a community against whom the extremists fomented unquenchable hatred.

In 1899 Gokhale was elected to the Bombay Legislative Council by the Municipalities of the Central Division of his Presidency. He soon came to prominent notice by his speeches against the Land Alienation Bill, introduced to restrict the Maratha peasant's power of alienating his lands. Gokhale, who knew the lives of the peasantry well, took the view that the restriction would only reduce the peasant's responsibility and self-respect, and that the best course was to create co-operative credit societies. How far Gokhale was correct it is hard to say. The Land Alienation Bill did produce good results where introduced; at the same time the Bombay government adopted his suggestion and introduced co-operative credit societies all over the Presidency and with marked success.

In 1902 Mr. Gokhale succeeded Mr. (afterwards Sir) Pherozeshah Mehta on the Imperial Legislative Council. Of this body he remained a member until his death some thirteen years later; and it was at Simla and Calcutta that his reputation reached its zenith. It was, however, clear that he could not in his new office continue his work as a professor at the Fergusson college, and after eighteen years of most onerous service he resigned. It was a grave step to take. His experience and reputation as a political leader and orator had given him very great influence over college students and, as he knew, that influence was sound and moderate. Nevertheless there was no alternative. He gave up his post, which had brought him in the small salary of seventy-five rupees a month and took instead the even smaller pension of thirty rupees a month.

When Gokhale joined the Indian Legislative Council, Lord Curzon was viceroy and dominated by his vast energy and ability every department of the administration. So successful had been his financial policy that in spite of disastrous famines he had a handsome surplus at his disposal. He proposed to spend much of this in restoring and beautifying the historic monuments of India. Gokhale's view was that all such surpluses should be returned to the taxpayers by reduced taxation. There was much to be said on both sides. It is true that the peasants, who paid the land revenue, were extremely poor, and nowhere more so than around Gokhale's home. Still the division of the surpluses among the hosts of peasantry would benefit each one very little; whereas the Government of India were trustees of some of the most magnificent structures in the world. These had been badly neglected and Lord Curzon restored them to their ancient splendour. Any tourist who visits the Taj Mahal, the sites of former Delhis, the mosque of Babur at Panipat, the fort at Agra, etc., etc., will, I think, glorify the great viceroy's name. Gokhale further attacked the salt tax and here he was more successful as I have already said. Salt taxes have always been hateful and in pre-revolutionary France the salt tax (*la gabelle*) was detested. Another of Gokhale's demands was the reduction of military expenditure. The army was, he said, too big and the officers were overpaid; but the army only numbered 280,000 men. It had to police a country more than half the size of Europe as well as guard hundreds of miles of frontier from the incursions of lawless and ferocious barbarians. The officers in the British army were so badly paid that none of them could stay in their regiments without private means. I do not, therefore, think that there was any real justification for this criticism. The fact was that neither Gokhale nor the Indian government understood the situation. The administration was so poor that once when I was on Lord Sandhurst's staff he complained to me that he had just had to refuse the money for whitewashing a traveller's bungalow! Yet the country was not really so poor as that. What was needed was a broader basis of taxation. When Sir Guy Fleetwood Wilson widened the basis of taxation, revenues poured into the treasuries.

In 1905 Gokhale did the greatest thing in his life. He founded the "Servants of India Society." It was created in imitation of the Society of Jesus and was originally an autocracy under Gokhale. It is now controlled by a body of three with a president and a secretary. Its object was to collect together a group of disciples who would voluntarily abandon all ordinary ambitions and pledge themselves to a life of toil and poverty in the cause of their country. It was a great conception and worked admirably so long as Gokhale lived. Afterwards it was affected by the rapid growth of the extreme Congress party.

In 1908 came the Minto-Morley reforms and their initiation was undoubtedly due to the influence that Gokhale, when in England, had acquired over Lord Morley. He also threw himself into the cause of elementary education. Towards that end he introduced in 1911 an Elementary Education Bill; but, as usual, the government had no money and many of the non-official members refused to support it. Another cause that he championed was that of the indentured Indians. These unfortunate persons were lured by crimps to distant colonies and there abominably treated. I am glad to say that I was myself a member of the Legislative Council of the Viceroy, when Sir William Vincent many years later decreed the abolition of the system.

The partition of Bengal and the treatment of Indians in South Africa were other subjects of Gokhale's tireless oratory. It was when he was eloquently defending the cause of South African Indians that he first met Mr. Gandhi, who was working on their behalf in Cape Colony. On the latter's invitation Gokhale went to Africa. Backed as he was by the Indian government he was able to make proposals that first the government of India and then Mr. Smuts accepted; but Gokhale did not live to see this triumph. He had long been suffering from diabetes, and the ever increasing tasks that he assumed as a member of the Public Services commission, as head of the Servants of India Society, as member of the Legislative Council, as president of the Congress, as representative of the South African Indians, aggravated the disease. On February 19, 1915, the great orator and political leader passed away. His last words spoken in Marathi to his comrades of the Servants of India Society were:

"This side of life has been good to me. It is time that I should go and see the other."

The death of Gokhale caused widespread grief among his followers and great regret among his English friends. Although he was politically opposed to the English officials, he always got on with them very well. Lord Kitchener, whose army estimates he tried so hard to reduce, was very fond of him and loved to chaff him. The magnificent Lord Curzon, who hated criticism, forgave it in Gokhale and was so impressed by his abilities, his self-restraint and his eloquence that to show his appreciation of his critic's services, he obtained for him a Companionship of the Indian Empire. Yet it was not only great men such as these who came under the wand of the magician, but all who met him. Once, when I was judge of Poona, I thought it my duty to call on Gokhale; but as it was a purely formal call I did not intend to stay more than five minutes. He received me with such courtesy and his graceful Marathi speech was so delightful to listen to, that thirty-five minutes passed before I left his little house in Bhamburda. The fact was that if he loved his country dearly, he also loved his fellow men and he could not but be charming to all of them. Whatever his faults may have been, and they must have been very few, they will surely be forgiven him for his abounding love of humanity.

THE RIGHT HONOURABLE V. SRINIVASA SASTRI

THE RT. HON. V. SRINIVASA SASTRI

G. K. GOKHALE'S CHOSEN SUCCESSOR

BORN 1869

BY C. F. ANDREWS

THERE is hardly anyone in India whose integrity of moral character is held in higher esteem than that of Srinivasa Sastri. People may differ from him in politics, but his sincerity is never questioned. This fact tells us in a very few words much about the man himself.

G. K. Gokhale had a true insight when he saw the latent powers of Sastri and thought of him as a possible successor. For there is in him a remarkable combination, which Gokhale also possessed, of intellectual honesty and high idealism; a readiness to face adverse facts, a sceptical frame of mind, a refusal to be led by sentiment. Though these two great Indian leaders came from different parts of India, they both met together on a common political platform, accepting, as an axiom, what Gokhale called the "inscrutable providence" whereby, as he affirmed, only in conjunction with Great Britain could India regain her freedom.

Again, in religious matters the sceptical attitude had predominated with both of them rather than the emotional; yet it would be wrong to speak of either as lacking in religious principles. Their high moral austerity has been itself of a religious nature. For Gokhale always had reverence for ideals and Sastri has the same. While in the field of scientific enquiry Gokhale exhibited the stronger mind of the two, Sastri, on the other hand, has revealed greater intuitive genius. He has more of the bent of a philosopher. He represents in India that cultured humanist tradition which can be seen perhaps at its best in Walter Lippman's writings. It has also its counterpart in Hu Shih in modern China.

Srinivasa Sastri was born on September 24, 1869, and is thus almost exactly the same age as Mahatma Gandhi, whose birthday was October 2 in the same year. A weak constitution has made it often very difficult for him to put forth all his strength without suffering for it afterwards. Yet, with remarkable fortitude, he has been able to exercise his will power in such a manner as to carry through very arduous work. Born in the highest caste of Hindu society, he displayed, as a child, all the traditional ability of the Brahman culture of the South. But his early career, at school and college, although brilliant in scholarship, did not leave behind it any immediate token of the world reputation which was to come to him almost unbidden in his later career.

After his University course was over Sastri worked his way steadily forward in the sphere of education which he had taken up as his own life profession. At last he was appointed to the Headmastership of one of the celebrated high schools in the South of India. It would almost have seemed that his career had then reached its own fulfilment. But G. K. Gokhale discovered his hidden genius and called him to higher service.

Gokhale had just reached the pinnacle of his political fame by his opposition to the redoubtable Lord Curzon. Both in finance and University administration he challenged Lord Curzon's figures, and was proved to be an even greater master of his subject than the brilliant

Viceroy himself. The latter was large-hearted enough to admire his doughty opponent, and Gokhale's fame was henceforth in the ascendant. When Lord Minto came out to rule in Lord Curzon's place and John Morley was at the India Office, Gokhale in many notable ways became the power behind the throne.

Then, at the height of his career, the deplorable fact was brought home to him that owing to an incurable disease his days on earth were numbered. Nothing daunted he put up a gallant fight right on to the end. Yet all the while, as his strength declined, he was aware that he must act soon or not at all. So he threw his moral and spiritual energy into the work of founding a society, which was to be named after him and carry on his ideas. Ever since 1905, this thought of a new foundation had been much in his mind. He called it "The Servants of India Society." All the last efforts of his brief life which could be spared from direct political activity were devoted to the organisation and endowment of his new Order.

The members of Gokhale's Society were to undertake, after a full probation, a life service. They were to dedicate themselves to the attainment of Swaraj for India as an "equal partner within the British Commonwealth." This last clause revealed the essential moderation of Gokhale's mind. It also made his Society accept the middle position in Indian politics. From the outset, it began to attract most of all men with that outlook.

It is commonly reported that after Mr. Gokhale's visit to South Africa in 1912, where he had been far-sighted enough to recognise at once the original genius of Mr. Gandhi, his mind began to waver as to the final selection of his successor in the Servants of India Society.

There was a time—so we are told—when a single word from Gokhale himself might have persuaded Mahatma Gandhi to join the Society as a life member. But that word was never spoken. For it became evident that Gandhi's gifts were of a different order. It is true that he had already taken Gokhale as his political Guru. His devotion to him was profound. Furthermore, his own readiness to sacrifice himself was quite unbounded. He was willing not only to join the Servants of India Society, but to serve it in the humblest capacity. But for him to have taken that course would have brought injury to his deepest convictions; and every year spent in India revealed clearly that his work had an individuality of its own which demanded absolute freedom for its development.

On the other hand, Sastri's genius was, in a very remarkable way (as I have shown) akin to that of Gokhale. Both of them had dedicated the earlier part of their lives to the teaching profession; both of them had very scholarly minds, with a desire for accuracy in the smallest details that was almost fastidious in its sensitiveness; both were moderate in their political opinions.

Though Gokhale died too soon to make the final choice of his own successor, the members of his Society were able, in close co-operation with Mahatma Gandhi himself, to settle the question by general consent. For, after a very long discussion at which Gandhi was present, the decision was unanimously reached that Sastri should succeed Gokhale as President of the Society, and that Gandhi should be left free to follow his own inner guidance. The years that followed have amply proved the wisdom of that long-considered verdict.

It has been necessary to dwell thus upon the Servants of India Society because it was this that brought Srinivasa Sastri out of his comparative obscurity, and gave him at once an All-India standing as G. K. Gokhale's successor.

The Government of India recognised the importance of the step that had been taken by the Society in electing Sastri as their new President, and almost from the very first the Viceroy, Lord Hardinge, took him into his confidence.

These were the crucial years of the World War, when every help was needed from men of the highest character who could represent Indian opinion. In less difficult times it is quite possible that Srinivasa Sastri with his innate modesty would have remained in retirement at Poona, absorbed in research work and chiefly occupied in his own fruitful studies. But the War made such a leisured life impossible for him, and Sastri himself discovered in the Council Chamber his own powers of oratory and also the rapidity of his mind in public debate. He came to Delhi with Gokhale's reputation behind him, and he was able amply to fulfil the part which his leader had marked out for him.

One of the most dramatic speeches that Sastri ever made was in opposition to the Rowlatt Act, when he protested with prophetic fervour against the attempt made by the Government to push it through in the teeth of public opinion. It was a strangely disturbed Sastri that spoke that day with such vehemence and fire. For on ordinary occasions he would appeal to the ultimate logic of persuasive argument; but then he spoke at a white heat. He solemnly declared that if the officials took the fatal step, which they were contemplating, they would surely repent of it afterwards. Those who had known Sastri on ordinary occasions, as he pursued the even tenor of his way, could hardly believe that such volcanic fires lay hidden beneath the surface. Very rarely do those fires break forth, but when an eruption does take place those in authority are foolish if they take no notice of them.

It speaks well for the Viceroy at Delhi that Sastri's denunciation of the Government policy was taken in good part. Its honesty was transparent, and

MR. SASTRI AT HOME

An informal portrait of Mr. Gokhale's successor taken with his wife at their home in Madras.

when the Government of India at a later date required a representative at the Imperial Conference in London he was chosen.

Sastri's work in London brought with it his first introduction to the problem of Indians abroad, which was destined to occupy the most fruitful years of his later life and to win him the well-deserved title of India's first ambassador in foreign parts.

At this Imperial Conference, in 1921, he came into conflict with General Smuts, the Prime Minister of South Africa. A great amount of heat was engendered; for Sastri's position in demanding equal citizenship for Indians domiciled in the dominions was quite unassailable; and General Smuts's argument, that for economic reasons this could not be granted, rang hollow. Everyone present knew perfectly well that the "colour bar" lay behind it.

That struggle for equal Indian citizenship was now to form the chief subject of Srinivasa Sastri's political career. His tour round the world, visiting all the dominions (except South Africa, which refused to accept him on that occasion) had this end in view. He was present also, while on the same tour, as India's representative at the Washington Conference in the United States. Secretary Stephen Porter described to me, when I was at Washington in 1930, the deep impression which Mr. Sastri had made on the delegates on that occasion.

In later years I had the opportunity of going round from one dominion to another, and it was a very great pleasure to me to find how much his visit had been appreciated. His noble bearing, his complete impartiality, and his wonderful eloquence had struck everyone. He did more than any other Indian statesman to raise the name of his country in those dominions.

In the same way the poet, Rabindranath Tagore, achieved a similar result both in Europe and America, while he delivered his lectures and read his poems. Mahatma Gandhi's world fame, as the hero of Satyagraha, was to come later.

My next recollections of Sastri are those in London, in 1923, where we used to meet each other every day at the time of the "Kenya Conversations." Here again Sastri was India's first ambassador, as he presented to the Colonial Office, on behalf of the Government of India, the case for full citizenship and racial equality.

Lord Delamere, as Sastri's opponent, exercised great influence in London society. He had been the joint author of a sweeping attack on Indian moral character in a Government Economic Report, which the British parliament had afterwards publicly to disown. His rooted dislike of Indians as settlers was notorious. Sastri had thus to meet both an influential opponent and a very highly organised campaign, whose aim was to stop all Indian immigration into East Africa. "Durban has closed the back door into Africa," the European statement ran, "and Mombasa must close the front door."

Along with this proposed restriction of Indian immigration went the reservation of the Kenya Highlands for Europeans. These two demands, together with the refusal to accept a common electoral roll under any conditions, displayed in flagrant manner a racialism which drove Sastri almost to desperation. He felt that the British constitution itself, on which he had pinned his faith, was being torn in pieces in order to appease a small number of settlers who had become infected with this racial virus. "If Kenya is lost," he cabled to India, "all is lost." This word of his became proverbial.

During those days of storm and stress Sastri himself was attacked by a very serious illness. He was forced to go into a nursing home in the centre of London, where the doctors ordered absolute rest; for heart disease had been the cause of all the trouble and his life itself was in danger. But nothing on earth would keep him at that time from fulfilling his duty to his country. Everything he held dear in life was at stake and he could not lie resting in a nursing home with any peace of mind. So he insisted on speaking at a great public meeting in the Queen's Hall; but this only brought on further illness. The whole period for him was a time of agonising struggle to maintain the Indian cause in an atmosphere where everything seemed to be directed in high quarters against it. His bitterness increased day by day along with his heart trouble. In the end he went back to India a physical wreck and it was a year before he recovered.

When the White Paper was published it was found that on two out of the three main issues—the franchise and the reservation of the Highlands—the Indian cause was defeated. Only on one point was there a decision in India's favour, namely, on that of immigration into East Africa; for it was finally decided by the Colonial Office that no restriction on Indians, bearing a racial character, would be imposed by law. Free entry into Kenya would be continued and this meant free entry into Uganda. Since Tanganyika was mandated territory, that door into Africa remained open also. Yet this freedom of entry, though important, was scant comfort when racial discrimination had been practically accepted by the White Paper in other directions.

On account of his great services to the British Commonwealth Srinivasa Sastri was now made a Privy Councillor and entitled to be called the Right Honourable. But this could in no way compensate for the patent fact, that in a British Colony like Kenya, under the direct control of the British parliament, his own fellow-countrymen were treated as inferior in status and a colour bar had been established. The noble record of British statesmanship for racial equality, going back over nearly a hundred years, had thus been broken in order to favour a very tiny body of white people. These British settlers had the vast unoccupied areas of the dominions open to them, from which Indians were practically excluded. The injustice of such favouritism is obvious and matters have been made still worse by a recent order in Council which has ratified this reservation of the Highlands.

The shock that Srinivasa Sastri then received changed the whole course of his life in the years that followed. It made him ready to respond at once to the appeal to go out to South Africa when the time came; and here, undoubtedly, he won the greatest success of his long career on behalf of Indians abroad.

The story of Sastri in South Africa can be told from personal recollections, for I was with him during a considerable part of the time. He hesitated much at first. He could not forget that at the Imperial Conference of 1921 General Smuts had been his strong opponent, and also that it had been intimated to the Government of India that a visit from him during his tour to the different dominions would not be welcome. He felt, therefore, that the deputation would lose rather than gain by his own presence on it.

In this Sastri was mistaken; and I tried hard to reassure him. When he reached South Africa he found out at once that his fears had been without foundation, for not only did General

Smuts receive him in a friendly manner, as though the past had all been forgotten, but Sastri also proved himself to be by far the most popular speaker on the deputation when any public speaking was required.

Soon after the first Cape Town conference Sastri was nominated, with universal consent, to be the first Agent-General to South Africa. Mahatma Gandhi himself expressed the voice of the nation by suggesting his name to the Viceroy as the most acceptable person to fill that office. Again he shrank back from it—this time chiefly on the ground of ill health. But he was prevailed upon to go out and try what he could do.

During the interval between the Round Table and his arrival as Agent-General I had remained on in Natal at his special request and, when he at last reached Durban, he induced me to remain with him still longer. It was then that I came to know the deeper sides of his character, and also how sensitive he was to the criticisms which were being continually levelled against him because of his "moderation."

While the altitude of the Transvaal tried his heart and was therefore bad for him, when he got to Cape Town, on the sea-level, and also to Durban, the climate suited him, and he was able to recover his strength. His popularity was so great that crowds flocked to hear him wherever he spoke in public. He was able to achieve, in a short time, what it would have taken anyone else years to accomplish.

At Pretoria, I remember, when he spoke at a public meeting in the Town Hall, how the whole of one portion of the large auditorium was taken up by the older boys from Pretoria High School. On the morning after the meeting the headmaster gave a lesson to his class on what he considered to be the best way of speaking English correctly—taking his examples from Sastri's lecture.

At Johannesburg the Dean of the cathedral invited him to deliver a lecture on India and took the chair himself, pointing out the iniquity of the colour bar and its utterly un-Christian character. He became Sastri's close personal friend.

These were only some of Sastri's triumphs. Among his own Tamil people in Durban, who formed the bulk of the domiciled Indians, he was entirely at home. They loved him with an intense affection, and when he started a movement to build a college for Indian students in their city, the Indian subscriptions mounted up to £20,000 and the college was called Sastri College in his honour.

The conference in London with regard to the new Indian constitution saw him there, as a delegate, both at its first and second session. By some strange act of official negligence his name was left out of the final Indian Committee which was to sit in a consultative capacity along with the Joint Parliamentary Committee while it hammered out the proposed reforms. It was semi-officially announced in the newspapers that Sastri's name was left out because of his ill health; but I knew for certain that he had been saving up all his strength in order to be there on that last occasion when the details were being determined. I went to the India Office and made known what I had been personally told about Sastri's keen desire to be present; but the matter had been already decided. Since on certain main issues the advice of the leading Indian members was rejected, it may perhaps have been well that he did not undertake that winter journey to London all to no purpose.

When I met Sastri, on my return from South Africa some years later, he was

ROUND TABLE CONFERENCE

The scene at the first Plenary Session of the India Round Table Conference at St. James' Palace, London, 1930.

staying at Poona, living on milk and lettuce, and spending much of his time in meditation. I said to him, with a laugh, that he seemed determined to die as a *Sannyasi!* He was extremely pleased with the idea and answered: "Do you know, that was just what an astrologer foretold about me when I was quite young!"

Though he has not yet reached this *Sannyasi* stage of retirement, his travelling days are nearly over. Everyone was highly delighted and gratified when he accepted the office of Vice-Chancellor at Annamalai University in his own province. The duties are by no means overwhelming, and he is able to live the life of meditation and study that he has always yearned after.

May he thus go on to a ripe old age both for the benefit of India, his Motherland, and also for the good of the world!

SIR PHEROZESHAH MEHTA

SIR PHEROZESHAH MEHTA

A VETERAN INDIAN LEADER

1845–1915

BY NAOROJI DUMASIA

The character and genius of Pherozeshah Mehta, the brilliant Parsi who declared that he was an Indian first and Parsi afterwards, occupy a remarkable and in some respects a unique place in the gallery of great Indians whose careers adorned the closing years of the last century and the beginning of the present one. That sudden flowering of nationalist genius has drawn the wonder and comment of innumerable observers. Undoubtedly, it was a phenomenon which owed its birth to the working of the freedom-breathing spirit of English literature, deeply imbued as it is with the ideals of liberty, democracy, and the rights of man, upon the natural genius of a people whose intellect is bred to a high degree of sensitivity by an ancient heritage of culture. The advent of English education in this country, effected by Macaulay's historic Minute, may be said, indeed, to have planted the first germ of nationalist aspiration in the Indian soul and to have begun the ferment of development which to-day is shaping slowly but inevitably into the birth of a new Indian nation.

Among the first fruits of that quickening was a galaxy of patriotic stalwarts whose names are familiar to every Indian—Dadabhai Naoroji, Pherozeshah Mehta, Dinsha Wacha, Telang, Budruddin Tyabjee, W. C. Bonnerjee, Gokhale, Ranade, and later, Surendranath Bannerjea, Bipin Pal and Tilak. These great souls, each of whom might have been the man of a century of nationalist endeavour, together with such Englishmen as William Wedderburn, Charles Bradlaugh, Sir Henry Cotton and Alexander Hume, Father of the Indian National Congress, names imperishably enshrined in Indian hearts, first blazed between them the trail of nationalism in India.

It has been said that after Dadabhai Naoroji, whom Mehta himself openly acknowledged as his political guru and to whom, indeed, he paid glowing tribute to the end of his days, Pherozeshah was by far the acutest and most far-seeing political thinker of his time. From early youth he displayed a rare genius for leadership which combined bold courage with amazing capacity for painstaking study. In his instantaneous grasp of a situation, swift decision, the unerring nature of his judgment, the inflexible resolve, boundless enthusiasm and energy with which he fearlessly pursued his decisions, and the almost electric nature of the personality with which he swayed his fellows, Pherozeshah displayed from the beginning of his career to the end of his days powers and qualities that marked him out a born leader of men, a national genius who must have stood out in any country.

To full-bodied conceptions of India's political future, beyond which the most ardent apostles of Indian freedom have not gone to-day, Mehta brought the leaven of a common sense acutely alive to practical realities and the conditions by which Indian political aspirations had to be governed in his day, as indeed they still are in our own. It was this realisation, coupled with characteristic intolerance of visionary policies and a fiery enthusiasm for first principles and logical endeavour, which made Pherozeshah Mehta the eminently constructive nation-builder he showed himself to be, and which turned his most fruitful activity into the channel of civic improvement rather than into the wider field of political reform.

Not that he did not have his dreams of Indian liberty and national evolution. His speeches are alive with visions which still provide the goal of Indian patriotism. Indeed such was his far-sighted wisdom in every field of thought connected with the improvement and future of this country that in most matters we are still achieving the signposts he set half a hundred years ago.

It is one of the more remarkable characteristics of this man that in all the days of a career, crowded at first with the struggles of a young lawyer striving to build up a practice in circumstances which practically slammed the doors in the face of Indian legal ambition, then with the showering briefs of a successful lawyer eagerly sought after by a clientele that flocked from all parts of the Presidency, and at the same time with the responsibilities of civic leadership at a time when the foundations of Bombay's municipal government were being laid, he was able to think so clearly that he never made an important pronouncement which he had subsequently to modify or recall, never undertook a policy or action which he had cause seriously to regret or deplore. The perspicacity of his mind betokened logical thought which instinctively rejected the false, with unerring accuracy winnowed the grain from the chaff, and created for him that reputation for being right which was his greatest asset in commanding the following he did and the unquestioning obedience accorded to him by his fellows. He never spoke without careful thought, and he thought back as well as forward. A thorough appreciation of essentials and realities enabled him to eschew error to a degree that won him in his own lifetime fame of almost legendary quality, and invested him with the halo of an arch guru in the field of civic politics which Time has only burnished.

While his contemporaries devoted themselves to the task of rousing the political consciences of their countrymen and of the people of England to the political needs of this country, Pherozeshah Mehta, who might if he cared have striven far more powerfully in this field, realised that the fundamental essential for the exercise of national freedom is capacity for its exercise. This undoubtedly accounts for the wholehearted zeal with which he threw himself into the field of municipal administration and devoted his life to the task of reforming, or rather of creating, the civic government of India's "First City."

It is worth noting here that Pherozeshah Mehta never regarded himself as anything other than a son of the soil. The thought that the Parsis might be regarded as foreigners who had no place or voice in shaping or influencing the destiny of the native population never entered his mind. And when on one important occasion some of his friends ventured to express a different opinion Pherozeshah made a historic statement in the name of his community which settled that issue for good and all so far as the Parsis were concerned. In a day when the community, which once led the vanguard of Indian nationalism, laid the foundations of Indian commerce and industry, and built the original structure of India's economic prosperity, has fallen on lean times and is relegated to the position of a minority whose voice is lost in the tumult of India's million-mouthed nationalism, that pronouncement by this great Parsi, who never

THE GATEWAY OF INDIA

The famous archway on the landing quay of Bombay Harbour, erected temporarily for the visit of King George V and Queen Mary in 1911, and later built permanently to commemorate their visit

paused to doubt whether he was an Indian or not before dedicating his life to the land of his birth, is worth recalling. Here it is:

"To ask the Parsis to isolate themselves and their interests from those of the other natives of this country is to preach something not only equally selfish, but a great deal more short-sighted and unwise. In our case, it would be almost suicidal policy. Its ultimate effect would be only to reduce us to insignificance. We are a power in this Presidency as a small but enlightened and enterprising portion of the natives of this country, and, as such, participate in its greatness. Isolated as Parsis, pure and simple, holding ourselves aloof from the other natives of the country, without common interests, common sympathies, and common co-operation, we might still remain an interesting community, but of no account whatsoever in the great march of events moulding the lofty destinies of this magnificent land."

In his birth and the conditions which surrounded his childhood and early youth Pherozeshah was distinctly fortunate. He was born on August 4, 1845, of a respectable middle class Parsi family. His father was a partner in the firm of P. & C. N. Cama which traded with China and London. Being in fairly affluent circumstances he was able to bring up his family in an atmosphere of comfortable living. Pherozeshah went to school at Ayrton's, a famous institution conducted by an English solicitor of those days, thence to another nursery of Bombay's early builders known as the

CENTRE OF BOMBAY'S MUNICIPAL LIFE

Municipal Buildings in Bombay opened in the year the Bombay Legislative Council sent Sir Pherozeshah as their representative to the Supreme Legislative Council; a recognition of the services he had rendered to the city.

"Branch School" and, passing the Matriculation examination, he joined Elphinstone College, of which Sir Alexander Grant, a famous educationist, was head.

His notice was soon attracted to the tall broad-shouldered Parsi youth who played and studied with equal zest and ability and the liberal-hearted Englishman developed keen interest in Pherozeshah, in whom he seems to have foreseen the makings of the stalwart character and high-souled man he later became. Pherozeshah graduated in 1864, and six months later took his M.A. with honours.

About this time Mr. Rustomjee Jamsetjee Jeejeebhoy, second son of the first Parsi baronet, announced an offer of a lakh and half of rupees "to enable five Indians to proceed to England for the purpose of qualifying themselves for practice at the Bar in India." By the good offices of Sir Alexander, Pherozeshah secured one of the five places. He did not enjoy the benefit of this scholarship for long, however, for six months after he landed in England Mr. Rustomjee's fortune disappeared in the great share mania crash of 1865 in which so many of Bombay's richest men and business houses were utterly ruined.

Pherozeshah spent nearly four years in England. They were profitable years, bringing him into intimate contact in a degree impossible to-day with English life and thought with their highly stimulating influences upon mind and character, and providing opportunities for the formation of friendships with half a dozen other Indians sojourning for similar purposes in England, all of whom rose later to positions of eminence in their country's life. Among these were Jamsetjee Tata, Mun Mohun Ghosh, Budruddin Tyabjee, W. C. Bonnerjee, Hormasjee Wadya and Jamsetjee Cama. Pherozeshah's most inspiring contact of those days, as he himself confessed throughout his life, was with Dadabhai Naoroji, already engaged even then in fighting the battle of India. Naoroji was closely connected with the London Indian Society and the East India Association, and through him Mehta had the advantage of being early trained in the atmosphere of these institutions to expression and development of those patriotic feelings which receive a peculiar stimulus in alien surroundings. It was at the meetings of these bodies that Bonnerjee and Mehta came to know each other better and laid the foundations of a life-long friendship. Among other activities Mehta read a memorable paper before the East India Association on "The Educational System of Bombay." The address was a powerful plea for the extension of higher education in India, urging the establishment of a thoroughly co-ordinated and liberally financed scheme of state education from primary schools to technical colleges and universities. In this the young man displayed sagacious perspicacity and foresighted wisdom, which have been amply vindicated by the bitter experience of more than half a century of unfruitful educational endeavour in this country.

The paper was well received, and won for the young law student a reputation for mature thought and able expression. His contacts increased and with them his mind widened into a happily liberal outlook, singularly free from narrow prejudices. He had been called to the Bar at the Easter term in 1868, and in September of the same year Pherozeshah sailed for India.

In Bombay it was some time before he could establish himself in the profession he had chosen. Legal practice in those days was almost the exclusive preserve of some half-dozen English barristers of formidable reputation and forbidding mien. But there could be no keeping out such a pugnacious spirit as Pherozeshah's, armed as it was with forensic powers bordering on genius and a pertinacity which knew neither defeat nor fear. Pherozeshah literally fought his way into local practice and by display of eminently capable legal ability soon won the respect of those who were inclined at first to obstruct his entry. As the fame of his advocacy spread briefs poured in from all parts of Gujerat and Kathiawar and further afield till, between travelling to mofussil courts and engagements in his home town, Pherozeshah was the busiest and most prosperous lawyer of the day in the entire Presidency. Offers of judgeships and various other legal incumbencies could not tempt him from his resolve to pursue his profession, even when briefs were rare and his income barely sufficient to enable him to make ends meet by judicious management.

His first notable appearance was in a case which has become one of the classic *causes célèbres* of Bombay legal history, the Parsi Towers of Silence case. His brilliant advocacy in this matter, upon which public attention was concentrated to an unprecedented degree, won him the respect of the hitherto aloof English members of the Bombay Bar and the enthusiastic support of his own wealthy and influential community. The famous Mr. Anstey, with whom Pherozeshah was briefed as junior counsel in the case, remarked of him afterwards that the young man had "all the germs of future eminence in him." The even more sensational Surat Riots case, resulting from the introduction of a new licence tax, clinched his reputation, and after it he had no further need to struggle for forensic success.

His qualities were brought out in more striking degree and his reputation for shrewd judgment and patriotic

AN OLD VIEW OF BOMBAY

When Sir Pherozeshah was a child of eight the first Indian railway was opened at Bombay—the Great Indian Peninsula. Above is the general view of Bombay from Malabar Hill at that time—April, 1853.

FROM MALABAR HILL TO-DAY

Bombay to-day—the second largest Indian cit; d one of the greatest ports in the world. Much of its splendid development it owes to Sir Pherozeshah.

wisdom established still more firmly by the part he played in the acute controversy aroused about this time by the notorious clause of the East India Bill dealing with the right of Indians to enter the Civil Services. The principle laid down by Sir Stafford Northcote in this Bill was devised to overcome the difficulties experienced by Indians desirous of entering the services as a result of the circumstance that the entrance examinations were held exclusively in England. The clause provided for the introduction of a system of selection in appointing Indian aspirants to the services without their having to undergo the examination in open competition. This obnoxious subterfuge, opening the door, as it did, to favouritism and discrimination, aroused Pherozeshah's strong indignation and he poured it forth with unhesitating vehemence. "In itself," he declared, "it embodies a measure of such pernicious tendency that it will sow fruitful seeds of discord between races among whom they are already by far too abundant." Those who know their India to-day can doubtless testify how that prophecy has been fulfilled.

Further evidence of the fearless independence of his character was provided in 1877 when, at a public meeting of the citizens of Bombay specially convened, a resolution was proposed for the formation of a volunteer corps composed exclusively of Europeans. Indignant at the implied slight, Pherozeshah Mehta moved an amendment pointing out that "it is not advisable to resolve on the formation of a volunteer corps composed exclusively of Europeans in a public meeting of the inhabitants of Bombay." In an admirable speech which aroused the admiration of his fellow countrymen and the indignation of the European community, Pherozeshah declared that it was nothing short of a public outrage and an affront to Indian self-respect to convene a meeting of all the communities of the city merely to place before them a resolution for the formation of a corps from which all except Europeans were expressly excluded.

He had held strong views on the need for military training in this country and was a stout opponent of the Arms Act, in regard to which he expressed himself in a manner so admirable that a relevant passage may be appropriately quoted. The speech was delivered at the fourth session of the Indian National Congress at Allahabad in connection with a keenly debated resolution relating to the Arms Act which had been opposed by Telang himself.

Said Pherozeshah:

"You cannot, and ought not to, emasculate a whole nation. It may be said that the time may come in future when these restrictions will be removed. But remember that when once the Indian people become emasculated, it will be a very long time indeed before you can get them to recover their manliness and their vigour. That is my ground for supporting the proposition; and I say it is a practical ground. Perhaps a good many of you remember the case of James II who, when in his hour of peril, appealed to the Duke of Bedford (whose son had been murdered by the King) for help, to whom the old nobleman replied, 'I had once a son whom I could have sent for your assistance. But I have not got him now.' In the same way, in some hour of need India might have to say something similar to England. I entirely recognise all the reasonable, and, to a certain extent, alarming difficulties which have been raised; but I say that, if you strive to follow a really far-sighted policy, you will realise from the lessons of history that it can never be wise to emasculate a nation."

Promising as were these essays of the Bombay Parsi in the wider field of Indian politics and imperialist policies, Pherozeshah clearly regarded them as providing occasion for forays in which his powerfully patriotic spirit found vent and expression rather than as the venue of his life's work. It is not that he did not aspire in the same degree as the other Indian nationalists of his own day, but rather that he saw the vast gap that lay between aspiration and capacity so far as the mass of the Indian people was concerned, and the colossal work of preparation that had to be done before demands could be put forward for political power or emancipation with the elementary but essential justification of fitness for fruitful exercise of such power and liberty.

Another important consideration which appears to have influenced the course of his life and interests at this stage of his career was the need of a steady income. While not extravagant, Pherozeshah's nature demanded comfortable living and professional activity was in consequence a matter of indispensable necessity. This made it virtually impossible for him, from sheer lack of the necessary leisure, to enter the large field of Indian politics in the only manner in which a man of his genius and character could consider doing that. Thus it came about that his powerful personality was projected into the sphere of municipal government. There his masterful nature and practical inspiration soon expressed themselves in a manner for which the City of Bombay must remain eternally grateful. Beyond question the best work of his life was

G.I.P. TERMINUS

The Great Indian Peninsular Station, Bombay, one of the most up-to-date stations in the world.

done in the Corporation of Bombay, to which his friends and admirers later loved to refer as the "Kingdom of Bombay." Of that "Kingdom" Pherozeshah Mehta, for something like forty years, was unquestioned "King."

Some have compared his municipal career in Bombay to that of Joseph Chamberlain's historic service to the city of Birmingham. A truer estimate would rank it considerably higher, since Pherozeshah may be said to have been the father of Bombay's municipal charter, the founder of its glorious tradition of civic efficiency, and its chief guide and mentor in laying down the principles of its municipal administration. So completely did his personality and views govern Bombay's civic life that his presence came to be regarded as indispensable by his fellow councillors as well as by the public whenever any matter of importance was on the *tapis* for discussion, and it became almost a tradition that decisions should go with the views of Pherozeshah Mehta.

He began his municipal career in the early 'seventies, in circumstances that could hardly be regarded as auspicious, with a spirited defence in the face of an angry population of Mr. Arthur Crawford, who as Municipal Commissioner had laid himself open to the charge of reckless expenditure. In the pursuit of municipal ideals and efficiency, which everybody admired, Mr. Crawford, whose name is commemorated in Bombay's chief municipal market, had not paused to consider the trivial matter of the Corporation's financial capacity. Heavy deficits angered the public, which forgot the amenities it enjoyed and heaped abuse upon the Commissioner.

The incident affords striking illustration of Pherozeshah Mehta's fearless independence and far-seeing intelligence. Amid the yells and hisses of an indignant mob which filled the Framjee Cawasjee Hall, he stood up and defended Mr. Crawford and seizing the opportunity to point a moral, laid down a scheme of municipal reform which was later embodied by an approving Government in more elaborate detail in the Municipal Act of 1872. Thus he became the father of municipal government in Bombay. When sixteen years later the Act of 1888 further amended the municipal constitution of Bombay, it was again his handiwork, and it was rightly regarded by the citizens of Bombay as the Magna Charta of their municipal freedom. To put it briefly, by the Act of 1888 Pherozeshah established the principle of the Bombay Corporation's right to manage its own affairs and it became the superior administrative authority in the City's civic life, "the ultimate tribunal whose decision must be final and binding."

In the midst of all this preoccupation in the comparatively restricted sphere of civic affairs, Pherozeshah yet found time for interest in all India issues. When Lord Lytton's Government proposed a reactionary measure for the control of the Press by censorship on the plea that undesirable influence on public opinion was being exercised as a result of "angry recriminations, exaggerated generalisations, pompous historical allusions, petulant expressions of offended vanity or disappointed hopes," he characterised the measure as offensive in the highest degree, unnecessarily repressive and contrary to all principles of good government. Happily, Lord Lytton's successor, Lord Ripon, was a man of different mould and this fine English gentleman, one of the best Viceroys who ever ruled in India, did all in his power to undo or mitigate the harsh effects of his predecessor's regime. His greatest contribution to Indian progress was the introduction of a scheme of local self-government, a beneficent measure which has rightly earned the country's

CENTRE OF INDIAN COMMERCE
A scene in the busy modern city of Bombay.

lasting gratitude. It won unstinted admiration from Pherozeshah Mehta, who saw in it the first step towards ideals long cherished by him for the political development of India. In grateful recognition Pherozeshah Mehta joined with other Indian leaders in getting up a memorial for extension of Lord Ripon's regime as Viceroy. The petition, however, was ignored.

Two guiding principles inspired Pherozeshah Mehta throughout his long political career; firstly, that British rule was the best possible thing that could have happened to India; and secondly, that it was essential for the better administration of India that Indian affairs should become a party issue in the British Parliament.

In regard to the former he once declared, "If I entertain one political conviction more than another, it is that this country in falling under British rule has fallen into the hands of a nation than which no other is better qualified to govern her well and wisely." In the course of his presidential address at the Calcutta session of the Indian National Congress in 1890 he said again:

> "I have no fears but that English statesmanship will ultimately respond to the call. I have unbounded faith in the living and fertilising principles of English culture and English civilisation. It may be that at times the prospect may look dark and gloomy. If the interests of the services are antagonistic to and prevail over the interests of the Indian people, it is still only one side of the shield. All the great forces of English life and society, moral, social, intellectual,

political, are, if slowly, yet steadily and irresistibly, declaring themselves for the choice which will make the connection of England and India a blessing to themselves and to the whole world, for countless generations."

"England," he said again, "must raise India to her own level or India will drag her down to hers."

In the year 1885, Pherozeshah Mehta and his friends in Bombay felt the need for a political organisation that could express their thought, and the Bombay Presidency Association was born. He was its first president and remained in that capacity till he died. In the year of its birth the Congress held its first session in Bombay under the presidency of Pherozeshah Mehta's old friend and companion in England, W. C. Bonnerjee.

Of the Congress itself, which had its birth in this City, Pherozeshah Mehta was a member from the very beginning. He presided, as we have seen, over its fifth session in Calcutta and in his address made a striking plea for the expansion of provincial councils on an electoral basis. Fifteen years later, as Chairman of the Reception Committee for the second Bombay session of the Congress under Sir Henry Cotton's presidency, Pherozeshah made a spirited defence of expenditure, amounting to some fifty thousand rupees on the Congress Camp, which had been adversely criticised by a section of Congressmen. In reply to the charge that it was money wasted on a *tamasha* he declared that "there is no purpose more important, no mission more sacred than the one which Congress fulfils in the three short days to which it confines its session," adding that the purpose of that session, "to present our petition of rights, our appeal and our prayer for a policy of wisdom and righteousness, for several of retrograde measures inconsistent with such a policy, and for the adoption of means steadily ensuring the gradual development of free political progress, broadening slowly down from precedent to precedent" more than justified the expenditure. "If we did nothing more than make this petition and prayer we shall not have spent our monies in vain," he concluded.

In 1886 Lord Reay appointed Pherozeshah a member of the Bombay Legislative Council, a position of which he availed himself to push through Bombay's civic charter, the Municipal Act of 1888. He remained a member of the Provincial Legislature till his death and evinced such practical wisdom seasoned with criticism that was invariably so constructive and reasonable that the Government, his colleagues as well as the public, regarded his services as of the utmost value. Fearless in defence of popular interests and in the expression of his views, a trenchant critic of official policy, he did not hedge his enthusiasm with reservations when he found occasion to praise the administration.

He frequently came into violent conflict with official policy. One of the most memorable of these occasions occurred in connection with the Bombay Land Revenue Bill, which he opposed with all his strength and eloquence. When he found that the Government were resolved to carry the measure through, he created a sensation by walking out of the Chamber. This dramatic, and at that time unprecedented, step raised a furore in the Press, and Pherozeshah defended his action in three brilliant letters which he wrote to *The Times of India*, that journal having led the attack against him.

When in 1892 Provincial Councils were enlarged on the elective basis, Pherozeshah Mehta was the first non-official member in the whole country to be returned—he was unanimously chosen by the Bombay Corporation, which he continued to represent as long as he lived. Brilliant as was his career in every arena of public life, it was no surprise to anybody when in the year 1893 the Bombay Legislative Council exercised its right to send one representative to the Supreme Legislative Council by choosing Pherozeshah Mehta for that post of honourable burden. It was a happy choice. His forensic fame, the brilliant services he had rendered to the City of Bombay, his position of commanding power in its civic affairs, his admirable discourses in the Congress which had won universal recognition as examples of statesmanlike sagacity, his work in the Bombay Council and the great reputation he enjoyed for personal integrity of character and fearless independence, had combined to establish him as an all-India personality, the most commanding figure of his day in the country. His election was hailed as likely to be highly beneficial to the Government as well as to the country. This was in 1893. The following year he was awarded a C.I.E. in the New Year Honours List—a distinction which was hailed even by his critics as a fitting honour well bestowed. One vernacular paper regarded it as "a crumb thrown to the Congress party." Referring to it *The Times of India*, which was one of his stoutest critics, remarked: "Mr. Mehta has of late shown an increasing independence of the reckless rhetoricians who pretend to serve their country by embarrassing and abusing the men who are governing it, and we may be sure he always will be an outspoken as well as an able critic of the Government both here and in the Supreme Council."

RESIDENTIAL QUARTERS

Modern flats and houses on Malabar Hills, Bombay.

In that body Pherozeshah appears to have found the proper *métier* for the expression of his towering genius, and all who remember his career in the Viceregal Council are agreed that he achieved his most brilliant political expression there. His outspoken views and trenchant criticisms did not always find favour with the Government, but they inspired a wholesome respect for popular interests in the mind of a bureaucracy accustomed till then to have its own way without protest or dispute. The officials of that august body were not accustomed to such plain speaking as they got from the honourable member for Bombay; and Pherozeshah was charged with introducing "a new spirit" into the Chamber. His condemnation of the notorious Police Bill, a piece of legislation of a most reprehensibly repressive character, as a piece of legislation than which he could not conceive anything "more empirical, more retrograde, more open to abuse, or more demoralising" delighted his admirers and nationalists generally throughout the country, and aroused in equal proportion the ire of its promoter, Sir Antony MacDonnell. Pherozeshah did introduce a new spirit into the Viceregal Council, a spirit which refused to echo official views, to support dumbly official policies and which actually presumed to criticise and condemn them. Among his most memorable utterances in any legislature were three budget speeches he delivered in the Supreme Legislative Council—the first particularly, which made history with its masterly criticism of the financial policy of the "most distinguished service in the world."

One other field in which he laboured long and fruitfully was the Bombay University Senate. As we have seen, he displayed keen interest in education even as a young man and as his power and influence grew, he spared no endeavour to fight the battle of education in the Bombay Council and in the Imperial Council too. His budget speeches invariably contained demands for more expenditure on education which he declared was India's primary, principal and most urgent necessity.

Though not personally connected in any way with individual enterprise, Pherozeshah Mehta was an ardent advocate of *Swadeshi* long before the movement was born, and in company with some friends, including Telang, started a soap factory. Despite solicitous attention from its originators, however, the enterprise came to an untimely end, Pherozeshah humorously remarking of it afterwards that it was a case of self-sacrifice in a good cause, for they lost every pie they had put into it.

His brilliant services in so many fields of national endeavour naturally earned him the esteem and gratitude of his countrymen, as well as official recognition. Public addresses were voted to him by the citizens of Bombay and Calcutta in 1895, the Bombay Corporation elected him to two successive terms as its President in 1884 and 1885—a distinction which remains unique in the annals of that body—and in 1905, the year of the visit to this country of the Prince of Wales, the Bombay Corporation manifested its gratitude and esteem once again by electing him President for that year too. That year was crowned by the conferment upon him by His Majesty the King Emperor of the title of Knight Commander of the Indian Empire. It was a signal honour, and opinion was unanimous that it was richly deserved by one whose record of public and national service was so uniformly brilliant, whose merit towered in eminence that dominated the whole country.

About this time elements of hostility began to make their first appearance against this great public servant. In

1907 a certain Mr. Harrison resolved with European support to bring about Sir Pherozeshah Mehta's defeat at the municipal elections. At the same time extremists in Congress circles initiated a movement against his moderate counsels and prudent leadership. Mr. Harrison's notorious caucus failed, but left behind it a trail of embittered feelings which lasted many years. The extremists' move resulted in the breaking up of the Congress session held that year at Surat—but failed to shift the organisation's adherence from the policy and principles enunciated by Sir Pherozeshah Mehta, who continued to dominate the counsels of the Congress throughout his lifetime. This outstanding dominance —it came to be said that the fear of Mehta was the beginning of wisdom in the Congress—placed him in a position of peculiar responsibility, particularly in the regime of such a Governor as Lord Sydenham. He had on the one hand to keep his countrymen within the bounds of loyal agitation, and on the other to retain in sufficient degree the confidence of official authority. However, his tremendous personality and a reputation established by years of wise counsel, unquestionable patriotism and proved service, helped him to steer clear of shoals on either side and it is a real tribute to his genius for leadership that not only did the Congress accept his principles after the Surat incident, but that Lord Morley, then Viceroy, was persuaded to adopt a policy of encouragement towards the reconstituted Congress.

It was largely the influence of his views which determined the nature of the now historic Morley-Minto Reforms, and it is worth noting in passing that the changes introduced as a result of that instalment of political enlargement in

WHERE THE PEOPLE OF BOMBAY GATHER

A general view of the bandstand and the car park and traffic island.

India, vindicated fully the wisdom and practical nature of Pherozeshah Mehta's lifelong advocacy of trust in the essential honesty of the British people.

Sir Pherozeshah now tended to abstention from Congress politics and the nationalist movement generally, doubtless because he found widening divergence in its outlook from views which he held very strongly. He continued, however, to express himself with all his old force and eloquence on matters of public import, and among other utterances put forth a strong condemnation of the principle of communal representation introduced by the newly enacted Morley-Minto Reforms.

Two years later, in 1913, he made a notable pronouncement on the treatment of Indians in South Africa, which had induced Mr. Gandhi to start the passive resistance struggle that launched him on his road to mahatmic fame and all-India leadership surpassing any dictatorship in history.

Sir Pherozeshah Mehta always displayed a peculiarly jealous regard for the rights of Indians abroad, far in excess of even Mr. Gandhi's zeal, for it is well known that he did not approve at all of the settlement of the South African dispute with which Mr. Gandhi was satisfied. Sir Pherozeshah roundly declared that there could be no compromise on the principle that Indians must have the open door throughout the Empire, and he maintained that there could be no justification whatever for any part of the British Empire to deny to other parts the right of equal citizenship pertaining by Royal proclamation to all subjects of the Crown.

In 1910 he proceeded on holiday to England and spent several months renewing innumerable old friendships, making new associations, seizing opportunity to meet the official arbiters of Indian affairs and to express, with all his firm brilliance, the Indian points of view on all the issues of the day.

On his return to India he continued to display the same zeal in all matters of public importance, but ill-health curtailed much of his personal activity in these fields. He appeared, however, before the Public Services Commission and gave evidence which that body seems to have valued highly. The appointment of Lord Willingdon as Governor of Bombay now enabled the tried veteran to exercise a wholesome influence in the administration of the Province to the development of which he had contributed so fruitfully. Lord Willingdon made it a practice to consult him on every public matter and appointed him Vice-Chancellor of Bombay University, which in its turn honoured him with the Degree of Doctor of Laws.

One of his last contributions to the life of Bombay was the establishment of an English daily newspaper owned, staffed and managed entirely by Indians—with a view doubtless to providing a wholesome corrective to popular as well as official opinion against the views and influence of the Anglo-Indian organs. *The Bombay Chronicle* thus came to birth in 1913, and on its front page it still acknowledges its debt to the man to whom it owes its origin by stating that it was "Founded by Sir Pherozeshah Mehta in 1913."

The first issue of *The Bombay Chronicle* came out in April, 1913, and the paper made rapid headway under the powerful patronage of Sir Pherozeshah and his friends. Mehta, in particular, took the keenest interest in the journal and even went to the length of personally managing its affairs.

Two years earlier Sir Pherozeshah Mehta had helped to found the Central Bank of India with similar objectives as inspired the founding of *The Bombay Chronicle*, namely, the provision of a

MEMORIAL TO SIR PHEROZESHAH MEHTA

The fine statue of this great civic benefactor by Derwent Wood. It stands in front of the Bombay Municipal Buildings.

purely Indian banking house, financed, staffed, managed and controlled by exclusively Indian interests. These activities, it is hardly necessary to point out, were in keeping with his life-long ideal of *swadeshi*. The Bank's first director was a young Parsi who had already displayed conspicuous ability in European banking houses, Mr. S. N. Pochkhanawala. Under his driving power and ambitious planning the Central Bank prospered rapidly and when two years later a severe financial crisis developed out of wild orgies of speculation and overwhelmed the Credit and Specie Banks, ruining innumerable persons and businesses, the Central Bank was one of the few banking houses to weather that disastrous storm. Its subsequent development under the direction of Mr. Pochkhanawala made banking history in India and when its able Manager was honoured with a knighthood a few years ago, the Indian financial and commercial world acclaimed the event as richly merited. When Sir Sorabji Pochkhanawala died in 1938, the Central Bank was well established as one of the soundest institutions of the kind found anywhere in the world to-day and one of the foremost in India. Nobody would have been more pleased by this happy fulfilment of a dream than Sir Pherozeshah, who was responsible more than any other individual for its foundation, who watched over its first years with the anxious care of a father for his first-born and who regarded it as the foundation, guarantee and nursery of all his *swadeshi* dreams and ambitions.

Two years later he invited the

EXTENDING THE CITY

The Oval and part of the new town-planning scheme to relieve overcrowding. In the background is Bombay's business centre.

Congress to Bombay and secured the consent of Sir S. P. Sinha, who had not yet been raised to the peerage, to preside over it. Arrangements were well under way for holding the session when on November 5 Sir Pherozeshah Mehta passed away, after having been ill for some time.

A statue erected out of public subscription at a cost of Rs80,000 stands in front of the Municipal building to commemorate the services of this great man to the city and people of Bombay. Lord Hardinge, then Viceroy, paid a singular tribute to him in a telegram to Lord Willingdon:

"I should like," he said, "to associate myself with the people of Bombay who are meeting to-day to express their grief at the loss of Sir Pherozeshah Mehta. He was a great Parsi, a great citizen, a great patriot and a great Indian." A fitting epitaph, indeed!

Those who are interested in the life of this great Indian and would like to study it in fuller detail should read the excellent biography in two volumes written by Sir H. P. Mody.

MOHANDAS KARAMCHAND GANDHI

MOHANDAS KARAMCHAND GANDHI

GREATEST FIGURE IN MODERN INDIA

BORN 1869

BY H. S. L. and M. G. POLAK

PART I. INDIA AND SOUTH AFRICA—PREPARATION

IN every period of man's activity there have appeared significant figures to whom history later points as the leaders of a new age. Such men are dynamic, purposeful, prophetic and dangerous to the established order and habit of their time.

Such a figure is Mohandas Karamchand Gandhi, known to the world as Mahatma Gandhi, born on October 2, 1869, in the small state of Porbandar, Western India, where his grandfather, father, and elder brother were prime ministers. His father later became prime minister of the Kathiawar States of Rajkot (to which Mohandas was taken as a boy of seven) and Vankaner.

Mohandas was the youngest child of a large family. Though well known and influential, it was of humble stock. Unlike many of his distinguished contemporaries, Mohandas Gandhi came not from the first, or Brahman, caste of Hindus, but from the Bania sub-caste of the third, or Vaisya, caste. Nor were the Gandhis in any way noted for scholarship. Kaba Gandhi, the father of Mohandas, "had no education, save that of experience." In his academic education Mohandas never went beyond the matriculation examination of London University. For his mother he had a beautiful and steadfast love. Her gentleness of character, her natural wisdom and her deep religious sense made a profound impression upon him from his earliest years. Probably this love was one of the deepest emotions of his life and gave him the tenderness that is so much a part of his otherwise Spartan disposition. It was in this background that his early years were spent.

Following the custom of his day and country, he was betrothed when he was seven, and was married at thirteen, to a girl slightly younger. Although still children they shared the same sleeping room, and as soon as the boy was physically capable, consummation of the marriage took place, much to his own horror and disgust in later years. His reactions to that period of his life, with its tormenting unrest, brought a strong antipathy to the expression of sex-life. When the fires of early manhood had died down, he vowed himself to celibacy for self-discipline, a fact that coloured all the after years. He fully believed that his child-wife was his own to mould as he liked, irrespective of what she herself desired. Fortunately she possessed a personality and a will not easily subdued to his pattern, and she has always retained some peculiar quality and an independence of her own.

Being of a Vaishnava family, largely influenced by Jainism, he was strictly vegetarian. Yet, as a youth, he was tempted secretly to eat meat and so break the caste-rules; and this for two reasons. The first was his own delicacy of physique and an intense desire to become a strong, healthy man. The second was his earnest desire for India

GANDHI AS A YOUTH
Mohandas Gandhi as a boy of about seventeen when he first went to England.

it is of the very essence of the Divine in man. Though he saw deceit and falsehood all around him, and knew that it was accepted as the standard of life by people occupying positions of authority and influence, he was never afterwards tempted to yield to it, even when to have done so would have brought advantage and no condemnation.

For healing he always had a great love and some aptitude, and when, at the age of seventeen, his family in conclave suggested his going to England to study law, he begged to be allowed to study medicine instead. This, however, was not permitted; law was chosen for him. But the love of healing remained, and though he could not study in the orthodox schools of medicine, he gratified his desire by studying various forms of Nature-cure treatment and by experimenting with these on his own person and on his friends and relatives. Some of these experiments produced remarkable results, possibly not only

to be a free and forceful nation. He reasoned within himself, after listening to the talk of other young people around him, that Englishmen walked over the land as conquerors; they had power to command others; they were meat-eaters; therefore, if India wished to free herself from the domination of the foreigner, she must cultivate strength; and meat-eating was the first step in this direction.

The taste of flesh was, however, obnoxious, and flesh-eating soon ended. But he had done more than break his caste-rules. For the first and last time he consciously lied.

Gandhi has repeatedly called himself a Truth-seeker and has learned, in the course of his search, that truth is a condition of being, not a quality outside of oneself or a moral acquisition; that

THE YOUNG MAN
A picture of India's future leader taken in his early twenties.

MR. AND MRS. GANDHI

An early photograph taken in their home of Mohandas Gandhi and the wife he married as a child.

due to the treatment, but to his devoted and instinctive nursing.

One such striking case was his cure of two plague patients in South Africa, when twenty others, who were treated by the orthodox methods, died. Another equally remarkable cure was that of his wife, who in middle life developed pernicious anæmia and was given up by the doctors as a hopeless case, unless recourse could be had to meat juices and other special treatment. This being refused, the doctor in attendance left the case, and Gandhi's Nature-cure methods were resorted to. Soon an improvement in the general condition of the patient was noticed, the treatment continued, and she recovered. Before leaving India for his studies abroad his mother persuaded him to take a solemn vow before a Jain monk never to touch wine, women, or meat. This vow he kept religiously despite the many temptations that were thrust upon him.

His first days in England were an agony; he was homesick and unhappy. Everything was strange—the people, the houses, the method of life, the idiom of the language and, worst of all, the food. He felt an intense longing for home and its familiar sights, sounds, and smells. But to have returned straightway, as his misery tempted him to do, would be an impossible act of cowardice. So he suffered and endured. Frequently starving himself, so as to be sure that he did not betray his vow, he gradually settled down, made some friends, started his studies, and set himself to acquire some of the so-called accomplishments of polite society. He reclothed himself, adopting the dress of the day—even to the extent of investing in a silk hat. Strange how clothes have played a symbolic part in the life of this man! He has never just accepted clothes, but used them as an indication of an inner conviction. In after years, having identified himself with the poor, in whose face he sees God, he has worn the peasant's loin-cloth.

SOUTH AFRICA, 1906

Mohandas Gandhi as a Sergeant-Major of the Indian Volunteer Stretcher Bearer Corps, organised by him in Natal during the Zulu rebellion.

He tried to learn to dance, but had no ear for rhythm and, failing in his attempt, gave it up. He also tried to learn to play the violin, but he was not, and never has been, an artist, except in the art of life itself; and he soon abandoned the bow and strings. He turned his attention to dietetics, always, of course, along vegetarian or fruitarian lines, and became, both in England and later in South Africa, an ardent propagandist.

In studying these early years of Gandhi's life, it becomes easier to understand his later developments. One can see in them all the seeds that later flow-

TRANSVAAL OFFICE

M. K. Gandhi with some of his South African supporters outside his own office in the Transvaal in 1905.

ered into full bloom. His innate love of truth, desire for the freedom of his Motherland, love of simple things and simple people, passion for purity even to austerity, tried courage, and quiet moral strength—all these qualities were struggling within him to find suitable expression in a field of labour big enough to call them into play.

Of his law studies, little need be said. He was a conscientious worker, read the prescribed books, and was duly called to the Bar by the Inner Temple, which later disbarred him because of his conviction in the Indian civil disobedience movement. He never applied for reinstatement. His studies completed, he returned to India. On his arrival at Bombay he was greeted with the tragic news that his mother had been dead some little while. The news had been kept from him so as not to render him unhappy whilst alone in a strange land. Overwhelmed by grief, for a time he felt that the background of his life had collapsed. To add to his distress, his caste people excommunicated him because of his journeying to a foreign land, and, though he performed the usual ceremonial purification rites, orthodox prejudice kept him outside the caste-fold. This caste denial left no resentment; rather, it taught him how artificial were the barriers of caste, and he came to realise intensely the cruelty of seeking to restrict human fellowship. He gained strength from his tribulations.

After some hesitation and anxiety he commenced practice in the Bombay courts. His first case was a trial, not so much of his knowledge and ability as of his courage. To speak in public had always been an ordeal for him, and now to have to conduct a case, even the placing of the bare facts of it before the Court, was more than he could do. He rose to speak, but became tongue-tied. Baffled, he begged to be relieved of his case and hastened from the Court in shame and anguish, vowing never to appear again until he had learned to master himself and could use his brain and body as the instruments of his will. The family fortunes were too slender to allow him to stand apart and study the art of advocacy; he felt compelled to earn money, and he returned to Rajkot to assist his brother in a small legal business already established. There his wife gave birth to their first living child. Gandhi, however, was not destined for a life set in a normal key, and soon the call came to him to move on.

It is interesting to glance back over the lives of great men and to see how circumstances, apparently insignificant in themselves, take them in hand and compel them to a desired end. They seem almost to be a plaything in the hands of a Player; but the Player knows the end of the game, the plaything only obeys the urge that so often seems blindly to move him forward.

The first great period of Gandhi's adult life, covering the years 1893 to 1914, now opens. A small hurt to self-esteem, a disappointment in Porbandar, the offer of a commission to go to South Africa for a year to represent professionally an Indian firm which had an important case pending in the South African Republic, and the first step was taken upon his path of destiny.

Of South Africa and its problems he knew practically nothing. His political sense had not as yet been developed, and of the position of Indians there he had never thought. His clients were wealthy, and he may have believed that South Africa was a land of sunshine and plenty.

He arrived in Durban in 1893, having no reason to expect other than good and decent treatment. Though he had had a foretaste of racial arrogance in India, it was not until he arrived in South Africa that he felt its full force and understood the grave nature of the colour-bar, that even yet prevails there. It is not, therefore, surprising to find that, having made some study of the disabilities and grievances of his countrymen in Natal and the neighbouring Republic, he was prevailed upon by them (when his professional task was completed to the satisfaction of both parties) to stay in Durban and help them to secure redress and improve their status.

He made it a condition that he should receive no payment for his public work, but asked for his countrymen's support in his legal practice, if they had confidence in his professional ability. Throughout his stay in South Africa, and until he renounced practice in 1908 in order to devote himself entirely to the service of his countrymen there, he enjoyed to the full the confidence of a large *clientèle*, but always he devoted a considerable proportion of his earnings to charity and to the public needs of the Indian community.

Of his professional work he says: "I realised that the true function of a lawyer was to unite parties riven asunder. The lesson was so indelibly burnt into me, that a large part of my time during the twenty years of my practice as a lawyer was occupied in bringing about private compromises of hundreds of cases. I lost nothing thereby—not even money, certainly not my soul."

The Indians had originally been taken from the United Provinces, Bihar and Madras (mostly Hindus), to South Africa in 1860, under indenture, at a time when the Colony of Natal was threatened with bankruptcy through an inadequate supply of native African

MAKING SALT

Salt preparing on Gandhi day at the Chaupatty Shore—a symbolic gesture instigated by the Mahatma.

SPINNING KHADDAR

One of Gandhi's followers spinning the Indian cotton-cloth, whose use he advocated rather than foreign materials.

labour. The economic situation had been saved and prosperity had been restored and largely increased through the labours of these indentured Indians, in whose wake and primarily to supply whose needs, upon the insistence of the Government of India, there had followed in due course, at first from Mauritius and later from Bombay, Gujarati merchants and traders (mostly Moslems). All alike were denied citizenship rights and were dubbed contemptuously "coolies" (Gandhi himself being known as "the coolie lawyer") by the white colonists.

In the course of time some of these Indians had entered the South African Republic. At first no difficulties had been raised but, as time passed, trade jealousy, aided by colour prejudice, resulted in "anti-Asiatic" legislation and administrative practice by the Boer Government, involving race-segregation and the denial to Indians of civil rights enjoyed by the white immigrants. The British Government constantly protested to the Boer authorities against their anti-Indian policy. It is conceivable that Gandhi may have, all unconsciously, received his first suggestions regarding the method of civil disobedience when, the Boer Government having refused to issue any more trading licences to Indians, the British Agent at Pretoria recommended them to tender the licence-fees and, if the licences were still refused, to trade without them. Later, when the Government threatened to prosecute for trading without licences, the British Agent warmly approved of the advice given to the traders to pay no bail or fines, but to go to jail.

During this time repeated representations, many of them drafted by Gandhi himself, were made by the Indian community against this oppression, and it is on record that the Indian grievances against the Republican Government were included in the British *casus belli*, Lord Lansdowne declaring at Sheffield, in 1899: "Among the many misdeeds of the South African Republic I do not know that any fills me with more indignation than its treatment of these Indians."

In Natal, where Gandhi had founded and was actively working as the Hon. Secretary of the Natal Indian Congress, the situation was not much better under responsible government. He was largely instrumental in inducing the Colonial Office, under Mr. Joseph Chamberlain, to refuse acceptance of the Asiatics' Exclusion Act, passed by the Natal Legislature, on account of its breach of the Imperial policy against racial legislation; but he and his countrymen could not prevent the virtual disfranchisement of the Indian population (excepting the few already on the voters' roll) on the ground that they did not enjoy the franchise in India.

Soon a strong anti-Indian movement was in full swing in the colony, and he was accordingly deputed to go to India in 1896 to represent the Indian grievances to the Government and people. Partly because of misrepresentations in the Natal press of his activities and partly because of the circulation of a report that the ships bringing him and a number of Indian indentured labourers to South Africa in the following year were carrying large numbers of skilled workers from India to take the place of white workers, an unruly demonstration was made against him on arrival at Durban; he was physically assaulted, and he escaped with difficulty in a policeman's uniform.

When the Boer War began, in 1899, Gandhi, loyal British subject and proud of the British connection, reminded his countrymen that, if they demanded rights, they must also bear responsibilities. The Indian community accordingly offered their services in any capacity, however menial, and at last,

WALKING ON THE SEASHORE

The Mahatma in a light-hearted mood taking his daily exercise. He is accompanied as is usual by a small boy whom he is prodding playfully with his stick.

against great opposition, induced the military authorities to accept an Indian Ambulance Corps, whose principal leader was Gandhi. Though the authorities did not require the Corps to enter the firing-line, it repeatedly did so in the great emergency that arose, and Gandhi records that it carried from the field of Chieveley the body of Lord Roberts' son. The Indian contribution to the campaign was praised by General Buller and widely appreciated, even by former political opponents. Gandhi and the other Indian leaders received medals for their services when the Corps was disbanded.

In 1901 Gandhi, refusing costly gifts from his compatriots, returned to India for reasons of health, with the intention of settling in Bombay. But Fate willed otherwise. When, a few months later, Mr. Chamberlain went out to South Africa to lay down the lines of permanent settlement of the British-Boer controversy, the Natal Indian community called urgently to Gandhi to return in order to help them to make the necessary representations on their behalf for citizenship rights. He responded from a strong sense of duty and led the Indian deputation to Mr. Chamberlain. Shortly afterwards, when the Colonial Secretary went to the Transvaal, Gandhi was summoned there by the Indian settlers, whose representation he drafted and, at their request, he settled in practice in Johannesburg, where he felt that he could be of the maximum service to his compatriots. To their dismay they found that not only was the Boer anti-Indian legislation and administration—against which the British Government before the war had so energetically protested—maintained; it was tightened up and added to under the Crown Colony *régime*.

In order to protect the community against inroads upon their few remaining rights, Gandhi helped to set up the Transvaal British Indian Association, of which he became the Hon. Secretary and the draftsman of its many powerful memorials. The Association had repeatedly drawn attention to the neglect by the Johannesburg Municipality of sanitary conditions in the Indian location, where the majority of the Indians resided. When, therefore, in 1904, plague broke out there, Gandhi refused to allow the major responsibility for the outbreak to be thrust upon his countrymen and demanded that it should be placed where it properly belonged. Closing his office he devoted himself to sanitary work and evacuation and to the nursing of the victims, for which he received the acknowledgment of the medical officer of health.

But the mischief was done. In addition to the generally prevalent anti-Asiatic prejudice, trade-jealousy was aroused once more by the distribution of a large part of the Indian trading population from the burnt-out Johannesburg Location to other towns in the Transvaal, creating the impression of an "Asiatic invasion." Pressure was now brought to bear by the white trading community upon the authorities to protect the Colony from this "invasion," and, in due course, the anti-Indian campaign bore fruit.

Two events of importance at this stage of Gandhi's career occurred. The first was his taking over of the full financial responsibility for the International Printing Press and the weekly newspaper, *Indian Opinion*, to which he had already generously contributed by both purse and pen. The paper became an invaluable propaganda organ for the South African Indian population and for Gandhi's own views on matters affecting it. Towards the end of 1904 he had transferred both the press and the paper to the Phœnix settlement, near Durban, which he had established as the result of his conversion to the Ruskin ideal of the "simple life" after reading "Unto This Last." He had already made deep studies of the Sermon on the Mount and the *Bhagavad Gita*, and had been much influenced by Tolstoy's writings. Here he set up a little colony of Indian and European friends and colleagues who lived and worked happily together in public service. During the later Passive Resistance struggle the paper helped greatly, under Gandhi's guidance and inspiration, to preserve unity among his countrymen, to encourage the Hindu-Mohammedan collaboration for which he has always stood, and to explain to the outside world the motives underlying the struggle and its objective.

In 1906 there occurred the Native Rebellion in Natal. In this new emergency the Indian community, under Gandhi's leadership, offered a stretcher-bearer company to the Government, who accepted it, with Gandhi as its sergeant-major. The company rendered valuable service and upon its disbandment at the end of the rebellion the community received the warm thanks of the Government.

In 1902 the Transvaal Government, upon an assurance to the Indian community that this would be the final identification requirement, had induced the leaders to agree to the exchange of the old Boer residential licence receipts for immigration permits to male Indians bearing the owner's right thumb impression.

Scarcely, however, had Gandhi returned to Johannesburg after the rebellion, than a draft ordinance was published, cancelling, in breach of Lord Milner's earlier undertaking, the permits issued to the Asiatic settlers. It required

THE WOMAN'S SIDE

Mrs. M. Sanger and the Mahatma discussing problems connected with Indian women's social welfare.

men and women alike to satisfy the authorities afresh of their *bona fides*, by making application for certificates of registration bearing a full set of finger impressions, previously demanded only of convicted prisoners.

A mass meeting of protest was held in Johannesburg, which he addressed and which, at Gandhi's instance, took an oath to adopt Passive Resistance and to go to jail rather than accept a law that was regarded as an insult to the Indian community and to the Motherland. As a result of energetic representations the Indian leaders secured the exclusion of women from the proposed legislation, but they failed to persuade the Government to drop the measure, which was ultimately passed by the Legislative Council. As the ordinance was of a differential character, it was reserved for the royal assent.

With a view to prevent this, Gandhi and a colleague were sent to England as a deputation. In consequence of their activities in London, the South Africa British Indian Committee was set up there, with Lord Ampthill as its president, and in the end the royal assent was refused.

This result, whilst welcomed as a great victory for right and justice by the South African Indian community and by the public in India, was deeply resented by the white population of the Transvaal. Within a few months responsible Government was accorded to the Colony, and the first important measure passed by the new legislature was the almost textual re-enactment of the disallowed ordinance. The royal assent was, notwithstanding the strong protests of the Indian community and of the Government of India, given in view of the new constitutional status of the Colony, and the historic Passive Resistance Campaign was immediately launched by the Indian community under Gandhi's guidance. Gandhi and a number of other leaders were arrested, convicted and imprisoned; but the campaign continued to gather force, until the Botha Government decided to negotiate with Gandhi through General Smuts, the Minister of the Interior. An agreement was reached, upon the basis of voluntary registration. According to Gandhi's statement to his compatriots immediately upon his release and uncontradicted at the time by the authorities, when the voluntary registration was successfully completed the "Black Act" (No. 2 of 1907) was to be repealed, and the voluntary registration certificates were to be validated.

A few of his countrymen failed to appreciate the subtle distinction between the voluntary and the compulsory giving of finger impressions and charged him with betrayal of the cause, threatening his life if he attempted to register. Undeterred, he was proceeding to the registration office to be the first to do so when he was set upon by a Pathan and nearly killed. Upon regaining consciousness, however, and before receiving medical attention, he made his application, thus rallying his compatriots.

The dismay of Gandhi and his people, therefore, was great when, at the end of the period fixed for voluntary re-registration, which was duly completed, the Government introduced and passed new legislation validating the voluntary certificates and giving them equal effect to the few that had been issued under the "Black Act," but omitting all provision for repeal of that Act. At a public meeting, held in Johannesburg, the new Act was denounced, the voluntary certificates were consigned to the flames, and Passive Resistance was renewed in July, 1908. Many hundreds of Indians (including Gandhi repeatedly, as well as his wife and other members of his family) suffered imprisonment, and many Indian homes and businesses were broken up. The struggle did not actually cease until June, 1914, when, after many fluctuations of fortune, the "Black Act" was finally repealed, as was the £3 annual tax upon ex-indentured Indians in Natal; Indian marriages, upon whose validity the courts had cast doubt, were legalised for immigration purposes; and the status of the Indian community was, for the time being, at least stabilised.

Three episodes in particular stand out in the campaign. The first was Gandhi's second mission to England, in 1909, upon his return from which he published his confession of faith in a pamphlet entitled "Hind Swaraj" or "Indian Home Rule." A parallel mission carried on propaganda in India, under the guidance of Mr. G. K. Gokhale, gaining support from Government and public alike, and resulting in the stoppage of indentured labour for Natal in 1910 and in a strong protest in 1913, by the Viceroy, Lord Hardinge, against the Indian treatment in South Africa.

The second was the great march into the Transvaal, led by Gandhi, in 1913, of Natal Indian indentured labourers, to court imprisonment as a protest against the failure of the Union Government to carry out its undertaking to Mr. Gokhale, during his visit to South Africa in 1912, to repeal the £3 tax.

The third was Gandhi's refusal, when he was on the point of resuming the struggle because of General Smuts' unwillingness to introduce the necessary remedial legislation, to take advantage of the Government's embarrassment during the general strike of European workers in the Transvaal, early in 1914.

Finally, won over by the passive resisters, by Gandhi's able advocacy of Indian rights, and by the representations of a high official deputed by the Government of India to assist in a settlement, the long drawn-out struggle was brought to an end, and Gandhi, amid the applause and with the goodwill of all sections, of the population, European and Indian, felt at last free to return to the Motherland to begin the public work for which his soul had long thirsted.

ROUND TABLE CONFERENCE, 1931

Mahatma Gandhi leaving St. James' Palace with other Indian Delegates.

DURING THE DISCUSSION

The scene inside St. James' Palace. Lord Sankey is in the chair. Mahatma Gandhi on his left and Pandit Malaviva next to him.

Part II. The Mahatma

He went first to England, arriving there on the eve of the outbreak of the Great War. Immediately he set himself to the task of organising among the resident Indian community an Ambulance Corps for service at the Front. But ill health prevented his accompanying it and, upon his recovery, he was obliged to proceed to India, where he arrived, in 1915, just before the death of Gokhale.

Soon after his arrival, and in pursuance of a promise made to Gokhale, Gandhi began a year's tour of his Motherland, after an absence of fourteen years. His overseas work against powerful odds and his great personal sacrifices had already established him firmly in the hearts and imagination of his countrymen, many of whom endowed him with the qualities of a superman, and the title of Mahatma (Great Soul) was conferred upon him by the people.

Gandhi's first work after the tour was to establish near Ahmedabad an Ashram, or retreat, where a little group of men and women settled who had accepted his general principles. Here were tried out the methods of the simple collective life that had been begun in South Africa, without restrictions of class, creed, or caste. Soon a problem arose that tested the fundamental tenets of the settlement—some untouchables sought admission to it. Gandhi consulted his followers and it was agreed that the untouchables should not be refused. As a result, the financial support of the orthodox, upon which the Ashram had greatly depended, was withdrawn, and he found himself without resources. When he realised this, he declared: "We will then have to leave here and live in the untouchable quarter with them." However, the situation was saved by a timely anonymous gift that enabled him to continue his work.

Meanwhile the agitation against indentured labour emigration to British colonies overseas had been steadily growing and its suspension was demanded. Gandhi, who had in South Africa fought the system, which had been denounced by Sir W. W. Hunter as "semi-slavery," now led the attack upon it once more, as degrading to India. All shades of opinion were united in support of this campaign. Success was reached in 1917, and, shortly after the War, indentured labour emigration was finally prohibited.

People had by now begun to turn instinctively to Gandhi for help and leadership in obtaining redress of grievances. Complaints of the conditions of the indigo-cultivators in Champaran (Bihar) were brought to him. He went into the question, collected the facts, and sought an interview with the planters to discuss the matter; but he received scant sympathy or courtesy from them and, regarding him as a stranger, they requested his non-intervention. Nor were the authorities any more helpful. He proclaimed an open campaign against the methods of indigo cultivation and, disobeying an order to leave the district, was arrested. But his detention was of short duration. In court he gave a closely reasoned statement as to his position in Champaran, and telegraphed an appeal to the Viceroy to intervene, with the result that the proceedings were withdrawn and he was enabled to set up a private inquiry into the Champaran ryots' grievances. Ultimately a committee of inquiry was set up by the

MAHATMA GANDHI WITH MRS. NAIDU

Lieut.-Governor of Bihar, to which he was appointed. It found substantially in favour of the ryots and made important recommendations to which effect was duly given. So began the work that he had long hoped to undertake of agrarian reform and the improvement of village conditions.

A labour dispute in the Ahmedabad mills led to his first public fast. Gandhi had extracted from the strikers a promise to stand firm and to do so without violence of word or deed. Too much, probably, was expected of them; they began to falter, and the strike looked like collapsing. To rally them again he took a tremendous resolution, vowing not to touch food until the strike was settled. He said afterwards that he realised that he had by his action placed an unfair burden upon the mill-owners, many of whom were his friends; for so great a following had Gandhi that they were compelled to come to terms rather than let ill befall him. Thus the strikers won, if not all they asked for, a considerable part of it, and a new weapon in dealing with public affairs was forged—that of suffering in one's own person for the sins or errors of others. It implied no new doctrine, but as a method of securing redress of a collective wrong it had not been used before. It struck the public imagination. *Satyagraha* (Soul-force) was now to be pitted against physical force: would it prove a mightier power? Much was said and written about it and the method and circumstances of its exercise, and the influence which Gandhi had already gained over the minds and hearts of men grew rapidly.

No sooner was the mill strike over than a new struggle began which put into operation *Satyagraha*. In Kaira district the crops failed, famine conditions threatened, and many cultivators were unable to pay the tax demands. Gandhi was called to their aid. He drafted a petition, and therein exercised the statutory right to ask for suspension of revenue collections; but the petition failed. Then Gandhi advised the sufferers and their sympathisers to refrain from attempting to pay; they should not sell their all and thus permanently impoverish or ruin themselves. "Refuse to pay," he said; "even those of you who can, and take the consequences at the hands of the Law." News of the struggle spread over India; money was sent to help the fight. Time passed, and the peasants began to lose nerve under the threats of the officials and at the sight of their cattle and goods seized and sold. Standing crops in some cases were attached and Gandhi grew anxious as he saw the wavering of the people. Again something urgent had to be done. He therefore suggested to some of his followers that they should remove the crops themselves from a field that had been attached. He knew that this might mean their being arrested, but all were willing to test it out. They were arrested and given short terms of imprisonment. Fortunately the struggle ended soon by an agreed compromise. But the Kaira struggle was a great step in the awakening of the masses of India to a sense of their rights and their own ability to secure redress. They were not to sleep again.

Of Gandhi's passion for unity amongst his countrymen much could be said. By pleading, by argument, by suffering and by example he sought most earnestly and diligently to weld into one strong whole the two main streams of Indian life, Hindu and Moslem. By his work for the Khalifat movement, under the leadership of the Ali brothers, he hoped to bring this desired end nearer, apart from the merits of the movement itself. It has to be confessed, however, that in this he has not been successful, though many Moslems have enrolled under his banner and that of the Indian-National Congress, and many call him brother.

Killing he has hated in any guise. That it was done as organised warfare could not exalt it in his eyes. But to refrain from the fight through cowardice was to him a greater crime than that of war itself. One did not then refrain from killing out of love, but because of fear for one's own person. So once again, and after much heart-searching, he led a recruiting campaign in the latter part of the Great War, on the ground that the quickest and straightest way to win Swaraj was to help to defend the Empire. Simultaneously, he addressed to the Viceroy an eloquent plea for a fuller understanding of India's national sentiment and a due recognition of her place in the British Commonwealth of Nations.

Under the continued strain that he had put upon himself for so long, his health gave way and he came near to death. His doctors were baffled by his illness and urged him to take milk as being the only food suited to his enfeebled condition. He had, however, for some time observed a vow not to take it, as a food calculated to stimulate the passions. With great subtlety, Mrs. Gandhi prevailed upon him to listen to the doctors by reminding him that his vow was against cow's milk, but not against the milk of the goat. From then dates the Goat as the symbol of Gandhi's abstemiousness in diet.

Soon after his recovery came the Rowlatt Act, against which British India, towns and villages alike, was united. A *hartal* (general cessation of work) at the opening of the struggle was proclaimed and widely observed throughout the country. Thus his work of rousing and uniting India continued.

Young India, a weekly newspaper, became his mouthpiece. His method of work had undergone no radical change from that of South Africa, but his field of action was now enlarged, and when his nation-wide non-co-operation movement was started, the ground had been well prepared.

In 1920, whilst the Khalifat agitation was still in progress, the Punjab disorders occurred, as a result of post-war economic distress and in protest against oppressive administration. When the news became known of the manner in which they had been suppressed by Sir Michael O'Dwyer's Government, culminating in the Jallianwala Bagh shooting at Amritsar, bitter indignation was voiced all over India. An official committee of inquiry was set up, but the Indian National Congress, which had appointed a sub-committee of its own, under Gandhi's chairmanship, refused to collaborate. The sub-committee's report, after meticulous examination of witnesses, was accepted by Indian opinion in preference to the milder one of the official committee. When the matter came up for discussion in the House of Commons, General Dyer's action was condemned; but in the House of Lords, on the contrary, it was vindicated. This unfortunate result was deeply resented in India. Gandhi joined forces with those who, as a protest against what was regarded as British injustice and indifference to Indian sentiment and self-respect, were urging the boycott of the councils set up under the Montagu-Chelmsford reforms. He enunciated four stages in the programme of non-co-operation: (1) to give up titles and honorary offices; (2) to refuse to serve the Government in paid appointments or to participate in any manner in the working of the existing machinery of Government; (3) to decline to pay taxes in support of it; and (4) to ask the police and the military to withdraw co-operation from the Government.

He himself returned his Kaisar-i-Hind medal, and he pursued an energetic campaign in support of his views in *Young India*. At a special session of the Congress his resolution to adopt non-co-operation throughout British India was carried by a large majority, though the minority was substantial and influential. His commanding influence over the Congress was finally established at the ensuing regular session. Had the movement succeeded as he had hoped, it would undoubtedly have gone far to paralyse the Government. But the "plan of campaign" did not work out as he had foreseen. Whilst jail became a familiar place to large numbers who followed him both in precept and in practice, the mass of the people, unprepared for the sacrifice and the self-discipline demanded of them, were unable to carry on the struggle with fortitude and calm. Internal troubles arose, many of the leaders doubted the political wisdom of remaining out of the legislatures, and on various occasions mob-violence occurred. Gandhi was horrified by these evident failures of his passionately-held doctrine of *Ahimsa* (non-violence), and he called off the civil disobedience movement against which, he felt, God had set His face.

He was convinced that the masses were as yet unprepared for a great non-violent struggle for freedom. Moreover, he had begun to realise increasingly that seasonal unemployment and intemperance were playing havoc with the vitality and the economic resources of the people. In addition, they were weakened by social divisions. He accordingly began to devote himself to the preaching of the use of the *charka* (hand-loom) and the spinning and weaving of *khaddar* (cotton-cloth) as a discipline and a primary means of improving village-welfare; the abolition of the liquor-traffic; and the removal of untouchability. He has lately organised a movement for mass-education, so far as possible on a self-supporting basis, by methods combining training of the hand and the mind. But for him education is first a question of character development.

In 1924, the year in which he fasted at Delhi to obtain Hindu-Moslem unity, he was unanimously elected president of the Congress and he enunciated vigorously his economic and social programme. He also spoke fervently of his belief in India's political goal as that of an equal member among the interdependent countries of the Commonwealth.

In place of *Young India*, which disappeared during a later non-co-operation campaign, he brought out the weekly *Harijan*, in order to advocate primarily the abolition of untouchability, but it was also used as his channel of communication regarding his many activities and interests, including his replies to correspondents from all over the world.

By 1929 a new atmosphere of intense emotion had developed with the growing self-consciousness of Nationalist India. There were now three main parties in the country: the Central Government, in whom was vested power, subject to the British Parliament; the Congress, full of spirit, restless energy, intense patriotic feeling and strong racial resentment; and the Moderates, widely experienced, but with little influence over the masses. At the Lahore Congress a notable difference of opinion occurred between Gandhi and Pundit Jawaharlal Nehru, the then president of the Congress and spokesman of Young India. The latter pressed for a declaration of complete independence (Purna Swaraj); the former insisted upon an interpretation of the term in the sense of Dominion Self-Government. In the end, no hard and fast definition of Swaraj was or has since been made by the Congress, though Gandhi, as late as the beginning of 1937, once more proclaimed his belief in Dominion status for India, as defined by the Statute of Westminster, as a fulfilment of India's political ambitions. He remains of the opinion that she can achieve the substance of independence whilst continuing, as an equal member, within the British Commonwealth of Nations (*Harijan*, June 24, 1939).

Gandhi has always possessed a strange instinct for the use of dramatic gesture and symbolism, often with spectacular results. One such was his decision to start a new non-violent campaign to secure the abolition of the salt-tax, which was held to oppress the very poor. He and some colleagues, early in 1930, accordingly set out for the seashore at Dandi in order to break the law by preparing salt, a Government monopoly, and he was arrested and imprisoned. His example was followed, and soon civil disobedience was prevalent once more throughout the country and repressive measures were adopted by the Government.

Another illustration of his gift for symbolic dramatisation was the public burning of foreign cloth, at his instance, partly to hit the Government's revenues and partly in aid of the *swadeshi* (home industries) movement. The familiar "Gandhi cap," part of the Congress uniform of *khaddar*, is another instance, for it is a replica of the convict's cap worn by him in the Transvaal jail.

It had, however, already been realised, both at Delhi and in London, that the time was ripe for further constitutional advance in India. A Round Table Conference was called in London, but the Congress at first refused to partici-

CROSSING THE FRONTIER

Mahatma Gandhi and a band of followers fording the Swat River.

pate in its deliberations. Lord Irwin, however, took steps soon after Gandhi's release from prison, to invite him to a meeting at Delhi, and shortly afterwards the Gandhi-Irwin Pact was announced (March 3, 1931), civil disobedience being suspended. The Pact was ratified at the Karachi session of the Congress.

Gandhi proceeded to London as its sole representative at the second Round Table Conference. In London, again in symbolic mood, he insisted upon living in a working-class district in order to be among the poor, and upon wearing his *khaddar* loin-cloth and shawl even when he visited King George V at Buckingham Palace. His heart, however, was not in the deliberations of the Conference, to which he made little effective contribution, but where he claimed to represent the impoverished masses and the "depressed classes" of India. He felt restless that he was adding little to the welfare of his "fellow-villagers" at home. He, however, took repeated occasion to deliver his message of non-violence to the Western world.

Upon his return to India, early in 1932, he found the stage set against all his hopes. Charges of breach of the Pact, under Lord Irwin's successor, had been made by the Congress leaders and several of his closest colleagues had already been arrested or imprisoned before his arrival. He, too, was arrested and imprisoned, in an atmosphere of mutual suspicion, upon his announcing the resumption of civil disobedience.

One of the matters outstanding at the end of the Round Table Conference was the question of the representation of the minority communities. Owing to the inability of the Indian leaders there to agree upon quotas and methods of representation, the Prime Minister issued his Communal Award. Gandhi took deep offence at the segregation of the depressed classes from the rest of the Hindu community, and undertook a "fast unto death" whilst still in jail, until the leaders of the community generally and of the depressed classes reached an agreement, which was subsequently adopted by the British authorities. Much resentment was, however, aroused in Hindu circles, especially in Bengal, at the limited representation left to the general Hindu body of electors after the claims of the depressed classes had been met. Criticism, too, was widespread in more thoughtful circles at the use of the fast by Gandhi in circumstances that bore the appearance of moral coercion, since nobody would willingly become responsible for the Mahatma's death.

After Gandhi's release, some time later, when the civil disobedience movement had collapsed, he continued to devote himself to social and economic reform work. He gradually withdrew from political activities and ultimately resigned his membership of the Congress. But it had learnt to depend upon his advice and guidance, and he has remained its unofficial leader and its referee and arbiter in great emergencies. This was particularly notable at the time when, with his strong support and after a reassuring pronouncement by the Viceroy, the new Indian constitution came into force, early in 1937, by the establishment of autonomy in the British Indian Provinces, in most of which Congress Governments were set up.

A further occasion of the demonstration of his powerful influence was when a change of Premier was brought about in the Congress Government in the Central Provinces after reference to him by the Working Committee of the Congress.

A striking illustration, however, of the unique position that he holds as the acknowledged leader of the Indian nationalist forces is the fact that, after the re-election of Mr. S. C. Bose as President of the Congress by the Provincial Congress Committees, quite recently, in spite of Gandhi's support of another candidate, the annual session of the Congress that followed almost immediately reiterated its complete confidence in him, resolved to support his policies, and virtually instructed Mr. Bose to appoint a Working Committee that would enjoy Gandhi's confidence. Mr. Bose, however, failed to secure the support of Gandhi's nominees, and resigned the Presidentship, the new President, Dr. Rajendra Prasad, being an old colleague of the Mahatma's and the new Working Committee being composed entirely of his supporters.

The most recent symbolic episode in Gandhi's career was his "fast unto death" early in 1939, at Rajkot. He determined upon this in order to compel the ruler of that small State to abide by what he contended the latter had undertaken in the appointment of the personnel of a committee to make proposals for constitutional reform in the State. He consented to abandon the fast after the dispute had been referred for an opinion to the Federal Chief Justice by the Viceroy, whom Gandhi had requested to intervene as the representative of the Paramount Power. In the result his contention was upheld; but to the general astonishment he subsequently renounced the advantages of the award as having been obtained by the coercion of the ruler and being thus "tainted with *Himsa* (violence)."

Two characteristic expressions of Gandhi's independence of judgment here call for notice. The first is his advice to the Congress leaders, in the face of Mr. Bose's demand to present Britain with an ultimatum in the prevailing international

THE FAST AT RAJKOT

Early in 1939 Mahatma Gandhi decided to embark on a "fast unto death." He did this as a protest against the ruler of Rajkot who, he insisted, had not carried out certain promises in connection with reforms in the government of his state. The Viceroy intervened, and the matter was referred to the Federal Chief Justice. Gandhi then abandoned his fast. His opinion was subsequently upheld.

DISCUSSING THE MATTER WITH A FELLOW TRAVELLER

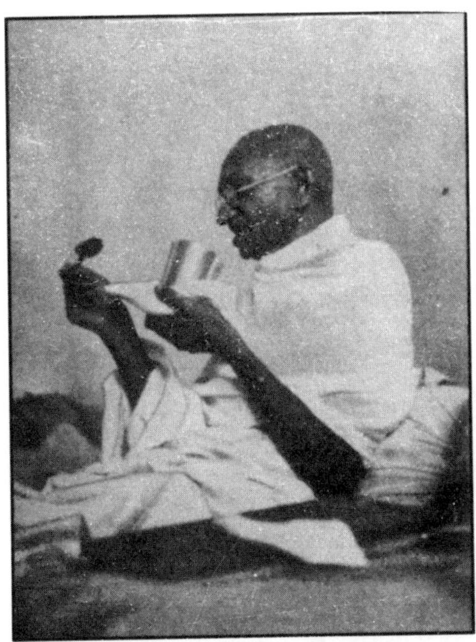

THE LAST MEAL BEFORE THE FAST

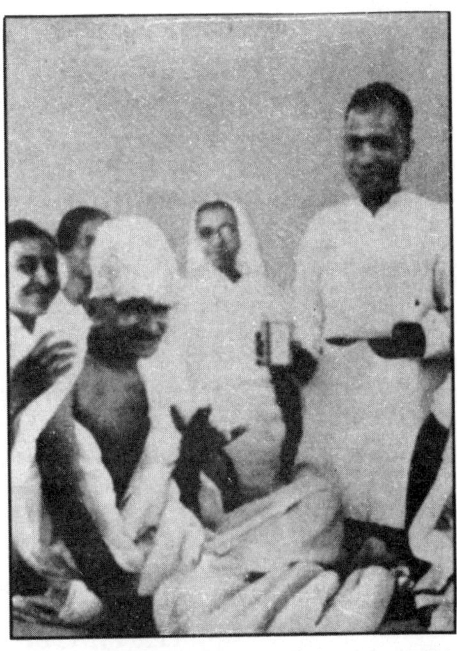

THE MAHATMA BREAKS HIS FAST

THE HATER OF VIOLENCE

A picture taken of the Mahatma in 1939 still vigorously preaching his doctrine of non-aggressive methods and unity of effort.

crisis in order to compel her to grant India's freedom, that it would not be proper or generous on her part to take advantage of Britain's embarrassment in the international field, and his insistence that India must secure her substantial independence on her own merits and by her own united efforts.

The other is his uncompromising denunciation of widespread corruption within the Congress organisation and of the departure of large numbers of Congressmen from the method of truth and non-violence, laid down by the Congress at his instance as the fundamental tenet of its policy.

These are summarised in the following passage from a letter from Gandhi to Bose, in reply to the latter's proposed ultimatum, under threat of a new intensive civil disobedience campaign, just before his resignation, expressing Gandhi's profound disbelief that such a campaign could be conducted without violence:

"I smell violence in the air I breathe. Our mutual distrust is a bad form of violence. The widening gulf between Hindus and Moslems points to the same thing."

It is too early yet to estimate finally Gandhi's influence upon his Motherland or upon world events; but it may be truly said that to him, more than to any predecessor or contemporary, is due the vivid national consciousness of India to-day and the growing respect in which she is held abroad. To many he is a strange enigma, an aggregate of inconsistencies, and his subtlety of argument is often incomprehensible and baffling. But of his courage, his integrity of purpose, the splendour of his idealism, his deep patriotism, and his fine example of public conduct and personal sacrifice there is an all but universal recognition.

PUNDIT MOTILAL NEHRU

PUNDIT MOTILAL NEHRU

A MAKER OF MODERN INDIA

1861–1931

BY C. F. ANDREWS

PUNDIT MOTILAL NEHRU belonged to that older generation of great men in India, of which Rabindranath Tagore is to-day one of the very few now living. It is a curious fact that Motilal's birthday came on exactly the same day of the year and month as that of the poet: for he was born on May 6, 1861.

Among his contemporaries, in Allahabad, Pundit Madan Mohan Malaviya comes nearest to him in age. Dr. Brajendranath Seal, that giant of massive learning in Bengal, who has just passed away, was somewhat younger. Sir Prafulla Chandra Roy, the renowned chemist, is about the same age as Rabindranath Tagore. Sir Jagadish Chandra Bose was a contemporary. Sir Nilratan Sarkar, who is still with us, belongs to the same generation. Lala Lajpat Rai in the Punjab was younger. Many names might be recalled in other provinces, but space will hardly allow it. What I have tried to point out is that the "sixties" of last century produced a larger number of eminent men than the years that followed. It must not be forgotten that Mahatma Gandhi himself comes just within this period.

Kashmiri Brahmans, to which class Pundit Motilal Nehru belonged, are well known all over the north of India both for their intellectual powers and fine appearance. They are, by birth, what may truly be called an aristocratic race, and easily recognised as such. Motilal was typical of this distinguished class and in his old age he gained the reputation of being the "aristocrat of the Assembly." His spotless *khaddar* dress, with his white Kashmiri shawl, suited him perfectly, and his portrait is rightly given the place of honour in his son's Autobiography. The fine features—which I have mentioned—and the fair complexion run through the whole family, and have descended from father to son.

Although, as a boy, Motilal took little interest in his school and college studies he was from an early age keenly interested in the subject of law. He came out first as "Gold medallist" in the High Court Vakil's examination and showed at once his marked ability. His father had died three months before he was born, so that he never knew what it was to have a father. But his elder brother, Nandlal, who was much older than himself, took the place of a father towards him during his school and college days and afterwards introduced him into his own practice at the Bar. This brother, however, died very early in Motilal's legal career and thus he was soon thrown upon his own resources.

According to the immemorial custom of India, Motilal was now obliged to bear the burden of all the members of the family who were settled in Allahabad. This meant very hard work at his legal profession, from morning to night, building up his practice. But he thoroughly enjoyed it and very rapidly climbed the ladder which led to success.

All the facts which I have thus briefly related are to be found in the remarkable Autobiography written by his son, Jawaharlal, who was for many years his only child. Much later in life two daughters were also born to him, and these three made up his family. But under the same roof there were a large number of cousins and near relatives, who formed a joint family together in the spacious house called Anand Bhavan.

It was there, at Anand Bhavan, that I first met Motilal Nehru more than thirty years ago. A family residence of this type is like the ancestral house of a clan in the Highlands of Scotland. Everyone who is a near relative, and also the servants who grow up in it, regard themselves as members of the joint family. The memory of my first meeting with Pundit Motilal Nehru is very dim to-day; but I can easily picture the house where he lived and his very handsome appearance. Delhi and Allahabad were closely associated in their intellectual life in those times. There was a close fellowship also between Moslems and Hindus within the different intellectual groups. The common Urdu language, in which very great pride was taken by both Hindus and Moslems, bound them together. The Western culture, which had come also into fashion, was another link common to this very small circle of English-educated people. The members of leading families met continually, especially at marriages. My own educational work soon brought me into touch with Allahabad and also with Anand Bhavan.

Motilal Nehru was from the first quite lavish in his hospitality. More and more he had adopted, after each visit to Europe, the expensive standard of living common in the West. Exceedingly foolish stories about his Western habits were spread widely over the north of India, which were ridiculous to those who knew him in his own house; for whatever he did in this direction, as events proved, was merely on the surface, and could be thrown off at a moment's notice. He frankly admired the character of the Englishmen he met who had been trained in the English public schools. Therefore he sent his only son to Harrow, and never regretted that action. But all through his life he was far too deeply wedded to his own country and its traditions to make him ever forget his birthright.

When I first came to know him intimately was in the autumn of 1919 at Amritsar and Lahore, where we met together during the first days of the Congress Enquiry into the Punjab disturbances and the acts which had been committed under martial law.

His son, Jawaharlal Nehru, had come up alone, in the first instance, immediately after martial law had been withdrawn and the entry into the Punjab had become possible. We had lived together for some time at Harkishen Lal's house in Lahore before any one else arrived. Each day, when we came back from one disturbed area after another, we used to compare notes in the evening. Then Motilal Nehru himself came, as soon as he was free from his engagements. Mahatma Gandhi soon followed, when the order against him was withdrawn. It was painful to witness how shock after shock went home, when they both examined, as trained lawyers, the evidence which we put before them. Some of the worst things that were done under martial law were not done in Amritsar or in Lahore, but in the Gujranwala district, in villages whose names even were quite unknown. It was a lesson that I never forget to notice how very carefully they sifted the evidence, and at once put aside as untrustworthy all that I had collected, at second-hand, on hearsay only.

Long before this Enquiry was over, the more urgent call suddenly came to me to go out to Kenya and South Africa.

I was very sorry to go away, but before I left the Punjab a golden opportunity had been given me of seeing at first-hand those two leaders of India, as they then were, closely associated together in this common investigation on behalf of those who had suffered under martial law.

That memorable year 1919, in Indian history, changed once and for all the mode of life of Pundit Motilal Nehru. Before this time, as we have seen, he had made some of his closest friends in Europe, and also among the ruling classes in India who were British by race and tradition. He greatly admired that tradition, while holding himself free to criticise it. He had also many friends among the aristocracy of India. His whole mind had been steeped in law and constitutional government. Though he had been for some time a member of the Congress, he had always represented the Right rather than the Left. But Amritsar shook the very foundations of the faith on which he had built up his life hitherto; and when he presided over the National Congress, which was held at Amritsar that very year, 1919, he felt that the parting of the ways had come between him and his old liberal friends. Then, when at last the call came to join the Non-Co-operation Movement, under the leadership of Mahatma Gandhi, he was fully prepared to accept it. He did this slowly and deliberately, realising all the consequences which it involved.

He would have been the first to acknowledge that, in his own home, there were those on both sides of the family—the women no less than men—who were eager to help him to make this great decision to join Mahatma Gandhi. Then, as soon as he had made it, the whole family became united. Jawaharlal's mother and wife and daughter took part in the struggle side by side with Motilal Nehru himself and his son.

Yet there was a marked difference from the very first that soon revealed itself. Motilal Nehru, as I have just said, was quite obviously inclined to the Right in all his actions and decisions. Even after he had joined the Non-Co-operation Movement this continued. So, after the first flush of the new venture of Non-Co-operation was over and it became logically evident to him that he could win more power by entering the Central Legislative Assembly, he was prepared to do this along with his great friend C. R. Das of Bengal. He was thus led materially to differ from Mahatma Gandhi. Those who followed the latter were called No-changers. As a parallel organisation, the Swaraj Party was formed by Motilal Nehru and C. R. Das. The parliamentary methods of obstruction, which Parnell and his Irishmen had so brilliantly tried out at Westminster, were put into execution at Delhi.

The next time I met Pundit Motilal Nehru was at Juhu, near Bombay, where Mahatma Gandhi was recovering from his very serious operation in the Sassoon Hospital at Poona. He came and stayed at Juhu for some time in order to be near Mahatmaji and talk things over; and I had many opportunities of seeing the lighter side of his character as the two leaders together made great fun of one another. Mahatmaji was convalescent and recovering health. He was thus in a joking mood with everyone. The whole Nehru family was in residence at Juhu during those extraordinary days, while Motilal and Gandhi talked out—as it seemed to me, almost interminably—the pros and cons of "Council Entry." Neither convinced the other; but, meanwhile, in the intervals between these long conversations, I had got to know Pundit

Motilal Nehru very much better than I had ever done before. I was also able to witness and appreciate his deep admiration for Mahatma Gandhi as a man. As a "Mathama" he was far less interested in him; but that made everything between them more human. He would chaff Gandhi mercilessly and nothing pleased him better. I wish I could remember some of the jokes, which were of a very elementary character, but they have quite passed from me. Just one I recollect, how he called Mahatma Gandhi "a bit of a dandy" because of his spotlessly white *khaddar!* Behind all the merriment, however, was a firmness on both sides which became at times crucially painful because the two minds, so strongly dissimilar, would not always work together. Yet the affection between them became all the deeper because of their very differences.

The portrait drawn by Jawaharlal of his father is one of the finest descriptions in his Autobiography.[1] "There was in him," he writes, "a strength of personality and a measure of kingliness. In any gathering where he was present he would inevitably be the centre and the hub. Whatever the place he sat at table, it would become, as an eminent English judge said later, the head of the table. He was neither meek nor mild. Consciously imperious, he created great loyalty as well as bitter opposition. It was difficult to feel neutral about him; one had to like him or dislike him. With a broad forehead, tight lips, and a determined chin he had a marked resemblance to the busts of the Roman Emperors in the museums in Italy. There was a magnificence about him and a grand manner, which is sadly to seek in this world of to-day.

"I remember," he adds, "showing Gandhiji a photograph of him, where he had no moustache, and till then Gandhiji had always seen him with a fine moustache. He started almost on seeing this photograph and gazed long upon it; for the absence of the moustache brought out the hardness of the mouth and chin; and he said with a somewhat dry smile that now he realised what he had to contend against. The face was softened, however, by the eyes and by the lines that frequent laughter had made. But sometimes the eyes glittered."

In all my own memories of him this gentler side predominated, and I remember him chiefly by his lavish fund of humour and his eagerness to engage in a bout of wit and merriment especially with Gandhiji himself. Yet no one admired Gandhi more than Motilal Nehru. "That humble and lonely figure," he wrote about him, "standing erect, on the firm footholds of faith unshakable and strength unconquerable, continues to send out to his countrymen his message of sacrifice and suffering for the Motherland."

On other later occasions it has been my privilege to see these two together, each great in his own way, but strongly dissimilar; and it has made me understand more clearly how this affection for Mahatma Gandhi has descended from father to son. Indeed, the whole Nehru family has joined in it.

The great event in the earlier days of Non-Co-operation, for which Pundit Motilal Nehru and Chittaranjan Das were responsible, became known as "Council Entry." They had argued out to the bitter end with Mahatmaji the value of the movement, if they went boldly into the Councils as Parnell the Irish leader did fifty years ago in England, and thus obstructed the Government within the legislatures.

At last Mahatmaji gave way; and at the next elections the Swaraj Party, as it was called, was fully organised and every-

[1] *An Autobiography, pages* 130 *and* 131, *published by John Lane, Bodley Head, London.*

where carried the polls. When Motilal Nehru was chosen to be leader of the opposition in the Central Assembly at New Delhi, as the head of the Swaraj Party, he felt himself once more entirely in his own element. He was no longer like a fish out of water. His whole legal training and his knowledge of assemblies had all along made him anxious to engage in a battle royal with the Imperial Government, using its own weapons to defeat it. He was quite certain that he could bring it down to its knees.

In this opinion he was more or less justified; for the Government suffered outwardly defeat after defeat at his hands. Indeed, on all the larger issues, it could only rely on its own official and nominated members, and these, by themselves, were not sufficient to form a majority. But his triumphs proved to be Pyrrhic victories after all, because as soon as ever any Government measure was defeated it was at once certificated by the Viceroy. There was also a majority ready in the Upper House to reverse the decision of the Assembly.

A subtle danger, meanwhile, attacked the Swaraj Party. For every possible inducement was given to its members to serve on one Committee after another, or to take this post or that, bringing certain emoluments with them. When these were accepted, the full force of a revolutionary method of procedure was continually frustrated.

During these difficult years, Pundit Motilal Nehru undertook almost alone the immensely arduous task of drawing up a form of constitution, by which India should have full Dominion Status within the British Commonwealth. His son, Jawaharlal, could not endure the limited terms on which this constitution was being framed, because they did not make absolutely clear that India's full independence was the goal. A considerable amount of friction arose between father and son on this issue and a compromise was reached at last with great difficulty, whereby the offer to accept this "Dominion Status" constitution would expire at the end of the year 1929.

It will not be possible to write much about the later years of his life during which he had to suffer imprisonment for taking an active part in the Civil Resistance Movement along with many other members of his family. Long before he took part in the struggle he had been afflicted for very many years with an acute form of asthma, which caused him great physical pain and put a severe strain upon his heart. But his utterly resolute temperament would not allow him for a moment to stand by while others suffered, even though he was already to all intents and purposes an invalid and had reached his 70th year.

In the jail, his illness rapidly grew worse, and it was obvious that prison life was doing him untold injury, because he could get no proper treatment for his asthma and heart trouble, under jail conditions. Yet he became immediately angry if anyone suggested that he should be released because of his infirmities. He went to the length of sending a telegram to the Viceroy, Lord Irwin, saying that he did not wish to claim any exemption. But on the doctors' imperative orders he was discharged after exactly ten weeks' imprisonment.

Then came the fifth arrest of his only son, Jawaharlal. The old father pulled himself together and declared to every one present that he was going to be ill no longer. For a time his indomitable spirit prevailed; but after a short period the blood came back into his sputum in greater quantities than ever. Therefore, he was urged to go to Calcutta for the purpose of taking a sea voyage along with a friend who was a doctor: but his condition so quickly grew worse that he could not make his journey any further than Calcutta. Yet even then his will was quite unconquerable, and he carried forward every part of his civil resistance just as before.

He returned to Allahabad, and his son Jawaharlal was discharged a little while before the others in order to be with him. Mahatma Gandhi had also been discharged at Yeravda and many others among the Congress leaders. These came to Allahabad and were able to meet him, one by one, for the last time before his death.

"I am going soon," he said to Mahatma Gandhi, "and I shall not be here to see Swaraj. But I know that you have won it."

The end came on February 6th. For many millions, in every part of India, it seemed as if a dear personal friend had been taken from them. His son writes:

MRS. VIJAYALAXMI PANDIT

Daughter of Motilal Nehru and herself prominent in politics.

"I was dazed all that day, hardly realising what had happened, and a succession of events and large crowds kept me from thinking. Great crowds in Lucknow, gathered together at brief notice—the swift dash from Lucknow to Allahabad sitting by the body, wrapped in our national flag, and with a big flag flying above—the arrival at Allahabad, and the huge crowds that had gathered for miles to pay homage to his memory. There were some ceremonies at home, and then the last journey to the Ganga with a mighty concourse of people. As evening fell on the river bank on that winter day, the great flames leapt up and consumed that body which had meant so much to us, who were close to him, as well as to millions in India. Gandhiji said a few moving words to the multitude and then all of us crept silently home. The stars were out and shining brightly when he returned, lonely and desolate."

Messages came pouring in from every side—from those who had been his most stalwart opponents in the Assembly, from the Viceroy and Lady Irwin, as well as from those dear companions who had stood side by side with him in the civil resistance campaign.

"This tremendous volume of goodwill and sympathy" wrote Jawaharlal, "took away somewhat the sting from our sorrow; but it was, above all, the wonderfully soothing and healing presence of Gandhiji that helped my mother and all of us to face that crisis in our lives."

Looking back after all these years, it has now become evident to thinking men all over the world that the good fight which Motilal Nehru fought was carried through to the end with a chivalry and courtesy towards his opponents that made his cause truly great and noble. His name is honoured to-day in India, not only by his fellow countrymen, but also by every European. In his own career, as a statesman he stands out more prominently than ever, as one who brought the debates of the Central Assembly at Delhi to a higher parliamentary level than has ever been reached before or since. Certainly no one has ever been so great as he, as Leader of the Opposition. In this, and in a thousand other ways, he has been one of the "Makers of Modern India."

PUNDIT JAWAHARLAL NEHRU

The Ex-President of Congress in a characteristic attitude delivering a speech.

PUNDIT JAWAHARLAL NEHRU

THE CHAMPION OF THE INDIAN PEOPLE

BORN 1889

BY C. F. ANDREWS

PUNDIT JAWAHARLAL NEHRU has made any description of his own personality comparatively simple because he has published one of the most revealing books of modern times, which tells us the story of his own life. It is a natural temptation, therefore, for one who is writing about him to draw largely from the book itself. But while I shall not fail to make use of what he has himself written, I shall seek at the same time to add other features from my own recollections.

Yet, before doing so, I would wish to dwell for a moment on the *Autobiography* itself, which has proved such an amazing success. It was issued from the press in London in April, 1936, and by August of the same year the eighth impression had been printed off. These first sales were mainly in England, and it was there that its great reputation was made. The equally large sales in India came later. New editions are still being published, which show that the book will continue to live when others are forgotten.

It was the entire frankness of what was written, together with the profound interest of the story he told, that gained Jawaharlal his very large and important reading public. He had the great advantage of being able to speak to the intellectual classes—especially at the Universities—in the very phrases and terms which they themselves used. He wrote as one of themselves. He told Englishmen exactly what they wanted to know about India in his own transparently clear style, and made them feel that India was not merely a land of saints and mystics but also of quite human and fallible people like himself, who were definitely lined up to fight against Hitler and Mussolini along with any freedom-loving Englishman, if only the latter would allow the same freedom to India that he demanded for himself.

"Here's a man we can understand," was the remark that a young civilian made on his first voyage out to India. "He's one of ourselves after all, and talks to us in our own language."

Probably more was accomplished in a few months by this one volume to swing round liberal opinion in the West than had been accomplished by the many years of political struggle that had gone before.

It is true that the strong impression which had been made by these multiple editions could hardly be lasting. Europe to-day is in such a turmoil and confusion that even the most liberal-minded Englishmen are inclined to cry out, "We have no time for India." But the pendulum is bound to swing back later and some new incident will bring India once more into the forefront of the picture. Then the same people, who had read the book before with such eagerness, will turn to the copy which is on their shelves and read through over again Jawaharlal's prophetic warnings.

Another point must not be overlooked. The remarkable photographs which have been reproduced have themselves proved to be a revelation to the ordinary reader. The frontispiece of Pundit Motilal Nehru, the father of the author, looking in his "toga" like someone out of the ancient Roman Empire; the face of the author himself, showing the markedly strong and clear-cut character that lies behind it; above all, perhaps, the tender portraits of the mother, wife and daughter of the author, disclosing a perfect refinement mingled with true womanly courage—all these tell their own story. Every English reader, as he turns over the pages, becomes in his heart of hearts ashamed that persons such as these should have been obliged to go to prison in order to make their voices heard. Thus the portraits have given rise to some very painful thinking. They have shown that all is not right in India. This last factor, as I know full well, has very deeply touched the women of England, who have recently gained, by a hard struggle, their own political rights. The women's influence in England to-day is no less important than that of the men, and their full weight is being thrown more and more on the side of Indian freedom.

One of Jawaharlal Nehru's most bitter opponents in the United Provinces, a diehard and a reactionary, paid him in my hearing a compliment, which is well worth quoting at this point. For it sums up a great deal.

"Whatever," he said, "we may think of young Nehru's socialistic doctrines and his Bolshevist ideas, the efficient way in which he handled the Allahabad Municipality, as Chairman, was beyond all praise."

This practical efficiency in all he undertakes and his clean contempt for shoddy work, have won him esteem from those who have heartily disliked his politics. The same people have also admired the out-spokenness with which he has been ready at all times to acknowledge faults of character and weakness of purpose within himself and others. This feature in his character has won him universal respect.

Among the multitudes of his own people, who love him with a devotion second only to that of Mahatmaji himself, the same quality of supreme honesty tells for very much. It endears him to them. But along with this, the conviction that he has never hesitated for a moment to suffer with them, and on their behalf, tells for even more. In the United Provinces there has grown up, year by year, a simple loyalty of devotion towards him among the villagers that is absolute in character.

I recollect his telling me once, at Allahabad, with a certain amount of dry humour, the story of the way in which he tried to train the ignorant villagers of his own province in the pure doctrine of non-violence, which they persistently failed to understand.

"What would you do," he asked a group of village leaders, "if you saw me taken prisoner before your very eyes and then handcuffed by the police?"

"We would rush in and rescue you," they replied at once in chorus.

"No, no," said Jawaharlal, "that's just what you mustn't do! You must keep perfectly calm and quiet. You mustn't move a step."

They would stare at him with a singularly puzzled look and he would patiently go on to tell them that even if they saw him beaten with *lathis*, they were not to use any violence in return. For these things were only to be expected.

"But we couldn't bear it," they shouted.

"You've *got* to bear it," was the answer.

And so the lesson in *Ahimsa* would have to begin all over again until it was learnt by heart.

The greatest strain of all came, in the United Provinces, when his own aged mother was injured by the police.

PUNDIT JAWAHARLAL AS PRESIDENT

A photograph taken of Jawaharlal Nehru when he was President of Congress. He is seen on the extreme right presiding over a Special Meeting of the All-India Convention Subjects Committee. Facing the camera are K. Munshi, Mrs. Hansa Mehta, Jairamdas Daulatram.

Jawaharlal himself was in prison at the time.

He frankly acknowledges, in his book, that if he had been on the spot, his Ahimsa might have been put to too severe a strain!

The deeply touching faith which these villagers repose in him I have witnessed personally again and again in all sorts of ways.

At the first, on his return from London and Cambridge, they had little chance of coming into very close contact with him; for he was incessantly occupied with various city engagements in Allahabad and also with his lawyer's work at the Bar. But from the moment when he gave himself up, heart and soul, to the Non-Co-operation Movement and placed himself with absolute loyalty and devotion under the leadership of Mahatma Gandhi, this old life of his began to be changed. The villagers now were made more and more his chief concern.

He worked with them, lived with them, and thus learnt to understand their tragic struggle against overwhelming odds. He knew them now at close quarters. So he won their hearts and they won his.

The book that he has written gives many touching indications of this, from which I would quote the following passage:

"There they were, these people, looking up with their shining eyes, full of affection, with generations of suffering and poverty behind them, and still pouring out their gratitude and love, and asking for little in return, except fellow-feeling and sympathy. It was impossible not to feel humbled and awed by this abundance of affection and devotion."

Mainly on account of his personal leadership and that of his own devoted companions, the *Kisan*, or Peasant Movement, in the United Provinces has become strongly organised and powerful. The only province that comes near it is Bihar, where Rajendra Prasad has won a similar confidence among his own countrymen.

It is of the utmost importance to realise this radical change which has come over the whole Congress Movement since the leadership was given into the hands of Mahatma Gandhi nearly twenty years ago. Before that time even leaders like Jawaharlal Nehru and his father thought in English, spoke in English, regarded the Congress itself as an organ of English opinion which had to deal chiefly with what was called "Educated India" and its disabilities. But just at the crucial moment, when everything was at stake and a leader for all India was needed, Mahatma Gandhi came to the front in such a manner that for the time being he united all the progressive forces in a compact body and received the whole-hearted allegiance not only of Motilal and Jawaharlal Nehru, but also of men like C. R. Das, J. M. Sen Gupta, Dr. Ansari, Maulana Muhammad Ali, Madan Mohan Malaviya, and others, whose outlook hitherto had been confined for the most part to the rights of citizenship for the small educated minority to which they belonged. The ninety per cent. of village India had only come indirectly into their political horizon.

But Mahatma Gandhi, living himself the life of a poor peasant, soon changed all that and brought those who sought his political support face to face with realities. The village now became the centre of the picture: its needs were India's needs; its language must be India's language.

Jawaharlal Nehru was among the very first to recognise this drastic change that was coming over the whole scene. He began to work out, with some compunction, what it would mean in detail to his own manner of living. Quite inevitably it would imply giving up many expensive habits and coming nearer to the level of those for whom he was now destined to work day and night.

It is easy to see from his autobiography how at first he half resisted some of these practical conclusions. When I was with him in Lala Harkishen Lal's house in Lahore, in 1919, after the humiliations under martial law, the change had only just begun. But what he met with in the Punjab—the horror of it—hastened the process, as did also the golden opportunity of seeing a great deal of Mahatma Gandhi during those days. No one could be with him at that time, in his entire physical exhaustion combined with amazing spiritual strength, without searching himself through and through.

But there was an honest revolt also, which this book by Jawaharlal clearly indicates. There was in him no blind worship. For he is a "modern," with no liking whatever for the extreme ascetic practices of Mahatma Gandhi. Mere fasts and penances do not attract him. They only irritate him, when they take the strange forms that mediæval saints practised. For they seem to him to be irrational. Thus his twentieth century mind had prevented him hitherto from carrying out to the full many of the things which seem to appeal with irresistible force to Mahatma Gandhi.

And yet the massive simplicity of Gandhi draws Jawaharlal all the while nearer and nearer to his own standard. He quotes more than once that striking phrase where Gandhi describes his aim as "*Complete identification with the poorest of mankind, longing to live no better than they.*"

If a sheer record were taken of all that Jawaharlal has suffered in the last twenty years, since Non-Co-operation was started, it would be seen to come not far short of Gandhi's own extreme privations which have brought him so close to the hearts of the poor people.

No one, for instance, can fail to be struck by the way in which the moment

Jawaharlal has been set free from prison he is at once courting another arrest by some action which he cannot avoid if he would be true to his own principles. To give an example, the Bihar Earthquake happens soon after he is set free. So, after making a challenging speech in Calcutta directly after his release, he takes the next train and is on the spot, toiling night and day among the terror-stricken village people. Only then, when he has done all he possibly could, does he return home. "I got back," he writes, "dead tired after my tour. Ten strenuous days had made me look ghastly and my people were surprised at my appearance. I tried to begin writing my report, but sleep overcame me. So I spent at least twelve out of the next twenty-four hours in sleep. Next day, Kamala and I had just finished tea, when a car drove up and a police officer alighted. I knew immediately my time had come."

It is a hard doctrine, this "complete identification with the poorest of mankind," which Mahatmaji has laid down as the true "democratic test." Yet who can doubt that those who come nearest to it in practice are able finally to win the loyalty and love of the masses of simple village people in India, who judge by deeds not words?

"Whether Gandhiji," writes Jawaharlal, "is a democrat or not, he does represent the peasant masses of India; he is the quintessence of the conscious and subconscious will of those millions. It is perhaps something more than representation: for he is the idealised personification of

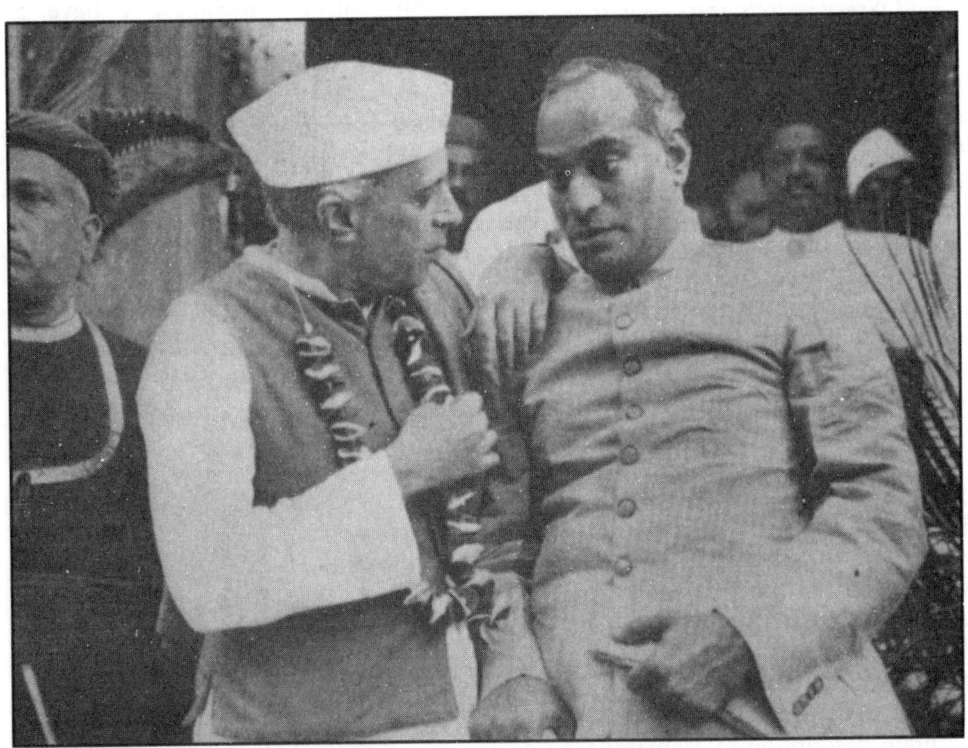

WITH MR. V. V. GIRI

A serious discussion between Pundit S. Nehru and the Hon. V. V. Giri during a meeting in Bombay.

THE LEADER
Pundit Nehru addressing a Congress Meeting at Lucknow.

those vast millions. Of course, he is not the average peasant. A man of the keenest intellect, of fine feeling and good taste, wide vision; very human, and yet essentially the ascetic, who has suppressed his passions and emotions, sublimated them and directed them in spiritual channels; a tremendous personality, drawing people to himself like a magnet, and calling out fierce loyalties and attachments—all this so utterly unlike and beyond a peasant. And yet withal he is the great peasant, with a peasant's blindness to some aspects of life. But India is peasant India; and so he knows his India well and reacts to her lightest tremors, and gauges a situation accurately and almost instinctively, and has a knack of acting at the psychological moment."

In every phrase of this remarkably accurate description of Mahatma Gandhi we can see how the author has been attracted by the extraordinary appeal that Gandhi makes to all the leading spirits in India who come within the close range of his personal influence and are ready to respond to its call.

"I have been," writes Jawaharlal in another remarkable passage about himself, "a queer mixture of the East and West, out of place everywhere, at home nowhere. Perhaps my thoughts and approach to life are more akin to what is called Western than Eastern, but India clings to me, as she does to all her children, in innumerable ways. I cannot get rid of that past inheritance of my recent acquisitions. They are both part of me, and, though they help me in both the East and the West, they create in me a feeling of spiritual loneliness not only in public activities, but in life itself. I am a stranger and alien in the West. I cannot be of it. But in my own country also, sometimes, I have an exile's feeling."

Yet out of all this inner conflict there

AT LUCKNOW
Speaking into a microphone as he presides over the meeting.

WOMEN TAKE THEIR PART IN NATIONAL LIFE

A procession of the All-India Women's League in Calcutta. Pundit Jawaharlal, whose sister was a member of Congress, encourages Indian women to take part in political affairs.

has come the power which has made him the one great driving force in national India, second only to Mahatma Gandhi. His attitude towards the latter oscillates but always comes back to the same centre. He is severely critical, yet at the same time won over to admiration and affection. He is continually repelled, and yet he realises that in the very things that jar upon him lies the secret of Gandhi's power with the vast multitudes of simple village people.

On one salient point there is no difference between them. For they both realise that only by infinite sacrifice and suffering can India's freedom be attained. And Jawaharlal knows absolutely that this one frail man, who has so often put his own life at stake, has won his way to India's heart as no one else has ever done, and that he alone can lead India forward to the final goal of Swaraj.

This increasing consciousness of the fate of the multitudes, in India, of poverty-stricken people has also drawn Jawaharlal Nehru irresistibly towards what he calls "Socialism." But in using this general word he is no doctrinaire, and has nothing but contempt for "arm-chair" economists, who seek to gain a cheap notoriety by using catch phrases. He knows intimately the difference between Indian conditions and those of the West. What changes are to be made in India must be made from the standpoint of Indian economy, not that of Europe.

Yet, while he recognises these practical differences, he is desperately in earnest about the immediate need in India of revolution in the economic and social system now prevailing. Whether it is in the petty Indian States, or in the large landlord areas, or in the mill centres, the concentration of arbitrary power in the

AT LUDHIANA

The men's procession during the All-India States' People's Conference at Ludhiana in 1939.

hands of a single person, who for all practical purposes has powers of life and death over thousands of helpless people, has become intolerable to him just in the same way that the imperialism of foreign rule has become intolerable also. He has seen this vision of the suffering peasant in India and other lands, and in a socialist co-operative endeavour, whereby the land and the instruments of production are placed at the service of the community, he sees the way out of this inveterate evil.

He quotes the moving lines of the American poet, E. Markham, from "The Man with the Hoe":

IN CALCUTTA

Pundit Jawaharlal Nehru being driven through the crowded streets in a flower-decked carriage.

"*Bowed by the weight of centuries he leans*
Upon his hoe and gazes on the ground,
The emptiness of ages on his face,
And on his back the burden of the world.

"*Through this dread shape the suffering ages look.*
Time's tragedy is in that aching stoop,
Through this dread shape humanity betrayed,
Plundered, profaned and disinherited,
Cries protest to the powers that made the world,
A protest that is also prophecy."

Strangely enough, at this very point, Jawaharlal, having gone thus far with Mahatma Gandhi, and having half accepted his hard doctrine of "complete identification with the poorest of mankind," parts company with him as to the methods to be employed for bringing the present evils to an end.

Mahatmaji, on his side, is willing to allow the rajah and the money-lender, and the Zamindar and the mill-owner to go on with their personal rule over those who are economically in their power provided the one religious quality of divine charity (which he would call *Ahimsa*) can be introduced into their despotic sway and thus cause it to become, for the time being at any rate, a "Rama Rajya"—a Kingdom of God upon earth. But Jawaharlal, on the other side, can see no lasting remedy in such a personal change in the heart of a single rajah, or Zamindar or mill-owner.

A RECENT STUDY OF PUNDIT JAWAHARLAL NEHRU

He regards the whole system of despotic power, whether brought about by capitalism or imperialism, as an evil in itself. He believes that some form of co-operative ownership of land and of the instruments of production must in the end lead to more equitable and stable results.

Thus the soul of Jawaharlal is vexed within him when he sees Mahatma Gandhi holding out the hand of cordial friendship and even partnership to those whose very function in society he believes to be destructive of elementary justice. Gandhiji, on the other hand, has his eyes fixed on the inner conversion of the rajah and the landlord and the money-lender and the capitalist which may lead them to a voluntary surrender of their power.

SEEKING GANDHI'S ADVICE

Jawaharlal Nehru climbing the stairs to the Mahatma's apartment to consult with him.

Looking back over what I have now written, I can see that I have attempted an impossible task in trying to compress into one brief article the life story of one of the greatest living personalities of the modern age. Nevertheless, if I have left a vivid picture of the inner struggle of one who is still young in years though old in wisdom and sorrow, I shall be content.

SIR FAZL-I-HUSAIN

SIR FAZL-I-HUSAIN

THE PUNJAB'S POLITICAL LEADER AND REFORMER

1877–1936

BY SIR GEORGE ANDERSON, C.S.I., C.I.E.

THE early career of Fazl-i-Husain ran along normal lines. After graduating from the University of the Punjab, and later of Cambridge, he was called to the Bar and subsequently built up a good, though by no means an exceptional, practice in the Punjab. In common with many other Indian politicians he took a deep interest in education, and the fortunes of Islamia College, Lahore, owed much to his perseverance and loyalty. He was for many years a member both of the Senate and Syndicate of Punjab University; and he also represented that university on the Legislative Council of the province. In politics he was what may be termed a progressive nationalist and he soon earned the reputation of being a staunch critic and opponent of the old-time bureaucracy. Had events pursued a different course he might, along with many others of his political associates, have found himself in gaol as a political offender. Had this been his lot, he would assuredly have met his fate with stoical indifference and with cynical contempt.

The institution of the Montagu-Chelmsford reforms, however, marked the turning point of his career. In 1921 he became Education Minister in the Punjab and, after a few years, he was transferred to the post of Revenue Member. He later served for five years as Education Member in the Government of India. Thus he held high office continuously for a period of fifteen years. Subsequent to his retirement in 1936 he returned to his home in Lahore and at once busied himself in the politics of the province. Had his life been spared, there can be little doubt that he would have been the first Premier of the Punjab.

Such, in brief, is the story of Fazl-i-Husain. But, eminent though his services undoubtedly were, his record, by itself, was scarcely such as to justify his inclusion in this series of the *Great Men of India;* and there are further considerations which deepen our perplexity as to his correct place in the history of India.

Though he was often effective in debate and though at times he spoke with force and persuasion, especially in the vernacular, he was not possessed of oratorical talent. His voice was lacking both in power and resonance, and the thread of his argument was often broken by violent fits of coughing. He was incapable of inspiring others by the magic of the spoken word or by playing on the emotions of his listeners. It was not by set speeches that he could lead men to action.

Nor was he either an erudite scholar or a profound thinker. No learned book bears his name, and what little he wrote was largely ephemeral. Even the official files of the Lahore and Delhi secretariats contain little under his signature that betokens one who exercised, and whose memory to-day continues to exercise, widespread influence over men and things.

Though he was by no means lacking in kindness and though on many occasions he displayed great magnanimity and forbearance, often towards those who had little claim to expect generosity at his hands, he was scarcely an engaging personality. He was very reserved in his relations with others. Towards the end of his life, when his malady became ever more critical, he was extremely loath to leave his home and to seek the companionship of his fellow men. Though his circle of acquaintances was a very wide one, he had but few intimate friends. He made no personal appeal such as did Louis Botha, or does Stanley Baldwin. But he had more friends than he would have cared to admit; he certainly had more enemies than he had earned.

Let it also be remembered that for years before his death, at a comparatively early age, he suffered from a grievous malady which sapped his vitality. Scarcely a month passed but he was confined to his bed, and his temperature always appeared to be above normal. But his patience and optimism were heroic. While he resented commiseration, he rarely complained. Yet he continued to persevere until almost his last moments in planning for the future of India, and especially of the province which he had served so well. But in spite of his fortitude it became ever more evident to others that it would be hazardous to place much reliance on a life which had become so precarious.

In order to appreciate Fazl-i-Husain's correct contribution towards the life and progress of India it is necessary first to bear in mind the time and the place in which he lived.

It is difficult to regard the political reforms which bear the names of Mr. Edwin Montagu and Lord Chelmsford as providing an opportunity for anybody, however ingenious, to justify himself as one of the *Great Indians;* and, indeed, Fazl-i-Husain himself took no pains to conceal his view that those reforms were at best an unsatisfactory compromise. But it was his genius and his political sagacity that enabled him to regard a difficult period of transition as the very time when preparations should be made for the next advance. That was the time when it should be proved that Indians were worthy of responsibility, and when all classes and communities should be encouraged and trained to make their full and effective contributions towards the development of the new India. The new India should not connote merely a particular class or community.

A narrow view of his policy would indicate, as many indeed held, that he thought merely of collecting the loaves and fishes for the benefit of the Moslem community. He undoubtedly spent much of his time in drawing up detailed figures regarding appointments and in fighting strenuously for communal percentages and quotas, but rarely did he seek appointments for particular individuals or even for those who were within his own circle. His object was rather that India should be enriched by the advance of all communities and should thereby live more abundantly.

Similarly, he was quick to realise, and was tenacious in the belief, that the strength and health of India lay in the countryside. The vast rural population of India should therefore be aided and encouraged to release themselves from the grave limitations imposed upon them by their own ignorance and by past neglect. If the life of India was to become pure and vigorous it should be strengthened by the attainments and self-reliance of those living in the villages.

Firm and steadfast in these beliefs, Fazl-i-Husain soon found welcome supporters from within the ranks of the bureaucracy with whom he was then brought into contact. Perhaps more than in any other province in India, the services in the Punjab have retained that

YOUNG MOHAMMEDANS IN SCHOOL

The School in the Mosque at Lahore. Here the boys receive a general education as well as studying the Koran.

A PUNJAB VILLAGE

A large proportion of the Punjab people are engaged in agriculture and live in villages such as this. It was for their betterment Sir Fazl-i-Husain chiefly worked.

devotion to the land and to the dwellers on the land, which had been implanted years before by Henry Lawrence; and that tradition has continued to be both potent and widespread. The life and training of many young civilians have pivoted round their settlement duties, which brought them into intimate contact with the lives and conditions of village folk. A further contact was provided by the feats of engineers who had built the great canals of the province, and by the resource of those who had come to live in the canal colonies. The Punjab was also "the sword-arm" of India; and many of those who had fought in the Great War had returned with their vision widened by contact with men and things in other lands. The influence of those men was permeating village life throughout the province.

Fazl-i-Husain was not himself the initiator of any great scheme of rural development. Indeed, the broad outlines of such a policy had been constructed and much had already been achieved. But it was he who saw the great opportunity and converted rural reform into a political reality.

There is much in his political career which resembles that of perhaps the most eminent and imaginative of English statesmen. After the memorable struggle with Robert Peel on the repeal of the corn duties, the Tory Party lost the services of most of its experienced supporters, and Benjamin Disraeli found himself at the head of a party bereft of leaders. It therefore became his lot to build up what ultimately became the modern Conservative Party and to impregnate it with his ideals; but he had to do so with most unpromising material. The landowning classes have rarely been favourable to reform, whether it be religious or social, political or economic; and those classes in England were then smarting with indignation over what they conceived to have been the great betrayal. And in those early days Disraeli could scarcely have been regarded as one fitted to lead the land-owning aristocracy of England.

The distinguishing feature of Disraeli's policy was his intense love of England, especially of its countryside. He thought much of the strength and the might and the power of England, and these had sprung from the villages of England; the bowmen of Agincourt, the sea-dogs of Devon, the Ironsides of the eastern counties, the men who had fought and triumphed at Minden, Quebec and Waterloo. But Disraeli saw that with the dwindling of the countryside the strength and vitality of the race would be sapped. And he thought even more of the soul of England. With the uncontrolled industrialisation of England there would inevitably ensue the sweated labour, the unhealthy conditions of vast industrial cities, a people stunted both in physical and in mental vigour. The very fibre of the race was at stake.

Fazl-i-Husain found himself in a somewhat similar position. His very acceptance of office had estranged him from most of his old political associates, who were brooding over what they also considered to have been their betrayal; and his very political astuteness enraged them almost beyond endurance. He had therefore to face a bitterly hostile legislative council and it was not long before he had to withstand, though successfully, a formal vote of no-confidence. And though there had been a large influx of rural members, few of these could be

THE PEOPLE OF THE PUNJAB

A group of Punjab village folk, typical people of this great agricultural province—the most important wheat growing area in India.

expected to stand up with success against opponents who were experienced in the thrust of debate and in political organisation. Mere voting strength, by itself, cannot prevail for long; it can quickly crumble in face of personal interest and intrigue as well as of alluring enticements from political opponents. To say the least, the prospects were far from promising.

Patience, imperturbability, attention to detail and, above all, political astuteness were the main gifts that Fazl-i-Husain brought to bear on his difficult task. He was himself an untiring worker, and everybody associated with him was also expected to work; to every one was given his allotted task. But for that task each had to be trained, and trained in the manner which his leader had devised for him. Diligence in voting was not enough.

As Fazl-i-Husain once expressed himself in his playful manner, he believed far more in tutorial classes than in mass lectures; in other words, the careful preparation for debates was of far greater importance than eloquent orations during debates. The real secret of his success was that even for discussion with an individual, and even more with a committee, he was always prepared. He knew exactly what he wanted and, what is more, he had carefully planned the very lines along which discussion should take place. The many who took part in such discussions will remember the untidy scraps of paper and the illegible hieroglyphics which prompted his memory and guided the trend of discussion. Every discussion, however unimportant it may have seemed to others, was to him a matter of supreme importance. And so it was that he usually got his way, and that not by peremptory commands but as a result of discussion. What was even more satisfactory, other people, and even the writer of this article, also began to produce untidy scraps of paper.

But this endless round of discussions did not consist merely of interviews and committees with particular objects in view; he frequently gathered unto himself groups of his political supporters, often those who seemed to be of little value beyond the casting of their votes. But even they had to be taught to understand the barest rudiments of his policy. To them he expounded with infinite patience the pros and cons of each topic in turn; and how cavalierly would he brush aside any hasty expression of opinion before, as he put it, the right of holding an opinion had been earned by industry and thought!

He was at his best in preparing for a debate in the Legislature. He seemed to know by instinct the course which each debate would take. He knew that so-and-so would represent a particular point of view, and that point of view had to be countered. And often, by some astute move, would he lure his opponents into an untenable position to be exploited when his turn came to wind up the debate. Everything as far as possible had been pre-ordained, and so it was that he usually had his way also in debates.

Leaders had also to be brought into the foreground, but whence were they to be found? Fazl-i-Husain had a good eye for latent capacity. Perhaps his most faithful follower was Chaudhri (now Sir) Chhotu Ram, the leader of the Jat community in the eastern part of the province. His diligence and readiness of speech quickly responded to the encouragement which he received. There were also Captain (now Sir) Sikandar Hayat Khan, who later officiated with much distinction as Governor of the province and is now the first Premier of the Punjab; Malik (now Sir) Firoz Khan Noon, who served for many years as a minister in varying capacities and is now High Commissioner for India in London; and Sir Shahab-ud-din, who has been for many years President of the Legislature and has done much to model its practice and procedure on that of the House of Commons.

The most difficult task, however, was to ensure that the party should betoken its name, that it should seek to become national and to unite rather than divide the different sections and communities of the province. In its early days it took the form, perhaps inevitably, of being too exclusively a Moslem party, and political controversy was therefore conducted largely on communal lines. But by degrees the lines of cleavage tended to broaden and recruits from other communities were gladly enlisted. The fruits of Fazl-i-Husain's labours were reaped when the first Premier of the province was able to form a government, which was broad-based both in its leaders and in its rank and file. The anxious time of preparation had not been in vain.

The educational policy of Fazl-i-Husain was in close accord with his political policy; the encouragement of backward areas and of backward communities were its watchwords. It was natural therefore that he should pay particular attention to the needs of the countryside, and a rapid expansion of education in the villages was clearly indicated. But, in achieving that objective, he suffered from a dual handicap resulting from his past record and from his past inclinations.

It is a platitude that education should be a means of uniting and not of dividing the rising generation; but unfortunately the bane of education in the Punjab is its communal bias. Bearing in mind the acuteness of communal strife, it is tempting Providence that, from the age of early childhood until the time of early manhood, children should be educated in the narrowing atmosphere of a communal institution, but such had become very largely the accepted practice in the Punjab. It speaks much for the moral courage of Fazl-i-Husain that he strove to shake off early and valued associations and to do what he could to encourage the members of his community to send their children to publicly managed schools and colleges rather than to communal institutions. He therefore founded a large number of Government high schools throughout the province, and the support which he received from his community is indicated by the fact that in most of those schools there was a preponderance of Moslem pupils. The seed that he thus sowed is beginning already to bear fruit, and there is a growing desire among more thoughtful minds that the schools should be rescued from communal thraldom.

In the sphere of primary education Fazl-i-Husain had a more straightforward task. His policy was that of rapid expansion by means of schools maintained by local bodies. Hence it has come about that, whereas in Bengal the number of pupils attending *maktabs* approximates 800,000, the number in the Punjab is negligible. But it is doubtful whether Fazl-i-Husain realised sufficiently that, in view of the changing political situation, the position of local bodies needed review. He was apt in that respect to live in the past when he and his associates, in their struggle against the bureaucracy, regarded official interference with the activities of local bodies as anathema. Indian politicians, not unnaturally, have been slow to grasp the fact that ministerial responsibility and local independence go ill together. But an Education Minister must find it difficult to carry out his responsibility to the Legislature in the matter of education so long as almost unsupervised control is vested in inexperienced and sometimes corrupt local bodies. It is possible, however, that Fazl-i-Husain was aware of this anomaly and that he preferred to ease matters, as he often did, by personal discussions with those concerned rather than by introducing contentious legislation. He was a past-master in judging the pace of political advance and in gauging when the time for action had become ripe.

He was not content, however, with mere numerical progress. He was well aware of the grave defects from which education, especially in rural areas, was suffering. The writer of this article well remembers how, shortly after he had taken over the duties of Director of Public Instruction and Fazl-i-Husain himself had become Education Minister, a bulky file of papers was placed before him. It contained a mass of opinions indicating that as the distinction between Vernacular and Anglo-vernacular middle schools had become so slight, the Vernacular side of education should be merged in the Anglo-vernacular. The issue appeared to have been prejudged, and therefore the papers were forwarded with little comment to the minister. They were quickly returned with the observation that immediate discussion was imperative. In the course of that discussion the instructions of Fazl-i-Husain were both trenchant and decisive. He expressed in forcible terms the view that the abandonment of the Vernacular system would be fatal in many directions, notably in the further impoverishment of the countryside and in the further congestion of the schools and colleges in the towns.

As a result of his memorable intervention, the whole trend of educational policy as affecting rural areas was revolutionised. The number of Vernacular middle schools was rapidly advanced, farms and gardens were attached to them, teachers in agriculture were trained; and later, the whole teaching of the schools was brought into harmony with rural conditions and requirements.

But Fazl-i-Husain was not content. He saw clearly that if these schools were to hold their own with their Anglo-vernacular counterparts, they should lead to higher studies of a rural type. Unfortunately, he soon ceased to be Education Minister and the question was held in abeyance. The manner in which such higher studies should be provided has since become clearer owing to the increased attention now being paid to the urgent need of rural development. Schemes of rural reform, however, if imposed from without, are unlikely to achieve any lasting success; an indigenous agency is imperative. Social workers, both official and non-official, should be given training in a rural atmosphere; and for that training the preliminary teaching in Vernacular middle schools should provide an admirable foundation. As soon as suitable training in the rural social services has been instituted, Fazl-i-Husain's policy in rural education will have come to fruition.

Such is our appreciation of Fazl-i-Husain's place in Indian history. Though it was not gained by spectacular achievements, it was greatly to the benefit of India, and especially of the Punjab, that he lived and worked during the difficult, though important, period of transition which had been introduced by the Montagu-Chelmsford reforms.

Fazl-i-Husain's great contribution to the political development of India was that he believed heart and soul in discussion; especially since real and effective discussion is so often lacking in the life of India. In the schools and colleges teaching consists mainly of a succession of monologues by the teacher, which the students rarely understand and in which they themselves take but little part. Political programmes, again, are framed mainly by means of high-sounding resolutions passed unanimously and without discussion by gigantic meetings, in which the rank and file are expected only to assent and to applaud.

As has been shown in this article, Fazl-i-Husain's methods were different. He was a great political teacher, and few teachers have taken such devoted care over the training of their pupils. If it be true that genius consists in an infinite capacity for taking pains, then undoubtedly Fazl-i-Husain was a genius. A good teacher is not necessarily a profound thinker, and still less a great speaker; but rather one who can expound clearly and, far more important, can make his pupils think for themselves and do their full share of the work. As a result of Fazl-i-Husain's teaching, there is far more political thought and political reality in the Punjab than elsewhere in India.

IRRIGATION IN THE PUNJAB
The Lower Chenab Canal irrigating 1,800 *square miles.*

MAHOMED ALI JINNAH

MAHOMED ALI JINNAH

ORGANISER OF MOSLEM UNITY

BORN 1876

BY USMAN AHMAD ANSON

THE Government of India Act, 1935, will go down in the constitutional history of India as an event of the first importance. In itself it was an epoch-making event. But the years which preceded and followed it saw the operation of those processes which made Mahomed Ali Jinnah the unquestioned leader of the bulk of ninety million Moslems of India, and crystallised the policy which is associated with the name of Jinnah and of the All-India Moslem League. This, though the oldest political organisation of Moslems, had considerably lost strength and following owing to numerous and important secessions from its ranks. But on the eve of the introduction of the new Government of India Act, Mahomed Ali Jinnah revived and re-organised the Moslem League, and for all practical purposes set it on its feet again. Now he is the accepted and undisputed leader of the Moslem community and is its highly esteemed and deeply loved "Qaid-i-Azam." This was no sudden rise to greatness by a lucky combination of favourable circumstances, but the consummation of a long record of selfless service and devotion to the cause of India's freedom, and to the cause of the community to which he belongs and which has been and is bound to be a large and powerful factor in the shaping of the country's destiny.

Mahomed Ali Jinnah at the present day stands solely for the rights of the Moslem community. This fact is exploited by other parties and their leaders for making the allegation that Jinnah has become a reactionary and is an obstacle in the path of the country's freedom. That this is deliberate and calculated calumny on one of the most fearless and courageous patriots which India has produced will appear from a simple record of his career. Mahomed Ali Jinnah entered political life as a nationalist and a radical, but slowly and surely the force of events and tendencies and, above all, the uncompromising attitude of the majority veered him more and more towards his own community and the guardianship of its interests. It can be said without fear of contradiction that the Moslem community has not fared very well under the new reforms and if any organisation has greater claim on Jinnah's services than another, it is the All-India Moslem League. So far from being a stigma on Mahomed Ali Jinnah, his dissociation from the Indian National Congress and complete identification with the fortunes of the Moslem League is an object lesson to the students of history who may be interested in the reactions of minorities in politically unfree countries.

Sixty-three years ago there was a Christmas of special significance to the Moslems of India. It was the Christmas of the year 1876. It fell on a Sunday and whatever blessings and happiness it might have brought to the followers of the Christian faith, it certainly brought a blessing to the Moslems of India and happiness into a Moslem Khoja family of Karachi. On that day was born Mahomed Ali Jinnah to gladden the hearts of his lucky parents, being their first son. His father belonged to a mercantile community and was himself a wealthy merchant. But, luckily for Indian Moslems, he decided for his first son, Mahomed Ali, upon a career different from what the traditions of his community demanded. If he had followed the usual practice, Mahomed Ali would have been in his early years initiated into business and would have ended perhaps as a millionaire, perhaps a knight and a leader without any following. India would have lost a stout patriot, Moslems an able leader, and history one of its most interesting figures. But luckily his father chose to give him a liberal education and make him a barrister.

Mahomed Ali Jinnah had his early education at Karachi. In 1892, at the tender age of sixteen, he was sent out to England by his parents. Fortunately for himself and for India the contacts which he made at this impressionable age were of the healthiest character and necessarily played their part in the formative process which made the Jinnah of later years. Above all he met about this time Dadābhai Naoroji, who saw with his experienced eye that this lad of 17, if properly influenced and guided, would go far indeed. Dadabhai Naoroji, already a veteran of mature years, was at that time President of the Indian Society in London. His is the first name in the list of patriarchs of the Indian Nationalist Movement. Beginning his connection with the Congress from its very outset, he continued to serve it till the evening of his life, and took it through the whole gamut of evolution, from the humble position of being a people's organ seeking redress of administrative grievances, to that of a National Assembly working for the definite object of attaining Swaraj. He singled out the young Jinnah there and then for rôles which would have done credit to any man. Jinnah returned to India in 1896 after qualifying himself for the Bar, and was called to the Bar in 1897.

When Mahomed Ali Jinnah returned to India he was a raw youth totally inexperienced in the ways of the world. But he was soon to have his first taste of hardship and real worry. For some time things in business had been going none too well for his father and, on his return, he found him involved in heavy financial ruin. It was naturally a hard blow to the young Jinnah who, until now a favourite of fortune, was suddenly faced with unexpected poverty. Fired, however, by a generous anxiety to keep his beloved father from feeling the sting of his misfortune, he set out to conquer the world equipped with nothing but his youth, his courage and his ambition.

About the year 1897 Jinnah went to Bombay, where he expected a wider field for the exercise of his talents. The first three years were of severe hardship. But after that period his buoyant patience bore fruit. Through the kind offices of an old friend Jinnah was granted permission to read in the chambers of Mr. Macpherson, then acting Advocate-General of Bombay. It was a very courteous concession, in fact, the first of its kind to be granted to an Indian. This may be described as his start on the path to success, because with his gifts he was bound to profit very largely from this opportunity. After a short time his career became just one continuous record of successive triumphs. To-day he is considered to be a great lawyer, in fact, one of the greatest that India has produced. We may have had jurists greater than Jinnah, but surely no greater advocate. His fine advocacy became his greatest asset in the legal profession, and this, combined with his other qualities, makes him one of the greatest lawyers.

He is gifted with a unique and

characteristic style of speaking which he has carried into every sphere of life in which he has taken a part. As a speaker Mahomed Ali Jinnah has the triple assets of a magnetic presence, an impressive delivery, and a voice which while lacking in volume has an arresting timbre. His small mannerisms, gestures and the inflection of his tone, which would be at best insignificant in a smaller man, all play their part in creating that final impression which is Jinnah the public speaker. But, though occasionally he has attained a moment of wholly unconscious yet stirring eloquence, he has the cogent force of a brilliant advocate rather than the glowing fervour of a fiery orator. And it is not on a public platform, but at a round table conference that he finds full scope for his unusual powers of persuasion, luminous exposition, searching argument and impeccable judgment. Perhaps his long connection with the Bar and the legislature has had something to do with moulding the style that has become his own. His great powers as a debater have earned him the name of "parliamentary juggler." But I am anticipating. Let us go back to his entry into politics and his activities in the cause of India's freedom, which form one of the noblest chapters in his career.

Mahomed Ali Jinnah was from the outset destined to play a prominent part in politics. His rich gifts clearly marked him for such a rôle. In his political creed we find him deeply influenced by two outstanding personalities of the time. It has been mentioned elsewhere that he came into contact with Dadabhai Naoroji at a very tender and impressionable age when he first went out to England. The second figure in Indian politics which was a source of inspiration to Jinnah was Gopal Krishna Gokhale, who occupies a place of great honour and respect in the roll of India's worthy sons. He combined in himself two of the rarest gifts—a heart fired by great fervour and sincerity and an intellect of the highest order. Accordingly we

ALL-INDIA MOSLEM LEADERS' CONFERENCE

A photograph taken outside Mr. Jinnah's bungalow in Bombay where a meeting had been held.

MR. JINNAH AT LAHORE

In 1936 Mr. Jinnah visited Lahore to seek a solution to the Civil Disobedience Campaign then in force in that city. He is seen at his reception at the station about to address the crowd.

find the impress of Gokhale's personality on the movement which he nurtured with his thought and service. He was the model which Jinnah placed before himself. On one occasion, in an unguarded moment of self-revelation, Jinnah said, "It is my ambition to become the Moslem Gokhale." The true significance of these words can only be realised by those who know how secretive he is in his inner thoughts and in the revelation of his true likes and dislikes. In the light of this avowal it is interesting to recall Gokhale's own prediction about his gifted comrade. "He has true stuff in him," he said, "and that freedom from all sectarian prejudice which will make him the best ambassador of Hindu-Moslem unity." This estimate of Jinnah, generous as it sounds, is only a just tribute to his true and tried patriotism.

In 1906 Jinnah was already a rising lawyer and coming politician. We find him playing his unostentatious part in the activities of the time as Private Secretary to his old master Dadabhai Naoroji who, at the historic sessions of the National Congress at Calcutta, for the first time enunciated the glorious ideal of Self-Government for India. Jinnah had already joined the ranks of the National Congress, fired no doubt by the virile patriotism of men like Badruddin Tyabji and the lion-hearted Pherozeshah Mehta. Incidentally it is interesting to note that his maiden speech at the Congress Session was on a motion relating to Waqf Alal-aulad—a measure that was later to bring his name into such prominence. Interesting, too, and suggestive in view of succeeding events, is it to find this future leader of the Moslems present as a sort of cross-bencher at the conference of Hindu and Moslem leaders convened at Allahabad in 1910 under Sir Wamilli Wedderburn's benign direction to consider a somewhat premature and artificial *entente cordiale* between the two communities still so sharply divided by a gulf of mutual dislike and distrust.

The year 1910 has yet another importance in our present chronicle. In that year the Moslems of the Bombay Presidency elected him as their representative to the Supreme Legislative Council. At first sight it might seem incompatible for a staunch nationalist like him to represent a purely sectarian interest. But his conduct throughout convincingly proved that national and Moslem interests were not necessarily opposed to each other, and it gave the lie to the belief that anyone who tried to reconcile the two would be torn between conflicting loyalties. In the Council, Mahomed Ali Jinnah invariably lent his willing support to every liberal measure involving the larger national issues—measures like Gokhale's Elementary Education Bill and Mr. Basu's Special Marriage Bill, against which there was violent opposition from many quarters.

About this time Jinnah rendered a great service to Moslems and earned their lasting gratitude. For some time past Moslem opinion had been clamouring for a measure to counteract the effect of certain Privy Council decisions based on an interpretation of Mohammedan Law considered to be wrong and injurious. That opinion finally crystallised into the Waqf Validating Bill of 1913, to introduce which Jinnah was specially nominated for an extra term by the Viceroy, Lord Hardinge. He showed great skill and tact in piloting through such an intricate and controversial measure—the first instance of a Bill passing into law on the motion of a private member. It won him not only the wondering admiration of his colleagues but also his first meed of general recognition from his co-religionists all over India, who, while still regarding him as a little outside the orthodox pale of Islam, were soon to seek his advice and guidance in their political affairs.

After this there was a short break in Jinnah's work as a legislator. During the three years that followed he was for a considerable time in England. His first trip was in 1913, when about the middle of April he proceeded to Europe in search of a long, idle holiday. Once in England, however, there was no rest for this tireless worker. He was drawn at once into the tangled web of the Indian Student-world, whose cause he espoused with great zeal and understanding. Within a few weeks of his arrival in London he founded the London Indian Association, which forms an excellent focus for the otherwise scattered energies and activities of young India in a foreign land. At his instance a Committee was appointed by the India Office to inquire into the legitimate grievances of Indian students suffering from restrictions which hindered their admission into educational centres.

He returned to India in the autumn of the same year, but had to go to England again in May, 1914, as member of the All-India Congress Deputation concerning the proposed reform of the India Council. On this he had already moved resolutions at the Karachi sessions of the Congress a few months earlier and at the Agra sessions of the Moslem League, with which organisation his connection had just begun and will be considered at length in due course. It was no small compliment to Jinnah that he was chosen to be the spokesman of articulate India before the representatives of the British Parliament and the British public. The leading English journals published numerous interviews, and his concise and lucid statement of the Indian

WITH THE MAHATMA

Mr. Jinnah consults with Mahatma Gandhi during discussions on Hindu-Moslem unity, an ideal dear to them both.

case which appeared in the London *Times* attracted widespread attention and comment.

In the autumn of 1916 Mahomed Ali Jinnah was once more elected by the Moslems of Bombay to the Viceregal Council. Ever since then he has almost continuously been connected with the Imperial Legislature of India, in the deliberations of which body he has taken a leading part, contributing in no small measure to raising the standard of its debates and heightening the general quality of its work. His association with the Central Legislature of India, through all its phases of evolution, has been so long and intimate that it has become difficult now to think of the one without the other. There is hardly any important enactment of the Legislature in the shaping of which he has not had a share. To-day he is considered a power in the Assembly. What is the secret of his power? He is, of course, a powerful debater. But that is only one of the reasons for his great strength and influence. The other reason is his independence and honesty, which have all through the years characterised his work in the Assembly. As he never puts himself under the slightest obligation to the Government Benches, he can always be counted upon to have a free judgment on all matters and give expression to it without hesitation or reserve. Although he receives more than his share of requests to put in a word of recommendation here and a word there, he has steeled himself against such weakness lest it may interfere with the independence of his action on more vital issues involving much greater consequences. The purpose of his smallest move in the Assembly is to work for the good of the people, whose interests he places above everything else. It is for history to determine the relative importance of men; but, judging from Jinnah's work as a legislator alone, we find the value and volume of his services second to none. His latest contribution was the part he played in sending the Shariat Bill to the Statute Book.

One of the most unfortunate and tragic events for Moslems in Indian history was the Mutiny of 1857. The actual incidents—brutalities perpetrated on both sides—were painful enough, but the memories which it left behind were even more so. Moslems had to shoulder the major share of the blame for this unfortunate outbreak and consequently had a more bitter taste of the retribution that followed. The result was that the Moslem community as a whole became apathetic towards politics and things in general. For several decades they continued to look with suspicion upon their new rulers and similarly in their turn were held in suspicion.

After the National Congress was founded in the eighties of the nineteenth century, Moslem attitude towards it was marked by the same apathy and suspicion which characterised their entire outlook. But this unhealthy state of affairs could not last indefinitely. Gradually Moslems began to have a growing realisation that the sister community was stealing a march on them in politics just as it had already done in education. So in December, 1906, the first political meeting of Moslems was held under the presidentship of Nawab Viqarul-Mulk in which the idea of a Moslem League was mooted, and finally an organisation of that name was set up with the object of voicing current Moslem opinion and aspirations. But it was soon found to be too narrow and too nebulous in its scope and aims to keep pace with the intense and growing national consciousness. About the middle of 1912 some important Moslem leaders met in a conference at Calcutta to reconsider a remodelling of the Constitution of the League on more progressive and patriotic lines.

Mr. Syed Wazir Hasan, who was honorary secretary of the League at the time, was sent round on an extensive tour to ascertain the views of Moslems in every province regarding so momentous a change of policy and perspective. In the following December a special meeting of the League Council was called, presided over by His Highness the Aga Khan, to consider the draft of an entirely new constitution. It was ultimately adopted with great enthusiasm at the memorable sessions of the All-India Moslem League held at Lucknow on March 22, 1913—a date that inaugurated a new era in the political history of Moslem India.

A reference has been made earlier to the fact that Mahomed Ali Jinnah was closely associated with Congress activities from the very beginning of his public career. So, pledged to the greater national welfare, he had with characteristic independence and honesty kept himself apart from the Moslem League movement which was till then frankly and exclusively sectarian in its sympathy and purpose. He was, however, invited to attend the Calcutta Conference, and also the later Council meeting—an act of courtesy which was in itself a graceful acknowledgment of his ability and merit. He gave his informal and valuable support to Clause D of the new constitution which materially embodied the Congress ideal of:

"*Attainment under the ægis of the British Crown of a system of Self-Government suitable to India through constitutional means, by bringing about, amongst others, a steady reform of the existing system of administration by promoting national unity, by fostering*

KARACHI WELCOMES MR. JINNAH

The picturesque procession was arranged to welcome Mr. Jinnah to Karachi, where he went in 1938 to attend the Moslem League Conference.

public spirit among the people of India, and by co-operating with other communities for the said purpose."

But up till now he was not a regular member of the organisation. This came about in England, where he had gone for a holiday in 1913. In the autumn of that year on the eve of his departure for India he was approached by Maulana Mohammad Ali and Mr. Wazir Hasan to enrol himself formally as a member of the All-India Moslem League. His deep interest in the organisation, to whose expanded outlook he had contributed so signally by his example, was unquestionably there, but, before enrolment, he made it clear to his two friends that loyalty to the Moslem League and the Moslem interest would in no way and at no time imply even the shadow of disloyalty to the larger national cause to which his life was dedicated.

The years that followed are of special interest, because during this period Jinnah worked ceaselessly in the cause of complete friendship and understanding between the Hindu and Moslem communities with his characteristic sincerity and energy. His efforts were so richly rewarded that he came to be looked upon as an ambassador of Hindu-Moslem unity. To-day certain individuals and bodies cannot repeat too loudly or too often that Jinnah is a communalist and an anti-nationalist. But any fair-minded person who takes the trouble of informing himself about past history and the succession of events which drove him to his present policy cannot help being struck by the injustice of such a description.

The tragic and untimely death of Gopal Krishna Gokhale in February, 1915, brought Hindus and Moslems together in a bond of common loss and sorrow. It was increasingly felt that the time was now ripe for a more direct and definite rapprochement between the two great communities that had recently exchanged cordial expressions of good-

THE STREETS OF KARACHI DURING THE PROCESSION

will and fellowship from afar. The Indian National Congress was to hold its sittings that year in Bombay. Mahomed Ali Jinnah, supported at that time by all the leading local Moslems, sent an invitation to the All-India Moslem League to hold its next annual sessions in Bombay during the national week in December. The story of that invitation and its startling sequel is painful in its shameful and subterranean intrigue. In the hour of such grave and bitter crisis this dauntless soldier of unity rose to the heights of an invincible patriotism. With a proud and splendid indifference to all personal suffering and sacrifice, heedless alike of official dissuasion or disfavour, the aggressive malice and machinations of his opponents or even the temporary injustice of his distant friends, Mahomed Ali Jinnah strove with an incomparable devotion and courage to create that supreme moment in our national history which witnessed the birth of a new India, redeemed and victorious in the love of her united children. An eye-witness of the grand culmination of events describes the scene in the following words: "Seldom has the pageant of time unrolled a scene so touching, so thrilling, so magnificent with drama and destiny as was enacted on the afternoon of December 30, 1915, when amidst the tears and applause of a gathered multitude the veteran heroes of the National Congress entered in a body to greet and bless their comrades of the Moslem League."

The new year dawned cloudless for this valiant fighter of national battles, bringing him some of the highest awards of his professional and public career. He added much lustre to his forensic reputation by his masterly conduct of two sensational law-suits involving respectively Mr. Horniman, the trusted friend, and Mr. Tilak the beloved tribune of the Indian people.

At this point we have to deviate a little from the thread of our narrative. About this time there was a growing surprise and reproach in the minds of his followers that so ardent an apostle of Self-Government should hold himself aloof from the recently organised Home Rule Movement which was rousing the country like a clarion call to freedom. It may have been partly due to a lingering sense of allegiance to the old school of politics in which he had been trained; or perhaps it may have been due to the habitual caution of a nature slow to commit itself to new and far-reaching responsibilities. However, the news of Mrs. Besant's internment in the June of 1917, which evoked unparalleled demonstrations throughout India, moved Mahomed Ali Jinnah to a prompt and militant decision. He immediately joined the Bombay Home Rule League. He could not remain in it as an ordinary member, but undertook, as its President, the delicate task of guiding its fortunes and guarding its interests through that troubled period of its indignant activities.

In the meantime the bonds of unity and affection in which Hindus and Moslems had been bound grew stronger and stronger. This was perhaps the most gladdening phase of a period almost heart-breaking in its disappointments. The Indian nation which had stood valiantly with its rulers in the War in the hope of winning back its freedom was soon to be rudely disillusioned. The War ended successfully for the British but, instead of bringing to Indians a realisation of their hopes, it inaugurated an era of repressive rule. Unfortunate incidents happened with astounding rapidity. The intense agitation which greeted the Rowlatt Bills and the iron hand with which the Government dealt with it will remain a sore wound in the heart of the Indian nation. Then Jilianwala Bagh: the "creeping orders" and the reign of Terror ushered in by martial law in the Punjab—and all this so soon after the War—finally destroyed any hopes which Indians might have entertained of the Government.

In this hour of their humiliation the two communities turned to each other for goodwill and affection. As a result of this understanding their policy and aims at this time were identical. The Congress espoused the cause of Khilafat, and the Moslem League fought shoulder to shoulder with the Congress in the great drive for National Freedom and Independence. In 1921 the fourteenth session of the All-India Moslem League was held in Ahmedabad with Maulana Hasrat Mohani as President. This was the seventh and last of the series held with the Congress sessions. Prominent among Congress leaders who attended the League Sessions were Messrs. Gandhi, Vijayragharacharia, Patel, Hakim Ajmal Khan and Dr. Ansari. It was a very well attended and a very successful session. Moslems were taking a complete share in the Non-Co-operation and Civil Disobedience movement started by Mahatma Gandhi and also in the suffering and sacrifice which it entailed.

A series of unfortunate incidents sounded the death-knell of the movement for the time being and of the Hindu-Moslem unity. The happenings at Chauri Chaura in the U.P., and similar incidents in Bombay and Madras compelled Mahatma Gandhi to suspend the movement which he had been unable to keep non-violent in character. All the leaders were arrested and lodged in jails. Soon after this started the series of communal riots which gradually spread to all parts of India and to this day mar the life and politics of the country.

It is not necessary for the purpose of the present narrative to try to assign or apportion blame for the riots, which will remain a disfiguring page in the history of this period. Here we are only concerned with the effect which they produced. They succeeded in shattering the Hindu-Moslem unity for which Jinnah and his band of supporters had worked so sincerely. They also succeeded in driving Jinnah out of politics, at least for the time being. The natural reaction of an inward and sensitive nature like his was deep disgust commingled with pain and sorrow. The Moslem community, in its lack of any definite policy or programme, could only be compared to a derelict vessel adrift on a stormy sea, and this condition of the community was reflected in the Moslem League.

Forces were now at work which were to turn Jinnah more and more towards the exclusive leadership of Moslems. The process, however, took the whole of the last decade to complete itself—running as it did the whole gamut from complete Hindu-Moslem unity in 1921 to an absolute break at the present day.

The announcement of the Statutory Commission in November, 1927, and the declaration of the policy and the principle underlying it stunned India by its utter lack of sympathy with Indian opinion, evoking intense and unanimous resentment. For a short time a common indignation brought together on a common platform the accredited leaders of all communities and classes, representing the most diverse interests and most divergent modes of political thought. Mahomed Ali Jinnah led the campaign of protest started in Bombay against the constitution and programme of the Statutory Commission. In his speech, delivered at the meeting of the citizens of Bombay held on December 3, Jinnah said, "I expect and I have every hope that they (Moslems) will not lag behind the Hindus in any way, but will work with you Hindus, Parsis and Christians, and go through the ordeal as a united people."

Subsequent events soon made it clear that this apparent unity and agreement was confined to the condemnation of the Simon Commission and of those who had appointed it. When it came to the formulation of a positive programme, the two principal parties were found to cling tenaciously to their respective policies and all efforts to bridge the gulf were unsuccessful. The Congress and the Hindu Mahasabha produced the Nehru Report as representing their ideas on the lines to be adopted by the proposed constitutional changes. This could not satisfy the Moslems, whose policy and demands had been taking shape for some time and were finally embodied in Jinnah's fourteen points.

The history of these points is important as it contains the clue of Jinnah's present policy and demands for the Moslems of India. The nucleus of the famous fourteen points is really the formulation of Moslem demands by Jinnah in respect of the forthcoming changes in the Indian Constitution at three successive sessions of the All-India Moslem League in the years 1924, 1925 and 1926. These related to the following:—

(1) Effective representation of minorities without reducing the majority in any province.

(2) Separate electorates.

(3) No disturbance in the Moslem majority in the Punjab, Bengal and N.W.F.P. by any territorial redistribution.

(4) Religious liberty, etc.

(5) Machinery for enforcing liberty of religion.

These proposals were criticised by the Hindu leaders, who insisted that Moslems should postulate in their scheme joint electorates with safeguards for rights and interests of Moslems. Accordingly Mahomed Ali Jinnah issued invitations to representative Mohammedans in all parts of India, who met at Delhi on March 20, 1927, and put forward what have come to be known as the Delhi Moslem Proposals. These accepted the principle of joint electorates if, *inter alia*, the following conditions were accepted:

(1) Sind should be separated from the Bombay Presidency and constituted into a separate province.

(2) Reforms should be introduced in the N.W.F.P. and in Baluchistan on the same footing as in any other province in India.

These proposals were substantially accepted by the All-India Congress Committee Meeting held in Bombay in May, 1927, and were later embodied in the resolution adopted at the open session of the Indian National Congress at Madras in December, 1927. The response thus made by the Congress to the Moslem proposals was considered by the session of the All-India Moslem League at Calcutta in December, 1927, and the Council of the League was authorised to appoint a sub-committee to confer with the Working Committee of the Indian National Congress for the purpose of drafting a constitution for India and of taking part in the National Convention which was going to be held in Delhi in the following March as proposed by the Congress.

The idea of drawing up an agreed constitution led to the summoning of the All Parties Conference at Delhi on February 11, 1928. This was the first and the last meeting of this conference in which the Moslem League representatives were present. The basis of rapprochement brought about by the Congress resolution at Madras and the response made by the League at Calcutta was thrown completely overboard. The All Parties Conference now struck altogether a new line, and its deliberations continued, unattended by League representatives, till at last the Nehru Report was ready for consideration.

The basic principles of the communal settlement embodied in the Nehru Report were contrary to those on which Moslem opinion had hitherto expressed its willingness to come to an agreement. The only occasion on which the League gave its consideration to the Nehru Report was when it was invited to send a delegation to the All Parties Convention at Calcutta in December, 1928. The proposals submitted by the League delegates were summarily rejected by the Convention. Thus ended the efforts to bring about a settlement between the Hindu and Moslem communities.

What took place at the two Round Table Conferences in London is comparatively recent history. Mahomed Ali Jinnah and other Moslem leaders took their stand on the demands contained in the Fourteen Points. Hindu leaders, and specially those of the Hindu Mahasabha, declared that the Nehru Report had already gone too far and there was no room for the slightest further concession. The one man who could have brought about a settlement was Mahatma Gandhi. But he contented himself with signing a blank cheque for the Moslems, leaving it to themselves to cash it if they could from the Hindus. The interminable quarrels and recriminations which were a feature of the whole business were brought to an end by the announcement of the Communal Award.

The Hindu-Moslem problem to-day remains as unsolved and insoluble as ever. Hindu-Moslem unity, for which Jinnah had striven so vigorously, became a fact in 1920. But once again Time has changed that victory into defeat. False hopes of a settlement were raised a number of times, but it is still very much out of sight. There was a lengthy correspondence between Jinnah and Gandhi on the one hand, and Jinnah and Nehru on the other. There were talks also between the same gentlemen with the same result. Pandit Jawaharlal Nehru's letters, which may be taken to represent fairly the Congress attitude towards this matter, dismiss the points raised by Jinnah as too trivial to bother about at a time when the country and the world are faced with problems of much greater moment. It has, however, not occurred to Pandit Nehru and others of the Congress that the triviality of these demands is just one more reason they should be done with and the way cleared for meeting the greater issues.

At present Mahomed Ali Jinnah is about sixty-three years of age, and in spite of his delicate health his great devotion to the cause which he is serving enables him to do an amount of work which would be the wonder and despair of a much younger man. It will be an apt ending to this short account of the life and achievements of this remarkable man to give a pen portrait of him by Mrs. Sarojini Naidu: "Never was there a nature whose outer qualities provided so complete an antithesis of its inner worth. Tall and stately, but thin to the point of emaciation, languid and luxurious of habit, Mahomed Ali Jinnah's attentuated form is the deceptive sheath of a spirit of exceptional vitality and endurance. Somewhat formal and fastidious, and a little aloof and imperious of manner, the calm hauteur of his accustomed reserve but masks for those who know him a naïve and eager humanity, an intuition quick and tender as a woman's, a humour gay and winning as a child's. Pre-eminently rational and practical, discreet and dispassionate in his estimate and acceptance of life, the obvious sanity and serenity of his worldly wisdom effectually disguise a shy and splendid idealism which is of the very essence of the man."

THE RT. HON. SIR AKBAR HYDARI, NAWAB HYDER NAWAZ JUNG BAHADUR, P.C.

Prime Minister of Hyderabad.

The Rt. Hon. SIR AKBAR HYDARI, P.C.

A MAKER OF MODERN HYDERABAD

BORN 1869

BY ROBERT BRYAN

THE state of Hyderabad stretches over an area nearly equal to that of Italy, on the high Deccan plateau that separates the Arabian Sea from the Bay of Bengal. Its size alone gives it and, ever since Asaf Jah, the Mogul emperor's viceroy in the Deccan, defeated the forces of Delhi in 1724 and asserted his independence, has given it, great importance in the history of India; moreover, it is the only great Moslem state south of the River Narbada. There were periods, however, throughout the nineteenth century when the state, laxly administered, declined in power and prestige. But with the coming of more modern ideas it has achieved that measure of re-organisation and enlightened progress which has enabled it to take its rightful place in the New India that is so rapidly taking shape. Among the makers of modern Hyderabad, Sir Akbar Hydari will always take an honoured place.

Mohamed Akbar Nyzarali Hydari was born in Bombay, of prosperous merchant stock, on November 8, 1869. His father, in pursuit of business interests, had made six voyages to China; on his mother's side were relatives who had travelled to England and elsewhere. From the first he knew an enlightened home in which narrowness of mind was conspicuous by its absence. His family was of the Jamaat Sulaimani (Bohra) sect of Moslems; the shaping of his views in later life may have been influenced by the fact that he was descended neither from the Moslem conquerors of the thirteenth century onwards nor from converted Hindus. The Bohras, moving eastwards for trading purposes in the ninth and tenth centuries, had settled on the Konkan coast as merchants—not warrior-conquerors. Though devout Moslems, their descendants do not inherit militant fanaticism; and in Akbar Hydari this characteristic, to be seen in so many Indian Moslems, has never been present.

Akbar Hydari was educated at the Jesuit College of St. Xavier in Bombay, where he took his degree at the age of seventeen. He had studied widely: English literature, economics, Latin, history, and above all the Law. With the example of his uncle, Badruddin Tyabji, who had won fame as a judge, before him, he planned for himself a legal career; he was prominent in debate at countless club and society debates. His family, however, thought otherwise; a career in the financial service was, they told him, to be his fate. He has told how he considered that he "hadn't a ghost of a chance" as he sat for the examination, for the subject, he thought at the time, was alien to him; but his name was first on the list of successful candidates, so, again to quote his own words, "I entered the Finance Department with tears."

That was in 1888, and by 1903 he had risen, by way of a variety of posts, to be Controller of Central Treasuries. Assistant Accountant General in the United Provinces in 1890, Deputy Accountant General at Madras (the first Indian ever to hold the post) in 1900, Examiner of the Government of India Press Accounts in 1901, these were some of the posts he held before entering the service of Hyderabad State in 1905. It is true that by the closing years of the last century Indians were being admitted in increasing numbers into the government service, but it was still the exception rather than the rule that they should achieve positions of great responsibility; in the circumstances then prevailing, Akbar Hydari's rise in these early years of his career was spectacular. He proved himself a sound as well as far-sighted administrator, notable for the lucidity with which he expressed his views and arguments.

The achievements with which his name is, to date, chiefly associated occurred later when he was finance and railway member of the Hyderabad State Executive Council; but his time in British India helped him to formulate those principles upon which his subsequent actions have been based. Particularly as Examiner of Government Press Accounts he travelled widely throughout India, coming into contact with all aspects of the vast Indian community. Slowly but surely his conception of a land where Hindu and Moslem should appreciate each other's good qualities took shape. Long afterwards he was magnificently to express this conception in a presidential speech to the All-India Mohammedan Educational Conference at Calcutta:

"It will not be the growth but the death of Indian Nationalism if the Moslems of India fail to be impressed by the greatness of Asoka, Chandragupta, or filled with pride and joy at the immortal frescoes of Ajanta and the sculptured monuments of Ellora, or fail to derive fresh inspiration from the glorious songs of Jayadev and Tukaram, or find food for deep and satisfying thought in the discourse of Sri Krishna and Gautama the Buddha. It will not be the growth but the death of Indian Nationalism if the Hindus are not filled with pride at the architectural splendours of the Moguls and the Adil Shahis, at the political achievements of great rulers like Sher Shah and Akbar, at the fine heroism of noble queens like Chand Bibi and Nur Jehan, at the liberal statesmanship of devoted ministers like Mahmud Gavan and Abul Fazl, at the wide learning of scholars like Al Beruni and Faizi or at the inspiration of poets like Amir Khusru and Ghalib. It will be a sad day indeed if the minds of Hindu and Moslem alike are not stirred with the high and noble aims of the Viceroys like Mayo and Ripon, of administrators like Munro and Elphinstone, of friends of India like Fawcett and Bright, of missionaries like Hare and Miller. For all these and many more, whether Hindu, Moslem or Christian, loved India and worked for her."

He was a man of great authority and prestige when he spoke those words, but even when a young and comparatively unknown servant of the Government of India he had voiced the same sentiments. The concluding paragraph of an article which he contributed in 1901 to a volume on Indian Social Reform reads as follows:

"I can conceive no nobler work to which an Indian can consecrate himself than that of cementing the hearts of the diverse races and nationalities of our vast continent into a solid and united whole, bound by a union that is not merely a superficial one or that merely enables the Hindu and the Moslem, the Parsi and the Christian, to regard each other on sufferance or even with a species of benevolent neutrality, but a living and active union whereby they come to look upon each other as brothers working for the cultivation and progress of their common heritage."

From 1905 to 1920 Akbar Hydari served the state of Hyderabad, first as

Accountant General, then from 1907 as Financial Secretary and finally from 1911 as Secretary to the Home Department. His financial acumen bore fruit in the reorganisation of the state finances so that each state department was given a separate triennial contract. Under the previous centralised system enterprise was stifled, for no department ever knew how much in any given year would be allotted to them to spend; Akbar Hydari opened up by this measure new channels through which the great wealth of the state could flow. Tolerant to additional expenditure where it was likely to have a constructive effect, he insisted also on the building up of reserves to deal with such matters as famine and flood. Famine when it visits the Deccan is perhaps more terrible than anywhere else in India. Less frequent than in more barren parts of the peninsula, it strikes more terribly, for in the Deccan there are more mouths to feed. Akbar Hydari's famine reserve fund has done much to mitigate its horrors.

Akbar Hydari had married in 1893 Amena Tyabji. It was with her aid that he fought against the rigours of the Purdah system. If there can be no doubt of his devotion to the Moslem creed, there can be as little of his liberal interpretation thereof. His wife, at his encouragement and with his support, was the first Moslem woman to appear in public in Bombay out of purdah, and in Hyderabad she set the same example. Presiding at the first Hyderabad Educational Conference in 1915, Akbar Hydari said: "That country can never be educated or progressive whose women are steeped in ignorance. . . . If the mothers who give our children their first lessons in life—lessons which must inevitably influence their entire future—are devoid of education, how can we be

MEETING OF THE LEGISLATIVE COUNCIL

Sir Akbar Hydari, presiding, announced the command of H.E.H. the Nizam for the formation of a Reform Committee.

ROYAL WEDDING

Sir Akbar Hydari (extreme left) at the marriage of the Nizam of Hyderabad's second son, Prince Muazzam Jah Bahadur.

sure that when the children go out of their hands they will be blessed with real education and morals?" To many to-day this statement may seem so obvious as to be a truism, but it must be remembered that Akbar Hydari is a Moslem and a servant of the premier Moslem state in India, and that what he was maintaining ran contrary to the orthodox Moslem tradition of many centuries.

Akbar Hydari made his reputation in Hyderabad as a financial expert; he increased it in other ways in the years after 1911 when he was in charge of the Home Department. To him the state owes the setting up of its archæological department. Within the borders of the state lie the caves of Ajanta and Ellora, the ruins of the great fortress of Daulatabad, the remains of the architectural glories of Bidar and Gulbarga, and many other relics of the Bahmani and later dynasties. Too long had these been neglected; their care, and researches into their origins, became, under Akbar Hydari's influence, a chief concern of the state.

It was in these years that he conceived the idea of a state university, the main concern of which would be to teach through the vernacular and by so doing to confer upon Indian students for the first time the supreme advantage of acquiring Western learning through the medium of a familiar idiom. The Osmania University at Hyderabad—the result of this idea—is certainly one of his chief claims to fame. Urdu is the language in which all general subjects are taught, and a bureau has been set up for the translation of Western text-books and of Western scientific and literary researches into this language. The Osmania was the first university in India conceived upon this principle. Its success has been considerable; the students benefit enormously from pursuing their studies in a familiar medium; and among its repercussions has been an advance in elementary education throughout the state. There is one, perhaps unavoidable, handicap. India has no single language; and Urdu, although intelligible to millions in the north, is not the "vernacular" of the majority of the population of Hyderabad. Specifically the university is not intended primarily for Moslems; the aim is that all communities in the state should benefit equally from it. Nevertheless, local students who are Moslems must start with a big initial advantage. The problem of language, if any attempt is made to get away from a sectarian basis in education, is common to all India, and it cannot be said that the Osmania University has solved it; at least, however, it has proved that there are tangible advantages to students in conveying higher education in a mother tongue.

In 1920 Akbar Hydari reverted for a brief period to service in British India as Accountant General in Bombay, but in the following year he returned to service in Hyderabad as Finance and Railway Member of the State Executive Council, a post he held until 1937 when he was appointed President of that body. In the ten years after 1921 the financial policy which he had earlier instituted bore fruit. The state treasury proved itself capable of shouldering the burden of large irrigation, famine relief and other schemes so successfully that the state was able without difficulty to float loans in the Indian market at 3½ per cent.; and in 1930 it took over from private ownership 1,200 miles of railway, paying out of income a sum equivalent to more than eight million pounds sterling. As Finance

HIGH COURT, HYDERABAD

One of the fine modern buildings erected in the city of Hyderabad is the High Court, lying to the west of the Afzalganj Gate.

Member, Akbar Hydari enhanced the reputation that he had won as a subordinate. He was knighted in 1928.

In the realm of education his interests had for long ranged beyond the borders of the state he served. If the Osmania University was his favourite child, he was keenly interested also in the Universities of Dacca, Calcutta, Bombay and Aligarh. He was president of the All-India Mohammedan Educational Conference in 1917, and he played a prominent part in 1921 in countering the attempts of the brothers Ali to win over the Aligarh University to Non-Co-operation. He was by 1925, as far as education was concerned, an all-India figure, incurring praise as well as condemnation from extreme congressmen and also, through his broad-minded views, from the extreme section of orthodox Moslems. He was made at various times a fellow of Bombay, Dacca and Aligarh Universities, as well as of the Osmania. As a political figure and statesman he first emerged into real prominence on the all-India stage in the course of the events that culminated in the first Round Table Conference in London in 1930-32. From that period his rôle has been a leading one.

The discussions and events that from 1930-37 led up to the formulation of a scheme of federal government for India and the putting into effect of Provincial Autonomy, formed a large part of the background to his career. He headed the Hyderabad Delegation to the Round Table Conference, and was the state's representative on the Select Committee on Indian Constitutional Reform appointed by the British Parliament in 1933. In 1934 he was Chairman of the Committee of Indian State Ministers.

Even when Hyderabad had been feeble of purpose and ill-governed, as it was for part of the nineteenth century, it was a force with which the British Government had always seriously to reckon. The support of the same state, well and efficiently governed, may be said to have been essential to the success of any federal scheme. From the first, Sir Akbar Hydari made it clear at numerous meetings in London of the Round Table Conference that he considered some sort of federation in which representatives of the states should sit in the Central Government with representatives from the provinces was essential to India's future, and he made it equally clear that he saw the necessity, and was prepared for, a surrender of some of the powers which, within their own borders, the various states exercised.

He was not alone in these views. The representatives of Mysore and Gwalior—to name two states—shared them, but his influence was immense and probably decisive in persuading the whole body of states to accept the federal idea. His point of view is put clearly in an article written by him early in 1937:

"The idealism which inspired the States at the early stages of the discussions to accept the idea of an organic association of an all-India legislature had not died down. The ideal of a self-governing India . . . could not be achieved for British India alone, and the States' readiness to throw into the common scales some of their own powers and authorities in order to assist that realisation, testifies to the inherent greatness of their traditions which permitted, despite a long history of unconcern with the rest of India, the vision of all-India to be conceived."

The end of this passage is as significant as its beginning. What he advocated in these years was a complete break in the policy pursued by the Indian States at least since the Indian Mutiny. As he himself stated: "The acceptance by the majority of States of the idea of

THE OLD CITY—

Flower stalls in the old bazaar, Hyderabad. These and much of the buildings in the vicinity are condemned under the City Town Improvement Scheme. They will come down to make room for modern well-planned and built houses.

—AND THE NEW

Playing fields and new houses built under the Town Improvement Scheme in Hyderabad. The improvement of housing conditions for the people of Hyderabad is one of the schemes to which Sir Akbar has given close, personal attention.

THE OSMANIA HOSPITAL, HYDERABAD

federation . . . is almost revolutionary." He believed, when he went to the Round Table Conference, that such acceptance was right, that the previous attitude of the states had "led to the growth of an artificial unconcern with developments outside their territories," but from the start he was on his guard lest what the states gained might be more than counter-balanced by what they were asked to give up. He was throughout the representative of the chief Indian State who, out of loyalty to his ruler but also because he believed that Hyderabad and other states had much to give to a united India, was determined that their sovereignty should be reserved to them. He was prepared, eager for federation, but for federation on terms which would ensure the states' survival. Nor can he be blamed, in view of the speeches and actions of leading members of the Congress party, for insisting that adequate precautions be taken to make their survival reasonably certain.

It was on Sir Akbar Hydari's initiative that the problem of Berar, which had for long complicated relations between Hyderabad and the Government of India, was settled. This territory, lying to the north of the Nizam's dominions, had been ceded to the British in 1853, this arrangement having been modified —but in a typically high-handed way— by Lord Curzon in 1902, when it was leased in perpetuity by the Nizam to the Government of India. In 1926 a reconsideration of the whole question was requested, which the Viceroy, Lord Reading, refused on the ground that "No ruler of an Indian State can justifiably claim to negotiate with the British Government on an equal footing." Yet ten years later Sir Akbar Hydari achieved exactly that basis of negotiation. It is improbable that he obtained all that he desired; the administration of Berar is still carried on by the Government of the Central Provinces, but the right to be consulted on various specified matters has been reserved to the Nizam, his sovereignty over the territory has been recognised, and the perpetual lease has been abolished. What had in 1926 been denied entirely to Hyderabad was in 1936 to a considerable extent granted. By able diplomacy, well supported by his great reputation as a statesman of balanced integrity, Sir Akbar Hydari achieved that basis of negotiation on terms of equality which ten years earlier had been unthinkable.

Sir Akbar Hydari's claim to greatness, to a secure place in Indian history, must be based mainly upon two characteristics: upon his broad-mindedness and upon his ability to look ahead. The former is shown most notably in his attitude to what in India are almost twin subjects, religion and education. Though a profound believer in Islam, he could yet realise that others might be entirely justified in believing equally profoundly the precepts of the great Hindu or Parsi teachers, the teachings of Christ or Gautama; and such realisation is extremely rare in profound believers of any description. Where religious tradition, as in the case of purdah, seemed to him anti-progressive, he discouraged it; where it tended to provoke civil discord, he endeavoured always to suppress it. The value of such an attitude in a Moslem state with a preponderantly Hindu population is not lightly to be underestimated.

And in educational matters he acted and advised always on the same principles. The Osmania University has, it is true, been criticised; but criticism cannot obscure the intention behind its inception. Of that intention there can be no doubt. In Akbar Hydari's own words: "Do not, I pray you, regard movements of this kind (Osmania University) as in any way separatist, or provincial or sectarian. They are based upon the first principles of self-respect, reverence, and respect for your cultural traditions which are

THE TOWN HALL, HYDERABAD

not the insidious enemies but the strongest supporters of a National Evolution." In all his dealings with, and advice to, educational bodies outside as well as inside Hyderabad State he made clear his conception of the main function of education in India: to fuse the various creeds, castes and social units of the Peninsula into a community, mutually forbearing, mutually helpful.

It is in the political sphere that his ability to look ahead is most noticeable. It must be remembered that in 1930, when he attended the first Round Table Conference, he had been, with one small interval, a servant for 25 years of the premier Indian state, and that he had been largely instrumental in raising that state to a position of power, prosperity and great prestige. This did not prevent him from realising that in the interests of a future united India the position of Hyderabad and of all the other Indian States must be modified; and in a united India he profoundly believed. Subject only to the operation of paramountcy—to the right consistently upheld but where a state was well-governed, sparingly if sometimes arbitrarily exercised—of the Government of India to interfere where necessary with their affairs—the states had for long enjoyed immunity from the turbulent problems that were always arising in British India. Sir Akbar Hydari realised that it was their duty to take a part in those problems and to surrender some of their privileges in order to do so. Only thus could India as a whole prove to the British its ability to govern itself.

It has been said that in later years his conviction of the practicability of federation wavered, that he was prepared for, if not reconciled to, the abandonment of the whole scheme. For the latter assertion there is little justification, and for his caution the attitude of

THE DURBAR HALL, PUBLIC GARDENS, HYDERABAD

the more extreme elements—both communal and political—in British India afforded considerable excuse. A mixture of realist and idealist, he saw no reason why Congress should take all and give nothing. In his conception of a united India there was room for the democratic lion to lie down with the lamb of modified autocracy. He could hardly with a clear conscience have continued to serve a state had he felt otherwise. Moreover he was convinced that any violent change from one system to the other must lead to a state of chaos out of which no good would come. He insisted, therefore, on safeguards which would insure the future integrity of the states with as much insistence as his opponents demanded that such safeguards should be non-existent. His conception of the India of the future differs in fact widely from that held by Pandit Jawaharlal Nehru or Subhas Chandra Bose. The latter envisage an India independent, radically changed, freed from the British connection. Akbar Hydari conceives of an India equally independent but a partner in the British Commonwealth of Nations—an India in which the old and new shall be blended, the best traditions of the former and the more fruitful ideas of the latter being preserved. But in spite of all their differences he and Pandit Nehru do agree on one fundamental—on the need for an India that is in truth united.

Sir Akbar Hydari has been honoured by his ruler, and he was made a Privy Councillor in 1936; his judgments are respected, even by those whose point of view is radically different from his own, throughout the length and breadth of India. Tolerant, ever ready to listen, capable both of giving and receiving friendship, subtle in diplomacy but with a subtlety that is based on conviction and not on pliability, he has sought not only the good of his state but of India as a whole. For this alone, and because on many occasions his influence has been decisive for progress, he would deserve to rank among the great Indians of history

SIR TEJ BAHADUR SAPRU

SIR TEJ BAHADUR SAPRU

GREATEST AUTHORITY ON INDIAN CONSTITUTIONAL LAW

BORN 1875

BY C. F. ANDREWS

My first meeting with Tej Bahadur Sapru was in Allahabad nearly thirty-four years ago, when I went there late in the cold weather of 1906. He was then just 31 years old, for he was born on December 6th, 1875. My own work at that time was in Delhi at St. Stephen's College, near to the Kashmir Gate, and I had heard much about the intellectual brilliance of the younger school of political thinkers in the centre of the United Provinces.

Just before paying this visit to Allahabad I had received some rather painful public attention owing to a series of letters which I had written to the daily papers, protesting against a very bitter attack made on the educated classes as "seditious" and "disloyal" people. Therefore, when I visited Allahabad soon after, the leading barristers, who were members of the Congress, cordially invited me to join them at an evening function where we could talk freely concerning the strained relations between the two races. I looked forward to this meeting with eagerness, and was not disappointed. At Delhi I had found a lamentable backwardness in all political matters. This lack of interest, combined with a somewhat indolent attitude, appeared to me to be entirely undemocratic. The educated classes were suppressing their real opinions and allowing things they disliked to continue by a mere passive acceptance of them.

All this had troubled me considerably since I had come out to India. So when this evening function took place at Allahabad, with Tej Bahadur Sapru in the chair, my mind was full of the subject, and I spoke strongly about the evil which must necessarily result where ever mutual frankness was impossible between two different races.

Some of the older among those present defended the order of things that then prevailed. "We cannot help ourselves," they said to me. "We are obliged to say one thing to people like you, and another thing to the officials."

"Do you always act in this manner?" I asked with a shock of surprise.

"We cannot help it," was the answer, "for we are a subject people." Words like these made me feel almost desperate and I spoke out my mind quite freely.

The incident, small as it is, has remained vividly with me ever since; and I can picture the scene even to-day. The only one who stood by me and shared my strong indignation was the chairman, Tej Bahadur Sapru. He acknowledged at once the deep-seated wrong of it all, and offered no defence. He condemned it with a sincerity of shame that revealed his own character. While doing so, he used one argument that went right home to me and evidently touched many of those present who were far more orthodox than he was. He declared that as long as they were content to remain in social and domestic bondage they weakened their claim for political freedom. That truly valid argument has been used not only in India, but in every country that seeks to obtain Swaraj. Mahatma Gandhi has employed it with great effect in order to bring about the removal of untouchability.

When the meeting was over, Sapru

came up to me and shook my hand very warmly and thanked me most cordially for what I had said. He had evidently been deeply moved. After that we talked together long into the night, and I felt that we had become friends.

He was by far the clearest thinker whom I had ever met so far in India, and my mind went along with his all the way as I recognised his rugged honesty of purpose. It was also quite easy to see that he was a strong conservative by nature in spite of the radical background of his idea.

The greatest contrast to him, in almost every direction, was Pandit Madan Mohan Malaviya, the champion of Hindu orthodoxy. He was far more intimately associated with the Congress than Sapru was; he was also intensely religious, while Sapru was sceptically minded in all religious matters. Malaviya used to model his long English speeches on Gladstone, who was his master. They were full of oratorical appeals, and on that account were regarded in India as a triumph of English eloquence. They did not move me personally because I had got past the age when such a style was impressive. People, however, who could hardly understand his English used to listen with rapt attention just as they would listen to Surendrenath Banerjea in Bengal. They were moved, not so much by what he said as by the flow of words which came pouring out of his mouth.

Sapru's English speeches were of an entirely different character. They were always terse and closely tc the point, without any superfluous words. He brought into them the forensic style with which he would plead a case in court. He was a debater rather than an orator, and did not even care to sway the multitudes by emotional appeals. Though radical in outlook, he was always somewhat of an aristocrat and too intellectual to be popular. In many ways his keenly critical mind was a hindrance to him in politics and prevented him from ever successfully leading a party.

It is interesting to me to review the present from the background of those days, and to note how far these two leaders in Allahabad, Malaviya and Sapru, who are so different in character, have drifted apart both in thought and action. We can see this not only in the political field, but even more with regard to social customs. Yet on one side they have become united, for each of them remained a constitutionalist at heart, even during the period of Non-Co-operation which followed the World War. Sapru left the National Congress as soon as ever the Non-Co-operation movement began. Even before that he had never had any sympathy with the earlier extremist position during the years 1907-1916, when the Congress was divided; and he refused to non-co-operate in 1920.

Malaviya, on the other hand, who also had never sided with the extremists in earlier days, continued to hang on as a member of the Congress, often in a minority of one, long after Non-Co-operation had been accepted as a national programme. Yet with regard to social custom his orthodoxy had remained almost entirely unshaken. The only point where it immediately gave way, at the trumpet call of Mahatma Gandhi, was with regard to "Temple Entry." Here, with a bravery that few of us were able to realise at the time, he had changed his whole manner of life and become the most ardent champion for the removal of untouchability.

Sapru, as I have already shown, had all along been a rebel at heart in these social and caste matters. He had spoken out in quite unorthodox fashion against many anti-social practices, such as child marriage, etc. Indeed, he had remained a rebel as a Hindu right up to the end. But, to-day, caste itself has moved so far forward that his earlier rebel actions would now be considered (at least in the North of India) to be quite normal and common-place.

Perhaps here is the best place to describe something of his character as I have known him. First, as I have already noted, there is a rugged independence, combined with a strong and rooted dislike for anything violent or unconstitutional. Quite regardless of consequences in speaking out the truth, even where he has to suffer for doing so, he is by his exact legal training almost over-conservative in action. Secondly, along with a very warm heart towards his own intimate circle of friends, he has deep down in his nature a close family love for all those who are nearly related to him, which makes his home in Allahabad a delightful place to stay in. Then again, he is a much travelled man, to whom Europe is almost as familiar as India. While intensely a lover of his own country and of the Urdu language (in which he writes as a master) he has become also a citizen of the world. One of his greatest relaxations is to take part in some literary contest in Urdu.

To return to the incident at Allahabad in 1906, I went on direct from there to Calcutta, in order to attend the session of the National Congress, over which Dadabhai Naoroji was presiding. There I saw for the first time Bepin Chandra Pal, Aurobindo Ghose, and others who were the new leaders in Bengal. That was my earliest education in Bengali politics, and it came almost as a shock to me after my experience in Delhi. For I had been living—so I now found out—in a "backward tract" in Delhi, where the old submissive temperament was still somnolently passive and inert. Allahabad had been a "half-way house;" but here, in Bengal, revolt was in the very air. The English style of dress the polished English speech (which still prevailed at Allahabad) had all been thrown aside. The Bengali dress and language were everywhere dominating. Whenever men spoke to me in English it was to tell me about the injustice of the Partition. Lord Curzon had accelerated this transformation by his imperious challenges. Poets, like Rabindranath Tagore, had composed songs of revolution, and all Bengal was singing them. A full Swadeshi movement was carrying the whole country by storm. There was a world of difference between the Bengali oratory of Bepin Chandra Pal as he addressed a huge crowd in Calcutta, and the clear-cut, incisive English speech, fastidiously accurate, of Tej Bahadur Sapru, in a select gathering at Allahabad.

After the Congress was over I met Sapru again and talked about the future with him. About that time, or a little later, I began to form one clear opinion of him, namely, that his mind was wedded to Law and not to Politics. The latter would only interest him as far as it brought up problems of the Indian Constitution. For he was not by temperament a general practitioner at the Bar, though he took up civil and criminal cases as a matter of practice and was a keen lawyer. But his heart had always been in constitutional law; and on this subject he could speak with an authority greater than that of any contemporary lawyer in India.

I must hurry on to refer to his work on the Imperial Legislative Council during the latter part of the War. No one probably rendered more active help to the Government of India as an adviser at that critical juncture: for Sapru was as blunt of speech as he was independent of character.

Let me give one small incident at this point from my own experience, for it illustrates Sapru's kindness and also his independence. There had been an evil system called "Indentured Indian Labour" whereby the British Colonies had been allowed to recruit labourers from the United Provinces, Bihar and Madras. The Government of India had become convinced at last of the evils of such recruiting and had agreed to abolish the whole indenture system. But later on they had weakly accepted a compromise and agreed to continue it for another five years in order to suit the planters. I had been to Fiji and Natal and had told Sapru about the evils I had seen and heard, and he was as indignant about them as I was.

We held a public meeting in Allahabad. Mr. H. S. L. Polak was to speak about South Africa, and I was to speak about Fiji. Both of us were staying with Sapru, who was helping the cause in every way possible. Then, suddenly, I was taken ill with a cholera-attack of a very virulent kind which seemed at one time to be nearly fatal. Never can I forget the kindness of my host on that occasion and the incessant care that was taken of me by the doctor whom he called in to treat me. It was impossible for me to attend the meeting, but Sarojini Naidu read a message from me and Sapru himself spoke strongly condemning the Government compromise. Polak also told the vast audience about the evils of indenture in Natal. That important public protest in Allahabad, along with others of the same character, helped to sound the death knell of the whole indenture system.

During those days which I spent in Sapru's house my friendship with him was cemented by the long illness from which I suffered. That special occasion afterwards played a prominent part in his own life, because it gave him a new interest in Indians abroad and made him the true champion of their cause at the Imperial Conference in 1923. He will always be remembered in India on account of his indignant challenge to General Smuts, who had refused to allow any citizenship to Indians domiciled in South Africa.

"We claim, along with you," said Sapru, "equal citizenship in the same Empire. We are *not* willing to be relegated from King George's dining-hall to King George's stables."

Rarely has the case for equal citizenship been put more forcibly than that. This one remark about King George's stables left a deep impression. On this racial question no one has spoken out with more burning indignation than Sapru, and he has nobly maintained the *izzat* of India on this and other occasions.

At the end of the same year, 1923, Sapru presided over the All-India Liberal Conference at Poona. He expressed there, also, his wrathful indignation at the inferior racial treatment of Indians abroad. While he had been unable, as we have seen, to identify himself any longer with the Congress, he had remained absolutely at one with Mahatma Gandhi with regard to this scandalous treatment of Indians abroad. On such a subject all parties in India are combined, and all take the same attitude. The Government of India has sided with them, and the Indian States also. Hindus, Moslems, Parsis and Christians alike are of one mind in rejecting the inferior status imposed on Indians in Kenya and South Africa.

Another opportunity of seeing a good deal of Sir Tej Bahadur Sapru was in Lord Reading's time, when he was Law Member. He followed Sir Sankara Nair, who had resigned after the Punjab disturbances. No more difficult post could have been offered anyone at such a critical time and it required resolution on his part to accept it. I know from personal experience how greatly the Viceroy relied on his counsel, and how frank Dr. Sapru was in offering unpalatable advice.

Whenever I went to Simla during those difficult years I used to stay with the Law Member. On one occasion he put to me a pointed question, which had evidently come from the highest authority, in order to elicit my opinion. It ran as follows: "How would you meet this new movement called Non-Co-operation?"

I replied at once, almost without thinking, "Co-operate in social uplift work, such as Prohibition, and on all questions with regard to Indians abroad."

Looking back, as I can now do, it seems to me that this advice was practical. As long as a sense of good humour remained, and also a sense of decency and humanity, the movement could be conducted on both sides in a gentlemanly manner, even though suffering was inevitable. But in the later stages, when good humour was lost, the conditions of the struggle went rapidly from bad to worse.

Though Dr. Sapru retained a profound respect for Mahatma Gandhi's character, it was easy for me to see that he could not appreciate his ideas. These remained almost a sealed book to him, and any profession of civil disobedience definitely annoyed him as a constitutional lawyer. I was constantly absent in South Africa from 1924 to 1927. Dr. Sapru had already retired from the Viceroy's Council, and as I was abroad I saw very little of him for some years. He remained in India and accomplished some very valuable work on what was called the Reforms Committee. On different occasions, also, at a later date he did his utmost to act as "peacemaker," when there seemed some possibility of a successful intervention between the Congress leaders and the Government, which might satisfactorily conclude the Non-Co-operation struggle. Being a Liberal and a Moderate, the whole movement of which Mahatma Gandhi was the leader distressed him beyond measure and he was never reconciled to the mode of direct action which had been adopted.

Perhaps the saddest years in Sir Tej Bahadur Sapru's own political life were those which he spent in London during the almost interminable Committees and Conferences concerning the New Constitution from 1929 to 1934. He gave the best part of his time to this work and in the end was profoundly disappointed with the results. Not one of the main issues for which he had fought so strenuously was granted. In the end, the new Constitution, passed through Parliament, was an imposed Constitution and not one decided by conference and discussion. Strangely enough, it is not realised, in the midst of world confusion, how quickly the sands are running out, and also how impossible it is to answer with a clear conscience the new imperial claims from Germany and Italy, without drastically revising our own British policy towards India. For if India were really free and independent to-day, as South Africa and Canada are, it would be much easier to reply to Hitler and Mussolini with the world's moral approval.

In recent years, Sir Tej Bahadur Sapru has retired from public life. He has gone back to his own profession as a lawyer, which occupies most of his time and attention. His son has taken a leading part in the Council of State and has recently returned from Australia, where he attended the Sydney Celebrations. His political views are similar to those of his father and he takes after him in character. May both live long enough to see the fruits of all their labour!

H.H. THE RT. HON. SIR SULTAN MUHAMMAD SHAH AGA KHAN III

H.H. THE AGA KHAN

GREAT INDIAN LEADER AND WORLD STATESMAN

BORN 1877

BY NAOROJI M. DUMASIA

HIS HIGHNESS THE RIGHT HONOURABLE SIR SULTAN MUHAMMAD SHAH, better known to the world as Aga Khan the Third, carries upon his shoulders the weight of a leadership that may aptly be described as unique. Descended in direct line from the Prophet of Islam through Fatima, Mohammed's daughter by his first wife, Khadijah, and Ali, their son-in-law, the Aga Khan can also trace through Hosain, Fatima's son, who was married to the daughter of the last of the Kings of Iran, his blood to the oldest and most renowned dynasties in the world's history. As the descendant of Mohammed, the Aga Khan inherits the spiritual leadership of one of the most important and influential of Islamic sects, namely, the Ismailis, who number millions in India alone and are spread in equally large numbers through more than half a dozen countries. As the heir to a royal tradition, but for the turn of destiny's wheel, he might to-day have been wearing a kingly crown, seated upon the throne of royal ancestors, who in their day made glorious contributions to the history of humanity and the progress of the world. It is only natural, therefore, that the Aga Khan should wield an influence in the councils of the nations such as few men have ever exerted, and that he should command a following which makes him a powerful factor in the realm of international relations.

Brought up to the vast responsibilities of a religious leader who is accepted, venerated and almost worshipped as father, mother, guardian, guide, philosopher and friend by millions of disciples throughout the world, from an age when the average child is occupied with toys and sweets, the Aga Khan has developed the qualities he inherited from a historic line of illustrious ancestors, in a degree that makes him one of the most remarkable men living. In the international breadth of his outlook, the influential part he has played during the past half-century in shaping the policies of the world's leading powers, the amazing extent of his humanitarian activities, and his benevolences which extend far beyond the confines of his spiritual leadership, the Aga Khan is a living embodiment of the description applied to him by Sir Samuel Hoare, former Secretary of State for India and leading British statesman, namely, that he is "par excellence a citizen of the world."

A born leader of men, the Aga Khan is a consummate student of the art of living, not in any vulgar, hedonistic meaning of that hackneyed and much misused phrase, but as a philosopher who has plumbed life's noblest purpose and conscientiously endeavours to secure fulfilment of that purpose, in his own life as well as in the existence of humanity at large. This is the true meaning and function of leadership and no man of our day understands it better and strives more steadfastly or with greater success to discharge its manifold responsibilities than this "Prince without territory," who wields an absolute sovereignty over the souls and bodies of millions which is all but incredible in this day of crownless monarchs, exiled kings and toppled thrones. Whether it be in the domain of politics, the field of sport or the narrower, but no less important, circles of society, in every civilised country in the world to-day the Aga Khan is a familiar, esteemed and dominant personality. An aura of good will and good works, an atmosphere of unfailing success, an indescribable talismanic air is associated with him wherever he goes, whatever he undertakes. It is a happy association, enhancing his power and influence, which are ever exerted to the promotion of human happiness and progress, and even when devoted to the furtherance of patriotic causes are still mindful of the larger human issues in a manner worthy of a citizen of the world and a leader of Islam.

It is not surprising that a personality so impressive and uniformly blessed should be invested in the popular mind with aspects and achievements that lift it to a superhuman level, that an atmosphere of legend should surround the man. The stories told about the Aga Khan are legion and they equal in imagination anything one may read in the *Arabian Nights*. He has been credited with fabulous wealth, "millions and millions of pounds in bullion and precious stones" and "treasure greater than all the wealth stored in the Bank of England," and the success which invariably attends his carefully planned activities—he never undertakes anything without having first foreseen and provided against every conceivable difficulty and obstacle—is doubtless responsible for the belief, more common than will be credited, that he commands the services of some genii like the classic Slave of the Lamp in the famous tale of Aladdin.

In point of fact, there is no need for artificial injection of romance into a life which is fascinating enough in its origin, career and achievement to provide material for half a dozen thrilling novels —which goes back in history to the Caliphs of Egypt, and beyond them into a dim and distant past before which the Bourbons and Brunswicks of Europe are but of yesterday. The blood of proud paladins who lorded it over the glories of Toledo and Cordova, Cairo and Baghdad, mingles in his veins with that of the famous "Assassins" of Freya Stark's book and the illustrious founder of Al Azhar, oldest university in the world, and of many another ancient hero whose name and deeds yet shine with golden glow across the curtain of countless centuries. The thing to remember about the Aga Khan is that he is a worthy descendant of a long and historic line, very much a man of the modern world, fully alive to his responsibilities as spiritual head of considerably more than a hundred million souls, a philosopher in the highest and noblest sense of the word, a polished statesman and diplomat, living in rich fulfilment of singularly gifted manhood, and striving purposefully each hour, each day, each year to see the world and humanity a little farther advanced on the road to progress.

To the British Empire he has been, and still is, one of its greatest assets, a veritable bulwark of protective influence in the perpetually disturbed and distracted countries that make the portion of the world which comes under the category and description of "the East." A scion of Persia's Royal House, he is the third of his line since his grandfather, the first Aga Khan, Lord of Mahallat (brave warrior and sagacious statesman, to whose services in Afghanistan in the deplorable days of Jalalabad, Kabul and Kandahar the British must acknowledge a debt of undying gratitude), was forced by circumstances and treacherous foes into exile and eventual settlement at Bombay, to be associated with India

AT HIS INSTALLATION

When a child of eight, H.H. the Aga Khan was installed upon the Gadi of Imams in Bombay. This picture was taken immediately after he had been proclaimed as the Hazur Imam of Ismailis. From "The Aga Khan and His Ancestors." By Naoroji Dumasia.

AS A YOUNG MAN

An early picture taken when the Aga Khan was spending a holiday at Monte Carlo.

EARLY DIPLOMATIC MISSION

Photographed in England where he came to attend the Near Eastern Conference.

IN BRITISH EAST AFRICA
A photograph taken at Nairobi when His Highness paid a visit to Africa.

and its people. The manner in which the Aga Khan has identified himself with the people of his adoption and fought for their interests entitles him in the fullest degree to be described as an Indian patriot and leader of the highest rank and ideals.

The story of the first Aga Khan's migration to India has been related in full detail in my recently published work, "The Aga Khan and His Ancestors" (*The Times of India Press, Bombay*), and records of the life of that dauntless warrior, to whose heroic courage and personal valour Nott and MacNaghten, Rawlinson, the Napiers and a score of British officers and statesmen in Persia, Afghanistan, England and India have paid glowing tribute, may be studied by the curious either in my work mentioned above, or in the records of the India Office in London and of the Governments of India, Bombay and Calcutta.

Hasan Aly Shah, grandfather of the present Aga Khan, was married to the daughter of Fateh Ali Shah of Persia. On the Shah's death he helped the grandson Muhammad to the throne, the son having been passed over in his father's lifetime. Twenty years later Hasan Shah was driven into rebellion by the machinations of an unscrupulous Prime Minister, found his way into Afghanistan in time to be of invaluable assistance to the British in the critical and disastrous period that followed upon the dethronement of Shah Shuja and culminated in the tragedy of Jalalabad, and on the conclusion of that campaign arrived in Sind with the British. Diplomatic relations between Persia and Britain having altered in the meantime, Hasan Aly Shah was unable to secure his return to Persia, and after spending some time in Karachi and Calcutta, settled down at Bombay with the consent and approval of the British authorities who accorded him a pension in gratitude for his valorous and valuable services. These services were augmented by the Aga Khan through the three succeeding decades with unstinted exertion of his vast influence among the turbulent tribes of India's North-Western frontier, and much valuable assistance during the nightmare months of the Mutiny of 1857. Later, in Bombay and elsewhere, he was an invaluable factor in quelling the periodic outbreak of communal violence that perpetually disturbed the peace of this country.

In Bombay Hasan Aly Shah soon became a familiar and popular figure, turning his interest with the characteristic ease of a versatile personality to the field of sport. He established a stud of the finest Arab blood and soon became a leading figure on the Indian turf, such as it was then. When King Edward VII as Prince of Wales visited India, he was entertained by the warrior hero of whom all England had heard, and in due course he formed friendships with the rulers of Indian states and leading Indian personalities. When he died in April, 1881, full of years, honours and experience so varied that a dozen average lifetimes could hardly contain it, he had laid the foundation of an environment in which his successors could build a position of leadership and patriotic Indian leader. A keen and erudite scholar in Persian and Arabic literature, a brilliant exponent of the religion of which he was leader and apostle, he extended his activities with singular zeal into the fields of politics, social reform and sport. He sat in the Bombay Council for making laws and regulations, as a member specially nominated (a rare distinction) by the then governor, Sir James Fergusson, and displayed fruitful activity in organising his own followers

WELCOMED AT MOMBASA

As head of the Mohammedan Community he was received with much enthusiasm.

endeavour. Hasan Aly Shah, son-in-law of a Shah of Persia, Viceroy of the great province of Kerman, ally of the British, warrior, statesman, sportsman and religious head of the far-flung Ismaili sect of Islam, was buried in a mausoleum at Mazagaon which the world knows to-day as "Husnabad."

He was succeeded by his eldest son, Aga Aly Shah, to whom Nasrudin, then Shah of Persia, sent condolences and special marks of honour recognising him as the Imam of the Ismailis and a Prince of the Ruling House of Persia. The second Aga Khan set about consolidating with striking success the position established by his father as an in Bombay, Sind and Kathiawar in the jamatkhans which exist till this day.

Having lost two wives he had married for the third time a grand-daughter of the Shah Fateh Aly and a niece of Shah Muhammad Aly. For some time after his marriage he resided in Baghdad, coming later during the lifetime of his father to Karachi, where the present Aga Khan was born, as already related, on November 2, 1877. When Hasan Aly Shah died in April, 1881, Aga Aly Shah moved to Bombay. Four years later Aga Aly Shah, Aga Khan II, was cut off suddenly in the prime of a life full of vigour and brilliant promise. His body was taken for burial at Kerbela and its internment in that Holy City of Islam was marked by all the honour and veneration due to the religious head of the great Ismaili sect.

At the time of his father's sudden death the present Aga Khan was barely eight years old. His mother, Lady Aly Shah, one of the most brilliant and outstanding women of our time, as towering of character as she was of person, realising the tremendous responsibility that devolved upon her with the death of her husband and the need to prepare her little son for the illustrious heritage that now descended to him, set about the task with characteristic resolve and thoroughness.

Shortly after her husband's death Lady Aly Shah was informed that the Government had decided to continue to her son the pension that had been granted to his grandfather, and a year later the honorary title of "His Highness" was bestowed on him, a manifestation of official regard for the family which is unique, since the Aga Khan was just nine years old at the time. Lady Aly Shah managed the estates and properties, looked after the enormous charities and benevolences of the Aga Khan's household and found time in the midst of these preoccupations to supervise personally the education of the young boy upon whom had devolved the vast burden of the responsibilities that belong to the "Pope of the Ismailians."

Till the Aga Khan attained the age of sixteen Lady Aly Shah controlled his affairs and the boy had to follow a régime almost Spartan in its severe simplicity. Humility and duty were the watchwords of his life from earliest boyhood, and they have remained so till to-day. Happily, his mother was a woman of extraordinarily liberal outlook, and the fundamental principle of her son's education was that his duty consisted not merely in fulfilling his obligations as a spiritual leader, but extended to every aspect of life and included the material well-being and progress of his followers. Persian, Arabic and English had to be learned, vast erudition in matters of religion had to be acquired and, in addition, there were all the other studies essential to the completion of a polished citizen of the world—literature, history, mathematics, philosophy, science, geography and the arts. It was hard work, and it speaks well of the Aga Khan's intellectual powers that not only was he equal to this formidable programme of education, but took immense delight in it. Despite the serious interruptions occasioned by the duties of his spiritual headship—he was installed on the Gadi of Imams at Bombay shortly after his father's death—he developed a precocious genius under the fostering eye of his gifted mother and the tutelage of men specially picked by her to teach him. The benefits of this rigorous schooling are perceptible to-day in the character of the Aga Khan, who combines in singular degree the qualities of a man of the world, a genial host and popular ornament of society, with those of a spiritual leader, sagacious politician, and the most universally loved sportsman of our day. The Aga Khan is best described as a philosopher, a man who has made a fine art of living, not, as I have remarked before, in the sense of getting the most pleasure out of life, but to the far more noble and essentially proper end that he extracts the utmost good out of life for the benefit not only of his followers and himself but of all humanity. He thinks always in terms of the world, his objective is the progress of humanity and at all times his thought, word and deed are inspired and directed by international ideals.

Those who know him only in one or other of his innumerable aspects are apt to misjudge his devoted enthusiasm.

AN EARLY FAMILY GROUP

H.H. the Aga Khan with his second wife, the Princess Theresa, and their son, the Aga Khan's present heir, Prince Ali Khan. From "The Aga Khan and his Ancestors." By Naoroji Dumasia.

Some accordingly regard him as a great and successful patron of the turf, who has made a life study of horse-breeding. So he has, indeed, and the fact that he holds the unique distinction of having won the Derby three times, twice in succession, is proof enough of the zeal with which he has followed this particular interest and hobby. For all that, it remains only one of his many interests. He can be equally zealous, as purposeful and devoted and has been as successful in regard to the League, as he showed during his term as President of that Council of the world's nations, the greatest, if also the most pathetic, effort of humanity to attain the status of true culture and civilisation. As a spiritual leader the Aga Khan's zeal is such that it fires his followers to a burning frenzy of worshipping admiration. As an educationist his enthusiasm is equally unbounded, and in the field of social reform he is far ahead of all his day.

As he grew up to manhood the Aga Khan increased his contacts with the leading minds of India and England. He was an associate of the men who laid the foundations of nationalism in India as well as of those whose enterprising genius for business and industry was responsible for the evolution of Bombay into the great port and city it is to-day. Not a leader can be mentioned of the past half-century in any country of the world with whom the Aga Khan has not come into contact, and more or less intimate association. In India he is numbered among the vanguard of its leaders, with the men who have made their contribution to the task of building the nation and vanished from the stage of life, as well as the men who in their several ways and lights are carrying on that work to-day. It is a singular characteristic of the Aga Khan that he has never at any time identified himself exclusively with any partisan movement, political group or school of thought, preserving at all times and in all his activities the liberality of outlook and breadth of statesmanship that may be expected in a citizen of the world and a leader whose followers are scattered in half a dozen countries. With the Royal House of England he has associations that began with Queen Victoria, developed into intimate friendship with King Edward VII and have remained on that level with his successors.

The Aga Khan takes a very serious view of his responsibilities, and never fails to discharge the humanitarian obligations that pertain to his position. The tale of his charities and benevolences would by themselves be sufficient to fill a volume. During the terrible famine that ravaged India in 1897 he carried out relief operations on a scale that can only be described as princely, opening vast camps in Cutch and Kathiawar, at Poona and Bombay, and in the plague epidemic that devastated the country shortly after the famine he played a foremost part in allaying public panic and helping the measures that were devised to fight the disease. It was then, years before Mr. Gandhi or any other Indian leader had given a thought to the condition of the masses of India, the so-called untouchables, that the Aga Khan displayed not merely lip-sympathy with the plight of these unfortunates, but embarked upon active measures to improve their lot with food, assistance and advice. He was the first to urge that mere removal of untouchability in itself can do little good to improve the condition of the Indian masses, but that the proper remedy is to improve their economic condition so that the benefits of better living, material comfort and happiness may be theirs. Unless these are first established there is little prospect, in the Aga Khan's view, of any permanent progress in India.

WITH HIS PRESENT WIFE

In 1926 *the Princess Theresa died and in* 1929 *the Aga Khan married Mlle. Andrée Carron, a beautiful and accomplished French woman.*

An ardent advocate of education, he was the first to raise a voice for the extension of facilities for the education of women in India, and the need to place them on a status of perfect equality with men. Child marriage, the purdah system, enforced widowhood and various other social evils, now engaging the attention of reformers and politicians, were attacked three decades ago by the Aga Khan, who declared that "the active influence of women in society under free and equal conditions is calculated not only to bring about practical improvement in the domestic realm, but also a higher and nobler idealism into the life of the State. The time has come for a full recognition that the happiness and welfare of the women themselves must be the end and purpose of all efforts of the Government and society towards improvement." It took two generations before that advice was even considered, but the changes of the past decade have fulfilled the Aga Khan's vision and one of his most cherished aspirations.

For the Moslems of India he pursued the ideal of education with equal zest. His efforts on behalf of and his benefactions to the Moslem University of Aligarh, one of the finest educational institutions of its kind in the whole world and a centre of Islamic culture comparable with the ancient University of Al Ahzar founded at Cairo centuries ago by one of his ancestors, fully entitle him to be classed among that institution's founders and most powerful patrons. From his first association with the University he gave it an annual grant of Rs6,000, which later he raised to Rs10,000. He has contributed with princely generosity to its funds and has worked with endless and efficient zeal to bring it to its present position of preeminence as a nursery of Islamic culture and a centre of Moslem education. The University on its part has fully acknowledged its debt to the Aga Khan and in 1936 gave expression to its gratitude by declaring in a formal address, presented to His Highness by the members of the Court of the University, that "So long as this University continues to function Your Highness' name will be remembered with reverence and affection by the Moslems of India." The address added, "We earnestly hope that under the fostering care and guidance of Your Highness this institution will develop into a Cordova of the East." The address, it is worth noting, greeted the Aga Khan "not only as the most respected, the most accomplished and the most trusted leader of the Moslem community, but also as a great statesman and educationist, owing to whose patriotic efforts our *alma mater* has established a position among the universities of the world." Towards the foundation of Aligarh the Aga Khan collected nearly thirty lakhs of rupees, towards which he himself made a substantial contribution in addition to his annual allowances and particular endowments.

As to his leadership among the Moslems of India, as far back as 1910 a joint address was presented to him at Bombay in the names of the Shiah and Sunni sects acknowledging in the most eulogistic terms his deep interest and valuable efforts on behalf of the Moslems of India and declaring that "he had endeared himself to every Moslem heart in India and they were proud to acknowledge him as their leader."

An even greater tribute to his position as a leader, not only of his own country or community, but of world standing, was provided when on February 5, 1924, a resolution was moved in the Council of State and adopted unanimously requesting the Government of India "to convey to the Norwegian Parliament the view of this House that

LEADING IN THE WINNER

In 1924 the Aga Khan realised the great ambition in the sporting world. He won the English Derby with his colt Blenheim. He is seen here leading in the winner.

His Highness Sir Sultan Muhammad Shah, Aga Khan, is a fit and proper person to be awarded the Nobel Prize for Peace this year in view of the strenuous, persistent and successful efforts that His Highness has made to maintain peace between Turkey and the Western Powers since the Armistice."

The suggestion, it is worth mentioning, emanated in the first place from Norwegian and Swiss newspapers which had advocated the right of the Aga Khan to be considered a worthy candidate for the distinction, and it met with enthusiastic support from representatives of every Indian community, including Sir Purshotamdas Thakurdas and the late Mr. V. J. Patel.

The Aga Khan's services to the cause of Indian political development are too well known to require more than passing mention here. From the days of the Morley-Minto Reforms to the Round Table Conferences at which the present Indian Constitution was so laboriously evolved, from the right of Indians to admission into the public services of their own country to their claims to equal treatment as citizens of the empire and subjects of the crown of England throughout the British Empire, His Highness has been an indefatigable champion and fearless exponent of Indian claims.

His efforts to establish communal peace and understanding in India, with a view to securing the co-operation of both the major communities in the important task of building up the new Indian nation, were being pursued with single-hearted zeal and unswerving purpose long before any other Indian leader had even thought of the problem. That they have failed to bridge a slowly widening gulf is no fault of the Aga Khan, whose reasonable and eminently practical proposals have fallen on ears that have steadily failed to respond to them. As recently as 1939 His Highness made yet another effort to heal the breach that divides Hindu and Moslem into two mutually suspicious and almost hostile camps. Above the reach of communal sentiment, this citizen of the world can see with clear gaze and profound pity the waste and tragedy of this communal misunderstanding. He has expressed again and again that every Indian must cultivate a national outlook such as will transcend individual and communal interests, so that Hindus, Moslems, Parsis, Christians, every son of the country, may be able to work together, harnessed in massive might to the chariot of Indian progress. It is an ideal he has not abandoned despite bitter experience of repeated failure and, if the dream ever comes true, the Aga Khan will have been largely responsible for bringing it to realisation. Although the major objective has not been achieved in this sphere of the Aga Khan's activities, his tremendous influence and the vast esteem in which he is held by all sections of the population have been exerted on innumerable occasions to avert communal clashes and restore peace where such disturbances have threatened or actually occurred.

His Highness was married the first time in 1898 to the daughter of his uncle, Aga Janjishah. Ten years later he married an Italian lady, the Princess Theresa Magliano, who was converted to Islam before the ceremony. By her His Highness had two sons, the elder of whom died in infancy. The second is Prince Aly Khan, the Aga Khan's present heir. Princess Theresa died in 1926, and three years later His Highness married a cultured French lady, Mlle. Andrée Carron, who is esteemed everywhere for her talent, beauty and virtues, and particularly beloved among the Aga Khan's followers in India, in whose welfare she has from the first displayed

AFTER THE MARRIAGE OF PRINCE ALY KHAN TO MRS. LOEL GUINESS IN PARIS

the keenest interest. A son, Sadruddin, was born to her in January, 1933.

I have not referred, except briefly in passing, to the Aga Khan's sporting interests and achievements. It is said that in this field he had three ambitions: to win the Viceroy's Cup at Calcutta, to win the Derby at Epsom and to win a golf handicap at St. Andrews. The world knows how he has achieved the first two—the second, indeed, in a manner which constitutes a record for the entire history of the Derby and one that may hardly be beaten—and anybody who knows the Aga Khan's amazing capacity for success will realise that he may yet achieve his last wish.

For the rest, nothing better could be written of the Aga Khan than that, throughout his fruitful years, he has loved righteousness and hated iniquity and achieved with unswerving pursuit of the noblest ideals a position which is unique in the world of men to-day. As religious leader, Indian patriot, devoted upholder of the British crown, philosopher, sportsman, shining social light, and fortune's favourite, he plays many parts and plays them all with spectacular success. An eminent authority has said of him that he possesses the wisdom of the entire League of Nations. He does. His secret is a simple one and explains equally his astounding sagacity, his genius for success and the amazing esteem and affection in which he is held by all sorts and conditions of people. No word escapes his lips that is not born of careful thought, he attempts no deed before he has reflected on all its possible consequences and a decision once made he bends the resolve of an inflexible will to its pursuit till achievement is complete.

BY COURTESY OF THE BRITISH MUSEUM

GAUTAMA BUDDHA

The Buddha in Earth-Touching attitude. A carving in sandstone of the Sarnath School, about 6th century.

GAUTAMA BUDDHA

THE FOUNDER OF BUDDHISM

c. 563–483 B.C.

BY CHARLES A. KINCAID, C.V.O.

GAUTAMA BUDDHA was born somewhere about 563 B.C. at Kapilawastu. He was a Kshattriya prince of the Sakya clan and his father was Suddhodana, the ruler or king of a strip of country thirty miles south of the foothills of the Himalayas and on the borders of Nepal. How the Sakyas came to occupy this land has been related in the following legend:

Once upon a time there was a king who reigned over a land called Potala. He fell in love with a beautiful princess and asked her hand in marriage. The princess accepted him, but added to her acceptance a curious condition. She would not marry the king unless he promised to appoint as his successor his youngest and not his eldest son. The royal suitor was too much in love to object. He married the princess, who bore him five sons. When the time came for appointing an heir to the throne, the king, bound by his promise, named

MARTIN HURLIMANN

BUDDH-GAYA

The Sacred Bo-tree at Buddh-Gaya under which the Buddha was sitting in deep meditation when he received enlightenment.

the youngest son as his successor. At the same time he banished his four eldest sons from the state and bade them seek their fortune elsewhere. The exiled princes set out and after a long and tiresome journey they came to a fertile land where lived an ancient sage called Kapila. They did reverence to him and begged him tell them whither they should direct their weary steps. The sage, pleased with their courtesy, counselled them to go no farther, but settle down near his hermitage. This they did, and built a city which in the sage's honour they called Kapilawastu or Abiding place of Kapila. They themselves took the title of Sakyas or the Brave Ones.

Suddhodana's father was a descendant of one of the four brave brothers and for many years he ruled happily over a prosperous, if somewhat restricted state. He was, however, greatly distressed that no son had been born to him, although for several years he had been married to two sisters Maya and Pajapati, the daughters of the king of Koli. His happiness was to come. During the full moon festival of the month of Ashalha or Ashad (June-July) queen Maya dreamt a strange dream. She dreamt that four great kings raised her and her bed, took her to the Manosila tableland and then moved aside. Their queens took their places and bathed her in the Anotatta Lake, and put her on a divine couch with her head to the east. A white elephant, bearing in its trunk a white lotus, appeared in the room and after circumambulating the bed three times, smote her side with its trunk and entered her womb.

Next day Maya told her dream to the king, who sent for his most learned Brahmans. They all agreed that the queen would have a famous son. If he stayed in the royal palace he would become a mighty conqueror. If he

A.S.I.

THE SERMON IN THE DEER PARK

In the Deer Park at Sarnath the Buddha preached his first sermon, the text of which was: "Sorrow; the cause of Sorrow; the removal of Sorrow; the way leading to the removal of Sorrow."

MARTIN HURLIMANN

SARNATH

e Great Stupa at Sarnath, near Benares, which was set up to mark the place where the Buddha first preached the Law and the Way.

renounced the world, he would become one of its wonders. He would be a great sage, who would guide all peoples to the goal of truth and justice.

The dream came true; for not long afterwards Maya realised that she was to become a mother. Following what is still the common practice of India, Maya decided with the king's permission to give birth to her baby in her mother's house in Devadaha, a small town not far from Kapilawastu. Unfortunately she either delayed her journey too long for reasons that have not come down to us or she miscalculated the date of her conception. On the way she felt the birth pains come on. It was impossible either to return or to continue the journey, for the party were about half-way between the capital and Devadaha. They halted near a wood known as the Lumbini Grove; but before the poor queen had time to lie down, she was delivered of her child standing. It is said that all nature rejoiced at its birth, that cool breezes blew everywhere and that a bright light flooded the whole world. However this may be, the birth brought but little pleasure to Maya. She and her child were carried amid great rejoicings to Kapilawastu, but only seven days after her delivery the poor mother died. Her sister, Queen Pajapati, adopted the baby as her own and gave him all a mother's care. He received the name of Gautama and possibly the name of Siddartha; but the latter may be a later appellation, for it means "He who has reached his goal."

Gautama grew up amid what were then deemed luxurious surroundings. Nothing sad or ugly was allowed near him. Beautiful maid-servants surrounded him and a host of men-servants waited on him and no doubt did their best to spoil him. When five years old, he went to a little school kept by a wise and learned Brahman, to which only the sons of Sakya nobles were admitted. Gautama soon attracted the teacher's attention by his superior intelligence, and he became in time most popular among the boys. His chief companions were his half-brother Nanda, his cousin Devadatta and a young Brahman called Udayin. Unfortunately Devadatta was bitterly jealous of Gautama's popularity and after a time grew to hate him, just as Duryodhana grew to hate Yudhishtira in the *Mahabharata*. A trifling incident brought matters to a head. One day when Gautama and Udayin were walking in the palace gardens they saw a flight of wild geese overhead. As they admired the graceful "V" formation in which wild geese are wont to fly, one of the birds, pierced by an arrow, fell at their feet. Gautama went to it, pulled out the shaft and dressed the wound. As he was thus engaged, a servant came up and told him that the goose had been brought down by the prince Devadatta and that he had been sent to pick it up. Gautama refused to let him and the servant returned empty-handed to his master. The prince himself came up and haughtily demanded his quarry. Gautama maintained that the bird was his because he had saved its life, while his cousin had only tried to kill it. Devadatta was furious; Gautama was no better than a preacher, he cried. A prince's duties included the chase, the use of arms and the defence of his country in battle. Since Gautama still refused to surrender the wild goose, Devadatta went away, muttering fearful threats against his cousin.

In spite of his threats Devadatta seems to have done nothing more than spread rumours that Gautama was a "mollycoddle," who cared nothing for field sports nor martial exercises. He was therefore unfit to succeed his father as the king of a free and warlike peop
The gossip reached Suddhodana's

MARTIN HURLIMANN

GREAT BUDDHIST SHRINE

The Great Buddha Temple at Buddh-Gaya. It was built, it is believed, just about two thousand years ago, and contains a much earlier shrine built by the Emperor Asoka.

CARVED PANEL FROM SANCHI

The upper portion shows the Sacred Bo-tree, the lower the miracle of the disciple who at Buddha's command walked on the water.

and he became rather alarmed about his son's future. He had him trained in riding, archery and swordsmanship. The youth took to these martial exercises in a way that delighted his teachers. Soon the king felt justified in issuing a challenge to the young nobles of his kingdom to try their skill against the royal heir. Edwin Arnold, following certain Sanskrit authorities, has described the contest as a *swayamvara* for the hand of the lady Yasodhara:

> "*So 'twas given forth that on the seventh day The Prince Siddartha summoned whoso would*
> *To match with him in feats of manliness,*
> *The Victor's crown to be Yasodhara.*"

This seems, however, to be an echo of the epics, wherein both Ramachandra and the Pandavas won Sita and Draupadi at a *swayamvara*. It seems more likely that the king wished by a public contest to establish his son's fitness for the Sakya throne. Gautama certainly proved it, for he beat his cousin Devadatta in archery, his half-brother Nanda in fencing and finally bent and strung his grandfather's bow, a feat deemed impossible of performance. As there was no longer any question of Gautama's royal qualities the king very properly thought that the sooner so splendid a youth continued the royal line, the better. Without delay he arranged his marriage and the lady chosen was Gautama's cousin Yasodhara, the sister of Devadatta. Once his senses were awakened by marriage the young prince found a keen enjoyment in worldly delights. The chroniclers have revelled in exaggerated accounts of the splendour of his palace and of the number and charms of his concubines. But this type of pleasure palls sooner or later, and although the prince's vigour enabled him to endure the strain without injury, a time came when his active mind wearied of the company of his beautiful wife and mistresses. The tale runs that the king deliberately kept from Gautama's eyes everything that was not young and beautiful. One day he saw, as he was driving down the road behind his four white horses, an old and feeble beggar. He enquired of his charioteer Channa the cause of the mendicant's weakness. To the prince's astonishment Channa explained that old age and weakness were the common lot of all mankind. Gautama returned home and questioned the king, who consoled him as best he could and drove away his son's melancholy by an unusually splendid banquet. Some days later the prince again drove out and saw a man in great pain lying on the road, and learnt from Channa that pain and sorrow awaited everyone, even royal princes. During a third drive Gautama met a dead man being carried to the burning ground. He received the explanation that all life at last ended in death. This legend is obviously imaginative. No child could grow to manhood, especially in a small state such as Kapilawastu, without seeing sick or dead men; and all children feel pain at some time or another. A far more likely cause of the change in Gautama was the reaction caused by worldly pleasure. It drove him back on his mind and started the enquiry common to nearly all young men, whether the religion taught them gave a satisfactory explanation of the origin and direction of life. If priests could really influence the gods, why did they not obtain immortality and the fulfilment of all their wishes? If they could not influence the gods of what use was their intercession? Indeed, of what use were the gods at all if they either could or would not help mankind? The climax came, when again driving with Channa, Gautama met an ascetic in an orange-coloured robe. His head was shaven and he seemed completely destitute, but in his face shone contentment and his eyes glowed with spiritual light. "Who is he?" asked Gautama.

"He is a *sanyasi* or anchorite" replied the charioteer. "He has renounced the world and lives only for the quest of truth."

Gautama was deeply impressed and within him the desire grew to become himself a *sanyasi* and live for the pursuit of truth. Not long afterwards Yasodhara bore him a son. The news rejoiced the king; for the royal line of the Sakyas would be thus continued. Gautama took a different view. He would now be immersed in the *Sansar* or married life. No more could he leave his palace and, dressed in an orange robe, wander in search of truth. He exclaimed bitterly "My son shall be called 'Rahula' or

A.S.I.

THE FOUR PRINCIPAL MOMENTS

A stele from Sarnath depicting the Birth, Enlightenment under the Bo-tree, the First Sermon, and the Attainment of Nirvana.

A.S.I.

THE CONVERSION OF NANDA
From a carving at Amaravati.

impediment," and this name was duly given to the baby boy. Yet at first Gautama was attracted by the beauty of his little son and enjoyed the congratulations showered on him by Suddhodana's subjects. This mood did not last long. The king gave a mighty banquet to his nobles with the usual accompaniment of dancing girls and music; but Gautama was now twenty-eight and was weary of such entertainments. When he left the banquet hall he found it impossible to sleep. At last he called Channa and bade him saddle his horse, as he could stay in the palace no longer.

Gautama, however, was human, and before he deserted his home he felt that he must look once more at Yasodhara, with whom he had lived so many years, and the baby Rahula, whom he had begotten. He returned to the threshold of his wife's chamber and saw her as she lay asleep on a pillow of flowers with one hand on her boy's head. An intense longing seized Gautama to embrace his child for the last time; but he realised that if he did so, he would wake his wife and that her clinging arms would chain him to the palace. Sadly he turned away, rejoined Channa and rode into the darkness a penniless wanderer. As he rode, he had an experience similar to that told of Christ; although whether Christianity or Buddhism is the source of the legend it is impossible to say. Mara, the spirit of evil, tried to induce Gautama to return home, promising him, if he did so, universal sovereignty. Gautama refused, but Mara followed him the whole journey, pressing on him glorious gifts, if he gave up his enterprise. Unmoved, the saintly prince reached his destination, which was the bank of the river Anoma. There he dismounted, took off his jewels, and ordered Channa to take them and his horse back to Kapilawastu. Channa protested, offering to become also an ascetic and serve Gautama.

The prince refused the offer saying: "How will my father and mother know what has become of me, unless you go back and tell them?" Channa reluctantly obeyed.

Gautama, left alone, cut off his hair, gave his rich clothes to a ragged passer-by and walked to Rajgriha, the capital of the Magadha kingdom, a mendicant anchorite. In the hills near Rajgriha were a number of caves, and several were occupied by Brahman teachers. Gautama attached himself to two of these in turn, wishing probably to probe fully the priestly doctrines before renouncing them. His first teacher Alara proved unconvincing, so Gautama left him for a second called Udraka. The latter proved no more satisfying than Alara. Both told him that it was only by penances that the priests obtained their superhuman powers. Gautama decided to leave them and test their doctrines by self-mortification. He withdrew to the forest of Uruvela near the existing temple of Buddha Gaya and there together with five devoted disciples, he for six years practised the severest penances until he nearly killed himself. His fame as an anchorite spread "like the sound of a great bell hung in the middle of the sky," yet he never came nearer his goal. At last as one day he dragged himself along he fainted from sheer exhaustion. He recovered and, fully satisfied that the priests knew nothing, he turned his back on their tenets and gave up for ever his self-mortification; but his disciples had only been attracted by his penances, so they abandoned him and returned to Benares.

Gautama was disillusioned and a likely prey for Mara the spirit of evil, who again attacked him and held before him visions of Kapilawastu, his familiar home, his beautiful wife Yasodhara and the comely boy whom he had deserted, and urged his return. Gautama, although sorely tempted, wandered on until he reached the banks of the Nairanjara river, where a kindly village maiden gave him a bowl of rice milk that she had meant to offer to the village gods. He sat down under a great tree, since known as the Bo-tree or tree of wisdom, and through the long Indian day he debated with himself what course to take. Worn out with starvation and exhausted by his thoughts he fell into

BY COURTESY OF THE BRITISH MUSEUM

SYMBOLISING HIS BUDDHAHOOD

A carved Buddha from Sarnath of the Gupta period. His hand was pointed downward "calling the earth to witness" his Buddhahood.

CAVES AT UDAYAGIRI

The Buddhist caves on Udayagiri Hill, not far from Bhubaneswar. They are the remains of a Buddhist Monastery probably founded by Asoka himself.

a trance-like sleep. Next morning he awoke fully refreshed and his mind clear. He had tested the doctrines of the priests and they had failed him. He had attained Bodhi or knowledge himself. He had become the Buddha or the Enlightened one. He would no longer examine the tenets of others. He would himself be a teacher and would lead mankind along the path of Truth. Having made this decision, Gautama went to a deer forest some three miles from Benares and began to teach his new faith. He soon gathered round him the curious of both sexes and even his five recreant disciples returned to him. At last, he selected sixty of his most fervent followers to spread his gospel. He himself went back to Rajagriha and converted Bimbisara king of Magadha, so that he repeated the famous formula:

"I take refuge in the Buddha; I take refuge in the doctrine; I take refuge in the order."

The conversion of a ruling prince made Gautama famous. Suddhodana heard that his son had found the Truth and was preaching the gospel of peace all over the world. He longed to see his son again and sent messengers to call him; but they were all converted, and instead of bringing back Gautama, stayed with the Master. At last a lifelong friend induced the prince to return to Kapilawastu; but he went as an anchorite, begging his food. His father went to meet him, shocked that the heir to the throne should walk the streets as a beggar. He brought his son back to the palace and showed him Yasodhara and Rahula. To the king's sorrow Rahula became a Buddhist monk and his throne was left without an heir. Yasodhara became the first of an order of nuns, founded later by her husband.

When Gautama was forty years old, he learnt that his father was dangerously ill, so he returned to Kapilawastu, reaching it in time to bid him good-bye. On Suddhodana's death, his widow became a Buddhist nun; and since there was nothing to keep Gautama in Kapilawastu, he spent the rest of his life wandering up and down northern India, spreading his doctrine. His chief trouble was the jealousy of Devadatta, who set up another order of monks, wherein the rules were harsher than those of Buddha. He even attempted to assassinate his cousin, but when he died soon afterwards, the monks of his order rejoined Buddha. Gautama continued his mission for forty-five years; but in his eightieth year he was attacked by a severe illness that he felt would be fatal.

MARTIN HURLIMANN

TEMPLE AT MARTAND

A Buddhist temple at Martand whose architecture clearly shows Greek influence.

MARTIN HURLIMANN

GIANT BUDDHA

The great Buddhist Chapel in the Ellora Caves with its magnificent seated Buddha.

Still he journeyed on, until he reached a grove outside Kusinagara, about one hundred and twenty miles north-east of Benares. There he lay down to rest for the last time. He had a long discussion with a Brahman philosopher named Subhadra and converted him. The effort proved too much for the weary old man. He turned to Ananda, who had been for many years his personal attendant and said: "You may think that the Word ends when the teacher goes, but it is not so. The law and the rules of the order which I have laid down will be your teacher." Making a last effort, he addressed a crowd of Buddhist monks, ending his address with the exhortation:

"Decay is inherent in all component things; work out your salvation with diligence!"

These were the Master's last words. He fell into a swoon and never again recovered consciousness.

BY COURTESY OF THE BRITISH MUSEUM

THE MASTER TEACHES

A Buddha with his first and middle fingers joined denoting discourse. From Sarnath.

Let us now consider what Buddha's teaching was. No more than Calvin or Luther did Gautama invent a new faith. He merely modified an existing one. The essentials of Hinduism he retained. The doctrine of metempsychosis or the wheel of life is still currently accepted by orthodox Hindus. He denied the efficacy of sacrifices and the power of the Brahmans. In other words he attacked priesthood and the Hindu gods, and substituted for them an ethical ideal. What happened? His followers in later years deified Buddha. He did away with penances and self-mortification, but he founded monasteries and nunneries, wherein harsh anti-sexual rules prevailed. Theoretically he abolished caste within the order, but this rule has only been observed in countries where no caste existed. Buddha himself paid special respect to converted Brahmans. He laid down eight principles: 1, Right Belief; 2, Right Aims; 3, Right Speech; 4, Right Actions; 5, Right Means of Livelihood; 6, Right Endeavour; 7, Right Mindfulness; 8, Right Meditation. As a norm of life these principles are the ideal accepted by every civilised religion. In fact Buddha would probably have been the last to admit that he was not a good Hindu. He would have claimed that he was a reformer merely. Yet if Buddha invented little new, how came it that his teaching spread all over Asia?

The personality of Gautama was certainly an important factor. By all accounts his person was kingly, his diction eloquent and his intelligence superhuman. Also, he led a revolt against a priestly caste, whose claims far exceeded their powers; and such a revolt is always popular. As late as the invasion of Alexander, Brahmanism was still triumphant. The Greek writers who wrote of the Macedonian's Indian campaign mentioned Gumnosophoi or Brahmans and the worship of the infant Heracles or Krishna at Mathura. But they neglected Buddhism. In 261 B.C. however, the great Asoka succeeded to the imperial throne of Pataliputra, founded by his grandfather Chandragupta, the friend of Alexander. Asoka had carried his arms successfully over all India and had perpetrated a fearful massacre in Orissa. Its memory haunted him all his life. In one of his edicts he inscribed the following passage:

"If a hundredth, nay a thousandth part of the persons, who were then slain, carried away captive or done to death were now to suffer the same fate, it would be a matter of remorse to His Majesty."

To escape from his remorse he became a Buddhist and set about converting India with the powers of an autocrat and the zeal of a missionary. He pressed on his subjects the rule of *ahinsa* or "non-killing" with far greater fervour than Gautama himself. He converted Ceylon, Burma and Siam to Buddhism and sent missionaries to the courts of his Greek friends Ptolemy of Egypt, Antigonus Gonatas of Macedonia, Magas of Cyrene and Alexander of Epirus. These missionaries effected no conversions, nevetheless their preaching may have sunk into men's minds. In 190 B.C. Demetrius, the Greek ruler of Bactria, invaded India under pressure from the Yueh-Chi and conquered a kingdom in the Punjab. His descendants became Buddhists, either because Hinduism did not admit foreigners, or because Buddhist ideas had become known through Asoka's missionaries and the old Greek Gods were no longer honoured. As time passed a section of the Yueh-Chi, known as Kushans, followed the Bactrian Greeks into India and conquered their possessions. From the conquered the Kushans learnt Buddhism and their greatest ruler Kanishka became as ardent a propagandist as Asoka. His missionaries converted China and Japan.

The next question arises why in spite of its successes abroad Buddhism is all but extinct in India. Buddhism flourished to the death of Harsha in 648 A.D. Then for two centuries a black curtain descended. When it was finally lifted the great peninsula was unrecognisable. It was dominated by a number of wild, romantic clans, the descendants of invaders from Central Asia. To men whose supreme joys were the hazards of the chase and the battle the doctrine of *ahinsa* seemed ridiculous. To kill panthers on foot, armed only with a sword, to die on the field of honour fighting against tremendous odds, was the only fit life and death for a Rajput soldier. The temper of these splendid warriors enabled the Hindu priests to effect a counter reformation. They told the listening paladins the tales of Ramachandra and Hanuman, of Bhima, Arjuna and above all Krishna. This last was the Rajput ideal. Renowned alike in love and war, he became the idol of the new rulers of India. Still they were not Hindus, and Hinduism did not accept converts. This difficulty was soon overcome. Skilful and learned men drew up genealogies, establishing the descent of the Rajput Ranas from one or other of the Epic heroes. Thus in no long time Hinduism recovered its old supremacy. It was fortunate for India that things fell out as they did. Had the Rajput swords not defended her, her fate would have been like that of Sind which the Arabs conquered and converted entirely to Islam, and India would have become a mere extension of Central Asia. As it was the Rajputs kept at bay Afghans and Moguls long enough for the Marathas to join in the defence of the ancient gods. Nevertheless even if Buddhism is all but dead in the land of its birth, in other countries its followers number at least five hundred millions.

F. HENLE

GOMATA RAYA

The gigantic statue of the Jain Saint at Sravana Belgola. So profound is his meditation that plants twine round his limbs unobserved.

VARDHAMĀNA MAHĀVĪRA

FOUNDER OF JAINISM

540–477? B.C.

BY MRS. RHYS DAVIDS, D.Litt., M.A.

WHEN I was asked to contribute an account of this great man among the great men of India, I was keenly aware of my unfitness, for my work is chiefly associated with another of India's great ones. And I refused. The request was renewed. It then seemed to me that the man I was asked to tell about was somehow near me and I had but to write as I was willed. That which came to me may not be on all fours either with the legends accepted by the one half of the Jaina world or with those accepted by the other half.[1] But while the one and the other are both purely "legends," too long orally handed down to be accepted as sober records of historical fact, I for my part have not invented a single phrase.

But this I would say first. In the books I have read on the beginnings of the Jain movement there is for me an insufficient depicting of the religious soil from which that movement, with its Founder, sprang. It has been called, and rightly called, a reform movement,

[1] *The Svetâmbaras and Dīgambaras.*

SRAVANA BELGOLA

Courtyard of the Jain Temple. Sravana Belgola was founded by Bhadra Bahu, a Jain sage converted, it is believed, by one of Mahavira's own disciples.

but I have not seen treated with right emphasis that which, in the generating soil, was calling for reform. So much is made of the legend of a prehistoric line of founders of a proto-Jainism, of which my subject is held to be a latest outcome, that little if any attention has been paid to that which is, for the culture of our day, an historic fact, namely, that a reform movement is begotten and determined, not by a fancied cosmic necessity for a line of teachers carrying out an independent plan, but by a certain evolution in man's religious quest, born in a certain land at a certain time, which, for the wise man, shows symptoms of needed correction and expansion. Thus we see Jesus rising to show that man, in the new conditions of the Roman domination and "pax," was not regarding his fellow-man *as just that*, as "neighbour," as "brother." And Islam largely arose because of the polytheism the Founder witnessed at Mecca and the growing polytheism in the church of Christendom. Similarly, the Founder of the Jain movement was a man urged by an inspiring call to rectify something he saw amiss in the accepted religious mandate of his day.

Now this mandate had been for perhaps some two centuries that *volte-face*, that inversion in the Nature-theism of the Vedic hymns, best called Immanence:—the perception of Deity less in powers of nature, and more in the essential nature of man. Learners in Brahman schools were told: "This immortal fear-less Brahman, this art *thou!* Worship Brahman as the self (or as I prefer to say, as the spirit). Seek to know that Self." That this was no alien creed to Vardhamāna we can see surviving in the Jain scriptures centuries later: "A wise man who knows that women are a slough, as it were, will get no harm from them, but will wander *searching for the Self*." (*Uttarâdhyayana.*) I have nowhere seen noticed the interesting parallel there is here with the first public injunction recorded as given by the Founder of Buddhism: "What have you, gentlemen, to do with a woman?[1] Were it not better that you sought thoroughly after the self?" Both records clearly hint that both teachers were followers of the Brahman teaching of Immanence. Yet both teachers, as such, set on foot a line of reformed teaching, not running counter to Immanence, but supplying something in which they deemed it lacking. And there has come to me that which claims to tell what this was.

This:— that those two reform movements sprang up, not in the region known as Central, the Majjhima-desa, where Brahmanism was strongest and best, but further east, east of where Delhi now stands, in the land alleged by scholars to be, as to Brahman teaching, more corrupt, does not invalidate the need of making clear what was calling for reform. The local conditions may have made reform yet more needed: that is all.

I would add again, if it be said, that had the Founders felt that reform was needed in just that accepted cult of Immanence, they would have made this clear—as they do not—in their recorded teaching, I would answer: the man who is charged with, inspired by, a mandate of help for his neighbours, may, or may not, have discerned just how that mandate applies to the prevalent cult of his country and age. He is too near; he cannot see the application of it in perspective as we can. Or, if he did see it, the religious values of his own after-men will have greatly changed by the time his own Sayings and those of his helpers came to reach the form in which

[1] *They had asked him, had he seen a thief they were seeking.*

MOUNT ABU

The Dilwara Temples, Mt. Abu, are among the oldest, most complete and loveliest Jain temples. These carved ivory pillars are certainly the finest thing of their kind in India.

TOWER OF FAME, CHITORGARH

Carved Jain figures on the lower part of the famous Tower of Fame. Many of the great Rajput chiefs followed the teachings of Mahavira.

we read them to-day. In the days of those after-men a new polytheism had sprung up in northern India, in India generally; and, even if the Founder had pointed out wherein he found the cult of his day faulty, it is only too likely that later editors will have failed to keep alive the original point of his teaching.

And now to come to the Man himself.

"For those who know nothing of the subject it is best to remind them that Mahā-vīra (great hero) was not the personal or family name of the Founder of Jainism. This was Vardhamāna, a word meaning, not merely increasing, multiplying (the meaning given in Jain exegesis), but also growing, becoming. It was a name by no means unique in India then or now. I have preference for this more organic meaning, as significant of what I tried to do in the religious mandate in India of the sixth century B.C. I saw the man as able, in growing, that is spiritually growing, to win to a More, to a Better in the man he was. I saw the man as capable of such growth, if not now, then in the future. Herein is man's will active. He seeks the Better in all he does, the Better, that is, as he sees it. It may be a Worse. But for him it is a Better. Sooner or later he will find out whether it be so indeed. He knows there is a More in his manhood, even if he mask it as a more in what he gets.

"Now I was he who first worded a departure from acquiescence in the worth of the Immanence as then taught in India by the preponderant Brahman teaching. Brahmans were teaching the mandate first taught by a forgotten seer of the preceding age, perhaps two centuries earlier. This was, that man in very essence is divine, and as being such would one day attain full Godhead. This was taught as in a way true of man even here and now. It was herein a dangerous teaching, for it treated the future as present; it told man he was, even now, as God: 'That art thou!' It was herein a lie in all but the basis. It passed over the fact of man's very imperfect, childlike state. It valued him in the present as he can only become in the future, when he could be said to be 'grown up.'

"I saw man as in a More, and in that only. I saw teachers holding in worth the unfit as the fit, the unhonoured as the honoured, the man as he may be not different from the man as he was as yet, even in the best.

"And I willed to differ from the Brahmans and teach a new mandate of effort in becoming.[1] I knew that herein I should be departing from the teaching of my colleagues. For I too was Brahman and a teacher. I was not Kshattriya, as is usually believed. I was of the Kaśyapa clan, and that was Brahman, as you know well, who know of many other Kaśyapa, or Kassapa Brahmans. I came to hear, in a later rebirth in India, of a legend which had grown up, of how the Ruler of the next world caused me in embryo to be shifted from a Brahman mother, Devânandā, to a Kshattriyan mother, Triśalā (Ācāranga Sūtra, III, 5). This was due to a growing worth in the Kshattriyan status and the will to show this taking shape in what folk told about me.

"I accepted the Immanence then taught as a More in the man, but I was dissatisfied with it, as were others known to me. And I persuaded these to will to make a new start in the wiser way of not merely seeing, in it, a great uplift for each man, but of working for this, in the effort to win what could be attained but was yet unattained. I saw this in the will to master the body in all its many wayward passions and hindrances in the way of the greater welfare. I had the idea that through the body man's will took effect in a Less, when that body was not kept under perfect control. I was, to this end, depending

[1] *It should be noted that the 'sets' of thoughts in Jain scripture called bhāvanās and translated 'meditations' or 'reflections' really mean '(ways of) making-to-become.'*

DILWARA TEMPLES

Part of the famous carved ceiling.

MARTIN HURLIMANN

THE HOLY MOUNTAIN

Jain Temples on Satrunjaya, Palitana. Here is a whole city of temples dating from the eleventh century down to the present day. It is a great centre for all devout Jains and thousands come yearly on pilgrimage.

on the *tapas* of my day, the method of austerities, or ascetic exercises in the unpleasant:—fasting, exposure to heat or cold, or pain, endurance in effort to sustain, whereby the man, with a subservient body, might more freely will. It was he I willed to see dominant, not the mind—that came in later. It was the very man, who *had* the body, whom I wanted to free from bondage to the body.

"That in thus scourging the body I might weaken effort as much as I forwarded it I did not well see. I have now come to know better, and hold that to harm the body must involve a weakening of it, and so weaken the use the man, in seeking the Better through it as vehicle, can make of it. In moderation the idea was sound, and it was the search for advance in the More toward the Most in man's essential nature that stimulated me. But there was danger, that these painful exercises would preoccupy man's will with a Less. I only saw that unless man's will was an obedient slave it would be a worse instrument. Now severe austerity would bring about this control.

"It was here that I treated will in the wrong way. Man wills his welfare, but when it is will in becoming a More than he was, he needs must be strong. He becomes a new man when he can turn all his strength, bodily and mental, into his efforts. I did well to stress the greater need in current teaching for the putting forth of effort in man's religious quest. Affirmation as to his nature was not enough. But man, as now in a Less, will become man in a More (let alone a Most) only when effort can be constructive, not destructive. My company were willing welfare, but to what extent we concentrated on *tapas*, we were training the will in a Less.

This we did not see. We were exercising will in a Worse.

"After teaching a few years I had many followers. Two of these I held in high worth: Gautama, a Brahman, with whom I had myself been a learner, and Maskari, called Gosāla (of the cowstall).[1] These were true helpers, seeing a More in me as I saw in them men in a More. They too were in favour of *tapas*, but not in excess. They accepted the teaching of Immanence, holding that man had in himself the highest welfare, and the will to win it.

"Remember that when I say 'will,' I bear in mind that our word for it was *manas*. We used it as you use will. Its meaning was not merely mind, as was the word *citra;* it was purpose, which is mind and will in one. Striving with *manas:* this is all man can do as yet.

"I held women in high worth. They were with me in my teaching from the first. I was a married man and had children, though none save one daughter grew up. (*Ācāranga Sūtra, II,* 15.) The worthy women I met were honouring the will in our company to make effort in becoming the New—surely this is ever woman's experience. I arranged that they of my company who willed to do so should make tours. But not women; that did happen, but only later. We toured around Vesālī, and met many who approved of our object. It was men in the world to whom I looked; I did not seek to make men leave the world. It was my wish to see them coming to will a More in their daily life and business. My very will was in this, worthing man at his trade, his field-work, his care for the less fortunate, his warding the sick, his seeing the More in the child, his seeing the More in his fellow-man than he seemed to be, his will in the man of the To Be.

"Moreover, I had heed to man in the Unseen. I could be aware of such myself. It was from the Unseen that I was mandated to teach the New. I was one day meditating on these things and I was hesitating, lest the teaching of the More in man might be undermined by my disapproving in one respect. Then I seemed to hear a voice as it were within which said: 'Man needs the very More in the will in effort, if he is to become what he can become. Word effort!' I believed that man was in more than one world, and that he would return to earth again, in a More-will to word the new he had come to learn.

"I came in time to hear of other men, two or three, also wanting to teach that which they found lacking in the current teaching of Immanence, but they had not kept in view the More that is in man, and I found them worthless. They taught a Less in man, his being not real, his turning to monkhood, and they thus tended to keep man in the Less. I too had had the will to leave the world, and I have been shown as having done this. It was then a new idea: that in leaving the world a man could get quicker to the More in himself.

"Monasticism was not always in Indian life. Brahmans left the world when elderly, but not the man of other classes, let alone before he was elderly. Man had work to do, food to get, and he would have been much blamed had he left the world when still strong. But the idea was beginning to take hold of men that they should leave the world early, and not only if they were Brahmans. This may have been due to the cult of Immanence, for in that it saw a More in man, it showed him to himself as not called upon to be merely earthman. Seeing himself as in a way the Highest, he could be only concerned with the highest things if he would be true to his nature. He was world-forsaker in order to be 'one who had

[1] *In Palī, Makkhali.*

BY COURTESY OF THE BRITISH MUSEUM

MAHAVIRA AND FOUR ATTENDANTS

A bronze figure of the tenth century from Madras.

become Brahman' (*Brahmabhūta*) so far as he yet could.

"Now men of other new messages were as such welcome to me till I found I could not rate highly their departures. Then, when I was already elderly, I heard of the men of the Śākyas (whom your world calls Buddhists). They did not approve of *tapas*, and this made my followers unwilling to welcome them. I wanted to meet their leader, who, as I heard, accepted the Immanence-teaching about the man, but held that the one thing needful in it was that man should not be held as being, nor as not being, but as becoming. I tried to see him, but failed, for the men in my company were silent about his movements, and so we never met. I valued their care of me, but it was a care of the sect, not of the man. I was then in weaker health and could no longer go on tour. Will was there but not strength. The much *tapas* had weakened me prematurely. And Gawtama did not know how I wished to see him.

"In the scriptures compiled by Gawtama's men of a later date, I am told there is recorded a conversation between him and one of my followers: one Upāli whom I can just remember. In this, Gawtama is shown insisting to Upāli that, of the three modes of *karma* or deeds, the mode of *manas* is more effectual in its results on man's life for good or evil than is the mode of bodily action. What I really taught was that bodily action is the vehicle of mind or purpose and, in the result of that purpose, responds to it. I never taught that body was the agent. Herein I have been misrepresented, as is the fate of all teachers of the More. I am not saying that Gawtama misrepresented me. It was my disciples who did that. Have you not yourself found it true that '. . . *it is the disciple who wounds him worst of all.*'[1]

[1] *Rudyard Kipling. Cf. "My Outlines of Buddhism," p. 5.*

"The man who values will or *manas* will value the More in will. The will in man will yet take him far, and the will in becoming, when he realises it is this, will take him further still.

"Very will was with me till the end, but it lay less in austerities, for I had learnt how they shortened our term of usefulness, nor had they otherwise compensated me. The notion of *karma* was beginning to dominate the man of India. He had learnt the notion, not from me, but from other teachers, who saw in deeds done a sort of seed sown, which could not be, as plants, rooted out save by *tapas*, and this was foolish. The better *karma*, better actions, were enough to kill the effects of the earlier less worthy *karma*, so far as the doer himself was concerned.

"I taught this with emphasis, but my men were no longer listening to what I taught. They saw me weak and ageing, and they tended me as a father who has to see his sons rating him as no longer wiser than they. They honoured me as teacher, but they no longer heeded what I said. Their value was in the teacher of a past day, not in the teacher grown wiser of the later years. I hold in worth the teaching that is new. The older teaching may be very true, but it should be valued as something that is in process of becoming.

"I was in good health till one day I had the wish to mandate the men of Vesālī. I went, but I had become weak—too weak for the walk—we all walked, holding it amiss to use beasts to draw us. The journey was too much for me and the end came.

"Man in his care for animals has gone to strange lengths. He has had the idea that he might be reborn as one, and that hence it might be well not to treat them unworthily. I never held with this idea, nor with the idea that noxious animals should not be killed. I had a firm belief that man could not be reborn save as man. Men have credited me with all sorts of theories in this, as in other things. On my shoulders got laid the childish ideas of the Many. Man in the More has much to suffer from his fellows, but he has also been their helper and therein lies comfort.

The man of will is ever in the greater well-being, since he wills it and finds it in his work. He may suffer ill in many ways, yet is he happier than the unwise, for he knows he is in the way to win to the perfect Man."

BY COURTESY OF THE BRITISH MUSEUM

RISHABHA AND MAHAVIRA

The first and last Tirthankaras.

MARTIN HURLIMANN

THE LION CAPITAL

*Four lions supporting the Wheel of the Law on the inverted lotus flower was **Asoka's Royal Standard.** The lion capital found at Sarnath is the **most perfect and most lovely example.***

ASOKA

THE GREAT KING AND MISSIONARY

REIGNED *c.* 273–232 B.C.

BY DAVID BURY

FAR back down the corridor of the years we perceive the figure of Asoka like an image in a shrine, encrusted with legends. But even these owe their lustre to the fire within, to the saintly personality that, after twenty-three centuries, illumines our imagination with the serene radiance of a star. For his life is that of the hero-saint, the king who, having all, renounces everything and receives abundance magnified again. The triumph of abnegation, the apotheosis of humility.

Let us try to deduce, from the broken fragments of evidence that are all that remain to us, what manner of man he was.

We must begin with a legend. It is recounted that the Emperor Asoka was a mighty warrior and hunter; that his dominions extended from horizon to horizon; and that in all the unnumbered leagues over which he held sway, no man was hated more. His iniquities multiplied and his pride offended heaven until the day when his guards took hold of a wandering Buddhist saint and for no other crime save that of poverty cast him alive into a cauldron of boiling filth. But lo! a miracle. For the sage, having taken refuge in the Buddha, was unharmed; the cauldron burst asunder and was transformed into a lotus flower supporting the saint in an attitude of meditation within its brazen petals.

The astonished emperor demanded from his prisoner the secret that could thus preserve him in the midst of adversity, offering him in return rewards to the extent of half his kingdom. Then the saint explained that he required nothing at all but that if the emperor was willing to listen he would instruct him in the way of perfection. And Asoka humbled himself and became a disciple and lived righteously, and when the time came when the emperor desired that his kingdom should also enjoy the advantages of the teachings of Buddha, the spirits of the air united in such numbers that the sun itself was darkened and in a single day built temples or stupas of immeasurable splendour throughout the land.

This charming legend contains, as do most legends, the seeds of truth. Whether or not it required such a spectacular miracle to transform the emperor's policy, we have records from Asoka himself indicating that he undoubtedly did suffer a change of heart. It is probable that he was never such a tyrant or libertine as the legends would have us believe. That, after all, is a literary licence that deepens for contrast the colours of every hero. But he was certainly a powerful warrior.

His grandfather, the famous Chandragupta, first of the Maurya dynasty, inspired by the example of Alexander (whom, legend says, he went to visit), set up a great Empire soon after Alexander's death, successfully repelled an invasion by Seleukos Nikator, secured his north-west frontier against the Greeks, and then conquered almost the whole of what we know to-day as British India. A territory along the east coast, between the Mahanadi and the Krishna rivers, inhabited by the Kalinga, remained independent. The remaining enormous kingdom he left, after twenty-four years of government and consolidation, to his son, Bindusara Amitragata, who reigned for a quarter of a century. At his death, about the year 272 B.C., his son Asoka ascended the throne where for eight years he reigned very much as his father and grandfather had done before him. He was one of several sons and it is probable that his father selected him as *Yuvaraja* or Crown Prince regardless of age or priority but because of his especial ability to govern. During his father's lifetime he was first Viceroy of the North Western Provinces which embraced the territories west of the Indus, Kashmir and the Punjab, and then of Western India. Its capital was Taxila, a great and glorious city, famous as a centre and headquarters of culture. Next, he was Viceroy of the Western Provinces, of which the capital was Ujjain, reputed to be the oldest town in India and a renowned seat of Hindu learning. Asoka's early administrative career was thus spent in two centres of learning, and here he must early have absorbed some part of the principles that remained quiescent until they were activated by later events. According to a Sinhalese legend Asoka was at Ujjain when the news came of his father's death. The curtain rises on his reign with a visionary procession from Ujjain to Pataliputra, his grandfather's capital, there to be crowned three years after his accession and lift his dynasty out of a darkness into immortal light.

We have no record of the early years of his reign, but we can imagine the constant labour it must have been to maintain order in a domain so vast that the vibrations from the king's accession were enough to cause splits and fissures in its unwieldy structure. The country, however, must have been quiet when, in the ninth year of his reign, the king set out with his armies to conquer the Kalinga people and thus extend his territory from sea to sea.

Of that war we have no exact description. Like all other wars it was bloody, wasteful and pointless; nor can all the panoply of elephants and horsemen and cow-hide bucklers and homeric bows with arrows three yards long make it any more heroic. But it was successful, in that the Kalingas were incorporated into Asoka's kingdom and it marked the turning point in Asoka's life. The horrors of that campaign caused a stirring of the king's conscience. He caused his feelings about the event to be inscribed on a rock face and for official purposes henceforth withdrew his name of Asoka and substituted the name Priyadarsin—the Humane One.

Here is the famous Edict:

His Majesty King Priyadarsin in the ninth year of his reign conquered the Kalingas.

One hundred and fifty thousand were thence carried away captive, one hundred thousand were there slain, and many times that number perished.

Ever since the annexation of the Kalingas, His Majesty has zealously protected the Law of Piety, has been devoted to that law, and has proclaimed its precepts.

His Majesty feels remorse on account of the conquest of the Kalingas, because, during the subjugation of a previously unconquered country, slaughter, death and taking away captive of the people necessarily occur, whereat His Majesty feels profound sorrow and regret.

There is, however, another reason for His Majesty feeling still more regret, inasmuch as in such a country dwell Brahmans and ascetics, men of different sects, and householders, who all practice obedience to elders, obedience to father and mother, obedience to teachers, proper treatment of

THE SPIRIT OF THE FOREST

Amidst the carvings on the Sanchi gateways depicting scenes from the life of the Buddha, the royal standard of Asoka and the crest of his house, comes this vigorously executed figure of a wood-nymph or fairy clinging to the boughs of a mango tree. The reason for the introduction of a forest deity is not certain.

ASOKA PILLAR, DELHI

It stands in the grounds of the old palace of Firoz Shah at Delhi. The inscription has been marred by the breaking of the pillar.

friends, acquaintances, comrades, relatives, slaves, and servants, with fidelity of devotion.

To such people dwelling in that country happen violence, slaughter, and separation from those they love.

Even those persons who are themselves protected, retain their affections undiminished: ruin falls on their friends, acquaintances, comrades and relatives, and in this way violence is done (to the feelings of) those who are personally unhurt.

All this diffused misery is matter of regret to His Majesty. For there is no country in which are not found countless communities of Brahmans and ascetics, nor is there any country where the people have faith in one sect only.

The loss of even the hundredth or the thousandth part of the persons who were then slain, carried away captive or done to death in Kalinga would now be a matter of deep regret to His Majesty.

Although a man should do him an injury, His Majesty holds that it must be patiently borne, so far as it possibly can be borne.

Even upon the forest tribes in his dominions His Majesty has compassion, though advised to destroy them in detail, and though the power to harm them is in His Majesty's hands. They are warned to this effect: "Shun evil-doing, that ye may escape destruction." For His Majesty desires for all animate beings security, control over the passions, peace of mind and joyousness.

And this is the chiefest conquest, in His Majesty's opinion, the conquest by the Law of Piety.

The conquest by the Law of Piety was a greater one than anybody realised. The king's change of heart was in itself an astonishing thing but its effects were even more astonishing.

In the year of the Kalinga campaign he joined a Buddhist community as a lay disciple and from that time resolved to dedicate his life and all the resources of his position as emperor to the promulgation of this doctrine which was to bring peace and happiness to his subjects. For two and a half years he limited his possessions to the eight essentials: three pieces of yellow cloth for a garment; a girdle to bind and a needle to mend it; a razor for his head; a strainer lest he should inadvertently destroy life in his drinking water; and a begging bowl. For two and a half years he lived a curious double life. His entrance into the monastery could not, of course, mean an absolute departure from his life as emperor, and indeed we find that he accomplished his difficult task well since he was able to absorb his precepts as a disciple and put them into operation as an autocratic ruler.

For the first two years he confesses that he displayed little zeal as a convert, and then, towards the end of the eleventh year of his reign, his faith received some sudden stimulation and he records his findings:

> "Work I must for the public benefit—and the root of the matter is in exertion and dispatch of business, than which nothing is more efficacious for the general welfare. And for what do I toil? For no other end than this: that I may discharge my debt to animate beings, and that while I make some happy in this world they may in the next world gain heaven."[1]

To this end he organised a widespread missionary scheme. Under the general guidance of his younger brother Mahinda and his sister Sanghamitra ("Friend of the Church") preachers in groups of five were sent all over Ceylon, to the kingdoms of South India, to Mysore, to the Bombay Coast, to the Mahratta

[1] *Rock Edict No. VI.*

THE PILLAR AT LAURIYA

Crowned again by the inverted bell-shaped lotus surmounted by a single lion.

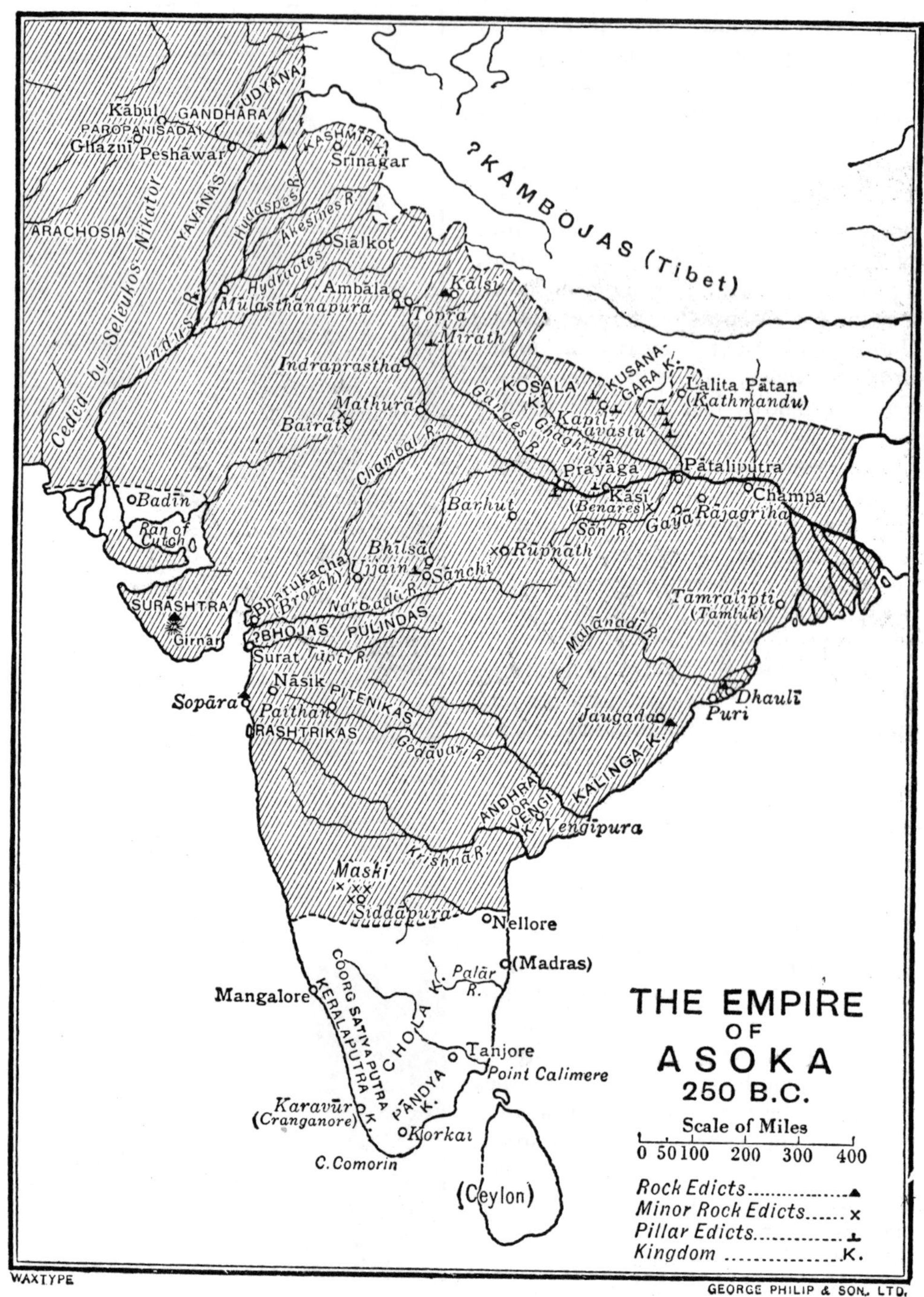

INDIA IN THE TIME OF ASOKA

country, to the Himalayas and Kashmir, and to Pegu. Of those nameless zealots we know little except that they laid the foundations upon which Buddhism in India securely rests to-day. From its beginnings, two and a half centuries before, as a sect of Hinduism, limited in its practice to no more than a part of the Ganges valley, Buddhism was broadcast over the length and breadth of India in a few years—a scattering that has produced one of the world religions for its harvest.

Ceylon was most easily converted, possibly because its king, Tissa, was a personal friend and sympathised with Asoka's ideals, and also on account of the island's previous association with the Buddha. Thence Asoka's victorious missionaries conveyed with much ceremony a branch of the sacred Bo tree from Buddh Gaya—that tree in whose shade the Holy One sat when he achieved enlightenment.

But the emperor's altruism was not confined to missionary work. In his own dominions he tried as best he could to make them a green and pleasant land. He planted fruit trees and trees valuable for their shade; he organised a system of rest houses at intervals along the roads all over his country; he caused deep wells to be dug and gave every encouragement to researches in medicine as well as arranging for supplies of curative herbs and roots to be easily available for his subjects.

By the thirteenth year of his reign, Asoka's philanthropical fervour was burning at its fiercest. In order that no one of his subjects should lack the benefits of the new Guide to Life, the king appointed "Censors of the Law of Piety," whose business it was to go about the country as teachers and living exemplars. They were in control of all charitable works and offices; they had power (and were encouraged to use it)

SANCHI STUPAS

At Sanchi (Bhopal State) is the best known of all the Asokan relics.

to prevent wrongful imprisonment or punishment; and they watched over and protected the interests of the poor and aged.

"Commissioners," records the king, "have been appointed by me to rule over many hundred thousand persons of the people and to them I have granted independence in the award of honours and penalties, in order that they may in security and without fear perform their duties and bestow welfare and happiness on the people of the country and confer benefits upon them.

"The commissioners will ascertain the causes of happiness and unhappiness and will, in accordance with the Law of Piety, exhort the people of the country that they may gain both this world and the next."[1]

"My agents, whether of high, low or middle rank, themselves conform to my teaching and lead the people in the right way, being in a position to recall to duty the fickle minded. . . ."[2]

Gradually the fantastic extravagance of the court was abolished and an ordered regime begun. In the eleventh year of his reign the emperor ceased from hunting and the ban on the slaughter of animals was soon extended to those intended for sacrifice and spread to every four-footed creature whose carcase is not eaten or otherwise utilised by man. On certain days the capture of fish was prohibited and various other detailed specifications concerning the branding and mutilation of animals became law, showing, from their wording, the care with which each individual case must have been considered.

From time to time he caused Edicts to be engraved on rock faces (or in some cases on pillars) throughout his dominions. That these were more than merely public notices is shown by the form in which they are cast and by the fact that, as will be seen below, they contain the essentials of his teachings. It must be assumed that Asoka intended them to be permanent records for posterity.

In addition, however, to these fragmentary remains (for we must also infer that the inscriptions are by no means complete) he caused an incredible number of buildings to be erected. One legend ascribes to Asoka the erection of no less than eighty-four thousand *stupas* apart from palaces and cities of immeasurable splendour. A stupa was originally designed to enshrine a relic of the Buddha or of a saint; but frequently they were more like cenotaphs; that is to say, empty but built in honour of the illustrious dead. The most famous of these is at Sanchi and consisted originally of a solid dome of brick and stone 106 feet in diameter on a cylindrical plinth 14 feet high and 117 feet across. On the top was a stone railing 34 feet across enclosing a square altar, the whole edifice rising to more than 100 feet.

The pillars upon which he carved certain of his edicts were masterpieces of the stone-cutter's art if we are to judge by the two that still stand at Bakhira and Navangarh. Made from a single block of polished sandstone they rise to an all-over height of 60 and 40 feet respectively, each tapering to a carved abacus on which squats a stone lion.

What carvings and architecture remain to us are for the most part stone copies of the original. This explains why the less tractable material develops a lightness and intricacy bordering upon the fantastic. Yet because of the intrinsic artistry of its creators, the sculpture of Asoka's period never seems overdecorated, and its wildest fancies

[1] *Pillar Edict No. IV.*

[2] *Pillar Edict No. I.*

CARVED GATEWAY

It is believed that while Asoka built the original Stupa, this was later covered over, while his wooden railings and gateways were faithfully copied in stone three centuries later.

STEPS AND RAILING

The steps leading to the colonnade or procession path round the stupa.

are always organised and restrained by basic pattern and rhythm.

And all this was done in the name of the Law of Piety. But what was this law?

Professor Rhys Davids has summarised it from the edicts and it will be seen to form the framework of an essentially practical, *non-religious* philosophy. Herein is revealed the quality of the emperor, for his beliefs were founded on basic ethical principles rather than on the forms of worship pertaining to an individual deity.

1. No animal may be slaughtered for sacrifice.

2. Tribal feasts in high places are not to be celebrated.

3. Docility to parents is good.

4. Liberality to friends, acquaintances and relatives, and to Brahmans and recluses is good.

5. Not to injure living beings is good.

6. Economy in expenditure and avoiding disputes is good.

7. Self-mastery, Purity of heart, Gratitude and Fidelity are always possible and excellent even for the man who is too poor to be able to give largely.

8. People perform rites or ceremonies for luck on occasions of sickness, weddings, childbirth or on starting on a journey—corrupt and worthless ceremonies. Now there is a lucky ceremony that may be performed—not worthless like these, but full of fruit—the ceremony of the Law. And therein is included right conduct towards slaves and servants, honour towards teachers, self-restraint towards living things, liberality towards Brahmans and recluses. These things, and others such as these, are the lucky ceremony according to the Law. Therefore should one—whether father or son or brother or master—

THE PROCESSION PATH

The colonnade or passage for circumambulation round the stupa.

interfere and say "Thus should it be. Thus should the ceremony be done to lasting profit. People say liberality is good. But no gift, no aid is so good as giving to others the gift of the Law, as aiding others to gain the Law."

9. Toleration. Honour should be paid to all, laymen and recluses alike, belonging to other sects. No one should disparage other sects to exalt his own. Self-restraint in words is the right thing. And let a man seek rather after the growth in his own sect of the essence of the matter.

10. The Law is good. But what is the Law? The having but little in one's own mind of the Intoxications (arising from lusts, craving after a future life, ignorance and idle speculations); doing many benefits to others; compassion; liberality; truth; purity.

11. Man sees but his good deeds, saying: "This good act have I done." Man sees not all his evil deeds, saying: "That bad act have I done, that act is corruption." Such self-examination is hard. Yet must a man watch over himself, saying: "Such and such acts lead to corruption—such as brutality, cruelty, anger and pride. I will zealously see to it that I slander not out of envy. That will be to my advantage in this world; to my advantage, verily, in the worlds to come."

Only in one Edict does he commit himself—as it were—as an avowed

THE EAST GATE

One of the elaborately carved gateways depicting scenes from the life of Buddha. Again the original gateways erected in Asoka's time would be of wood. These gateways replaced them some time in the Gupta era.

follower of the Buddha; but that, of course, does not mean that other avowals were not made that are now lost.

In 249 B.C., the twenty-third year of his reign, Asoka made a pilgrimage to the Holy Places in his kingdom. Five huge engraved pillars marked his passage from Pataliputra northwards through Muzaffarpur and Champaran to the foothills of the Himalayas. There he turned westward to erect another pillar at the Lumbini Garden where the Venerable One was born. Thence his guide and mentor Upagupta conducted the emperor to Kapilawastu where Buddha spent his childhood; to Sarnath where the Master preached, to Sravasti where he lived for many years and to Gaya where grew that sacred tree whose branches shaded the Master at the dramatic crisis of his life. Finally they came to Kusinagara where the Buddha died, and at every place the emperor made oblation, erecting monuments and endowing colleges for the further dissemination of the Word.

But already the mists of time begin to obscure the glimpses we have of that legendary figure. Like a ruined bridge across a river of unknown breadth, the facts upon which we can erect structures of truth become fewer and more widely spaced. About 242 B.C., in the twenty-eighth year of Asoka's reign, he took stock of himself and his work. The result was the inscribing of what are now known as the Seven Pillar Edicts and these inscriptions form a sort of epilogue or postscript to the Rock Edicts. These are the last words. He reiterates his convictions concerning the Law of Piety and recapitulates his ordinances concerning the election of the Censors, the treatment of animals and the propagation of the Law.

About two years later Asoka retired without abdicating from active government. In pursuance of the logic of his creed and aware that no layman may attain Nirvana, the emperor assumed the yellow robe for a second time. He was no longer a lay disciple but a devout subject of the Ten Precepts binding upon ordained monks. The administration of his kingdom was carried out by ministers or regents and the *Yuvaraja* that was to succeed him; although Edicts were still issued by his authority. An emperor in monastic robes governed India. That silhouette, stripped of the pomp of royalty, is the last glimpse we have of him.

Of the rest of his life, except for the publication of certain supplementary Pillar Edicts, we know nothing. The last eight years of his reign are absolutely without record. Only the bare date of his death (232 B.C.) has been handed down and that he was succeeded by two grandsons,

THE GREAT STUPA, SANCHI

STUPA NO. 3

A closer view of one of the stupas which shows plainly the plan on which it was built.

Dasaratha, who ruled the eastern, and Samprati, who ruled the western part of his vast kingdom.

He had attempted a tremendous task during his lifetime and it was not his fault that he failed. For he had tried to convert his myriad subjects to his ideas by his own example and he was too much of a visionary to see that "the opinions he favoured with his patronage were enfeebled and corrupted by his favour."[1]

While he lived and shone, his empire remained a single unwieldy entity; but after his death it crumbled and declined and only half a century was to pass before the Maurya dynasty became extinct. But although Asoka's counsels were, like so many reformers', those of perfection and are more honoured than practised, his personal character has survived across the centuries and we are able to recognise the humanity, the wisdom, the tolerance and the sympathy of one of the most striking personalities in the history of the world.

Rhys Davids: *Buddhist India.*

THE IMAGE SHRI SANKARACHARYA

SHRI SANKARACHARYA

HIS PHILOSOPHY AND TEACHING

FLOR. 8TH CENTURY A.D.

BY HIS HOLINESS JAGADGURU SHRI SHANKARACHARYA of PURI

Editorial Note:—The illustrations of this article show some of the finest examples of Hindu art and architecture of the ninth and tenth centuries. A revival of Hindu culture and consequently of art occurred during and immediately after the time of Sankaracharya due in a large degree to his teachings.

EVEN the veriest tyro in matters pertaining to Human History (in its various departments) cannot be unaware that the History of Human Progress is not a mechanical process of continuous advancement but has always been marked by what may be accurately described as alternations of ebbs and flows, that each Era of Progress in the history of mankind (as well as of any and every country) invariably began after a period of stagnation and in consequence of the tremendous momentum given to mankind (or that particular country) by the advent of something like a superman who brought a new ideology or revived an old but long-forgotten ideal, set it in motion not so much by dint of his extraordinary spiritual, intellectual and other powers as with the compelling force of his virile and magnetic personality and was personally responsible—by his spirituality, his erudition, his philanthropic activities and other lofty traits of character. Then followed the acceptance of his ideology, his ideals and his ideas by huge masses of humanity eager for and ready to follow a great leader of such supreme eminence and dominating personality. Each such epoch began, after a long period of concentrated and incessant activity, to slacken and slow down, show signs of exhaustion and fall into a steady decline, to be followed by a long period of rot and even retrogression and consequent suffering and then again another such resuscitation, renaissance and rejuvenation with a fresh or a revived ideology for Humanity's progress.

It would almost seem as if, in parallelism to the physical law which is well known to mathematicians and physicists in the sphere of dynamics, there were an identical psychic law at work in the realm of human psychology too, to the

ANCIENT INDIAN DANCE

Fresco on a wall near Vitthalaswami Temple, 16th century.

effect that "Action and Reaction are equal and opposite" and that the alternations in question were in obedience to such a law. At any rate, this is the lesson which history (with its peculiar knack of repeating itself almost as if with deliberate intent to teach us the otherwise unlearnable and unpalatable truths of life) actually teaches us to infer.

The psychology behind this phenomenon and its modus operandi are very simple, i.e. that the initial momentum given by a great epoch-making personality and continued by a few generations of his immediate successors dies out in due course, that the ordinary masses cannot grasp, retain, carry on and keep alive the ideology of the founder of the movement but can only keep up and mechanically follow the outer details of instructions given by him and that the mere letter of the law (divorced from the spirit underlying and motivating it) leads not merely to a natural and inevitable reaction thereagainst but even to blind and unreasoning rebellion against the basic truth itself, thereby necessitating the advent again of a magnetic world-personality capable of harmonising and resynthetising the fragments and shreds which alone then remain of the movement!

Thus it was that, after the Mahabharat war wherein the central figures were Man (as represented by the great hero Arjuna) and Mankind's Preceptor (in the person of God's own Incarnation the Lord Shri Krishna) and after a period of ordered and righteous rule by Arjuna's descendants, the momentum given by the Lord himself in respect of the correct synthesis and harmonising of the Karma Kanda (the path of Works), Bhakti (Faith, Devotion and Worship) and Gnan (Illumination) seemed to have spent itself; people lost their grip over that doctrine of Harmony and Synthesis and the Ideology and the spirit behind the Vedic injunctions relating to the Karma Kanda and kept up only the external forms and rituals thereof; and confusion, corruption and hypocrisy reigned everywhere.

Such a state of affairs was naturally bound to and did actually give rise to the reaction and revolt which culminated in the advent of the Lord Buddha, who not merely denounced and thundered—as Isaiah, Jeremiah, Hosea and other prophets of Israel did—against the letter of the law as symbolised by an incessant round of rituals and ceremonials divorced from the underlying spirit thereof, but (owing to the very vigour of those condemnations and his ignoring of all other aspects of the question) was understood by the great masses of the people to have gone to the other extreme and denied even the very existence of God and the need for religion and its ministrations (as if it were possible to separate the spirit from the flesh and adhere to the former without its manifesting itself through the latter in the shape of the injunctions and prohibitions relating to the outer life).

It was, of course, perfectly right and proper that He should have denounced the people's addiction to mere formalism and ritualism and called their attention to the spirit that ought to have motivated every deed of theirs; but the reaction set up by Him did not restore the equilibrium, but followed the law of dynamics already referred to and proved wholly "equal and opposite!" At any rate, His disciples and followers made it a complete revolt against the Vedic Law and denied not only God but even the Individual Soul, thereby laying the axe at the very root of even the ethical doctrines—divorced from religion—which their Master, the Buddha, had laid so much stress on.

It is well known that the Lord Jesus Christ Himself—like the Lord Shri

MARTIN HURLIMANN

SHIVA TEMPLE, CHIDAMBARAM

The tank of the great Shiva temple. The temples of Chidambaram are among the oldest in Southern India, dating from the tenth century.

Krishna in the Bhagavad Gita—had taught His disciples all the three paths (i.e. of Works, of Faith, and of Wisdom) and not only found no conflict between them but actually synthetised them and kept them in perfect balance in His own personal life—as well as in His teachings. But, amongst the very first generation of His Apostles, we find natural temperamental leanings towards one path more than to the other two. Thus, St. Peter and St. James emphasise the Law of Works; St. John concentrates on Faith and Devotion and indeed defines God most beautifully with the soul-stirring definition "God is Love"; and St. Paul inclines to the path of Gnan (Wisdom) and, even while dealing with Faith, speaks of "the faith that is born of understanding." All three were perfectly correct; but, unfortunately, the followers of the three paths during later days have not merely shown their own natural temperamental predilections but carried on an incessant and virulent dialectical crusade against the other two paths without even a sense of proportion and kept up, to the present day, an interminable controversy based on their inability to balance the three paths as the Lord Jesus Himself had done!

Now it is perfectly true that a life of mere external ritualism without the internal spirit that ought to underlie and actuate the outer life, is a *Fraud*, is described by the Lord Shri Krishna as *Mithlyachara* (hypocritical conduct) and ought to be condemned. But it is impossible for humanity (the great masses thereof, at any rate) to keep to mere doctrinaire ideology and ethical ideals without manifesting them in the shape of outer forms and rituals. And every attempt to denounce the latter and keep the former alone alive is a result of lop-sided psychology and has always been, in the light of history, an abject, utter and all-round failure! In fact, nothing short of a resynthesis and a reharmonising of the three paths can really satisfy the Spiritual, Psychic and Physical requirements of humanity.

VIRUPAKSHA AND MALLIKARJUNA TEMPLES

Two temples at Pattadakal, dating from the seventh and eighth centuries. Virupaksha is a perfect example of the earliest Shiva temple built at the time Sankaracharya's teaching was having its greatest effect.

CARVED PILLARS

Two carved pillars from Pattadakal. The left-hand pillar shows scenes from the Vishnu legends.

Thus it was that the lop-sided and dry-as-dust doctrine of mere theoretical "Morality" which (without a living religious philosophy and a religious scheme of life to make it bearable to the normal human mind) was placed before the people by decadent Buddhism, soon began to pall on their minds and jar on their hearts and was followed by another swing of the pendulum in the shape of the *Mahayana* (i.e. Eleusinian profligacy and debauchery amongst the Holy Orders of the Monks and Nuns founded by the Lord Buddha Himself) and that, too, in the name of Upasana (i.e. service and worship of God whose very existence they had denied but whom they could not possibly do without).

The pseudo-philosophy of decadent Buddhism which denied the individual Soul, having paved the way for such immoralities in the name of the Lord Buddha's ultra-ethical school, there was a reaction therefrom towards rigid orthodox Vedic ritualism under the lead and guidance of the redoubtable Shri Kumarila Bhatta; but, in as much as His system enjoined incessant Vedic ceremonial, but refused to recognise God and the Soul and thus ignored both the Bhakti and the Gnana paths, it too was lop-sided and was consequently incapable of meeting humanity's cravings and

FROM PATTADAKAL

The right-hand pillar shows incidents from the story of Shiva and Parvati.

psychic requirements in those two directions.

It was at such a strange and stirring, critical and epoch-making juncture in the history of the world in general and of India in particular, when everything seemed to have gone into the melting-pot and there was utter chaos all round, that it pleased Bhagawan Shri Sankara (the Almighty Lord of the Universe) to think the time ripe for His own incarnation on earth, fulfilling the prophecies contained in the sacred scriptures, reharmonising the three paths, restoring the long-lost balance (between Works, Faith and Wisdom) and thereby bringing back "Peace on Earth and Goodwill amongst Men."

His life on earth was a very brief one (of only 32 years in all) but full of incessant and benevolent activity, whereby He traversed every part of India, preached the Vedantic doctrine throughout the length and breadth of the land, subdued and subjugated all hostile disputants, reconverted them to the ancient Vedic faith during his own short space of life on earth, established four monasteries in the four cardinal directions for propagating and diffusing that faith and keeping it perpetually alive, and reascended to Heaven.

He has been credited with the destruction of Buddhism or rather the *exiling* of it from India. This is not historically true. For, while we find his Sootra Bhashya (commentaries on the Vedantic Aphorisms of Vyasa) condemning the muddled "philosophy" of decadent Buddhism, we never find Him speaking

MARTIN HURLIMANN

KAILASA TEMPLE

Carved elephants on the pedestal of the Chief Temple.

derogatorily of the Lord Buddha himself; nay, on the contrary, He actually describes the latter in terms of the highest reverence as Yoginam Chakravarti (the greatest amongst Ascetic Adapts). And the real historical truth of the matter is not that *He* killed Buddhism or drove it out but only that, by honestly and categorically admitting the ethical and psychic beauties of Shri Buddha's own teachings (while controverting and disproving the later Buddhists' distortions thereof), He made it unnecessary for the Buddhists to continue their separate existence (except as an integral part of Sanatani—orthodox—Vedic Hinduism). It was thus really a unique process, not of extermination but of reabsorption of the Buddhists into their own original fold.

Even as regards the six denominations of Orthodox Hinduism, which were terribly at loggerheads with one another, He adopted His usual procedure of *Samanvaya* (i.e. reconciliation, synthesis and reharmony) and is therefore known to the present day as the Shan-Mata-Sthapanacharya (the Founder of the six faiths). He achieved this unique distinction by removing all internal feuds amongst the six denominations of His day and by reconciling and reharmonising them with the Vedas on the one hand and with one another on the other.

This is why, while the other Acharyas are all regarded as propagators of particular denominations of the Vedic Religion, Shri Sankaracharya alone is reverenced as the Reviver and Ecclesiastical Head of the Vedic Religion itself. In fact, He was the Historic Personage who was responsible for orthodox Hinduism and orthodox Hindu India as we now know them.

And He is, too, the one and only Philosopher of the East whom the greatest metaphysicians and psychologists of the modern Western world—including Berkeley, Kant, Hegel, Fichte, Thomas Hill Green, Professor Mackenzie (of University College, Cardiff), etc., of the Idealistic School of Philosophy) and great mathematicians and physicists of Europe (like Sir James

LORD OF THE DANCE

The magnificent image of Shiva as Lord of the Dance. From the inside of the Meenakshi Temple, Madura.

Jeans, etc.) claim philosophical and scientific kinship to.

We do not, in this article, propose to go into a detailed study of His philosophy but shall (without citing texts, etc.) merely call our readers' attention to the following analysis of the "Goal of Human Life" and the "Nature of the Soul" as expounded by Shri Sankaracharya.

It is manifestly inconceivable that, even after a thorough-going—nay, all-pervading—search amongst all human beings throughout the boundless length and breadth of the whole Universe (with their infinite variety of emotional tendencies, intellectual capacities, temperamental idiosyncrasies, consequential view-points, resultant views, etc.), one can ever come across even a single individual who—however illiterate or unintelligent he (or she) may be—has never asked others or at least wondered within his (or her) own mind:

"What am I? What is my goal? Whence have I come? Whither am I going? And which is the right path that will lead me from where I now am to where I am to go?" and so on and so forth.

Those who, being unceasingly impelled by such Nature-prompted queries which clamour from within for a satisfactory answer, pursue them and go on doing so until they have at last unravelled the Great SECRET of LIFE and solved these problems, are counted as the world's great thinkers, seers, prophets, sages, and so on, while those who occasionally feel such questions arising from within themselves but do not tackle, persevere in their enquiry into and solve them, get relegated to the world's list of the non-wise and the non-thinking herd! This is all that contra-distinguishes the wise man from the unthinking one!

Of this historical and psychological truth of everyday experience, however, there cannot be the least doubt, namely, that there *can* be no man or woman who has never even felt these questionings at all and the inherent inner urge to solve them, if possible.

It is this most momentous (because most clamant, most irresistible and most universal) of all problems which every system of philosophic thought seeks to tackle, which all religions do actually—each in its own way—solve, and which, in the present writer's carefully considered judgment (based on an unbiased, conscientious and prayerful study of all religions and philosophies), the Lord Shri (Adi) Sankaracharya's teachings have not merely solved but also thrown the most detailed, convincing and illuminating *Light* on.

This enquiry is really of the utmost and the highest importance. For, so long as we do not correctly understand whence we have come, where we are and whither we are proceeding, surely it must be very difficult—if not positively impossible—for us to determine the path and the means which will take us from our present station to our destination! How then can we hope to tread that path and adopt that means and thereby enable ourselves to ultimately reach that Goal?

Any attempt to determine the Path and the *Means* without first determining the *Goal* of life must naturally and necessarily—nay, inevitably—partake of the nature of a huge and perpetual lottery! And, as every gambler must know from bitter personal experience and as every thinking human being can readily see, there are always many more blanks than prizes in all lotteries! And, consequently, no person who, owing to lack of forethought (as to the Goal of Life and the Path thereto), has no planned scheme to guide him through life and its vicissitudes and thus turns

SHIVA, PARVATI AND RAVANA

Rock carving from the Kailasa Temple, Ellora. Ravana attempts to undermine the mountain. Parvati clutches Shiva's arm in fear but Shiva merely presses with his foot and holds the impious Ravana captive in the dungeon he has made for himself.

his everyday life into an incessant lottery, can have the least justification for wondering why so much more misery than happiness (if any) falls to his lot!

It is thus absolutely essential that we should first get into grips with this problem of the Goal of Life, solve it and lay it aside before we can tackle the question of the Path to that Goal. And, in doing so, it is also indispensable that we should make a conscious, persistent and successful effort to cast off and clear our minds of all prejudices and prepossessions (including what may be called natural or unconscious partialities and angularities engendered by hereditary, temperamental, personal, environmental and other such factitious factors which ought not to be allowed to distort our vision and warp our judgment). And we should tackle the great problem of life, not as partisans (nor even as advocates) but merely as earnest, sincere and humble enquirers after the real Truth and Seekers after Correct Knowledge.

Now, it is a truism and an elementary axiom that one's Goal must necessarily be related to, depend on and result from one's own individual outlook on the one hand and one's capabilities on the other. In other words, the real Nature and potentialities of the individual Soul must naturally have a great deal—if not everything—to do with the determination of one's Goal. It is from this standpoint therefore that we are called upon to—and do herewith—commence our whole study of Life with a systematic enquiry into the Nature of the Soul and connected matters regarding

THE SEVEN PAGODAS

Carved elephant and Rath at Mamallapuram. These monoliths, some of the most magnificent rock carving in India, date from the seventh and eighth centuries.

THE SHORE TEMPLE

One of the finest examples of the Shiva temple of the eighth century. Like the other temples at Mamallapuram it is not built, but carved out of solid stone.

"whence we came," etc.—in fact, into the very question which we began this philosophical study with.

In order to avoid unconscious errors and to arrive at correct and accurate conclusions hereon, it is desirable for us to start this enquiry with a correct definition of what exactly we mean by the Nature of the Soul.

It needs no elaborate argumentation to demonstrate—and we may therefore take it for granted—that, by that phrase, we do not mean all the qualities, properties, and characteristics which may be found associated—directly or indirectly—with the Soul from time to time on account of temporary and external causes and circumstances of the moment, but only such essential, innate and inherent traits and characteristics as, after thorough and careful investigation, are found to be naturally and permanently associated with the Soul—nay, to be inextricably intertwined therewith in such a manner and to such an extent that, when a quality which is alien thereto comes over it (or is forced into it) as a sort of encrustment in consequence of some extraneous and temporary cause or another and seems—for the moment—to have driven out its natural characteristics, even such a quality does not and cannot continue for ever in association therewith but goes on gradually decreasing, finally goes off altogether and quietly yields place to the natural characteristic and inherent tendency which it had not really driven out at all but only driven under for a short while!

For instance, if we ask ourselves whether cold or heat is the nature (i.e. the natural property) of water, we may feel nonplussed for a moment because of our frequent experience both of cold water and of hot water; and we may, at first, feel inclined to say that both heat and cold are its natural properties and that neither of them is its inherent and sole characteristic! But a little reflection will suffice to convince us that, inasmuch as water becomes (or is made) hot, owing to association with fire, the sun's rays, sulphur springs, etc., and when water that has been boiled (to a terrible degree of heat) is separated from the external heating agent (i.e. fire, etc.), even that water begins to give off its heat, becoming gradually cooler and cooler and finally—of itself—turns absolutely cold altogether, cold and not heat is therefore the real, natural property of water and that all the heating in the world will not prevent its natural characteristic (viz. cold), which we have artificially suppressed, from reasserting itself, driving out the enemy or alien quality (i.e. heat) and manifesting itself once again as the real, natural, inherent and inalienable trait and characteristic of water!

This is why a stranger coming to a reservoir of water which has been rendered hot by sulphur springs, and so forth, and finding it to be hot, at once exclaims: "Why is this water so hot?" This very question (WHY) is the clearest possible proof that heat is not the natural property of water and that, when and where it is found in association with it, it needs an explanation!

If we remember this definition of what we have termed the Nature (or natural property) of things and apply it to the question: "Is joy or sorrow the true Nature of our Soul," we can readily realise the really axiomatic character of the Vedantic doctrine that Joy (and not Sorrow) is the real Nature of our Soul. For, when one is unhappy and weeps, every onlooker at once asks: "Why do you weep?" and, in reply thereto, the weeper has always an explanation to give as to *why* he weeps! Here again the very question "WHY?" and the need for an explanation prove that every unhappiness needs an external cause of the moment and is not the real Nature of the Soul!

Over against this we have also this additional fact to reckon with, namely, that no one ever asks another: "Why do you not weep?" thereby proving that all misery needs an external cause of the moment and an explanation, i.e. is unnatural, while Happiness is Natural and needs no explanation!

And if we remember that, whatever may have caused it, every sorrow—like the heat of hot water—naturally decreases by mere efflux of time (unless kept alive) and goes on diminishing until at last it goes off and is even forgotten altogether (or survives at best as a faint memory which one needs to be reminded of), we can easily see how complete and perfect is the analogy between our sorrows and the heat of hot water and how perfectly obvious is the truth and accuracy of the Vedantic doctrine that the Soul's own real Nature is Bliss (and not misery).

There is another method too, by which we can quite easily realise the correctness of this Vedantic doctrine. It is this, namely, that just as a fish's inability to live away from water, and its incessant panting and struggling therefor when separated therefrom, prove that water is its natural element, similarly the fact that we cannot live without Happiness, that we always pant and struggle therefor and that continuous and absolute separation therefrom causes even death (by suicide or by heart-breaking, etc.), proves indubitably that Happiness is our natural element and is therefore always striven for by us and that the contrary is unnatural and therefore abhorred.

Again, it is because health is natural and disease is unnatural and requires a *cause* (for coming into being) and an explanation (for being understood by others and even by ourselves) that everyone prefers and seeks the former and dislikes and wishes to avoid the latter! Similarly, it must be because Joy is our Nature and every sorrow needs a cause and an explanation that all of us like and pant for the former and hate and endeavour to shun the latter!

With the help of this elementary and fundamental principle, which is really universal and all-comprehensive in its applicability, we can study and solve the whole Problem of Life in all its seemingly ever-changing aspects and baffling phases. There may be—and actually are—innumerable and tremendously different—nay, even irreconcilably antagonistic—opinions as to the means to the attainment of complete, perfect and absolute Bliss, but there can be no difference of opinion about the fact that all sentient beings (without even a single exception) naturally seek Happiness and not misery. The Soul's natural characteristic, therefore, is Joy and not sorrow.

And inasmuch as all of us naturally seek absolute, unlimited and unadulterated Happiness, we may proceed further and infer that the real Nature of our Soul is perfect Beatitude, i.e. pure, illimitable, indivisible and absolute Bliss without even the least admixture with even an infinitesimally tiny particle of sorrow!

After arriving at this general conclusion, we can now go on to a more detailed study of the Nature of the Soul, but on the same principle and on the same line

THE PENANCE OF ARJUNA

Part of the great bas-relief at Mamallapuram. The elephants and figures are actually life size. The carved figure of Shiva with the ascetic Arjuna is hidden in the deep shadow on the left.

of reasoning, i.e. that those sub-items which go to make for Joy, which we cannot do without and which we are incessantly in search of are also constituent characteristics of our Soul.

The first item hereunder for us to consider is the fact that we all desire to live for ever and not to die. Is this not a clear indication that Eternal Life (and not Death) is our real Nature?

And then there is also the eloquent and tell-tale fact that all disease and, much more therefore, Death, needs an explanation. When anyone's death is reported, everyone at once asks: "Why? what happened? What did he die of?" and so forth.

In fact, when a man in the seeming prime of health and strength dies suddenly and the doctors themselves are unable to trace the cause of that death, they find themselves driven to infer that he must have been poisoned or at least that he "must have had" heart-disease and that his heart must have failed suddenly! What else is this but a proof that Death needs an external cause and an explanation? (i.e. is not a natural property of the Soul). In other words, the Soul is—by Nature—Eternal.

When, however, we hear that a person —nay, even a new-born babe—continues to live, none of us ever asks: "Why does he continue to live?" The very question is absurd and inconceivable! This too shows that, while death needs a cause and an explanation, continued life requires none. In other words, Immortality is a natural trait of our Soul.

The second item for us to ponder over hereunder is that we are always curious to know things and feel unhappy or at least baffled, perplexed and worried when we do not understand them. On the line of reasoning explained already and followed by us hitherto, this can only mean that Knowledge (and not Nescience) is our real nature.

This is why the Upanishads and Bhagavad Gita have likened our Soul in its present predicament to the cloud—hidden Sun who—although of the nature of Pure Effulgence—has been rendered invisible to us by the clouds separating him from our eyes! In fact, they declare that the Wisdom—Sun who is the real nature of our Soul—has got clouded off from our visions by a cloud of Nescience.

They further enjoin that, just as we do not really create fire, electricity, etc., but only adopt suitable scientific processes (e.g. friction, etc.) judiciously selected for the purpose and thereby force the unmanifested fire, electricity, etc., around us everywhere in Nature to manifest themselves, exactly so is it the purpose of Education to draw out the latent (i.e. unmanifested) capabilities and potentialities within us and give them free and full scope for play (and not to put anything *into* us from without!)

Thus Knowledge can never be put in from outside but only drawn out from within. If, however (by unpsychological and therefore reprehensible processes of cramming, etc.), it be actually put in, even then it cannot endure within us but—like the heat of hot water—must throw itself off and go on diminishing until it goes off altogether! And this would mean that all our endeavours to impart (or obtain) knowledge are really wasted labour! This is, in fact, true of all cramming. But, true Education (in the sense described, i.e. of drawing out the unmanifested knowledge from within us and making it manifest itself) suffers from no such disability and is alone therefore worth striving for.

In fact, the very meaning of the word "Education" is to draw out. The contrary process (i.e. of putting things in) would deserve to be called not Education but only injection!

A few years ago the scientific and

philosophical Western world was shocked into acceptance of this great Vedantic Truth (as to knowledge and not ignorance being the Nature of the Soul) by the peculiar instance of a little French girl, who, after passing through a critical illness and being reclaimed from the very jaws of death, was found to have forgotten her mother-tongue (French) entirely, but to be able to speak—fluently and in the highest literary style—in about a dozen foreign languages which she had never (in her present life, at any rate) had the least occasion to read or even to hear!

After a thorough, careful and searching investigation of all the facts pertaining to that historic occurrence, they came to and announced the conclusion that no other explanation of that incident was conceivable except that the Soul is naturally a store-house of all knowledge (including the knowledge of languages), but the various branches thereof are barred by different doors (so to speak) from manifesting themselves, that Experience and Education are the keys which unlock those portals and that, in that particular case, something must have happened within the ailing girl's brain, which had resulted in the shutting off of the one and only thitherto-open door (i.e. to French) and the opening of about a dozen previously closed doors. The natural characteristic of the Soul is thus the Light of Perfect Knowledge and not the Darkness of Ignorance.

A third factor which contributes to our Happiness can be traced from this fact of universal experience, namely, that not only human beings but all sentient beings (including parrots, rats and even the tiniest insects, worms, etc.) seek independence and hate dependence. This proves that Liberty (and not subjection or bondage) is the true nature of the Soul.

There is a fourth factor too, i.e. that, while all of us naturally wish to be guided by our own desires and views and not be subject to or dependent on the wishes and opinions of others in any respect what-

GATEWAY TO THE GREAT TEMPLE, TANJORE

soever, we also all—at the same time—desire all others to follow our wishes! In other words, we all naturally—nay, instinctively—seek to *rule* over others. This clearly means that, whether we know and believe in the existence of God or not, we all hanker for the attainment, by ourselves, of that attribute —of absolute suzerainty over all—which all the Religions which postulate His existence declare to be His and His alone! And, on the same line of logical inference as we have hitherto uniformly adopted, this can only mean that Sovereignty (and not non-rulership) is the natural characteristic of our Soul.

In fact, if we now go over, recount and analyse the conclusions which we have arrived at in the course of this simple psychological analysis of our own feelings, desires and aspirations, the inference becomes irresistible that the five attributes—i.e. the major one of Pure Joy and the four sub-items of Eternal Existence, Perfect Knowledge, Absolute Liberty and Complete Suzerainty—which we have found to be the natural characteristics of each Individual Soul are really, all of them, God's own attributes and that, consciously or unconsciously, we are unceasingly striving to attain Godhood, and this too because we are ourselves, by nature, divine !

Having thus realised what may be described as the psycho-structural oneness of God and Man, let us now proceed further and study what may be termed the chemico-structural relationship between Him and ourselves.

Hereon we have to meditate on the wonderful fact that all the Religions in the world which postulate the existence of God, agree in definitely declaring not merely that He governs or controls the Universe but also—in the simple and beautiful words of the very first verse of the very first chapter of the very first book of the Bible—that "In the beginning, God created the heaven and the earth."

Now the question which naturally arises in every enquirer's mind on reading such passages is: "Yes, but what was the material out of which He created the whole world!" And the only natural—nay, possible—answer is that He must have created it out of the only material which was in existence at the time, i.e. Himself! And this ultimately means that God, the Individual Soul and the whole world are chemically one and the same substance.

There is thus, for the believer in God's Creatorship of the world (in the popularly accepted and well-known sense of the term), absolutely no escape from the natural and inevitable corollary to that doctrine, i.e. that God, the Individual Soul, and the Universe are—chemico-structurally speaking—the same in chemical substance. And, as we have already seen, they are the same in psychological content too.

In this connection, it is interesting to note that, whereas the Bible, the Koran and other Scriptures of the theistic religions of the world speak of God as having Created the whole Universe and leave it to us to infer therefrom that God Himself is the material out of which it must have been created, the Taittiriyopanishad and other Hindu Scriptures, in their accounts of the world's creation by God, categorically narrate that He willed, not to make or create many things but only that He would become many and manifest Himself and that He actually did so! There is thus no conflict between the Vedantic doctrine and the Bible, etc., hereon, but only this distinction, that the former has specifically stated what the latter have left us to infer!

It is thus obvious that, because the real nature of the whole Universe is Pure Joy, Eternal Existence, Perfect Illumination, Absolute Liberty and Complete Suzerainty (which are, every one, of them, God's own characteristics) and because it is also chemically identical with God, it therefore incontrovertibly follows that the whole universe is actually nothing but an infinite series of different manifestations of God—in fact, is really Divine and that all the difference consists in the degree of manifestation and the form, the shape, the colour, the external properties, functions, values, etc., thereof.

All theists believe, too, that God is omnipresent, i.e. that He pervades and permeates the whole Universe. Most of us, however, fail to realise the real connotation and the inescapable implications of this belief, to wit, that His very Omnipresence, too, proves our Oneness with Him!

Now it is everybody's common-place experience that, when a potter makes a pot of clay, a weaver weaves a piece of cloth, a goldsmith manufactures an ornament of gold, and so forth, it is only the clay, the yarn, the gold, etc.—and not the potter, the weaver, the goldsmith, etc.—that pervade and permeate the entire material of the pot, the cloth, the ornament, etc., respectively! In other words, it is not the maker but the material which pervades and permeates the particular creation in question.

Similarly, although it is perfectly true that God Himself has actually created the Universe, yet it is not as its Creator, but only in His capacity of the material thereof that He can pervade and permeate it! Such in brief is the philosophy of Shri Sankaracharya, who argues that, whatever its outer form, shape, functions, value, etc., may be, every ornament emanating from pure gold must itself be pure gold in its actual substance and everything emanating from God must necessarily itself be God.

Having thus arrived at the conclusion that our Goal as well as our own real nature is God (with His five-fold attribute of Pure Beatitude, Eternal Existence, Perfect Illumination, Absolute Liberty and Complete Suzerainty), we need not go into a detailed disquisition here and now as to questions of detail arising hereout of, but may content ourselves with stating that, in order to attain (i.e. really to realise) that Godhood which is really our own inherent inner nature, we should direct our minds to a conscious endeavour and planned scheme for understanding the real situation (i.e. our own inner Divinity), for tracing and recognising the factors that tend to keep us back from a realisation thereof and for correctly determining and successfully adopting the means which will enable us to throw off and free ourselves from all the obstacles and encrustments which conceal our own real nature from ourselves and thereby to realise our Godhood in the actual practical everyday life from moment to moment in the shape of Pure and Perennial Joy, absolute and ineffable, all-pervading and all-permeating.

May God Grant It!

DETAIL OF CARVING, SOMANATHAPUR

THE IMAGE OF RAMANUJA

RĀMĀNUJA

WHO PREACHED A GOSPEL OF DIVINE LOVE

c. 1037–1137

BY RAO BAHADUR V. RANGASWAMI AIYANGAR

THOSE who have faith in a Providence, which watches over human destiny, will not admit that the appearance of a man, when he is most wanted, is fortuitous. The Srīvaishṇava Society entertained this belief and, later, when Rāmānuja's full plan of work for it was unfolded, saw in his birth an incarnation. To grasp the timeliness of his arrival in the *milieu* of the eleventh century A.D. in South India a knowledge of the antecedent circumstances is necessary. The spread of Sanskrit culture in the peninsula brought in its train the active labours of northern religious missions. Brahmanism was not the only religion which established itself, in its protean forms, in the Dravidian area. So did Buddhism and Jainism. The dawn of the Christian era saw the three creeds in peaceful emulation. Later came a Hindu reaction, the fruit of a counter-reformation, which burnt out the evils of ceremonialism and blind formalism, against which and moral and spiritual bankruptcy the heterodox cults of the Buddha and Mahāvīrā were protected. The tables were turned. The spiritual poverty of the developed creeds of Buddhism and Jainism, and their elaborate systems of scholastic philosophy, seemed arid and atheistic to the neo-Hinduism, which cut channels for the religious emotion in fervid devotion to God, viewed as Siva or Vishṇu. The early centuries of the Christian era saw the growth, side by side, of a powerful poetical literature in Tamil, in which men who were specialists in religious emotion expressed the mystic raptures of the devotee, who

VITTHALASWAMI

Detail of carving on the base of the temple, sixteenth century.

seeks or has found God, along with old philosophical concepts. In form, in a common hostility to atheism and religious indifference, in their surpassing fervour, their mastery of language and thought, their instinctive comprehension of the popular mind, their proficiency in the technique of poetry and music, and in the possession of a background of Sanskrit learning for their devotional outpourings, the saints, Siva or Vaishṇava, were alike. With the collapse of the common enemies, the sacred song-makers were ready for internecine war, based on the rival loyalties to Vishṇu and Siva.

The tolerance of ruling powers, born of policy as well as of the eclectic spirit of Hinduism, was strained by the rivalries. The emulation had one result: immense activity in temple building and popularisation of the worship of idols. The movement is synchronous with the epoch of Pallava supremacy (the second to the eighth centuries A.D.). On the Vaishṇavite side, the saints, who led this movement, are collectively known as the twelve Ālwārs. The most eminent of them, and the most philosophical, was saint Nammālwār or Satakopa, the author of a thousand hymns, known as the Holy Word (*Tiruvāi-moli*). The tenets of Srivaishnavaism, religious and philosophical, are clearly manifest in these devotional songs, and particularly in those of Satakopa.[1] Their services in reclaiming from infidelity and indifference hosts of common folk, to whom their songs appealed as none of the sacred canon preserved in Sanskrit could have done, are beyond praise. Justice, more than gratitude or parochial feeling, accounts for the loving description of the Vaishṇava collet (*Prababandham*) as the Tamil Veda, and the Srivaishṇava student of Vedānta as a *Ubhaya-Vedāntin*, i.e. the follower of two Vedantas.

In the *Liber Pontificalis* of Srivaishṇavism, the Ālwārs are succeeded by a new group of teachers, who gathered where the former had sown, and who are known as the *Āchāryas*. The task of the new leaders was to consolidate the work of their predecessors, organise the sect internally, and provide it with the means of resisting present and future assaults. The need for the last had already arisen. Sankara (*c.* A.D. 800) had presented a reasoned exposition of the philosophy of Monism, and supported it by argument and scriptural warrant. He provided a powerful artillery for Monism by writing elaborate disquisitions (*bhāshyas*) on the entire sacred canon, comprising the ten major Upanishads, the *Bhagavad-gīta*, and the *Brahmasūtra*, not to mention a commentary to the "Thousand Names of Vishnu," an ancient prayer section of the Great Epic (*Mahābhārata*), in which he interpreted each name of the Supreme Being so as to confirm his philosophy.

The essence of his teaching, which reflected his erudition, remorseless logic, and literary power, was briefly this: The soul (ātman) is one with the Soul (Brahman), which is eternal, infinite, one and indivisible, unchangeable, and attributeless. It is the one and only reality. All else is merely the result of an illusion (Māyā) born of ignorance (Avidyā). The phenomenal world is illusory and unreal, like a mirage, or a dream. The soul (ātman) being the Soul has its qualities. In the inner self lies the knowledge of the reality and unreality which, fully comprehended, ends the illusion, and the fetters of seeming rebirth or suffering. One may attain this knowledge even in life as a *jīvanmukta*. To such a person the limitation of thought, feeling or morality, or

[1] *Vide R. Rāmānujachari, "The Philosophy of Saint Satakopa" (Journal of the Annamalai University).*

SRIRANGAM

The tank of the Jambukeswar Temple at Srirangam, the city where Rāmānuja lived and taught.

duty will not apply. Complete deliverance, such as his, is attainable only from a knowledge of the highest Brahman. The *mukta* (freed) awaits the dissolution of the mortal body, in complete indifference to his surroundings, and in unruffled calm, like the Buddha after attaining *Nirvāna*, and death only completes the delivery.

A succession of thinkers elaborated the Monism of Sankara, with learning and dialectical skill only inferior to their Master's, and by the end of the tenth century the system of Advaita (Monism) appeared to be proof against assault. The accession of the powerful dynasty of the Cholas to supremacy in the peninsula, with its marked partiality for the worship of Siva, added another danger to the integrity of Srivaishnavaism. The early Āchāryas (teachers) of the community, who witnessed the advance of Advaita and Siva-worship, as the contemporaries of the imperial Cholas, were content to be on the defensive. The first of them, Nāthamuni, was a mystic, the author of two lost works on Yoga, and the editor of the collect comprising the four thousand hymns of the Ālwārs, which he caused to be recited as part of the service in the Vishnu temples of the country. His grandson, Yāmuna, was a philosopher and poet, as well as a saint and administrator, who ruled, with splendour, the Srivaishnavas from Srirangam, where he fixed his abode. He was a master of dialectic, and tried to stem the rising tide of Monism by controverting the theories of illusion (Māyā) and ignorance (Avidyā) which are basal to Advaita.[1] Sankara had rejected the *Pāncharātra*, on which Srivaishnavaism based its worship and doctrine of *avatāra*, and *Prapatti*, in another tract.[2] He contributed to the ancient controversy as to the identity of the Supreme Being with Vishnu in a third,[3] which is lost. To show that the *Bhagavad-gītā* supported the Bhaktimāirga he composed a brilliant summary of it in verse. While he utilised much old material now lost to us, he produced no work, which in range, depth or power could be set against the magistral commentaries of Sankara on the cardinal texts of Vedānta. That he was unable to accomplish this was the one cause of grief to the learned and pious saint. To obtain a successor in the leadership of Srivaishnavaism, who would rectify the omission, was the subject of his supplications to the Lord.

The prayer was seemingly answered, and the aged Yāmuna realised it before he passed away, in the middle of the eleventh century, at an advanced age. A grandson of his had settled at the holy shrine of Vishnu at Tirumalai with his sisters. One of them was married early in the century to a young and devout Brahman scholar from a township, Bhutapuri (modern Srīperumbudūr), a day's journey from Kānchi (Conjeeveram), an ancient cultural and political capital of the peninsula, and then the seat of a Chola viceroy. The lady gave birth to a boy, who received the name of Rāmānuja. The date of the nativity is traditionally placed in Sāka 939 (A.D. 1017), but another tradition which states that Rāmānuja was only a hundred when he died in Sāka 1059 (A.D. 1137) harmonises better with the chronology of the events of Rāmānuja's life and the history of the time.

Rāmānuja was a comely and precocious child. Under his father's tuition he absorbed the traditional learning of the day, religious and secular, and was married when he was seventeen. The father (Kesava-Somayāji) died soon after. Rāmānuja then moved, with his widowed mother and wife, to Kanchi,

[1] *Atma siddhi, samrit siddhi,* and *Isvara siddhi.*
[2] *Āgama prāmānya.*
[3] *Mahā bumsa nivnaya.*

to study the Advaita system under a distinguished professor named Yādava-prakāsa, who had shown his independence and originality by criticising Sankara's interpretation, and offering an alternative interpretation on a crucial point.

The studies continued for six years, during which the relations between teacher and disciple were strained. The cause was the inconvenient acuteness and erudition, as well as the sturdy independence, of Rāmānuja, which made him challenge now and then the teacher's interpretations of the *Brahmasūtra*, which appeared uncogent. This won him a great name in the schools. The irate teacher organised a pilgrimage, with his pupils, to Kāsī, and when they had traversed part of the way, Rāmānuja learned with distress that there was an intention of doing away with him. In alarm, he parted from the company, wandered in the wilderness, and got back to Kānchi, with help which he attributed to divine intervention. He resumed his studies under Yādava-prakāsa, when the latter returned, and before he was twenty-two came to be regarded as the rising champion of his sect. The aged Yāmuna had chosen him as his successor, and summoned him to Srīrangam for a personal communion. Rāmānuja responded, but met not Yāmuna but the funeral cortège of the Master on the outskirts of Srīrangam.

Deeply dejected, he returned to Kānchi to resume his studies, and preparation for the duties which he knew awaited him. The oral transmission of the different elements of Srīvaishṇava doctrine was with different scholars, to whom he successively applied for initiation, so as to become the repository of all the authentic tradition of his sect. In the course of this search for enlightenment, he found himself considerably embarrassed by his domestic life, which

STREET SCENE IN SRIRANGAM TO-DAY

became distasteful to him on that account. His mother was now dead, and Rāmānuja made the great renunciation, as many others had done before him (e.g. the Buddha), after providing for his wife. He received the insignia of monastic life (*Sanyāsa*) at the Vishnu temple of Kānchi, where he had been doing daily service. His age at the time was probably thirty, but by common consent he was the greatest man among his community. His entry into the ascetic order made his position unchallengeable. Pressed by the disciples of Yāmuna, he moved at last to Srīrangam, and began, as the chosen successor of that venerable teacher, an apostolate, which extended to over seventy years, during the whole of which he remained in the full possession of his physical and mental powers.

The first task of the new leader was to perfect his own position in the apostolic succession of inspired teachers. The next was to organise the worship and ritual in the many Vishnu temples of the country, and make them again spiritual centres. Both tasks he steadily accomplished, making extensive tours to every centre in which his community had settled. The third and most difficult task he set himself to was to provide his sect with a philosophical literature that could challenge comparison with Sankara's famous works. With the thoroughness that was characteristic of all he did, he mastered old statements of the doctrine of his school, in writings now lost but then available, such as the extensive gloss (*vārttika*) of Bodhāyana, and the great commentary of Dramidācharya on the *Brahmasūtra*, and similar works by Tanka, Guhadeva, Kapardin and Bhāruchi, who are now only names to us. The disappearance of the old works increased the sense of obligation on Rāmānuja to provide a commentary, which would enshrine whatever was of value in the older interpretation, and which would possess qualities that would enable it to live.

The composition of the great commentary was a work of years. But when it was completed it took rank immediately among the greatest works of its class. Its title *Srī-Bhāshya*, which contains a verbal play, suggesting an aspect of Rāmānuja's cult (dependence on Srī for intercession), besides describing its beauty as a piece of philosophical composition, was recognised as well deserved. No contemporary was fit to be ranked with him as an expounder of philosophy, and his rivals were the great dead, like Sankara.

He also provided a commentary to the *Bhagavad-gītā*, which gave a turn to its interpretation different from Samakara's. For the ordinary run of his disciples and future students he summarised his views of the drift and teaching of the *Brahmasūtra* in three shorter works, viz., Vedarthasngrahu, which discussed with some fulness the passages in the Upanishads, supporting or apparently opposed to his philosophy. For the guidance of the community, and consistently with his view (opposed to Sankara's) that, so long as one was alive, his duties (karma) could never be given up, he prepared a manual of eternal duties, named *Nityam*. These constitute his entire output with the exception of three prayers (*Gadyatraya*), which he recited in the course of his daily worship at the shrine of Vishnu and Srī at Srīrangam. All his works are in Sanskrit. A young disciple and relation composed, under his command, a short commentary (known as the "Six Thousand") on the hymns of Satakopa, the greatest of the Ālwārs. Another young disciple produced a commentary on the Thousand-names of Vishnu (*Vishnu-sahasra-nāma*), which was fuller than Sankara's commentary

VITTHALASWAMI

Temple of Vishnu, Vijayanagar, which was still unfinished when the city fell in 1565.

A.S.I.

VISHNU-SURYA

Vishnu as the sun at noon, supporting the heavens. He is represented as an eight-armed Aryan warrior king. With one hand he holds up the sky. He holds his discus, mace, sword, shield, his trumpet and the conch in his other hands. Relief from Mamallapuram.

on the text, and not less learned. The Upanishads were not separately commented on, since their leading texts were discussed fully in the *Srī-bhāshya*. At last the successor of Yāmuna had provided his sect with an array of authoritative philosophical works, not inferior in learning, depth or subtlety or logical power to the great treatises on Advaita philosophy. With characteristic restraint, his comments on the *Brahmasūtra* were made non-sectarian, and it is noteworthy that the essential doctrine of salvation by surrender (*Prapatti*) is not brought into the *Srī-bhāshya*.

The success of his teachings was immediate and widespread. It was due to the emphasis which Rāmānuja laid on the untenability of the idealistic view of illusion and ignorance, as obscuring the vision of the oneness with the Universal Soul, and the rejection of the world and its phenomena as unreal and illusory. It was strengthened by his constructive effort, rebuilding the theory of Monism, so as to allow of differentiation of Īswara through his modes (*Prakāra*), without implicating His divisibility, and his affirmation that matter and spirit (*achit* and *chit*) were no less eternal than Īśwara. The ultimate oneness and reality of the Absolute is conceded. But it is coupled with the assertion of the separate existence, within God, of *chit* and *achit* (souls and matter), and their equal eternal character and reality. God is a synthetic unity, consisting ot elements animate and inanimate. Though equally ultimate, matter (achit) and soul (chit) are dependent on Īśwara, their relations to Him being like that of body to soul. The soul is a mode of the Supreme and, like Īśwara eternal, real, intelligent, self-conscious, atomic, imperceptible, and changeless. God has both a causal and effectual relationship with soul and matter. It is the indivisibility (non-duality, *advaita*) of the effectual part from the causal, which gives the name Visishtādvaita to Rāmānuja's system of philosophy. The three are in a quiescent condition, when Īswara withdraws them within Him, in the *Pralaya* (dissolution) following each cyclic age (*kalpa*), but they maintain their individuality even in that latent condition, being only unable to manifest it till Īśwara starts His creative activity again, as part of his sport (*līlā*) or wish (*icchā*). Then subtle matter (*achit*) takes on its grosser forms, souls (*chit*) rediscover their intelligence and enter into relations with gross matter; but the union takes place in rigid accordance with the past action (*karma*) of the soul before the dissolution (*Pralaya*). Souls are masters of their own destiny, and are free to redeem themselves by their efforts by overcoming their bonds of Karma (*Karma-pasa*). This freedom is subject to intervention by divine grace—a concept of the union of Infinite justice with Infinite mercy. The way of release is by devotion-cum-reason (*Bhakti*). To Rāmānuja, Bhakti is not blind love, or faith, but a reasoned devotion to God, which springs from good action in the past, and which is attainable only by a good life of arduous discipline. Rāmānuja thus fuses into his conception of Bhakti, the Jñāna or wisdom of the Advaita. With the dawn of light, through the operation of this Bhakti, comes release (*moksha*) from rebirth and suffering. The released soul does not lose its individuality. Life eternal, in perpetual communion with God, is its lot, equally with those souls (chit), like Viśvakshena or Garuḍa, who have never been allowed to come within the grip of rebirth (*Nitya-muktas*). The freed soul differs in this state from the Lord only in its powerlessness to create, withdraw from the world, or rule it as He alone can do.

CONJEEVERAM

Temple at Conjeeveram—the old Kanchi, where Ramanuja studied under Yadavapraksa.

On the side of religion the concept of one God, who is the Reality, is coupled with His description as the embodiment and abode of all conceivable good qualities. He is Vishnu or Narayana, as depicted in the Vishnu and Bhagavata Puranas. As in the *Pancharatra* system, the Supreme Lord is conceived as "coming down" in incarnations, so as to be accessible to the yearning souls.

On the ethical side, the conception of God as the embodiment of justice, whose will is expressed by the law of Karma, which he will not set aside even in *Pralaya* and creation, involves a denial of the easy and convenient view that the *jīvan-mukta* (of Advaita) might set himself above a moral law. God impels souls towards righteousness as the "inner mentor" of souls (*antar-yāmin*), and salvation is only for the righteous. Bhakti itself is the gift of a righteous life. The suppliant (*Prapanna*) gets the inner urge for his total surrender to the Lord, because of the righteousness to which he has been impelled by the Lord's mercy, which fills him with an intense craving for His grace. The guidance of the inner guide (antar-yāmin) is no less useful than that of a saintly teacher (*āchārya*).

The supplication of the teacher on behalf of the pupil adds to its effectiveness, even as the intervention of Śrī is the source of Divine Grace. Even vicarious service is helpful in the work of redeeming the soul.

The balm which the teaching of Rāmānuja must have brought to those who found their God either denied or turned to an abstraction, and felt themselves converted into a helpless identity of the Supreme Soul, as well as those who were unable to reconcile the doctrine of illusion with the insistent call of experience to reject it, must have been powerful. To the yearning soul Rāmānuja held out the hope of communion with a loving and just God. He not only gave men a God but, in Max Müller's telling phrase, he gave the Hindus the souls they had lost. Salvation was not a mere apprehension of the Infinite, but the attainment for eternity of His supreme status. All souls gravitate or move towards God.

To the comprehensive philosophy, which vindicated the rights and obligations of the free soul, Rāmānuja attached a religious side, which gave wide scope for spiritual emotion. He provided for the diffusion of his message of hope among the millions a church organisation dedicated to the service of redemption. The idea of God as immanent in all high thought and endeavour, by whomsoever the effort was made, unfolds a limitless tolerance which overrides the barriers of caste and creed. By demonstrating the compatibility of his views of redemption with the old tradition he reassured its defenders. Spiritual statesmanship could go no further.

It now remains only to tell briefly the story of his apostolate. The effect of his personal influence, his discourses and writings and, above all, his example was to increase the strength of his following. Twelve thousand disciples, 700 ascetics and 74 select leaders are said to have been in his *entourage*. A powerful community, united by spiritual leadership and common convictions, was forming within the wider society of the Chola Empire. When the years of trial to the empire (A.D. 1045-1070), in which five kings had ruled, were over, the throne came to a mature statesman and soldier, Kulottunga I (A.D. 1070-1117). A centralised government, assisted by a trained bureaucracy, was coming into existence again in the empire. Such an organisation could ill brook the existence of divided loyalties among its subjects, and of a state within the state. The irritation caused by the condition of such a society under Rāmānuja was not improbably the real cause of a persecution, foreign to the disposition of a king who encouraged continued patronage of Vishnu shrines. This policy is said to have been started by the great Chola Emperor. The tradition that it was Kulottunga I who started it is no more improbable than the similar treatment of the early Christians in the Roman Empire under virtuous rulers like Marcus Aurelius, Decius and Diocletian. A test of obedience, extreme and novel, was applied to the Srīvaishnavas. They were ordered to subscribe to the brief statement that there was no God greater than Siva. The penalty for non-compliance was plain.

Rāmānuja fled to the uplands of Mysore, where a new power was rising, which challenged the Chola Empire, viz. the dynasty of Hoysāla Ballālas, under an enterprising and warlike prince named Bityideva (Sanskrit, Vittal Deva). To him Rāmānuja went for asylum (*c.* 1197). A saint, who was also obnoxious to the dynasty's powerful enemy, was doubly welcome. Rāmānuja remained in Mysore for about twenty years, during which the king became his staunch disciple, receiving the name of Vishnuvardhana. Hosts of converts were made to Srīvaishnavasm. Five great shrines of Vishnu were dedicated, including the great temple of Nārāyana at Yadugiri (Melkote).

The enraged Chola Emperor, finding that Rāmānuja had escaped him, and resenting the spirited reply of a teacher and a pupil of Rāmānuja, who had answered the summons, had blinded him and turned him out into the street, where the older man died of pain. It was well to keep out of the dominions of so rancorous an enemy. Rāmānuja, though guiding his flock in the Tamīl country from Mysore (as it was left to itself by the Emperor once his rage was sated), kept away till Kulottunga I died (A.D. 1117). Then he returned to Srīrangam to resume his ministry, till his death in A.D. 1137.

The only incident which marred the repose of his last years was another outbreak of fanaticism. The crown prince (later Kulottinga II) desecrated (A.D. 1127) the Vishnu shrine at Chitrakutam (Chidambaram). Rāmānuja caused the discarded image to be removed to the Tirumalai hills, where another shrine was built for its reception. There it remained, for four hundred years, till the desecrated shrine at Chidambaram was reconsecrated by an emperor of Vijayanagara.

For another ten years Rāmānuja lingered. His work was done. Persecution had added moral strength to his community. In numbers, organisation and devotion to their faith the Srīvaishnava community was stronger than it ever was. Every Vishnu temple resounded with the benediction: "May the divine commands of Rāmānuja ever gain in strength!"[1] It only remained for the great apostle to follow the many Cholas who had predeceased him. Amidst sorrowing disciples, with mind unclouded and concentrated on Him whose reality and beneficence no one had comprehended better than he, the scholar-saint found the release for which he had taught every one to work and pray. By precept and by personal example he had shown, in his own life of dedicated service to God and human redemption, the qualities which he had wrested from the Monist for the God of Mercy whom, for over a hundred years, he had served faithfully and well.

[1] *Rāmānujarya divyājñā vardhatamahbi vardhatām.*

MARTIN HURLIMANN

THE GOLDEN TEMPLE

The Pool of Nectar dug by Guru Ramdas at Amritsar, and in the background the famous Golden Temple of the Sikhs.

GURU GOVIND SINGH

THE GREAT SIKH TEACHER

1660–1708

BY SARDAR K. M. PANIKKAR

GOVIND SINGH was the tenth and last of the Sikh Pontiffs (Gurus), and was born at Patna in Bihar where his father, Guru Tej Bahadur, had accompanied one of the Rajput generals of the Mogul Emperor.

Tej Bahadur, on his return from Patna, defied the Emperor Aurangzeb by espousing the cause of some persecuted Kashmiri Brahmans who had approached him for his help. In other ways also he had come into conflict with the imperial authorities in the Punjab. The Emperor summoned the Guru to Delhi; and, after the usual offer of Islam or death, Tej Bahadur was executed in 1675, and his body was publicly exposed in the streets of Delhi. At the place where the execution took place now stands the Gurudwara of Shish Ganj.

Govind Singh succeeded his father as Guru at the early age of fifteen. Tej Bahadur had left his son supreme and uncontested power over a united community, strong not only in its religious devotion, but in a rare combination of discipline and martial spirit. He had also bequeathed to his son a tradition of implacable hostility towards Moslems in general and the Mogul Empire in particular, as his last wish was that his son should avenge the ignominy with which he had been put to death in Delhi.

The community, to the spiritual and temporal headship of which Govind had succeeded at this early age, was no

THE CAPITAL OF THE SIKHS

Amritsar, once just a village given to Guru Ramdas it is said by the Mogul Emperor Akbar, and established as the capital of the Sikhs by Arjun, the son of Ramdas.

MARTIN HURLIMANN

MARBLE ENTRANCE TO BABA ATAL TOWER

longer the pietist sect which Nanak (1469-1539) had founded. Nanak, like Kabir, Ramanand and others whom he accepted as his predecessors, was content to gather round him men of cognate spirit and to preach to them the message of love and humility. But under his successors, more especially Gurus Ramdas, Arjun and Har Govind, the teachings of Nanak underwent a gradual and unseen but fundamental change. The disciples of the Guru were gradually differentiated from the rest of the community and became in time a numerous and powerful sect.

Guru Ramdas dug the sacred pool, later known as Amritsar or the pool of nectar, in one of the villages given to him, it is said, by the Mogul Emperor. Arjun, his son and successor, organised the rudiments of a temporal government and accustomed his followers to the secular authority of the Guru and taxation through his officer. He also established his capital at Amritsar and assumed regal dignities. But it was Har Govind, the son of Arjun, who transformed what was till then merely a religious community into a martial people. He himself appeared in Durbar fully armed and was surrounded by numerous armed retinue. His followers also began to allude to him as "Sachi Padshah," or the "True King"—a mystic title which combined spiritual authority with temporal sovereignty.

At the time of Govind's succession to the pontificate in 1675, the community had gained many adherents in the eastern Punjab. It had also acquired considerable prestige among the Hindu population in the Province by its continuous fight against the authority of the Moslem rulers.

There was a further factor which gave additional importance to the grow-

MARTIN HURLIMANN

BABA ATAL TOWER

The tower which is situated in the Garden of the Golden Temple is dedicated to Atal Rai, younger son of Guru Har Govind. The lower room is painted with frescoes representing scenes from the life of Nanak.

ing Sikh community. For over 600 years the Hindus in the Punjab had been subjected to Moslem rule. During that long period, not only had their political independence vanished, but their manliness of spirit had been practically extinguished. Punjab, as the doorway of Hindustan, was the one area which had been continuously under Moslem rule. Nanak himself had been greatly moved by the degradation of his race, and in one of his songs he bewailed:

"You wear a loin cloth, sacrificial mark and a rosary,
And yet you earn your living from those whom you call mlechas;
You perform the Hindu worship in private,
Yet, oh my brothers, you read the books of Mohammedans and adopt their manners."

The gradual transformation of Nanak's sect into a martial community gave to the Hindus of the Punjab a new hope, a new feeling of self-respect; and in times of persecution, as already alluded to in the case of the Kashmiri Brahmans, they turned to the Gurus of the Sikhs for help and support.

On Govind's succession to the Guruship, his chief followers decided that it was not safe for one so young to be exposed to the enmity of the Mogul Emperor. He was, therefore, quietly taken to Anandpur, a small settlement which the late Guru had founded at the foot of the Himalayas. For practically 20 years Govind lived in obscurity in this retreat, devoting himself to the study of Hindu classics and religion and preparing himself for the high responsibility which had fallen on him.

The Daswin Padshah Ka Granth, or the "Book of the Tenth King," which is the contribution of Govind to the Sacred Book of the Sikhs, shows how deeply he studied the scriptures of the Hindus, not so much for religious inspiration as for imbibing in the fullest measure the national tradition and culture of his race. He kept strictly to the teachings of the earlier Gurus about the unity of God, the inhumanity of caste and the meaninglessness of accumulated custom. But alone of the Gurus after Nanak, he was not only a genuine Hindu in outlook, but a profound student of the books, traditions and literature of his Aryan forefathers.

Another aspect of his study at the time which is well brought out by the Chandi-ki-Charitr, Chandi-ki-Var, and other contributions to the Daswin Padshah ka Granth, is the emphasis on the martial exploits of ancient heroes in the Hindu *puranas*. Chandi-ki-Charitr is the story of the Goddess' fight with the forces of evil described with all the realism of the most thrilling martial poetry. Govind in fact went to the *puranas* to find inspiration for his people in the fight that he planned for them during his years of retirement.

He came out of his retirement in 1695, and proclaimed his mission to the world, not only as the Pontiff of his community, but as a national leader of a revived Hindu nation. This mission he explained in Vichitra Natak or the Strange Drama, a composition of his own in which the Almighty is said to declare to him:

"I extol and cherish thee as my own son. I send thee to form a separate new faith. Go and spread it, the light of righteousness, and refrain people from senseless acts."

And again:

"For this purpose was I born,
And to spread this religion the Lord appointed me:
'Go and spread righteousness everywhere,
And seize and destroy the wicked and the tyrannical.'

MARTIN HURLIMANN

ENTRANCE TO THE GOLDEN TEMPLE

For this purpose was I born,
And this let all the virtuous understand:
To advance righteousness, to emancipate the good,
And to destroy all evil-doers, root and branch."

This it may be noticed *en passant* is a literal translation of a famous passage in the Bhagavat Gita where Krishna says:

Paritrānāya sadhūnām vināçāyaca duskrtām Dharmasamstāpanārthāya sambhavāmi yugē yugē.

The first active step Govind took in order to give effect to his ideals was to organise the Sikhs into a disciplined and closely knit body under his own uncontested authority. For this purpose on the 1st of Baishak, 1699, he announced the establishment of the Khalsa (literally the "liberated"), and laid down that, in order to be one of his true followers, a disciple must take Pahul and wear the five "K.s," being Kesh, Kara, Kank, Katch and Kripan. These five are in themselves extremely symbolic.

The kesh is the hair which a Sikh is not allowed to shave or shear. Kara is an iron bangle which is to be worn on the hand. Kank is the comb which is to be worn on the hair. Katch is short trousers and kripan is the sword.

These, apart from the kripan, are all symbols of *diksha*, or dedication, according to Hindu religion. The kesh especially represents a vow, and it has been the oldest symbol of dedication in India. The comb is in order to keep the hair clean. The iron bangle represents the determination to eschew all luxury, and the katch, which must always be worn, perpetual readiness. The kripan, or long sword, proclaims the martial purpose of the dedication of the Sikhs. In short, the five "K.s," as they are called, were devised by Govind to impress on the Hindu mind the dedication of the Sikhs to the supreme task of liberating their people.

The Pahul, or the so-called baptism, was the process by which the different Hindu castes which formed the following of the Guru were united into one community. Govind realised that it was caste that stood in the way of any unification of the Hindus and that mere declarations against the inequity of the system would not break down its rigours. He therefore considered it essential that there must be a symbolic act which united the different castes into a single community. The Pahul is in no sense a baptism. It is the genuine Hindu tradition of samskar, or a *rite de passage.* The Pahul made the Sikh a *dwija.* It was a second birth.

He further laid down the motto that a true Sikh who was his follower must wholly dedicate himself to the faith and to him as the Guru. The Sikhs must be prepared for Kirtnash (loss of fame), Kulnash (loss of family), Dharmnash (loss of orthodox religion), Karmnash (loss of karma) in their devotion to the Khalsa and its chief. They were asked to add the suffix "Singh" or "lion," by tradition the suffix of the martial classes of the north, to their names. By these teachings he made the Khalsa a disciplined army under the control of one dominating mind dedicated to the service of God.

The community which he established was in essence a theocracy which exacted unqualified submission to the will of the sovereign Pontiff who was not only the Guru of his disciples, but also the Sachi Padshah or "True King" of the community. The strength that this organisation gained caused jealousy among the petty chiefs of the hills neighbouring Anandpur; and they combined under Bhim Chand to crush this rising power which threatened the allegiance of their own subjects.

In the battle that ensued at Bhangani, the Guru's forces were successful, and his prestige rose greatly in consequence. But the triumph was only short lived as Govind had soon to meet a more powerful foe. Disquieting reports of the growth of this new power, so near his own capital, had reached the Mogul Emperor, Aurangzeb, who was engaged on his campaign against the Marathas in the Deccan. The Viceroys of Sirhind and Lahore were ordered to march against Govind. The imperial armies besieged Anandpur in 1701; and after undergoing great privations, Govind, who had been deserted by most of his followers till there were not more than forty left to bear his standard, secretly left Anandpur.

For the next seven years, in effect till the death of Aurangzeb, Govind had no peace. He was hunted and harassed by the Mogul armies, betrayed by friends and allies and shunned by those who hailed him first as the Saviour. Two of his sons fell on the battlefield. Two were bricked alive at Sirhind by the Mogul governor. Most of his followers, borne down by privations, deserted, and only a handful were left with him. But the courage of Govind, made dauntless by his supreme sense of mission, never for a moment faltered.

In 1706, when his fortune seemed to have touched its nadir, the Guru wrote the celebrated epistle *Zafar Nama*, literally the Epistle of Victory, to the Mogul Emperor, in which he proudly remarked:

> "What is the use of putting down a few sparks (meaning the murder of

MARTIN HURLIMANN

SIKH TEMPLE, LAHORE

The Punjab is the home of the Sikhs. Here is the entrance to the Sikh temple in Lahore, the headquarters of Ranjit Singh, last great ruler of the Sikh Empire. He covered the dome of the temple at Amritsar with copper gilt, giving it its name of "Golden Temple."

his sons) when the flame of power is
burning more fiercely than ever?"

He denounced the emperor for all the wrongs he had done; and, as became a religious leader, proudly proclaimed that he feared none but the King of Kings in whose presence the Emperor himself would have to answer for the tyranny he had exercised in this world. Aurangzeb was unmoved by the denunciation of an infidel, and sent a peremptory order to the Guru summoning him to his presence. But before even the order reached Govind, Aurangzeb passed away, and the Mogul Empire, which the personality of the great emperor had kept together, was rent by the dissensions of a war of succession.

This was Govind's opportunity. After seven years of incessant warfare which had reduced his following and crippled his material resources, the opportunity was now offered to him to intervene effectively in the affairs of the Empire itself. Bahadur Shah sent for Govind; and the Guru, supported by a numerous following which again gathered around him with this change in his fortune, appeared in the Mogul camp. A military command is said to have been given to him; and he marched with the imperial troops to the Deccan where, on the banks of the Godavari, he was stabbed to death when asleep by a Pathan youth whose father had been killed by Govind in a private quarrel.

Govind was only forty-seven when he died, and the schemes which he had evolved in the retreat at Anandpur during his earlier days remained unfulfilled at his death. But the work he had done during the twelve years of his active ministry from 1695 to 1707 entitle him to be considered one of the truly great men of mediæval India.

Perhaps the greatest achievement of Govind was his declaration that the mission of the Gurus had ended with him, and that the Sikhs in future were to seek the guidance of God only in the collective voice of the community and in the sacred writings of the ten Gurus. By this momentous decision he saved the community from a hereditary theocracy. The final authority in all matters of the *panth* was left to the community itself, which was enjoined not to recognise any spiritual authority beyond that of the Granth Sahib, or the Sacred Book containing the teachings of the ten Gurus, or any temporal authority over the *panth*, except that of the community itself.

The history of the community before him had convinced Govind that succession to the Pontificate was the easy source of schism. It was also obvious to him that since his own sons were dead, an undisputed succession to the Gaddi was impossible at that critical juncture. Govind, therefore, had no successors, and the Sikhs today acknowledge no spiritual authority beyond the Sacred Book and the collective conscience of the community.

It would be a mistake to think that Govind's influence as a teacher was confined to the Sikh community. There is ample evidence in his writings to show that it was the helpless and defenceless condition of the Hindus that acted as the supreme motive of his action. The Khalsa was to him the instrument for reviving the martial spirit of the Hindus and of reviving them as a nation. The Daswin Padshah ka Granth not only glorifies the deeds of the ancient Hindu Heroes, but draws upon them for inspiration for the present. The kripan itself, which he adopted as the symbol of the Sikhs, was said to have been touched by Bhawani (the Mother-Goddess) after tantric ceremonies performed by a Brahman ascetic from Benares. Chandi-ki-Charitr, as well as the glorification of

MARTIN HURLIMANN

THE ALTAR IN THE SIKH TEMPLE AT SIALKOT

the deeds of Rama and Krishna, in the writings of Govind shows that he aimed at the resurrection of the Hindus as a people, while keeping his own disciples strictly to the religious tenets of Nanak and his predecessors.

The political effects of Govind's twelve years of activity were also considerable. The Mogul authority in the vital province of the Punjab was completely shattered at the time of Aurangzeb's death. The military tradition of the Khalsa, which he emphasised and perfected, practically eradicated the vestige of Moslem authority in the 150 years that followed his death. The Punjab, which had for 700 years been entirely under Moslem occupation, again became a Hindu province under the successors of Govind; and undoubtedly what made this possible was the strength, solidarity and the national ideals which Govind gave to the Hindus in general and his own Sikh community in particular.

BY PERMISSION OF THE BRISTOL CORPORATION

RAJA RAMMOHAN ROY

From a painting in the Bristol Art Gallery..

RAJA RAMMOHAN ROY

FOUNDER OF A UNIVERSAL RELIGION

1772–1833

BY P. K. SEN

THE real biography of Rammohan is to be read in his life work, a life full of sustained strivings in various fields—social, political and religious; full of courage, sincerity and singleness of purpose, of indomitable energy and fiery enthusiasm such as has seldom been equalled in any part of the world. Much of this is happily reflected in his prolific writings in the English, Bengali, Sanskrit, Persian and Urdu languages, and thus remains as a heritage to generations unborn. For the purpose of this biographical sketch it is more appropriate to dive into his mind than to deal with the events of his life, save in so far as it may be necessary to furnish a framework for the picture.

Rammohan was born in the village of Radhanagar, near Krishnagar, in the district of Hoogly, on the 22nd May, 1772.[1] He came of a respectable Brahman family. His great-grandfather, Krishna Chandra Banerji, saw service under the Nawab of Bengal and was honoured with the title of "Roy Roy," afterwards contracted into "Roy," which has since been retained as the designation of the family in place of the caste name "Banerji."

Braja Benode, the third son of Krishna Chandra and the grandfather of Rammohan, served the Nawab Siraj-ud-Doula in a distinguished capacity; but, on account of some ill-treatment accorded to him, he quitted the employment and spent the rest of his life at home. He had five sons, of whom Ramkanta, the fifth, was the father of Rammohan. Rammohan's paternal ancestors were Vaishnavas noted for their piety and devotion. His maternal ancestors were staunch Shaktas. Very early in life Rammohan showed signs of conspicuous talent, and Ramkanta spared no pains to give him an excellent education. He received his early instruction in the village school, where he made some progress in Bengali. But Bengali was not of much consequence in those days. Persian was still the Court language, and a knowledge of it was indispensable. He received private tuition in Persian at home under a Maulvi, and later on he was sent to Patna, then a great centre of Islamic learning, for a proper study of Arabic and Persian. There he read Euclid and Aristotle in Arabic, and also made a study of the Koran and Koranic literature. He was then sent for study of Sanskrit to Benares, where he did not take long to become well-versed in the literature, law and philosophy of his people, specially the Upanishads. While this education made him an ardent admirer and advocate of the monotheistic religion inculcated in the Upanishads, it shook his faith in the popular Hindu religion of the day.

On his return home he fearlesssly attacked the meaningless ceremonialism and the priest-ridden idolatry which prevailed all round in the name of Hinduism. This led to an estrangement between him and his father, and made him leave his paternal roof. In search of truth he went out on travel, which was not confined to India alone

[1] *There is some uncertainty as to the year and date of his birth. The year most frequently accepted is that given on his tombstone, namely,* 1774. *His biographer, Miss S. D. Collet, gives certain reasons for preferring the earlier date, which is accepted here. See Miss Collet's "Life and Letters of Raja Rammohan Roy."*

but extended to far-off Tibet. After about three years of travel Rammohan returned to his father—when he was about twenty years old—and on his return was taken back with great kindness and affection. It appears, however, that intellectually and spiritually the paternal roof proved inhospitable, and we learn from his friend and contemporary, William Adam, that Rammohan, after relinquishing idolatry, "was obliged to reside for ten or twelve years at Benares at a distance from his friends and relatives."

The death of his father in 1803 led him to remove from Benares to Murshidabad, the old Mogul capital of Bengal. There he published his first work, entitled Tuhfat-ul-Muwahuddin, or "A gift to Monotheists"—a treatise in Persian with an Arabic preface. This work shows in a considerable measure the influence on Rammohan's mind and style of writing of his studies in Islamic scriptures at Patna. In matter, it is a deistic dissertation on the futility of all existing religions and the fatuities of religious leaders. In form, it is cast in a logical mould and abounds with logical and philosophical terms. It is an essay seeking to establish that the real root of all religions is faith in one Supreme Being, and that all the rest is mere excrescence.

Rammohan now entered service under the East India Company as a clerk in the Collectorate under Mr. John Digby, the Collector at Rangpur. He was subsequently promoted to the post of *Dewan*, "the principal native officer in the collection of revenue." Rammohan commenced the study of English in his twenty-fourth year (1796). In his twenty-ninth year (1801) he could speak it well enough to be understood. During his stay at Rangpur, Rammohan carried on religious controversies with the Pundits, wrote tracts in Persian, translated portions of the Vedanta, studied the Tantras and made a study of the Kalpa Sutras and other Jaina scriptures. Thus it was a time of strenuous preparation for his future work. Besides these, he used to hold vigorous religious discussions every evening at his residence, in which he used all the weapons of his armoury in exposing the absurdities of idolatry.

After about ten years Rammohan retired from service with a view to finding more time for the work which lay nearest his heart. Leaving government service he went home to stay with his mother awhile. But his controversies with the Pundits and his persistent attacks on the popular Hinduism of the day roused the animosity of his neighbours, who subjected him to endless persecutions. Eventually, these brought about the displeasure of his mother, Tarini Devi, who obliged Rammohan to quit the house. He then went to Raghunathpur, a neighbouring village, where, living in a society sunk in idolatry, superstition and nameless ritualism, this votary of the spirit-God worshipped from day to day The One without a second, in spirit and in truth, and in the grand solitude of his independence.

There was one fateful event that happened during this period which left an indelible impression on Rammohan's mind and acted on him as a powerful impetus later in life, to the everlasting benefit of his country. Rammohan had an elder brother, named Jaganmohan, who died in 1811. His wife, who was devotedly attached to him, burnt herself on his funeral pyre. Rammohan had tried to dissuade her from it, but had failed. When, however, she actually felt the flames on her person she made an attempt to get up and escape. But the orthodox relations, dreading such escape as almost an act of heresy and sacrilege, managed to keep her pinned down to the pyre by means of bamboo poles while, with the noise of tom-toms and other instruments, they drowned her frantic shrieks. Rammohan, though a witness of this awful scene, failing to help her out of such a tragic end, was stricken with pity and remorse. He there and then took the vow that he would never rest till the inhuman practice of Suttee was abolished.

How faithfully he kept this vow and with what consummate energy and skill he accomplished his great object will appear from the following testimony of the Rev. J. Fox, a noted Englishman of the day: "There is no doubt that it was greatly through his firmness, his enlightened reasonings, and his persevering efforts, that the Government of Bengal at last thought themselves enabled to interdict the immolation of widows. His arguments and his appeals to ancient authorities held sacred by the Brahmans, enlightened the minds of many of them, and made the merciful intervention of Lord William Bentinck and his Council no longer regarded by them, and by persons connected with the East India Company at home, as an interference with the religions of the Hindus." So great was the agitation engineered by the blind Hindu orthodoxy of the day in favour of its retention that, but for Rammohan's indefatigable exertions and powerful moral support, it would hardly have been possible for Lord William Bentinck, the then Viceroy and Governor-General of India, actuated as he was by the most humane sentiments and the best of intentions, to abolish the Suttee. In 1829 the Suttee Act was

STAPLETON GROVE HOUSE

In September, 1833, the Raja arrived at Bristol to rest and recuperate after the strain of his stay in London. In this house he was taken suddenly ill and died, September 27.

passed and the inhuman practice put down for ever.

The year 1814 saw Rammohan settled down at Calcutta and there he soon began his life work in right earnest. There was in those days in and about Calcutta a galaxy of foreign intellectuals who have by their labours left their mark on the Indian social and educational history of the day—men of the calibre of Colebrooke, H. H. Wilson, Macaulay, Sir William Jones, Sir Hyde East, Adam, and the like. The last mentioned of these played the part of an active comrade and coadjutor with Rammohan later on. Thus the atmosphere was congenial to Rammohan and favourable for his work. He had now set his heart on waging war against the current idolatry and superstition, and on reviving the unidolatrous Hindu monotheism of old. With this object he first published, at considerable expense, the Sanskrit original with annotations of a few of the Upanishads. In the year 1815 he published the Vedanta Sutras in Bengali. In 1816 came the Abridgment of the Vedanta in Bengali, Urdu and English and also translations of the Kena and Isha Upanishads into Bengali and English. In 1817 followed translations of the Katha and Mundaka Upanishads into Bengali and English, and in 1818 a translation of the Mandukya Upanishad into Bengali. In 1817 there also appeared in English "A Defence of Hindu Theism" and "A Second Defence of the Monotheistical System of the Vedas." These publications, appearing in quick succession one after another, caused a great commotion in the orthodox camp. Criticisms and controversies followed; but Rammohan was not to be silenced. The next four or five years saw Rammohan vigorously engaged in refuting with consummate skill the arguments in support of Hindu symbolism and priestcraft.

This was but one phase of his polemical activities. Another important phase was his controversy with Christian missionaries. In order to study the Christian scriptures in their original, Rammohan began to learn Greek and Hebrew with the help of his friend Adam. The friendship that sprang up between Rammohan and Adam remained unshaken even to the day that Rammohan drew his last breath. With the help of his friend and one Mr. Yates, another Christian missionary, Rammohan commenced translating the four Gospels into Bengali. This undertaking proved rather eventful—Adam made a public avowal of his conversion from Trinitarianism to Unitarianism! This was sarcastically described by the scandalised critics of the day as the "fall of the second Adam."

In 1820 Rammohan published "The Precepts of Jesus, the Guide to Peace and Happiness," being a compilation from the four Gospels of the essential teachings of Jesus, with all that savoured of dogmas and miracles studiously left out. This raised a storm of opposition. Contrary to expectation, it was the Baptist missionaries of Serampore who attacked him most vehemently. In fact, this opposition came as the greatest surprise of his life. Nothing daunted, Rammohan published in close succession three "Appeals to the Christian Public in Defence of the Precepts of Jesus." In these he surpassed himself in the accuracy, clearness and perspicuity of his exposition, in the thoroughness and depth of his research, in the dignity of his self-restraint, and in his transparent sympathy and charity towards his opponents. Indeed, his writings on this subject will go down to posterity as a model for all controversialists.

While his main objective was religious reformation, a life so true and devout, a genius so versatile could not but flow

THE RAJA'S MAUSOLEUM
The Indian mausoleum which has been raised over the Raja's grave in Arno's Vale Cemetery, Bristol.

into other channels of activity. And so it came to pass that there was hardly any field of reform that Rammohan did not traverse, hardly any effort in which he was not the first and foremost in India's renaissance. In upholding the cause of education and social reform, in advocating the rights of woman, in pressing for the inherent right of citizens to freedom of speech and to a free press, in claiming for the submerged castes the right to better treatment, and for the agriculturists the right to freedom from rack-renting, in demanding equal treatment to the white and coloured races, Rammohan was always to the fore and brought to bear upon these questions his vast erudition, his logical acumen and his polemical skill.

Rammohan turned the public mind from its apathy and indifference to womenfolk and demanded on their behalf "a fair opportunity of exhibiting their natural capacity." The time had not yet come for actually initiating a measure for the education of women. The function of the pioneer everywhere is to kill prejudices, provoke thought, turn people's minds in the right direction and thus clear the path to reform and progress. This Rammohan did in ample measure for women. The high esteem and sympathy with which he regarded women is evident throughout his writings on their behalf.

In his "Brief Remarks Regarding Modern Encroachments on the Ancient Rights of Females," published in 1822, Rammohan sought to elucidate "the interest and care which our ancient legislators took in the promotion of the comfort of the female part of the community; and to compare the laws of female inheritance which they enacted, and which afforded that sex the opportunity of enjoyment of life, with that which moderns and our contemporaries have gradually introduced and established, to their complete privation, directly or indirectly, of most of those objects that render life agreeable." He directed his attention to the general Hindu Law of inheritance. His "Essay on the Rights of Hindoos over Ancestral Property according to the Law of

ORIGINAL RESTING PLACE
Original grave of the Raja in the grounds of Stapleton Grove House.

Bengal" (1830) would do credit to any trained lawyer and jurist deeply trained in the history of Hindu Law.

The beginnings of educational enthusiasm in India may be traced to Rammohan as the pioneer. He conducted the journals the *Sambad Kaumudi*, in Bengali, and the *Mirat-ul-Akhbar*, in Persian, for the dissemination of useful knowledge of a historical, literary, and scientific character, politics not excluded. He turned the Bengali language into a powerful medium of expression for all purposes of national uplift. He wrote text books in Bengali on Grammar, Geography, Astronomy and Geometry. He lent his support to all movements and organisations which were calculated even indirectly to help forward the cause of education. It did not matter to Rammohan whether the schools and colleges were to be started under Christian missionary enterprise or not. It was the diffusion of useful knowledge—scientific, literary and moral—that he cared for. Later on, when Dr. Duff, the great educationist, arrived in India and found the forces of prejudice arrayed against him, it was Rammohan who actively helped him to secure pupils and even attended the Bible classes himself in order to dissipate the fears of the guardians in regard to proselytism. Besides this, he established and maintained at his own expense an English School, where Devendra Nath Tagore, the second great leader of the Brahma Samaj, received his early instruction.

Rammohan's name will always be remembered with gratitude for the distinguished part he took in the famous controversy of the so-called Anglicists *versus* the Orientalists as to the pattern of education to be pursued in India. Himself a profound Oriental scholar he would yield to none in his regard and respect for Oriental learning. But his eagle eye perceived its limitations and saw the future fraught with danger, if education were pursued after a purely Oriental pattern. In a country where metaphysics and philosophy had almost been overdone and men had developed a morbid feeling that "we are such stuff as dreams are made of," what was wanted was a wholesome antidote of Western methods of education in natural sciences and a more practical view of life. At the same time he was not unconscious that the Vedanta, rightly handled, would help his countrymen to emerge from superstition and idolatry and embrace pure Theism. It was with this purpose that he founded the Vedanta College for the kind of instruction which the Vedanta alone could give.

The efforts of Rammohan for the introduction of the English system of education did not fructify till two years after his death. In 1835 was passed the famous Education Decree inaugurating the present system of English education.

Rammohan may well be called the Father of Indian Politics. But his political horizon was not confined to India. His politics were truly cosmopolitan and sprang out of a consuming love of freedom which brooked no barriers of race, creed, colour, or country. Hence, whether it was the people of Naples that had failed to extort a constitution from their despotic king, or the people of Ireland that had failed to get justice and fairness from the British Government, Rammohan's active sympathies were always with the oppressed. Similarly, when he saw the triumph of liberty in the success of the French revolution of 1830, or in the establishment of constitutional government in Spain, his heart rejoiced with them in sympathy, which he did not fail publicly to express. Indeed, it was his intense love of freedom, freedom not only for himself but for all, that accounted for this cosmopolitanism in his politics. In the words of his lifelong friend Adam, "He would be free or not be at all. . . . Love of freedom was perhaps the strongest passion of his soul—freedom not of action merely, but of thought."

Nearer home in matters that affected freedom he proved an intrepid fighter and an unfailing champion of liberty In 1823 was passed a Press Ordinance which provided that thenceforth no one was to publish a newspaper without having first obtained a licence from the Governor-General in Council. Rammohan took a fearless stand against this Ordinance curtailing the freedom of the Press, and presented a memorial, signed by leading gentlemen of the town of Calcutta, praying for its repeal. This memorial has rightly been described by his biographer, Miss Collet, as "the Areopagitica of Indian history." The Memorial, however, did not succeed in its object.

In 1827 was passed a new Jury Act. The mischief of the Act lay in the fact that thereby there had been introduced "religious distinctions into the judicial system of the country." He was the first to protest against it, and sent petitions for presentation to both the Houses of Parliament signed by many leading Hindus and Mohammedans. In 1828 the Executive Government of India passed a regulation authorising its revenue officers to dispossess the holders of rent-free lands at their own discretion, without any judicial decree having been sought or obtained against the validity of the title to such lands. Rammohan instantly placed himself at the head of the landholders of Bengal, Bihar and Orissa and in a petition of protest addressed to Lord William Bentinck, Governor-General, condemned such arbitrary and despotic proceedings. The representation failed. The matter was carried to England where, too, it proved unsuccessful. But it points to the promptitude with which Rammohan exposed the black spots in the administration, of which he was as ardent a well-wisher as he was of his own people.

No less important were his answers to the numerous questions put to him during his sojourn in England by the Select Committee of the House of Commons on a variety of subjects vitally affecting good government. They show the breadth and accuracy of the Raja's knowledge of the administration of this country, and the unfailing sympathy for his people which breathed through them. In his answers on the Judicial and on the Revenue systems of India he had to touch upon a vast variety of topics, such as appointment of native assessors in the civil courts; the separation of judicial from revenue functions; the separation of judicial from executive functions; the codification of the criminal and other laws of India; the proportion of Indian revenues expended in England, in other words, the drain of Indian money to foreign countries without any hope of return—subjects which present problems still unsolved. It was only a Rammohan who could have dealt with all these questions with the same insight and authority as he did the Vedanta and the Precepts of Jesus!

Side by side with this incessant quest after knowledge, freedom, happiness for all, there was the insatiable hunger and thirst of his soul after the bringing together of people of all races and creeds in one catholic worship of the common Father of all. That was to be the crowning act of his life. To that end he had to go through much preparation, much thought and research, much estrangement from his near and dear ones, till in 1830, on the 23rd January, he was able to throw open the doors of the first Temple of Universal

Worship of The One without a second —an epoch-making event. The Trust Deed, dated January 8, 1830, is a unique document. It marked the advent of Universalism in actual worship in the Temple "to be used occupied enjoyed applied and appropriated as and for a place of public meeting of all sorts and descriptions of people without distinction as shall behave and conduct themselves in an orderly sober religious and devout manner." The worship was to be so conducted as would not only tend "to the promotion of the contemplation of the Author and Preserver of the Universe," but also "to the promotion of charity morality piety benevolence and virtue and the strengthening of the bonds of union between men of all religious persuasions and creeds." Thus the Trust Deed was not a mere legal document. It heralded the beginning of the Brahmo Samaj which in the fulness of time was to take its stand on universal brotherhood and universal worship of the common Father of all.

Later, under Devendra Nath Tagore —the next leader of the Brahmo Samaj —was evolved a congregation with a covenant and a public declaration of faith. It was left to the genius of Keshub Chunder Sen, the third great leader, fifty years after, to form it into an organised Church which recognises in all prophets and saints a harmony, in all scriptures a unity and through all dispensations a continuity.

As far back as 1817 Rammohan had written to his friend Digby of his intention to visit England. An opportunity now presented itself. The titular Emperor of Delhi, Akbar the Second, successor to the House of Timur, was anxious to place some grievances of his before His Britannic Majesty for redress. And who could plead his case better than Rammohan? He accordingly appointed Rammohan as Imperial Envoy to the Court of Great Britain and invested him with the title of Raja as a mark of dignity and distinction attaching to the position of Envoy. To Rammohan the visit to England was imperatively indicated for more reasons than one. The advocates of Suttee were going to appeal to the King in Council against the Suttee Act which, according to them, was an unwarranted interference with the religious practices of the Hindus. Rammohan felt that his presence in England would be necessary to vindicate the Government of Lord William Bentinck and to show up the hollowness of the contention that the inhuman practice of Suttee had religious sanction behind it. There was also the Charter of the East India Company, which was shortly to come up for renewal. Rammohan was anxious in that connection to do his part for safeguarding and enlarging the rights and privileges of his people. All these, added to his insatiate thirst for a study of the peoples and politics of the West, pointed to the time as specially opportune for carrying out his long-cherished desire. He sailed from Calcutta in the *Albion* on the 15th of November, 1830, and landed in Liverpool on the 8th of April, 1831. His fame had preceded him. As a God-fearing man of cosmopolitan sympathies, as an intrepid fighter and reformer, as a man of vast learning and erudition, as one who spoke and wrote with authority as the mouthpiece of India's aspirations, indeed as the herald of Indian renaissance, he was already known in the West.

The actual impressions of his visit on English minds and the relations it established between the East and the West far exceeded expectations, and opened a new epoch. In the words of Professor Max Müller: "For the sake of intellectual intercourse, for the sake of comparing notes, so to say, with his

Aryan brothers, Rammohan Roy was the first who came from East to West, the first to join hands and to complete that world-wide circle through which henceforth, like an electric current, Oriental thought could run to the West, and Western thought return to the East, making us feel once more that ancient brotherhood which unites the whole Aryan race, inspiring us with new hopes for a common faith, purer and simpler than any of the ecclesiastical religions of the world, and invigorating us for acts of nobler daring in the conquest of truth than any that are inscribed in the chronicles of our divided past." Wide and varied as were his interests, the period of the Raja's sojourn in Europe coincided with some of the momentous events of British history. Apart from the mission from the King of Delhi, to which he faithfully attended and in which he attained success in a large measure, he threw himself with all the earnestness of his soul into the great political movements of the day. He presented to the House of Commons the counter-petition, numerously signed from India, against the renewal of the Suttee atrocities and had the satisfaction of being present when the Suttee appeal preferred by the die-hards of India was rejected. As a recognised authority on Indian affairs he was invited to give evidence before the Select Committee of the House of Commons appointed to consider the renewal of the East India Company's Charter. He did not personally appear before the Select Committee, but by means of a series of "Communications to the Board of Control" gave his authoritative views on the revenue and judicial systems and the condition of the people in India which were duly embodied in the Blue Books. By the Statute that followed, embodying the last renewal of the Company's Charter, the East India Company was changed from a trading concern into a political organisation. He followed with intense interest the passage of the Reform Bill through all its stages and saw England passing from a practical oligarchy to a truer democracy. He saw the Act pass which abolished slavery throughout the British dominions. In fact, as his biographer puts it, he saw the New England being born out of the heart of Old England and "in him the New England first became acquainted with the New India." He made many friends, and was received into many an English home not only as a distinguished guest but as a friend.

Public honours came thick and fast. The East India Company entertained him at a dinner attended by eighty distinguished guests, the chairman presiding. At the Coronation of George IV he was honoured with a place amongst foreign ambassadors. The Raja was also introduced to an audience of the King (William IV) and was most graciously received. On his visit to France in autumn, 1832, he was received with great royal consideration by Louis Phillippe, with whom he had the honour of dining more than once. The Royal Asiatic Society and the British and Foreign Unitarian Society invited the Raja with great cordiality to take part in their annual functions.

But all this incessant strain told on the Raja's health. Early in September, 1833, the Raja arrived at Stapleton Grove, near Bristol, to rest and recoup his tired nerves at that retreat. There, however, he was suddenly taken ill on the 18th, and after a short illness passed to his eternal rest on the 27th September, 1833.

His earthly remains lie interred in Arno's Vale Cemetery at Bristol, where a graceful Indian mausoleum has been raised over them by his grateful countrymen.

BY COURTESY OF ADVAITA ASHRAMA, CALCUTTA

SWAMI VIVEKANANDA

SWAMI VIVEKANANDA

FOUNDER OF THE RAMAKRISHNA MISSION

1862–1902

BY NICOL MACNICOL, D.Litt., D.D., M.A.

SWAMI VIVEKANANDA, one of the most notable figures in the social and religious development of modern India, was a Bengali bearing the secular name of Narendra Nath Dutt. He was born in Calcutta on the 9th of January, 1862. He was by birth a Kayastha, a member of a caste of writers, belonging to the middle class of the Indian social order. Of his mother he often spoke with a sense of deep indebtedness. "It is my mother," he declared, "who has been the constant inspiration of my life and work." His father seems to have been much influenced by the atmosphere of the new India of his time, an India that was coming under the powerful influence of the scientific outlook of the West. He abandoned his ancestral faith, but we are told that when his son showed him on one occasion the Christian Bible he said, "If there is a religion it would be in this book."

The young man received a good education, graduating from a Christian College in Calcutta. The influence of Herbert Spencer was at that time very powerful over the quick and assimilative minds of the students of Bengal, and Narendra seemed likely to follow in this respect in the footsteps of his father. "The analytic and scientific method of the West," we are told by one of his disciples of a later day, "laid hold on him." We can see that even then he was aware of a conflict within him between his reason and his passions, a conflict that throughout all his tumultuous life was never fully resolved. There was much in him, it is evident, that drew him towards a life of sensuous enjoyment. "He could box, swim, row, and had a passion for horses. He was the favourite of youth and the arbiter of fashion." Especially he seems to have possessed the ear of a musician and a voice that, whether he used it, as a young man, to sing the songs of Bengal or, later, to deliver his orations to American audiences, charmed those who listened to it. Madame Calvé described his voice as "an admirable baritone having the vibrations of a Chinese gong." On the occasion of his first meeting with Paramhamsa Ramakrishna the young man, who was then eighteen years of age, was asked to sing. He did so, with the result that his future Master, emotionally intensely sensitive as he was, passed, we are told, into an ecstasy.

But there was another aspect of his experience besides that of "a young artist prince of the Renaissance."[1] From his youth up, he himself tells us, two dreams visited him. In one he saw himself "the possessor of riches, honours, power and glory." "But the next instant," he goes on, "I saw myself renouncing all worldly things, dressed in a simple loin-cloth, living on alms, sleeping at the foot of a tree." When the tumult of his restless life was dying down and the end was at hand he delivered this verdict—"More and more the true greatness seems to me to be that of the worm doing its duty silently from moment to moment and hour to hour." There was little of the silent worm about Vivekananda at any period of his life, but perhaps one can under-

[1] *Romain Rolland, "Prophets of the New India" p.* 173.

stand better the clamorous energy of his career if one remembers that always this ideal lay behind it and never ceased to beckon him.

To understand the spiritual discord of which Narendra Nath Dutt was already aware we must have some conception of the atmosphere which he breathed as a student in Calcutta. India, in the decade during which he was at College, was entering upon the gradual process of its awakening to a new interest in its national and spiritual heritage. The period of docile submission to the forces that for some time had been invading India was passing. Restlessness and self-questioning were stirring the minds of many, but with as yet little confidence as to the direction in which advance should be made. It was not surprising that this ferment should have its centre in the eager and questing spirit of the Bengali people. A generation had passed since the death of Raja Rammohan Roy, the first of the great men of modern India, and a different temper from his was now abroad in the land. The Samaj Movement, of which he was the initiator, was beginning to lose its impetus and to exhibit symptoms of a divided purpose. Narendra had come for a while under the influence of the Brahmo Samaj leaders, but their rationalistic theism and their Puritan ethics did not long satisfy him, not even when these were modified by the emotionalism of Keshub Chunder Sen and were proclaimed with his powerful eloquence. Another influence more truly Hindu and more attuned to the mood of this young paladin, and to the nationalist pride beginning to stir the hearts of many like him, was about to lay its grasp upon him and bring his hesitations to an end.

This influence was that of an unlettered Brahman ascetic called Ramakrishna, who by the spell of his personality was drawing to himself great numbers of those who, in Calcutta and the country round about, were looking for a guide to lead them out of their perplexities. This is not the place in which the story of this remarkable man can be told. Max Müller first made him and his teaching known to the West, and his extraordinary qualities have not ceased since then to interest and attract students of Oriental mysticism. What concerns us is to understand what it was in him that brought this young seeker so completely into subjection to his spirit. At what date Narendra first saw his Master seems to be somewhat uncertain. It may have been when, at the age of 18, he, with some student companions, met him in the house of a friend, and the seer perceived the great qualities in him and set himself to win him. The story of the struggle in Narendra between the advanced views he had imbibed in the halls of the Brahmo Samaj and the very different message of this Hindu who followed old ways and claimed to have reached through them truths hid from the learned, need not be related here. How it ended may be told in the words of one of Narendra's fellow-students, afterwards a distinguished teacher and scholar, Brajendra Nath Seal.

He is describing, more than twenty years afterwards, the change that was wrought at this time in his friend by the influence of Ramakrishna. "I watched," he says, "with intense interest the transformation that went on under my eyes. The attitude of a young and rampant Vedantist—cum Hegelian—cum Revolutionary like myself towards the cult of religious ecstasy and Kali-worship may be easily imagined; and the spectacle of a born iconoclast and free-thinker like Vivekananda, a creative and dominating intelligence, a tamer of souls, himself caught in the meshes of what appeared to me an uncouth, supernatural mysticism, was a riddle which my philosophy of the Pure Reason could scarcely read at the time." What he saw of this change and of its source in Vivekananda's Master who had brought it about in his disciple seemed to this observer to prove that Vivekananda obtained somehow "the firm assurance he sought in the saving grace and power of his Master" and that in the strength of this assurance he went forth preaching and teaching his message.

We need not, however, accept the explanation of onlookers as to the change wrought in Narendra by the man whom he always called his Master and of whom he wrote: "If there has ever been a word of truth, a word of spirituality that I have spoken anywhere in the world, I owe it to him." He himself tells us how in the early days of their acquaintance he asked Ramakrishna, "Do you believe in God?" and the reply he received was, "I see Him just as I see you here only in a much intenser sense." This was what the young man's restless spirit was seeking. "Religion," he says, "consists in realisation—not in reasoning about its doctrines but in experiencing it." Two ideals that he found in this religion of realisation were, first, renunciation and, second, the unity of all religions. As regards the former he could affirm of Ramakrishna, "That man was the embodiment of renunciation." He could equally have said that he was the embodiment of religious universalism.

It is not necessary, nor, perhaps, possible to present Vivekananda's religious beliefs as a consistent whole. What is important is to note the power that they had over him and how he sought to proclaim them as a message both for India and for the world. Dr. Brajendra Nath Seal, who has already been quoted, sums up this message as "the creed of the Universal Man and the absolute and inalienable sovereignty of the Self." It was, in fact, a combination of the two ancient Hindu doctrines of Jñana and bhakti, or, in Western terms, it was a combination of an absolute monism which affirms that all is one, and at the same time of a devout approach to a God who can be worshipped. We can, however, best form a judgment in regard to his creed by his own proclamation of it and the conclusions for life and practice that he himself deduced from it.

The whole of the life that was granted to him from this time on was devoted to the task that his Master bequeathed to him. Ramakrishna died on August 15, 1886, and soon thereafter Vivekananda, along with other disciples of the Master, constituted themselves, under his leadership, into an order of sannyasis or world-renouncers. The name that the head of the order himself adopted was Vivekananda, suggesting a combination of "discrimination" and "joy" as his special characteristic. The next six years were spent by him mainly as a wandering ascetic in preparation for the work that was to come. Words that he is said to have uttered at Benares during this period may be taken as representing what was passing within his mind. "I am going away," he said, "and I shall never come back till I can burst on society like a bomb and make it follow me like a dog."

That opportunity came to him when, his years of preparation completed, he emerged at Madras at the close of 1892, ready to go forth in the name of India to America "in behalf of the people and the poor." He left Bombay on May 31, 1893, travelling by way of Japan to Chicago, where was to be held a "Parliament of Religions" in connection with the World's Fair in that city. He had only the vaguest idea, it would seem, of what he was going to take part in, but there was a fire within him that drove him on. "It is," he said, "as if I were about to blaze forth. There are many powers in me.. It appears to me as if I could revolutionise the world." His confidence in himself proved to be fully justified. Clothed in a dazzling robe of red silk and wearing the yellow turban of the sannyasi his imposing figure at once drew all eyes and the power of his eloquence completed his conquest. What his audiences thought of him may be indicated by what the *Boston Evening Transcript* testifies. "At the Parliament of Religions," we are told, "they used to keep Vivekananda until the end of the programme to make people stay till the end of the session." When people grew tired and wanted to go away the chairman would intimate that Vivekananda would be the last speaker. "Then he would have the peaceable hundreds perfectly in tether. They would sit smiling and expectant waiting for an hour or two of other men's speeches to listen to Vivekananda for fifteen minutes."

He remained in America till August, 1895, and during that time he accomplished an immense amount of work and gathered to himself a considerable number of disciples. He had, as he wrote in a letter just before his return home, "planted a seed." "It is already a plant," he goes on, "and I expect it to be a tree very soon. I have got a few hundred followers. I shall make several sannyasis and then go to India, leaving the work to them."

His letters to his friends in India during these years indicate how his hopes soared and died down again with his changing emotions. Sometimes he was weary of being treated as if he were "a circus turn." "I think I have had enough," he wrote after he had been a year in the country, "of newspaper blazoning and the humbugging of a public life." But the burden of his letters to his disciples in India is a reiteration of the charge to "work, work, work." He felt increasingly, as he travelled about the land, the need that India should exchange its apathy for energy if it was to be lifted from poverty and degradation. "I do not believe," he wrote, "in a God or a religion that cannot wipe the widow's tears or bring a piece of bread to the orphan's mouth." One can see signs, as we read his letters from his exile, that the strain of his labours was having an inevitable effect even upon his strength and courage. So he breaks out on one occasion: "I see a greater Power than man or God or devil at my back. I want no one's help." Before he set out from India on this journey he had said in Madras that "the Hinduism of the Rishis must become dynamic," but the force he was daily expending in his speeches (every lecture, it is said, "was a torrential improvisation") could not but exhaust him, and this was the more inevitable in that he was carrying with him all the time the disease of which he died. In addition to his lectures he found time to write his chief work, an exposition of *Raja Yoga*—a book which is said to have attracted such different personalities as William James and Leo Tolstoy.

The Swami, before finally leaving America, paid several brief visits to England as well as to Switzerland. Of his experience in England he said, after his return to his own land: "No one ever landed on English soil with more hatred in his heart for a race than I did for the English. . . . There is no one among you who loves the English people more than I do now." While he was there he paid his homage of reverence to Max Müller, in whom he perceived what was to him the summit of all attainment, "a soul that is every day realising its oneness with Brahman." There also he found new disciples, some of whom proved the most devoted of all his followers. One of these was Margaret Noble, of whom Romain Rolland writes: "The future will always unite her name of initiation, Sister Nivedita, to that of her beloved Master, as St. Clare is to St. Francis, although," he goes on, "the imperious Swami was far from possessing the meekness of the Poverello."[1] She outlived her Master, giving herself to a life of service in Calcutta and conducting a school for girls in her own house. The Swami so succeeded in her case in Hinduising her thoughts and her habits that she shared in his worship of "Kali the Mother" and indeed went far beyond him in glorifying Hinduism and Hindu life. Mr. M. K. Gandhi in his Autobiography gives us a glimpse of this devoted disciple when he saw her in Calcutta in 1902. "I was taken aback," he writes, "by the splendour that surrounded her, and even in our conversation there was not much meeting-ground." But if to him and to Mr. G. K. Gokhale this lady seemed "volatile" we find no indication of that in the years of service that she gave to her adopted land. And when in 1911 she died there was a remarkable demonstration of reverence for her among the Hindus of Bengal.

Along with his little group of disciples the Swami landed in Colombo in January, 1897. By that time his name was famous throughout all India and the story of his Western triumphs had done much to restore to India the sense of self-respect that was slowly being recreated. In consequence, his journey north from Colombo to Madras and Calcutta was a triumphal progress. Vivekananda's energies had revived again after the weariness and depression into which he had sometimes fallen. "My day is done," he had said; but now, refreshed in body and stimulated by the enthusiasm of his welcome back to India, his hopes blazed up again and a new plan of campaign was announced in Madras. He still cherished great expectations from his work in America and England. But it is in England that it seems to him now that his religious ideas will root themselves most deeply. "Before many years elapse," he declares, "a vast majority of the English people will be Vedantists. There is a greater prospect of this in England than in America. You see Americans make a fanfaronade of everything which is not the case with Englishmen."

But now he is looking mainly to victories in his own land and work on behalf of his own people. He had gone to the West in the hope of raising a large sum of money which he might use for the uplift of his people from their poverty and degradation. In this he had not obtained any great success. Now he turns his reinvigorated energies to arousing in his own fellow-countrymen the spirit of help and of compassion for the poor. "I consider," he told them, "that the great national sin is the neglect of the masses and that is one of the causes of our downfall. No amount of politics would be of any avail until the masses of India are once more well educated, well fed and well cared for. . . . I want to start two central institutions at first, one at Madras and one at Calcutta, for training young men as preachers."

Accordingly a few months later the Ramakrishna Mission was established. Vivekananda did not find it easy at first to persuade his fellow sannyasis from among Ramakrishna's disciples that his aims were in accordance with the sannyasi tradition or that his methods were such as Ramakrishna would have approved. The Swami was not, however, to be overborne. He burst forth passionately—"Hands off! Who cares

[1] *Romain Rolland, op. cit. p.* 305.

for your Ramakrishna? Who cares for *your* Bhakti and Mukti? Who cares what the Scriptures say? I will go into a thousand hells cheerfully if I can rouse my countrymen to stand on their own feet and be men inspired with the spirit of karma-yoga. I am not a follower of Ramakrishna or anyone; I am a follower of him only who serves and helps others without caring for his own Bhakti or Mukti." Needless to say this masterful sannyasi got his own way.

Two monasteries were opened, one at Belur near Calcutta, the other at Mayavati near Almora in the Himalayas. Soon the monks found more than enough opportunity for the exercise of their compassion in caring for the victims of famine and plague. Such philanthropic work and the training of young disciples in the principles of Vedanta were the main tasks laid upon the members of the Mission. Vivekananda was himself the chief teacher and, when his health permitted, the chief organiser of the service of the poor and the suffering. The Vedanta he taught was, indeed, a Vedanta of a new pattern. His was to be a "practical Vedanta." "Spread far and wide," he said, "the worship of Sri Krishna roaring the Gita out with the voice of a lion. And bring into daily use the worship of Sakti—the divine Mother, the source of all power."

But his waning strength demanded a rest and a change of climate and, accordingly, in June, 1899, he set out on his second journey to the West. It was very different from the earlier one. He delivered some lectures, but the early fire was sinking, and he evidently was aware that his work was nearing its end. "The battles are lost and won," he wrote to one of his disciples. "I have bundled my things and am waiting for the great Deliverer. Shiva, O Shiva, carry my boat to the other shore." The climate of California suited his need and under its influence "his athletic will relaxed its hold."[1] In December, 1900, he returned to India and, in spite of the increasing grasp upon him of the diabetic malady from which he had suffered so long, he continued to make plans for the progress of the work of the Mission. But on July 4, 1902, in Belur Monastery the sannyasi, in the language of Hinduism, attained samadhi.

To look back across the forty years of the Swami's life from that day when the last silence fell is to be impressed anew with the amazing amount of effort that he concentrated within the brief period given to him, as well as with the influence that these forty years have exercised. This man, compact of energy both of speech and action, will continue to be remembered as a bizarre and significant figure dominating his time and leaving an enduring influence behind him. He initiates a new era in the Indian development, the passing of the age of reason, with Raja Rammohan Roy as its distinguished representative, and the inauguration in its stead of a period of romanticism. Swami Vivekananda's very violence of utterance is a token of the change. Like his fellow-romantic of the West, Nietzsche, he revolts with passion against the enervation that reason brings. He admits, it is true, that reason has its place for the detection and destruction of elements of superstition in the Hinduism he desires to purify, but his aim is to lead his people to a region that is beyond reason.

What Vivekananda was seeking to do was to achieve a new thing by means of the old instruments that belong to the heritage of the Hindu. He desired to awaken the manhood of his people. He saw one thing clearly and it always had

[1] *Romain Rolland, op. cit. p.* 355

primacy in his purpose—the need for a recreated vitality in a nation drained of its vigour through the centuries. But he must bring this about by means of the ancient traditions of Indian thought. He was therefore an Advaitist, but an Advaitist who at the same time would have the individual man made strong. Thus he would both have and have not. "Will itself," he says, "is phenomenal and cannot be the Absolute." And yet what can the individual accomplish apart from his will? It is difficult to find a place for the individual in such a vacuum as the Brahman of the Advaitist is. Thus the two aspects of his thought stand side by side, the one an exalted theory, the other a practical necessity. Man is all, and yet he is himself as well, over-against the All.

It is clear that, as in the case of the great Sankaracharya, he had two levels of religious living between which he vacillated, the austere and passionless Advaita on the one hand, and the worship of "Kali, the Mother" on the other. He belonged by family tradition to the Hindu sect of Sāktas, just as his Master, Ramakrishna, did also. He realised that the dark and the terrible, because they are elements in life, must also be elements in religion. As we have seen, he was not content with the rationalistic religion of the Samajists, but, passing beyond them, found himself in the strange and terrifying company of the deity of destruction. If God is the All, then the most revolting things must be included in His being. When Sister Nivedita went to her Master with her hesitations on the subject of the blood shed before Kali his only reply was: "Why not a little blood to complete the picture?" His fellow Hindu, Mahatma Gandhi, was not able to view the Kali Ghat with such equanimity. In a poem addressed to the goddess with the appeal, "Come, Mother, come," Vivekananda says,

Who dares misery love
And hug the form of Death,
Dance in Destruction's dance,
To him the Mother comes.

Thus he found in this grim Mother an object of worship that could satisfy him when his heart could not be content with the empty name of Brahman. Kali for him, as for many others in Bengal in that period of awakening patriotism, was in fact a symbol of India, the motherland.

Yet another element in the message of which this prophet felt himself to be the bearer was the unity of all religions. This follows naturally from the view that everything is God. The religions of the world, therefore, "are but various phases of one Eternal Religion." This belief he inherited from his Master, Ramakrishna, who did not hesitate to contemplate the vision—terrible as even he perceived it to be—that "all three are of the same substance, the victim of the sacrifice, the block and the executioner." With this way to "harmony," Vivekananda was in full agreement. "I accept all religions that were in the past," he writes, "and worship with them all." "Acceptance—not even toleration which is an insult and a blasphemy."

With such words as these the Swami, if he did not always satisfy, at least aroused. It is as an arouser, an enemy, in spite of his Advaitism, of negation, an awakener of his sleeping fellow-countrymen to living issues, that we should view this remarkable Indian figure. In his robe of red and his great yellow turban he caught for a brief space the eyes of the American people and produced at least a temporary realisation in the West of India's great heritage of thought and aspiration. But the Swami's abiding significance lies in what he accomplished among his own people, kindling a flame from the dying embers of their past and awakening in them hope for their future.

THE EXILED YAKSHA

An illustration to the Megadutha, by A. N. Tagore. Modern Bengal School.

KALIDASA

FLOR. *circa* A.D. 400

THE SHAKESPEARE OF INDIA

BY DENIS CLARK

"HISTORY in the ordinary sense of the word is almost unknown in Indian Literature"; so wrote Professor Max Müller, and this is particularly true of those great ones, poets and sages, whose works were written and are still preserved in Sanskrit. The causes of this apparent carelessness may be touched on lightly. They were, first, the impermanence of the recording materials used and, second, the fundamental Hindu belief in the absolute unimportance of the individual, compared with the world soul. So, very often, little enough remains to tell us what manner of men these were, whose works we still read and admire. They are voices no more; but voices that speak when nearly two thousand years have passed by are not easily denied.

If ever man won immortality by what he thought and wrote rather than what he *was*, Kalidasa is he. Plays, poems are all that remain; no tomb, no sculptured inscription, no city even, whose proud citizens may point and say, "That is where Kalidasa lived and worked." So little is known about the great poet-dramatist that it is still disputed as to where or *in what century* Kalidasa existed. Some, Wilson among them, believe him to have been one of those "nine gems" which adorned King Vikramaditya's court, that he lived and wrote about 56 B.C., when Vikramaditya reigned at Ujjayini in Central India; that warlike Vikramaditya who defeated the encroaching hordes of Sákais or Scythians, established the Malavas as a formidable tribe, and inaugurated the glorious Vikram *Samvat* or era. Except that he gave his royal patronage to several artists and writers, including Amarasimha, compiler of a *Kosha* or Sanskrit dictionary, very little more is discoverable about this monarch. His obscurity is not, perhaps, very surprising when we remember how the great Samudragupta, who conquered all India from Oxus to Ceylon between A.D. 330 and 380, was not even remembered by name until his identity was slowly pieced together by minutely laborious researches into inscriptions and coins during the last century.

But Bhan Dhaji, and many others, argue that it was not in this King's reign that the "Indian Shakespeare" penned his Sanskrit masterpieces. They bring strong evidence to prove that his time was during the reign of Chandragupta II, or even of Harshavadhana (both of whom bore the title of Vikramaditya), who ruled in A.D. 606, so that here at once lies latitude of more than six hundred years' uncertainty as to the Kalidasian period.

That Kalidasa lived under a King Vikramaditya is vouched for by almost the opening words of his drama, "The Fatal Ring," wherein the *Sutradhana* or stage manager says to his wife, the actress: "This, madam, is the numerous and polite assembly of the famed hero, our king Vikramaditya, who is himself an eminent dramatic critic. To-day we are to do justice to *Abhijnana-Sakuntalam*, the new historical play of Kalidasa."

Endless discussion has arisen as to which city might claim the poet, all the more confused since he cannot certainly be said to represent the best of a period or school of poets, as did his English prototype, Shakespeare, or to be some great pioneer of verse, as Chaucer was. Shakespeare belongs to Stratford-on-Avon, and London to Marlowe, Donne and Greene; but where and to who Kalidasa? Legend relates that Kalidasa finally went to Ceylon, there to die at the hands of a courtesan in a brawl such as caused Marlowe's end, and that King Kumaradasa, his friend, in his grief caused himself to be burned on the pyre by his side; but there are many legends. Despairingly, it has even been suggested that Kalidasa was not one poet alone but several poets, who lived in the reigns of several different kings, each one employing the title which earned such renown. This seems the most improbable theory of all, for throughout Kalidasa's work runs a potent characteristic, a wonderful, all-surpassing power of description and glorification of Nature, of the beauty of forest, field and sky, stamped with such soulfelt sincerity of expression as can only belong to one man, and that man a prince among poets.

> "*Wouldst thou the young year's blossoms and the fruits of its decline*
> *And all by which the soul is charmed, enraptured, feasted, fed,*
> *Wouldst thou the Earth and Heaven itself in one sole name combine?*
> *I name thee, O Sakuntala! and all at once is said.*"

So Rabindranath Tagore, greatest modern poet of India, explains, has Goethe, the master-poet of Europe, summed up his criticism of Kalidasa's *Sakuntala* in a single quatrain. . . "In Goethe's words *Sakuntala* (Kalidasa's most famous drama) blends together the young year's blossoms and the fruits of maturity; it combines heaven and earth in one." Indeed the theme of all Kalidasa's work interprets that curious, strong blending of the flesh and the spirit, the erotic and the esoteric, which are so characteristic of his age and creed. Nymphs of unblemished, unimpeded charms disport round *yogis* of centuries old asceticism. Sometimes the gods, in wilful malice or sport, send them direct to tempt sage men from their vows. Clouds embrace rocks, streams the strong roots of trees. All nature is called to Kalidasa's service to depict in parable the amorous joys of mankind.

The *Rajatarangini* describes Vikramaditya Sákari (Chandragupta II, another conqueror of the Sákais) as a keen patron of learning. It was he who made a poet, one Matrigipta, king of Kashmir for his skill. In none of his works does Kalidasa show any familiarity with Kashmir, yet Kashmir and Dhara too lay claim to the honour of calling him their own poet. But Chandragupta made Ujjayini his capital, and Kalidasa's poems more than once refer with such affection to this state that it seems more than probable that it was there and under that monarch that he lived. In the *Svayamvara* (bridegroom selection) scene of his *Raghuvamsam*, the poet puts into the mouth of a minor character a description of the king of Magadha, who is most probably Chandragupta Vikramaditya (A.D. 380-413):

> "*In Maghada he rules, his people's joy,*
> *Whose blazing wrath burns up his stubborn foes.*
> *Alone he's Spouse of Earth, though thousand Kings*
> *Usurp the style. . . .*"
>
> (P. D. L. Johnstone.)

Remains then, not for the first time, the poet's immortal lustre long after the monarch's temporal power has passed away. Vikramaditya's countenance, his prowess and his dominion, alike lie forgotten but for disputed rumours of deeds, of a gracious patron of letters: but the work of the man he favoured, the poet he fostered, lives till this day, the delight and wonder alike of East and West, translated in many tongues, performed on the stages of Europe's foremost capitals. Dr. Keith, famous scholar of Sanskrit literature, ranks Kalidasa higher than Ovid or Propertius, and compares him with Tennyson. Some people, he says, criticising Kalidasa's *Malavikagnimitra*, one of his earlier epic poems dealing with the love story of King Agnimitra, deny that he is its author owing to its inferiority to the rest of his work. But such inferiority was merely due to the poet's youthful inexperience, he explains, just as in Alfred Tennyson's earlier work. Both were poets "not so much on inspiration and genius as of perfect accomplishment based on a high degree of talent."

Through the mists of antiquity certain characteristics of Kalidasa the man still shine through for us. "We may be sure, for example (writes Mary B. Harris in her work *Kalidasa, Poet of Nature*), that he was a man of culture and acquainted with the fine arts. This we infer from the number and character of his allusions to painting and music, in his lyrics and dramas." He was a nature student and nature lover, as are most of his race; the great word-artist of nature whose talent is seen at its highest mark in his poem "The Seasons," which also gives rein to the poet's other supreme characteristic of intricate eroticism interwoven with nature. In this poem about the six seasons, described in six books of one hundred and fifty-three cantos, the Indian year's different periods are reviewed in intimate detail, and their inner meaning for lovers clearly explained. The verses abound in parallels; the summer moon fills with jealousy as she beholds the ivory skins of nude, lovely maidens; the wild freshets provoked by the rains embrace the staggering forests which stand on their banks; the clouds swoop down to caress the mountain rocks. Creepers are clinging arms; crimson Asoka flowers, passionate lips; jasmine petals are flashing teeth, and so on.

This eroticism is at its peak in the poem *Kumarasambhava*, wherein in the eighth canto Kalidasa describes the love transports of Parvati and Siva, together in wedlock after numerous trials and privations. The tremendous ascetic has been won over at last, by Parvati, lovely of body; but not before she has undergone discipline too. Kalidasa's descriptions here go far beyond anything attempted, tolerated or probably even imagined by Western minds, yet it is of a part with the rest of the poet's work; supreme, natural consummation of a union well won. It is this poem in particular, to which many spurious stanzas have been added at different times by more modern poets, which has given rise to the legend mentioned earlier that Kalidasa's name covers the writings of several. But the master's work is easy to be distinguished from the verse of his imitators.

The well-known poem *Meghaduta*, or "The Cloud Messenger," contains some of the most beautiful descriptions of Indian scenery ever written. It relates how Yaksha, servant to Cuvera, God of wealth, is punished for allowing his master's garden to be invaded by Indra's elephant by banishment to the remote solitude of Mount Ramagiri. Here he languishes, and eight months of his wretched exile have already passed at the time the poem begins. Observing a cloud floating northward, low overhead, Yaksha addresses it in his lonely grief, imploring it to carry a message to his beloved wife in distant Alaca. This gives Kalidasa opportunity to describe the scenery on its route. The peacock will dance at this sign of approaching rain:

"*Pleased on each terrace dancing with delight*
The friendly peacock hails thy grateful flight:
Delay then, certain in Ujayin[1] *to find*
All that restores the frame or cheers the mind.
Hence with new zeal to Siva homage pay,
The God whom earth, and hell, and heaven obey:

For at his shoulders like a dusky robe,
Mantling impends thy vast and shadowy globe:
Where ample forests, stretched its skirts below,
Projecting trees like dangling limbs bestow;
And vermeil roses fiercely blooming shed
Their rich reflected glow, their blood-resembling red."

H. H. WILSON.

Most of the poem consists of such vivid descriptions as those quoted of the country the cloud will pass over. Fortunately for the exiled Yaksha, Cuvera got to hear of his impassioned prayer and remitted the rest of his exile, uniting him once again with his wife. The slightly pompous Augustan couplets of Mr. Horace Hayman Wilson's translation scarcely do justice to the original poem, which consists of one hundred and fifteen stanzas, each of four lines, the number of syllables in the Sanskrit line being nearly double that of the metre adopted by its English translator. Some idea of the stately sonorous beauty of Kalidasa's original medium may be obtained by reading the following example taken from *Sakuntala*, which describes the King Dushyanta's speculations as to the causes of his melancholy when he sits in the place where once Sakuntala had been.

[1] *Note favourable reference to Ujjayini*

"*Ramyàni Viskya Madhrámscanisamya Sabdān*
Paryutsuki—bhavati yat sukhitopi jantuk
Tac cetasá smarati núna mabodhapúr-vam
Bhávasthiráni jananantarasauhridani."

To fully appreciate Kalidasa's three famous plays, the *Malavikagnimitra*, *Urvasi* or "Won by Valour," and *Sakuntala*, it is necessary to recollect the tradition from which they sprang. Legend relates that India's first actual drama was composed by Pavan, with a main plot obtained from the *Ramayana*. Pavan engraved his play on a smooth, flat stone, till, displeased with his work, he threw it into the sea. Long afterwards an interested prince sent divers down to take a wax impression of what was carved and lay hid. So, legend tells, the first play arrived in India. It is more likely, however, that, as almost everywhere else in the world, drama in India was slowly developed from some equivalent of Europe's mummers or Passion Plays, enacted by priests or temple acolytes for the people's instruction. Such simple, significant religious plays go back to remote antiquity in, for instance, Tibet. In India the principal message most often to be conveyed was that of man's conquest over temptation and self, frequently typified by *rakshas* or other supernatural powers of darkness, and the force of tribulation towards his purification. Behind the great play *Sakuntala* lie the mighty epics, the *Mahabharata* and the *Ramayana;* and behind the *Ramayana*, going back to 1200 B.C., lie the *Sutras*, *Brahmanas*, and, at last, the mystic, questing *Rig Veda:*

"*Who knows the secret? Who proclaimed it here,*
Whence, whence this manifold creation sprang?

The gods themselves came later into being—
Who knows from whence the great creation sprang?"

MAX MÜLLER'S *Translation.*

Who knows whence sprang the poet's fire and skill? But that tradition of suffering well sustained, which leads at last to a fortunate ending, inspires the theme of Kalidasa's play, with, for backcloth, his ardent love of nature—nature the refuge of the Thinking Man, be he ascetic or poet.

The action of *Sakuntala* opens with King Dushyanta of the Lunar race, descendant of Puru, driving in his chariot through the woods. He is in pursuit of an antelope and is about to strike down the hard-pressed beast with his arrow when the voice of a hermit intervenes, bidding the king desist from his wanton slaughter. The king now observes that the part of the woods where he is is blessed by the presence of saints. Fawns feed unafraid on its lawns, and the smoke of aromatic, ceremonial fires rises to hang in the trees. Of a sudden he hears girlish voices. Sakuntala, daughter of a nymph sent down from heaven by Indra to tempt the sage Visvanitra, dwells here with her foster-father, Kanva the hermit, and friends of her age and sex. These damsels are tending the flowers of the grove, talking and laughing, when a bee trespasses on Sakuntala. Laughing, she calls for assistance—and Dushyanta springs to her help, entranced!

Kanva has gone on a pilgrimage to Gujarat. Unguarded by him, encouraged by her companions, Sakuntala, "eastern, subtle, evasive," falls under the spell of Dushyanta's virile attraction. Her passion is amply reciprocated. When the king learns of her descent from the Kshatriya Visvanitra all scruples disappear and they go through the simple form of *gandhava* marriage.

But Dushyanta is forced to return to his court. Before Sakuntala can join him there she unluckily omits to offer certain hospitable rites to a formidable ascetic Durvasas, who lays a curse on the girl. Only as long as she wears Dushyanta's token gift, Durvasas tells her, shall the king remember her face. Sakuntala goes to the court of the king, where he lives surrounded with dancing girls, pleasure gardens, and all luxury can provide. When she comes before him, she is abashed, for Dushyanta does not know her at all. She finds she has dropped her ring in a wayside stream.

Shocked by his distant reception she returns to the forest, resuming her quiet, frugal life. Her son is born there, a lovely, lion-hearted child whom she names Bharata. But, meanwhile, two fishermen have discovered the token ring in the belly of a trapped fish; and so it comes back to the king. At once Dushyanta remembers his *gandhava* marriage and everything that has passed. Frantically, full of penitence, he sets out to seek Sakuntala. He must travel far and undergo many privations before he finds his young wife. But at last he comes on the infant Bharata playing under a tree. Soon Sakuntala joins them, and so at last their blissful reunion occurs and he carries her back to his court. Thus, briefly, ends the beautiful drama of Sakuntala. The plot is slender enough, but that is not what makes this play. Its true glory, as in all Kalidasa's work, lies in its wonderful imagery, its splendid erotics and conjuration of every marvel of nature. Moreover, as Frazer says: "*In the Sanskrit alone can the lines be traced on which the poet's fancy modelled a form such as grew to life in 'Sakuntala,' who spoke in a music, each note of which was skilfully attuned to her own gentle grace.*"

BY COURTESY OF THE BRITISH MUSEUM, LONDON

KABIR

Kabir working as a weaver in Benares.

KABIR

1398–1518?

BY DR. HARI PRASAD SHASTRI

The fifteenth century, which covers the main period of Kabir's life, was marked by disorder and great social agitation.

Mohammad bin Tuglak (1325-1351) left the Moslem Empire in India in a state of chaos. Reducing the people to a state of great poverty and misery through his maladministration and fanatical religious intolerance, he left behind him a country in the grip of famine, plague, and rebellion.

In 1398 Timur invaded India and put to the sword thousands of innocent men, women and children, and carried away most of the wealth of the country that he could lay his hands on. The beautiful city of Delhi was reduced to ruins; Meerut was sacked and everywhere in the north of India, through which the Moslem conqueror passed, there was nothing but ruin and chaos.

Hindu India was not shown the beautiful side of Islam. The great personality of the prophet of Arabia remained a sealed book to them. It can be imagined what they thought of Islam.

F. E. Keay gives the following account of India under Moslem rule, immediately before the birth of Kabir: "During the period of the Sultanate of Delhi, the Hindu religion had been exposed to constant danger. The more ruthless sovereigns, or governors of provinces, often carried out wholesale massacres and destroyed Hindu Shrines, while even milder rulers often used force to bring about their people's conversion. The *Jiziya*, a tax on non-Mohammedans, was generally enforced. . . . Yet in spite of persecution, Hinduism flourished. . . ."

The destruction of their temples and the outrages on their sacred traditions by the north-western invaders did not shake the faith of the Hindus in their religion. In many instances, it was a period of great religious upheavals. The bhakti or devotional school of thought acquired strength and a great wave of devotion of the heart to Vishnu or Hari swept through the land.

Shankaracharya, the supreme exponent of Hinduism, had stressed the importance of bhakti as a means to purify the heart; but his main theme was knowledge or gnosis which alone, according to the Vedic doctrines, leads to the inner enlightenment and ultimate deliverance of the soul from the bonds of nescience.

Rāmānuja (A.D. 1100), a southern teacher of great erudition and a monk of pious character, developed the school of Devotion in his Commentary on the Upanishads, the Gita and the Vyas Suttras. His doctrine is called VISISHTADVAITA, or qualified monism, according to which the universe is the body of God, and His Spirit animating the Universe is the Essence of man. Even in the final reunion with Hari, the spirit retains its individuality. Sri Krishna, the teacher of that most wonderful scripture, the Bhagvad Gita, and the cowherd of Brindavana, is regarded as the supreme incarnation of Vishnu. Ram, the ideal man and king, is also regarded as an incarnation. Man loves his personality and clings to it with tenacity. In Krishna and Ram the Hindu mind found the very ideals of perfection and wisdom that it loved.

Northern India adopted the bhakti school of thought, and the bleeding soul of the Hindus of that time found consolation in the wisdom of compassion, benevolence and self-surrender to Krishna or Ram. Men, women and children found aesthetic, moral and spiritual food in the personality of Krishna and received the spiritual upliftment and ecstasy which made them forget the horrors of their environment and in some cases brought real and abiding peace to their hearts. What more does the spirit of man need?

Poets of outstanding ability and of a cosmopolitan outlook on life sang of Krishna and Ram in their sweet and immortal songs in the Hindi language, the language of the masses.

Many of these spiritual singers were contemporary with Kabir, and it is certain that the child Kabir, born in 1398, heard these sweet devotional lyrics when he was rocked in the cradle by his mother.

Vidyapati, Umapati, Mirabai, and others poured forth their burning love, pure as the waters of the Ganges and the Jumna, and men of every walk of life took up these songs and sang of Radha-Krishna and Seeta-Ram.

The school of bhakti abolished the rigid caste rules, and it was commonly held that anybody who worshipped God belonged to God—irrespective of his caste and birth.

> "*Jat pant puche na koi*
> *Har ko Bhaje so karka hoi.*"

A shoe-maker, Rai Das, was hailed as a saint and worshipped by all on account of his self-transcending love of God.

The Hindu saint whose influence moulded the life of Kabir was Ramanand (1400-1447). A great teacher was Swami Ramanand. His holy life was a source of inspiration to many. Among his disciples were numbered Sena, a barber, Dhanna, a peasant, and Rai Das, a leather worker.

Having travelled through Northern India teaching the doctrine of devotion, Karma, reincarnation and personal piety, Ramanand lived in the holy city of Kashi (Benares) when Kabir was a child. Hundreds flocked to him every morning to join him in his devotion.

One of the results of the contact of Hinduism and Islam was the development of the Sufi school in Islam, which was free from fanaticism and had a close resemblance to the system of Rāmānuja. The Sufi singers mixed freely with the Hindu bhaktas and fraternised with men of other cults.

Sanskrit scholarship received a great reverse during the Moslem rule. The precious books of the Hindus were burned publicly, and the scholars were forced to leave their monasteries, which were committed to the flames. Now the Hindi literature grew up, in the development of which Kabir took a prominent part.

Though the India of the time of Kabir was characterised by misrule and chaos, yet there was great religious activity and literary upheaval in the vernacular.

Benares has ever been the seat of learning and religious fervour in India. Its gorgeous temples, the slow current of the Ganges, the processions of monks, the debates of scholars and the stately flights of steps cannot but impress the mind of one who lives there as well as even the casual visitor. Kabir is said to have passed his boyhood in this city of Lord Shiv, in which Shakya Muni Buddha "turned the wheel of Law" some 1,500 years before Kabir.

Like the lives of other great religious teachers of the past—excepting Mohammed—the life of Kabir is full of legends. The following account may be taken as reasonably correct.

A.D. 1398 is the traditional date of the

birth of the Saint Kabir. According to tradition, Kabir was born in Benares itself, though the *Benares Gazatteer* gives Belhara, a village in the district of Azamgarh, as the place of his birth.

A Brahman virgin widow is said to have given birth to the child who was subsequently called Kabir. The birth is said to have been miraculous. All followers of Kabir admit that Kabir was brought up in the house of a Moslem named Nur Ali or Nura, a weaver, whose wife was named Nima. It is said that a Hindu monk named Ashtanand, who had a knowledge of the real parentage of Kabir, took care to teach him Hindu ideas and ideals when he was a child.

Kabir was a precocious child. He was sent to a Moslem teacher. But he was not satisfied with the teachings given and left him.

From his childhood the religious quest seems to have been his favourite pursuit. The traditional accounts of the birth of Creation and other such matters did not satisfy him.

Kabir Kasauti, an old work taken as authentic by the followers of Kabir, says that in his childhood he did not identify himself definitely with either Hinduism or Islam, and gave offence to many. While playing, he often cried: "Ram, Ram" or "Hari, Hari." The Moslems warned him and said that he was a kafir, an unbeliever. Kabir replied saying: "He who uses violence or rules others, who drinks intoxicants, or seizes the goods of others is a kafir."

He put the tilak (the sacred mark) on his forehead; and used the Janeu (sacred thread). The Brahmans expostulated: "This is not thy religion. Thou hast made thyself a Vaishnavite and callest on Vishnu, Narayan, Hari, Govind; this is our religion." He answered one of their leaders:

BENARES

A general view from the river of the Sacred City of the Hindus, where Kabir lived, learned, worked and taught.

"On my tongue Vishnu, in my eyes Narayan, and in my heart Govind dwells. . . . My meditation is with Hari."

When Kabir was hardly a youth, Ramanand was preaching his doctrine of absorption in God through pure devotion and benevolence. Evidently Ramanand Swami was a magnetic personality. He had thousands of selfless disciples and was held in great esteem by those who knew him. Ramanand was in love with rituals and preached bhakti as the means to God-realisation.

Kabir heard him in the streets of Benares and was profoundly impressed with his teachings and personality. Knowing well that a teacherless mystic is not fitted for a life of higher devotion and contemplation, Kabir applied to Ramanand for initiation. It was after hesitation and trial that Kabir was accepted as a disciple by Ramanand.

It is stated by some writers that Kabir was a *sufi* and a disciple of some Moslem teacher. Professor Wilson, a great authority on the subject, does not hold this view.

Kabir served his teacher personally with devotion, and learned from him not only the theoretical side of the Hindu doctrine, but also the mystic Yoga which he seems to have practised with great patience. Kabir was not a pundit; probably he did not know Sanskrit at all. Having listened to the philosophical controversies that were held between the Benares pundits and his Guru, Kabir acquired a thorough knowledge of Vedanta and Sankhya.

In his private life Kabir continued to work as a weaver, spending a part of his earnings on charity and hospitality to the sadhus and part on Nura.

Once he mysteriously disappeared for a while, then suddenly reappeared, full of light, peace and joy.

Kabir married a woman named Loi. Her name figures in many of his songs. We see a reference to Kabir's marriage in the *Adi Grantha*, the Sikh holy book:

> "*His first wife was ugly, of low caste,*
> *of ill-boding feature . . .*
> *The present wife is beautiful, intelligent, of auspicious features, easily child-bearing.*"

(Quoted by G. H. WESTCOTT.)

There are several references by Kabir in his songs to his son Kamal; some traditions credit him with two sons.

During the early days of his devotion, Kabir encountered much opposition from his family. His mother often reproached him with neglecting his work and insisted on his giving up his religious devotions and study. His outspoken criticism of the rituals, of both Hinduism and Islamism, brought on him the wrath of his fellow-citizens and caused annoyance to his family. After his father's death the burden of supporting the family fell on Kabir. His mother opposed him and wanted him to mind his family affairs only.

Kabir's household affairs undoubtedly suffered on account of his devotion to religious contemplation and the service of his teacher. In a verse he refers to this and says:

> "*O thou who art ever compassionate*
> *to the poor,*
> *I have put all my family into the*
> *boat which is under thy care.*"

In another verse, Kabir makes the following reference to his mother:

> "*Kabir's mother is distressed and*
> *weepeth, saying, O God, how*
> *shall I support my children?*
> *Kabir hath relinquished weaving and*
> *has made God's house his only*
> *support.*"

A true seeker after God is above all dogmatism, sectarianism and fanaticism. We find Kabir in the company of a Moslem teacher, Taqi of Jhusi, near Allahabad, participating in his devotions.

Taqi gave his full spiritual blessings to Kabir and kept a friendly eye on him throughout his life they say.

Kabir's wife, Loi, suffered for want of rice and vegetables in the household, her husband having neglected them. In fact, Kabir was passing through those mystic experiences in which the worldly objects seem to receive no attention from a mystic. She complained of the monks in whose company he passed his time. To this complaint, Kabir replied:

"*These devotees are the support of the drowning,*
Hear, O mis-guided Loi!
Kabir is under the protection of these devotees."

Kabir obtained the full inner illumination "By the grace of my Guru Ramanand." Now all doubts were gone and he saw one Infinite Reality within and without. He became a saint, a liberated being. He had seen God as his own spiritual Self.

Kabir lived a life of voluntary poverty and simplicity. Having seen the eternal beauties of the inner world, the spiritual life, he was in perfect peace and joy. Nothing could add to or subtract from the spiritual joy of his God-vision. He found in the life of contemplation, as Aristotle says, all he needed. The following song is noteworthy:

"*Kabir says, I have neither a thatched roof, nor hut,*
Neither have I a house nor a village.
I think Hari will ask "Who art thou?"
I have neither caste nor name. . . .

. . . .

I have never been acquisitive; Thy name alone,
O Hari, is enough for me."

Kabir says, My heart is full of happiness. . . . Though Kabir lived in poverty he treated his uninvited guests with hospitality. Sometimes Loi borrowed salt and rice to feed a guest. Anybody who knocked at his door was received with joy and given hospitality.

To a certain section of the people Kabir was an impostor and they treated him with contumely.

Sometimes Kabir was called a thief, panderer and dancer. He says:

"*O Ram, thou art my only refuge!*
I have no need to bow to any man!

. . . .

I am free from fellowship or partnership with any one.
Honour or dishonour are just the same to me.

. . . .

Kabir says, The honour of Hari is real.
O give up all, and praise only Ram."

Tradition says that Kabir travelled far into Central Asia and met many Moslem teachers there. But there is no historical evidence to establish this. In the following song we find a reference to his intended visit to Mecca:

"*I was going on a pilgrimage to the Ka'abah, on the road the Lord went with me.*
The Lord began to quarrel with me: 'By whom has this pilgrimage ever been ordered?'"

Kabir travelled extensively in India. Many followed him, a few became his disciples. When he was in Gujrat, a Raja, called Solankhi, went with his Rani to do honour to the Saint and beg the blessing of a son. Kabir replied in the hymn:

"*The world is so mad that no one cares for devotion to God. One comes and begs for a son: My Master, grant me this boon. Another is ill, and asks relief from it. Some come and want the boon of a beauteous bride. Not one comes to buy the Truth. All the world believes a lie. Kabir says, Hear, O Sadhus, what can one make of the blind?*"

Among the disciples of Kabir, his wife Loi, his son Kamal, and one

Dharmadas are prominently mentioned. One Surat Gopal Sahib is also mentioned as one of his chief disciples.

Kabir was summoned by Sikandar Lodi, the reigning sovereign of Delhi, to answer to the charges of infidelity preferred against him both by Hindus and Moslems. The Moslems complained that the weaver outraged the ears of the faithful Moslems with his cries of "Ram, Ram," in the streets. The Hindus complained that he unlawfully used the tilak and Janeu (sacred thread).

When brought before the king, Kabir refused to make obeisance.

After a short conversation the king was convinced of the innocence of Kabir and let him go. But his enemies remained unsatisfied. They approached Taqi, who had influence over the Court, and Taqi pronounced Kabir a political danger, hated both by Hindus and Moslems. Charges of moral turpitude were also made against the saint. It was said that he associated daily with low caste reprobates and women of bad character.

Kabir was again brought before the king and it is said that a few of his close associates were among his accusers. Kabir was fearless and without any bitterness towards them. Death or life is the same to one who has known God. Kabir's answer to the charge of immorality is as follows in his own words:

"*That I know all to be one, what cause of grief is that to others?*
If I am dishonoured, I have lost my own honour: others need pay no heed.
Mean I am, with the mean I would be numbered. . . .
For honour and dishonour I care not; he whose eyes are opened, he will understand.
Kabir says, honour is based on this: renounce all else, sing only Ram. . . ."

(Quoted by ADMAD SHAH.)

The doctors of Moslem law (Qazi) demanded that Kabir should live as a true Moslem and threatened death if he did otherwise. Kabir was not to be daunted. He had overcome all fear of death. He answered: "Know only One Lord animating the hearts of both Hindus and Moslems. He is not the monopoly of either of them. I worship Him in any form I see Him."

They asked him why he called himself Kabir which, in Islam, is one of the names of God. Kabir answered:

"*My name is Kabir; all the world knows this.*
In the three worlds is my name, and happiness is my abode.
Water, air, the seasons, thus I created the world.
The unstruck wave thunders in Heaven, and Soham keeps time.
I made manifest the seed of Brahma . . . God, men and rishis (sages) do not find my end. Kabir's saints alone can find it. . . . Hear, O Sikandar, I am a Pir of both religions."

Kabir was condemned as a heretic and having been bound with chains was thrown into the river. The tradition says that "the bonds could not hold him nor the water drown." He was thrown, bound in chains, before infuriated elephants. But the elephants did not hurt him as Kabir "was protected by the power of the name of Hari."

Kabir lived to the age of 120, and voluntarily gave up his body in a town near the holy city of Benares. "Ram is in Benares and also in every other place," said Kabir when his disciples asked him to go to Benares to die.

Tradition says that a dispute arose as to the disposal of Kabir's body, between the two rivals—Hindus and Mohammedans. An appeal to arms seemed imminent. A passing holy man appeared and bade the rivals to raise the sheet that covered the saint Kabir's body. They did so, and to their great surprise, found beneath a heap of fresh and fragrant flowers.

KABIR BEFORE A KING

An old mural painting at Amritsa—the figure of Kabir is marked with a K.

Kabir wrote in Hindi, an off-shoot of Sanskrit. Evidently he was not versed in Sanskrit—which was, long, long before Kabir, a highly-developed language. Kabir's Hindi is simple and his style is attractive. He invented many new metres and wrote verse in so graceful and flowing a language that we can call him one of the fathers of Hindi poetry. The great Hindi poets, Keshav Das, Sur Das, Tul'si Das, and Behari Das, who compare favourably with Dante and Shakespeare, were indebted to Kabir.

Most of the verses of Kabir are hymns of devotion, mysticism and discipline. He seldom uses flowery language. Like the great Chinese poets of the Tang and Sung periods Kabir is a poet without making efforts to be one. In his simple, natural way poetry flows from him like water from a fountain. Kabir rises to great heights when he tries to describe the indescribable spiritual experiences.

> "*On this tree is a bird: it dances in the joy of life.*
> *No one knows whence it is: nor what the burden of its music may be?*
> *Where the branches throw a deep shade, there does it have its nest; and it comes in the evening and flies away in the morning and says not a word of that which it knows.*
> *No one can tell me of this bird that sings within me. . . . .*
> *It dwells within the unattainable, the infinite and the Eternal, and no one marks when it comes and goes.*
> *Kabir says: 'O brother Sadhu! Deep is the mystery. Let wise men seek to know where rests the bird.*"

(Translated by TAGORE.)

An oft-quoted verse of Kabir which shows the profundity of his vision is:

"That body in which Love does not dwell is a crematorium; that heart which is without Love is as the blacksmith's bellows, breathing but lifeless."

In some of his songs he is rugged like Walt Whitman, and very unconventional:

"If union with God can be obtained by going about naked
All the beasts of the forests would be saints!
If God is not seen within, it matters not whether we walk clad in goat skin or nude.
If spiritual release can be obtained by shaving, then all sheep should be taken as saved.
If continence leads to God-vision, then all eunuchs are saints.
Kabir says, Hearken, O Sadhus,
There is no release without Ram's name."

Kabir was a great singer. Dressed as a poor wandering devotee, drunk with the love of God, he used to go about with a hand-drum, pouring forth his heart in his songs. He composed thousands of songs, many of which are orally known, but not yet included in any anthology.

Many of the songs attributed to Kabir are not his. Some Punjabi songs are credited to him, but it is very doubtful whether Kabir wrote in that dialect. The songs contained in the Bijak of Kabir are his own composition. *Kabir Kasauti* is taken as one of the genuine works of Kabir. Most, if not all, of the *Sakhes* or rhyming couplets, conveying the inner realization of the saint, are his own. The couplets are of unsurpassed beauty. A few of them are given below:

"A Guru should be as a knife grinder, removing the rust of a lifetime in an instant."

"My Lord is a great trader, in merchandise he deals; neither weights nor scales he needs, but in his own hands this great world he weighs and feels."

"He who sows for you thorns, for him you should sow flowers; you will have blossoms at the time of Spring; he will regret to find thorns."

"He may drink the cup of love who gives his head to God; the covetous cannot give all, but only take the name of love."

"The tree does not keep its fruits for its own use, nor the river its water; for the benefit of others has the Sadhu incarnated as man."

"The gardener comes to the garden and seeing him, the buds cry out, 'The full-blown flowers are culled to-day, to-morrow our turn will come.'"

(Translated by REV. WESTCOTT.)

Kabir had four chief disciples and eight more to whom he imparted his inner teachings. Each of them has composed songs, attributing them to Kabir. It is, therefore, not easy to say which of the songs credited to Kabir are by him. *Sukh Ni Dhan* (Treasure of Happiness), *Guru Mahatmya* (Greatness of the Guru), and *Amarmul* (Root of Immortality) contain the spiritual teachings of Kabir, but they are not his compositions. Dharma-Das, a disciple of Kabir, is perhaps the author of one of them. The dialogue between Kabir and the great Hath Yogi teacher, Gorakhnath, containing many deep spiritual truths, is not Kabir's composition as the language is more modern and the style not so simple as that of Kabir.

The basis of Kabir's teachings is the strict monotheism of the Upanishads. He places the Lord of the Universe in the heart of man as his higher Self, where alone the soul can discover Him. The following quotations from Bijak establish Kabir's monotheism:

"*He is one; there is no second.*
Ram, Khuda, Shakti, Shiv are one.
By the One name I hold fast: Kabir proclaims this aloud."

In the *Adi-granth* of Mahatma Nanak, probably a disciple of Kabir, Kabir is reported to have said:

"*The one Name, like the tree of life, saveth mankind.*
That One living God is everywhere present, and there is no second."

Kabir is a follower of the pure Advaita School of Vedic thought as interpreted by the greatest of the Indian philosophers, Shankaracharya. Kabir worshipped the self-conditioned aspect of the attributeless God, through His own power called Maya. He held that the worship of the self-conditioned leads to the contemplation and realisation of the Absolute. Kabir describes Him as compassionate, most lovable, omniscient and the saviour, with whom man can hold intercourse in his being.

Kabir says:

"*He Himself is the tree, the seed, and the form.*
He Himself is the flower, the fruit and the shade. . . .
He is the breath, the word, and the meaning."

Kabir admits Maya, the principle of limitation which, though unreal, yet is the root cause of the false knowledge of duality.

Kabir finds Love or bhakti the easiest way to realise the Infinite within one's own Self. He is positive that God can be seen only in the being of man and that then the whole Universe becomes a mirror reflecting the bliss and beauty of God.

Many of the most beautiful hymns of Kabir are the expressions of his heart's devotion to the Lord immanent and yet transcendent. The name of God dearest to Kabir is Ram. He sometimes calls Him Hari and when he speaks of His mystic names uses the sacred word *Om*. The repetition of the name of Ram, according to the Saint, removes all the sins of man and makes him fit to see God in his heart. Kabir says in his Bijak:

"*Hardly a friend have I at all:*
What more shall I say, O brother. . . .
Sitting in the air, studying Yoga, Vedas, rites and astrology, they are demented.
. . . Kabir says the hope of the Yogi and the Jangam is withered.
If they repeat, like the bird Chatrik, the name of Ram, their abode in bhakti is sure."

Kabir called compassion the greatest virtue, and non-attachment to sense-objects the key to inner tranquillity in which Ram is mirrored as our soul. Mind, free of all earthly desires, devoted to the service of the *guru*, rises to the divine state, through love of Ram.

"*Without the guru there is no release.*"

Kabir loved his guru Ramanand as God and he recommends this practice to his disciples.

Meditation on the transitoriness of the world and the incertitude of life are the favourite themes of Kabir. Unless one recognises this axiomatic truth, one is not fitted for the life of Yoga. Kabir is a great moralist and bases the fabric of his ethics on the two above-mentioned principles. As long as one loves the world of duality, one cannot overcome sin.

Kabir describes the six Chakras (centres of consciousness) in the human body minutely, and advises a Yogi to meditate on the name of Ram in the Chakras. Peace and celestial vision, music of the devas, rambles in the inner gardens of beauty supreme, are some of the experiences resulting from the meditation on the Chakras. The following song expresses Kabir's experiences of the inner world of the Chakras:

"*Where Spring holds sway the twelve months through, few have conceived the perfection there.*
Where light as rain pours down in ceaseless streams, where the forest grows green in all its eighteen regions—
Where unrestrained the waters well up within, and the cleansing air bears away all foulness—
No trees are there, yet heaven is bright with blossoms.
Shiv and Brahma desire to drink its perfume."

According to Kabir the human body is the Universe in miniature and the trained mind can see in it the regions of saints, celestial beings and other spheres of unsurpassed beauty and divine music. Kabir locates the Supreme Being, Ram, in the Chakra situated in the crown of the head which he calls Sat-Loka. It may be stated that all this is described in the pre-Buddhist mysticism of India.

Unlike other Hindu saints, Kabir condemns idol-worship and sees no meaning in rituals and pilgrimages. He has little patience with asceticism either. No wonder he incurred the hostility of the orthodox by his sharp condemnation of the outer practices of Hinduism. He did not favour the Moslems either and condemned their Namaz and recitation of the Quran:

"*Qazi, what is the book you discourse on?*
Are you not jangling and wrangling always; nothing of wisdom do you know,
Leave these distractions, meditate on Ram, O foolish mind."

(REV. KEAY.)

Kabir condemns the caste system of the Hindus. To him a Brahman who reads the Vedas and a cultivator who tills the ground are equal. All mankind is one family and God is the supreme head of it.

"*If birth from a Brahman mother makes you a Brahman,*
Why did not you come by any other way . . . ?
Saith Kabir, renounce family, caste, lineage; become an ant and thou canst pick up and eat the sugar."

The doctrines of Karma and transmigration, the basic Hindu teachings, are upheld by Kabir:

"*The soul assumes many forms, according to its merits.*
After birth and death it again comes to a body."

Kabir believes in man's ability to see God, in this very life. We can see from his words that he claims to have seen God, the fountain-head of all Joy, Truth and Beauty. Here is the personal testimony of Kabir as translated by Tagore:

"*I have known in my body the Sport of the Universe:*
I have escaped from the error of this world.
The inward and the outward are become as one sky; the Infinite and the finite are united; I am drunk with the sight of All!"

. . . . . .

In another song quoted in the *Adigranth* of Nanak, Kabir says:

"*I have met God who dwelleth in the heart.*
When a stream is lost in the Ganges,
It becometh the Ganges itself.
Kabir is similarly lost in God by invoking Him;
I have become the true One and need not go elsewhere."

Kabir advocates recourse to a Guru and fellowship of holy men. The time passed in the society of fellow-disciples and holy men is best spent. It is essential that we should avoid the society of the worldly-minded and cultivate fellowship with the spiritually-minded.

The goal of the soul, according to Kabir, is reabsorption into God and to become the soul of the Universe. It was not a theoretical doctrine to the saint; he had realised it in his life and he proclaimed it to all who came to hear him. Kabir does not desire wealth, fame or honour as these are all unreal.

"*I shall not die like the rest of the world.*
I have now met Him who remaineth.
The soul is not born, though men think it is; it is free from birth and death.
When the idea of birth and death departeth from man's mind, he shall forever be absorbed in God. . . .
As my attention is fixed on God, I no longer expect to suffer transmigration;
Even in life I am absorbed in the Infinite."

Students of the Hindu Upanishads will see that Kabir speaks the language of the rishis of the Himalayas.

Kabir is one of the rare Hindu saints who speak the language of the Quran and he quotes, approvingly, many of its teachings. His acquaintance with Islam is not superficial. He often mentions Adam and Eve and his references to the Moslem customs are significant. He disapproves of the rite of circumcision and discourages pilgrimage to Mecca.

"*They fast all day, at night they slaughter the cow.*
Here murder, there devotion; how can this please God?
O Qazi, thy One God is in thee, thou beholdest Him not by thought and reflection.
Thou gainest nothing by reading and study, O madman, since thou regard'st Him not in thy heart. . . .
If thou prayest with deception in thy heart,
What availeth thee thy pilgrimage to Mecca?"

Whether Kabir founded the Order called Kabir Panth is open to doubt. He was most anxious to see the unrighteous and the ignorant restored to the path of devotion and compassion, and he often said that the chief duty of a holy man is to help others to the path of virtue and unity with God. Kabir was indifferent to wealth and loved simplicity. The order called Kabir Panth is rich and the life of its Chief is far from being simple.

There are two main sections of the Order: One has its headquarters at Kabir Chaura at Benares, and the other at Chattisgarh, in the Central Provinces of India.

The immediate successor to Kabir, at Benares, was Surat Gopal Das, one of the favourite disciples of the saint, who is said to be the real founder of the Order. The last head of the Order, at Benares, was Ram Bilas. The head of the Order is elected, and the qualifications he is supposed to have are piety, learning and ability to teach the doctrine of Kabir.

There are two shrines to Kabir in the Benares headquarters; one is in the custody of the Hindus and the other is in the hands of Moslems. There is a shrine dedicated to Kamal also. The ritual consists of singing the hymns of Kabir, silent meditation, *arti* and distribution of *prasad.* There are many centres of the Order in the various parts of Northern and Central India and the Province of Bombay. Some of the centres are wealthy. The monks attached to the Order travel about singing the songs of their first Guru. They are supported by the Centre and in the rainy season they return to their monastery for study, meditation and instructions by the Mahant (abbot).

The Order of Kabir is above the caste system of the Hindus and he who joins the fraternity gives up all caste prejudices. The Shudras, or the untouchables of India, are welcome to the Order and the Order has done much to elevate the lot of these unfortunate followers of the Hindu Dharma.

The followers of Kabir are strict vegetarians and abstain from the use of alcohol.

The influence of Kabir is noticeable in many sects of India. The Sikhs of the Punjab, the noble followers of the Guru Nanak, perhaps one of the disciples of Kabir himself, acknowledge Kabir as one of the great Mahatmas and sing his hymns daily. The Vairagis, the Udasees and others are all lovers of Kabir and read his literature. Kabir is quoted by the Moslem Sufis freely. In the mystic circles of the Yogis he is regarded with reverence and his exposition of the Chakras is used by them.

In the Himalayan regions, the home of the Upanishadic learning and the abode of the high Sanyasins, Kabir is not mentioned at all. There is no known centre of the Kabir Panth in these sacred places. Perhaps the reason is that Kabir's hymns are in Hindi, and the Himalayan Sanyasins study the Vedantic doctrine in Sanskrit. Kabir was not a dialectician, whereas the Hindu monks love logic and metaphysics.

Kabir was an avadhut. Having realised God as his Self he lived in ecstasy and like Sur Das his songs welled forth from his being, without any conscious effort on his part. Men like Kabir are not in favour of Orders and are alive to the future contradictions and inconstancies that such Orders are likely to create.

There are fifty articles of the Kabir Panthi doctrine, a few of which are quoted below:

THE TWO SHRINES AT MAGHAR

The Hindu shrine is in front, with the small Sadhu's tomb, and a corner of the Moslem math can be seen in the distance.

1. One must devote oneself to the contemplation of the One all-pervading, attributeless Brahman, called Sat Purush. Brahman is known only by means of the Sat Guru.

2. Brahman and Kabir are one. If any one thinks that Kabir and Brahman —Guru and God—are not one, he will not find God.

3. One ought to serve one's Guru with body, mind and wealth, place reliance on his word and obey him. He who thinks there is any difference between Guru and God will find that all his devotion and meditation will be in vain.

4. One ought to love and serve one's fellow Sat-sangees. All devotees of God are worthy of great respect.

5. One ought to count all living creatures as one's own body and treat them with kindness. One ought to refrain from giving any pain, at any place or any time, to any living creature.

6. All intoxicating drinks are forbidden.

7. The only way to salvation is the Essence of the Word (Sar Sabda).

8. Without true love, devotion is fruitless.

9. Without liberality no one can attain salvation.

10. Do not curse any one, nor speak evil, nor think unkindly of any one.

11. So long as one thinks much of one's body, and nourishes it, as if it were real, one cannot give full obedience to one's Guru.

Let me conclude this short article on Kabir with the following Sakhis:

"My song is new: none understands
the strain.
Whoever has perceived this word;
he is a King of Kings."

. . . .

"O Kabir, deck Thyself in the garments of love, and dance.
To him is given honour, whose body
and soul live Truth."

BY COURTESY OF THE BRITISH MUSEUM

TELLING THE STORIES OF KRISHNA

Uddhava, the messenger of Krishna, talking to the Gopis. Kangra School: about 1820.

TUL'SI DAS

WHO SANG THE SONGS OF RAMA

1532–1623

BY KISSANE KEANE

ONE day during the early half of the seventeenth century, in the city of Benares, a poet laid down his pen for the last time and closed his eyes on this world. A great man had died. To-day, more than three hundred years after his death, his work lives on, wielding enormous influence among the people for whom it was written, and familiar to scholars the world over, who recognise it for the work of an inspired genius.

Tul'si Das, or, as it is sometimes written, Tulasi Dasa, was both a great poet and a great religious reformer. Though he founded no new sect but accepted, and re-interpreted, the established Hindu theology, yet his teaching claimed the attention not only of his contemporaries but grew yearly in power and influence until, at the present time, it is followed by some ninety or a hundred million Hindus of Upper India, who base their religious and spiritual beliefs, and their theories of moral conduct, upon his doctrines. In the direct succession of master and pupil, Tul'si Das came seventh in descent from Ramananda, a teacher of the Vedanta doctrine of Rāmānuja, who established a schism of his own, giving to his disciples the significant name of the "Liberated," admitting all castes equally to the fellowship, and teaching

BY COURTESY OF THE BRITISH MUSEUM

BRINGING OUT THE BOW OF SHIVA

From the Ramayana: Chamba School: about 1800.

BY COURTESY OF THE BRITISH MUSEUM

DASARATHA AND JANAKA

Janaka, father of Sita, discussing his daughter's marriage with Rama. From the Ramayana: Chamba School: about 1800.

the people in their own tongue. This revolution in religious ideas paved the way for Tul'si Das, who accepted these doctrines but developed them in a manner essentially his own.

Tul'si Das was indeed a poet of the people. He wrote in the vernacular—claiming the right of common speech as a medium for religious teaching—and wrote with extraordinary vigour and power, illustrating his imaginative conceptions with vivid descriptions, drawn from his observation of Nature, and with poetic similes, always beautiful and apt but never reaching beyond the understanding of the ordinary man. He was, moreover, a man of experience. In spite of his brilliant gifts of language and of vision, in spite of his friendships with famous men of the time like Todar Mall, finance minister to Akbar, and Man Singh of Amber, his native countrymen knew him for a simple man who had lived among them freely; praying, teaching, begging, sharing with them the ordinary joys and sorrows of daily life. Into his works he put the wisdom of his experience, his concepts are sane and lofty, the words he uses to clothe them are direct, colourful and arresting. It is small wonder that his people throughout successive generations have acknowledged him as their poet and their guide.

There are, unfortunately, only a few facts about the poet's life that can be authoritatively ascertained. It seems that he was born in 1532 under the auspices of an unlucky star. Children born in "Abhuktamula" were supposed to be destined to destroy their fathers out of the wickedness of their own natures, and were generally abandoned by their parents. Tul'si Das himself says that this is what happened to him. He was then picked up by a wandering

Sadhu and travelled over India with him as his disciple, getting what education he could, and learning no doubt the story of Rama which he was afterwards to write. He was by birth a Sarayupaina Brahman and the names of his mother and father and immediate relations are known at any rate to tradition.

He married a wife to whom he became deeply devoted. Her name was Ratnavali, and she was brought up very piously to worship Rama in her father's house. A son was born to Ratnavali and Tul'si Das, but died before growing to manhood. After this it seems that Ratnavali returned to her father's house, and it is said that when Tul'si Das, anxious and distressed, followed her there, she would not be persuaded to go back with him, but told him that he must devote himself to the worship of the holy Rama. Tul'si Das then abandoned house, home and family life and became an ascetic, a wandering Vaishnava. He made the city of Audh his headquarters where, at the age of forty-three, he started to write his great work, the Ramayana. Later, some difference of opinion about a point of discipline arose between the poet and his fellow-believers and he moved to Benares to continue his writing and teaching. He lived to a great age, and though, as an old man, he was attacked by plague he recovered from this disease but died shortly afterwards in the year 1623.

So many legends have grown up around the life and the name of Tul'si Das that it would be impossible to quote them all. Many of them may be based on truth, others are obviously fabulous. It may be worth while to note briefly one or two of these stories which are given wide credence among the poet's followers and have acquired the authority of tradition.

It is said that Tul'si Das, as an old

BY COURTESY OF THE BRITISH MUSEUM

THE MARRIAGE OF RAMA AND SITA

From the Ramayana: Chamba School: about 1800.

BY COURTESY OF THE BRITISH MUSEUM

ATTACKED BY THE DEMON HOST

Rama and Sita with Lakshman in their retreat in the forest are attacked by Khara and Dashan, sons of Ravan. From the Ramayana: Kangra School: about 1858.

man, came on one of his travels to his wife's village and called for hospitality at his father-in-law's house without knowing where he was. His wife, also an old woman now, tended him, and after a while recognised her husband's voice. She could not decide whether to make herself known to him or whether to say nothing, since he was now an ascetic and her presence might be only an embarrassment to him. However, watching him at his food she discovered that he carried about with him on his travels various luxuries like pepper, camphor, condiments and other delicacies, and it seemed to her that he could not be as strict an observer of ascetic discipline as she had thought. She then made herself known to him, exhorting him either to allow her to stay with him, since he already took about with him his worldly goods, or else to abandon all and devote himself altogether to spiritual things. Tul'si Das, much moved, departed and gave away everything he had to Brahmans, while his wife became even more pious and devout than before.

At the beginning of his greatest work, the Ramayana, he defends his use of the vernacular for his writings and there are also stories told of his replies to Pandits who questioned this preference for the common tongue when, as they knew, he was learned in the pure Sanskrit language. Once he likened his work to an earthen vessel filled with ambrosia and compared the flowery unimportance of his Sanskrit-writing contemporaries to jewelled cups filled with poison; another time he asked them who would wear silken clothing when the useful protection of a coarse woollen blanket was more necessary.

There is one miracle told of Tul'si Das which is said to have converted thousands of people to lives of holiness. It was at Benares that the poet, hearing a repentant murderer calling on the name of the Lord Rama, blessed him and gave him alms and food. The Brahmans of Benares, however, were troubled about this and wanted to know how so low a man as a murderer could be forgiven his sin, and why the poet declared him purified. Tul'si Das agreed to prove to them that the power of the name of Rama was enough to bring salvation to the faithful. He told them that the sacred bull of Siva would eat out of the murderer's hand as proof that his crime was absolved. The man was taken to the temple where the bull at once took food from his hands. Tul'si Das was proved right and thereby illustrated the great mercy of Rama towards all sinners who would repent.

There are many more famous legends long connected with the poet's name, such as that of the grateful ghost who introduced him to the God Hanuman, who in turn allowed him a vision of the Lord Rama and Lakshman; that of Rama himself, disguised as a handsome, dark watchman, guarding the poet's house with bow and arrow; that of the Brahman widow on her way to the funeral pile, whose husband he restored to life; that of the poet's imprisonment by the emperor for refusing to work a miracle and produce the God Rama before the court, his delivery by Hanuman's army of monkeys and the Emperor's subsequent promise to leave Rama's holy abode, the city of Delhi, and build a new city and fort elsewhere. All these, and others as fascinating, have become part of the poetic tradition asso-

BATTLE BETWEEN VANA AND KRISHNA

From the Mahabharata: Kangra School: about 1858.

ciated with the life of Tul'si Das. At the moment, however, it is perhaps of more importance to turn to a short study of his work.

Some twenty works have been, at one time or another, attributed to the pen of this poet, but only twelve—six of greater importance and six of less—are certainly his. The most famous, and undoubtedly the greatest of these, is the *Ramayana*—The Lake of the Deeds of Rama. The influence of its teaching, as of the beautiful language used, has permeated every class of the Hindu community; appreciated alike by young and old, it is as familiar among the highest as among the humblest in the land. It is an epic poem dealing with the life and deeds of the Lord Rama, and into the poetic structure are woven the doctrines of whole-hearted worship, faith, incarnate divinity and individual mortality—in fact, all the tenets and teaching of the poet himself. His characters are living, heroically drawn people, who, though dignified with sublime powers, are nevertheless endowed with poignant human qualities that enable them to enter fully into the complex emotional situations of life.

The language varies with the content and is used at times as a definite sound-value to echo the sense. It can be gentle and tender and most moving if the poet is describing death or leave-taking; it can be easy and charming if he is concerned with childhood or the tranquillity of Nature; or it can be majestic, stirring and rugged in the passages dealing with storm, battle, or calamity.

He uses a multitude of similes of a simple and direct kind, drawn almost entirely from Nature: "Monarchs give honour to the lowest of their servants, in the same way as fire tops itself with smoke and a hill with grass"; "At sight of him the kings all cowered down as partridges shrinking beneath the swoop of a hawk"; "Obedient to the will of its lord, the gallant steed was as beautiful as a peacock, that dances in response to a thunder-cloud, whose dark mass is irradiated by the stars of heaven and the fitful lightning."

It is, of course, not possible in a short extract to give a complete idea of so infinitely varied a style. The best known quotation from the Ramayana is probably the description of the rainy season and its passing, a passage of superbly balanced poetry. I shall, however, quote another passage of descriptive action which is written in a tenser and more vital manner. The occasion is the breaking by Rama of the great bow of Shiva. Janak, the king, has declared that only the man who can bend the bow shall wed his beautiful daughter Sita. Many warriors have already tried and failed. In front of the crowd and all the kings and princes the young Rama draws near the great bow:

"*Rama first looked at the crowd who all stood dumb and still as statues; then the gracious Lord turned from them to Sita, and perceived her yet deeper concern; perceived her to be so terribly agitated, that a moment of time seemed an age in passing. If a man die of thirst for want of water, when he is once dead, of what use to him is a lake of nectar? What good is the rain when the crop is dead? What avails regret when a chance has been lost? Thinking thus to himself as he gazed at Sita, the Lord was enraptured at the sight of her singular devotion, and after making a reverential obeisance to his Guru, he took up the bow with most superlative ease; as he grasped it in his hand, it gleamed like a flash of lightning; and again as he bent it, it seemed like the vault of heaven. Though all stood looking on, before any one could see, he had lifted it from the ground, raised it aloft and drawn it tight, and in a moment broken it in halves; the awful crash re-echoed through the world."* [1]

After a few stanzas describing the joyful excitement of the people, the gods, and the kings, the poet goes on to describe the beauty of Sita, who, with rapture in her heart, brings forward the wreath of victory: "As she drew near and beheld Rama's beauty, she stood motionless like a figure on the wall, till a watchful attendant roused her, saying —'Invest him with the ennobling wreath.' At the word she raised the wreath with both her hands, but was too much overcome by emotion to drop it; till as the lotus, flower and stalk, shrinks at the moonlight, so her hand and arm drooped in the glory of his moonlike face. At the sight of his beauty her handmaids broke into song, while Sita let fall the wreath upon his breast."

[1] *This and the previous extracts are from F. S. Growse's translation of "The Ramayana."*

The *Kavittavali* is another long work dealing with the life of Rama, but from another point of view. It emphasises the majestic and heroic side of Rama's character and is full of stirring adventure and action. There are some fine and wild descriptions of battle and a fear-inspiring picture of a mighty fire in the crowded city of Lanka. The book ends with a great victory, followed by a number of hymns in praise of Rama.

The *Gitavali* is a work of an altogether different nature. Though it, too, is devoted to the career of Rama, the largest part of the book describes the

BY COURTESY OF THE BRITISH MUSEUM

RAMA AND HANUMAN GOING INTO BATTLE

From the Ramayana: Kangra School: about 1800.

childhood and early life of the God and his baby brothers. The narrative flows along easily and gently, sounding the notes of tenderness and natural affection throughout. As the children play about the courtyards, learning to walk, to chatter, to understand what they see, and as their mothers watch over them, delighting in their pranks and guarding their first footsteps, one remembers again that Tul'si Das described life as he knew it. Many a countryman of his, reading the simple and poetic tale, must have felt that it was an account of his own or his son's infancy. A brief extract may serve to give an idea of the work:

"*Full of happiness Kausalya caresses her little darling. She lets him cling to her finger as she teaches him to walk in the fair courtyard of the palace. Runu jhunu, runu jhunu, sweetly tinkles the bell-girdle on his waist, sweetly tinkle the anklet bells on his feet, as she helps him along. On his wrists are bracelets . . . a spotless, saffron-coloured little silken coat adorns his dark limbs. His bonny face is a picture, with two little teeth peeping out behind his dawn-rosy lips and stealing away the hearts of all. . . . As he hears his mother snap her fingers he crows with delight, and when he lets go her finger from his hand she is filled with dismay. He tumbles down and pulls himself up upon his knees, and babbles with joy to his brothers when his mother shows him a piece of cake: and she, as she looks at all his pretty baby ways,*

BY COURTESY OF THE BRITISH MUSEUM

ALIRUDDHA'S BATTLE WITH THE DANAVAS

Kangra School: 1858.

is drowned in love, and cannot bear her happiness. . . . Saith Tul'si Das, the man who loveth not this sweetness, hath no soul, and his life in this world is vain."[1]

The poet takes on a very different character in his *Vinaya Pattrika*—the Book of Petitions. He writes as a suppliant addressing his petitions, or hymns, firstly to the lower gods of heaven and finally to the Lord Rama himself. It is conceived in a spirit of humility and prayer. Tradition has it that it was the God Hanuman who advised Tul'si Das to write as a complainant in the court of the Lord himself, so that the court would be empowered to punish the Evil Spirit of the Age who had threatened the poet with death unless he would stop teaching the increase of piety among the people.

The *Krishnavali* is a work about the authenticity of which the opinion of scholars is divided. It is a collection of songs in honour of the God Krishna and is written in a slightly different dialect and in a completely different style from the other works from the poet's pen.

A collection of verses, mostly selected from Tul'si Das' other works, and having very little connection with each other, is called the *Dohavali*. It is possible that it was compiled as an anthology by a later admirer, or, since it is partly composed of original verses, it may have been drawn up by the poet himself, (some say at the request of his friend, the great Todar Mall) as a kind of short religious guide. Another vexed question is the authenticity of a work called the *Sat'sai* which shares a number of verses with the *Dohavali* and seems in the other verses to betray the hand of an

[1] *This translation is by G. A. Grierson.*

BY COURTESY OF J. C. FRENCH, ESQ.

ALLIANCE BETWEEN RAMA AND SUGRIVA

From the Ramayana: early 18th century.

imitator although the teaching is in accord with Tul'si Das' principles and seems in fact to be a systematic exposition of his religious theories.

Among the lesser works there is the *Ramajna* which is a collection of omens, or commands of the holy Rama. It is consulted as a religious guide and as a means of divining the outcome of anything to be undertaken. The *Vairagya-Sandipini* is a religious poem dealing with the true nature and greatness of a holy man and the attainment of perfect peace. It is written in a tone of calm devotion and assurance and is full of noble precepts. Of peace the poet writes:

"*The adornment of the night is the moon, the adornment of the day is the sun. The adornment of the servant of the Lord is Faith, and the adornment of that Faith is Perfect Knowledge. The adornment of meditation is total Self-surrender to the Lord, and the adornment of Self-surrender is pure and spotless Peace.*"

Of the Holy Man he says:

"*Very cool is he, very pure, free from all taint of earthly desire. Count him as free, his whole existence rapt in Peace.*"[1]

The *Ram Lala Nahachu* and the *Barawe* are shorter poems, again celebrating incidents in the life of Rama or aspects of his character; while the *Parbati Mangal* and *Janaki Mangal* are both marriage songs, the former describing the wedding of the beautiful and

[1] *Translation by G. A. Grierson.*

BY COURTESY OF THE SECRETARY OF STATE FOR INDIA

THE BREAKING OF THE BOW

From the Ramayana. From the Johnson Collection in the India Office, London.

innocent daughter of the Himalayas with the fearful Shiva, and the latter relating the story of the betrothal and marriage of the young Rama to his bride, Sita.

There is a short poem by Tul'si Das on the death of his friend Todar Mall. It has been translated by G. A. Grierson, and as it is a specimen of the poet's style which is complete in itself I give it here.

"*Lord of but four small villages, yet a mighty monarch whose kingdom was himself: in this age of evil hath the sun of Todar set.*

The burden of Ramas's love, great though it was, he bare unto the end; but the burden of this world was too great for him and so he laid it down.

Tul'si's heart is like a pure fount in the garden of Todar's virtues; and when he thinketh of them, it overflows, and tears well forth from his eyes.

Todar hath gone to the dwelling-place of his Lord, and therefore doth Tul'si refrain himself; but hard it is for him to live without his pure friend.

As a theologian, Tul'si Das was a man of vision and as a poet he was able to immortalise his own interpretation of the Hindu religion. He upheld the view that there is one Supreme Being who, out of his great mercy, put off his divinity for a time, to become incarnate in the person of Rama, and so to procure salvation for the infinitely sinful nature of man. The God, therefore, returning once more to heaven to live forever in perfection, has experienced the life of a man and can understand and sympathise with the trials and temptations of humanity. The Supreme Being is the only representative of true existence, being in itself an eternal, complete and absolute unity. Tul'si Das, however, does not allow this conception of divine perfection to be reduced simply to an abstraction. He insists on imbuing even the most Holy with the attributes of personality, and presents his God, not a relentless and avenging tyrant, but as a loving, merciful and all-knowing spirit. Teaching the universal fatherhood of God he lays stress upon the doctrine that grows from this, namely, the universal brotherhood of man.

It is impossible to exaggerate the influence that the great works of Tul'si Das have had upon the lives and learning of his own countrymen. Above all, the *Ramayana* as a creation in literature and as an exposition of a religion, stands supreme; it is known and loved by every Hindu from the Punjab in the west to eastern Bengal, and from the Vindhyas northward to the ranges of the Himalayas.

BANKIMCHANDRA CHATTERJEE

BANKIMCHANDRA CHATTERJEE

BY DR. M. M. BHATTACHARJEE

1838–1894

Bankimchandra Chatterjee's name is almost a household word in Bengal, but the available materials for his biography are rather meagre. The history of his early life is almost unknown. His father, Jadavchandra Chatterjee, was born in 1794. Though Bengal was then under the government of the East India Company, traces of Mohammedan administration still continued in the province, and Jadavchandra learnt Persian—a knowledge of which was then considered to be a passport to office. But he could read the signs of the times and soon took to the study of English. He was intelligent and hardy, and is said to have walked the whole distance from Calcutta to Cuttack, where his elder brother was an officer in the Government department for the collection of salt-tax. He was soon provided for, and he took to his work with zest. There was a welcome change in his career when he was appointed Treasurer at Midnapore in 1836. In 1838 he was appointed a Deputy Collector at Hoogly.

This was the year when Bankimchandra was born in the village of Kantalpara in the district of 24-Parganas (June 27). It also witnessed the birth of three other distinguished men of Bengal, viz. Keshabchandra Sen, the theistic reformer; Hemchandra Banerjee, the poet, and Krishnadas Pal, the public man. Bankim had two elder brothers and a younger one. His school life was partly spent at Midnapore where his father was a Deputy Collector. Though almost nothing is known about his juvenile habits, tastes and activities, tradition mentions that Bankim was not fond of games.

The Hoogly College was a noted educational centre in those days, and Bankim joined it in 1847. Here it was that his merit first attracted notice. The College produced many distinguished scholars, but it was believed that none of them could stand comparison with Bankim except Dwarkanath Mitra, who distinguished himself later as a very brilliant judge of the High Court of Calcutta. Bankim had studious habits, and the range of his studies was far beyond the average. In 1857 he joined Presidency College where Keshabchandra Sen was a contemporary of his.

In the same year there broke out in India the Sepoy Mutiny, which had far-reaching consequences. It led to the transfer of the government of the country from the East India Company to the British Crown, and made for stable and efficient administration by stamping it with its British character. An acquaintance with Western ideas and culture gradually came to be regarded as a desirable qualification in those who were to be entrusted with the administration of this country. The University of Calcutta, modelled on that of London, was founded in 1857 for the spread of Western culture, the movement for which had received the support of Lord Macaulay and Raja Rammohan Roy.

Bankimchandra attended lectures on Law and probably some other subjects in Presidency College, Calcutta. He sat for the examination for the B.A. degree held by the newly-established

University in 1858, and was declared to have passed it along with another candidate. He was thus one of the first two graduates of the premier University of India.

Bankim was appointed to the Bengal Executive Service in the same year in which he took his degree, and was posted at Jessore as a Deputy Magistrate and Deputy Collector in August, 1858. His official career, which covered a period of thirty-three years, was rich in experiences of various kinds, and brought him reputation as an able administrator and a shrewd dispenser of justice. His impartiality was indisputable, and he neither cared for cheap popularity nor feared the frowns of his superior officers.

Details of his official activities would here be out of place. He had to live outside Calcutta, in places which were not always easily accessible in his day, and transfers were frequent from one station to another. His work was onerous and at times risky. At Khulna he came into prominence in connection with the suppression of the river dacoits and the steps taken against some turbulent indigo-planters. In 1867 he was appointed Secretary to the committee for the revision of the pay of ministerial officers, and this was considered as a recognition of his merit by Government. At Berhampur he had a tussle with Colonel Duffin, a European army officer who was in command of the troops stationed at the place. A law-suit was brought against him by Bankimchandra, which created a sort of sensation. He was connected with a literary society at Berhampur, and it was here that his plan of founding a Bengali periodical materialised in 1872, with the publication of the *Bangadarshan*. His father died in 1881. In 1882 Bankim was transferred to Jajpur in Orissa, and during his return journey he had the bitter experience of an encounter with a gang of dacoits. Bankimchandra retired in 1891, when he was only 53. The same year Government conferred on him the title of Rai Bahadur as a personal distinction, and in 1894 he was made a Companion of the Most Eminent Order of the Indian Empire. He had been suffering from diabetes for some time, and died prematurely on April 8 of this year, when he was only 56.

His literary career had begun with his youthful contributions to the Bengali periodical *Sambad-Prabhakar*, and continued till 1893. It is strange that his earlier work—published before his graduation in 1858—should have given no promise of his future greatness as a writer of Bengali fiction, for it comprised articles and poems in Bengali (*Lalita* and *Manas*) and stories in English (*The Adventures of a young Hindu* and *Rajmohan's wife*). His novels were all written during his official life when he had to live laborious days. The first two, *Durgeshnandini* and *Kapalkundala*, were published in 1865 and 1866 respectively, when he was a Deputy Magistrate at Baruipur in the district of 24-Parganas. His pen had no rest during the remaining years of his life. The novels were published in quick succession, till by 1887 all the fourteen had come out, along with other prose works. Little was produced after this date. *Krishnakanter Will* had been brought out in 1878 and the famous *Ananda Math* in 1882.

Bankimchandra's place in the history of Bengali fiction may be called unique. The novel as a work of literary art really owes its existence in Bengal to him. Before Bankim, fiction was represented only by Bengali translations of a few Sanskrit dramas and stories as well as of some Persian and Arabic tales. Most of them were didactic and moralistic. Rhetorical embellishment, detailed description of natural scenery, tiresome portrayal of human beauty, lengthy accounts of impossible exploits were their usual stock-in-trade. Plot architecture and characterisation were almost unknown. Most of the characters were pure abstractions—personifications of virtues or vices—far removed from reality. Two works of fiction however stand on a different footing. Both were realistic studies of contemporary society, and both castigated social vice. Of these two, *Nababababubilash* was published in 1823, and pointed the way to *Alaler Gharer Dulal* which came out in 1858. They were both written by publicists who had come under the influence of Western ideas and were inspired with a reforming zeal. Though full of obvious defects, they answer to the description of a novel more than any other previous works. *Alaler Gharer Dulal* reveals greater power of characterisation, and has, in spite of its digressions, a sort of artistic unity. It has been rightly called the first Bengali novel. It is also a landmark in the evolution of Bengali prose. The style of previous writers like Rammohan Roy, Isvar Chandra Vidyasagar and Akshyakumar Dutt, bore traces of Sanskritic influence, and compound words and verbose expressions were far too common in their composition. There was no likelihood of ordinary people being ever attracted by it. But *Alaler Gharer Dulal* was written in a colloquial style which was intelligible to all. Another literary man, Kali Prasanna Singha, was also marked out as a writer of colloquial prose. *Nababababubilash* avoided the Sanskritised style, but resorted to foreign words and a peculiar diction which was uninviting to the reader. The tendencies noticeable in these writers and, specially in the author of *Alaler Gharer Dulal*, were further developed in Bankimchandra. In his hands the novel ceased to be a mere didactic story, and became a work of art with an æsthetic appeal. In place of loosely-strung incidents, we have well-knit plots with complications and dénouement. In plot-architecture Bankim still remains supreme among Bengali novelists. It is true that his plots sometimes suffer from a lack of artistic compactness, but this is probably due to the fact that many of his novels were published in a serial form in monthly journals. The author found it desirable to revise his work in some cases. Studies in the depth and complexity of character by Bankimchandra have no parallel in the abstractions of the earlier writers. Undoubtedly Bankim was not fond of realism. The past attracted him much more than the present, and he relied on History or on imagination for his stories in most cases. But there is no lack of psychological verisimilitude. He had to forge his medium of expression, and in doing so he steered a middle course between the highly Sanskritised diction of Vidyasagar and others, and the colloquial style of *Alaler Gharer Dulal*. Bankim's language has the stamp of his genius and possesses a rare charm. It combines "the strength, dignity and soft beauty of Sanskrit with the nerve and vigour of the vernacular." It is indeed difficult to decide which is more admirable—the beauty of his descriptive passages or the creation of his sublime imagination—the dignified Ayesha, the warrior-saint Jeebananda, the cultured and magnificent Debi Chaudhurany, the heroic Pratap, supreme in self-sacrifice.

Bankim flourished in an age when the need of education was keenly felt in Bengal, and a number of distinguished educationists appeared to supply it. Isvar Chandra Vidyasagar, Bhudeb Mookerjee, Rajnarain Bose, Akshyakumar Dutt—to name only the more prominent of them—devoted their talents and energy to the spread of education. Ignorance, according to them, was the cause of the national decadence which had set in. The educationists emulated the example of European missionaries who had founded schools for Indian children and sometimes worked in a spirit of rivalry with them, as they were suspected of having secret designs for the propagation of Christianity in this country. Preparation of text-books in Bengali and rtanslation from Sanskrit interested many. Bankim, too, was inspired by educational idealism, but his activities did not flow along the strict academic channel. Spread of culture amongst all classes became his aim, and he sought to realise it through the medium of his Bengali journals and novels which could reach a large number of people. Naturally, he was more familiar with Hindu culture, but he tried to inculcate upon his countrymen not this only, but also the more recent speculation of Western philosophers and the teachings of Western science. Positivism, utilitarianism, the doctrines of liberty, equality and fraternity found in him an admiring exponent in Bengali. But in his days very few, even amongst those who had imbibed Western ideas in the University, took any interest in these cults, though there were many who were dazzled by the glamour of Western civilisation. Aping of Western manners and mode of living went hand in hand with rank superstition, unscientific thought and outlook, and a grevious lack of curiosity. Bankimchandra attempted to stir their consciousness, and also to stimulate their moral sense.

Speculation and theory, creed and dogma—in fact, ideologies of all sorts—have an angularity which is uninviting except to those who have gone through the requisite mental drill. Before they can appeal to man as such, their angularities have to be rounded off, their aloofness must disappear and they must be ready to take their proper place in the scheme of things. Rigid truth, simply because of its stiffness, may not be wholly true. It must be humanised, so that it may establish contact with human consciousness and have a human appeal. The principle of truth must, in other words, be realised in beauty. The novels of Bankim furnish an illustration of this. The fruits of his studies, his wisdom and experience of life appear there in a supremely attractive setting—transformed into images of imperishable beauty, their stiffness removed and their ordinary meaning suffused with a new significance.

This leads to a discussion of the question how far Bankimchandra's literary craftsmanship has suffered on account of his desire to teach. Didacticism is antagonistic to art, but works which enshrine ideas and culture, high thought and noble sentiment, are not necessarily didactic. Everything depends on the manner in which these have been pressed into the service of art, and on the extent to which they have stimulated the creative activity of the artist. The crux of the matter is whether Bankim, the author, is distinguishable from Bankim, the exponent of culture, savant and thinker; whether his philosophy is separable from the pleasure derived from his works. Is he a preacher of doctrines, a collector of interesting historical information, a portrayer of fascinating manners of bygone days, or a "maker" with an æsthetic appeal whose

"*imagination bodies forth*
The forms of things unknown,

and whose pen

"*turns them to shapes*
And gives to airy nothings
A local habitation and a name.

Has he that white heat of imagination which transforms his knowledge and experience beyond recognition, tinges them with a light that never was on sea or land and makes them undergo a "sea-change into something rich and strange?" Here opinions must differ. Probably a majority of discriminating readers will incline to the view that in novels like *Debi Chaudhurani* and *Anandamath*, disquisitions on ideals—political and moral—are rather obtrusive, in *Rajsinha* and *Sitaram*, *Mrinalini* and *Chandrasekhar* historical matters assume undue prominence and in *Kapalkundala* and *Durgeshnandini* appear attractive sketches of the life and manners of romantic ages that have passed away. Few will deny pre-eminence to *Krishnakanter Will* and *Bish-Briksha* as consummate works of art.

To a large extent, the appeal of Bankimchandra's fiction is based on revival of the past. Institutions, civilisations and cultures that have disappeared, and which differed immensely from what we see around us, have an element of mystery and romance and whisper strange things across the silence of centuries. The mediæval times with their gay and spectacular life thus furnish an irresistible attraction. Gorgeous royalty, military aristocracy in full panoply, priests in saffron robes, the motley crowd, gaily caparisoned war-horses and tuskers, the camp, the battlefield, the splash of colour, the stir of variegated life—these certainly fill the canvas in some of the novels of Bankimchandra. It is probably this aspect of his work that is responsible for his comparison with Sir Walter Scott. There is however this difference while Scott was captivated mainly by the externals of mediæval society, Bankim was more interested in the inner life of the past. He dived deeper than the Scotch novelist, and collected treasure to which there is no parallel in the latter. Scott was, on the other hand, a much closer student of antiquities—of ballads, folk-lore, traditions, annals—and the range and accuracy of his historical knowledge were much greater. Time was not probably ripe for historical studies on an adequate scale in this country in the middle of the last century, and Bankimchandra's short-comings may be due to want of opportunity. But he certainly more than made up for them by his capacity for deeper comprehension and his readiness to imbibe and interpret the message of the past. His exposition of the doctrine of the *Geeta*, analysis of the character of the hero of the Mahabharat, synthesis of cultures in *Dharmatattwa*, etc., are examples.

Bankimchandra has been called a classicist. Undoubtedly his work is marked by lucidity of thought, clarity of vision and judgment, and sense of proportion. There is no idea which cannot find clear, concise and adequate expression in his language, and there is never any doubt about his meaning. Emotional abandon, which is sometimes associated with Romanticism, is not to be noticed in him. He is no uncertain thinker, no faltering guide. His cogency of argument is unparalleled, and one can almost see the inner working of his mind—the stages through which he reaches the conclusion from the data. There is no beating about the bush, no dimness of suggestion, no excessive subtlety of analysis and disquisition which ultimately loses itself in a mist of verbiage. While these literary characteristics must be traced to qualities of soul and an unerring æsthetic sense, not a little must have been due to the discipline of the life he lived. Harmony of conflicting instincts and faculties was its main feature. It was not exclusively devoted to any single pursuit—abstract thinking, religious musing, or even literary creation. When carried to excess, each has been known to lead to some aberration and to detract from mental equilibrium even in men of talents. Bankimchandra had many interests. He was a man of affairs, and had to work strenuously throughout his life in responsible and difficult positions. He had to mix with all sorts of people, including bureaucrats, lawyers, police officers, landlords, traders, and ryots. And in the midst of multifarious work, he had to collect his energies for serious study and literary work. Bacon wisely says, "whosoever hath his mind fraught with many thoughts, his wits and understanding do clarify and break up in the communicating and discoursing with another; he tosseth his thoughts more easily, he marshalleth them more orderly, seeth how they look when they are turned into words." Again, "they (studies) perfect nature, and are perfected by experience, for natural abilities are like natural plants that need proyning by study, and studies themselves do give directions too much at large, except they be bounded by experience."

Bankimchandra's name is indissolubly linked with the Indian national anthem "Bande Mataram," and outside Bengal he is perhaps known chiefly as a political visionary, a man whose main concern was the emancipation of his country, and who was the source of Indian nationalism. Though he dreamt golden dreams of the future of his fatherland, Bankim was neither a Mazzini, nor a Milton. He was somewhat of a social reformer, a pugnacious controversialist in defence of Hindu culture, a stern mentor of aspirants to literary fame, but not a politician nor a statesman.

Apart from his habits and temperament there were the government servants' conduct rules which forbade him to take an active interest in politics and even to write on political matters. He was a servant of the state, and as such he could not very well be also its critic. A hard-worked officer who had to do multifarious duties, he had neither the opportunity nor the leisure to concern himself with questions affecting the destiny of millions of people. Thus we look in vain for his views on concrete problems like India's position in the British Empire, her economic condition and desirable constitutional changes in the country.

Political struggle—even political speculation—is the outcome of political consciousness which again is the product of various factors. Spread of education, economic uplift, a legitimate pride in cultural heritage and grievance against the ruling class are some of them. British administration in Bankim's days was paternal and had obvious defects, but it had given satisfaction to people who had faith in British Justice. Poverty and ignorance had limited their vision, and they had no conception of a better system of government. Political activity had not, therefore, commenced in Bengal in the days of Bankimchandra, except in a very qualified sense. This is again another reason why he had avoided political controversy. Bankim had really no political programme in view. His complaint was not so much against the machinery of government in the country as against the frailty and defects of his own countrymen. A far-sighted thinker, he knew that nations by themselves are made, that political systems and institutions have their roots far deep in man's inner worth. It is this which gives birth to, and sustains them. Nothing counts but strength—moral, intellectual and spiritual—which is another name for virtue. Without it, liberty, howsoever won, cannot long be enjoyed. Its absence means sure decadence and wasting away. As an Indian savant points out, "He had an unerring vision of the moral strength which must be at the back of the physical force. He perceived that the first element of the moral strength must be complete self-sacrifice." Bankim had sublimated patriotism into an ethereal virtue. His message thus transcends political considerations, and may be described as spiritual. If devotion to spirituality is not a disqualification in a statesman, Bankim can well be regarded as one.

He asked his countrymen to avail themselves of the opportunity afforded by the British Government to shake off their age-old weakness and to gain strength. In their struggle for progress they may look upon England as helper and guide. Not only has she given this country security against foreign invasion and internal tranquillity but has also unlocked to it the treasures of Western science. If knowledge is a form of power, intellectual strength may be acquired by India through discipleship to England. For spiritual force, he has asked Indians to turn to their ancient systems of culture. These are clearly expounded in *Debi Chaudhurani* and *Anandamath*, and again in *Dharmatattwa* and in his commentary on the *Geeta*.

Bankim has often been called an apostle of Neo-Hinduism. This is probably a half-truth, and therefore misleading. But even if it represent the whole truth, it is wrong to suggest that his work has rendered a disservice to the cause of Indian nationalism. The human mind rises to higher and more abstract conceptions through the realisation of what are less comprehensive and more palpable, which form the lower rungs of the ladder. The idea of the nation is modern and somewhat abstruse. Indians had in the past known religious and cultural ideals but not nationalism. Their revival might be expected to be helpful to the growth of national consciousness. The latter has actually been, in many cases, preceded by some form of cultural or religious renaissance. What eventually made itself felt as the powerful Irish Nationalist Movement had its beginnings in the Gaelic Revival. Nationalism in Turkey, ultra-modern as it appears in some respects, meant at first an insistence on old culture and language. Bankim's attempt to spread the message of ancient India thus prepared the ground for Indian Nationalism, and was a step in the right direction.

It has been pointed out that though Bankim's teachings were valuable and served as an inspiration, his best literary work owes little to them. And it is by this that he will live in the memory of posterity. The time is not distant when the political significance of his work will disappear, the fascination of forgotten history revived in it will fade, and the use made in it of the teachings of ancient India will cease to impress. Already the bourgeois Hymn to the Mother

"*Rich with thy hurrying streams,*
Bright with thy orchard gleams,
Cool with thy winds of delight,
Dark fields waving, Mother of might,
Glory of moonlight dreams,
Over thy branches and lordly streams,
Clad in thy blossoming trees,
Mother, giver of ease——"

is almost drowned in the tremendous, deafening proletarian slogan—"Inquilab Zindabad." But other forces are at work which will soon hold our attention and stir our imagination. A higher synthesis of thoughts and ideologies, under which must be subsumed current narrower thoughts, will inspire creative efforts in future. But Bankim, the maker of our literature, who has also shaped our language, will always be remembered with loving admiration.

ROMESH CHUNDER DUTT

ROMESH CHUNDER DUTT
AND THE REVIVAL OF INTEREST IN INDIAN CULTURE
1848–1909

BY SIR ATUL CHANDRA CHATTERJEE

EDITORIAL NOTE

Romesh Chunder Dutt worked above all things to revive the national pride and interest in India's artistic and literary past. For this reason we illustrate this article with examples of Indian art dating from two of the most brilliant periods in the country's cultured past—the Gupta period, and the renaissance of Hindu art in the eighth, ninth and tenth centuries.

ROMESH CHUNDER DUTT was born in Calcutta on August 13, 1848. He was fortunate in the time and circumstances of his birth. There were many signs of a spiritual and intellectual awakening in Bengal after the torpor that had settled on the people of the province in the eighteenth century. A revival was in progress in the study of Sanskrit and the basic literature of the Hindu religion and philosophy. The movements started by Rammohan Roy were producing wide and lasting effects on the social, religious and educational life of the whole of India. Christian missionaries and Hindus alike had started educational institutions on Western lines in Calcutta and throughout the province of Bengal. Social reform awoke much interest and was supported by many orthodox Hindus. The organisation of public opinion on these questions led to similar movements in political and economic matters. While there were as yet no signs of an artistic or industrial revival, literature was becoming a living force and there was a distinct effort towards the development of new literary forms. Bengali prose was the creation of the early nineteenth century and Bengali poetry also breathed a new life.

These circumstances moulded the life and character of Romesh Chunder. His great-grandfather, Nil Moni Dutt, was a leading citizen of Calcutta in the days of Clive and Warren Hastings and became the founder of the well-known Rambágán Dutt family. Rasamoy, the eldest son of Nil Moni, distinguished himself in business and public service, and was noted for his scholarship and breadth of outlook. His death in 1854 was followed by the conversion to Christianity of all his surviving sons and their families. A grand-daughter of Rasamoy was the gifted Toru Dutt, who, though she died at the early age of twenty-one, secured for herself a permanent rank among the poets in the English language. To quote the words of Mr. H. A. L. Fisher, "In her all too brief life she mastered Sanskrit and wrote in French and English with a grace, a facility and an individual distinction which have given her rank among the authentic voices of Western literature."

This interest in literature and the more serious aspects of life was not confined to the Christian branch of the Dutt family. Isán Chunder, who was the son of a younger brother of Rasamoy, was also educated on Western lines and maintained a life-long interest in literary pursuits. He was employed as a Deputy Collector and was posted in different districts in the course of his duties. His family moved about with him. Romesh was his second son, and inherited from his father both a love for rural life in Bengal and an interest in poetry and literature. The father was drowned in 1861, and Romesh was then entered at Hare School in Calcutta.

His mother had died two years earlier, and the care of Romesh and his brothers developed on an uncle, Soshee Chunder Dutt, who also was a scholar and an author of many books. "A stern integrity and unswerving uprightness, and uncompromising independence marked his character." There can be little doubt that Soshee Chunder Dutt exercised a far-reaching influence in shaping the thoughts and ideas of Romesh.

Matriculating from Hare School in December, 1864, Romesh studied at Presidency College in Calcutta for three years. In March, 1868, he sailed for England to compete for the Indian Civil Service, which had been thrown open in 1854 to all British subjects including Indians, but until then only one Indian, an elder brother of the poet Rabindranath Tagore, had been successful. It was natural for a bright and ambitious young man like Romesh to aspire to pass into this service. In those days a voyage to England for a young Indian was an adventure very different in character from what it is now. Romesh was accompanied by two friends, Surendranath Banerjea and Bihari Lal Gupta, who had the same objects in view as Romesh. The life of Surendranath has been treated elsewhere in this book. His name subsequently became a household word in India as an orator and as one of the creators of Indian nationalism of to-day. Bihari Lal also had a successful career in the Indian Civil Service and rose to the position of a Judge of the Calcutta High Court.

When these three young men left Calcutta, only Surendranath had the consent of his parents, while Romesh and Bihari had actually run away from home without the knowledge of their people. The position was truly described by Romesh himself in a letter to his brother: ". . . For we have left our home and our country, unknown to our friends, unknown to those who are nearest and dearest to us, staking our future, staking all, on success in an undertaking which past experience has proved to be more than difficult. The least hint about our plans would have effectually stopped our departure. . . . Shall we achieve that success? Or shall we come back to our country impoverished, socially cut off from our countrymen, and disappointed in our hopes, to face the reproaches of our advisers and the regrets of our friends?"

In London the three young men worked hard attending classes at University College and taking private lessons. They passed the open competitive examination in 1869, Romesh standing third in order of merit, and all three were assigned to the province of Bengal. During the two years which Dutt spent in England on probation he travelled extensively in the British Isles, enjoying the natural scenery as well as the historical and literary associations of the places visited by him. He did not fail to take an appreciative measure of the social and political problems of England, but then as ever his main interest lay in India. The following quotation from a letter written by Romesh at the end of his probationary period in England is a prophetic vision of India's future advancement: ". . . We in India have an ancient and noble civilisation, but nevertheless we have much to learn from modern civilisation. Our children's children will live to see the day when India will take her place among the nations of the earth in manufacturing industry and commercial enterprise, in representative institutions, and in real social advancement. May that day dawn early for India."

On the way home, in the summer of 1871, the three friends travelled through France, Germany, Switzerland and Italy, Shortly after his return to India, Romesh

MARTIN HURLIMANN

THE BUDDHA AT TAXILA

A statue of Buddha from Taxila. It shows the Greek influence on Indian sculpture. The Buddha's robe, the modelling of his face and the attendant angels are in the traditional Greek Classical style.

BY COURTESY OF THE VICTORIA AND ALBERT MUSEUM, LONDON

HEAD OF A BODHISATTVA

Another example of the Græco-Buddhist School, from Gandhara, Gupta Period.

published "Three Years in Europe," an account of his sojourn and travels in Europe. Written in a clear and attractive style the book secured many readers, both Indian and European.

From 1871 to 1883, Romesh Chunder served the usual period of training as a junior officer in the Indian Civil Service in Bengal. This comparatively lengthy training furnished him with opportunities for valuable work among the people entrusted to his care. He received commendation for good work in the Bengal famine of 1874, and two years later he specially distinguished himself in the restoration of order and prosperity in Dakhin Shahbazpur, an island in the mouth of the Ganges inhabited mostly by Bengali Moslems where a hundred thousand people had been drowned in one night by a cyclone and a storm wave. This terrible calamity had been accompanied by the destruction of all dwelling-houses, the removal of land and boundary marks and the dispersal of all movable property including the cattle which had survived the inundation. All administrative machinery in the area had naturally disappeared, and a widespread cholera epidemic caused further misery to the surviving inhabitants. The situation must have tested to the full the tact, energy and administrative ability of young Romesh Chunder. In one of his later works Dutt paid a well-merited tribute to the co-operation he received from the suffering people. "The Musalman population of Dakhin Shahbazpur, a sturdy and self-reliant race, faced the worst season with admirable courage and helped themselves under the most trying circumstances."

Even in these early stages of his official life Romesh Chunder gave ample evidence of the independence of his character and the sanity of his judgment. In upholding the interests of the people in his charge he did not shrink from incurring the displeasure of the European indigo planters of Bengal, a powerful body at that time. When Sir Ashley Eden was relinquishing the office of Lieutenant-Governor of Bengal, Dutt published in the *Statesman* a frank and candid review of his career which contained the following sentences: "The good he did to the oppressed raiyats over twenty years ago—the good which he is trying to do to the cultivators now, will live and bear fruit. His personal rule, his attempts to crush a young press, however wayward, his efforts to stamp out the young aspirations of Bengal—will all vanish with him." As early as 1875, Dutt had published his little book on "The Peasantry of Bengal," dealing with the agrarian problems of the province. The Permanent Settlement of 1793 had not safeguarded the interests of the tenant-cultivators, and the subsequent legislation down to the well-known Act of 1859 had proved only partially effective. Agrarian disturbances occurred from time to time. Dutt's remedy may be stated in his own words: "There is then one, and only one way left before the Government: to estimate the importance of the general rising correctly—to grapple with the problem intelligently—to newly create the status of the zamindar and the raiyat in a definite manner—to enact a Permanent Settlement between the zamindar and the raiyat as a Permanent Settlement has been enacted between the zamindars and the Government." This wise suggestion coming from a young official was naturally resented by the land-holding classes, but the agitation thus started on behalf of the peasants ultimately led to the passing of the Bengal Tenancy Act of 1885.

In 1883 Dutt was appointed to the charge of the district of Backerganj and was there for two years. Previous to this he and two other Indians had acted as District Officers for periods of three months or less, but this was the first instance in the whole of India that an Indian was placed in charge of a district for a considerable length of time. A few months earlier the *Pioneer* (then the spokesman of official Englishmen in India) had observed, "The administration of districts means the government of the country. . . . People have pleaded for the employment of natives in all other ways, but the warmest partisans of the movement have generally conceded that it would be premature to put natives in charge of districts." The district, too, to which Dutt was posted was "one of the heaviest and most turbulent in all Bengal and the period was one of excitement, for the Ilbert Bill agitation greatly exercised the public mind and embittered the public feeling during these years." It may be mentioned that this Bill—which sought to equalise the powers of Indian and European magistrates in the trial of Europeans accused of criminal offences—was largely the result of the official positions which had been attained by Dutt and his Indian colleagues in the I.C.S.

Dutt's work in Backerganj won the whole-hearted approbation of Indians as

BY COURTESY OF THE VICTORIA AND ALBERT MUSEUM, LONDON

THE SANCHI TORSO

This figure in red sandstone stood before the Western Gateway of the Sanchi Stupa. Gupta Period.

well as of the Government, and fully established the fitness of qualified Indians for the duties of a district officer. It was also during these years that Dutt submitted a full report on tenancy legislation in Bengal which was characterised by Sir Antony MacDonnell (perhaps the highest authority in that generation on the tenancy problems of Northern India) as a "most valuable contribution to the literature of the subject." Dutt's report displays in a remarkable manner his knowledge of the agrarian conditions of the province together with his sympathy for the cultivation classes.

In 1887, after his return from a period of leave, Dutt was sent to take charge of Mymensing, another difficult and troublesome district. The area was over six thousand square miles, and the population over three millions. Communications except by river were undeveloped, and the great and rapid increase in jute cultivation had given rise to many new and complicated problems of administration. Here again, Dutt's work was entirely successful. Then followed similar but shorter periods of service as District Officer of Burdwan, Dinajpur and Midnapur. Everywhere Dutt maintained cordial relations with the people in his charge, preserved the rule of law, and often composed troublesome disputes between rival landholders or between landlords and tenants. His energy and enthusiasm were also directed to the improvement of education, communications and public health. He was specially interested in the development of local government, but though always an ardent advocate of reform, he was also a believer in the principle of "gradualness." In 1882, when the subject was being discussed by Lord Ripon's government, Dutt observed, "While therefore it is most desirable to try to induce the people to have a practical share in the administration of local matters, it is also essential, to the very success of the scheme, that they are not suddenly entrusted with a task which may be at first beyond their ability." At a later date Dutt put forward suggestions for the creation of small self-governing bodies to include groups of villages, with elementary powers and responsibilities. This was the beginning of the system of "union panchayats" which has since been developed in several provinces with very beneficial results.

In 1894 Romesh Chunder was appointed to be a divisional Commissioner, again the first Indian to hold this post in the British service. There was criticism of this appointment by some short-sighted Englishmen, but all Europeans associated with Dutt, whether as colleagues, superior officers or subordinates, acknowledged his eminent fitness, and during the four years that Dutt worked as a Commissioner he amply proved that it was in the best interests of the Government to make the fullest use of Indians of merit in high administrative posts. In 1895 Dutt was moved to Orissa as Commissioner and was at the same time Political Agent for the Indian States in that province. Here again, his success as the intermediary between the Government and the rulers of a number of states in varying stages of social and political progress showed that racial considerations should not be a bar to the employment of Indians in the "Political" department of the Indian Government.

In October, 1897, soon after completing the minimum period required to earn a full pension, Dutt resigned from the Indian Civil Service. He could have served for another nine years and might have reached a much higher official position. Although singularly qualified for secretariat work, Dutt was never posted in the Secretariat, and it was not until nearly twenty years after Dutt's

MARTIN HURLIMANN

THE TRIMURTI ELEPHANTA

The three Faces of Shiva in the Elephanta Caves, Bombay. The front face is Shiva the Creator; the left face is Shiva the Destroyer; and the right Shiva as Vishnu the Preserver. About eighth century.

retirement that an Indian was appointed as Secretary to a provincial government. It is not, however, true that Dutt retired from official service with a feeling of unfair treatment. As has been well observed, "An official career had always been his second love only; other ambitions, literary and national, had always exercised a far stronger attraction for him."

We have seen how well Romesh Chunder performed the exacting and strenuous duties of an officer in executive charge of heavy and important posts. Throughout this period, however, he had been able to carry out much literary work, some in English and some in Bengali, his own mother-tongue. This was rendered possible only by his marvellous industry and capacity for organising the time at his disposal.

Literature was to Dutt a means "for revivifying the national mind of India and restoring to her sons their lost faith in her past." He believed that only in this way would Indians learn again to have faith in themselves. With this object he published in 1877 a history of the literature of Bengal. It was the first scientific study of the intellectual life of Bengal from the twelfth century down to his own time. This pioneer effort has since been superseded by much scholarly work on the origin and history of the Bengali language and literature, but credit will always be given to Romesh Chunder for revealing to his countrymen and to the world at large that Bengali has a literature dating from very early days, full of interest not only to the student, but also to all who want to understand the inner life and thought of the people of that province.

About this period Romesh Chunder came under the influence of the great Bengali writer, Bankim Chatterjee, and was persuaded by him to begin writing in his own language. Dutt was always interested in history, and in the following few years he composed and published four historic novels in Bengali. Although he did not reach the level of Bankim in diction, style and craftsmanship, these novels of Romesh were of great literary merit. In later years Romesh produced two social novels which furnish a faithful and critical picture of contemporary rural life in Bengal. These books had a wide circle of readers in Bengal, and some of them have been translated into other Indian languages and also into English.

In 1886 Romesh published a complete translation of the *Rig Veda* in the Bengali language. This was a task entailing immense industry and courage, and received the commendation both of his own countrymen and of European scholars. Bankim Chatterjee, himself a fine Sanskrit scholar and literary critic, praised the thoroughness, accuracy and rapidity with which Romesh Chunder had completed the work and predicted that it would bring him lasting fame.

In 1889 and the two following years Dutt wrote and published his most ambitious work in the English language, "The History of Civilisation in Ancient India." In this work Dutt laid no claim to original research, but put together in a methodical order the results of the labours of other scholars. Here again Dutt was a pioneer. As Grierson wrote at the time, it was a work "which we have all been wanting for years. . . . It is just the thorough and at the same time delightful book which one would expect from R.C.D." The book, published in three volumes, was the first attempt in the English language to give a clear and connected estimate of the origin, growth and the many aspects of Hindu life, literature, religion and philosophy. It was very favourably reviewed by competent critics, Indian and European, and was for a quarter of a century the standard work on the subject.

After his retirement from the Indian Civil Service, Romesh Chunder lived in England for seven years with occasional trips to India. He accepted an appointment as Lecturer in Indian History at University College, London, but his time was mainly occupied in pursuing the literary and political aims which had actuated him to retire from service. In 1898 and the following year appeared the "Great Epics of Ancient India," a condensed translation in English verse of the Mahābhārata and Rāmāyana. Dutt felt that these ancient Indian epics were not accessible to Europeans in a readable form, because in the course of centuries they had been overlaid with a mass of dull and didactic episodes and legends. He believed that the main incidents of the Epics would bear an unabridged translation into English verse, and that, linked together by short notes, they would present the entire stories in a form and within limits which might be acceptable. There can be little doubt that these translations will prove to be the most enduring literary effort of Romesh Chunder. They display a striking command of vigorous, flowing and idiomatic English, a fine sense of rhythm and a real power of poetic imagination.

On the political side, Dutt's object during his residence in England was

BY COURTESY OF THE VICTORIA AND ALBERT MUSEUM, LONDON

CAPITAL OF A PILLAR FROM MATHURA, SECOND CENTURY A.D.

to educate the British public in general and persons of influence in particular in Indian matters, and to win their sympathy and support in favour of India's political advancement. We have already given indications of what Dutt hoped would be the ultimate position of India in the comity of nations, but he always stressed the fact that "the people of India are not fond of sudden changes and revolutions. They do not ask for new constitutions issuing like armed Minervas from the heads of legislative Jupiters." In *England and India*, published in 1897, he dwelt on the lack of representative government in India and the small share given to Indians in the higher offices of the public services. In December, 1899, he had the high honour of presiding over the fifteenth session of the Indian National Congress held at Lucknow. His presidential speech, sober and moderate in tone, dealt mainly with economic and agrarian topics, but questions of fiscal and administrative reforms were also surveyed.

The cardinal basis of Dutt's political philosophy was his belief that the principal need of India was the raising of the standard of life of the Indian masses. Realising that the vast majority of the population subsisted on agriculture, he devoted his attention mainly to agrarian problems. In his view "agricultural labourers and their families in India generally suffer from insufficient food from year's end to year's end. . . . Agriculturists who have lands are better off. . . . But a severe land tax or rent takes away much from their earnings and falls on the labouring classes also." The causes of this poverty and the inability of the Indian peasant and his hired worker to resist the climatic calamities which bring about famines were, in the opinion of Romesh Chunder, first, the gradual decay of Indian industries (he wrote and spoke before the recent development of Indian factory industries) simultaneously with the growth of the Indian population and, secondly, the fiscal policy of the Government which hardly left the bare necessities for the tillers of the soil. He believed that in so far as recent tenancy legislation in Bengal had passed on to cultivators some of the benefits secured to the landholders of the province by the Permanent Settlement, the Bengal tenants were better off than those in the rest of India. He was firmly of the opinion, however, that the land assessment in Southern and Central India was excessive and that the revisions were too frequent. He advocated the extension to these areas of the system in vogue in the northern provinces, and he also urged a large development of irrigation works. In the light of the subsequent history of these questions Dutt's recommendations seem moderate enough although to Lord Curzon and others at the time they had seemed almost revolutionary. India owes the immense progress that has taken place in the last forty years in the land revenue policy of the government very largely to the earnest and energetic pioneer work of Romesh Chunder.

During these years of political work in England Dutt did not confine his attention only to the land revenue question. He interested himself in all the problems of the day, such as the law of sedition, the separation of the judiciary and executive, currency reform and "home charges," and in the important question of constitutional progress.

Romesh Chunder returned to India early in 1904 and in the autumn of that year he entered the service of the Baroda State, first as Revenue Minister and later as Dewan. His Highness the Maharaja Gaekwar, an enlightened and progressive ruler, desired to utilise the ripe and wide experience of Dutt in the promotion of reforms in the state. On his side, Romesh Chunder was keen to prove that the administrative and legislative reforms which he had advocated throughout his life were practicable and could be introduced in an Indian state as well as in British India. It is not necessary to give a detailed account of the reforms effected by Dutt in Baroda with the full approval of the ruler. On his recommendation the judiciary was separated from the executive, an Executive Council of Ministers was constituted, many oppressive taxes and customs duties were abolished, the system of revenue assessment was improved, local self-government was developed, free and compulsory education was extended to the whole state, and measures were adopted for the development of cottage as well as factory industries. This was no mean achievement when it is remembered that during the five years which he spent in Baroda, Dutt also maintained a full and active interest in British Indian affairs. In 1907 the Government appointed the Royal Commission on Decentralisation in India. Dutt was the only Indian member of the Commission and was able very materially to influence its recommendations. He was in England for nearly a whole year from the spring of 1908, and he freely placed his counsel and criticism at the disposal of Morley when he was shaping his well-known constitutional reforms.

Dutt returned to Baroda in June, 1909, as the Dewan of the State, and resumed his work there with his usual earnestness. But his health had been undermined by his manifold and incessant activities. He fell ill during a Viceregal visit to Baroda and died on November 30, 1909. He was survived by his wife and all his children, five daughters and a son.

We cannot do better than close this sketch of Romesh Chunder with the following estimate recorded by His Highness the late Maharaja Gaekwar:

"His mental grasp, the power of will, and the habit of industry gave Romesh Dutt the unmistakable character of a man fashioned in a large mould. There was nothing small about him. It was well and truthfully said that among any company of leading men in any part of the world he would have stood high."

BY COURTESY OF THE BRITISH MUSEUM

TERRA-COTTA RELIEF FROM MATHURA, GUPTA PERIOD

DR. SIR MOHAMAD IQBAL

DR. SIR MOHAMAD IQBAL

THE GREAT POET OF ISLAM

1873–1938

BY SIR ABDUL QADIR

WITH the dawn of the twentieth century there arose, on the sky of Indian literature, a star that has just passed out of our sight, after having shone with a lustre peculiarly its own. That star was the poet Iqbal, or to give him his full name and titles, Dr. Sir Mohamad Iqbal. He departed from this earth on the 9th April, 1938, mourned by his countrymen throughout the length and breadth of India.

He was born on the 22nd February, 1873,[1] at Sialkot, a well-known town on that border of the Punjab which adjoins Jammu, the winter capital of the State of Jammu and Kashmir. He belonged to a family of Kashmiri Brahmans who had embraced Islam some generations back, thus combining in his person some of the best characteristics of his race as well as of the religion adopted by his forefathers.

Iqbal received his early education in the town of his birth. His father, though not very learned, had a great love of learning and had many scholarly friends—among them was Maulvi Syed Mir Hassan, whose ripe scholarship was recognised later by the title of *Shamsul Mema* conferred upon him by Government. Syed Mir Hassan was the teacher of Arabic and Persian at the Murray College, Sialkot, and it was from him that Iqbal got his love of these languages and their literature.

In 1895 Iqbal migrated to the Government College, Lahore, to study for his B.A. and M.A. While there, he had the good fortune of being a pupil of Professor T. W. (afterwards Sir Thomas) Arnold. He showed a special aptitude for philosophy, which was appreciated by Professor Arnold, and thus arose between them an affection which lasted all their lives.

Soon after taking his M.A. degree, Iqbal was awarded the Mcleod Arabic Readership at the Oriental College, Lahore. A few years later he was appointed a lecturer on Philosophy in the Government College, where he worked with great success, till he made up his mind in 1905 to go to England to qualify for the Bar and to work as an advanced student of Philosophy at Cambridge. Professor Arnold was in England at the time and with his advice Iqbal carried on research on Persian Mysticism,[2] and wrote a thesis on this subject which earned for him not only a degree from Cambridge but also a Ph.D. from the University of Munich. He had to put in a short residence at Munich and to show that he had acquired a knowledge of the German language.

He was called to the Bar in 1908, and on his return to India started practice as an Advocate, at Lahore. His old College offered him a Professorship of Philosophy, but he was advised by some of his friends to stick to the legal profession and he accepted that advice. His taste for philosophy and literature, however, continued to absorb his atten-

[1] *This is the correct date, as announced in the* Daily Inqlab, *Lahore, the 7th May,* 1938, *on the authority of the brother of the deceased. In some other papers,* 1876 *had been given as the year of his birth, but the* Inqlab *was asked to publish the date found in the records of the family.*

[2] *The thesis on "Persian Mysticism" was subsequently published in the form of a book.*

tion. The law, being a jealous mistress, did not smile on him to the extent which his ability and gifts demanded, but the loss to Law was the gain of Literature.

Having said something about the formative period of Iqbal's life, let us turn to his work as a poet. An inclination to write Urdu verse was shown by him at a very early stage of his student life. Before he came to Lahore he had written some *Ghazals* in Urdu, which he sent for correction to the famous poet Dāgh, of Delhi, who was then a shining light of the Court of the late Nizam of Hyderabad. After seeing Iqbal's poems a few times, Dāgh is said to have written to him that his verses did not need correction. At Lahore Iqbal took part in a *Mushaira* where some well-known poets were present, and his verses at once elicited praise from them. Some time after that he recited a poem on the natural beauties of the Himalayas at a meeting of an Urdu Literary Society, where it was greeted with unanimous applause.[1] As soon as he became known in literary circles as a rising poet, he was invited every year to the great annual gatherings of the Anjuman Himayet-i-Islam of Lahore, an institution responsible for religious and educational work among the Moslems of the Punjab. The recitation of his poems like the *Taswir-i-Dard* (The Picture of Pain), the *Shikwa* (A Complaint—addressed to God), and the *Jawab-i-Shikwa* (Answer to the Complaint), brought him into great prominence as a writer of Urdu poetry.

The Urdu poems of Iqbal may be divided into three different periods, as follows:—

(1) Those written before he went to England in 1905;

(2) Those written in Europe, till 1908;

(3) Those written after 1908, till the poet began writing Persian verse and practically gave up Urdu writing for some time.

They were collected and published by the author himself in 1924 under the title of the *Bang-i-Dira* (The Sound of the Caravan Bell). This rather unusual name owes its origin to the fact that his song is meant to awaken his countrymen from their slumber and to lead their caravan to progress. The publication of this book gave Iqbal a lasting title to fame as a master of Urdu verse. A second edition of the book was called for in 1926 and a third in 1930.

It was by chance that Iqbal discovered that he could express his thoughts in Persian verse with the same facility as in Urdu. This discovery was made when he was once asked in England to compose verses in Persian. That suggestion resulted in a few fine verses the next day, and thus the genius of Iqbal found a vehicle better suited than Urdu for the expression of his philosophic ideas. The first poem in Persian was the *Asrar-i-Khudi* (Secrets of Self), published in 1915.

By the publication of this book the fame of Iqbal spread beyond the borders of India to Iran and Afghanistan and to parts of Turkey and Russia, wherever Persian was spoken or read. It also led to his becoming known in England and America, when the translation of the *Asrar-i-Khudi* by Professor R. A. Nicholson of Cambridge was published in 1920. Some portions of the book were translated into German and Italian, presumably through this translation, and thus the poet acquired an international reputation.

The *Asrar-i-Khudi* was followed by another Persian poem, the *Ramuz-i-Bekhudi* (Mysteries of Self-Denial). It was a sequel to the *Asrar*, which lays

[1] *This poem was first published in the "Makhzan," a well-known literary journal of that time, in which most of the early Urdu writings of Iqbal appeared.*

stress on the development of the Human Ego or Personality and holds up Power and Courage as the ideals to be followed by Man to accomplish his great Destiny. The *Ramuz* inculcates the subjection of the Personality, with all the power it has developed, to the Law, which places the service of humanity as the highest goal for the ambition of Man. It may be noted that the author, as a Moslem, puts forward the Law of Islam as the best solution of the difficulties of mankind.

After the *Ramuz* came the *Payam-i-Mashriq* (Message of the East), a collection of Persian poems in the style adopted by Goethe in his "West Ostlicher Diwan." This was followed by the *Zabur-i-Ajam* (The Psalms of Persia) and the *Jawid Nama*, named after Jawid, the young son of the poet. It is an allegorical representation of a flight to the Upper World by the Soul of the Poet, in the company of the Soul of the great mystic Jalalud din Rumi, the style of whose famous *Masnavi* has been followed by Iqbal in his Persian writings and whom he regards as his guide in the realm of the spirit.

While Iqbal was busy with his Persian writings, there was a growing demand on the part of the admirers of his Urdu verse that he should make further contributions to Urdu poetry. He responded to this call by giving to the world two more collections of Urdu poems called the *Bal-i-Jibril* (i.e. The Wings of Gabriel), published in 1935, and the *Zarb-i-Kalim* (i.e. The Stroke of the Rod of Moses), published in 1936. The theme running through these Urdu poems is mainly the same which found expression in the "Secrets of Self" and other Persian works. Their importance, therefore, is more for the Message of Action which they contain than for the purely imaginative and poetical elegance which characterised his first collection of Urdu poems.

The last book published by Iqbal in his lifetime was again in Persian. It was a small book with a longish name—*Pas chi bayed Kard ai aqwam-i-Sharq* ("What should we do, O Nations of the East?") —a protest against the aggressive pressure of Western nations on Oriental people.

One more book must be mentioned to complete the list of Iqbal's poetical works and that is the *Armughan-i-Hijaz* (A Present of the Hedjaz). This collection of Iqbal's quatrains and some miscellaneous pieces of poetry was ready for the press, when he departed from this world in 1938. It has been published after his passing away.

The poet always felt a great love for Arabia and all that it stands for, and had, it is said, a keen desire to visit it. Owing to ill health this desire remained unfulfilled. Perhaps this collection was meant to be the present he would have taken to the Hedjaz, but it is more likely that it is meant as a present of the Hedjaz to the world, as the verses contained in it express in poetical form many of the principles of human conduct which have been taught by Arabia, through her great Prophet.

Though the fame of Iqbal rests mainly on his poems, his well-known book, in English prose, known as "Reconstruction of Thought in Islam," deserves special mention and is a valuable contribution to religious philosophy. It contains six lectures delivered by Iqbal at Madras, at the instance of a Literary Trust there. They show a knowledge of Western philosophy combined with a mastery of the thought of Islam. This book has been greatly admired by scholars in the West. It was due mainly to this work that Iqbal was selected by the Oxford University for the Rhodes Lectureship and was invited to deliver a series of lectures at Oxford. He accepted the invitation, but the engagement had to be subsequently cancelled owing to the failure of his health.

The popularity achieved by Iqbal in his lifetime has scarcely a parallel in India, so far as any writer of Urdu is concerned. The only other instance of great popularity in India, combined with international reputation, is furnished by the well-known master of Bengali verse, Dr. Rabindranath Tagore. The two poets had considerable admiration for one another. They have a resemblance in some respects and differ in others. They are both lovers of their country and of the East in general. They have also breadth of mind enough to love humanity as a whole. They are both visionaries and dream of a better future for the world. Their methods of approach, however, to their common goal differ. The path of Tagore is of peace and tranquillity, while that of Iqbal is that of stress and struggle. He gives to mankind a message of action and, in the words of Mr. Abdullah Yusuf Ali, "would din into the ears of a lethargic world the watchwords of swiftness, forcefulness and unflinching assertion of Personality."[1]

Tagore and Iqbal are both fond of mystic introspection, but with this difference, that the one treats it as a goal in itself, while the other uses it as an urge to dynamic energy and a warning against the effects of mysticism as an opiate. In his opinion many of the difficulties of the East are due to her failure to use the God-given powers of man to captivate nature and to subordinate it to his own use. This aspect of Iqbal's philosophy has been aptly described by Mr. Yusuf Ali as "a mystical protest against mysticism."[2]

A question often raised for discussion, in connection with Iqbal's favourite doctrine of the development of the Ego, is whether it was inspired by the writings of the German philosopher Nietzsche. There is, no doubt, a marked resemblance between the latter's doctrine of the Superman and the theory of Self preached by Iqbal, and one can easily understand the tendency to accept the existence of a connection between the thought of Nietzsche and Iqbal. A closer examination of Iqbal's writings, however, shows that, though he was influenced to some extent by his study of Nietzsche, his real source of inspiration for the message that he gave to the world was the spirit of Islam as understood and interpreted by him. Nietzsche did not believe in religion; while Iqbal believed religion to be the only source of life and strength. The two thus differed as to the fundamental principles on which their respective philosophies were based. An interesting article published in the October number of the well-known Urdu journal, called *The Urdu*, from the pen of Dr. Abdul Hakim, Professor of Philosophy at the Osmania University of Hyderabad, throws light on this subject and may be read with advantage by those interested in this question. While frankly admitting that Iqbal appears to have been attracted at one time by the writings of Nietzsche, Dr. Hakim brings out the features which distinguish the two thinkers from one another, and in summing up his analysis refers to the ideal of the "perfect man" being a familiar one in the writings of several old Islamic thinkers. The following translation of a passage from his article is interesting:—

"To search for Man before searching for God, which is a distinctive feature of Iqbal's poetry, is a common factor between Nietzsche and Iqbal. The thought of Islamic Sufism was not unfamiliar with this form of thought.

[1] *From a paper on "The Doctrine of Human Personality in Iqbal's Poetry," read by Mr. Abdullah Yusuf Ali (Retired I.C.S.), before the Royal Society of Literature, London, on the 9th Nov., 1938.*

[2] *In the paper before the Royal Society of Literature referred to already.*

The famous work of Abdul Karim Jabali, entitled 'The Perfect Man,' presents a philosophy of the same kind in a metaphysical colouring. Several verses in the *Masnavi* of Rumi and in his *Divan* breathe the same spirit. Above all, man, as depicted by the Qoran, capturing the powers of the Universe, is the fountain head of this kind of thought. With the lapse of time this trend disappeared. The emphatic re-assertion of this idea once more by Iqbal, in his poetic language, has so impressed the Moslems that it sounds as a newly-born theory of life."

It is difficult to say that the view expressed by Dr. Abdul Hakim sufficiently disposes of the striking resemblance between the thought of Nietzsche and Iqbal, but there can be no doubt that whatever may have been the impressions left on the mind of Iqbal by his study of Nietzsche they were radically modified by his study of the religious philosophy of Islam.

We may pass on now to the discussion of another question, on which there has been a considerable difference of opinion among the admirers of Iqbal. A number of those who liked his earlier Urdu poems which breathe a spirit of Nationalism, regret that in later years he changed his outlook, and, instead of being an exponent of the aspirations of the Indian nation as a whole, he became content with a restricted patriotism, confined to the welfare of the Moslem community. I think, however, that this criticism is based on a superficial reading of Iqbal's poetry and on an inadequate comprehension of the stages through which his poetical thought passed in the course of its gradual evolution.

It is true that some of the earlier poems expressed in glowing words his love for his homeland. Poems like the *Naya Shivala* (The New Temple), or the National Song of Indian Children, are the best instances of writings in the nationalist strain, but it should not be assumed that his love for India or her people had decreased when his outlook broadened and his heart began to throb in sympathy with Eastern countries outside India and, later still, when his feelings extended to humanity as a whole. It was a natural widening of the circle. After local and provincial sympathies came a feeling for his country. With a knowledge of the conflict between the East and the West, and of the dominating influence of the latter, came a deep sympathy with the East in her desire for freedom. This was followed by a vision that was broader still, a realisation of the dangers to which Western civilisation was exposed and his warnings to the West, culminating in a strong belief in the destiny of man and of the great heights attainable by him.

In my opinion it could be safely said that Iqbal was not only "the Poet of Islam"—a title often used in conjunction with his name—but also "the Poet of India" and "the Poet of the East" and "of Humanity." His frequent use of Islamic terminology and metaphors and of allusions based on Moslem literature was mainly due to the suitability of such terms to the themes about which he wrote, while the stress laid by him on certain Islamic principles was due to the fact that he honestly believed that the solution of the difficulties of modern civilisation was possible by the adoption of those principles.

The influence exercised by the writings of Iqbal on his contemporary writers is noteworthy. At first there was a reluctance in some quarters to recognise his eminence as an Urdu poet. It was in the United Provinces, which are regarded as the home of Urdu, that a prejudice against Iqbal originally existed, mainly on the ground that the Urdu used by Iqbal was Persianised and that there were indications here and there of what may be called Punjabisms in some words or expressions used by him. This prejudice disappeared, however, with the rising tide of his fame, when it was pointed out by his admirers that for the Persianised style there was the distinguished precedent of *Ghalib*, and that the few Punjabisms, coming from such a masterly pen, must be taken to be permissible.

Gradually there was a general recognition of the beauty of his thought and of the forceful words in which it was presented. With this recognition there came a tendency, among his younger contemporaries, to imitate his style and to adopt his mode of expression. His favourite theme of awakening the powers of the "Self" now finds its echo in the effusions of a large number of writers and so does another subject which he has done much to popularise, that is, the conflict between Capital and Labour. Iqbal had studied the doctrine of Karl Marx and had been considerably impressed by it. He has many poems sympathising with the hard lot of the labourer and the peasant and denouncing Capitalism.

I have been very much struck recently by the large number of poems appearing in Urdu newspapers and magazines against Capitalism and in favour of Labour. They are often recited in public gatherings, not only at political meetings, as part of a political creed, but also in purely literary societies. This trend in Urdu literature may be said to owe its origin to the writings of Iqbal.

Capitalism is not the only "ism" which has been adversely criticised by Iqbal. He is equally strong in his attacks on Imperialism. Even Democracy has not been spared by him, and he exposes some of its vulnerable points. He says, for instance, in one of his poems, that "Democracy is a system in which heads are counted but not weighed." In another poem his assault on Democracy is less reasoned and more satirical. He says:

"*Beware of the system of democracy,*
And follow the lead of a man of ripe experience,
Because the brains of two hundred donkeys
Cannot produce the understanding of one human being."

In this connection it may be interesting to mention an occasion when these lines were quoted against the poet himself. He had been persuaded to stand for election to the Legislative Assembly of the Punjab and was being opposed by a rival candidate. The latter issued a poster, on the top of which these lines appeared in bold letters, thereby throwing on the poet the burden of explaining why he was ready to take part in a democratic body, following a system denounced by him in such sweeping terms. It is obvious, however, that this epigrammatic *dictum* was not meant to be taken too literally. The same may be said of the lines in which he referred to the League of Nations as a body of "Stealers of Shrouds" forming an association "for a partition of the graves of dead nations." This nickname obtained so much vogue that for a long time the League was referred to as a Society of Shroud Stealers in the Indian Press.

Though literature always remained the main occupation of Iqbal, yet for a time he took part in politics as well. By his temperament and constitution he was not much suited to politics. Left to himself, perhaps, he would not have cared to step into this thorny field. Some of his admirers, however, obliged him to stand for the Legislative Council as a representative of Lahore and he did so. Without much effort on his part he was elected, as he was popular, and his friends exerted themselves earnestly on his behalf. This success, however, did not lead to any tangible result and his connection with the Council ceased after the expiry of the term of three years. On two other occasions he had a contact with politics, firstly when he was called upon to preside over the annual Session of the All-India Moslem League, and the other when he went to England as a Member of the Second Round Table Conference in 1931. Of these two occasions the Moslem League Session deserves a special mention, because it was in his address there that the idea of two separate administrative areas in India, one for Hindus and one for Moslems, was offered as a solution of the unfortunate differences between the two great communities. This idea did not find favour at the time in any quarter, but it is significant that it has found many adherents since, and there is now a party of young Moslems pressing it on the attention of the Government and the Communities concerned under the title of "the *Pakistan* Movement."

Another field of Iqbal's activity that deserves notice is Education. We have seen that he started life as a practical educationist, but his connection with this line terminated when he first left for England. This did not, however, mean that his interest in this work ended. As a Member of the Senate and the Syndicate of the Punjab University and for many years as the Dean of its Oriental Faculty, his advice on educational work was sought and availed of by those engaged actively in the work of education. He was one of the three scholars invited by the late King Nadir Khan of Afghanistan to advise him as to the proposed re-organisation of the Department of Public Instruction in his territory. His two companions were the late Syed Sir Ross Masud, then Vice-Chancellor of the Moslem University at Aligarh, and Syed Sulaiman Nadvi. They went to Kabul and formulated a scheme for the education of the Afghans. It was unfortunate that soon after their return from Kabul King Nadir Khan was assassinated, and the scheme could not be enforced at the time; but I understand some of the improvements recommended by them have been now adopted and some others are under consideration.

Iqbal's real service to the cause of education is not to be measured so much by what he actually did for it from time to time in official or non-official capacities, but should be estimated on the ideals of education placed before us in his poems. This aspect of the question is admirably dealt with in a book called "Iqbal's Educational Philosophy,"[1] by Mr. K. G. Saiyidain, Director of Public Instruction in Kashmir State, who was formerly the Principal of the Training College at Aligarh. As is aptly observed in the Introductory Chapter of this book, "the emergence of an outstanding creative thinker, who has a distinct message to impart and new values to present before the world, is a phenomenon of the greatest interest for the educationist, and the more his ideas catch the imagination, the understanding and the enthusiasm of his contemporaries, the greater must be his influence as an educative force."

So many notices on the life and work of Iqbal by well-known scholars have appeared in various literary journals that it is not possible to refer to them here, but a brief reference may be made to an interesting review of the poet's work by Mr. Amiya Chakravarty (Oxon).

1 *"Iqbal's Educational Philosophy," published by Arafat Publications, Model Town, Lahore.* 1938.

Mr. Chakravarty is a distinguished scholar of English literature, who has made a special study of post-war poetry. Before going to Oxford he was at Santiniketan, Tagore's Indian University. He also had the benefit of travelling with Tagore as his secretary on one of his extensive tours. Writing to the *Voice of Islam* of Singapur,[1] Mr. Chakravarty thus begins his impressions of his visit to Iqbal, a few months before the latter's death:

"In Iqbal's house there was little obvious modernity; in fact, an odd air of indifference oppressed you as you waited to be ushered into his presence. With rare charm, taking the stem of his hubble-bubble out of his lips, he would greet you, raising himself on his couch where he lay reclining in Oriental fashion, clad in the garment of the Punjabi gentleman. His smile would put you at ease; in flawless English he would begin discussing on modern themes as to the manner born."

To this impression of his personal contact with Iqbal, appearing at the beginning of Mr. Chakravarty's article, may be added a passage—occurring about the end of it—where he thus sums up his evaluation of Iqbal's poetry:

"Passionate faith in Islam and artistic skill give a striking power to his verse—it goes to the heart—and young Islam knows why. If some notes are strident, and even lack an all-India appeal, they will be forgotten; the ultimate evocative power lies in his profound humanity."

Before concluding, I should like to relate an interesting account which I have heard of the way in which Iqbal, who never tried to seek official favour, got his knighthood. This was before he went to the Legislative Council and the Round Table Conference, and had nothing to do with politics or any services rendered to Government. It came his way in an unusual manner, purely as a recognition of his literary eminence, and as such reflects credit on the recipient as well as those who moved that appreciation of his merits should be shown in this form. I am told that a European traveller once came on a visit to Lahore and was a guest at Government House. He expressed to the Governor his desire to go and see Iqbal. The Governor asked his guest as to how he came to know about the poet. The reply was that during his travels in Iran and in parts of Russia he found people reading the Persian poems of Iqbal and admiring them. He wondered why the Government of his own country had not done anything to recognise his worth. The Governor invited Iqbal to Government House to meet the traveller and listened to the conversation that went on between the two. Though the Governor knew Iqbal before, he had no idea of the extent of his knowledge or of his reputation abroad, and he was so impressed that he sent up a proposal for a distinction to be conferred on him. This proposal was accepted and the poet was knighted. In certain circles there arose a misunderstanding about Iqbal when this honour was announced. They thought that this meant that he had surrendered his independence by accepting this honour from the Government, but their apprehensions were eased before long, when they found that his pen ran as freely as ever and his criticisms were as strong as before.

He remained true to the ideal which he had set before himself—of expressing his views about men and things, about systems of Government without fear or favour, according to the light within him.

The last few years of his life were spent under the shadow of a deep sorrow

[1] *"The Voice of Islam" of Singapur, for January and February,* 1939, *pages* 19–23.

caused by the death of his wife, followed by a long spell of bad health. His weakened health, though a handicap, was not allowed by him to interfere with his literary pursuits or his accessibility to his friends and visitors. The end came somewhat unexpectedly after a short illness, on April 21, 1938. His last resting-place is near the Shahi Mosque, at Lahore. He had a funeral which princes might envy and his death has been mourned throughout India and even abroad, at hundreds of meetings, and the grief of the sorrowing nation has been demonstrated in different forms. At Lahore a strong committee is at work to raise funds for having a library to commemorate him. At other places institutions called after him have been started, to make the study of his works their special object. Numerous literary societies bearing his name have also been formed, in different parts of India, at which papers are read and poems recited to keep up the awakening produced by his writings. He is no longer with us but his work lives and will be a source of inspiration for generations to come.

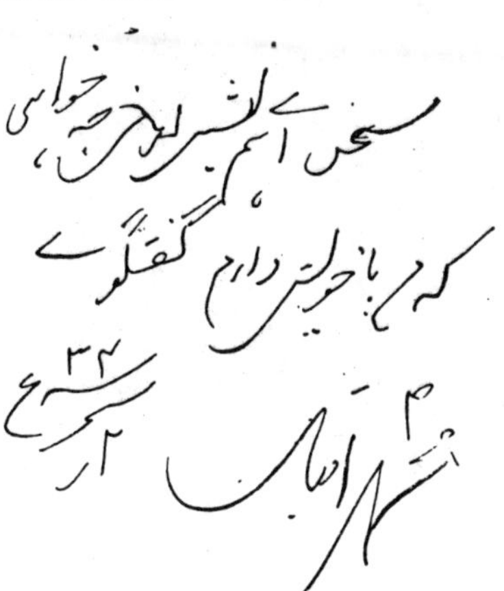

THE AUTOGRAPH OF SIR MOHAMAD IQBAL

BOURNF AND SHEPHERD, CALCUTTA

SIR RABINDRANATH TAGORE

RABINDRANATH TAGORE

INDIA'S GREATEST LIVING POET

BORN 1861

BY DR. K. S. SHELVANKAR

WITH the exception of Gandhi, Rabindranath Tagore is the most famous Indian of our time. His name is known to the educated all over the world—from Japan to Scandinavia and from Moscow to Buenos Aires. In his own country he is venerated as a poet and philosopher in the tradition of the ancient rishis. The admiration he evokes has perhaps never been expressed more rapturously than by Keyserling, who said of him that he is "the most universal, the most encompassing, the most complete human being I have known."

The Tagores are one of the first families of Bengal. They are not only great hereditary landowners (zamindars) but are noted for their munificent patronage of art and literature. Originally Banerjis, they are believed to have settled in West Bengal about the eighth century A.D. In the seventeenth century they received the appellation of Thakur, which means "respected lord," or seigneur. The name was later anglicised as Tagore.

The Tagores were intimately connected with the social and cultural development of Bengal in the last century. Both the poet's father, Devendranath, and Dwarakanath, his grandfather, were leading members of the Brahmo Samaj. Founded by Raja Rammohan Roy, this sect propagated theism, and was strongly opposed to the idolatry and ritualism practised by the majority of Hindus. But for the tireless labours of Devendranath and Dwarakanath Tagore, it is safe to say that the Brahmo Samaj would not have exercised the far-reaching and many-sided influence it has had on modern Indian life.

Defiance of orthodoxy appears indeed to be one of the characteristic traits of the Tagore family. At some time in the past they are supposed to have broken caste rules by eating with Moslems. This offence cost them their place in the Brahman community; and notwithstanding their great wealth and prestige, they are still "looked down upon with a certain contempt as *pirilis*." No strictly orthodox Brahman would either eat or intermarry with them. Dwarakanath brushed aside the then prevalent taboo against sea voyages and was one of the first Hindus to visit England. Devendranath evinced the same independence of spirit. But he was less hostile to orthodox Hinduism than either his father or the founder of the Brahmo Samaj, and in his later years his countrymen united to accord him the title of *Maharshi*, "Great Sage."

Besides Rabindranath, its most dazzling star, and his father—who wrote a remarkable autobiography—and his grandfather, the Tagore family has supplied India with an astonishing galaxy of talent. Dwinjendranath, the poet's elder brother, was a philosopher and essayist of distinction, while Jyotirindra, another brother, was an artist who earned the praise of such discerning critics as Sir William Rothenstein. A third brother was the first Indian to enter the Civil Service. Abanindranath and Gaganindranath, the poet's nephews, were artists of international renown. Recent and contemporary art in India owes an incalculable debt to them.

Rabindranath was born on May 6, 1861, in the rambling old mansion at Jorasanko, in the heart of Calcutta, where the family had lived for generations. It was a world in itself, this house, so vast and full of life it was. Here Rabindranath spent a none too happy childhood. He lost his mother when very young. His father was a remote figure, austere and inaccessible, not often to be seen or spoken with. In these circumstances, the child's early upbringing devolved largely on the trusted servants who play such a significant, if inconspicuous, rôle in aristocratic Indian households.

For schooling of the usual kind, Rabindranath had from the beginning a wholesome dislike. He was sent to the Bengal Academy, and then to St. Xavier's, "but his resolute refusal to be educated stood proof against authority and blandishment, and he was allowed to study at home." He showed as little enthusiasm for private lessons as for the more formal discipline of the class-room. His mind was at once too eager and too dreamy, too independent and too sensitive to fall readily into the conventional ruts.

His father was an incessant traveller, and took the boy with him on his wanderings. Rabindranath spent some time in the villages around Calcutta, making his first acquaintance with the lush fields and the drifting sails and the simple peasant folk of rural Bengal; and in the course of a leisurely journey to the north-west he was able to steep his senses in the sights and sounds of the variegated pageant that is India, from the mouths of the Ganges to the distant frontier.

He paid his first visit to England in

THE POET AND THE IDEALIST

Sir Rabindranath talking with Jawaharlal Nehru.

THE SPRING FESTIVAL

Students at Santiniketan welcome the spring with traditional Indian dances—dances which have their parallel in every country in the world.

1877. He was at a Brighton school for a while, then joined University College, London. When he returned to India, after about a year's absence, he brought back with him some unpleasant memories of England and a knowledge of Sir Thomas Browne's *Religio Medici* which he had studied with Henry Morley.

Travel scarcely interrupted his literary output. He had begun to write verse almost as soon as he could walk; his work appeared in print before he was fifteen; and before he was eighteen he had published nearly seven thousand lines of verse and a great quantity of prose. In the *Bhanu Singh* poems (first published in *Bharati*, in 1877) he reproduced the themes and melodies of the old Vaishnava poets with such success that many a scholar was misled into lauding them as newly-discovered masterpieces of Bengali literature.

There is very little of value in these early effusions. Rabindranath himself attached little importance to them, if we may judge from the pieces he selected for the first collected edition of his poems (1896).

The prose work of this period has at least the virtue of displaying a comprehensive sweep of interest. In 1878 one number of *Bharati*—a magazine edited by his brother—contains articles on *The Saxons and Anglo-Saxon Literature*, *Petrarch and Laura*, *Dante and his Poetry*, and on *Goethe*, all by Rabindranath. An essay entitled *The Hope and Despair of Bengalis* is notable for adumbrating a theme which was to exercise him a good deal in after years—the necessity of East and West to each other. In *Letters of a Traveller to Europe* he described his experiences in the West and maintained that the social morality of Europe was in some respects superior to that of the East.

In his early twenties, Rabindranath passed through a moment of mystical illumination—the first of many similar experiences—which left a deep impress on him. We must relate it in his own words. "One morning," he writes in his *Reminiscences*, "I happened to be standing on the verandah. The sun was just rising through the leafy tops of those trees. As I continued to gaze, all of a sudden a covering seemed to fall away from my eyes, and I found the world bathed in a wonderful radiance, with waves of beauty and joy swelling on every side. This radiance pierced in a moment through the folds of sadness and despondency which had accumulated over my heart, and flooded it with this universal light."

Evening Songs have perhaps no intrinsic merit, but they mark an important stage in Rabindranath's development. They were soon followed by *Morning Songs*, a much better book, in which the poet gave exultant and tumultuous expression to his new-found sense of inner freedom. *Nature's Revenge*, his first important drama, embodied one of the key-thoughts of all his life—the joy of attaining the Infinite within the finite. *The Love of Rahu*, in *Pictures and Songs*, is held by some to be perhaps his greatest poem. But the whole of this phase must be regarded as mainly experimental in character. It ended with the publication of *Sharps and Flats* (1887), which is remarkable for the beauty of its sonnets, some of them among the loveliest in any language.

In the meantime, Rabindranath, after a holiday in Karwar on the west coast, returned to Calcutta and married Shrimati Mrinalini Devi (December, 1883). In addition to his other work, he actively participated in the attempts to start a Bengali Literary Academy and contributed frequently to various periodicals, including *Balika*, a magazine for boys. He was rapidly establishing himself as the best of the younger literary men of Calcutta, the "Bengali Shelley." Always strikingly handsome, he dressed at this time "with much eccentricity and exquisiteness." He is said to have introduced among educated Bengalis the fashion of wearing long wavy hair and the "Napoleon beard." "My recognised cognomen was the Lisping Poet," he says, in his *Reminiscences*.

These years saw, too, the ripening of a friendship with Bankimchandra Chatterjee, the famous Bengali novelist—a friendship unfortunately broken by a long spell of estrangement following on a controversy over the Neo-Hindu movement and the death of his older brother Jyotirindra's wife. Rabindranath was profoundly affected by this loss. "From now onwards the thought of death is very present in his poetry."

In 1887 he withdrew to Ghazipur, in the United Provinces, intending to devote himself to the single-minded worship of his muse. Here he wrote *Manasi*, his first fully mature work, savagely satirical in parts; but the life of semi-retirement amid the famed roses of this provincial town palled on him before long. He determined to leave Ghazipur and travel along the Grand Trunk Road to Peshawar in a bullock-cart. But the plan was thwarted by his father's wish that he should go to Shileida, on the Ganges, and take charge of the family estates. "The poet was just a little afraid at the name of Work, but at last he consented."

At Shileida, Rabindranath spent some

of the happiest years of his life. Poet though he was, he showed himself not incapable of practical efficiency in the management of the estate. He was in intimate touch with the common people, and gained a first-hand knowledge of the rural problems of India, both in their technical and human aspects. He was surrounded by the Bengal landscape that he loved so well and delighted to describe —its fields and its canals, "its ducks and its reed beds." And he had the leisure and peace of mind necessary for the complete unfoldment of his genius.

This period was rich in achievement. Not only did Rabindranath contribute for four years a ceaseless stream of essays, short stories and poems to *Sadhana*, but he now revealed himself as a dramatist of the first rank. *Sacrifice* has been described as the greatest drama in Bengali literature; while *Chitrang ada* "is one of the summits of his work, unsurpassed, and unsurpassable in its kind." His lyrical powers, too, were at their height. *Sonar Tari*, a volume which exposed him to the charge of mysticism, was followed two years later by *Chitra*. "In no other book has he attained to more single-minded adoration and celebration of beauty. . . . The greatest poem of all (in *Chitra*), *Urbasi*, is perhaps the greatest lyric in all Bengali literature, and probably the most unalloyed and perfect worship of Beauty which the world's literature contains."

Sadhana, "incomparably the best periodical Bengal has ever known," ceased publication in 1896, and with it the first purely æsthetic phase of

CLASSES IN THE OPEN AIR

A group of boys and their master at Santiniketan. Pupils and students work as much as possible in the open air.

THE LIBRARY, SANTINIKETAN

At Santiniketan, Sir Rabindranath's School near Bolpur, Bengal, the study and revival of Indian culture in all its forms go hand in hand with Westernised and most modern methods of education.

Rabindranath's life came to an end. His restless spirit sought for some more solid and significant belief than Art for Art's sake. Besides, political preoccupations were beginning to weigh on him. Bengal, like the rest of India, was witnessing a national revival; British rule was being assailed with increasing vehemence; and Rabindranath, who had till then preserved an aristocratic detachment, found himself drawn more and more into these popular movements. Inevitably, he became a leader of the Indian Renaissance.

Opposed as he was to foreign rule, he was even more strongly critical of the servile and cringing attitude of so many Indian politicians of the time. He exhorted them to cease blaming the British raj for all the ills of India and to turn their zeal into channels of educational and social reform that lay well within their power. In order to resurrect for his countrymen ideals in harmony with the national genius, he delved into India's past. He lectured on the Upanishads and on the civilisation of Aryan India; he extolled the valour and self-reliance of Mahrattas, Sikhs and Rajputs; and he endeavoured to popularise these themes not only by the use of the colloquial idiom, as in *Kshanika*—in itself a revolutionary departure—but by the adoption of a simple ballad form in *Katha* and *Kahini*.

But the most enduring memorial of

this time is Santiniketan. The world-famous school, on a site two miles out of Bolpur, whither the Maharshi was wont to repair for communion with Nature, was founded in 1901. Here Rabindranath hoped to recapture the meditative calm of ancient India and provide an environment where the mind of the young "might expand into love of Beauty and of God." Some of the best educational methods of the West were copied at Santiniketan. Before many years had passed the school came to be looked upon as a model institution. Among those who gave devoted service to it were a number of eminent Indian scholars and artists; and, in addition to the poet himself, some of his English friends, notably W. W. Pearson and the Rev. C. F. Andrews.

The next few years were as busy as they were full of grief. Rabindranath's wife died in November, 1902. His second daughter was ill with consumption. In a vain attempt to save the child he took her to Almore, in the Himalayas, where he nursed her for many anxious months. She died in 1904. In 1905, his father, the venerable Devendranath, passed away; also, two years later, at Monghyr, his first son—"he was a very sweet boy." The suffering caused by these successive bereavements is reflected in his poetry, in *Smaran* and in *Kheya*. It was, however, during these years that he wrote most of his novels, including *Gora*, "a long story with the fullness of detail of the Russian novel."

The partition of Bengal had now become a burning issue. The whole country was seething with excitement. Indian nationalism, in one of its crucial struggles with the Government, had no more effective champion than Rabindranath. He made innumerable speeches and wrote innumerable articles. The songs he composed were sung by patriotic youths in every province. He started national schools, formed village committees and was active in a hundred other ways. Yet, in the midst of all this, disillusionment grew on him. He despised the politicians, and their endless petty squabbles wearied him. So, suddenly, he resigned from the political committees and organisations with which he had been associated and withdrew to Santiniketan.

Watched by the police and abused

USING THE OLD INDIAN BOWS AND ARROWS

by many of his countrymen, he lived here in strenuous retirement during the next few years. Political and social problems definitely yielded place in his mind to religion. He would often talk to the boys in his school on religious subjects, and these talks were subsequently collected and issued in a series of volumes entitled *Santiniketan.* He wrote a group of symbolical plays—*Autumn Festival. The King of the Dark Chamber*, and *The Post Office;* and he wrote *Gitanjali.*

This was not his first book of religious poetry. *Naibedya* had come out in 1901. But *Naibedya* was as much an experiment in form and patriotic hymnology as a lyrical expression of religious sentiment. The inspiration of *Gitanjali* is clear and unsullied. It is the authentic voice of one who, through much suffering, had attained joyous serenity. Some passages in it, Maeterlinck said, "are among the loftiest, most profound and most divinely human ever written."

In 1911 Rabindranath emerged from his seclusion and plunged once more into public work. He exerted himself to heal the breach between the different sects into which the Brahmo Samaj had been split for many years. His efforts were of no avail and he went back to Santiniketan. The next year his jubilee was celebrated in Bengal with immense éclat. Shortly after, he sailed for England, happy, but tired and ill.

He had taken a short holiday in Europe in 1890. And before that, when he was about twenty, he had set out for England to study law, but had turned back at Madras because his companion, an older nephew, suffered so much from sea-sickness that it was impossible for him to continue the voyage, and Rabindranath was in no mood to face the rigours of English life for the second time without a friend at his side. Arriving in London in the spring of 1912, he found himself just as lonely and wretched as on his first visit in 1877. "Everyone seemed like phantoms. . . . Then it occurred to me to try to get into touch with Rothenstein." At Rothenstein's he met Yeats, Stopford Brooke, Nevinson and others who at once recognised the profound beauty of his poems, even in translation. An English publisher was found for them. A special edition of *Gitanjali* was brought out, and had a splendid reception from the public. "Not since Fitzgerald's *Omar Khayyām* won its vogue has any Eastern poetry won such acceptance."

After a visit to America, Rabindranath returned to Santiniketan in the autumn of 1913, universally recognised as one of the foremost poets of the age. Within a few weeks of his arrival the Nobel Prize for Literature was conferred on him. Calcutta University hastened to crown him with academic laurels. In 1914 he was knighted. During these years, when his fame was spreading over the world, he wrote *The Gardener*, *The Crescent Moon*, *The Cycle of Spring*, *The Home and the World*—a long novel—and *Balaka*, "the greatest of his books." In 1916 he delivered a series of lectures on "Nationalism"—in Japan—and on "Personality," in the United States.

The Great War intensified the loathing with which Rabindranath had always regarded the nationalism and militarism of the West. But also it gave a fillip to the national awakening in India. Political tension was even more acute than in the days of the Bengal Partition; and following on the shootings at Amritsar in 1919, Rabindranath felt compelled to resign his knighthood as a gesture of protest.

It was about this time that Mr. Gandhi came into Rabindranath's life. He and some of his disciples stayed for a while at Santiniketan on their return from South Africa in 1915. Much as the poet admired the politician-saint, there were deep differences between them—differences which rose to the surface when Gandhi launched the non-co-operation movement. Rabindranath was profoundly opposed to it. He condemned its narrowness of spirit; he feared its further consequences; he deplored the effect it was having on the lives of the young; and he derided the glorification of the *charkha*.

He was fiercely attacked for this attitude but would not be shaken from it. Quietly he pursued what he held to be the true ideal of nationalism and internationalism by founding the Institute of World-Culture—*Viswa-bharati*—and by starting a Department of Rural Reconstruction—Sriniketan—to develop the village welfare work that he had begun in 1914.

Meanwhile his popularity abroad was on the increase. A cult of his work sprang up. In the decade between 1920 and 1930 he undertook no less than seven extensive lecture tours in the West, in Europe and America, and throughout the East. He was everywhere welcomed with enthusiasm, and made countless friends and admirers. But towards the end of this period, a reaction set in. Mysticism and religiosity came to be identified with his name, and his reputation suffered. In 1930 he visited the Soviet Union and was favourably impressed by much that he saw there. His Hibbert Lectures on *The Religion of Man* were delivered in 1931. To mark his seventieth birthday a memorial volume was presented to him with contributions from Einstein, Heinrich Mann, Bertrand Russell and many others.

Rabindranath's literary achievement is prodigious; it overshadows everything else. It should be recorded, however, that he was not only poet, playwright and novelist, but a musician, actor, painter, composer, philosopher, journalist, teacher, orator, and a host of other things—and distinguished himself in each of these very different rôles. There is a no more versatile, prolific and gifted genius in history.

He drew his inspiration chiefly from two sources: the Sanskrit poets of the classical age and the mediæval Vaishnava lyrics. They represent two of the central traditions of Indian history—the secular, aristocratic tradition and the religious fervour of the masses. Blending these with the lofty mysticism of the *Upanishads*, Rabindranath achieved a distinctive synthesis which is as perfect an expression as it is perhaps possible to have of the spirit of India. Besides, as a craftsman, a master of words, he exercised an enormous influence on the languages of India, particularly on Bengali, which became in his own lifetime, and largely through his own work, a vigorous and flexible tongue equal to the needs of the present century.

Though Rabindranath shrank from the rough and tumble of politics, he had a vivid awareness of the plight of his country under foreign rule. He constantly inveighed against a system which destroyed freedom and condemned millions to miserable and poverty-stricken lives. There is reason to think that of late he has grown more conscious than ever of the importance of doing away with imperialism and the greed and violence ingrained in it. But he has never ceased to urge with all his eloquence that the subject nation, struggling for independence, should not acquire the aggressive vices of its rulers, but seek to understand other peoples and discover ways of co-operating with them in the common cause of civilisation. During the last few years he has been in very poor health. His intellectual powers, however, are unimpaired, and from time to time he has raised his voice in indignant protest at the barbarism and bloodshed that have been released in many parts of the world.

SIR JAGADISH CHANDRA BOSE

SIR JAGADISH CHANDRA BOSE

AND HIS RESEARCHES INTO PLANT PHYSIOLOGY

1858–1938

BY PROFESSOR J. C. GHOSH, D.Sc.

SIR JAGADISH CHANDRA BOSE was born on November 30, 1858, in the village of Rarikhal in Bikrampur. His early days were spent in Faridpur, where his father, Bhagawan Chandra Bose, was posted as a Deputy Collector. The latter was a man of broad sympathies and of generous impulses, who ruined himself by his attempts to establish indigenous industries. Bose was fortunate in having such a wise and sympathetic father to guide him through his youth. His school education was completed in the St. Xavier's School; he also graduated from the same college, and it was the influence of Father Lafont which aroused his interest in experimental physics. Like the latter, Bose developed later a flair for experimental demonstration which has kept many audiences in rapt attention. When it was decided to send him to England, it was his mother who sold her jewels to find money for her son's education. Bose decided to study medicine in London. But after repeated attacks of malarial fever contracted in Assam prior to his departure for England, Bose had to give up the study of medicine and take up Natural Science. He joined Christ's College, Cambridge, and later took his degree both in Cambridge and in London, with physics, chemistry and botany. He had for his teachers Rayleigh, Livieng, Michael Foster, Francis Darwin, Dewar and Vines. They all remembered and helped him in many ways when Bose later returned to England to demonstrate the results of his investigations.

On his return to India, and on the recommendation of Lord Ripon, he was given a professorship in Physics in the Presidency College, Calcutta, in 1885. Being an Indian he was entitled to two-thirds salary, and as the post was an officiating one, only half of that was offered to him. He protested against this invidious distinction, and for three years refused to accept the cheques by which he was paid his salary. He married in 1887 the second daughter of Mr. Durgamohan Das, and the golden anniversary of their wedding was celebrated on January 27, 1937. Owing to the great financial difficulties under which the newly-married couple started their life, they had to take a house in Chandernagore on the bank of the river, from where he used to cross over every day to Naihati in a rowing-boat, which used to be taken back by his wife. Later in the early 'nineties he came down to Calcutta and shared a house in a large compound in Mechuabazar Street with his brother-in-law, Dr. M. M. Bose. At this period he was engaged in various scientific hobbies including photography and sound recording. One of the earliest models of Edison's phonograph was purchased by the College, and Bose was engaged in experiments in voice recording and production. His work in photography was taken up very seriously. On the lawn of his house a studio was erected and equipped. He used to go out on photographic excursions during the vacations. In the midst of all these scientific recreations he had kept up his interest in Hertz's experiments with electromagnetic waves, which had caused a great amount of interest in scientific circles while he was in England. On his thirty-fifth birthday in November, 1893, he decided seriously to devote himself to the pursuit of new knowledge, and from the following year he began to publish his series of investigations on the properties of electric waves.

Bose's research falls under three main groups. In the first period he deals with the properties of electric waves; in the second period with the study of the similarity in behaviour under the action of electric waves of a class of substances used for detecting such waves to that shown by living tissues. Thus he was led to the investigation of the response in the living and the non-living. From such studies he was finally led to investigate the physiological properties of plant tissues and to demonstrate the similarity of their behaviour to that of animal tissues.

In course of his electric wave investigations he devised an extremely compact form of generator of electro-magnetic waves, in which the radiating source was a sparking system between platinised spheres, which emitted radiation of wavelength of about 5 mm., which is about the limit of the shortest electro-magnetic waves which have so far been investigated. For his detecting system he used an improved form of coherer, which had been first used by Branly of Paris. The detailed study of the action of the coherer proved later on to be the turning point in Bose's career. The form of coherer first used by him consisted of a number of fine wire spiral springs, adjusted with a large number of regular contacts fixed in ebonite and under the control of a spring. A weak current flows through this, to which the spirals offer appreciable resistance. On the impact of electric radiation this resistance is appreciably diminished, resulting in a large deflection in a galvanometer which is used in the circuit as an indicating instrument. In the early forms of the coherer it was necessary to tap the latter in order to bring it back to its initial condition of high resistance. Bose later on devised other forms of coherer which showed the property of automatic recovery. The apparatus thus built up was not only very sensitive and regular in behaviour, but also very neat and compact; it could be packed up in a small suitcase and put up on the end of a writing-table. Compared to the large wavelength of the radiation used by Hertz and Lodge, which required the use of optical apparatus of enormous dimensions, and which gave rise to uncontrollable stray radiations by diffraction effects, Bose's small and compact apparatus at once attracted the appreciative attention of the leading European physicists, and its description appeared in text-books by Poincaré, in an Encyclopedia Britannica article by Sir J. J. Thomson, and in other text-books. With this apparatus Bose was able to demonstrate the optical properties of reflection, refraction, selective absorption, interference, double refraction and polarisation, rotation of the plane of polarisation, etc. It was found that a crystal named nemalite produced polarised electric waves by selective absorption in the same way as tourmaline does for visible light waves. Since the electric waves due to the comparatively large wave-lengths were not much absorbed by air and other media, Bose investigated the possibility of sending electric signals through long distances, and in a lecture experiment showed the possibility of sending signals over a distance of 75 feet with three solid walls intervening. Those who visited Bose in his house in Convent Road at this time could have seen him working with his apparatus for sending and receiving signals in the shape of the ringing of bells. In this apparatus flat metal discs on the top of long rods were used for facilitating the sending and receiving of signals, anticipating in some ways the use of antennæ in radio-telegraphy. The possibility of practical application of this method of sending signals did not escape the attention of interested people when Bose, in 1895, went to England and demonstrated to various learned societies the results obtained by the apparatus constructed by him. If one takes into consideration the very limited workshop facilities available in the Presidency College Laboratory in those days, one can well understand the chorus of appreciation with which distinguished physicists in Europe like Kelvin, Rayleigh, Thomson, Lippman, Cornu, Poincaré, Warburg, Quincke, and others received this demonstration.

We come now to the second period of his physical researches, which led to his postulation of the similarity in the response of the living and of the non-living.

In course of investigating the suitability of different materials as coherer, he found that in a certain class of substances the incidence of electric waves leads to a diminution of contact resistances, while in another class of substances—of which potassium and arsenic are representatives—an increase in electric resistance under radiation was observed. For this type of effect he introduced the term Electric Touch or Contact Sensitiveness in preference to the word then used: "Coherence." He further noticed that this contact sensitiveness diminished with constant impact of radiation and it recovered its previous sensitiveness if the receiver was laid aside for a long time. In fact all the characteristics of the behaviour of a living tissue under stimulation were exhibited. In the course of his investigations he, about the same time with Shelford Bidwell, investigated the change of conductivity of selenium cell under the action of light. The work of these two pioneers in this field is mentioned in a report which appeared recently in *Physikalische Zeitschrift* of the rapidly growing and technically important subject of photo-conductivity and contact rectification in semi-conductors. At the time of Bose's investigation the electron had just been discovered in the phenomena of gaseous discharge, but its application to the conductivity of solids had not been considered and Planck's Quantum Theory of Radiation was just being formulated. To explain the responsive variation of material bodies under different types of stimulation, Bose postulated his molecular stress and strain theory, viz., that every type of stimulus, be it electrical, mechanical, effect of radiation visible or invisible, produces a state of molecular strain in the substance. One of the most delicate methods of investigating this state is by means of electrical conductivity measurements. If left to itself the substance returns from its strained state and behaves normally again. The electric behaviour of a large class of substances under different types of stimuli was investigated and interpreted under the molecular stress and strain theory. One of the most successful applications of this was in explaining the disappearance of the latent image on an exposed photographic plate if it is not developed within a certain time. All these effects find an explanation in Pohl's investigation of photo-conduction and light absorption by alkali and silver-halide crystals, and its interpretation in terms of Franck's theory of photo-sensitised activity. Another interesting application of Bose's theory was the interpretation of binocular alteration of vision. A physicist cannot help regretting that Bose should have left this promising and then unexplored region of physical investigations—in which he could have been a pioneer—for physico-physiological investigations, where his appearance was resented by the orthodox physiologists and his work was much hampered by their opposition.

In 1900, Bose attended the International Congress of Physics in Paris, and read a paper on the generality of molecular phenomena produced electrically in living and non-living matter, in which he brought together a large amount of comparative observations on the similarity of response in the two classes of substances. It is interesting to note that he used the ferro-magnetic magnetite as specimen of non-living matter. It was shown in this and subsequent papers that many of the effects of stimulation shown by living tissues were also shown by non-living matter, thereby extending the degree of similarity in behaviour in living and non-living matter. In England, Bose's communications of his investigations had a mixed reception. Some of the physiologists, headed by the veteran Sir John Burdon Sanderson were opposed to the interpretation of the results of his experiments. As a consequence, his communication to the Royal Society was only read, but not published, and placed in the archives of the Society. It was at this juncture that some of the leading botanists who were office-bearers of the Linnæan Society, including Vines, Howes and Horace Brown, and who had seen his experiments, offered the hospitality of the Society for the reading and publication of his paper. In the course of these investigations, Bose became more and more interested in the response of plant tissues under different kinds of stimulation, and of their similarity to that shown by animal tissues.

Now began the third epoch of his investigations on plant response, which were communicated in a series of papers to the Royal Society in 1903, and it was proposed to publish them in the *Philosophical Transactions*. As he was now away from England, the opposition group was successful in holding up his papers on the ground that his results were so unexpected and so opposed to current theories that nothing short of the plant's automatic record would carry conviction. In the early days—when the investigations on the plants were commenced—the responses in plants were magnified by optical levers, which were first introduced by him in plant physiology, and recorded by following the movement of the spot of light on a drum with a pencil. This rebuff from the Royal Society spurred Bose to devise more and more sensitive apparatus for making the plant write its autograph. Of these the first, completed in 1911, was the Resonant Recorder which automatically recorded the velocity of nervous impulse in Mimosa petiole and by means of which time values as short as 1/1000 part of a second could be estimated.

Then followed, in 1914, his Oscillating Recorder for recording the exceedingly feeble pulsations of the leaflets of Desmodium Gyrans.

For measuring linear growth movements in plants he devised and brought to a high degree of perfection, in 1917, his Compound Lever Crescograph which conveniently shows a magnification of 5,000 times.

Not content with this magnification he constructed his Magnetic Crescograph which easily magnified one million times. It is rather interesting to note that this apparatus was the bone of contention between Sir Jagadish and Dr. Waller, who doubted its performance. Eleven Fellows of the Royal Society jointly testified to the claims of Sir Jagadish in a communication to the London *Times*, in 1920. At this time he was elected a Fellow of the Royal Society. In the same year he perfected his Balancing Apparatus, which can be adjusted to balance any rate of growth, thus keeping the recorder steady, until a change in the rate of growth takes place. This apparatus compares favourably with the Heliostatic movement of astronomical telescopes. In 1919 he was the first to introduce insulated microelectrodes for determining the electrical activity of deeper tissue cells under geotropic and other stimuli.

Then came the "Bubbler," or Photo-Synthetic Recorder, first used in 1922 for certain sap movement experiments, finding its final use in measuring the rate of photosynthesis in plants.

Another apparatus designed and perfected by him about the year 1927, is his Diametric Contraction Apparatus which can show diametric expansion and contraction in plants under the effects of heat or cold, poison or stimulants.

The main principles utilised in the above apparatus are: elimination of friction and unhampered movements of the recorders.

It is generally assumed that there are certain fundamental resemblances in the behaviour of all living cells by virtue of their possessing the same ground plan of protoplasmic structure. The fundamental properties of the protoplasm are contractability, conductivity, rhythmicity. In animal organisms these functions are taken up by specialised tissues such as muscles, nerves and organs composed of nerves and muscles. Bose's great problem was to discover similar functions in plant tissues.

Contractability in plants is demonstrated by his diametral contraction apparatus. He showed that plant tissues undergo change in shape under the action of electrical stimuli as animal muscles do. By means of the resonant recorder, which can measure intervals up to one-thousandth of a second, he demonstrated that the conduction of impulses in plant tissues follows the same laws as in animal tissues—the effect of the application of warmth, cold, depressant and exciting drugs and of homodromous and heterodromous electric currents producing identical effects. These experiments definitely opposed the then accepted theory of the hydraulic transmission of impulses in plants.

By means of his oscillating recorder he showed that the rhythmic pulsation of the leaflets of Desmodium and of other plants are of the same category as the pulsatile activity of an animal heart. He demonstrated that the source of pulsatile movements in Desmodium leaflets is light stimulus, the response being proportional to the quantity of light falling on the leaflets—light impulse of a short duration producing a single pulsation whereas stronger light or longer exposure producing multiple responses.

Another outstanding problem of plant physiology is the movement of sap in plants. The generally-accepted view at his time being that the movement is due to the action of purely physical forces such as capillarity, osmosis, transpiration and of a new type of force, root pressure. Bose, on the other hand, while not denying that these forces may be partially effective in causing sap movements, maintained that the principal factor was a vital phenomenon probably of a pulsatile character. He used to show a simple experiment where two wilted leaves—one dead and one living—coated with vaseline to prevent transpiration and detached from the parent plant to prevent the action of root pressure, showed very different activities when their stems are put in tepid water, the living one becoming erect in a very short time, while the dead one not responding at all. He devised some very ingenious experiments to explain this pulsating activity of the plant cells when transmitting sap through the tissues. Other important problems dealt with by him were the investigation of tropic movements in plants. His main hypothesis in explaining the opposite activity of different parts of plant tissues to the action of stimulating agents such as gravity and light, was that a stimulus of the same kind produced opposite effects in a given tissue, depending upon its intensity—weak stimuli producing positive and strong stimuli negative effects.

While in the midst of these investigations, Bose's period of service in the Presidency College was nearing its end and he had to retire in 1915, after he had completed his fifty-seventh year of age. For two years he continued his work, partly in a laboratory fitted up in his own house in Upper Circular Road and partly at Darjeeling. He felt that the time had come for establishing a research institute, where his work in biophysics could be carried on by a band of research scholars. As he was nearing the end of his period of service, it was discovered by the Government that though by his seniority he was entitled to the highest grade in the Education Service, his claims had been overlooked. He was gazetted to the highest grade with retrospective effect. The large amount received as back pay was credited to the account of the prospective Research Institute; also a legacy from an old, valued friend was received for this purpose. All these amounts were very carefully invested and had increased considerably by the time the Institute was started. To this were added some donations received from the public and an annual subvention from the Government. A plot of land to the north of his house was purchased, and a beautiful, well-planned research institute was built and opened on November 30, 1917.

The results of the investigations carried out in the Institute were published in the *Transactions of the Bose Institute* which first appeared in 1918. From time to time he summarised the results of these investigations in monographs, the last of which, entitled "Growth and Tropic Movements in Plants," appeared in 1929. As a member of the Committee for Intellectual Co-operation of the League of Nations, he used to visit Europe every summer for five years and came in contact with the leading intellectuals of the Western world. In 1928 he visited some of the leading university centres in Europe, where his lectures and demonstrations aroused a great deal of interest. Prof. Mölisch of Vienna (who died very recently) accompanied him to work in his Institute for six months. At the time of leaving the Institute he wrote a letter to *Nature* (April 13, 1930), testifying to the remarkable experimental work which was being carried out in the Institute. "I saw the plant writing down the rate of assimilation of its gaseous food. I also observed the speed of the impulse of excitation in the plant being recorded by the Resonant Recorder, which automatically records intervals of time as short as a thousandth part of a second. All these are more wonderful than fairy tales; nevertheless, those who have the opportunity of seeing the experiments become fully convinced that they are laboratory miracles revealing the hitherto invisible reactions underlying life."

Bose's great contributions to the study of plant physiology have been first the incomparable set of apparatus devised by him, his bold hypothesis of the similarity of reaction and of mechanism in plant and animal organisms, and his attempt to isolate these in the case of plants. Many valuable results have been established, but it cannot be said that the problems have received their final solution. Research fellowships and post-graduate scholarships are being endowed by the money left by him for the study of plant physiology and allied subjects. It is to be hoped that these bands of scholars, in co-operation with the workers of the Bose Institute, will continue with new enthusiasm the study of this vastly interesting subject of biophysics.

No account of Bose's life will be complete which deals only with his scientific activities. He was a man with many-sided interests and activities. In the early 'nineties he used to spend his vacations armed with a full-sized camera, photographing scenic beauty and sites of ancient Indian monuments. His Bengali prose writing has been declared by competent critics to be of high literary value, and sure of a permanent place in Bengali literature. His friendship with Rabindranath Tagore is well known, the latter being one of the first to recognise the importance of Bose's achievements. The new school of Bengali artists found an appreciative friend and helper in Bose. Paintings of Gaganendranath Tagore, Abanindranath Tagore and Nandalal Bose are to be found in his house and on the walls of the Institute building. His early biological training and his inheritance of the pantheistic outlook of ancient Indian culture penetrated deeply into his scientific thought. He is the first Indian scientist of eminence who has tried to align his scientific investigations to the traditional pantheistic view of Nature prevalent in this country. Future historians of science may find the introduction of this standpoint an important contribution of the Indian mind to the scientific conception of Nature. In a letter, written after receiving the news of the death of Sir J. C. Bose, Sir Michael Sadler remarks that "He was a poet among biologists. Shelley had he gone on with Science, and had he lived in the days of exact measurements, might have shared in his (Bose's) work."

THE BOSE RESEARCH INSTITUTE, CALCUTTA

SIR CHANDRASEKHARA VENKATA RAMAN
Working in his laboratory at Bangalore.

SIR CHANDRASEKHARA VENKATA RAMAN

HIS WORK IN X-RAY AND RADIO-ACTIVITY

BORN 1888

BY PROFESSOR J. C. GHOSH, D.Sc.

VENKATA RAMAN was born on November 7, 1888, at the town of Trichinopoly, which stands at the head of the Cauvery delta and which, with its picturesque rock crowned by a temple, is famous in South Indian history. His ancestors on the paternal side were Brahman landholders, owning and farming agricultural property in a small way at a village near Ayyampet in the district of Tanjore. The father, R. Chandrasekhara Iyer, was the first in the line to break away from the village and the traditional occupation and to seek the path of Western learning. At the time his second son Venkata Raman was born, Chandrasekhara Iyer was a pupil teacher in a local high school, studying for his bachelor's degree. The mother, Parvathi Ammal, was a scion of a Trichinopoly family of "Sastris" or Sanskrit Pandits; her father, it is said, had as a youth walked all the way from Trichinopoly to Nadia in Bengal to study "Nyaya" or law and had returned to his native town to practise in the local courts. In this ancestry on both sides we can trace the origin of the vigour of mind and of the adventurous and independent spirit coupled with a love of learning which characterise the subject of this biography. Soon after Venkata Raman was born, his father took his bachelor's degree in physical science and secured a position as a teacher in one of the local colleges. He was also deeply interested in South Indian music and learned to play it on the violin. It is not surprising therefore that, at a very early age, Chandrasekhara Iyer's children acquired a love of music, and that the mind of Venkata Raman turned naturally to the study of science.

Not content with a position of which the emoluments were insufficient to meet the needs of his growing family, Chandrasekhara Iyer decided early in 1892 to quit the Tamil country and seek his fortunes in the land of the Andhras. His friend, Mr. P. T. Sreenivasa Iyengar, who had preceded him and held the position of Principal of the Hindu College at Vizagapatam invited him to become Lecturer in Physics at the same College. The offer was accepted and Chandrasekhara Iyer moved with his family to Vizagapatam after making what was then a long and arduous journey. Here, in lonely houses on the seashore at Waltair, Chandrasekhara Iyer and Sreenivasa Iyengar lived near each other and worked, and here Venkata Raman grew up amidst scenes of picturesque natural beauty and in an atmosphere of scholarly life and endeavour.

Sreenivasa Iyengar was a brilliant scholar and teacher who took the English classes at the College, while Chandrasekhara Iyer taught physics and mathematics. The environment was thus favourable for the speedy recognition of young Venkata Raman's abilities and the provision of special facilities for its encouragement. At a very early age he acquired a remarkable mastery of the English language and developed an enthusiasm for scientific studies which was so all-absorbing as to leave no inclination for the study of less favoured subjects. While in the high school classes, Venkata Raman had learnt all the physics that could be found in such treatises as Ganot's *Physics*, and was eager for more. The strain of less congenial but nevertheless compulsory studies, however, told on his health, and the fœtid atmosphere of the town into which the family had meanwhile moved brought on serious illness. The young lad survived with some difficulty to pass the matriculation examination at the age of twelve. Two years later he passed the First Arts Examination of the University, securing a high position in the list in spite of the fact that physics did not figure amongst the subjects for study.

The scene then shifts to the Presidency College at Madras where the young lad enrolled as a University student. He soon attracted the attention of the professors, who were astonished by the maturity of knowledge shown by one who was scarcely old enough to be a student in the degree classes. A useful result of this impression was that the routine of lectures and practical classes was partly set aside in his favour, thus allowing more freedom for his chosen studies. The latter included especially mathematics and mechanics, thus laying the foundation for later excursions into theoretical physics. At the degree examination of 1904 he was the sole first class of his year in science and was awarded the University Gold Medal for physics, besides receiving the college prizes for English essay writing. For the next two years he was a student working for his M.A. degree, very happy at having no lectures to attend and free to improve his knowledge of mathematics, and to read such classics of physics as Helmholtz's *Sensations of Tone*, Rayleigh's *Theory of Sound* and Ewing's *Magnetic Induction in Iron and other Metals*. To this period also belongs Venkata Raman's first début as an independent scientific investigator. *The Philosophical Magazine* of London for November, 1906, contains his first formal paper on *The Unsymmetrical Diffraction Bands due to a Rectangular Aperture*. In this and other work of the same period, we see the beginnings of his career in research and his deep interest in the sciences of optics and sound which has survived unabated till the present time.

At that time the only superior service which was open to Indians of talent without necessitating a qualifying period in England was the Indian Finance Department. As there seemed to be no possibility of a scientific career, Raman decided to sit for the competitive examination for the Finance Department. Accordingly, he prepared for it during his second year M.A. course, reading books on literature, economics, history and other subjects. In the M.A. degree examination in January, 1907, Raman secured a first class, obtaining record marks in his subject. He next sat for the Finance Examination in February, 1907, and here again secured the first place.

For the next ten years, Raman was an officer of the Indian Finance Department, serving successively at Calcutta, Rangoon, Nagpur and again at Calcutta in diverse capacities. He acquired very varied experience and knowledge of such matters as currency and remittance operations, salary and pension audit, the theory and practice of life insurance, the management of savings banks, the issue of government loans and the preparation of official budgets. At a very early age he was put in independent charge of large offices and found that even in his official work there was some scope for the exercise of initiative, originality and scientific thoroughness. The unusual qualities of the young officer did not lack appreciation in the department. Indeed, on several occasions Raman received the thanks of his official superiors and of the Finance Member of the Government of India. He also received an invitation to join the Secretariat of the Department, but declined the offer for reasons that will presently be clear.

Though his official duties took up most of his time, Raman's zeal for scientific work never suffered diminution or eclipse. From the very first he was on the look-out for opportunities for carrying on the experimental investigations begun by him at college. Soon after he joined the service at Calcutta, he discovered the existence of the Indian Association for the Cultivation of Science in that city and sought an interview with the son of the original founder, Dr. Mahendra Lal Sircar, who was then secretary. To his great joy he obtained permission to work in its laboratories in the mornings and evenings, out of office hours, and made the fullest use of these opportunities. Even when he was transferred out of Calcutta, first to Rangoon and then to Nagpur, Raman continued his investigations, converting part of his house into a laboratory and working with improvised apparatus. Fortunately he was transferred back to Calcutta towards the end of 1911 and thus regained the facilities offered by the Science Association. The latter remained the chief centre of his activities for the next twenty years. The steady stream of original papers coming out from the laboratory of the Association soon established Raman's reputation as an investigator.

Raman's enthusiasm for scientific work and his success in original research despite many handicaps, could not fail to attract the vigilant eye of the late Sir Asutosh Mookerjee, the then Vice-Chancellor of the Calcutta University. When the Palit Endowment Fund was created and Sir Asutosh wanted a Professor capable of organising and directing research to fill the chair of Physics, he thought of the young finance officer and offered him the post. Although Raman knew that from a pecuniary point of view he would be a great loser, he did not hesitate to accept the offer. It may be worth while here to quote the speech made by Sir Asutosh Mookerjee on the occasion of the laying of the foundation-stone of the University College of Science in March, 1914:

> "For the chair of Physics created by Sir Taraknath Palit, we have been fortunate enough to secure the services of Mr. Chandrasekhara Venkata Raman, who has greatly distinguished himself and acquired a European fame by his brilliant researches in the domain of Physical Science, assiduously carried on under the most adverse circumstances amidst the distraction of pressing official duties. I rejoice to think that many of these valuable researches have been carried on in the Laboratory of the Indian Association for the Cultivation of Science, founded by our late illustrious colleague, Dr. Mahendra Lal Sircar, who devoted a lifetime to the foundation of an institution for the cultivation and advancement of science in this country. I shall fail in my duty if I were to restrain myself in my expression of the genuine admiration I feel for the courage and spirit of self-sacrifice with which Mr. Raman has decided to exchange a lucrative official appointment for a University Professorship, which, I regret to say, does not carry even liberal emoluments. This one instance encourages me to entertain the hope that there will be no lack of

seekers after truth in the Temple of Knowledge which it is our ambition to erect."

Raman joined the Calcutta University as its professor under the Palit Trust in July, 1917. On the death of Mr. Amrita Lal Sircar in November, 1919, he was elected as secretary of the Indian Association for the Cultivation of Science. These two positions, one of them salaried and the other honorary, supplemented each other most usefully. The professorship freed him from the vexatious necessity of earning his living at the desk of a Government office. His position at the Science Association enabled him to carry on research in the most congenial surroundings undistracted by the routine of teaching and examinations. The terms under which Raman held the Palit Chair did not require him to take part in the ordinary work of instruction at the University College of Science. Nevertheless he found it of advantage to undertake a fair share of this lecturing. The closer contact with the subject and with the students which such lectures gave was found to be highly beneficial and did not appreciably diminish the time and energy available for original research. It was these favourable conditions of work that were largely responsible for the outstanding successes of Raman during the fifteen-year period from 1917 to 1932.

The personal enthusiasm for research which led Raman to choose a life of scientific toil in preference to a lucrative official career soon overflowed and fertilised the minds and careers of a host of young men who came under his influence at the two institutions between which he divided his time. A school of research in physics rapidly grew up at Calcutta whose publications attracted wide attention, bringing recognition and honours for Raman, and advancement in life for his collaborators. This, in turn, enabled Raman to attract a larger number of highly-qualified workers and to secure further resources for the equipment of his laboratory. The atmosphere of high scientific endeavour thus created under Raman's leadership proved itself in the sequel to be favourable for the attainment of outstanding scientific success.

No account of this period of Raman's life would be complete which did not give some account of the great discovery made by him in 1928 and of how he was led up to it. The phenomena of light and colour had from the first been of the deepest interest to Raman and had been the subject of many researches by himself and his collaborators. His long residence at Waltair and at Madras had made him familiar with the varied colours of the sea in the vicinity of land. During his first brief visit to Europe in 1921, he travelled over the deeper areas of the Mediterranean Sea; noticing with surprise the intense blue colour of its waters, he became deeply interested in the question of its origin. It suggested itself that the colour was incidental to the process of the diffusion of sunlight in its passage through clear water, and experimental support was soon forthcoming in support of this hypothesis. This led, naturally, into an intensive study of the diffusion of light in liquids and other transparent substances. This subject and various issues connected with it occupied the attention of Raman and his collaborators continuously for several years following. Gradually, from these experimental studies, a new phenomenon emerged, namely that in the process of diffusion, light may also change its colour. This was observed as early as 1923, but it was not until towards the end of 1927 that it became clear that this was a universal phenomenon and was entirely distinct from the well-known effect of fluorescence exhibited by many chemicals. The final step was taken by Raman in February, 1928, when he used the light of the mercury lamp for these experiments, and found in the spectrum of the light scattered by various substances, new lines or bands not present in the incident beam of light. These new lines or bands are now known as the Raman lines or bands, and the spectrum containing them as the Raman spectrum of the substance studied.

To quote the words of a reviewer in a British scientific periodical, "the discovery of the Raman Effect in 1928 opened a view of research which has almost paralleled the early history of work in X-rays and radio-activity." Mathematicians hailed the discovery with delight, as they saw in it a confirmation of the new quantum mechanics which they had framed to replace the dynamics of Newton. Physicists and chemists also received the discovery with enthusiasm as it provided unlimited opportunities for experimental research and opened new pathways of investigation in their respective sciences. In scores of physical and chemical laboratories all over the world, and indeed in every civilised country, the experiments on the Raman Effect were repeated and applied to the solution of a variety of scientific problems. So great was the interest in the subject that it gave a new stimulus to the optical instrument industry; the leading manufacturers vied with each other in designing and producing spectrographs specially adapted for work in this field. In the ten years which have

WITH OTHER NOBEL PRIZE WINNERS

At the Galvani Congress, Bologna, Italy, 1937. *Raman, Heisenberg, Bohr, Richardson and Schrodinger, all of whom have received the Nobel Prize for Physics.*

elapsed since the discovery, several treatises, dozens of monographs and over seventeen hundred separate original papers have been published upon the Raman Effect in various parts of the world. This stream of original work continues to flow unabated year after year.

It is not possible in such a brief sketch to survey the numerous contributions to science which have secured for Sir C. V. Raman a position of acknowledged eminence in the world of science. He has not followed established paths, but made his own way into many different fields of research, and opened new roads of advance. The outstanding qualities of his work have been originality and versatility. He has been a theorist as well as an experimenter.

The research papers published in the last twenty years by Sir C. V. Raman and the collaborators in his laboratory during the period of his professorship include over 600 titles, and the topics with which they deal indicate an astonishing catholicity of scientific interests. The investigations concern themselves with subjects so diverse as the dynamics of vibrations and sound, the theory of musical instruments, special diffraction problems, meteorological and colloid optics, X-ray diffraction in liquids and solids, magnetism and magne-crystallic action, electro- and magneto-optics, dielectric behaviour and ultra-sonics. In all of these subjects, the researches of his school have notably influenced current progress. It is not feasible within any reasonable limits of space to review them even in broad outline.

The majority of investigators are individualists by nature, but a few are born leaders. Sir C. V. Raman belongs to the latter category. Impressive though his own personal contributions to science have been, his greater achievement is the work he has done in inspiring a whole group of investigators and creating a distinctive school of research in India. During the past twenty years, well over a hundred young men have been personally initiated into research by him. These young men have been drawn to his laboratories from all parts of India, and they have been encouraged to engage in independent research and to put forth their own individual efforts with just the right kind of stimulus and assistance from their teacher. This policy has proved remarkably successful in bringing out their highest qualities and securing for them academic distinctions. They occupy high positions everywhere in India on the teaching staff of the universities and colleges, and in the scientific services of the Government, and they have easily held their own in comparison with the products of foreign research schools. Much valuable scientific work is being done in India to-day by Raman's former students not only in pure physics, but also in its applications such as meteorology, seismology and soil physics.

One of the ambitions of Sir Venkata Raman has been to secure a prominent place for India on the scientific map of the world. As a step forward he realised that opportunities should be created in the country which would provide competent investigators, trained in India or elsewhere, with scientific careers, for the furtherance of their researches. Accordingly, it has been his ceaseless endeavour to create independent schools of research all over the country, to stimulate interest for research of a high standard in the universities and the scientific institutions and to staff them with men of proved ability in research. The Indian Association for the Cultivation of Science owes to his administration the permanently-endowed professorship of physics—now held by one of

THE INDIAN INSTITUTE OF SCIENCE, BANGALORE

his most distinguished pupils—a well-equipped research laboratory, a fine library, and a substantial annual grant from the Government of India which enables its work to be carried on. At the University College of Science, Calcutta, he has left a staff largely composed of his former pupils and collaborators, a finely-equipped department of physics, and a great tradition for his chair to be maintained by his successors. He has taken a very special interest in the welfare of the Andhra University and played an active part in the development of the University College of Science and Technology at Waltair. In his present sphere of activities at Bangalore, Sir C. V. Raman has been able, in a short time and at a minimum of expense, to build up a research centre in physics which has already to its credit a notable record of scientific achievement.

With the rapid increase in the volume of research work in fundamental sciences in India, the need for a periodical was keenly felt and was partially met by the issues of *Bulletins* and later of *The Proceedings of the Indian Association for the Cultivation of Science* by Sir C. V. Raman. From 1926 onwards, this periodical was issued under the name of *The Indian Journal of Physics* and contained the greater part of the research work of Indian physicists. On his removing from Calcutta to Bangalore in 1933, Professor Raman found it difficult to edit the *Journal* and to personally supervise the publications from at a distance, and he was therefore obliged to transfer its control to the men on the spot. At the same time, the creation of an active centre of research under his direction at Bangalore, and the increased productivity in research in many of the younger universities in India, prompted him to start the Indian Academy of Sciences in 1934. Under his fostering care the Indian Academy has, during the past four years, published its proceedings promptly at the end of every month, and has provided a medium in which a considerable volume of the scientific work done in India to-day is being regularly published.

The world has not been slow to recognise the importance of the achievement of Sir C. V. Raman as an investigator and a leader of scientific research. Scarcely had he completed six years as a professor of physics when the Royal Society of London elected him as its fellow in 1924. He was knighted by the British Government in 1929. He was the recipient of the Matteucci Medal of the Italian Society of Sciences in 1928, of the Hughes Medal of the Royal Society in 1930, and in the same year he was awarded the Nobel Prize for Physics. He has received *honoris causa* the D.Sc. degree of the Paris University, the LL.D. degree of Glasgow and the Ph.D. degree from Freiburg. The Universities of Calcutta, Bombay, Madras, Benares and Dacca in India have also conferred honorary doctorates on him. He is an honorary fellow or member of various learned societies, including especially the Royal Philosophical Society of Glasgow, the Zurich Physical Society, the Royal Irish Academy, the Deutsche Akademie of Munich and the Hungarian Academy of Sciences. He is also an honorary member of the Indian Mathematical and Chemical Societies and of the Indian Science Congress.

A remarkable fact about the life of Sir C. V. Raman is that he started his career as an investigator without any external stimulus and attained eminence as a scientist by his own individual effort, sustained by the work of his devoted pupils. The fact that he had no training in foreign laboratories endowed him with a power born from within and an originality in moulding the career of young men. In later years his ripe experience as a scientific leader was enriched by his frequent travels outside India, which have afforded him opportunities of visiting the leading research laboratories and of cultivating personal relations with the leaders of Europe and America. His first visit to Europe was in the summer months of 1921, when he attended the Congress of the Universities of the British Empire held at Oxford. In 1924 he was invited to open a discussion on the Scattering of Light at the Toronto meeting of the British Association and of the International Congress of Mathematicians. Following this meeting, Raman visited the United States to represent India at the Centenary of the Franklin Institute at Philadelphia. At the invitation of R. A. Millikan, he spent four months at Pasadena as a Visiting Professor at the California Institute of Technology before returning to India early in 1925. In the autumn of 1925 Raman again visited Europe, as the guest of the Russian Academy of Sciences, to represent India at the Bicentenary celebrations of the Academy in Leningrad and Moscow. In 1929 Raman was invited by the Faraday Society to open a discussion on molecular spectra at Bristol, and took the opportunity of visiting and lecturing at many centres of learning in Europe. He subsequently visited Europe in the winter of 1930 to receive the Nobel Prize at Stockholm; in 1932 to receive the honorary Doctorate at Paris; and in 1937, as an invitee to take part in the International Congress of Physics at Paris and Bologna.

The life of Sir C. V. Raman has been one of unswerving devotion to the pursuit of knowledge and of unceasing service to the cause of science and the promotion of research in India. The award of the Nobel Prize represents the considered judgment of the scientific world on the fundamental character and enduring importance of Professor Raman's contribution to science. It places his name in a select list of famous men, the record of whose discoveries is also the history of modern science.

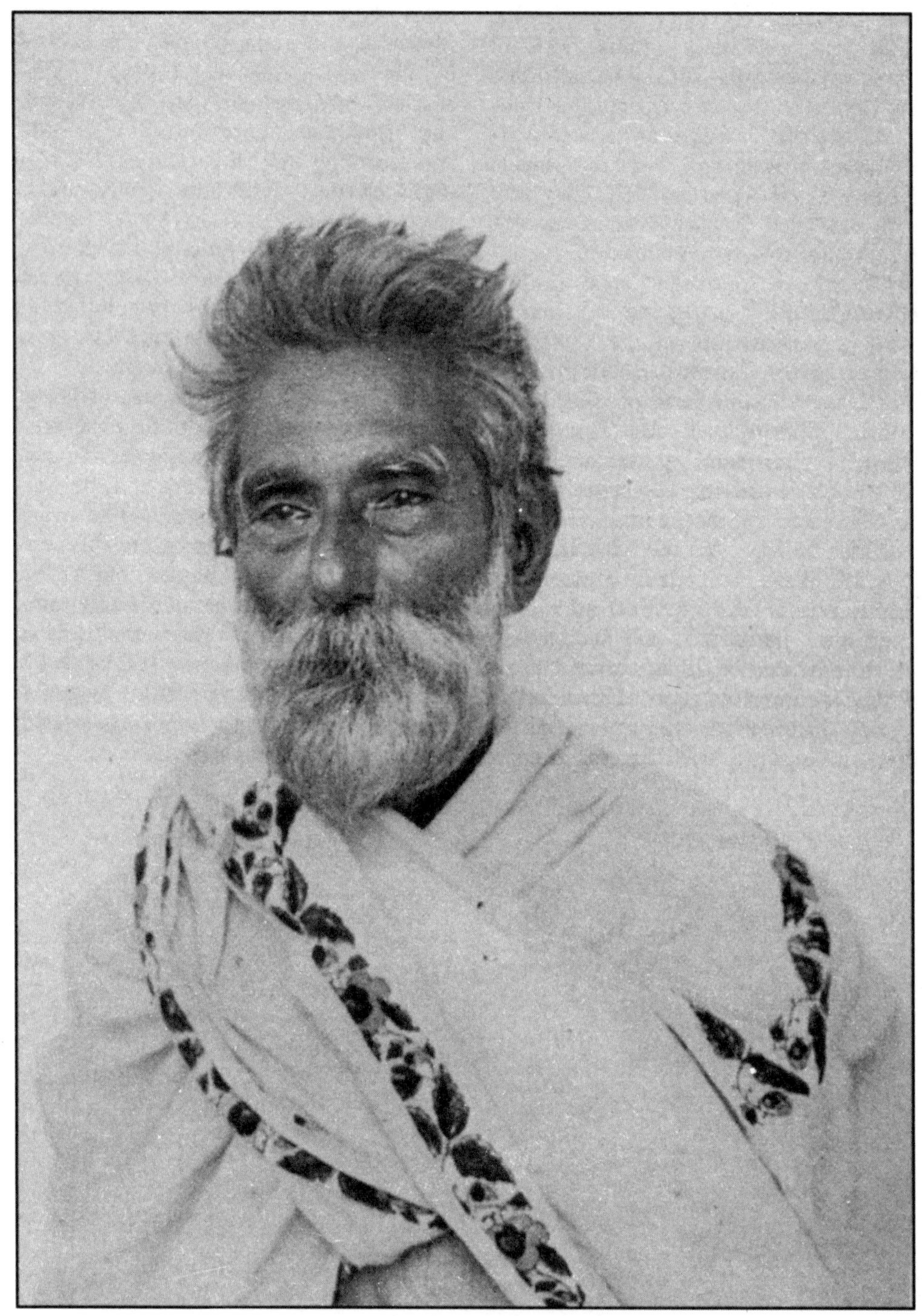

SIR PRAFULLA CHANDRA RAY

SIR PRAFULLA CHANDRA RAY

SCIENTIFIC GENIUS AND PATRIOT

BORN 1861

BY PROFESSOR J. C. GHOSH, D.Sc.

SIR PRAFULLA CHANDRA RAY was born on August 2, 1861. His father, Haris Chandra Ray, was a prosperous landed proprietor and a man of wide culture. He was not only proficient in Persian—then the court language in India—but also possessed a very considerable knowledge of classical English literature which he acquired at the Krishnanagor College under its distinguished principal, Captain Richardson.

Haris Chandra early imbibed the heretical ideas of the West, and Sir Prafulla relates in his autobiography how when almost a child, he learnt from his father that beef-eating was quite in vogue in ancient India and the very word for guest in Sanskrit is "Goghna" (one in whose honour the fat cow is killed). To his sons Haris Chandra was a friend and companion, inculcating in them the principles of rational thinking and the lessons of dutifulness and patriotism by way of telling anecdotes from lives of great men.

Up to nine years of age Ray was educated at his father's village school. In 1870 the family removed to Calcutta and he joined the Hare School. Unfortunately in a few years his health was almost wrecked by an obstinate attack of dysentery, and he had to leave the school. The years of physical suffering were, however, in his case, years of passionate home-study; and when, after convalescence, he joined the Albert School he was unquestionably the ablest student there.

He passed the Entrance Examination in 1879 and joined the Metropolitan Institution founded by Pandit Iswar Chandra Vidyasagar. He also attended lectures on chemistry and physics at the Presidency College and was greatly attracted by the manipulative skill of Sir Alexander Pedlar.

To the handicap of a fragile constitution was now added the equally serious one of poverty. The family estates were rapidly dwindling into insignificance due to debts incurred by his father, but this only stirred young Prafulla to greater efforts. While reading for his degree he was secretly preparing at home for the Gilchrist Scholarship Examination. It was an all-India competition, and his success in 1882 gave him the long-cherished opportunity for proceeding to Europe for higher studies.

He entered the University of Edinburgh in October, 1882, and his subjects of study were chemistry, physics, botany and zoology. In chemistry he came under Crum Brown, whom he learnt to esteem, and with fellow students like Hugh Marshall, Alexander Smith, James Walker, the atmosphere was such that he became passionately fond of chemistry. His studies for the B.Sc. degrees were interrupted for a time when he competed for a prize on the best essay on "India, before and after the mutiny." In this "he indulged in many bitter diatribes against the British Rule" and the essay was judged among those *Proxime accesserunt*. It did, however, one good thing—Ray discovered that he had the faculty of writing with facility, a faculty which he has used with great power in later life.

The essay written, he worked hard in his favourite subject of chemistry and obtained the D.Sc. degree in 1888 on the basis of a thesis in inorganic chemistry. He was honoured in due course by the award of a special scholarship by the Gilchrist Foundation and of the Hope Prize Scholarship, and also by his election to the position of Vice-President of the Edinburgh University Chemical Society. The simple life and the cheap living of those days in a Scottish University made an abiding impression on him. Students—left to fend for themselves at an early age and protected by poverty from vicious amusements—lived in an atmosphere of high endeavour, in which University education was of real value as a preparation for life.

He now tried to join the Indian Educational Service; but high honours at the University, strong testimonials from professors of repute and powerful recommendations from well-wishers like Sir W. M. Muir and Sir Charles Bernard were of no avail at the India Office in London.

He returned to Calcutta in 1888 and, after a year of waiting, obtained the post of an assistant professor at the Presidency College, Calcutta on Rs. 250 a month. Persons with inferior qualifications were holding high appointments as professors in the Indian Educational Service, and he naturally felt the injustice that had been done to him. But he was determined to make the best use of his opportunities. In Europe the reputation of a professor depends more on his capacity for extending the bounds of knowledge rather than that for actual teaching. But in India this tradition was sadly lacking. From the very beginning of his career Dr. Ray felt it to be his mission in life to bring this tradition of Europe into the atmosphere of Indian Universities and to create an enthusiasm for research in his young students.

In 1896 he became famous through his discovery of mercurous nitrite, a compound of unexpected stability; and a stream of research work began to flow out from his laboratory, carried out either by himself or in collaboration with his senior students. His main interest centred round the formation and stability of nitrites. For example, besides mercurous nitrite he prepared in the pure state nitrites of alkaline earths, and showed that magnesium nitrite was the least stable, forming a link between the nitrites of zinc and cadmium and those of calcium, strontium and barium. He made the important discovery that ammonium nitrite was far from the unstable compound that it was supposed to be, and that it could be vaporised in vacuum at 78° in an undissociated form. He also isolated the amine-nitrites and studied their physical and chemical properties. An aqueous solution of pure nitrous acid was prepared which was found to react very slowly with urea—a fact which was utilised by Werner in postulating a new constitution for urea. In later years he studied in great detail organometallic compounds of sulphur, mercury, platinum, etc., and made many interesting observations. For example he prepared the compound

I-Hg-S-S-Hg-I

and showed that the crystals changed colour in light but reverted to the original form when kept in darkness.

Sir Prafulla believes that his greatest achievement has been the foundation of the Indian School of Chemistry and of the Indian Chemical Society. Of him as a teacher of youth, as a *Guru* inspiring him with high ideals and the spirit of conquest in the domain of knowledge, Rabindranath Tagore thus speaks:

"It is stated in the Upanishads that the One said, 'I shall be many.' The beginning of creation is a move towards self-immolation. Acharya Prafulla Chandra has become many in his students and has made his heart alive in the hearts of many. And that could not have been at all possible had he not unreservedly made a gift of himself. This power of creation having its inception in self-sacrifice is a divine power. The glory of this power in the Acharya will never be worn out by decrepitude. It will extend further in time through the ever-growing intelligence of youthful hearts; by steady perseverance they will win new treasures of knowledge."

After twenty-eight years' active service in the Presidency College, he retired from Government service in 1916.

The severance of connection with the College was extremely painful to him, but he found a larger sphere of work as Director of the Chemical Laboratories of the University College of Science founded by Sir Asutosh Mukerjee with the princely endowments of Sir Tarak Nath Palit and Sir Rash Behary Ghosh. For fifteen years (1921-1936), his salary has been entirely spent on improving the equipment of the laboratories and maintenance of research fellowships. In 1936 he retired from active service and was appointed Emeritus Professor of Chemistry in the University of Calcutta.

Great as he has been as a teacher, he has also proved a most successful man of action. He has been responsible for establishing many industrial enterprises, of which the creation of the Bengal Chemical and Pharmaceutical Works is the most remarkable. When, as a young D.Sc. of Edinburgh, he was trying to secure an appointment in the Education Department, the Director of Public Instruction told him once that if he was such a clever chemist why did he not start industries. The young professor felt that the cheap and innumerable raw materials of Bengal could be converted into costly finished products with the aid of the scientific knowledge that he commanded.

Unaided, and with a capital of a few hundred rupees saved from his small salary, he began the preparation of pharmaceuticals at his own home. His duties at college were exacting. His research work in the laboratory continued every day from 10.30 a.m. to 5 p.m., his health was much below normal, but the will to achieve success as an industrialist was unconquerable.

In a few years the house at 91 Upper Circular Road, except for the bedroom which he occupied, had the appearance of a factory. His pharmaceutical preparations soon secured a well-merited recognition and the business rapidly expanded. In 1902 the Bengal Chemical and Pharmaceutical Works were converted into a limited concern with a capital of 2 lakhs of rupees, and Sir Prafulla made over his share in the concern to a trust created for conducting a High School and other beneficent activities in his native district of Khulna. To-day the Bengal Chemical and Pharmaceutical Works, with his unfailing help and guidance, boasts of having the biggest sulphuric acid plant in Asia, and pays its manager something like Rs. 40,000 a year.

Students and friends of Sir Prafulla have always felt that the patriot in him has prevented the fullest realisation of his genius as a researcher and an industrialist. The one passion in his life has been an ardent love for his motherland. He has reiterated from hundreds of platforms his conviction that "researches can wait, industries can wait, but Swaraj cannot wait." This passion has been the dominating force in his life. His *History of Hindu Chemistry*, in two volumes, was the result of a long and painful research extending over a period of about ten years. It has earned for its author a great reputation and has been acclaimed as adding a very interesting chapter to the history of sciences and of the human spirit. In this self-imposed task Sir Prafulla was guided by the hope that a rediscovery of the past might bring confidence in the future. Time and again we find the scientist laying aside his test-tube and leading great movements for the relief of the distressed, and preaching new ideas for the moral and material progress of his fellow-countrymen.

A man of wide culture, interested in almost all activities of human life, he has come to occupy a unique position in the political and educational world of Bengal. Living a life of severe asceticism, spending whatever he has for the benefit of the poor and the oppressed, he has always justified the enormous confidence which his countrymen place in him. His work in connection with the North Bengal Flood of 1922, whose havoc is yet fresh in the memory of many, has thus been described by the special correspondent of the *Manchester Guardian*:

> "In these circumstances, a professor of chemistry, Sir P. C. Ray, stepped forward and called upon his countrymen to make good the Government's omission. His call was answered with enthusiasm. The public of Bengal in one month gave three lakhs of rupees, rich women giving their silk and ornaments and the poor giving their spare garments. Hundreds of young men volunteered to go down and carry out the distribution of relief to the villagers, a task which involved a considerable amount of hard work and bodily discomfort in a malarious country. The enthusiasm of the response to Sir P. C. Ray's appeal was due partly to the Bengali's natural desire to score off the foreign Government, partly to genuine sympathy with the sufferers, but very largely to Sir P. C. Ray's remarkable personality and position. He is a real organiser and a real teacher. I heard a European saying: If Mr. Gandhi had been able to create two more Sir P. C. Rays he would have succeeded in getting Swaraj within this year. . . . He is too warm-blooded and energetic a man to make a perfectly fair critic (of Government). But any man who feels aggrieved by his criticism has at least the satisfaction of knowing that unlike so many critics Sir P. C. Ray would never shirk taking on the job himself if the chances were offered him, and if he did take on the job he would like to put it through about as well as and perhaps a little better than anybody else."

He was made a Companion of the Order of the Indian Empire in 1911 and was knighted after the War. In 1934 he was elected an Honorary Fellow of the Chemical Society of London. Sir Gowland Hopkins and Prof. C. Matignon were the other two recipients of this high honour on this occasion. This appreciation of his services by his fellow chemists of the British Empire has touched him deeply.

In 1932, Sir P. C. Ray published an autobiography,[1] and this short sketch may well be concluded with the following extract from the review of

[1] "*Life and Experiences of a Bengali Chemist*," *by Prafulla Chandra Ray. London, Kegan Paul & Co. Ltd.*, 1932.

this book by Prof. H. E. Armstrong in *Nature*:

"A more remarkable career than that of Sir P. C. Ray could not well be chronicled. The story told is not only fascinating, it has an altogether special value as a presentation of a complex mentality unique in character, range of ability and experience. . . . In part the study of a life overfull of action, of unusually varied occupations and interests, in no small degree it is also a dispassionate statement and discussion of pressing Indian social problems. . . . From beginning to end the message of the book is one of the highest endeavour—pulsating with vitality and intellectual force."

SIR SYED AHMAD KHAN

SIR SYED AHMAD KHAN

FOUNDER OF ALIGARH UNIVERSITY

1817–1898

BY SIR ABDUL QADIR

To be treated cruelly by your brethren,
but to live for their good;
To be pierced by the arrow and to remain
fond of the arrow;
To live anxious to serve your nation,
And to die with that anxiety in your
heart.
You may aspire to be a Syed Ahmad,
If you can live up to his ideal of life.
(Translation from Hali's Elegy on
Syed Ahmad).

IN the touching words which have been cited above (in translation) Hali, the famous Indian poet, has truly described the life of the late Sir Syed Ahmad Khan. These words are particularly applicable to the crowning years of Sir Syed's life, when he devoted all his time and energy, after his retirement from Government service, to social, religious and educational work and when reforms advocated and introduced by him met with a lot of opposition and harsh criticism. He was not, however, daunted by such treatment, and by dint of his sincerity and perseverance, he gradually succeeded in winning the sympathy and support of a large number of his countrymen and co-religionists. He founded the well-known Moslem College at Aligarh, which has now grown into a flourishing University. He also originated the movement of independent religious thought among the Moslems of India.

Syed Ahmad Khan lived for more than four score years. His life can be conveniently divided into four approximately equal periods. The first twenty years (1817–1837), representing his youth and early education, were not very eventful, except that during this period he had the benefit of living in an environment which was helpful in laying the foundations of some of the best traits of his character. The next period of twenty years (1837–1857) began with a modest start on the rungs of the official ladder in the service of the British Government. He secured substantial advancement in his career by dint of his ability, honesty and devotion to duty. It was during this period that the perilous events of 1857 occurred. He was serving at Bijnaur at the time, and was instrumental in saving the lives of a number of English men, women and children, for which he earned their lasting gratitude and a pension for life from the Government. In the third period of twenty years (from 1857–1877), he performed, with conspicuous success, his duties as a judicial officer at different stations in the United Provinces, and also began to take an active interest in promoting the cause of education by founding societies for this purpose wherever he went. It was during this period that he decided to go to England, on long leave, and to acquire a first-hand knowledge about the educational institutions there, in order to start work in India on similar lines. The fourth period (1877–1898) was the most important of all, as his unique experience and his intense zeal for helping his co-religionists and his countrymen were utilised by him for rendering a unique service in various spheres of nation building, which will be always remembered with sincere gratitude and which earned him the title of the Grand Old Man of India.

Syed Ahmad Khan was born at Delhi on October 17, 1817. The Syed family to which he belonged was distinguished not only for its piety and learning but also for the position of eminence it had enjoyed under the Moguls. His ancestor, Syed Hadi, came to India from Herat. The paternal grandfather of Syed Ahmad, Syed Jawad Ali Khan, was an army commander in the reign of Alamgir II, and was granted the title of *Jawad ud Daula*. On the mother's side Syed Ahmad was equally well-connected. Khwajah Faridud Din Ahmad, his maternal grandfather, was the Prime Minister of Akbar II. The Mogul emperors who occupied the throne of Delhi towards the end of the eighteenth century had very little of their empire left in their hands, but they retained all the pomp of the old Court. Syed Ahmad, in his youth, constantly visited the palace and received robes of honour from the Emperor on several occasions.

It is interesting to note that while his noble ancestry and early associations with the Mogul Court gave Syed Ahmad Khan his charm of manner and his dignified behaviour and marked him out as a born leader of men, he combined with it a sincere spirit of humility. He also had a deep reverence for religion. This feature he inherited from his father, Syed Muhamad Taqi, who attached great importance to the things of the spirit and preferred the life of a recluse and a Sufi to official honours and rank. Though the love of religion in Syed Ahmad Khan took a practical turn in his maturer years and induced him to preach changes and reforms, which were objected to by the orthodox sections of the Moslem community, there can be no doubt that his love of religion was deep and genuine. He owed his early education to his devout mother. He had no regular schooling, and learnt no English except a small number of words which he picked up later in life and could use on occasions. His father died in 1836, and early next year he entered the British Service, as a *serishtadar*, a Reader in a Court. It is said that his family people did not approve of the step taken by him, as Bahadur Shah, the last of the Moguls, had conferred on him the titles of his grandfather and would have given him some position in his Court. It seems the far-seeing eye of Syed Ahmad Khan had already dimly discerned that the Mogul power was completing the stages of its decay and that the British Government was taking its place.

Syed Ahmad's good work soon attracted notice, and after about four years of service he was appointed a Musasif, a judicial officer, now known as a sub-judge. He tried to use his moments of leisure in improving his mind by private study, and in 1844 he published the first result of his research in the form of a book called the *Asar-us-Sanadid*, or "The Traces of the Great."[1] Syed Ahmad Khan gave in this book interesting descriptions of the ruins of ancient Delhi; accounts of some of the saintly men who lived in Delhi, when Syed Ahmad Khan was young, are also given with great reverence, and accounts of some of the poets of Urdu and Persian are also added. It was translated into French by M. Garcin de Tassy, and it was mainly on the strength of this work that Syed Ahmad Khan was elected an Honorary Member of the Royal Asiatic Society in 1864.

It has been mentioned already that it

[1] *This work has gone through several editions. The reprint of this work that I have consulted was published in* 1876, *at the Naval Kishare Press, Lucknow, and it is stated in a note by the publisher that an earlier edition was printed at the Syed-ul-Akbar Press in* 1847.

was at Bijnaur, that he helped the English men, women and children of the place to escape in safety, by boldly going unarmed into the camp of Nawab Mahmud Khan, whose men, 800 strong, had surrounded the house in which the English people had taken refuge. He interceded with the Nawab on their behalf. The Nawab listened to his advice and agreed that they should quickly leave at the dead of night, after signing a document that they conferred that part of the country on the Nawab, if the English did not return to claim it. With the help of an escort from the Nawab and four of Syed Ahmad's horsemen the party left for Meerut, and safely arrived there. Syed Ahmad Khan remained in Bijnaur and provisionally administered the district on behalf of Nawab, but later some disturbances arose which made it necessary for him to flee for his own safety, and after running many risks he also reached Meerut.

After the fall of Delhi, Syed Ahmad visited his own home there and found that his uncle and cousin had been slain, and that his mother and an old woman servant of hers had found shelter in the house of the attendant of their horses. They had had no water for three days. He brought them water and finding the servant very weak gave it to her first, but soon after drinking a little of it, she died. He took his mother with him to Meerut, but the sufferings of this disastrous period had undermined her health and she died about a month after going to Meerut. The painful scenes witnessed by him left a deep impression on the mind of Syed Ahmad and considerably affected his attitude towards life. He set to work first of all to analyse the causes that had culminated in the events of 1857 and wrote a book called the "Asbabi-Baghawat-i-Hind," or "The Causes of the Indian Revolt."[1] It was translated from Urdu into English by Sir Auckland Colvin, with the co-operation of Colonel (subsequently Major-General) Graham, a friend and admirer of Syed Ahmad Khan. In that book he offered advice to the Government as well as to the people, and made it his aim to interpret them to one another in order to bring about a better understanding between them. Among the means he suggested for producing this result was education. According to him this was a cure for all the social and political diseases of India. As soon as he arrived at this conclusion he began work on that basis, as a practical man. He was stationed at Moradabad and he opened there a school for the study of modern history, in 1858.

In 1862 Syed Ahmad Khan was transferred to Ghazipur, where he and Colonel Graham met for the first time, and there grew between them a life-long and sincere friendship, which resulted in Graham writing a biography of Sir Syed, which is the best available account in English of the Syed's work.[2]

Graham was a military officer with a literary bent of mind, and was at that time stationed at Ghazipur, as an Assistant District Superintendent of Police. Syed Ahmad Khan enlisted his sympathy and support in establishing a society for translating useful books from English into Urdu. He had felt the need of such a society when he started his school at Moradabad, but the idea took a definite shape at Ghazipur, when a meeting of Europeans and Indians was held at the house of Syed Ahmad Khan. Graham, in a speech heartily supporting the

1 *Published in* 1858.

2 *"The Life and Work of Sir Syed Ahmad Khan," first puplished in* 1885. *The author brought out a revised and enlarged edition in* 1909. *There is a fuller and more comprehensive story of Sir Syed Ahmad's life in Urdu called the Hajat-i-Javid (or Life Eternal), written by Maulana Hali.*

proposal, said that he was sure that those interested in India's well-being would give their hearty aid to this society, because it would be "through the modern arts and sciences that this country will advance with the age." After an eloquent speech by Syed Ahmad Khan the society was formed and developed later into the Scientific Society of Aligarh, which did very useful work in enriching Urdu with translations of scientific works and of books on general knowledge.

From Ghazipur Syed Ahmad was transferred to Aligarh. His official connection with this district was an important turning-point in his future career. A number of well-to-do families of the landed aristocracy were residing in the district, and the heads of many families were men of culture, well versed in Eastern literature. Syed Ahmad's contact with them and their contact with him proved of great value. They were gradually infected by his zeal for engrafting a knowledge of Western arts and science on Oriental learning, and he found in them eventually a body of faithful helpers in his scheme of education.

The efforts for spreading education among his countrymen made by Syed Ahmad Khan received an encouraging recognition in 1866, when the Viceroy, Lord Lawrence, presented him with a gold medal and a copy of Macaulay's Works. In 1867 came another transfer. This time it was to Benares, a town sacred in Hindu tradition and a seat of ancient Hindu learning. Here, too, he continued his advocacy of the study of Western knowledge. There was a great prejudice at the time among Indian gentlemen against sending their sons abroad for their education, but Syed Ahmad Khan helped people to get over it. He sent his sons, Syed Mahmud and Syed Hamid, to England for higher education. He also decided to go himself on a visit to the country, to study its methods of education and its civic institutions. This was a bold and courageous step. His sons were lucky enough to be selected for State scholarships, and their expenses were thus provided for; but for his own expenses he had to raise a loan, to be subsequently discharged. He took long leave and sailed for England in 1869 with his sons. This enterprise was fully justified by the results achieved. Syed Mahmud returned after a successful career at Cambridge, qualifying for the Bar. His merits as a lawyer were soon recognised, and he was taken into the judicial service and eventually adorned the Bench of the High Court of Allahabad. The second son, Syed Hamid, went into the Police service and rose to the rank of a District Superintendent of Police. The old Syed himself had very interesting experiences and useful contacts which helped the great work of education and reform that he carried out after his return to India.

It so happened that the period of Syed Ahmad Khan's leave coincided with the furlough which his friend Graham was spending in England and they met one another very often. Lord Lawrence, who had known Syed Ahmad Khan in India and appreciated his public activities, was also in England, and made his stay very pleasant by calling on him frequently and introducing him to influential friends. He also met Lord Stanley of Alderley[1] who was known to be keenly interested in the welfare of Moslems and who was glad to meet a leading Indian Moslem. When Syed Ahmad Khan founded the Mohammedan

[1] *Lord Stanley's interest in Moslems began with his official career as British Ambassador at Constantinople. In his lifetime he was known only as a sympathetic admirer of Islam, but it transpired on his death that he had been a Moslem, as he left a will showing that in his latter days he had lived as a Moslem and wished to be buried according to Islamic rites. His wishes were carried out in this respect.*

Oriental College at Aligarh, Lord Stanley gave a handsome donation for that institution.

One of the most interesting contacts which Syed Ahmad Khan had in England was when he had an interview with Carlyle, the sage of Chelsea. Graham tells us that they talked long over "Heroes and Hero-Worship," especially about Mohammed. They also talked about Syed Ahmad's "Essays on the Life of Mohammed," a book which he had written in Urdu and a translation of which was being printed in England at the time, under his supervision. The publication of this book was one of the useful things accomplished by Syed Ahmad during his visit to England.[1]

Syed Ahmad Khan received the honour of being made a Companion of the Star of India in June, 1869, and was presented with the insignia of that Order by the Duke of Argyll, the then Secretary of State for India. About sixteen years after this he was knighted and became Sir Syed Ahmad Khan, K.C.S.I.

In the course of his travels, Syed Ahmad Khan found time to send graphic accounts of his journey to and his stay in England to the Scientific Society at Aligarh, which were published in Urdu in the *Aligarh Institute Gazette*. He mentions the interesting contact he had on board the SS. *Poona* with the famous French engineer, M. de Lesseps, who constructed the Suez Canal. He had many talks with him. He managed to carry on a conversation in Arabic, though the Arabic spoken by M. de Lesseps was a little different in pronunciation and idiom from the literary Arabic which Sir Syed could speak.

In 1870, Sir Syed returned to India and resumed his duties at Benares. His visit to England had given a definite shape to his plans for higher education in India, and he aimed at establishing a residential College on lines similar to those of the colleges at Oxford and Cambridge and to combine in it the learning of the East and the West, with a special emphasis on religious teaching. With this object he formed the Mohammedan Anglo-Oriental College Fund Committee in 1872.

Syed Ahmad Khan began to canvass for money to start the proposed college and met with a fair amount of encouragement. His plans matured about the middle of 1875, when Sir William Muir performed the opening ceremony of the institution, which began work with the formation of school classes at Aligarh. It developed into a college in a few years and attracted students from all parts of India. Thousands of them have passed out of the college and a large number of them have won distinctions in various spheres of life.

In 1876 Syed Ahmad Khan retired on pension, and made Aligarh his home for the rest of his life. He was now able to give his undivided attention to the development of the college, and aimed at raising it one day to the status of a university.

The foundation stone of the college buildings was laid on January 8, 1877, by H.E. Lord Lytton. An address setting out the aims of the college, was presented to him and elicited from him a reply highly appreciative of the efforts of Syed Ahmad Khan.

I do not think it is necessary to dwell at length on the growth of this famous institution or the anxious care with which Syed Ahmad Khan watched its development. He was fortunate in securing the services of very distinguished English scholars, among whom three names deserve special mention, i.e. Beck, Morison and Arnold, who may be called

[1] *The full name of this book was "A series of Essays on the Life of Mohammed and subjects subsidiary thereto," published by Trubner & Co., London, in* 1870.

the builders of the Aligarh College under the supervision of its great founder. Theodore Beck was a man who combined excellent scholarship with an unusual charm of manner. The period during which he was the head of the institution with Morison and Arnold as his right-hand men, is regarded the period of its prime. These three Englishmen treated the old Syed as if he were their father and he loved them as if they were his children. They mixed freely with the students and infected them with their own zeal for learning. Unfortunately none of the three is now with us, but they have left a lasting impression on the minds of those who came in contact with them. They trained the young men who came to Aligarh, and Aligarh in its turn trained them. They breathed the atmosphere which the old Syed had created there, and learnt to love the East. Some of the finest scholars of Urdu, Persian and Arabic among the contemporaries of Syed Ahmad were co-operating with him. A few of them adopted Aligarh as their home; others visited it frequently. The three young Englishmen could not remain unaffected by these contacts. Professor Arnold (afterwards Sir Thomas Arnold) had the greatest enthusiasm for Oriental literature. He began to study Arabic and learnt it so well that later on, when he returned to England he was a lecturer on Arabic at the School of Oriental Studies of the London University. It was under the inspiration of Syed Ahmad Khan that he got the idea of writing his memorable book, known as the "Preaching of Islam," which placed him in the front rank of literary men.

Morison (afterwards Sir Theodore Morison) had inherited a taste for literature from his father, who was a collaborator of Mr. (afterwards Lord) Morley, in some of the latter's publications. Morison succeeded Beck as Principal and made a great name as an educator. He rose subsequently to be a member of the Council of the Secretary of State for India. If Beck's career had not been cut off by his premature death at Simla, he would, perhaps, have achieved great distinction like his two colleagues.

Among the Indian scholars who gathered round Sir Syed, the most prominent were Hali, the famous poet and the author of the Urdu biography of Sir Syed; Shibli, the author of the *Siratun Nabi*, a scholarly work on the life of the Prophet of Islam, Maulvi Nazir Ahmad, the well-known master of Urdu prose; and Nawab Muhsinul Mulk, the great orator, who afterwards carried on the work of Sir Syed, when the latter and his son, Syed Mahmud, passed away.

Besides the work done by Syed Ahmad Khan for the M.A.O. College, his marvellous energy found vent in several other directions. He started the Mohammedan Educational Conference, which was meant as an adjunct to the college, and tried to popularise the cause of modern education among the Moslems and to combat the prejudices which many old-fashioned Moslems had against it. The Conference held its sessions every year at some important centre, and attracted a large crowd of educated Moslems to hear lectures on different aspects of education and to consider means of advancing it in all parts of the country. Many schools and colleges for Moslems sprang up through the efforts of this conference and there is no important place in India at which it has not held its sittings. It is still active and is continuing the educational propaganda among the Moslems.

Another of Sir Syed's activities deserving mention is the movement for social reform in his community. A periodical called the *Tehzib-ul-Akhlaq*, which was edited by him, was the organ through which his message of reform was conveyed to his readers from time to time, with great effect.

It was in his efforts for reform, and particularly when he stepped into the dangerous zone of religious reform, that Syed Ahmad met with strong opposition. Some orthodox people had looked askance at his proposed teaching of Western science and the social changes advocated by him, but had not adopted an openly hostile attitude towards him. But when he began to write his *Tafsir*, that is a commentary on the Qoran, with views in it which were considered unorthodox, the anger against him burst into a storm. His critics gave him and his followers the nickname of *nechari*, and regarded him as the founder of a new heretical sect. He had not, in fact, founded a new sect. The main difference between him and the orthodox theologians was that he advocated the adoption of rational explanations of religious doctrines, to reconcile religion with science, while they thought this to be a dangerous effort likely to undermine religion. The word *nechari* has really no bad meaning. It means one who follows Nature. Syed Ahmad had, in one of his writings, emphasised that Islam was in accordance with Nature. Thus the name began. But in the mind of the illiterate masses its implications were the worst that may be imagined. Some of the *Ulema* (theologians) denounced Syed Ahmad Khan as a *Kafir* (infidel), and one of them went the length of taking a document of denunciation to Mecca to have it signed by the *Ulema* there. He came back triumphantly with the seal of many Arabian *Ulema* fixed to the *fatwa* (a religious edict) and published it in India. When the attention of Syed Ahmad Khan was drawn towards it and some of his friends suggested the need of a strong comment on it in his own journal, all that the Syed wrote was a brief line to say that he was gratified that a sinful person like himself had been indirectly instrumental in enabling his opponent to acquire virtue by performing the pilgrimage to Mecca, in order to obtain the signatures on the edict. He quoted a line from Hafiz, the translation of which is as follows:

> "*Behold how blessed is my temple of idols,*
> *That it becomes the house of God, when it is destroyed.*"

The achievements of Syed Ahmad Khan as an educationist and a reformer are so famous that one is apt to lose sight of the fact that he was a distinguished writer of Urdu and a benefactor of Urdu literature. He not only influenced the work of men like Hali and Shibli, but directly and indirectly that of many others. As a writer of good prose, he is entitled to share with Ghalib the credit of introducing in Urdu the simple and impressive style which aims at writing as if you were talking freely to a familiar friend. He was, perhaps, the very first to make use of Urdu for public speeches and his example has since been followed by some of the ablest speakers in India.

A reference to another aspect of the life of Syed Ahmad Khan may be made before concluding this brief sketch of his career, and that is his attitude towards politics. It may be pointed out that politics were not a live issue at the time when he began his educational work. The idea of a political organisation for the assertion of Indian rights may be said to have its birth from the foundation of the National Congress in 1885, which was in its early youth, when Syed Ahmad Khan died. He was not, however, favourably inclined to it and considered it advisable that his co-religionists at least should not join it.

His main reason for this attitude was that he wished the Moslems to concentrate first on making up their deficiency in modern education. His advice proved useful on the whole and during his lifetime the bulk of the Moslem Community kept aloof from the Congress and from taking any part in politics. The organisation of the Moslems for safeguarding their political interests did not begin till 1906, when Nawab Muhsinul Mulk, on whom the mantle of Sir Syed as a leader of Moslem India had fallen, organised a strong and representative deputation of Moslems, led by H.H. the Aga Khan, to claim a suitable status for Indian Moslems in the future political developments of the the country. The All-India Moslem League was founded as an outcome of this move.

About this attitude of Syed Ahmad Khan towards the Congress there has been considerable misunderstanding. As soon as he gave his advice to his co-religionists, the Hindu press and certain Hindu leaders blamed him for opposing the interests of the country and encouraging separatism. They ignored the fact that he had always tried to bring Hindus and Moslems together wherever he was, and was also in favour of friendly contacts between all classes of Indians and their British fellow-citizens, as he honestly believed that the interests of India could be best served through such mutual understanding and co-operation. In his opinion the Congress movement had been started a little prematurely. In any case it was clear to him that the Moslems could not afford to neglect their educational progress by indulging in the exciting game of political struggle, and he advised them accordingly. It is not fair to infer from this that this was from lack of patriotism or his desire for Hindu-Moslem unity had cooled down. In one of his memorable speeches he had declared that the Hindus and the Moslems were to India what the two eyes of a human being are to his body, both equally important and indispensable to one another. In the constitution of his college he acted on this principle. The portals of the college have always been open to young Hindu students as freely as to Moslems, and hundreds of young Hindus have completed their education there and enjoyed its amenities. There have been many distinguished Hindu scholars on the staff of the college. Many Hindu princes and noblemen have been among the donors who have lent their financial support to the institution.

As regards Syed Ahman's patriotism, it may be stated that he was a forerunner of the great political leaders that came after him, in the matter of a fearless advocacy of the rights of Indians and the bold and spirited tone of his speeches during his brief connection with the Viceregal Council of those days, to which he was nominated in 1878 by Lord Lytton and re-nominated for two years in 1880 by Lord Ripon.

In conclusion, I may add my own impression of Sir Syed's wonderful personality. It was my privilege, in my young days, to meet him on a few occasions. The first time when I came in contact with him and spent a few days with him was when I attended the meetings of the Moslem Educational Conference, which was held at Shahjahanpur, in the United Provinces, in 1895. I went then to write a report of the proceedings of the Session for the *Punjab Observer*, a newspaper that was started that year to represent Moslem interests. Sir Syed was naturally interested in it and at the end of every sitting I went to him to gather some information and to verify some facts. The kindness with which he encouraged me and the gracious smile with which he met me every time have remained with me as precious memories. I was struck with his wonderful energy, though he was then an old man of 78. He sat for more than six hours every day in the Conference as its secretary, he gave numerous interviews to its members and visitors in the hours preceding and following the sittings, and with the exception of the time of meals, he was busy from early morning till late at night, unruffled and majestic.

I saw him again in 1896 at the sittings of the same Conference at Meerut. It was one of the best Sessions of the Conference. Syed Mahmud was there. Nawab Imadul Mulk Bilgrami was in the chair. Nawab Muhsinul Mulk and Maulvi Nazir Ahmed and a galaxy of other distinguished leaders were present and in the centre of this galaxy sat the veteran leader, Sir Syed, with his beautiful white beard, his red fez cap suiting his fair face. But there was one element of sadness. Sir Syed's health had been suffering from the strain of work and his doctors had allowed him to come to the Conference on condition that he would not speak at it. Thus the voice that had thrilled his hearers for years was silent even before its final silence came. It was a great disappointment to all in that Conference and it was a disappointment to Sir Syed himself. It was touching to see him trying to jump up and speak, whenever any interesting discussion was going on, but his friends begged him to keep silent.

I went, afterwards, to the tent in which he was staying, and heard him conversing with his friends sitting around him, and with the same vigour as before, and hoped that he would soon be his normal self again. That hope was, however, not to be fulfilled. He attended no conferences after this and a little more than a year later he breathed his last, in 1898, and his community and country deeply mourned his loss. Never before, in living memory, had the loss of any one been so widely felt throughout the country and meetings of mourning were held in every town. It was resolved that the most fitting memorial to him would be to raise the M.A.O. College at Aligarh to a University and to collect funds for the purpose. The movement gradually gained strength and became a success through the efforts of Sir Syed's able successor, Nawab Muhsinul Mulk, who enlisted the powerful sympathy of His Highness the Aga Khan. The Aga Khan led a deputation to different parts of India and collected funds for founding a Moslem University. This example was followed by the late Mrs. Annie Besant—who was greatly interested in the education of the Hindu Community—to start, with the help of the veteran Hindu leader, Pandit Madan Mohan Malaviya, a similar movement in favour of a Hindu University, and thus in due course the two Indian Universities at Benares and Aligarh came into existence.

The founder of the Aligarh University found his last resting-place within the precincts of the College he had created and loved. In a corner of the Mosque of the College there is a simple epitaph on his tomb, speaking of the services rendered by him. Beside him there is the grave of his son, Syed Mahmud, who did not live long after his father, though he served for some time as the Secretary of the College and then as the President of its Executive Council.

SIR ASUTOSH MOOKERJEE

SIR ASUTOSH MOOKERJEE

CREATOR OF THE MODERN CALCUTTA UNIVERSITY

1864–1924

BY DR. S. P. MOOKERJEE, M.A., D.Litt. (Hon.)

THE deluge of foreign conquest that swept through India one century after another could not obliterate all signs of her ancient culture and traditions. In the picturesque language of Macaulay, the night which descended upon the land was the night of an Arctic summer; the dawn began to reappear before the last reflection of the preceding sunset had faded from the horizon. The impact between Western and Eastern thought produced far-reaching effects on the development of Indian national life. In the inevitable clash and conflict of ideals there were many who came to despise everything Indian, and regarded Western culture as the only passport towards a better civilisation. There were many who, for reasons historical and cultural, were reluctant to follow the new path, and jealously guarded their old heritage. There were others who might well be described as master-builders, who were loyal to the imperishable foundations of their ancient knowledge and at the same time desirous of utilising the wholesome contributions of Western learning and skill. They recognised that if a strong and puissant nation was to emerge from this welter of tribes and babel of tongues, this clashing of cultures and creeds, a synthesis was necessary. India, especially Bengal, produced during the 19th century a band of eminent sons who were stirred by the vision of a new India, freed from the shackles of oppression and superstition, ignorance and poverty, and who dedicated their lives to the uplift of their country in diverse spheres of life, social, religious, economic, educational and political. It is in this setting of Indian life and conditions that the ideals preached by Asutosh Mookerjee and the work done by him for the intellectual advancement of his countrymen can be worthily appreciated. He did not think in terms of groups and factions. He organised a system of education in which room was found for all that was best in the culture of the East and the West, of the Hindu and the Moslem, of the Buddhist and the Christian, of Bengal and the rest of India—a system of education that was not the close preserve of favoured individuals or communities but was accessible to all. He devoted his life to the task of laying the foundation on which was to be reared the lofty superstructure of Indian nationalism—a nationalism free alike from the parochial outlook of the group patriot, the narrow conservatism of the blind admirer of old ways, and the denationalising tendency of the Westernised Indian.

Asutosh Mookerjee was born in Calcutta in June, 1864. His father, who was essentially a self-made man, was one of the earliest graduates in Arts and Medicine of Calcutta University. He was a man of unimpeachable character, of simple habits, straightforward in his dealings with men, independent and generous in disposition. He was an ardent lover of his own language and literature and more than sixty years ago wrote books in Bengali dealing with medicine and problems of health and welfare of women. Asutosh was brought up under the personal guidance of his father, and the great qualities of head and heart which the father possessed came as a natural inheritance to the son. Asutosh's mother belonged to the old generation of Indian women, who though not educated in the modern sense of the term, proved to be ideal mothers, broad-minded, God-fearing and essentially practical, wielding considerable influence in the affairs of the family. Her influence on Asutosh was profound and remained unabated till her death in 1914. His father died in 1889.

Asutosh was fortunate in coming into contact with several distinguished teachers, all of whom, though not known to fame, were men of learning and character, and served as worthy patterns of conduct and attainment to their pupils. He developed from his boyhood a passion for knowledge which almost knew no bounds. He was encouraged from his student days to collect books dealing with various subjects of study, a habit which grew steadily with the passage of years, and his was one of the richest and rarest private libraries in the whole of India. The range of his studies became wide and diverse, and he mastered with eagerness and facility literature, languages (Eastern and Western), philosophy, science, mathematics and law.

After completing his brilliant educational career, Asutosh eagerly sought for an opportunity for doing research work in mathematics, which was his favourite subject. He had made original contributions to it in his early career which had won the approbation of famous experts. In those days, barring a few isolated instances of distinguished special workers, research was generally unknown in India. Opportunities were seldom available to brilliant Indian youths for devoting themselves to the task of advancement of learning. No such facilities came to Asutosh, and he ultimately turned to the legal profession.

At the early age of 24 he became a Fellow of the Calcutta University and was soon elected to the Syndicate. He developed from a very early stage an unbounded zeal for serving the cause of education, if not as a teacher, at least as one of those who would be able to mould the policy of the University and thereby help to raise the intellectual status of his country.

A man of outstanding intellectual equipments, well versed in various branches of learning, fearless and industrious, a clear thinker and an eloquent expounder, he did not neglect the profession of law which he took up as his own. Before he completed his thirtieth year he specialised in legal studies and obtained the degree of Doctor of Law while he was a member of the Syndicate of the University. In his fortieth year he was elevated to the Bench of the Calcutta High Court, and for nearly twenty years he held this office with great distinction and merit. He was universally regarded as one of the greatest Judges in British India.

Asutosh was also connected with the public life of his province before he became a Judge. As a member of the Calcutta Corporation, of the Bengal Legislative Council and of the Imperial Legislative Council he brought to bear upon their deliberations the full force of his vigorous personality. As observed by a distinguished Indian politician whose sphere of work was far different from that of Asutosh, "his utterances were measured but always without any suspicion of falsehood or flattery in them. He was as loyal and courageous a defender of popular rights as the most aggressive of our patriots and politicians."

The greatest work of Asutosh lay, however, in the sphere of University education. As he himself once said, "It had always been my ambition to be allowed to do something—something great, as I flattered myself in my youthful dreams—for the good and glory of my Alma Mater." His monumental achievement was the transformation of the Calcutta University from a merely examining body to one of the greatest teaching universities in the East, manned and controlled mainly by Indian scholars. It was here that his broad statesmanship, his remarkable powers of organisation, his versatility, his administrative skill, his love for national culture and his courage and tact came into full play. From 1889 to 1924, when he died, he was a Fellow of the University. He was Vice-Chancellor from 1906 to 1914, and again from 1921 to 1923; but whether in or out of office, for more than thirty years he was the most dominant personality in the University. "Asutosh, in the eyes of his countrymen and in the eyes of the world," said Lord Lytton, once Governor of Bengal and a party to the famous Lytton-Mookerjee correspondence, "represented the University so completely that for many years Asutosh was in fact the University and the University Asutosh."

It was not an easy path that lay before Asutosh when he started to mould the University into a teaching and research institution. Libraries, laboratories and buildings had to be created and equipped; scholars, teachers and workers from all parts of India and from outside were collected and functioned under his inspiring guidance. Obstacles came from quarters expected and unexpected. There were occasions when everyone feared that all was lost, but Asutosh had an unconquerable faith in the cause he had made his own and his optimism always won the day.

If he encountered opposition, he received support as well. His policy and work attracted the notice of many philanthropic Indians, including Sir Rashbehari Ghose and Sir Taraknath Palit, whose munificent gifts led to the establishment of the University College of Science and Technology, to-day the pride of Bengal and India. He selected young, brilliant scholars who, after completion of their education in this country, were sent abroad for advanced study in diverse branches of knowledge. This system worked exceedingly well, for it helped to give the fullest possible scope to gifted young Indians for the proper utilisation of their powers and attainments. He also invited distinguished scholars from various parts of the world to visit Calcutta, and thus teachers and advanced students working here were brought into intimate contact with these master minds.

One of the greatest achievements of Asutosh was to give Bengali its due place in the University studies. The principle of adopting the mother-tongue as the medium of instruction was adopted after a prolonged discussion and controversy. Bengali was included as a subject for study and research in the highest University examinations, and the scheme for a systematic publication of important works in Bengali and other languages was taken up. His scheme of work included encouragement of study and research not only in the Indian and other languages, classical and modern, in Literature, Philosophy, History, Religion, Art and Archæology, but also in Economics, Commerce, Science (Pure and Applied, Physical and Biological).

The Earl of Ronaldshay, now the Marquis of Zetland, who was Governor of Bengal in 1921, referred to the remarkable achievements of the University and to Asutosh's scheme of expansion which received his unstinted support as Governor. Such plans of work, he said, gave him "a vision of Nalanda growing up in this the greatest and most populous city of the Indian Empire."

Asutosh succeeded in transforming the dry atmosphere of an examining body into a vigorous seat of learning vibrating with life and thought, inasmuch as he not only himself had a unique enthusiasm for learning but had the capacity to communicate such enthusiasm to all who surrounded him. As a famous professor of mathematics wrote of him in *Nature* after his demise, every earnest, intellectual worker, however humble or however eminent, would find in him a wise and understanding friend, and could talk to him as to a co-worker and an equal. To every band of men in quest after truth and light his help and encouragement were greatly and unselfishly given. For a quarter of a century in almost all the learned societies and academies in the city of Calcutta he was a dominant figure, giving appreciation where it was due and advice where it was needed.

His dream was to make his country intellectually free and pre-eminent, to see education spread from town to town, village to village, and home to home, an education that would not denationalise his countrymen, but would combine in it the best elements of Eastern and Western thought. It would be idle to hold that there were no imperfections in the work which he accomplished. Such imperfections would be inevitable in the execution of a colossal work affecting the progress of society not only during one's lifetime but for generations to come. The surest way of doing homage to Asutosh's memory will be for his successors to keep his great ideals in view and pursue the work of reconstruction in accordance with the ever-changing needs of the country.

His personal qualities created an undying impression on the minds of his countrymen. He lived a life devoid of all luxuries. In his daily life, in dress and behaviour, in his public dealings, he represented a characteristic simplicity and straightforwardness which won for him the esteem and regard of all. Though an official for twenty eventful years, he throughout maintained his nationalist outlook and had the full courage of his conviction. He dreaded nothing more than unnecessarily wounding people's feelings, although he never shrank from braving the frowns of the mightiest in the land when he considered such a course to be necessary in the interest of truth and justice. Outwardly he sometimes appeared to be rough, but he was gentle at heart and full of human sympathy and understanding. His accessibility was proverbial and streams of visitors used to pour at all hours into his house and his door was open to one and all without any distinction. People, high and low, old and young, rich and poor, came there "to seek advice and help from that man of stout heart and capacious brain." Everyone received a hearing and none got an empty assurance from him. If he thought it possible to do something good for anyone, he did it with all his might. There are to-day thousands of people of all classes and communities who revere Asutosh's memory in grateful and affectionate remembrance of what he had done for them. Just as he was a staunch friend who could be safely relied upon, so also was he a good hater but never of a vindictive disposition. Even his bitterest enemy could count upon his help, if he sought his assistance in a frank and straightforward spirit. He had a keen sense of humour and his characteristic laugh was a great asset to him. His capacity for work, so diverse in character, was simply amazing. His memory was prodigious and this contributed to his unfailing grasp of broad policies as well as minute details. A genuine friend of the student-community, he knew the name of almost every graduate of his University. There was hardly any one possessing brilliant attainments whose career he did not follow with deep interest. Though an orthodox Hindu, who never went abroad, he did not suffer from any irrational conservatism. He held advanced views on social reforms and made no distinction between man and man based on caste, creed or community.

Though fifteen years have passed since his death, he is yet too near us to admit of his many-sided character being viewed in its proper perspective. In daring, in determination, in massiveness of intellect, in powers of organisation, in strength of character, he belonged to that brotherhood of adventurers who in ages past had founded states and kingdoms. As Sir Michael Sadler said, he was one of the world's commanding personalities who could have ruled an empire. His star had placed him in India in the later years of the 19th and the earlier years of the 20th century, and he gave the best of his powers to education, because he believed that in education, rightly interpreted, lay the secret of human welfare and the key to every nation's moral strength.

In him the man of action and the man of imagination were not brought face to face under their old-world relation of hostility; they became allies, good and true. If his energy was dynamic, Asutosh was also a superb dreamer of dreams. As Rabindranath Tagore said, he had the courage to dream, because he had the power to fight and the confidence to win—his will itself was the path to the goal. Men, said the poet, are always rare in all countries through whom the aspirations of their people can hope to find their fulfilment, who have the thundering voice to say that what is needed shall be done, and Asutosh had that magic voice of assurance. He had that hope, that faith in the future, which can move mountains. In the wildest of storms his sheet-anchor would hold. He intensely hated that whining namby-pamby poverty of spirit which oftentimes masquerades as fatalism or philosophic indifference. His religion was the religion of Swami Vivekananda—Glory to God in the Highest and Service to Man. As years roll on the gap created by his demise becomes wider and wider. His life and career will serve to inspire generations of men in their onward march towards progress and constructive work, will banish from their minds fears and doubts, and will instil in them a spirit of unity and dauntlessness for the attainment of their cherished goal.

SIR SHAH MUHAMMAD SULAIMAN

SIR SHAH MUHAMMAD SULAIMAN

"UNIVERSALLY RESPECTED GENIUS OF INDIA"

BORN 1886

BY M. B. AHMAD, M.A.

THE "universally respected genius of India"—this was how the late Sir Anand Sarup Sahabji Maharaj, Kt., the founder of the well known Dayal-Bagh Model Industries at Agra, once referred to the Honourable Sir Shah Sulaiman, Chief Justice of the Allahabad High Court, when he requested him to open the Dayal-Bagh Industrial Exhibition at Allahabad in 1934. There are, indeed, very few people in India to whom this reference could be applied more appropriately, and there is hardly anyone whose versatile accomplishments simultaneously in the realms of Law, Education and Science deserve a similar tribute. The brilliant career of Sir Shah Sulaiman has been, and indeed shall remain, unique in the annals of Indian history. In whatever task or activity of life in which he has taken part he has achieved distinction, and shown that rare grasp of the subject which is so essential for its successful accomplishment. An account of the life of Sir Shah Sulaiman must necessarily be a catalogue of great achievements.

Shah Sulaiman was born in a family of lawyers and scientists which can boast of a physicist, like the author of *Shams i Bazigha*—a contemporary of Newton in India. His father, Shaikh Muhammad Usman, was a leading lawyer of the Jaunpur Bar, whose legal acumen and mastery of details are still remembered in that place with admiration. As a boy Shah Sulaiman took a keen interest in his studies. When I was a member of the University Moslem Hostel at Allahabad sixteen years ago I often used to hear old inmates speaking of a student whose devotion to, and concentration in, his work always remained the despair of the more turbulent among his contemporaries in their efforts to rag the college authorities for their insistence on "more work and less play." At the B.A. examination of 1906 he came first in the first class and won several medals.

In those days the Education Department of the United Provinces Government was ever on the look-out to encourage intelligent and promising young men in order to send them to England for higher education. A definite sum was kept apart for this purpose in the Provincial budget. In 1906 Shah Sulaiman was selected for a United Province State Scholarship and in that year he set out for Cambridge. He obtained the Mathematical Tripos in 1909 and the Law Tripos in 1910. In 1909 he sat for the Indian Civil Service examination, but was not among the selected candidates. His failure was, as has proved in the case of several others, a blessing in disguise. Among his contemporaries at Cambridge and Oxford those who passed the Indian Civil Service exam. have sometimes wondered whether it was the Civil Service that could always give them sufficient scope to bring their intellectual gifts into proper use. Shah Sulaiman did not make a second attempt to take the examination and preferred to be called to the Bar. He was awarded LL.D. by the University of Dublin in 1910.

In 1911, the year of the Imperial Durbar, Dr. Shah Sulaiman returned to India and practised as a junior to his father for a year, and then shifted to Allahabad in 1912.

The Rani of Sherkot's case, the Bamrauli case, the Dharampur case, and the Bhilwal case were his early triumphs as a barrister. He impressed Sir Henry Richards and Sir Grimwood Mears so favourably that he was offered a seat on the Bench at the early age of 34. Since then the record of Sir Shah and the versatility of his genius have been frequently before the public in many ways.

The Pre-emption Law in the United Provinces has largely been built up through his efforts. He was consistently a member of the Special Bench constituted by the late Chief Justice Sir Henry Richards since his appointment. He acted as Chief Justice when he was 43, and at the age of 46 became the permanent Chief Justice of the Allahabad High Court; five years later he was elevated to the Federal Court—a record in the British Commonwealth and perhaps in the Judicial world.

During his judgeship he was the senior member of the Peshawar Enquiry Committee which was appointed to enquire into the riots at Peshawar in 1930, and his recommendations were fully given effect to by the Government of India. He was also a member of the Capitation Rates Tribunal, along with Lords Dunedin and Tomlin, and on the recommendation of this Tribunal the Government of England agreed to bear a portion of the military expenditure in India.

As Chief Justice, Sir Shah's judgment in the Meerut Conspiracy case will stand as a landmark in the history of judicial administration in India. The case had taken two years in the Magistrate's Court and four in the Sessions Court, while the arguments in appeal in the High Court were expected to last for months. The hearing of appeal and the judgment were all finished in eight days.

Speaking of his judgment in Federal Court case No. 1 of 1938 Mr. J. H. Morgan, K.C., the well-known English constitutional lawyer, while delivering his Tagore Law Lectures at the Calcutta University said:

> "Now I have just been reading the judgments of the Federal Court at Delhi in that important case. One of those judgments stands out conspicuous and pre-eminent and may well prove to be Locus Classicus of the law on the subject. It is a judgment worthy of the highest traditions of the House of Lords as an Appellate Tribunal and of the Privy Council itself. I refer to the brilliant judgment of Mr. Justice Sulaiman. In depth of thought, in breadth of view, in its powers alike of analysis and of synthesis, in grace of style and felicity of expression it is one of the most masterly judgments that I have ever had the good fortune to read. Everyone in India interested in future development of the Constitution should study it."

A different episode which has made history in the United Provinces in maintaining the independence of the Judiciary was the refusal of Sir Shah Sulaiman in 1936 to answer questions put by the members of the Legislature about judicial acts performed by the Judges—especially the appointment of Official Receivers. The President of the United Provinces Legislative Council not only allowed such questions, but made a statement on the floor of the House disapproving of the attitude of the High Court. Sir Shah, however, maintained that under the Letters Patent the responsibility involved was not of the Government but entirely of the High Court.

It may not, perhaps, be quite appropriate for me here to write about the numerous judgments of Sulaiman which have made their own name, but

I can, with greater freedom, deal with Sir Shah's record in the educational reconstruction of his country.

In his early days at Allahabad Sir Shah was one of the original founders of the Moslem High School, President Madarsa i Subhaniah, Secretary of the University Moslem Hostel, member of the Courts of the Aligarh and the Allahabad Universities, and also of the Executive Council of the latter and of the Finance Committee of the former. As president of the United Provinces Moslem Educational Conference at Budaon in 1924 he revived the Educational Conference. In the following year he was chairman of the Reception Committee of the Educational Conference at Allahabad and in 1928 he presided at the All-India Mohammedan Educational Conference at Ajmer. In his address Sir Shah Sulaiman advocated a definite change in the educational policy and laid stress on the practical side of learning. He has consistently held the view that training in technical subjects, after the entrance examination, is an essential need of the country. His Convocation addresses delivered at the Universities of Dacca, Aligarh, Hyderabad and Agra do not contain bombastic expressions or the usual platitudes, but savour more of the Gandhian method of less talk and more work. Sir Shah, steeped in the technique of the Law Court, evidently discards irrelevant discussion.

Sir Shah Sulaiman's services to the University of Aligarh as Vice-Chancellor must ever remain a monument of industry, devotion and selfless work in the cause of education. In 1928 the controversy between the late Sahebzada Aftab Ahmad Khan and Dr. Zia Uddin Ahmad resulted in the appointment of the Rahmat Ullah Enquiry Committee. The members of this Committee recommended far-reaching changes and Sir Shah was, in the same year, appointed Vice-Chancellor of the University. All the rules and regulations—some of which had become obsolete—were, within the short space of six months, brought into line with modern requirements and in conformity with the recommendations of the Rahmat Ullah Committee. Only a lawyer of his ability could perform this task. His efforts further succeeded in obtaining a lump sum grant of fifteen lakhs from the Government of India in September, 1929.

The members of the teaching staff in his régime were asked to enter into definite terms of contract till the age of 55. Their vacations were cut short and they were induced to work for longer hours. Urdu was made an independent subject in the B.A. and also the medium of office routine.

Education for women, which had hitherto been advocated to a limited extent, was given definite scope for expansion. For the first time degree classes and the Teachers' Training College were opened for women in the University under separate Pardah arrangement. The sound finances maintained under Sir Shah's vigilant supervision, in spite of continued expanding expenditure, have helped the inception of schemes concerning the water-works, the Agricultural and the Technological Institute and the Housing Assessment.

While the buildings of the University have received an adequate share of his attention, his desire to make Aligarh a centre for higher scientific research has stimulated a healthy spirit of competition among the students.

Sir Shah has evidently accepted the Vice-Chancellorship at a considerable inconvenience to himself. He visits Aligarh at the week-end, without remuneration. This spirit of personal sacrifice reminds one of the days of

Sir Syed Ahmad Khan who had made Aligarh his life and blood. The University Court has given him *carte blanche* and full powers to deal with any situation. This is the highest tribute that could be paid by the members of the University Court. While there may be differences of opinion on a few details of administration the devoted industry of Sir Shah has, in the unanimous opinion of the observers, established Aligarh on a sound foundation, educationally and financially. The recent successes obtained by the Aligarh candidates at the various competitive tests are eloquent testimony of what is being done. Higher scientific and historical research has been given a fresh impetus which, I hope, will soon result in some concrete form.

Sir Shah's interests in education are not limited to any particular community. The Inaugural Address delivered by him at the Hindustani Academy, Allahabad, and his Presidential Address at the All-India Adult Educational Conference at Delhi deal with problems in a manner which reveals complete impartiality towards any one class of people. He is also President of the Delhi Anglo-Arabic College.

The mathematical tradition in Sir Shah's family has found prominent expression in his private researches.

Newton's law of gravitation, which achieved signal successes in explaining the motions of the earth, the moon and the planets, and helped in discovering two new planets, has been found to be somewhat inexact, as it fails to account for two important astronomical phenomena. Einstein's theory of Relativity, which has displaced the Newtonian Mechanics and revolutionised our ideas of space, time and motion is, however, based on certain postulates so extraordinary that they would not have been easily accepted but for the belief that their results are actually confirmed by observation. Newton's theory had implied an instantaneous action of gravitation even at long distances, so that it was wholly immaterial whether the source of gravitation was moving or was stationary. In mathematical language this implied that the velocity of gravitation was infinite.

Sir Shah has pointed out that there is no reason why the velocity of gravitation should be infinite. Starting with a finite velocity, he has shown that the Newtonian equations would require a slight correction on account of the motion of the source. By the application of the principle of retarded potential to Newton's law he has deduced an equation which is identical with Einstein's so far as the planets of the solar system are concerned. Accordingly he has obtained the same value for the rotation of the orbit of Mercury as Einstein has done, which the Newtonian theory was wholly unable to account for. But in the case of a high velocity, like that of light, his equation differs from Einstein's in a small term which, however, causes an appreciable difference. There appear to be only two astronomical phenomena in which the influence of the Sun's gravitation is exerted on light itself. Confident of the soundness of his theory, Sir Shah boldly predicted before the Solar eclipse of June 19, 1936, that in these two cases the values would be in excess of Einstein's, and announced their amounts.

Light rays coming from distant stars which happen to be just behind the edge of the Sun at the time of a solar eclipse are attracted by the Sun, and therefore slightly bent towards it as compared with their straight paths six months later when the Sun does not intervene between the stars and the Earth. Einstein's value for such bending of light is just double of that under Newton's law.

Sir Shah's value is even thirty per cent. more than Einstein's. Observations made at some previous eclipses have shown an excess over Einstein's value, which in the absence of any other theory was attributed to errors of observation. The results of the observations made by a Russian observer at the time of the 1936 eclipse have not yet been announced, and are awaited with great interest.

It is also found that lines in a spectrum of light coming from the Sun are shifted slightly towards the red side of the spectrum, when compared with the spectral lines of similar atoms observed in a laboratory. Newton's theory is wholly unable to explain any such shift. By means of its postulates Einstein's theory accounts for such shifting. But according to Relativity the spectral shift should be the same for light coming from all parts of the Solar disc, whether centre, circumference or any intermediate point. For some time past it has been observed that there is an excess of the shift for light coming from the edge of the Sun; but as this was unaccountable in Relativity it was ascribed to some unknown mysterious cause. Sir Shah's theory predicted that the shift for the light from the edge should really be about double of Einstein's value, and he published his prediction before the eclipse of 1936. The Government of India financed an expedition, led by Dr. T. Royds, of Kodikanal, to Japan to observe the total solar eclipse of that year. Dr. Royds' observations were announced in July, 1937. It was a remarkable confirmation of Sir Shah's prediction that the extent of the spectral shift of light from the edge of the Sun was actually found to be just double of Einstein's value. Sir Shah has since developed his theory further, and claims to have unified the three independent phenomena of gravitation, light and electricity.

Sir Shah Sulaiman's theory, which is now gradually obtaining recognition—even from orthodox quarters—is his signal and outstanding contribution towards the advancement of scientific knowledge.

JAMSETJI NUSSERWANJI TATA

JAMSETJI NUSSERWANJI TATA

FOUNDER OF INDIA'S GREATEST INDUSTRIAL ORGANISATION

1839–1904

BY SIR STANLEY REED, K.B.E., LL.D., M.P.

THE term "great" is often so loosely applied to the lives of men that we should ask ourselves what are the standards which justify it. Two may be suggested. They are, that to deserve this appellation a man must have powerfully influenced for good the generation in which he lived, and that his work should endure after his death. There is yet another condition: rightly to be judged, the life and work of any man should be considered in relation to the times in which he lived. Gauged by these standards, none can question the right of Jamsetji Nusserwanji Tata to be included in the Indian valhalla.

Consider first the times in which he lived. Of all the races inhabiting India the Parsis were quickest to appreciate the opportunities unfolded to the enterprising by the establishment of British rule. Hardened in the school of adversity, free from any caste restriction and therefore able to travel, broadened by the tolerance, if exclusiveness, of the Zoroastrian creed, the road to Bombay from their ancestral homes in the Naosari District must have seemed like the highway to London for the Scots—the path to opportunity and success. From Bombay they threw their tentacles East and West—to the rich China market in opium and cotton, to Britain for the importation of manufactured goods which India could not make herself. Jamsetji Tata entered this field at a great formative period. The liberalising influence of education in English poured new and heady wine into receptive minds, and he received his instruction in that great school, the Elphinstone College. Experience fell richly to him. His father's firm was one of those cosmopolitan houses so characteristic of Bombay, for associated with it was Premchand Roychand, one of the most fertile and enterprising spirits of the age. Enriched by money made in supplying the needs of the forces landed at Bushire in the little Persian war the House was well established, and Jamsetji was sent to China to open a branch in Shanghai. Returning thence, it was his lot to be immersed in the greatest boom of all times—the hectic flow of money which poured into Bombay for the purchase of cotton during the American Civil War. Chastening, too, was the lesson of the slump, when with the fall of Richmond fortunes disappeared almost in a night. He was in England at the time, loaded with securities of little or no value, and from that bitter experience learnt a lesson he never forgot—the importance of sound finance. Escaping the worst evils of the collapse, which brought down the towering figure of Premchand Roychand, the family fortunes were retrieved by profits from contracting for the supplies to the Abyssinian Expedition, which Napier financed with prodigal extravagance. Fortified with this rich experience and adequate funds, none could be better equipped to play a great part in the industrial renaissance of India.

But—and this is the distinguishing feature of his life—Jamsetji Tata was never content with the conventional part. The beginnings of the cotton textile industry were laid before he entered the field. Now it is not unjust to say that in his day, and the same is more or less true now, industrial progress in India tends to be imitative rather than creative. If one pioneer erects a mill, then a score follow in his wake; if a cement or a sugar factory is established then others spring up like mushrooms until the market is saturated or even glutted. Jamsetji Tata was always creative. When his contemporaries were satisfied with producing low-grade yarn for export to the China market and rough cloths for home consumption, he looked farther afield, and selecting Nagpur, in the Central Provinces, put down his mill in the centre of the cotton-growing lands and catered for the proximate market. The prosperity of the Empress Mills he established there against the advice of all his friends reads like a dream. His ambition was that the mills should pay a hundred per cent. In 1920 original holders of the scrip were receiving 360 per cent. At a time when most industrialists gave little thought to their workpeople after they left the mill at the close of the day's toil, he bent his mind to all the social activities which we call to-day by the generic title of welfare work. Later, he was to learn in the hard school of experience that it is far easier to establish a new factory than to resuscitate an old one, and the struggle to recreate the derelict mills he acquired at Coorla and in Admedabad took heavy toll of his energies; but he succeeded here as in everything else. The strain was so great that it possibly shortened his life.

Many men know how to acquire a fortune; it is given to fewer to understand how to use it. Money was never to Jamsetji Tata an end in itself. Not that he was indifferent to many things that wealth can bring. He loved travel; he was a splendid spender; although abstemious to the point of asceticism in the use of alcohol, he did not scorn the pleasures of the table. At a time when the successful Indian merchant of the day was well content to dwell in the family house in the overcrowded and not too healthy bazaar, he built himself an imposing mansion overlooking the breezy maidan. It was not until plague fell upon the city that the great migration to the heights of Malabar and Cumballa Hills and the suburbs set in. Although I was in close touch with him and his sons for many years, looking back I am astonished at the range of his activities. He looked upon the decaying silk industries of Mysore and brought Japanese experts to put them on modern lines. He fought successfully for cheaper freights to the Far East—with the result of stimulating Japanese competition in directions not altogether favourable. He argued with the Government of Bombay until the heavy "fines" on building in the adjacent island of Salsette were lightened. But in this phase of his life one enterprise stands out above all others—his unbounded confidence in the future of the city he had made his home.

"Romance brought in the 9.15," sang Rudyard Kipling when told that the age of romance was dead. Short as memories are, can any be insensible to the romance of the rise of Bombay? Look at the old maps and realise the few scattered islets, divided by the sundering tide, which was the Bombay inherited from Catherine of Braganza; read the annals of Bombay and learn how the people living on the verge of these pestiferous swamps rotted into early graves, and compare this with the Second City in the Empire of to-day, with its million and a half of souls! Nor is this a tottering city won from the sea resting on rotting piles like Venice; it is based for all time on the foundation of soil rent from the neighbouring hills or pumped by giant dredgers from the bottom of the muddy harbour.

In the use of this new-found land Jamsetji Tata played an heroic part. Wherever land could be had he bought it. He acquired for instance the greater part of the adjacent island of Trombay, with a view to making it a garden suburb. He would have reclaimed the tidal creek which separates Bombay Island from Salsette if he could have come to terms with the Government. He cast his restless eye on the sea-girt spit of land open to the western winds at Juhu, and would have made it an ordered Brighton, instead of the higgledy-piggledy collection of bungalows and shacks it is to-day. When new sites were available from the reclamations of the Port Trust and the land thrown upon the market by the creation of the Improvement Trust, many investors held aloof, afraid of the terms of the new leases. Not so Jamsetji Tata; he acquired and built in every part of the Island. And when a friend casually remarked that Bombay was without a first-class hotel, he growled in his deep-toned voice—"I will build one," and on the site of the basin where rowers were wont to take their skiffs for a stretch in the harbour, he raised, at a cost of a quarter of a million of money, the hotel which seizes the eye of the incoming passenger, and established a new standard of comfort for the visitor and resident alike.

Yet, embracing and beneficial as these activities were, they seem to me to be no more than the prelude to his great constructive work. Secure in possession of an ample fortune, with a big income from the Empress and other cotton mills,

TATA WORKS, CENTRAL PROVINCE

A general view of the Cotton Mills, Nadpur, one of the great Tata concerns.

he bent his mind to three major schemes. Though they came to fruition after his death, his was the inspiration, his the pioneer work.

The inspiration came in the late 'eighties when Lord Reay, the Governor of Bombay, in an address as Chancellor of the University, warned India that she was at the parting of the ways; higher education could no longer develop if the Universities remained purely examining bodies. It was imperative to evolve a teaching university. In passing, we may note that few lines of criticism are more misdirected than those which attack the foundations of the Indian educational system. They were laid to meet the immediate needs of the hour—the provision of educated and efficient administrative services—and they discharged that rôle admirably. The fault, if fault it was, lay in the fact that they became stereotyped; that when this need was fully satisfied, and India was hungry for scientific and vocational training the colleges and universities continued to concentrate on a literary education, producing a growing class of graduates for whom there was no economic outlet. Lord Reay's words fell on receptive ears and Jamsetji Tata decided to fill the gap. One of his dominant characteristics was his judgment of men. As he brought Bezonji Dadabhai, a Goods Superintendent on the railway, to organise and direct the Empress Mills, and A. J. Billimeria to take charge of his office organisation, so he selected B. J. Padshah, a college professor of unbounded enthusiasm and complete devotion to the welfare of India, to be his adviser.

Padshah was sent round the world to study post-graduate education in every land, and returned charged with the advantages of the Johns Hopkins institution at Baltimore. Sir William Ramsay was brought from Britain to lend the weight of his scientific knowledge and experience. A sum of thirty lakhs of rupees was set aside as foundation money. Long and wearisome was the path to achievement. It had not been trodden to the goal when Jamsetji Tata died; it was indeed then doubtful whether it would ever be brought to fruition. But his sons accepted the project as a trust; they decided to continue the offer of the original sum of thirty lakhs; and aided by a large grant from the Government of India and a generous gift of land and money from the Maharajah of Mysore, the foundation stone was laid in the pleasant station of Bangalore in 1911, and students were admitted to classes in General and Applied Chemistry, Electro-Technology, and Organic Chemistry. That was the origin and history of the Indian Institute of Science, the foremost institution for the teaching of higher science in the East.

Even the most casual survey of the industrial field carries the conviction that no country can become industrially great which does not possess an iron and steel industry; it is indispensable to the formation of a true economic cycle. India had practised for ages a smelting industry, whose calibre can be gauged from the famous Iron Pillar at Delhi, but like the industry of Sussex, it languished as the forests were drawn upon for charcoal and before the competition of the highly-organised industries of the West. A useful factory for the production of pig-iron was founded at Kulti in Bengal, but the attempt to produce steel was a failure, and the needs of the country were supplied from abroad. In the year 1899, one of those far-sighted Artillery Officers to whom India owes so much, Major R. H. Mahon, Superintendent of the Government Ordnance Factories at Cossipore, produced a prophetic report; he declared that the time had come for the establishment of iron and steel works on a considerable scale, that these should be on the most modern lines, and that the most favourable theatre for operations was Bengal. Jamsetji Tata seized on the idea with avidity, remitted the direction of the enterprise largely to his eldest son Dorabji (Sir Dorab Tata), and provided the funds for the prospecting activity from his own purse. Later, he established contact with two men who were destined to play a large part in the enterprise—Julian Kennedy, of the firm of Julian Kennedy, Sahlin and Co., and Charles Page Perin, a mining engineer of world-wide experience. Romance has been used to describe the rise of Bombay; it is equally applicable to the establishment of the iron and steel industry. Jamsetji Tata was not alone in the field of research. The prospector was abroad in the land and more than one financier fixed his gaze on the Indian scene. Whilst waiting for an interview with the Head of the Central Provinces, Dorabji drifted by chance into the Museum, and there noticed on the geological map a large area in the Drug district coloured to represent deposits of iron. Secretly he and his geological expert went to the scene and discovered a veritable hill of iron ore of the richest quality. That was enough. Good coking coal was found in the Jherria district, limestone and manganese were available in abundance, and the major problem was solved.

Those who know their India resent the idea that it is to the United States that we must look for the dramatic note in the growth of major enterprise. It is

WADALA DAM

The great reservoir near Poona; part of the Tata Hydro-Electric Scheme which supplies Bombay with electric energy.

MODERN BOMBAY

Buildings on the Ballard Estate, Bombay, a city which the House of Tata has helped enormously to develop.

struck far more sonorously in India. Here was the iron and the coal; it only remained to fix the site of economic assembly and manufacture, and to find the money. The latter was the greater difficulty of the two. British capital has played a great part in the development of India; but it has for the most part been on conservative lines. There was always money ready for established credit; there was little or none for the creation of new credits. The present generation little appreciates the difficulties under which the early industrialists laboured. They had first to risk their all; then to go cap in hand to their friends for financial support. Assuming this succeeded, then as soon as an asset was created it had to be pledged for working capital. No one dreamt that the unprecedented sum needed for an iron and steel industry could be found in the country itself. The scheme, ripe for exploitation after Jamsetji Tata's death, was literally hawked round London and New York without success; all the heavy preliminary expenses were met from the Tata House. In an hour of inspiration Dorabji Tata decided to appeal to his own countrymen. A new spirit was abroad. The Swadeshi movement—the movement for the development of India's immense resources—was at its height, and though it is over three decades ago I can recall the trembling anxiety with which Dorabji Tata came to my office (I was then editing *The Times of India*) to ask my support to the enterprise. The response was immediate. The public subscribed the whole of the capital required—£1,630,000—and when a further sum

THE BHIVA STATION

A general view of the Andhra Valley Hydro-Electric Scheme.

INSIDE THE STATION

The High-Tension room inside the Bhiva Station of the Andhra Valley Scheme.

of £400,000 was needed a single Indian Prince, the Maharajah of Gwalior, provided the money.

That was the origin of the Steel City which has grown up in the jungles of Chota Nagpur. The engineers literally went into the wilderness, a land of scrub jungle, thinly peopled with descendants of the aboriginal inhabitants of India, the Santhals. The land had to be cleared and levelled; the river dammed for water; a railway connection established with the main line and another to the Hill of Iron at Gurumaishini, where an almost inexhaustible supply of the finest ore was available. From these beginnings have grown the iron and steel works of to-day, the Tata Works, producing 1,200,000 tons of pig iron a year (1,000,000 tons of steel ingots), with a capital of Rs10,47,00,000 and employing forty-five thousand men, and the ancillary enterprises which have grown round it—the making of tin plates, agricultural implements, etc., and the sulphate of ammonia for which the Indian soil is hungry. It was a graceful act of the Government of India to change the name of Sakchi to Jamshedpur, and of the railway junction to Tatanagar.

Turn now to another enterprise with which the name of Jamsetji Tata is indissolubly associated. Bombay was the original, and still is the greatest, centre of the cotton textile industry. From the crest of Malabar Hill the curious could look forth and see the smoke rising from eighty chimneys, spreading over the Island a mephitic fog which hung like the pall of a "London particular" on a stilly morning. Ideally situated in many respects, with a magnificent harbour and every facility for exporting to the once

THE HEAD OFFICES OF THE TATA ORGANISATION, BOMBAY

JAMSHEDPUR

General view of railway sidings and the giant furnace sheds at the great Tata Steel Works at Jamshedpur.

profitable markets of China, Japan and the Levant, it labours under one disadvantage—remoteness from the coalfields. In the early days fuel came from South Wales and Yorkshire; then Natal entered the field; but with the development of the Indian mines indigenous supplies captured the market. That involved rail carriage of twelve hundred miles from Bengal, or the rail-cum-sea route with considerable loss from repeated handling. Yet in the Western Ghats immense resources in hydro-electric power lay dormant. A region of constant rainfall, in places up to three hundred inches, an immediate fall of eighteen hundred feet, and an established demand sixty miles away—what could the financier and engineer ask more? The successful working of a modest scheme at Sivasmudrum in Mysore, where the waters of the Cauvery River were harnessed to furnish hydro-electricity to drive the Kolar Gold Mines, had revealed the prospects of water power, and when this scheme was brought to the attention of Jamsetji Tata by David Gostling, a practising architect of imagination, it at once appealed to his fertile mind. As with everything else in the India ot those days, the wheels of Government moved slowly, and Government aid was essential to the granting of the necessary licences and the acquisition of the land. Little had been done save the preliminary work when Jamsetji Tata "crossed over." The burden of carrying his ideas to completion again rested on the shoulders of Dorabji. Here, again, finance seemed to be the rock on which the enterprise might founder. Arrangements were almost complete for the enlistment of London finance when the Governor of the day, Lord Sydenham, himself an engineer of repute, urged Indian capitalists to make the work their own. Again the response was amazing. When the Tata Hydro-Electric Company was launched in 1910 the capital of two crores of rupees was promptly subscribed.

The Tata Hydro-Electric scheme is complicated. There is a shallow lake at Lanavla to store the monsoon rains; then a supplementary reservoir at Walhwan connected with it by duct; and at a later stage comes the immense lake at Shirwata, whose waters are carried into Walhwan by tunnel, the magnitude of which may be indicated by the fact that the containing dam is as large as the famous Assouan Barrage on the Nile. Before the scheme was completed a demand arose for yet more power, and a site was found in the Andhra Valley, where the waters were stored in a single lake and carried to the turbines at the foot of the hills through a tunnel. This paved the way for the yet bigger scheme, damming the Nir Mulla River on the same lines as Andhra, and supplying the turbines through a tunnel. These connected works develop no less than 244,000 electrical horse-power, the whole of which is absorbed in the industries of Bombay, the electrification of the suburban and part of the main railway lines, and in Poona and the Island of Salsette. The total share capital of the associated companies is Rs9,05,00,000. Through this agency it may be claimed that Bombay is the most electrified city in the world, for the Bombay Electrical Supply and Tramway Company, acting as distributors, have carried electricity into the smallest dwellings, even to thousands of consumers each with no more than a single light.

Applying these activities to the canons of greatness suggested earlier, who can deny that Jamsetji Tata was entitled to the title of A Great Indian? He brought into industry a new concept. He was no imitator, but carved out a fresh field, going to the sources of supply of the raw material, cotton, and to the market. More, in an age of cheapness he sought

SIR DORABJI TATA

[illegible] material money could [illegible] the best was only just good [illegible] He was a pioneer in the work [illegible] industrial welfare, and had a vivid interest in the lives of his employees. Again, he had an abiding sense of responsibility to his shareholders. When he entered the textile industry the vicious system obtained of the managing agents drawing a commission of a quarter of an anna on every pound of yarn spun; it sometimes paid the agent to work full time even when the yarn had to be sold at a loss. Jamsetji Tata substituted the commission of ten per cent. on profits now general; no profits no commission.

Then when his fortunes were established he looked abroad to see how best they could be utilised for the advantage of his country. It was said of a great writer that he took the whole world of learning for his province. Of Jamsetji Tata it might equally be said that the whole field of industry came within his ambit. Those associated activities—the Indian Institute of Science to train the higher personnel; the iron and steel works to start the true economic cycle; and the hydro-electric stations to furnish cheap power and conserve the coal resources—left an enduring mark on his own generation. He did not live to see the coping stone placed on this work; but so well were the foundations laid, so determined the enthusiasm inspired in his sons and colleagues, that they pressed it to completion. Of him truly can the epitaph be writ—he wrought the people lasting good.